Charles Lever

Maurice Tiernay

The Soldier of Fortune

Charles Lever

Maurice Tiernay
The Soldier of Fortune

ISBN/EAN: 9783337136710

Printed in Europe, USA, Canada, Australia, Japan

Cover: Foto ©ninafisch / pixelio.de

More available books at **www.hansebooks.com**

MAURICE TIERNAY,

THE SOLDIER OF FORTUNE.

BY

CHARLES LEVER,

AUTHOR OF
"FORTUNES OF GLENCORE,"
"HARRY LORREQUER,"
"DAVENPORT DUNN,"
ETC. ETC.

NEW EDITION.

LONDON:
CHAPMAN AND HALL, 193 PICCADILLY.
1879.

NOTICE.

THE strangeness of some of the incidents, and the rapidity with which events so remarkable succeeded each other, almost deterred the writer from ever committing them to the press; nor was it till after much consultation, and some persuasive influence on the part of friends, that he at length yielded and decided upon so doing. Whether in that determination his choice was a wise one, must be left to the judgment of the reader: for himself he has but to say, that to ponder over some of these early scenes, and turn over, in thought, some of his youthful passages, has solaced many a weary hour of an age when men make few new friendships, and have almost as few opportunities to cultivate old ones.

That the chief events related in these pages—such, for instance, as every detail of the French invasion, the capture of Wolfe Tone, and the attack on Monte di Faccio—are rigidly exact, the writer is most sincere in the expression of his conviction; for the truth of incident purely personal, it is needless to press any claim, seeing that he was this hero—owns no higher name—than that of—a Soldier of Fortune.

MAURICE TIERNAY,

THE

SOLDIER OF FORTUNE.

CHAPTER I.

"THE DAYS OF THE GUILLOTINE."

NEITHER the tastes nor the temper of the age we live in
are such as to induce any man to boast of his family
nobility. We see too many preparations around us for
laying down new foundations, to think it a suitable occasion
for alluding to the ancient edifice. I will, therefore, confine myself to saying, that I am not to be regarded as a
mere pretender because my name is not chronicled by
Burke or Debrett. My great-grandfather, after whom I
am called, served on the personal staff of King James at
the Battle of the Boyne, and was one of the few who
accompanied the monarch on his flight from the field, for
which act of devotion he was created a peer of Ireland,
by the style and title of Timmahoo—Lord Tiernay, of
Timmahoo the family called it—and a very rich-sounding
and pleasant designation has it always seemed to me.

The events of the time, the scanty intervals of leisure
enjoyed by the king, and other matters, prevented a due
registry of my ancestors' claims; and, in fact, when more
peaceable days succeeded, it was judged prudent to say
nothing about a matter which might revive unhappy recollections, and open old scores, seeing that there was now
another king on the throne "who knew not Joseph;" and
so, for this reason and many others, my great-grandfather
went back to his old appellation of Maurice Tiernay, and
was only a lord among his intimate friends and cronies of
the neighbourhood.

That I am simply recording a matter of fact, the patent

of my ancestors' nobility, now in my possession, will sufficiently attest: nor is its existence the less conclusive, tha
it is inscribed on the back of his commission as a captai
in the Shanabogue Fencibles—the well-known "Clear-
the-way-boys"—a proud title, it is said, to which they
imparted a new reading at the memorable battle afore-
mentioned.

The document bears the address of a small public-house
called the Nest, on the Kells road, and contains in one
corner a somewhat lengthy score for potables, suggesting
the notion that his majesty sympathised with vulgar infir-
mities, and found, as the old song says, "that grief and
sorrow are dry."

The prudence which for some years sealed my grandfather's lips, lapsed, after a time, into a careless and even
boastful spirit, in which he would allude to his rank in the
peerage, the place he ought to be holding, and so on: till
at last, some of the Government people, doubtless taking
a liking to the snug house and demesne of Timmahoo, denounced him as a rebel, on which he was arrested and
thrown into jail, where he lingered for many years, and
only came out at last to find his estate confiscated, and
himself a beggar.

There was a small gathering of Jacobites in one of the
towns of Flanders, and thither he repaired; but how he
lived, or how he died, I never learned. I only know that
his son wandered away to the east of Europe, and took
service in what was called Trenck's Pandours—as jolly a
set of robbers as ever stalked the map of Europe, from
one side to the other. This was my grandfather, whose
name is mentioned in various chronicles of that estimable
corps, and who was hanged at Prague afterwards, for an
attempt to carry off an archduchess of the empire, to whom,
by the way, there is good reason to believe he was pri-
vately married. This suspicion was strengthened by the
fact that his infant child, Joseph, was at once adopted by
the imperial family, and placed as a pupil in the great military school of Vienna. From thence he obtained a commission in the Maria Theresa Hussars, and subsequently,
being sent on a private mission to France, entered the
service of Louis XVI., where he married a lady of the
Queen's household—a Mademoiselle de la Lasterie—of
high rank and some fortune; and with whom he lived
happily till the dreadful events of 17—, when she lost
her life, beside my father, then fighting as a Garde du
Corps, on the staircase at Versailles. How he himself
escaped on that day, and what were the next features in

his history, I never knew; but when again we heard of
him, he was married to the widow of a celebrated orator
of the Mountain, and he himself an intimate friend of St.
Just and Marat, and all the most violent of the Republicans.

My father's history about this period is involved in such
obscurity, and his second marriage followed so rapidly on
the death of his first wife, that, strange as it may seem, I
never knew which of the two was my mother—the lineal
descendant of a house, noble before the Crusades, or—the
humble "bourgeoise" of the Quartier St. Denis. What
peculiar line of political action my father followed I am
unable to say, nor whether he was suspected with or without due cause; but suspected he certainly was, and at a
time when suspicion was all-sufficient for conviction. He
was arrested, and thrown into the Temple, where I remember I used to visit him every week; and whence I
accompanied him one morning, as he was led forth with a
string of others to the Place de la Grêve, to be guillotined.
I believe he was accused of royalism; and I know that a
white cockade was found among his effects, and in mockery
was fastened on his shoulder on the day of his execution.
This emblem, deep dyed with blood, and still dripping,
was taken up by a bystander, and pinned on my cap, with
the savage observation, "Voila, it is the proper colour;
see that you profit by the way it became so." As, with a
bursting heart, and a head wild with terror, I turned to
find my way homeward, I felt my hand grasped by another
—I looked up, and saw an old man, whose threadbare
black clothes and emaciated appearance bespoke the priest
in the times of the Convention.

"You have no home now, my poor boy," said he to me;
"come and share mine."

I did not ask him why. I seemed to have suddenly
become reckless as to everything present or future. The
terrible scene I had witnessed had dried up all the springs
of my youthful heart; and, infant as I was, I was already
a sceptic as to everything good or generous in human nature. I followed him, therefore, without a word, and we
walked on, leaving the thoroughfares and seeking the less
frequented streets, till we arrived in what seemed a
suburban part of Paris—at least the houses were surrounded with trees and shrubs; and at a distance I could
see the hill of Montmartre and its windmills—objects well
known to me by many a Sunday visit.

Even after my own home, the poverty of the Père
Michel's household was most remarkable: he had but one

small room, of which a miserable settle-bed, two chairs, and a table, constituted all the furniture; there was no fireplace, a little pan for charcoal supplying the only means for warmth or cookery; a crucifix and a few coloured prints of saints decorated the whitewashed walls; and, with a string of wooden beads, a cloth skull-cap, and a bracket with two or three books, made up the whole inventory of his possessions; and yet, as he closed the door behind him, and drew me towards him to kiss my cheek, the tears glistened in his eyes with gratitude as he said—

"Now, my dear Maurice, you are at home."

"How do you know that I am called Maurice?" said I, in astonishment.

"Because I was an old friend of your poor father, my child; we came from the same country—we held the same faith, had the same hopes, and may one day yet, perhaps, have the same fate."

He told me that the closest friendship had bound them together for years past, and in proof of it showed me a variety of papers which my father had entrusted to his keeping, well aware, as it would seem, of the insecurity of his own life.

"He charged me to take you home with me, Maurice, should the day come when this might come to pass. You will now live with me, and I will be your father, so far, at least, as humble means will suffer me."

I was too young to know how deep my debt of gratitude ought to be. I had not tasted the sorrows of utter desertion; nor did I know from what a hurricane of blood and anarchy Fortune had rescued me; still I accepted the Pére's benevolent offer with a thankful heart, and turned to him at once as to all that was left to me in the world.

All this time, it may be wondered how I neither spoke nor thought of my mother, if she were indeed such; but for several weeks before my father's death I had never seen her, nor did he ever once allude to her. The reserve thus imposed upon me remained still, and I felt as though it would have been like a treachery to his memory were I now to speak of her whom, in his lifetime, I had not dared to mention.

The Pére lost no time in diverting my mind from the dreadful events I had so lately witnessed. The next morning, soon after daybreak, I was summoned to attend him to the little Church of St. Blois, where he said mass. It was a very humble little edifice, which once had been the private chapel of a Chateau, and stood in a weed-grown, neglected garden, where broken statues and smashed fountains bore evidence of the visits of the destroyer. A rude effigy of St. Blois, upon whom some profane hand had stuck a Phrygian cap of liberty, and which none were bold enough to displace, stood over the doorway; except this, not a vestige of ornament or decoration existed. The altar, covered with a white cloth, displayed none of the accustomed emblems; and a rude crucifix of oak was the only symbol of the faith remaining. Small as was the building, it was even too spacious for the few who came to worship. The terror which prevailed on every side—the dread that devotion to religion should be construed into an adherence to the monarchy, that submission to God should be interpreted as an act of rebellion against the sovereignty of human will—had gradually thinned the numbers, till at last the few who came were only those whose afflictions had steeled them against any reverses, and who were ready martyrs to whatever might betide them. These were almost exclusively women—the mothers and wives of those who had sealed their faith with their blood in the terrible Place de la Grêve. Among them was one whose dress and appearance, although not different from the rest, always created a movement of respect as she passed in or out of the chapel. She was a very old lady, with hair white as snow, and who led by the hand a little girl of about my own age; her large dark eyes and brilliant complexion giving her a look of unearthly beauty in that assemblage of furrowed cheeks, and eyes long dimmed by weeping. It was not alone that her features were beautifully regular, or that their lines were fashioned in the very perfection of symmetry, but there was a certain character in the expression of the face so different from all around it, as to be almost electrical in effect. Untouched by the terrible calamities that weighed on every heart, she seemed, in the glad buoyancy of her youth, to be at once above the very reach of sorrow, like one who bore a charmed fate, and whom Fortune had exempted from all the trials of this life. So at least did I read those features, as they beamed upon me in such a contrast to the almost stern character of the sad and sorrow-struck faces of the rest.

It was a part of my duty to place a footstool each morning for the "Marquise," as she was distinctively called, and on these occasions it was that I used to gaze upon that little girl's face with a kind of admiring wonder that lingered in my heart for hours after. The bold look with which she met mine, if it at first half abashed, at length encouraged me; and as I stole noiselessly away, I used to feel as though I carried with me some portion of that high hope which bounded within her own heart. Strange magnetism! it seemed as though her spirit whispered to me not to be down-hearted or depressed—that the sorrows of life came and went as shadows pass over the earth—that the season of mourning was fast passing, and that for us the world would wear a brighter and more glorious aspect.

Such were the thoughts her dark eyes revealed to me, and such the hopes I caught up from her proud features.

It is easy to colour a life of monotony; any hue may soon tinge the outer surface, and thus mine speedily assumed a hopeful cast; not the less decided, that the distance was lost in vague uncertainty. The nature of my studies—and the Père kept me rigidly to the desk—offered little to the discursiveness of fancy. The rudiments of Greek and Latin, the lives of saints and martyrs, the litanies of the church, the invocations peculiar to certain holydays, chiefly filled up my time, when not sharing those menial offices which our poverty exacted from our own hands.

Our life was of the very simplest; except a cup of coffee each morning at daybreak, we took but one meal; our drink was always water. By what means even the humble fare we enjoyed was procured I never knew, for I never saw money in the Père's possession, nor did he ever appear to buy anything.

For about two hours in the week I used to enjoy entire liberty, as the Père was accustomed every Saturday to visit certain persons of his flock who were too infirm to go abroad. On these occasions he would leave me with some thoughtful injunction about reflection or pious meditation, perhaps suggesting, for my amusement, the life of St. Vincent de Paul, or some other of those adventurous spirits whose missions among the Indians are so replete with heroic struggles; but still with free permission for me to walk out at large and enjoy myself as I liked best. We lived so near the outer boulevard that I could already see the open country from our windows; but fair and enticing as seemed the sunny slopes of Montmartre—bright as glanced the young leaves of spring in the gardens at its foot—I ever turned my steps into the crowded city, and sought the thoroughfares where the great human tide rolled fullest.

There were certain spots which held a kind of supernatural influence over me—one of these was the Temple, another was the Place de la Grève. The window at which my father used to sit, from which, as a kind of signal, I have so often seen his red kerchief floating, I never could pass now, without stopping to gaze at—now, thinking of him who had been its inmate; now, wondering who might be its present occupant. It needed not the onward current of population that each Saturday bore along, to carry me to the Place de la Grêve. It was the great day of the guillotine, and as many as two hundred were often led out to execution. Although the spectacle had now lost every charm of excitement to the population, from its frequency, it had become a kind of necessity to their existence, and the sight of blood alone seemed to slake that feverish thirst for vengeance which no sufferings appeared capable of satiating. It was rare, however, when some great and distinguished criminal did not absorb all the interest of the scene. It was at that period when the fierce tyrants of the Convention had turned upon each other, and sought, by denouncing those who had been their bosom friends, to seal their new allegiance to the people. There was something demoniacal in the exultation with which the mob witnessed the fate of those whom, but a few weeks back, they had acknowledged as their guides and teachers. The uncertainty of human greatness appeared the most glorious recompense to those whose station debarred them from all the enjoyments of power, and they stood by the death-agonies of their former friends with a fiendish joy that all the sufferings of their enemies had never yielded.

To me the spectacle had all the fascination that scenes of horror exercise over the mind of youth. I knew nothing of the terrible conflict, nothing of the fierce passions enlisted in the struggle, nothing of the sacred names so basely polluted, nothing of that remorseless vengeance with which the low-born and degraded were still hounded on to slaughter. It was a solemn and a fearful sight, but it was no more; and I gazed upon every detail of the scene with an interest that never wandered from the spot whereon it was enacted. If the parade of soldiers, of horse, foot, and artillery, gave these scenes a character of public justice, the horrible mobs, who chanted ribald songs, and danced around the guillotine, suggested the notion of popular vengeance; so that I was lost in all my attempts to reconcile the reasons of these executions with the circumstances that accompanied them.

Not daring to inform the Pére Michel of where I had been, I could not ask him for any explanation; and thus was I left to pick up from the scattered phrases of the crowd what was the guilt alleged against the criminals. In many cases the simple word "Chouan," of which I knew not the import, was all I heard; in others jeering allusions to former rank and station would be uttered; while against some the taunt would imply that they had shed tears over others who fell as enemies of the people, and that such sympathy was a costly pleasure to be paid for but with a life's-blood. Such entire possession of me had these awful sights taken, that I lived in a continual dream of them. The sound of every cart-wheel recalled the dull rumble of the hurdle—every distant sound seemed like the far-off hum of the coming multitude—every sudden noise suggested the clanking drop of the guillotine! My sleep had no other images, and I wandered about my little round of duties pondering over this terrible theme.

Had I been less occupied with my own thoughts, I must have seen that the Pére Michel was suffering under some great calamity. The poor priest became wasted to a shadow; for entire days long he would taste of nothing; sometimes he would be absent from early morning to late at night, and when he did return, instead of betaking himself to rest, he would drop down before the crucifix in an agony of prayer, and thus spend more than half the night. Often and often have I, when feigning sleep, followed him as he recited the litanies of the breviary, adding my own unuttered prayers to his, and beseeching for a mercy whose object I knew not.

For some time his little chapel had been closed by the authorities; a heavy padlock and two massive seals being placed upon the door, and a notice in a vulgar handwriting, appended, to the effect that it was by the order of the Commissary of the Department. Could this be the source of the Pére's sorrow? or did not his affliction seem too great for such a cause? were questions I asked myself again and again.

In this state were matters, when one morning, it was a Saturday, the Pére enjoined me to spend the day in prayer, reciting particularly the liturgies for the dead, and all those sacred offices for those who have just departed this life.

"Pray unceasingly, my dear child—pray with your whole heart, as though it were for one you loved best in the world. I shall not return, perhaps, till late to-night; but I will kiss you then, and to-morrow we shall go into the woods together."

The tears fell from his cheek to mine as he said this, and his damp hand trembled as he pressed my fingers. My heart was full to bursting at his emotion, and I resolved

faithfully to do his bidding. To watch him as he went,
I opened the sash, and as I did so, the sound of a distant
drum, the well-known muffled roll, floated on the air, and
I remembered it was the day of the guillotine—that day
in which my feverish spirit turned, as it were in relief, to
the reality of blood. Remote as was the part of the city
we lived in, I could still mark the hastening steps of the
foot-passengers, as they listened to the far-off summons,
and see the tide was setting towards the fatal Place de la
Grève. It was a lowering, heavy morning, overcast with
clouds, and on its loaded atmosphere sounds moved slowly
and indistinctly; yet I could trace through all the din of
the great city, the incessant roll of the drums, and the
loud shouts that burst forth, from time to time, from some
great multitude.

Forgetting everything save my intense passion for
scenes of terror, I hastened down the stairs into the street,
and at the top of my speed hurried to the place of execution. As I went along, the crowded streets and thronged
avenues told of some event of more than common interest; and in the words which fell from those around me,
I could trace that some deep Royalist plot had just been
discovered, and that the conspirators would all on that
day be executed. Whether it was that the frequent sight
of blood was beginning to pall upon the popular appetite,
or that these wholesale massacres interested less than the
sight of individual suffering, I know not; but certainly
there was less of exultation, less of triumphant scorn in
the tone of the speakers. They talked of the coming
event as of a common occurrence, which, from mere repetition, was gradually losing interest.

"I thought we had done with these Chouans," said a
man in a blouse, with a paper cap on his head. "Pardie.
they must have been more numerous than we ever suspected."

"That they were, citoyen," said a haggard-looking fellow, whose features showed the signs of recent strife,
"they were the millions who gorged and fed upon us for
centuries—who sipped the red grape of Bordeaux, while
you and I drank the water of the Seine."

"Well, their time is come now," cried a third.

"And when will ours come?" asked a fresh-looking,
dark-eyed girl, whose dress bespoke her trade as a flower-
girl, "or do you call this our time, my masters, when
Paris has no more pleasant sight than blood, nor any music
save the 'ça ira' that drowns the cries at the guillotine?
Is this our time, when we have lost those who gave us

bread, and got in their place only those who would feed us with carnage?"

"Down with her! down with the Chouane! à bas la Royaliste!" cried the pale-faced fellow; and he struck the girl with his fist upon the face, and left it covered with blood.

"To the Lantern with her!—to the Seine!" shouted several voices; and now, rudely seizing her by the shoulders, the mob seemed bent upon sudden vengeance; while the poor girl, letting fall her basket, begged with clasped hands for mercy.

"See here, see here, comrades," cried a fellow, stooping down among the flowers, "she is a Royalist: here are lilies hid beneath the rest."

What sad consequences this discovery might have led to, there is no knowing; when, suddenly, a violent rush of the crowd turned every thought into a different direction. It was caused by a movement of the Gendarmerie à cheval, who were clearing the way for the approaching procession. I had just time to place the poor girl's basket in her hands, as the onward impulse of the dense mob carried me forward. I saw her no more. A flower—I know not how it came there—was in my bosom, and seeing that it was a lily, I placed it within my cap for concealment.

The hoarse clangour of the bassoons—the only instruments which played during the march—now told that the procession was approaching; and then I could see, above the heads of the multitude, the leopard-skin helmets of the dragoons, who led the way. Save this I could see nothing, as I was borne along in the vast torrent towards the place of execution. Slowly as we moved, our progress was far more rapid than that of the procession, which was often obliged to halt from the density of the mob in front. We arrived, therefore, at the Place a considerable time before it; and now I found myself beside the massive wooden railing placed to keep off the crowd from the space around the guillotine.

It was the first time I had ever stood so close to the fatal spot, and my eyes devoured every detail with the most searching intensity. The colossal guillotine itself, painted red, and with its massive axe suspended aloft— the terrible basket, half filled with sawdust, beneath—the coarse table, on which a rude jar and a cup were placed— and, more disgusting than all, the lounging group, who, with their newspapers in hand, seemed from time to time to watch if the procession were approaching. They sat beneath a mis-shapen statue of wood, painted red like the guillotine. This was the goddess of Liberty. I climbed one of the pillars of the paling, and could now see the great cart, which, like a boat upon wheels, came slowly along, dragged by six horses. It was crowded with people, so closely packed that they could not move their bodies, and only waved their hands, which they did incessantly. They seemed, too, as if they were singing; but the deep growl of the bassoons, and the fierce howlings of the mob, drowned all other sounds. As the cart came nearer, I could distinguish the faces, amid which were those of age and youth—men and women—bold-visaged boys and fair girls—some, whose air bespoke the very highest station, and beside them, the hardy peasant, apparently more amazed than terrified at all he saw around him. On they came, the great cart surging heavily, like a bark in a stormy sea; and now it cleft the dense ocean that filled the Place, and I could descry the lineaments wherein the stiffened lines of death were already marked. Had any touch of pity still lingered in that dense crowd, there might well have been some show of compassion for the sad convoy, whose faces grew ghastly with terror as they drew near the horrible engine.

Down the furrowed cheek of age the heavy tears coursed freely, and sobs and broken prayers burst forth from hearts that until now had beat high and proudly.

"There is the Duc d'Angeac," cried a fellow, pointing to a venerable old man, who was seated at the corner of the cart, with an air of calm dignity; "I know him well, for I was his perruquier."

"His hair must be content with sawdust this morning, instead of powder," said another; and a rude laugh followed the ruffian jest.

"See! mark that woman with the long dark hair—that is La Bretonville, the actress of the St. Martin."

"I have often seen her represent terror far more naturally," cried a fashionably-dressed man, as he stared at the victim through his opera-glass.

"Bah!" replied his friend, "she despises her audience, voila tout. Look, Henri, if that little girl beside her be not Lucille, of the Pantheon."

"Parbleu! so it is. Why, they'll not leave a pirouette in the Grand Opera. Pauvre petite, what had you to do with politics?"

"Her little feet ought to have saved her head any day."

"See how grim that old lady beside her looks; I'd

swear she is more shocked at the company she's thrown
into than the fate that awaits her. I never saw a glance
of prouder disdain than she has just bestowed on poor
Lucille."

"That is the old Marquise D'Estelles, the very es-
sence of our old nobility. They used to talk of their
mesalliance with the Bourbons as the first misfortune of
their house."

"Pardie! they have lived to learn deeper sorrows."

I had by this time discovered her they were speaking
of, whom I recognised at once as the old Marquise of the
Chapel of St. Blois. My hands nearly gave up their
grasp as I gazed on those features, which so often I had
seen fixed in prayer, and which now—a thought paler,
perhaps—wore the self-same calm expression. With what
intense agony I peered into the mass, to see if the little
girl, her grand-daughter, were with her; and, oh! the
deep relief I felt as I saw nothing but strange faces on
every side. It was terrible to feel, as my eyes ranged
over that vast mass, where grief, and despair, and heart-
sinking terror were depicted, that I should experience a
spirit of joy and thankfulness; and yet I did so, and with
my lips I uttered my gratitude that she was spared! But
I had not time for many reflections like this; already
the terrible business of the day had begun, and the prisoners were now descending from the cart, ranging themselves, as their names were called, in a line below the
scaffold. With a few exceptions, they took their places
in all the calm of seeming indifference. Death had long
familiarised itself to their minds in a thousand shapes.
Day by day they had seen the vacant places left by those
led out to die, and if their sorrows had not rendered them
careless of life, the world itself had grown distasteful to
them. In some cases a spirit of proud scorn was manifested to the very last; and, strange inconsistency of
human nature! the very men whose licentiousness and
frivolity first evoked the terrible storm of popular fury,
were the first to display the most chivalrous courage in
the terrible face of the guillotine. Beautiful women, too,
in all the pride of their loveliness, met the inhuman stare
of that mob undismayed. Nor were these traits without
their fruits. This noble spirit—this triumphant victory of
the well-born and the great—was a continual insult to the
populace, who saw themselves defrauded of half their
promised vengeance, and they learned that they might
kill, but they could never humiliate them. In vain they
dipped their hands in the red life-blood, and, holding up

their dripping fingers, asked—" How did it differ from that of the people?" Their hearts gave the lie to the taunt; for they witnessed instances of heroism, from grey hairs and tender womanhood, that would have shamed the proudest deeds of their new-born chivalry!

" Charles Gregoire Courcelles!" shouted out a deep voice from the scaffold.

" That is my name," said a venerable-looking old gentleman, as he arose from his seat, adding, with a placid smile, " but for half a century my friends have called me the Duc de Riancourt."

" We have no dukes nor marquises; we know of no titles in France," replied the functionary. " All men are equal before the law."

" If it were so, my friend, you and I might change places; for you were my steward, and plundered my chateau."

" Down with the Royalist—away with the aristocrat!" shouted a number of voices from the crowd.

" Be a little patient, good people," said the old man, as he ascended the steps with some difficulty; " I was wounded in Canada, and have never yet recovered. I shall probably be better a few minutes hence."

There was something of half simplicity in the careless way the words were uttered that hushed the multitude, and already some expressions of sympathy were heard; but as quickly the ribald insults of the hired ruffians of the Convention drowned these sounds, and " Down with the Royalist" resounded on every side, while two officials assisted him to remove his stock and bare his throat. The Commissary, advancing to the edge of the platform, and, as it were, addressing the people, read in a hurried, slurring kind of voice, something that purported to be the ground of the condemnation. But of this not a word could be heard. None cared to hear the ten-thousand-time told tale of suspected Royalism, nor would listen to the high-sounding declamation that proclaimed the virtuous zeal of the Government—their untiring energy—their glorious persistence in the cause of the people. The last words were as usual responded to with an echoing shout, and the cry of " Vive la Republique " rose from the great multitude.

" Vive le Roi!" cried the old man, with a voice heard high above the clamour; but the words were scarce out when the lips that muttered them were closed in death ; so sudden was the act, that a cry burst forth from the

mob, but whether in reprobation or in ecstacy I knew
not.

I will not follow the sad catalogue, wherein nobles, and
peasants, priests, soldiers, actors, men of obscure fortune,
and women of lofty station, succeeded each other, occupying for a brief minute every eye, and passing away for
ever. Many ascended the platform without a word; some
waved a farewell towards a distant quarter, where they
suspected a friend to be; others spent their last moments
in prayer, and died in the very act of supplication. All
bore themselves with a noble and proud courage; and
now some five or six alone remained of whose fate none
seemed to guess the issue, since they had been taken from
the Temple by some mistake, and were not included in
the list of the Commissary. There they sat, at the foot
of the scaffold, speechless and stupified—they looked as
though it were matter of indifference to which side their
steps should turn—to the gaol or the guillotine. Among
these was the Marquise, who alone preserved her proud
self-possession, and sat in all her accustomed dignity;
while close beside her an angry controversy was maintained as to their future destiny—the Commissary firmly
refusing to receive them for execution, and the Delegate
of the Temple, as he was styled, as flatly asserting that
he would not reconduct them to prison. The populace
soon grew interested in the dispute, and the most violent
altercations arose among the partisans of each side of the
question.

Meanwhile the Commissary and his assistants prepared
to depart. Already the massive drapery of red cloth was
drawn over the guillotine, and every preparation made for
withdrawing, when the mob, doubtless dissatisfied that
they should be defrauded of any portion of the entertainment, began to climb over the wooden barricades, and,
with furious cries and shouts, threaten vengeance upon
any who would screen the enemies of the people.

The troops resisted the movement, but rather with the
air of men entreating calmness, than with the spirit of
soldiery. It was plain to see on which side the true force
lay.

"If you will not do it, the people will do it for you,"
whispered the Delegate to the Commissary; "and who is
to say where they will stop when their hands once learn
the trick!"

The Commissary grew lividly pale, and made no reply.
"See there!" rejoined the other—"they are carrying a

fellow on their shoulders yonder—they mean him to be the executioner."

" But I dare not—I cannot—without my orders."

" Are not the people sovereign?—whose will have we sworn to obey but theirs?"

" My own head would be the penalty if I yielded."

" It will be, if you resist—even now it is too late."

And as he spoke he sprang from the scaffold, and disappeared in the dense crowd that already thronged the space within the rails.

By this time the populace were not only masters of the area around, but had also gained the scaffold itself, from which many of them seemed endeavouring to harangue the mob ; others contenting themselves with imitating the gestures of the Commissary and his functionaries. It was a scene of the wildest uproar and confusion—frantic cries and screams, ribald songs and fiendish yellings on every side. The guillotine was again uncovered, and the great crimson drapery, torn into fragments, was waved about like flags, or twisted into uncouth head-dresses. The Commissary, failing in every attempt to restore order peaceably, and either not possessing a sufficient force, or distrusting the temper of the soldiers, descended from the scaffold, and gave the order to march. This act of submission was hailed by the mob with the most furious yell of triumph. Up to that very moment they had never credited the bare possibility of a victory; and now they saw themselves suddenly masters of the field—the troops, in all the array of horse and foot, retiring in discomfiture. Their exultation knew no bounds; and, doubtless, had there been amongst them those with skill and daring to profit by the enthusiasm, the torrent had rushed a longer and more terrific course than through the blood-steeped clay of the Place de la Grêve.

" Here is the man we want," shouted a deep voice. " St. Just told us t'other day that the occasion never failed to produce one; and see, here is ' Jean Gougon ;' and though he's but two feet high, his fingers can reach the pin of the guillotine."

And he held aloft on his shoulders a mis-shapen dwarf, who was well-known on the Pont Neuf, where he gained his living by singing infamous songs, and performing mockeries of the service of the mass. A cheer of welcome acknowledged this speech, to which the dwarf responded by a mock benediction, which he bestowed with all the ceremonious observance of an archbishop. Shouts of the wildest laughter followed this ribaldry, and in a

kind of triumph they carried him up the steps, and depo·
sited him on the scaffold.

Ascending one of the chairs, the little wretch proceeded
to address the mob, which he did with all the ease and
composure of a practised public speaker. Not a murmur
was heard in that tumultuous assemblage, as he, with a
most admirable imitation of Hebert, then the popular idol,
assured them that France was, at that instant, the envy of
surrounding nations ; and that, bating certain little weak-
nesses on the score of humanity—certain traits of softness
and over-mercy—her citizens realised all that ever had
been said of angels. From thence he passed on to a
mimicry of Marat, of Danton, and of Robespierre—tearing off his cravat, baring his breast, and performing all
the oft-exhibited antics of the latter, as he vociferated, in
a wild scream, the well-known peroration of a speech he
had lately made—"If we look for a glorious morrow of
freedom, the sun of our slavery must set in blood!"

However amused by the dwarf's exhibition, a feeling
of impatience began to manifest itself among the mob,
who felt that, by any longer delay, it was possible time
would be given for fresh troops to arrive, and the glorious
opportunity of popular sovereignty be lost in the very
hour of victory.

"To work—to work, Master Gougon!" shouted hundreds of rude voices ; "we cannot spend our day in listening to oratory."

"You forget, my dear friends," said he, blandly, "that
this is to me a new walk in life. I have much to learn,
ere I can acquit myself worthily to the Republic."

"We have no leisure for preparatory studies, Gougon,"
cried a fellow below the scaffold.

"Let me, then, just begin with monsieur," said the
dwarf, pointing to the last speaker, and a shout of laughter
closed the sentence.

A brief and angry dispute now arose as to what was to
be done, and it is more than doubtful how the debate might
have ended, when Gougon, with a readiness all his own,
concluded the discussion by saying—

"I have it, citizens, I have it. There is a lady here,
who, however respectable her family and connections, will
leave few to mourn her loss. She is, in a manner, public
property, and if not born on the soil, at least a naturalised
Frenchwoman. We have done a great deal for her, and
in her name, for some time back, and I am not aware of
any singular benefit she has rendered us. With your permission, then, I'll begin with her."

" Name, name—name her !" was cried by thousands.

" La voila," said he, archly, as he pointed with his thumb to the wooden effigy of Liberty above his head.

The absurdity of the suggestion was more than enough for its success. A dozen hands were speedily at work, and down came the Goddess of Liberty! The other details of an execution were hurried over with all the speed of practised address, and the figure was placed beneath the drop. Down fell the axe, and Gougon, lifting up the wooden head, paraded it about the scaffold, crying—

" Behold! an enemy of France. Long live the Republic, one and 'indivisible.'"

Loud and wild were the shouts of laughter from this brutal mockery; and for a time it almost seemed as if the ribaldry had turned the mob from the sterner passions of their vengeance. This hope, if one there ever cherished it, was short-lived; and again the cry arose for blood. It was too plain that no momentary diversion, no passing distraction, could withdraw them from that lust for cruelty that had now grown into a passion.

And now a bustle and movement of those around the stairs showed that something was in preparation ; and in the next moment the old Marquise was led forward between two men.

" Where is the order for this woman's execution ?" asked the dwarf, mimicking the style and air of the Commissary.

" We give it : it is from us !" shouted the mob, with one savage roar.

Gougon removed his cap, and bowed a token of obedience.

" Let us proceed in order, citizens," said he, gravely ; " I see no priest here."

" Shrive her yourself, Gougon ; few know the mummeries better !" cried a voice.

" Is there not one here can remember a prayer, or even a verse of the offices," said Gougon, with a well-affected horror in his voice.

" Yes, yes, I do," cried I, my zeal overcoming all sense of the mockery in which the words were spoken ; " I know them all by heart, and can repeat them from 'lux beatissima' down to 'hora mortis ;'" and as if to gain credence for my self-laudation, I began at once to recite, in the sing-song tone of the seminary—

" Salve, mater salvatoris,
Fons salutis, vas honoris;
Scala cœli, porta et via,
Salve semper, O, Maria !"

It is possible I should have gone on to the very end, if the uproarious laughter which rung around had not stopped me.

" There's a brave youth !" cried Gougon, pointing towards me, with mock admiration. " If it ever come to pass—as what may not in. these strange times?—that we turn to priestcraft again, thou shalt be the first archbishop of Paris. Who taught thee that famous canticle ? "

" The Pére Michel," replied I, in no way conscious of the ridicule bestowed upon me ; " the Pére Michel of St. Blois."

The old lady lifted up her head at these words, and her dark eyes rested steadily upon me ; and then, with a sign of her hand, she motioned to me to come over to her.

" Yes ; let him come," said Gougon, as if answering the half-reluctant glances of the crowd. And now I was assisted to descend, and passed along over the heads of the people, till I was placed upon the scaffold. Never can I forget the terror of that moment, as I stood within a few feet of the terrible guillotine, and saw beside me the horrid basket splashed with recent blood.

" Look not at these things, child," said the old lady, as she took my hand and drew me towards her, " but listen to me, and mark my words well."

" I will, I will," cried I, as the hot tears rolled down my cheeks.

" Tell the Pére—you will see him to-night—tell him that I have changed my mind, and resolved upon another course, and that he is not to leave Paris. Let them remain. The torrent runs too rapidly to last. This cannot endure much longer. We shall be among the last victims. You hear me, child ? "

" I do, I do," cried I, sobbing. " Why is not the Pére Michel with you now ? "

" Because he is suing for my pardon—asking for mercy where its very name is a derision. Kneel down beside me, and repeat the ' angelus.' "

I took off my cap, and knelt down at her feet, reciting, in a voice broken by emotion, the words of the prayer. She repeated each syllable after me, in a tone full and unshaken, and then stooping, she took up the lily which lay in my cap. She pressed it to her lips two or three times passionately. "Give it to *her;* tell her I kissed it at my last moment. Tell her——"

"This 'shrift' is beyond endurance. Away, holy father," cried Gougon, as he pushed me rudely back, and seized the Marquise by the wrist. A faint cry escaped her. I heard no more ; for jostled and pushed about by the crowd, I was driven to the very rails of the scaffold. Stepping beneath these, I mingled with the mob beneath ; and burning with eagerness to escape a scene, to have witnessed which would almost have made my heart break, I forced my way into the dense mass, and, by squeezing and creeping, succeeded at last in penetrating to the verge of the Place. A terrible shout, and a rocking motion of the mob, like the heavy surging of the sea, told me that all was over; but I never looked back to the fatal spot, but naving gained the open streets, ran at the top of my speed towards home.

CHAPTER II.

THE RESTAURANT "AU SCELERAT."

As I gained the street, at a distance from the "Place," I was able to increase my speed ; and I did so with an eagerness as if the world depended on my haste. At any other time I would have bethought me of my disobedience to the Pére's commands, and looked forward to meeting him with shame and sorrow, but now I felt a kind of importance in the charge entrusted to me. I regarded my mission as something superior to any petty consideration of self, while the very proximity in which I had stood to peril and death made me seem a hero in my own eyes.

At last I reached the street where we lived, and, almost breathless with exertion, gained the door. What was my amazement, however, to find it guarded by a sentry, a large, solemn-looking fellow, with a tattered cocked hat on his head, and a pair of worn striped trousers on his legs, who cried out, as I appeared, "Halte la!" in a voice that at once arrested my steps.

"Where to, youngster?" said he, in a somewhat melted tone, seeing the shock his first words had caused me.

"I am going home, sir," said I, submissively; "I live at the third story, in the apartment of the Pére Michel."

"The Pére Michel will live there no longer, my boy; his apartment is now in the Temple," said he, slowly.

"In the Temple!" said I, whose memory at once re-called my father's fate; and then, unable to control my feelings, I sat down upon the steps and burst into tears.

"There, there, child, you must not cry thus," said he; "these are not days when one should weep over misfor-tunes; they come too fast and too thick on all of us for that. The Pére was your tutor, I suppose?"

I nodded.

"And your father—where is he?"

"Dead."

He made a sign to imitate the guillotine, and I assented by another nod.

"Was he a Royalist, boy?"

"He was an officer in the Garde du Corps," said I, proudly. The soldier shook his head mournfully, hut with what meaning I know not.

"And your mother, boy?"

"I do not know where she is," said I, again relapsing into tears at the thought of my utter desolation. The old soldier leaned upon his musket in profound thought, and for some time did not utter a word. At last he said,—

"There is nothing but the Hotel de Ville for you, my child. They say that the Republic adopts all the orphans of France. What she does with them I cannot tell."

"But I can, though," replied I, fiercely; "the Noyades or the Seine are a quick and sure provision; I saw eighty drowned one morning below the Pont Neuf myself."

"That tongue of yours will bring you into trouble, youngster," said he, reprovingly; "mind that you say not such things as these."

"What worse fortune can betide me than to see my father die at the guillotine, and my last, my only friend, carried away to prison?"

"You have no care for your own neck, then?"

"Why should I—what value has life for me?"

"Then it will be spared to you," said he, sententiously; "mark my words, lad. You need never fear death till you begin to love life. Get up, my poor boy; you must not be found there when the relief comes, and that will be soon. This is all that I have," said he, placing three sous in my palm, "which will buy a loaf; to-morrow there may be better luck in store for you."

I shook the rough hand he offered with cordial gratitude, and resolved to bear myself as like a man as I could. I drew myself up, touched my cap in soldier-like fashion, and cried out, adieu; and then, descending into the street

hurried away to hide the tears that were almost suffo-
cating me.

Hour after hour I walked the streets; the mere act of
motion seemed to divert my grief, and it was only when
foot-sore and weary, that I could march no longer, and my
sorrows came back in full force, and overwhelmed me in
their flow. It was less pride or shame than a sense of my
utter helplessness, that prevented me addressing any one
of the hundreds who passed me. I bethought me of my
inability to do anything for my own support, and it was
this consciousness that served to weigh me down more than
all else; and yet I felt with what devotion I could serve
him who would but treat me with the kindness he might
bestow upon his dog; I fancied with what zeal I could
descend to very slavery for one word of affection. The
streets were crowded with people, groups were gathered
here and there, either listening to some mob orator of the
day, or hearing the newspapers read aloud. I tried, by
forcing my way into the crowd, to feel myself "one of
them," and to think that I had my share of interest in
what was going forward, but in vain. Of the topics discussed I knew nothing, and of the bystanders none even
noticed me. High-swelling phrases met the ear at every
moment, that sounded strangely enough to me. They
spoke of Fraternity—of that brotherhood which linked
man to man in close affection; of Equality—that made all
sharers in this world's goods; of Liberty—that gave freedom to every noble aspiration and generous thought; and
for an instant, carried away by the glorious illusion, I even
forgot my solitary condition, and felt proud of my heritage
as a youth of France. I looked around me, however, and
what faces met my gaze! The same fearful countenances
I had seen around the scaffold—the wretches, blood stained,
and influenced by passion—their bloated checks and
strained eye-balls glowing with intemperance—their oaths,
their gestures—their very voices having something terrible
in them. The mockery soon disgusted me, and I moved
away, again to wander about without object or direction
through the weary streets. It was past midnight when I
found myself, without knowing where I was, in a large
open space, in the midst of which a solitary lamp was
burning. I approached it and, to my horror, saw that it
was the guillotine, over which in mournful cadence a
lantern swung, creaking its chain as the night wind stirred
it. The dim outline of the fearful scaffold, the fitful light
that fell upon the platform, and the silence—all conspired
to strike terror into my heart; all I had so lately witnessed

seemed to rise up again before me, and the victims seemed
to stand up again, pale, and livid, and shuddering, as last
I saw them.

I knelt down and tried to pray, but terror was too
powerful to suffer my thoughts to take this direction, and,
half fainting with fear and exhaustion, I lay down upon
the ground and slept—slept beneath the platform of the
guillotine. Not a dream crossed my slumber, nor did I
awake till dawn of day, when the low rumbling of the
peasants' carts aroused me, as they were proceeding to the
market. I know not why or whence, but I arose from the
damp earth, and looked about me with a more daring and
courageous spirit than I had hitherto felt. It was May—
the first bright rays of sunshine were slanting along the
"Place," and the fresh, brisk air felt invigorating and
cheering. Whither to? asked I of myself, and my eyes
turned from the dense streets and thoroughfares of the
great city to the far-off hills beyond the barrier, and for a
moment I hesitated which road to take. I almost seemed
to feel as if the decision involved my whole future fortune
—whether I should live and die in the humble condition
of a peasant, or play for a great stake in life. Yes, said I,
after a short hesitation, I will remain here—in the terrible
conflict going forward, many must be new adventurers,
and never was any one more greedy to learn the trade
than myself. I will throw sorrow behind me. Yesterday's
tears are the last I shall shed. Now for a bold heart and
a ready will, and here goes for the world! With these
stout words I placed my cap jauntily on one side of my
head, and with a fearless air marched off for the very
centre of the city.

For some hours I amused myself gazing at the splendid
shops, or staring in at the richly-decorated cafés, where
the young celebrities of the day were assembled at breakfast, in all the extravagance of the new-fangled costume.
Then I followed the Guard to the parade at the "Carousel," and listened to the band, quitting which I wandered
along the quays, watching the boats as they dragged the
river in search of murdered bodies or suicides. Thence
I returned to the Palais Royal and listened to the news of
the day, as read out by some elected enlightener of his
countrymen.

By what chance I know not, but at last my rambling
steps brought me opposite to the great solemn-looking
towers of the "Temple." The gloomy prison, within whose
walls hundreds were then awaiting the fate which already
their friends had suffered—little groups, gathered here and

there in the open Place, were communicating to the prisoners by signs and gestures, and from many a small-grated window, at an immense height, handkerchiefs were seen to wave in recognition of those below. These signals seemed to excite neither watchfulness nor prevention—indeed, they needed none; and perhaps the very suspense they excited was a torture that pleased the inhuman gaolers. Whatever the reason, the custom was tolerated, and was apparently enjoyed at that moment by several of the turn-keys, who sat at the windows, much amused at the efforts made to communicate. Interested by the sight, I sat down upon a stone bench to watch the scene, and fancied that I could read something of the rank and condition of those who signalled from below their messages of hope or fear. At last a deep bell within the prison tolled the hour of noon; and now every window was suddenly deserted. It was the hour for the muster of the prisoners, which always took place before the dinner at one o'clock. The curious groups soon after broke up. A few lingered around the gate, with, perhaps, some hope of admission to visit their friends; but the greater number departed.

My hunger was now such that I could no longer deny myself the long-promised meal, and I looked about me for a shop where I might buy a loaf of bread. In my search, I suddenly found myself opposite an immense shop, where viands of every tempting description were ranged with all that artistic skill so purely Parisian, making up a picture whose composition Snyders would not have despised. Over the door was a painting of a miserable wretch, with hands bound behind him, and his hair cut close in the well-known crop for the scaffold; and underneath was written, " Au Scélérat;" while on a larger board, in gilt letters, ran the inscription :—

"Boivin Pére et fils, Traiteurs pour M. les Condamnées."

I could scarcely credit my eyes, as I read and re-read this infamous announcement; but there it stood, and in the crowd that poured incessantly to and from the door, I saw the success that attended the traffic. A ragged knot were gathered around the window, eagerly gazing at something, which, by their exclamations, seemed to claim all their admiration. I pressed forward to see what it was, and beheld a miniature guillotine, which, turned by a wheel, was employed to chop the meat for sausages. This it was that formed the great object of attraction, even to those to whom the prototype had grown flat and uninteresting.

Disgusted as I was by this shocking sight, I stood watch-

ing all that went forward within with a strange interest. It
was a scene of incessant bustle and movement; for now,
as one o'clock drew nigh, various dinners were getting
ready for the prisoners; while parties of their friends were
assembling inside. Of these latter there seemed persons
of every rank and condition; some, dressed in all the
brilliancy of the mode; others, whose garments bespoke
direst poverty. There were women, too, whose costume
emulated the classic drapery of the ancients, and who displayed, in their looped togas, no niggard share of their
forms; while others, in shabby mourning, sat in obscure
corners, not noticing the scene before them, nor noticed
themselves. A strange equipage, with two horses extra-
vagantly bedizened with rosettes and bouquets, stood at
the door; and as I looked, a pale, haggard-looking man,
whose foppery in dress contrasted oddly with his care-
worn expression, hurried from the shop, and sprung into
the carriage. In doing so, a pocket-book fell from his
pocket. I took it up; but as I did so, the carriage was
already away, and far beyond my power to overtake it.

Without stopping to examine my prize, or hesitating for
a second, I entered the restaurant, and asked for M. Boivin.

"Give your orders to *me*, boy," said a man busily at
work behind the counter.

"My business is with himself," said I, stoutly.

"Then you'll have to wait with some patience," said he,
sneeringly.

"I can do so," was my answer, and I sat down in the
shop.

"I might have been half-an-hour thus seated, when an
enormously fat man, with a huge "bonnet rouge" on his
head, entered from an inner room, and passing close to
where I was, caught sight of me.

"Who are you, sirrah—what brings you here?"

"I want to speak with M. Boivin."

"Then speak," said he, placing his hand upon his
immense chest.

"It must be alone," said I.

"How so, alone, sirrah?" said he, growing suddenly
pale; "I have no secrets—I know of nothing that may
not be told before all the world."

Though he said this in a kind of appeal to all around,
the dubious looks and glances interchanged seemed to
make him far from comfortable.

"So you refuse me, then?" said I, taking up my cap,
and preparing to depart.

" Come hither," said he, leading the way into the room from which he had emerged. It was a very small chamber; the most conspicuous ornaments of which were busts and pictures of the various celebrities of the Revolution. Some of these latter were framed ostentatiously, and one, occupying the post of honour above the chimney, at once attracted me, for in a glance I saw that it was a portrait of him who owned the pocket-book, and bore beneath it the name "Robespierre."

" Now, sir, for your communication," said Boivin; " and take care that it is of sufficient importance to warrant the interview you have asked for."

" I have no fears on that score," said I, calmly, still scanning the features of the portrait, and satisfying myself of their identity.

" Look at me, sir, and not at that picture," said Boivin.

" And yet it is of M. Robespierre I have to speak," said I, coolly.

" How so—of M. Robespierre, boy? What is the meaning of this? If it be a snare—if this be a trick, you never leave this spot living," cried he, as he placed a massive hand on each of my shoulders and shook me violently.

" I am not so easily to be terrified, Citoyen," said I; " nor have I any secret cause for fear, whatever you may have. My business is of another kind. This morning, in passing out to his carriage, he dropped his pocket-book, which I picked up. Its contents may well be of a kind that should not be read by other eyes than his own. My request is, then, that you will seal it up before me, and then send some one along with me, while I restore it to its owner."

" Is this a snare—what secret mischief have we here?" said Boivin, half aloud, as he wiped the cold drops of perspiration from his forehead.

" Any mishap that follows will depend upon your refusal to do what I ask."

" How so—I never refused it; you dare not tell M. Robespierre that I refused, sirrah?"

" I will tell him nothing that is untrue," said I, calmly; for already a sense of power had gifted me with composure. " If M. Robespierre——"

" Who speaks of me here?" cried the identical personage, as he dashed hurriedly into the room, and then, not waiting for the reply, went on—" You must send out your scouts on every side—I lost my pocket-book as I left this a while ago."

"It is here, sir," said I, presenting it at once.

"How—where was it found—in whose keeping has it been, boy?"

"In mine only; I took it from the ground the same moment that you dropped it, and then came here to place it in M. Boivin's hands."

"Who has taken care of it since that time?" continued Robespierre, with a slow and sneering accentuation on every word.

"The pocket-book has never left my possession since it quitted yours," was my reply.

"Just so," broke in Boivin, now slowly recovering from his terror. "Of its contents I know nothing; nor have I sought to know anything."

Robespierre looked at me as if to corroborate this statement, and I nodded my head in acquiescence.

"Who is your father, boy?"

"I have none—he was guillotined."

"His name?"

"Tiernay."

"Ah, I remember; he was called L'Irlandais."

"The same."

"A famous Royalist was that same Tiernay, and, doubtless, contrived to leave a heritage of his opinions to his son."

"He left me nothing—I have neither house, nor home, nor even bread to eat."

"But you have a head to plan, and a heart to feel, youngster; and it is better that fellows like you should not want a dinner. Boivin, look to it that he is taken care of. In a few days I will relieve you of the charge. You will remain here, boy; there are worse resting-places, I promise you. There are men who call themselves teachers of the people, who would ask no better life than free quarters on Boivin. And so saying, he hurriedly withdrew, leaving me face to face with my host.

"So then, youngster," said Boivin, as he scratched his ear thoughtfully, "I have gained a pensioner! Parbleu! if life were not an uncertain thing in these times, there's no saying how long we might not be blessed with your amiable company."

"You shall not be burthened heavily, Citoyen," said I; "let me have my dinner—I have not eaten since yesterday morning, and I will go my ways peacefully."

"Which means straight to Robespierre's dwelling, to tell him that I have turned you out of doors—eh, sirrah?"

"You mistake me much," said I; "this would be sorry gratitude for eaten bread. I meant what I said—that I will not be an unwelcome guest, even though the alternative be, as it is, something very nigh starvation."

Boivin did not seem clearly to comprehend the meaning of what I said; or perhaps my whole conduct and bearing puzzled him, for he made no reply for several seconds. At last, with a kind of sigh, he said,—

"Well, well, it cannot be helped; it must be even as he wished, though the odds are he'll never think more about him. Come, lad, you shall have your dinner."

I followed him through a narrow, unlighted passage, which opened into a room, where, at a long table, were seated a number of men and boys at dinner. Some were dressed as cooks; others wore a kind of grey blouse, with a badge upon the arm, bearing the name "Boivin" in large letters, and were, as I afterwards learned, the messengers employed to carry refreshments into the prison, and who, by virtue of this sign, were freely admitted within the gates.

Taking my place at the board, I proceeded to eat with a voracity that only a long fast could have excused; and thus took but little heed of my companions, whose solecisms in table etiquette might otherwise have amused me.

"Ar't a Marmiton, thou?" asked an elderly man in a cook's cap, as he stared fixedly at me for some seconds.

"No," said I, helping myself, and eating away as before.

"Thou can'st never be a commissionaire, friend, with an appetite like that," cried another; "I wouldn't trust thee to carry a casserole to the fire."

"Nor shall I be," said I, coolly.

"What trade, then, has the good fortune to possess your shining abilities?"

"A trade that thrives well just now, friend—pass me the flask."

"Indeed, and what may it be?"

"Can you not guess, Citoyen," said I, "if I tell you that it was never more in vogue; and, if there be some who will not follow it, they'll wear their heads just as safely by holding their peace?"

"Parbleu! thou hast puzzled me," said the chief cook; "and if thou be'st not a coffin-maker——" A roar of merriment cut short his speech, in which I myself could not but join heartily?

"That is, I know," said I, "a thriving business; but

3

mine is even better ; and, not to mystify you longer, I'll
just tell you what I am ; which is, simply, a friend of the
Citoyen Robespierre."

The blow told with full force ; and I saw, in the terrified
looks that were interchanged around the table, that my
sojourn amongst them, whether destined to be of short or
long duration, would not be disturbed by further liberties.
It was truly a reign of terror that same period! The
great agent of everything was the vague and shadowy
dread of some terrible vengeance, against which precautions were all in vain. Men met each other with
secret misgivings, and parted with the same dreadful distrust. The ties of kindred were all broken; brotherly
affection died out. Existence was become like the struggle
for life upon some shipwrecked raft, where each sought
safety by his neighbour's doom! At such a time—with
such terrible teachings—children became men in all the
sterner features of character ; cruelty is a lesson so easily
learned.

As for myself, energetic and ambitious by nature, the
ascendancy my first assumption of power suggested was too
grateful a passion to be relinquished. The name—whose
spell was like a talisman, because now the secret engine
by which I determined to work out my fortune—Robespierre had become to my imagination like the slave of
Aladdin's lamp; and to conjure him up was to be all-
powerful. Even to Boivin himself this influence extended;
and it was easy to perceive that he regarded the whole
narrative of the pocket-book as a mere fable, invented to
obtain a position as a spy over his household.

I was not unwilling to encourage the belief—it added to
my importance, by increasing the fear I inspired ; and
thus I walked indolently about, giving myself those airs of
" mouchard " that I deemed most fitting, and taking a
mischievous delight in the terror I was inspiring.

The indolence of my life, however, soon wearied me,
and I began to long for some occupation, or some pursuit.
Teeming with excitement as the world was—every day,
every hour, brimful of events—it was impossible to sit
calmly on the beach, and watch the great, foaming current
of human passions, without longing to be in the stream.
Had I been a man at that time, I should have become a
furious orator of the Mountain—an impassioned leader of
the people. The impulse to stand foremost—to take a
bold and prominent position—would have carried me to
any lengths. I had caught up enough of the horrid fana-
ticism of the time to think that there was something

grand and heroic in contempt for human suffering; that a man rose proudly above all the weakness of his nature, when, in the pursuit of some great object, he stifled within his breast every throb of affection—every sentiment of kindness and mercy. Such were the teachings rife at the time—such the first lessons that boyhood learned; and oh! what a terrible hour had that been for humanity if the generation then born had grown up to manhood unchastened and unconverted!

But to return to my daily life. As I perceived that a week had now elapsed, and the Citizen Robespierre had not revisited the "restaurant," nor taken any interest in my fate or fortunes, I began to fear lest Boivin should master his terror regarding me, and take heart to put me out of doors—an event which, in my present incertitude, would have been sorely inconvenient. I resolved, therefore, to practise a petty deception on my host, to sustain the influence of terror over him. This was, to absent myself every day at a certain hour, under the pretence of visiting my patron; letting fall, from time to time, certain indications to show in what part of the city I had been, and occasionally, as if in an unguarded moment, condescending to relate some piece of popular gossip. None ventured to inquire the source of my information—not one dared to impugn its veracity. Whatever their misgivings in secret, to myself they displayed the most credulous faith. Nor was their trust so much misplaced, for I had, in reality, become a perfect chronicle of all that went forward in Paris—never missing a debate in the Convention, where my retentive memory could carry away almost verbally all that I heard—ever present at every public fête or procession, whether the occasions were some insulting desecration of their former faith, or some tasteless mockery of heathen ceremonial.

My powers of mimicry, too, enabled me to imitate all the famous characters of the period; and in my assumed inviolability, I used to exhibit the uncouth gestures and spluttering utterance of Marat—the wild and terrible ravings of Danton—and even the reedy treble of my own patron, Robespierre, as he screamed denunciations against the enemies of the people. It is true these exhibitions of mine were only given in secret to certain parties, who, by a kind of instinct, I felt could be trusted.

Such was my life, as one day, returning from the Convention, I beheld a man affixing to a wall a great placard, to which the passing crowd seemed to pay deep attention. It was a decree of the Committee of Public Safety, containing the names of above seven hundred Royalists, who were condemned to death, and who were to be executed in three "tournées," on three successive days.

For some time back the mob had not been gratified with a spectacle of this nature. In the ribald language of the day, the "holy guillotine had grown thirsty from long drought;" and they read the announcement with greedy eyes, commenting as they went upon those whose names were familiar to them. There were many of noble birth among the proscribed, but by far the greater number were priests, the whole sum of whose offending seemed written in the simple and touching words, "ancien Curé," of such a parish! It was strange to mark the bitterness of invective with which the people loaded these poor and innocent men, as though they were the source of all their misfortunes. The lazy indolence with which they reproached them seemed ten times more offensive in their eyes than the lives of ease and affluence led by the nobility. The fact was, they could not forgive men of their own rank and condition what they pardoned in the well-born and the noble! an inconsistency that has characterised democracy in other situations beside this.

As I ran my eyes down the list of those confined in the Temple, I came to a name which smote my heart with a pang of ingratitude as well as sorrow—the "Pére Michel Delannois, soi disant curé de St. Blois"—my poor friend and protector was there among the doomed! If, up to that moment, I had made no effort to see him, I must own the reason lay in my own selfish feeling of shame—the dread that he should mark the change that had taken place in me, a change that I felt extended to all about me, and showed itself in my manner as it influenced my every action. It was not alone that I lost the obedient air and quiet submissiveness of the child, but I had assumed the very extravagance of that democratic insolence which was the mode among the leading characters of the time.

How should I present myself before him, the very impersonation of all the vices against which he used to warn me—how exhibit the utter failure of all his teachings and his hopes? What would this be but to embitter his reflections needlessly. Such were the specious reasons with which I fed my self-love, and satisfied my conscience; but now, as I read his name in that terrible catalogue, their plausibility served me no longer, and at last I forgot myself to remember only him.

"I will see him at once," thought I, "whatever it may cost me—I will stay beside him for his last few hours of

life; and when he carries with him from this world many
an evil memory of shame and treachery, ingratitude from
me shall not increase the burthen." And with this resolve
I turned my steps homeward.

CHAPTER III.

THE "TEMPLE."

At the time of which I write, there was but one motive
principle throughout France—"TERROR." By the agency
of terror and the threat of denunciation was everything
carried on, not only in the public departments of the state,
but in all the common occurrences of every-day life.
Fathers used it towards their children—children towards
their parents; mothers coerced their daughters—daughters, in turn, braved the authority of their mothers. The
tribunal of public opinion, open to all, scattered its decrees
with a reckless cruelty—denying to-day what it had decreed but yesterday, and at last obliterating every trace of
"right" or "principle," in a people who now only lived
for the passing hour, and who had no faith in the future,
even of this world.

Among the very children at play, this horrible doctrine
had gained a footing: the tyrant urchin, whose ingenuity
enabled him to terrorize, became the master of his play-
fellows. I was not slow in acquiring the popular education
of the period, and soon learned that fear was a "Bank"
on which one might draw at will. Already the domineer-
ing habit had given to my air and manner all the insolence
of seeming power, and, while a mere boy in years, I was
a man in all the easy assumption of a certain importance.

It was with a bold and resolute air I entered the restaurant, and calling Boivin aside, said,—

"I have business in the Temple this morning, Boivin;
see to it that I shall not be denied admittance."

"I am not governor of the gaol," grunted Boivin,
sulkily, "nor have I the privilege to pass any one."

"But your boys have the entrée; the 'rats' (so were
they called) are free to pass in and out."

"Ay, and I'm responsible for the young rascals, too, and
or anything that may be laid to their charge."

"And you shall extend this same protection to me,
Master Boivin, for one day, at least—nay, my good friend,
there's no use in sulking about it. A certain friend of

ours, whose name I need not speak aloud, is little in the
habit of being denied anything: are you prepared for the
consequence of disobeying his orders?"

"Let me see that they are his orders," said he, sturdily
—"who tells me that such is his will?"

"I do," was my brief reply, as, with a look of consummate effrontery, I drew myself up and stared him insolently in the face.

"Suppose, then, that I have my doubts on the matter—
suppose——"

"I will suppose all you wish, Boivin," said I, interrupting, "and even something more; for I will suppose myself
returning to the quarter whence I have just come, and
within one hour—ay, within one hour, Boivin—bringing
back with me a written order, not to pass me into the
Temple, but to receive the body of the Citizen Jean
Baptiste Boivin, and be accountable for the same to the
Committee of Public Safety."

He trembled from head to foot as I said these words,
and in his shaking cheeks and fallen jaw I saw that my
spell was working.

"And now, I ask for the last time, do you consent or
not?"

"How is it to be done?" cried he, in a voice of downright wretchedness. "You are not 'inscribed' at the
sécretaries' office as one of the 'rats.'"

"I should hope not," said I, cutting him short; "but I
may take the place of one for an hour or so. Tristan is
about my own size; his blouse and badge will just suit me."

"Ay, leave me to a fine of a thousand francs if you
should be found out," muttered Boivin, "not to speak of a
worse mayhap."

"Exactly so—far worse in case of your refusing; but
there sounds the bell for mustering the prisoners—it is
now too late."

"Not so—not so," cried Boivin, eagerly, as he saw me
prepared to leave the house. "You shall go in Tristan's
place. Send him here, that he may tell you everything
about the 'service,' and give you his blouse and badge."

I was not slow in availing myself of the permission, nor
was Tristan sorry to find a substitute. He was a dull,
depressed-looking boy, not over communicative as to his
functions, merely telling me that I was to follow the others
—that I came fourth in the line—to answer when my name
was called "Tristan," and to put the money I received in
my leathern pocket, without uttering a word, lest the
gaolers should notice it.

To accoutre myself in the white cotton nightcap and the blouse of the craft was the work of a few seconds; and then, with a great knife in my girdle, and a capacious pocket slung at my side, I looked every inch a "Marmiton."

In the kitchen the bustle had already begun, and half-a-dozen cooks, with as many under-cooks, were dealing out "portions" with all the speed of a well practised performance. Nothing short of great habit could have prevented the confusion degenerating into downright anarchy. The "service" was, indeed, effected with a wonderful rapidity; and certain phrases, uttered with speed, showed how it progressed. "Maigre des Curés,"—"finished." "Bouillon for the 'expectants,'"—"ready here." "Canards aux olives des condamnées,"—"all served." "Red partridges for the reprieved at the upper table,"—"despatched." Such were the quick demands, and no less quick replies, that rung out, amidst the crash of plates, knives, and glasses, and the incessant movement of feet, until, at last, we were all marshalled in a long line, and, preceded by a drum, set out for the prison.

As we drew near, the heavy gates opened to receive, and closed behind us with a loud bang that I could not help feeling must have smote heavily on many a heart that had passed there. We were now in a large court-yard, where several doors led off, each guarded by a sentinel, whose ragged clothes and rusty accoutrements proclaimed a true soldier of the Republic. One of the large hurdles used for carrying the prisoners to the "Place" stood in one corner, and two or three workmen were busied in repairing it for the coming occasion.

So much I had time to observe, as we passed along; and now we entered a dimly-lighted corridor of great extent; Passing down which, we emerged into a second "Cour," traversed by a species of canal or river, over which a bridge led. In the middle of this was a strongly-barred iron gate, guarded by two sentries. As we arrived here, our names were called aloud by a species of turnkey; and at the call "Tristan," I advanced, and, removing the covers from the different dishes, submitted them for inspection to an old, savage-looking fellow, who, with a long steel fork, pricked the pieces of meat, as though anything could have been concealed within them. Meanwhile, another fellow examined my cotton cap and pocket, and passed his hands along my arms and body. The whole did not last more than a few minutes, and the word "forward" was given to pass on. The gloom of the place—

the silence, only broken by the heavy bang of an iron-barred door, or the clank of chains—the sad thoughts of the many who trod these corridors on their way to death—depressed me greatly, and equally unprepared me for what was to come; for as we drew near the great hall, the busy hum of voices, the sound of laughter, and the noises of a large assembly in full converse, suddenly burst upon the ear; and as the wide doors were thrown open, I beheld above a hundred people, who, either gathered in single groups, or walking up and down in parties, seemed all in the fullest enjoyment of social intercourse.

A great table, with here and there a large flagon of water, or a huge loaf of the coarse bread used by the peasantry, ran from end to end of the chamber. A few had already taken their places at this, but some were satisfied with laying a cap or a kerchief on the bench opposite their accustomed seat; while others again had retired into windows and corners, as if to escape the general gaze, and partake of their humble meal in solitude.

Whatever restrictions prison discipline might have exercised elsewhere, here the widest liberty seemed to prevail. The talk was loud, and even boisterous; the manner to the turnkeys exhibited nothing of fear: the whole assemblage presented rather the aspect of a gathering of riotous republicans than of a band of prisoners under sentence. And yet such were the greater number, and the terrible slip of paper attached to the back of each, with a date, told the day on which he was to die.

As I lingered to gaze on this strange gathering, I was admonished to move on, and now perceived that my companion had advanced to the end of the hall, by which a small flight of stone steps led out upon a terrace—at the end of which we entered another and not less spacious chamber, equally crowded and noisy. Here the company were of both sexes, and of every grade and condition of rank—from the highest noble of the once court, to the humblest peasant of La Vendée. If the sounds of mirths and levity were less frequent, the buzz of conversation was, to the full, as loud as in the lower hall, where, from difference of condition in life, the scenes passing presented stranger and more curious contrasts. In one corner a group of peasants were gathered around a white-haired priest, who, in a low but earnest voice, was uttering his last exhortation to them; in another, some young and fashionably-dressed men were exhibiting to a party of ladies the very airs and graces by which they would have adorned a saloon; here, was a party at piquet—there, a little group, arranging, for the last time, their household cares, and settling, with a few small coins, the account of mutual expenditure. Of the ladies, several were engaged at needle-work—some little preparation for the morrow—the last demand that ever vanity was to make of them!

Although there was matter of curiosity in all around me, my eyes sought for but one object, the Curé of St. Blois. Twice or thrice, from the similarity of dress, I was deceived, and at last, when I really did behold him, as he sat alone in a window, reading, I could scarcely satisfy myself of the reality. He was lividly pale, his eyes deep sunk, and surrounded with two dark circles, while along his worn cheek the tears had marked two channels of purple colour. What need of the guillotine there—the lamp of life was in its last flicker without it.

Our names were called, and the meats placed upon the table. Just as the head turnkey was about to give the order to be seated, a loud commotion, and a terrible uproar in the court beneath, drew every one to the window. It was a hurdle which, emerging from an archway, broke down from over crowding; and now the confusion of prisoners, gaolers, and sentries, with plunging horses and screaming sufferers, made a scene of the wildest uproar. Chained two by two, the prisoners were almost helpless, and in their efforts to escape injury made the most terrific struggle. Such were the instincts of life in those on the very road to death!

Resolving to profit by the moment of confusion, I hastened to the window, where alone, unmoved by the general commotion, sat the Pére Michel. He lifted his glassy eyes as I came near, and in a low, mild voice said,—

" Thanks, my good boy, but I have no money to pay thee; nor does it matter much now—it is but another day."

I could have cried as I heard these sad words; but mastering emotions which would have lost time so precious, I drew close, and whispered,—

" Pére Michel, it is I, your own Maurice."

He started, and a deep flush suffused his cheek; and then stretching out his hand, he pushed back my cap, and parted the hair of my forehead, as if doubting the reality of what he saw ; when with a weak voice he said,—

" No, no, thou art not my own Maurice. His eyes shone not with that worldly lustre—thine do; his brow was calm, and fair as children's should be—thine is marked with manhood's craft and subtlety; and yet, thou art like him."

A low sob broke from me as I listened to his words, and the tears gushed forth, and rolled in torrents down my cheeks.

"Yes," cried he, clasping me in his arms, "thou art my own dear boy. I know thee now; but how art thou here, and thus?" and he touched my "blouse" as he spoke.

"I came to see and to save you, Pére," said I. "Nay do not try to discourage me, but rather give me all your aid. I saw her—I was with her in her last moments at the guillotine; she gave me a message for you, but this you shall never hear till we are without these walls."

"It cannot be, it cannot be," said he, sorrowfully.

"It can and shall be," said I, resolutely. "I have merely assumed this dress for the occasion; I have friends, powerful and willing to protect me. Let us change robes—give me that 'soutane,' and put on the blouse. When you leave this, hasten to the old garden of the chapel, and wait for my coming—I will join you there before night."

"It cannot be," replied he again.

"Again I say, it shall, and must be. Nay, if you still refuse, there shall be two victims, for I will tear off the dress here where I stand, and openly declare myself the son of the Royalist Tiernay."

Already the commotion in the court beneath was beginning to subside, and even now the turnkeys' voices were heard in the refectory, recalling the prisoners to table,—another moment and it would have been too late: it was, then, less by persuasion than by actual force I compelled him to yield, and, pulling off his black serge gown, drew over his shoulders my yellow blouse, and placed upon his head the white cap of the "Marmiton." The look of shame and sorrow of the poor Curé would have betrayed him at once, if any had given themselves the trouble to look at him.

"And thou, my poor child," said he, as he saw me array myself in his priestly dress, "what is to be thy fate?"

"All will depend upon you, Pére Michel," said I, holding him by the arm, and trying to fix his wandering attention. "Once out of the prison, write to Boivin, the restaurateur of the 'Scélérat,' and tell him that an escaped convict has scruples for the danger into which he has brought a poor boy, one of his 'Marmitons,' and whom by a noxious drug he has lulled into insensibility, while, having exchanged clothes, he has managed his escape. Boivin will comprehend the danger he himself runs by leaving me here. All will go well—and now there's not a moment to lose. Take up your basket, and follow the others."

"But the falsehood of all this," cried the Pére.

"But your life, and mine, too, lost, if you refuse," said I, pushing him away.

"Oh, Maurice, how changed have you become!" cried he, sorrowfully.

"You will see a greater change in me yet, as I lie in the sawdust beneath the scaffold," said I, hastily. "Go, go."

There was, indeed, no more time to lose. The muster of the prisoners was forming at one end of the chamber, while the "Marmitons" were gathering up their plates and dishes, previous to departure, at the other; and it was only by the decisive step of laying myself down within the recesses of the window, in the attitude of one overcome by sleep, that I could force him to obey my direction. I could feel his presence as he bent over me, and muttered something that must have been a prayer. I could know, without seeing, that he still lingered near me, but as I never stirred, he seemed to feel that my resolve was not to be shaken, and at last he moved slowly away.

At first the noise and clamour sounded like the crash of some desperate conflict, but by degrees this subsided, and I could hear the names called aloud and the responses of the prisoners, as they were "told off" in parties from the different parts of the prison. Tender leave-takings and affectionate farewells from many who never expected to meet again, accompanied these, and the low sobs of anguish were mingled with the terrible chaos of voices; and at last I heard the name of "Michel Delannois:" I felt as if my death-summons was in the words "Michel Delannois."

"That crazy priest can neither hear nor see, I believe," said the gaoler, savagely. "Will no one answer for him?"

"He is asleep yonder in the window," replied a voice from the crowd.

"Let him sleep then," said the turnkey; "when awake he gives us no peace with his prayers and exhortations."

"He has eaten nothing for three days," observed another; "he is, perhaps, overcome by weakness more than by sleep."

"Be it so! if he only lie quiet, I care not," rejoined the gaoler, and proceeded to the next name on the list.

The monotonous roll-call, the heat, the attitude in which I was lying, all conspired to make me drowsy: even the very press of sensations that crowded to my brain lent their aid, and at last I slept as soundly as ever I had done in my bed at night. I was dreaming of the dark alleys in the wood of Belleville, where so often I had strolled of an evening with Pére Michel; I was fancying that we were gathering the fresh violets beneath the old trees, when a rude hand shook my shoulder, and I awoke. One of the turnkeys and Boivin stood over me, and I saw at once that my plan had worked well.

"Is this the fellow?" said the turnkey, pushing me rudely with his foot.

"Yes," replied Boivin, white with fear; "this is the boy; his name is Tristan." The latter words were accompanied with a look of great significance towards me.

"What care we how he is called! let us hear in what manner he came here."

"I can tell you little," said I, staring and looking wildly around; "I must have been asleep, and dreaming, too."

"The letter," whispered Boivin to the turnkey—"the letter says that he was made to inhale some poisonous drug, and that while insensible——"

"Bah," said the other, derisively, "this will not gain credit here; there has been complicity in the affair, Master Boivin. The Commissaire is not the man to believe a trumped-up tale of the sort; besides, you are well aware that you are responsible for these 'rats' of yours. It is a private arrangement between you and the Commissaire, and it is not very probable that he'll get himself into a scrape for you."

"Then what are we to do?" cried Boivin, passionately, as he wrung his hands in despair.

"I know what I should, in a like case," was the dry reply.

"And that is?——"

"Laisser aller!" was the curt rejoinder. "The young rogue has passed for a curé for the last afternoon; I'd even let him keep up the disguise a little longer, and it will be all the same by this time to-morrow."

"You'd send me to the guillotine for another?" said I, boldly; "thanks for the good intention, my friend; but Boivin knows better than to follow your counsel. Hear me one moment," said I, addressing the latter, and drawing him to one side—"if you don't liberate me within a quarter of an hour, I'll denounce you and yours to the Commissary. I know well enough what goes on at the Scélérat,—you understand me well. If a priest has really made his escape from the prison, you are not clean-handed enough to meet the accusation; see to it then, Boivin, that I may be free at once."

"Imp of Satan," exclaimed Boivin, grinding his teeth, "I have never enjoyed ease or quietness since the first hour I saw you."

"It may cost a couple of thousand francs, Boivin," said I, calmly; "but what then? Better that than take your seat along with us to-morrow in the 'Charrette rouge.'"

"Maybe he's right, after all," muttered the turnkey in a half whisper; "speak to the Commissary."

"Yes," said I, affecting an air of great innocence and simplicity—"tell him that a poor orphan boy, without friends or home, claims his pity."

"Scélérat infame!" cried Boivin, as he shook his fist at me, and then followed the turnkey to the Commissary's apartment.

In less time than I could have believed possible, Boivin returned with one of the upper gaolers, and told me, in a few dry words, that I was free. "But, mark me," added he, "we part here—come what may, you never shall plant foot within my doors again."

"Agreed," said I, gaily; "the world has other dupes as easy to play upon, and I was getting well nigh weary of you."

"Listen to the scoundrel!" muttered Boivin; "what will he say next?"

"Simply this," rejoined I—"that as these are not becoming garments for me to wear—for I'm neither 'Pére' nor 'Frére'—I must have others ere I quit this."

If the insolence of my demand occasioned some surprise at first, a little cool persistence on my part showed that compliance would be the better policy; and, after conferring together for a few minutes, during which I heard the sound of money, the turnkey retired, and came back speedily with a jacket and cap belonging to one of the drummers of the "Republican Guard"—a gaudy, tasteless affair enough, but, as a disguise, nothing could have been more perfect.

"Have you not a drum to give him?" said Boivin, with a most malignant sneer at my equipment.

"He'll make a noise in the world without that!" muttered the gaoler, half soliloquising; and the words fell upon my heart with a strange significance.

"Your blessing, Boivin," said I, "and we part."

"Le te——"

"No, no; don't curse the boy," interposed the gaoler good humouredly.

"Then, move off, youngster; I've lost too much time with you already."

The next moment I was in the "Place"—a light misty rain was falling, and the night was dark and starless; the "Scélérat" was brilliant with lamps and candles, and crowds were passing in and out, but it was no longer a home for me—so I passed on, and continued my way towards the Boulevard.

CHAPTER IV.

"THE NIGHT OF THE NINTH THERMIDOR."

I HAD agreed with the Père Michel to rendezvous at the garden of the little chapel of St. Blois, and thitherward I now turned my steps.

The success which followed this my first enterprise in life had already worked a wondrous change in all my feelings. Instead of looking up to the poor Curé for advice and guidance, I felt as though our parts were exchanged, and that it was I who was now the protector of the other. The oft-repeated sneers at "les bons Prêtres," who were good for nothing, must have had a share in this new estimate of my friend; but a certain self-reliance just then springing up in my heart, effectually completed the change.

The period was essentially one of action and not of reflection. Events seemed to fashion themselves at the will of him who had daring and courage to confront them, and they alone appeared weak and poor-spirited who would not stem the tide of fortune. Sentiments like these were not, as may be supposed, best calculated to elevate the worthy Père in my esteem, and I already began to feel how unsuited was such companionship for me, whose secret promptings whispered ever, "go forward."

The very vagueness of my hopes served but to extend the horizon of futurity before me, and I fancied a thousand situations of distinction that might yet be mine. Fame— or its poor counterfeit, notoriety—seemed the most enviable of all possessions. It mattered little by what merits it were won, for, in that fickle mood of popular opinion, great vices were as highly prized as transcendent abilities, and one might be as illustrious by crime as by genius. Such were not the teachings of the Père; but they were

the lessons that Paris dinned into my ears unceasingly.
Reputation, character, was of no avail, in a social condition where all was change and vacillation. What was
idolised one day was execrated the next. The hero of
yesterday was the object of popular vengeance to-day.
The success of the passing hour was everything.

The streets were crowded as I passed along; although a
drizzling rain was falling, groups and knots of people
were gathered together at every corner, and, by their
eager looks and gestures, showed that some event of great
moment had occurred. I stopped to ask what it meant,
and learned that Robespierre had been denounced in the
Assembly, and that his followers were hastening, in arms,
to the Place de Grêve. As yet, men spoke in whispers,
or broken phrases. Many were seen affectionately embracing and clasping each other's hands in passionate emotion; but few dared to trust themselves to words, for none
knew if the peril were really passed, or if the power of
the tyrant might not become greater than ever. While I
yet listened to the tidings which, in half sentences and
broken words, reached my ears, the roll of drums, beating
the "générale," was heard, and suddenly the head of a
column appeared, carrying torches, and seated upon ammunition waggons and caissons, and chanting in wild chorus
the words of the "Marseillaise." On they came, a terrible host of half-naked wretches, their heads bound
in handkerchiefs, and their brawny arms bare to the
shoulders.

The artillery of the Municipale followed, many of the
magistrates riding amongst them dressed in the tricoloured
scarfs of officers. As the procession advanced, the crowds
receded, and gradually the streets were left free to the
armed force.

While, terror-struck, I continued to gaze at the countenances over which the lurid torch-light cast a horrid
glare, a strong hand grasped my collar, and by a jerk
swung me up to a seat on one of the caissons; and at the
same time a deep voice said, "Come, youngster, this is
more in thy way than mine," and a black-bearded
"sapeur" pushed a drum before me, and ordered me to
beat the générale. Such was the din and uproar that my
performance did not belie my uniform, and I beat away
mantully, scarcely sorry, amid all my fears, at the elevated
position from which I now surveyed the exciting scene
around me.

As we passed, the shops were closed on either side in
aste, and across the windows of the upper stories beds

and mattresses were speedily drawn, in preparation for the state of siege now so imminent. Lights flickered from room to room, and all betokened a degree of alarm and terror. Louder and louder pealed the " Marseillaise," as the columns deployed into the open Place, from which every street and lane now poured its crowds of armed men. The line was now formed by the artillery, which, to the number of sixteen pieces, ranged from end to end of the square, the dense crowd of horse and foot forming behind, the mass dimly lighted by the waving torches that here and there marked the presence of an officer. Gradually the sounds of the "Marseillaise" grew fainter and fainter, and soon a dreary silence pervaded that varied host, more terrible now, as they stood speechless, than in all the tumultuous din of the wildest uproar. Meanwhile, from the streets which opened into the Place at the furthest end, the columns of the National Guard began to move up, the leading files carrying torches; behind them came ten pieces of artillery, which, as they issued, were speedily placed in battery, and flanked by the heavy dragoons of the Guard; and now, in breathless silence, the two forces stood regarding each other, the cannoniers with lighted matches in their hands, the dragoons firmly clasping their sabres—all but waiting for the word to plunge into the deadliest strife. It was a terrible moment—the slightest stir in the ranks—the rattling of a horse's panoply—the clank of a sabre—fell upon the heart like the toll of a death-bell. It was then that two or three horsemen were seen to advance from the troops of the Convention, and, approaching the others, were speedily lost among their ranks. A low and indistinct murmur ran along the lines, which each moment grew louder, till at last it burst forth into a cry of " Vive la Convention." Quitting their ranks, the men gathered around a general of the National Guard, who addressed them in words of passionate eloquence, but of which I was too distant to hear anything. Suddenly the ranks began to thin; some were seen to pile their arms, and move away in silence; others marched across the Place, and took up their position beside the troops of the National Guard; of the cannoniers, many threw down their matches, and extinguished the flame with their feet, while others again, limbering up their guns, slowly retired to the barracks.

As for myself, too much interested in the scene to remember that I was, in some sort, an actor in it, I sat upon the caisson, watching all that went forward so eagerly, that

I never noticed the departure of my companions, nor perceived that I was left by myself. I know not how much
later this discovery might have been deferred to me had
not an officer of the " Guard" ridden up to where I was,
and said, " Move up, move up, my lad; keep close to the
battery." He pointed at the same time with his sabre in
the direction where a number of guns and carriages were
already proceeding.

Not a little flattered by the order, I gathered up reins
and whip, and, thanks to the good drilling of the beasts,
who readily took their proper places, soon found myself
in the line, which now drew up in the rear of the artillery
of the Guard, separated from the front by a great mass of
horse and foot. I knew nothing of what went forward in
the Place; from what I gathered, however, I could learn
that the artillery was in position, the matches burning, and
everything in readiness for a cannonade. Thus we remained for above an hour, when the order was given to
march. Little knew I that, in that brief interval, the
whole fortunes of France—ay, of humanity itself—had
undergone a mighty change—that the terrible reign of
blood, the tyranny of Robespierre, had closed, and that he
who had sent so many to the scaffold now lay bleeding and
mutilated upon the very table where he had signed the
death-warrants.

The day was just beginning to dawn as we entered the
barracks of the Conciergerie, and drew up in a double line
along its spacious square. The men dismounted, and stood
"at ease," awaiting the arrival of the staff of the National
Guard, which, it was said, was coming; and now the
thought occurred to me of what I should best do, whether
make my escape while it was yet time, or remain to see by
what accident I had come there. If a sense of duty to the
Pére Michel urged me on one side, the glimmering hope
of some opening to fortune swayed me on the other. I
tried to persuade myself that my fate was bound up with
his, and that he should be my guide through the wild
waste before me; but these convictions could not stand
against the very scene in which I stood. The glorious
panoply of war—the harnessed team—the helmetted dragoon—the proud steed in all the trappings of battle! How
faint were the pleadings of duty against such arguments.
The Pére, too, designed me for a priest. The life of a
"seminarist" in a convent was to be mine! I was to wear
the red gown and the white cape of an "acolyte!"—to be
taught how to swing a censer, or snuff the candles of the
high altar—to be a train-bearer in a procession, or carry a

4

relic in a glass case! The hoarse bray of a trumpet that
then rung through the court routed these ignoble fancies,
and as the staff rode proudly in, my resolve was taken. I
was determined to be a soldier.

The day, I have said, was just breaking, and the officers
wore their dark grey capotes over their uniforms. One,
however, had his coat partly open, and I could see the blue
and silver beneath, which, tarnished and worn as it was,
had to my eyes all the brilliancy of a splendid uniform.
He was an old man, and by his position in advance of the
others showed that he was the chief of the staff. This
was General Lacoste, at that time "en mission" from the
army of the Rhine, and now sent by the Convention to
report upon the state of events among the troops. Slowly
passing along the line, the old general halted before each
gun, pointing out to his staff certain minutiæ, which, from
his gestures and manner, it was easy to see were not the
subject of eulogy. Many of the pieces were ill slung, and
badly balanced en the trucks; the wheels, in some cases,
were carelessly put on, their tires worn, and the iron shoe-
ing defective. The harnessing, too, was patched and
mended in a slovenly fashion; the horses lean and out of
condition; the drivers awkward and inexperienced.

"This is all bad, gentlemen," said he, addressing the
officers, but in a tone to be easily heard all around him;
"and reflects but little credit upon the state of your discipline in the capital. We have been now seventeen months
in the field before the enemy, and not idle either; and yet
I would take shame to myself if the worst battery in our
artillery were not better equipped, better horsed, better
driven, and better served, than any I see here."

One who seemed a superior officer here appeared to
interpose some explanation or excuse, but the general
would not listen to him, and continued his way along the
line, passing around which he now entered the space between the guns and the caissons. At last he stopped directly in front of where I was, and fixed his dark and
penetrating eyes steadily on me. Such was their fascination that I could not look from him, but continued to stare
as fixedly at him.

"Look here, for instance," cried he, as he pointed to
me with his sword, "is that 'gamin' yonder like an artillery-driver? or is it to a drummer-boy you entrust the
caisson of an eight-pounder gun? Dismount, sirrah, and
come hither," cried he to me, in a voice that sounded like
an order for instant execution. "This popinjay dress of
yours must have been the fancy of some worthy shop-

keeper of the 'Quai Lepelletier;' it never could belong to any regular corps. Who are you?"

"Maurice Tiernay, sir," said I, bringing my hand to my cap in military salute.

"Maurice Tiernay," repeated he, slowly, after me. "And have you no more to say for yourself than your name?"

"Very little, sir," said I, taking courage from the difficulty in which I found myself.

"What of your father, boy?—is he a soldier?

"He was, sir," replied I, with firmness.

"Then he is dead? In what corps did he serve?"

"In the Garde du Corps," said I, proudly.

The old general gave a short cough, and seemed to search for his snuff-box to cover his confusion; the next moment, however, he had regained his self-possession, and continued: "And since that event—I mean, since you lost your father—what have you been doing? How have you supported yourself?"

"In various ways, sir," said I, with a shrug of the shoulders, to imply that the answer might be too tedious to listen to. "I have studied to be a priest, and I have served as a 'rat' in the Prison du Temple."

"You have certainly tried the extremes of life," said he, laughing; "and now you wish, probably, to hit the 'juste milieu,' by becoming a soldier?"

"Even so, sir," said I, easily. "It was a mere accident that mounted me upon this caisson; but I am quite ready to believe that Fortune intended me kindly when she did so."

"These 'Gredins' fancy that they are all born to be generals of France," said the old man, laughing; "but, after all, it is a harmless delusion, and easily curable by a campaign or two. Come, sirrah, I'll find out a place for you; where, if you cannot serve the Republic better, you will, at least, do her less injury than as a driver in her artillery. Bertholet, let him be enrolled in your detachment of the gendarme, and give him my address: I wish to speak to him to-morrow."

"At what hour, general?" said I, promptly.

"At eight, or half-past—after breakfast," replied he.

"It may easily be before mine," muttered I to myself.

"What says he?" cried the general, sharply.

The aide-de-camp whispered a few words in answer, at which the other smiled, and said—"Let him come somewhat earlier—say eight o'clock."

"You hear that, boy?" said the aide-de-camp, to me;

while with a slight gesture he intimated that I might re-tire. Then, as if suddenly remembering that he had not given me the address of the general, he took a scrap of crumpled paper from his pocket-book, and wrote a few words hastily on it with his pencil. "There," cried he, throwing it towards me, "there is your billet for this day, at least" I caught the scrap of paper, and after deciphering the words, perceived that they were written on the back of an "assignat" for forty sous.

It was a large sum to one who had not wherewithal to buy a morsel of bread; and as I looked at it over and over, I fancied there would be no end to the pleasures such wealth could purchase. I can breakfast on the Quai Voltaire, thought I: ay, and sumptuously too, with coffee and chestnuts, and a slice of melon, and another of cheese, and a "petite goutte" to finish—for five sous. The pau-ther, at the corner of the Pont Neuf, costs but a sou; and for three one can see the brown bear of America, the hyæna, and another beast whose name I forget, but whose image, as he is represented outside, carrying off a man in his teeth, I shall retain to my last hour. Then, there is the panorama of Dunkirk, at the Rue Chopart, with the Duke of York begging his life from a terrible-looking soldier in a red cap and a tri-coloured scarf. After that, there's the parade at the "Carousel;" and mayhaps something more solemn still at the "Grêve;" but there was no limit to the throng of enjoyments which came rushing to my imagination, and it was in a kind of ecstacy of delight I set forth on my voyage of pleasure.

CHAPTER V.

THE CHOICE OF A LIFE.

In looking back, after a long lapse of years, I cannot re-frain from a feeling of astonishment to think how little remembrance I possess of the occurrences of that day —one of the most memorable that ever dawned for France—the eventful 29th of July, that closed the reign of terror by the death of the tyrant! It is true, that all Paris was astir at daybreak; that a sense of national ven-geance seemed to pervade the vast masses that filled the streets, which now were scenes of the most exciting emotion. I can only account for the strange indifference that I felt about these stirring themes by the frequency with which similar, or what to me at least appeared similar, scenes, had already passed before my eyes.

One of the most remarkable phases of the revolution was the change it produced in all the social relations by substituting an assumed nationality for the closer and dearer ties of kindred and affection. France was everything—the family nothing; every generous wish, every proud thought, every high ambition or noble endeavour, belonged to the country. In this way, whatever patriotism may have gained, certainly all the home affections were utterly wrecked; the humble and unobtrusive virtues of domestic life seemed mean and insignificant beside the grand displays of patriotic devotion which each day exhibited.

Hence grew the taste for that "life of the streets," then so popular; everything should be "en evidence." All the emotions which delicacy would render sacred to the seclusion of home were now to be paraded to the noon-day. Fathers were reconciled to rebellious children before the eyes of multitudes; wives received forgiveness from their husbands in the midst of approving crowds; leave-takings the most affecting; partings, for those never to meet again; the last utterings of the death-bed; the faint whispers of expiring affection; the imprecations of undying hate—all, all were exhibited in public, and the gaze of the low, the vulgar, and the debauched associated with the most agonising griefs that ever the heart endured. The scenes, which now are shrouded in all the secrecy of domestic privacy, were then the daily life of Paris; and to this cause alone can I attribute the hardened indifference with which events the most terrible and heart-rending were witnessed. Bred up amidst such examples, I saw little matter for emotion in scenes of harrowing interest. An air of mockery was on everything, and a bastard classicality destroyed every semblance of truth in whatever would have been touching and affecting.

The commotion of Paris on that memorable morning was, then, to my thinking, little more than usual. If the crowds who pressed their way to " The Place de la Révolution" were greater—if the cries of vengeance were in louder utterance—if the imprecations were deeper and more terrible,—the ready answer that satisfied all curiosity was—it was Robespierre who was on his way to be executed. Little knew I what hung upon that life! and how the fate of millions depended upon the blood that morning was to shed! Too full of myself and my own projects, I disengaged myself from the crowds that pressed

eagerly towards the Tuileries, and took my way by less-
frequented streets in the direction of the Boulevard Mont
Parnasse.

I wished, if possible, to see the Pére once more, to take a
last farewell of him, and ask his blessing, too: for still a
lingering faith in the lessons he had taught me, continued
to haunt my mind amidst all the evil influences with
which my wayward life surrounded me. The further I
went from the quarter of the Tuileries, the more deserted
and solitary grew the streets. Not a carriage or horseman was to be seen; scarcely a foot-passenger. All Paris
had, apparently, assembled on the "Place de la Révolution;" and the very beggars had quitted their accustomed
haunts to repair thither. Even the distant hum of the vast
multitude faded away, and it was only as the wind bore
them that I could catch the sounds of the hoarse cries
that bespoke a people's vengeance; and now I found myself in the little silent street which once had been my
home. I stood opposite the house where we used to live,
afraid to enter it lest I might compromise the safety of
her I wished to save; and yet longing once more to see
the little chamber where we once sat together—the chimney-corner where, in the dark nights of winter, I nestled,
with my hymn-book, and tried to learn the rhymes that
every plash of the falling hail against the windows routed
—to lie down once more in the little bed, where so often
I had passed whole nights of happy imaginings—bright
thoughts of a peaceful future, that were never to be
realised!

Half choking with my emotion, I passed on, and soon
saw the green fields, and the windmill-covered hill of
Montmartre rising above the embankment of the Boulevards; and now the ivy-clothed wall of the garden,
within which stood the Chapel of St. Blois. The gate lay
ajar as of old, and, pushing it open, I entered. Everything was exactly as I had left it—the same desolation and
desertion everywhere—so much so, that I almost fancied
no human foot had crossed its dreary precincts since last I
was there. On drawing nigh to the chapel, I found the
door fast barred and barricaded as before; but a window
lay open, and on examining it closer I discovered the
marks of a recent foot-track on the ground and the
window-sill. Could the Pére Michel have been there?
was the question that at once occurred to my mind. Had
the poor priest come to take a last look and a farewell of a
spot so dear to him. It could scarcely have been any
other. There was nothing to tempt cupidity in that

humble little church; an image of the "Virgin and Child" in wax was the only ornament of the altar. No, no; pillage had never been the motive of him who entered here.

Thus reasoning, I climbed up to the window, and entered the chapel. As my footsteps echoed through the silent building I felt that sense of awe and reverence so inseparably connected with a place of worship, and which is ever more impressive still as we stand in it alone. The present, however, was less before me than the past, of which everything reminded me. There was the seat the Marquise used to sit in; there the footstool I had so often placed at her feet. How different was the last service I had rendered her! There the pillar, beside which I have stood spell-bound, gazing at that fair face, whose beauty arrested the thoughts that should have wended heavenward, and made my muttered prayers like offerings to herself. The very bouquet of flowers some pious hand had placed beneath the shrine—withered and faded—was there still. But where were they whose beating hearts had throbbed with deep devotion? How many had died upon the scaffold!—how many were still lingering in imprisonment, some in exile, some in concealment, dragging out lives of misery and anxiety! What was the sustaining spirit of such martyrdom? I asked myself again and again. Was it the zeal of true religion, or was it the energy of loyalty that bore them up against every danger, and enabled them to brave death itself with firmness?—and if this faith of theirs was thus ennobling, why could not France be of one mind and heart? There came no answer to these doubts of mine, and I slowly advanced towards the altar, still deeply buried in thought. What was my surprise to see that two candles stood there, which bore signs of having been recently lighted. At once the whole truth flashed across me—the Père had been there; he had come to celebrate a mass—the last, perhaps, he was ever to offer up at that altar. I knew with what warm affection he loved every object and every spot endeared to him by long time, and I fancied to myself the overflowing of his heart as he entered once more, and for the last time, the little temple, associated with all the joys and sorrows of his existence. Doubtless, too, he had waited anxiously for my coming; mayhap, in the prayers he offered I was not forgotten. I thought of him kneeling there, in the silence of the night, alone, as he was, his gentle voice the only sound in the stillness of the hour; his pure heart throbbing with gratitude for his deliverance, and prayerful

hopes for those who had been his persecutors   I thought
over all this, and, in a torrent of emotions, I knelt down
before the altar to pray.   I know not what words I uttered, but his name must somehow have escaped my lips;
for suddenly a door opened beside the altar, and the Père
Michel, dressed in his full vestments, stood before me.
His features, wan and wasted as they were, had regained
their wonted expression of calm dignity; and by his look
I saw that he would not suffer the sacred spot to be pro-
faned by any outburst of feeling on either side.

" Those dreadful shouts tell of another massacre," said
he, solemnly, as the wind bore towards us the deafening
cries of the angry multitude.   " Let us pray for the souls'
rest of the departed."

" Then will your prayers be offered for Robespierre, for
Couthon, and St. Just," said I, boldly.

" And who are they who need more the saints' intercession—who have ever been called to judgment with such
crimes to expiate—who have ever so widowed France, and
so desecrated her altars?   Happily, a few yet remain
where piety may kneel to implore pardon for their iniquity.
Let us recite the Litany for the Dead," said he, solemnly,
and at once began the impressive service.

As I knelt beside the rails of the altar, and heard the
prayers which, with deep devotion, he uttered, I could
not help feeling the contrast between that touching evidence of Christian charity and the tumultuous joy of the
populace, whose frantic bursts of triumph were borne on
the air.

" And now come with me, Maurice," said he, as the
mass was concluded.   " Here, in this little sacristy, we
are safe from all molestation; none will think of us on
such a day as this."

And as he spoke he drew his arm around me, and led
me into the little chamber where once the precious vessels
and the decorations of the church were kept.

" Here we are safe," said he, as he drew me to his side
on the oaken bench, which formed all the furniture of the
room.   " To-morrow, Maurice, we must leave this, and
seek an asylum in another land; but we are not friendless, my child—the brothers of the 'Sacred Heart' will
receive us. Their convent is in the wilds of the Ardennes,
beyond the frontiers of France, and there, beloved by the
faithful peasantry, they live in security and peace.   We
need not take the vows of their order, which is one of the
strictest of all religious houses; but we may claim their
hospitality and protection, and neither will be denied us.

Think what a blessed existence will that be, Maurice, my son, to dwell under the same roof with these holy men, and to imbibe from them the peace of mind that holiness alone bestows; to awake at the solemn notes of the pealing organ, and to sink to rest with the glorious liturgies still chanting around you; to feel an atmosphere of devotion on every side, and to see the sacred relics whose miracles have attested the true faith in ages long past. Does it not stir thy heart, my child, to know that such blessed privileges may be thine?"

I hung my head in silence, for, in truth, I felt nothing of the enthusiasm with which he sought to inspire me. The Pére quickly saw what passed in my mind, and endeavoured to depict the life of the monastery as a delicious existence, embellished by all the graces of literature, and adorned by the pleasures of intellectual converse. Poetry, romance, scenery, all were pressed into the service of his persuasions; but how weak were such arguments to one like me, the boy whose only education had been what the streets of Paris afforded—whose notions of eloquence were formed on the insane ravings of "The Mountain," and whose idea of greatness was centered in mere notoriety!

My dreamy look of inattention showed him again that he had failed; and I could see, in the increased pallor of his face, the quivering motion of his lip, the agitation the defeat was costing him.

"Alas! alas!" cried he, passionately, "the work of ruin is perfect; the mind of youth is corrupted, and the fountain of virtue defiled at the very source. Oh! Maurice, I had never thought this possible of thee, the child of my heart!"

A burst of grief here overcame him; for some minutes he could not speak. At last he arose from his seat, and wiping off the tears that covered his cheeks with his robe, spoke, but in a voice whose full round tones contrasted strongly with his former weak accents.

"The life I have pictured seems to thee ignoble and unworthy, boy. So did it not appear to Chrysostom, to Origen, and to Augustin; to the blessed saints of our church, the eldest-born of Christianity. Be it so. Thine, mayhap, is not the age, nor this the era, in which to hope for better things. Thy heart yearns for heroic actions—thy spirit is set upon high ambitions—be it so. I say, never was the time more fitting for thee. The enemy is up; his armies are in the field; thousands and tens of thousands swell the ranks, already flushed with victory.

Be a soldier, then. Ay, Maurice, buckle on the sword—
the battle-field is before thee. Thou hast made choice to
seek the enemy in the far-away countries of heathen
darkness, or here in our own native France, where his
camp is already spread. If danger be the lure that tempts
thee—if to confront peril be thy wish—there is enough of
it. Be a soldier, then, and gird thee for the great battle
that is at hand. Ay! boy, if thou feelest within thee the
proud darings that foreshadow success, speak the word,
and thou shalt be a standard-bearer in the very van."

I waited not for more; but springing up, I clasped my
arms around his neck, and cried, in ecstacy, "Yes! Pére
Michel, you have guessed aright; my heart's ambition is
to be a soldier, and I want but your blessing to be a
brave one."

"And thou shalt have it. A thousand blessings follow
those who go forth to the good fight. But thou art yet
young, Maurice—too young for this. Thou needest time,
and much teaching, too. He who would brave the enemy
before us, must be skilful as well as courageous. Thou
art as yet but a child."

"The general said he liked boy-soldiers," said I,
promptly; "he told me so himself."

"What general—who told thee?" cried the Pére, in
trembling eagerness.

"General Lacoste, the Chef d'Etat, major of the
army of the Rhine; the same who gave me a rendezvous
for to-morrow at his quarters."

It was not till I had repeated my explanation again and
again, nor, indeed, until I had recounted all the circumstances of my last night's adventure, that the poor Pére
could be brought to see his way through a mystery that
had almost become equally embarrassing to myself. When
he did, however, detect the clue, and when he had perceived the different tracks on which our minds were travelling, his grief burst all bounds. He inveighed against
the armies of the Republic as hordes of pillagers and bandits, the sworn enemies of the Church, the desecrators of
her altars. Their patriotism he called a mere pretence to
shroud their infidelity. Their heroism was the blood-
thirstiness of democratic cruelty. Seeing me still unmoved by all this passionate declamation, he adopted another tactic, and suddenly asked me if it were for such a
cause as this my father had been a soldier?

"No!" replied I, firmly; "for when my father was
alive, the soil of France had not been desecrated by the
foot of the invader. The Austrian, the Prussian, the

Englishman, had not yet dared to dictate the laws under which we were to live."

He appeared thunderstruck at my reply, revealing, as it seemed to him, the extent of those teachings, whose corruptions he trembled at.

"I knew it, I knew it," cried he, bitterly, as he wrung his hands. "The seed of the iniquity is sown—the harvest-time will not be long in coming! And so, boy, thou hast spoken with one of these men—these generals, as they call themselves, of that republican horde?"

"The officer who commands the artillery of the army of the Rhine may write himself general with little presumption," said I, almost angrily.

"They who once led our armies to battle were the nobles of France—men whose proud station was the pledge for their chivalrous devotion. But why do I discuss the question with thee? He who deserts his faith may well forget that his birth was noble. Go, boy, join those with whom your heart is already linked. Your lesson will be an easy one—you have nothing to unlearn. The songs of the Girondins are already more grateful to your ear than our sacred canticles. Go, I say, since between us henceforth there can be no companionship."

"Will you not bless me, Père," said I, approaching him in deep humility; "will you not let me carry with me thy benediction?"

"How shall I bless the arm that is lifted to wound the Holy Church?—how shall I pray for one whose place is in the ranks of the infidel? Hadst thou faith in my blessing, boy, thou hadst never implored it in such a cause. Renounce thy treason—and not alone my blessing, but thou shalt have a "Novena" to celebrate thy fidelity. Be of us, Maurice, and thy name shall be honoured where honour is immortality."

The look of beaming affection with which he uttered this, more than the words themselves, now shook my courage, and, in a conflict of doubt and indecision, I held down my head without speaking. What might have been my ultimate resolve, if left completely to myself, I know not; but at that very moment a detachment of soldiers marched past in the street without. They were setting off to join the army of the Rhine, and were singing in joyous chorus the celebrated song of the day, " Le chant du depart." The tramp of their feet—the clank of their weapons—their mellow voices—but, more than all, the associations that thronged to my mind, routed every other thought, and I darted from the spot, and never stopped till I reached the street.

A great crowd followed the detachment, composed partly of friends of the soldiers, partly of the idle loungers of the capital. Mixing with these, I moved onward, and speedily passed the outer boulevard and gained the open country.

CHAPTER VI.

"THE ARMY SIXTY YEARS SINCE."

I FOLLOWED the soldiers as they marched beyond the outer boulevard, and gained the open country. Many of the idlers dropped off here; others accompanied us a little further; but at length, when the drums ceased to beat, and were slung in marching order on the backs of the drummers, when the men broke into the open order that French soldiers instinctively assume on a march, the curiosity of the gazers appeared to have nothing more to feed upon, and one by one they returned to the capital, leaving me the only lingerer.

To any one accustomed to military display, there was little to attract notice in the column, which consisted of detachments from various corps, horse, foot, and artillery; some were returning to their regiments after a furlough; some had just issued from the hospitals, and were seated in charettes, or country cars; and others, again, were peasant boys only a few days before drawn in the conscription. There was every variety of uniform, and, I may add, of raggedness, too—a coarse blouse and a pair of worn shoes, with a red or blue handkerchief on the head, being the dress of many among them. The Republic was not rich in those days, and cared little for the costume in which her victories were won. The artillery alone seemed to preserve anything like uniformity in dress. They wore a plain uniform of blue, with long white gaiters coming half way up the thigh; a low cocked hat, without feather, but with the tricoloured cockade in front. They were mostly men middle-aged, or past the prime of life, bronzed, weather-beaten, hardly-looking fellows, whose white moustaches contrasted well with their sun-burned faces. All their weapons and equipments were of a superior kind, and showed the care bestowed upon an arm whose efficiency was the first discovery of the republican generals. The

greater number of these were Bretons, and several of
them had served in the fleet, still bearing in their looks
and carriage something of that air which seems inherent
in the seaman. They were grave, serious, and almost
stern in manner, and very unlike the young cavalry
soldiers, who, mostly recruited from the south of France
many of them Gascons, had all the high-hearted gaiety
and reckless levity of their own peculiar land. A campaign to these fellows seemed a pleasant excursion; they
made a jest of everything, from the wan faces of the invalids, to the black bread of the "Commissary;" they
quizzed the new "Tourlerous," as the recruits were styled,
and the old "Grumblers," as it was the fashion to call the
veterans of the army; they passed their jokes on the Republic, and even their own officers came in for a share of
their ridicule. The Grenadiers, however, were those who
especially were made the subject of their sarcasm. They
were generally from the north of France, and the frontier
country toward Flanders, whence they probably imbibed
a portion of that phlegm and moroseness so very unlike
the general gaiety of French nature; and when assailed
by such adversaries, were perfectly incapable of reply or
retaliation.

They all belonged to the army of the "Sambre et Meuse,"
which, although at the beginning of the campaign highly
distinguished for its successes, had been latterly eclipsed
by the extraordinary victories on the Upper Rhine and in
Western Germany; and it was curious to hear with what
intelligence and interest the greatest questions of strategy
were discussed by those who carried their packs as common soldiers in the ranks. Movements and manœuvres
were criticised, attacked, defended, ridiculed, and condemned, with a degree of acuteness and knowledge that
showed the enormous progress the nation had made in
military science, and with what ease the Republic could
recruit her officers from the ranks of her soldiers.

At noon the column halted in the wood of Belleville;
and while the men were resting, an express arrived an-
nouncing that a fresh body of troops would soon arrive,
and ordering the others to delay their march till they came
up. The orderly who brought the tidings could only say
that he believed some hurried news had come from Germany, for before he left Paris the rappel was beating in
different quarters, and the rumour ran that reinforcements
were to set out for Strasbourg with the utmost despatch.

"And what troops are coming to join us?" said an old
artillery sergeant, in evident disbelief of the tidings.

"Two batteries of artillery and the voltigeurs of the 4th, I know for certain are coming," said the orderly, "and they spoke of a battalion of grenadiers."

"What! do these Germans need another lesson?" said the cannonier. "I thought Fleurus had taught them what our troops were made of."

"How you talk of Fleurus," interrupted a young hussar of the south; "I have just come from the army of Italy, and, ma foi! we should never have mentioned such a battle as Fleurus in a despatch. Campaigning amongst dykes and hedges—fighting with a river on one flank and a fortress on t'other—parade manœuvres—where, at the first check, the enemy retreats, and leaves you free, for the whole afternoon, to write off your successes to the Directory. Had you seen our fellows scaling the Alps, with avalanches of snow descending at every fire of the great guns—forcing pass after pass against an enemy, posted on every cliff and crag above us — cutting our way to victory by roads the hardiest hunter had seldom trod; I call that war."

"And I call it the skirmish of an outpost!" said the gruff veteran, as he smoked away in thorough contempt for the enthusiasm of the other. "I have served under Kleber, Hoche, and Moreau, and I believe they are the first generals of France."

"There is a name greater than them all," cried the hussar, with eagerness.

"Let us hear it, then—you mean Pichegru, perhaps, or Massena?"

"No, I mean Bonaparte!" said the hussar, triumphantly.

"A good officer, and one of us," said the artilleryman, touching his belt to intimate the arm of the service the general belonged to. "He commanded the siege-train at Toulon."

"He belongs to all," said the other. "He is a dragoon, a voltigeur, an artillerist, a pontonièr—what you will—he knows everything, as I know my horse's saddle, and cloak-bag."

Both parties now grew warm; and as each was not only an eager partisan, but well acquainted with the leading events of the two campaigns they undertook to defend, the dispute attracted a large circle of listeners, who, either seated on the green sward, or lying at full length, formed a picturesque group under the shadow of the spreading oak-trees. Meanwhile, the cooking went speedily forward, and the camp-kettles smoked with a steam whose savoury odour was not a little tantalising to one who, like myself, felt that he did not belong to the company.

"What's thy mess, boy?" said an old grenadier to me, as I sat at a little distance off, and affecting—but I fear very ill—a total indifference to what went forward.

"He is asking to what corps thou belong'st?" said another, seeing that the question puzzled me.

"Unfortunately I have none," said I. "I merely followed the march for curiosity."

"And thy father and mother, child—what will they say to thee on thy return home?"

"I have neither father, mother, nor home," said I, promptly.

"Just like myself," said an old red-whiskered sapeur; "or if I ever had parents they never had the grace to own me. Come over here, child, and take share of my dinner."

"No, parbleu! I'll have him for my comrade," cried the young hussar. "I was made a corporal yesterday, and have a larger ration. Sit here, my boy, and tell us how art called."

"Maurice Tiernay."

"Maurice will do; few of us care for more than one name, except in the dead muster they like to have it in full. Help thyself, my lad, and here's the wine-flask beside thee."

"How comes it thou hast this old uniform, boy," said he, pointing to my sleeve.

"It was one they gave me in the Temple," said I. "I was a 'rat du prison' for some time."

"Thunder of war!" exclaimed the cannonier, "I had rather stand a whole platoon fire than see what thou must have seen, child."

"And hast heart to go back there, boy," said the corporal, "and live the same life again?"

"No, I'll never go back," said I. "I'll be a soldier."

"Well said, mon brave—thou'lt be a hussar, I know."

"If nature has given thee a good head, and a quick eye, my boy, thou might even do better; and in time, perhaps, wear a coat like mine," said the cannonier.

"Sacre bleu!" cried a little fellow, whose age might have been anything from boyhood to manhood—for while small of stature, he was shrivelled and wrinkled like a mummy—"why not be satisfied with the coat he wears?"

"And be a drummer, like thee," said the cannonier.

"Just so, like me, and like Massena—he was a drummer, too."

"No, no!" cried a dozen voices together, "that's not true."

"He's right; Massena was a drummer in the Eighth," said the cannonier; "I remember him when he was like that boy yonder."

"To be sure," said the little fellow, who, I now perceived, wore the dress of a 'tambour;' "and is it a disgrace to be the first to face the enemy?"

"And the first to turn his back to him, comrade," cried another.

"Not always—not always," said the little fellow, regardless of the laugh against him. "Had it been so, I had not gained the battle of Grandrengs on the Sambre."

"Thou gain a battle!" shouted half-a-dozen, in derisive laughter.

"What, Petit Pièrre gained the day at Grandrengs!" said the cannonier; "why, I was there myself, and never heard of that till now."

"I can believe it well," replied Pièrre; "many a man's merits go unacknowledged: and Kleber got all the credit that belonged to Pièrre Canot."

"Let us hear about it, Pièrre, for even thy victory is unknown by name to us poor devils of the army of Italy. How call'st thou the place?"

"Grandrengs," said Pièrre, proudly. "Its name will live as long, perhaps, as many of those high-sounding ones you have favoured us with. Mayhap, thou hast heard of Cambray?"

"Never!" said the hussar, shaking his head.

"Nor of 'Mons,' either, I'll be sworn?" continued Pièrre.

"Quite true, I never heard of it before."

"Voila!" exclaimed Pièrre, in contemptuous triumph. "And these are the fellows that pretend to feel their country's glory, and take pride in her conquests. Where hast thou been, lad, not to hear of places that every child syllables now-a-days?"

"I will tell you where I've been," said the hussar, haughtily, and dropping at the same time the familiar "thee" and "thou" of soldier intercourse—"I've been at Montenotte, at Millesimo, at Mondove——"

"Allons, donc! with your disputes," broke in an old grenadier; "as if France was not victorious whether the enemies were English or German. Let us hear how Pièrre won his battle at—at——"

"At Grandrengs," said Pièrre. "They call it in the despatch the 'action of the Sambre,' because Kleber came up there—and Kleber being a great man, and Pièrre Canot a little one, you understand, the glory attaches to the place where the bullion epaulettes are found—just as the old King of Prussia used to say, 'Le bon Dieu est toujours a cotè de gros bataillons.'"

"I see we'll never come to this same victory of Grand-rengs, with all these turnings and twistings," muttered the artillery sergeant.

"Thou art very near it now, comrade, if thou'lt listen," said Pièrre, as he wiped his mouth after a long draught of the wine-flask. "I'll not weary the honourable company with any description of the battle generally, but just confine myself to that part of it in which I was myself in action. It is well known, that though we claimed the victory of the 10th May, we did little more than keep our own, and were obliged to cross the Sambre, and be satisfied with such a position as enabled us to hold the two bridges over the river—and there we remained for four days: some said preparing for a fresh attack upon Kaunitz, who commanded the allies; some, and I believe they were right, alleging that our generals were squabbling all day, and all night, too, with two Commissaries that the Government had sent down to teach us how to win battles. Ma foi! we had had some experience in that way ourselves, without learning the art from two citizens with tricoloured scarfs round their waists, and yellow tops to their boots! However that might be, early on the morning of the 20th we received orders to cross the river in two strong columns, and form on the opposite side; at the same time that a division was to pass the stream by boat two miles higher up, and, concealing themselves in a pine wood, be ready to take the enemy in flank, when they believed that all the force was in the front."

"Sacre tonnerre! I believe that our armies of the Sambre and the Rhine never have any other notion of battles than that eternal flank movement!" cried a young sergeant of the voltigeurs, who had just come up from the army of Italy. "Our general used to split the enemy by the centre, cut him piecemeal by attack in columns, and then mow him down with artillery at short range—not leaving him time for a retreat in heavy masses——"

"Silence, silence, and let us hear Petit Pièrre," shouted a dozen voices, who cared far more for an incident than a scientific discussion about manœuvres.

"The plan I speak of was General Moreau's," continued Pièrre; "and I fancy that your Bonaparte has something to learn ere he be his equal!"

5

This rebuke seeming to have engaged the suffrages of the company, he went on : " The boat division consisted of four battalions of infantry, two batteries of light-artillery, and a voltigeur company of the ' Regiment de Marbœuf '— to which I was then, for the time, attached as ' Tambour en chef.' What fellows they were—the greatest devils in the whole army ! They came from the Faubourg St. Antoine, and were as reckless and undisciplined as when they strutted the streets of Paris. When they were thrown out to skirmish, they used to play as many tricks as school-boys : sometimes they'd run up to the roof of a cabin or a hut—and they could climb like cats—and, sitting down on the chimney, begin firing away at the enemy as coolly as if from a battery ; sometimes they'd capture half-a-dozen asses, and ride forward as if to charge, and then, affecting to tumble off, the fellows would pick down any of the enemy's officers that were fools enough to come near— scampering back to the cover of the line, laughing and joking as if the whole were sport. I saw one when his wrist was shattered by a shot, and he couldn't fire, take a comrade on his back and caper away like a horse, just to tempt the Germans to come out of their lines. It was with these blessed youths I was now to serve, for the Tambour of the ' Marbœuf' was drowned in crossing the Sambre a few days before. Well, we passed the river safely, and, unperceived by the enemy, gained the pine wood, where we formed in two columns, one of attack, and the other of support—the voltigeurs about five hundred paces in advance of the leading files. The morning was dull and hazy, for a heavy rain had fallen during the night ; and the country is flat, and so much intersected with drains, and dykes, and ditches, that, after rain, the vapour is too thick to see twenty yards on any side. Our business was to make a counter-march to the right, and, guided by the noise of the cannonade, to come down upon the enemy's flank in the thickest of the engagement. As we advanced, we found ourselves in a kind of marshy plain, planted with willows, and so thick that it was often difficult for three men to march abreast. This extended for a considerable distance ; and, on escaping from it we saw that we were not above a mile from the enemy's left, which rested on a little village."

" I know it well," broke in the cannonier ; " it's called Huyningen."

" Just so. There was a formidable battery in position there ; and part of the place was stockaded, as if they expected an attack. Still, there were no videttes, nor any look-out party, so far as we could see ; and our commanding officer didn't well know what to make of it, whether it was a point of concealed strength, or a position they were about to withdraw from. At all events, it required caution ; and, although the battle had already begun on the right—as a loud cannonade and a heavy smoke told us—he halted the brigade in the wood, and held a council of his officers to see what was to be done. The resolution come to was, that the voltigeurs should advance alone to explore the way, the rest of the force remaining in ambush. We were to go out in sections of companies, and spreading over a wide surface, see what we could of the place.

"Scarcely was the order given, when away we went— and it was now a race who should be earliest up and exchange first shot with the enemy. Some dashed forward over the open field in front ; others skulked along by dykes and ditches ; some, again, dodged here and there, as cover offered its shelter ; but about a dozen, of whom I was one, kept the track of a little cart-road, which, half-concealed by high banks and furze, ran in a zig-zag line towards the village. I was always smart of foot ; and now, having newly joined the 'voltigeurs,' was naturally eager to show myself not unworthy of my new associates. I went on at my best pace, and being lightly equipped— neither musket nor ball cartridge to carry—I soon outstripped them all ; and, after about twenty minutes' brisk running, saw in front of me a long, low farm-house, the walls all pierced for musketry, and two small eight-pounders in battery at the gate. I looked back for my companions, but they were not up—not a man of them to be seen. 'No matter,' thought I, 'they'll be here soon ; meanwhile I'll make for that little copse of brushwood ;' for a small clump of low furze and broom was standing at a little distance in front of the farm. All this time, I ought to say, not a man of the enemy was to be seen, although I, from where I stood, could see the 'crenelated' walls, and the guns, as they were pointed—at a distance all would seem like an ordinary peasant house.

"As I crossed the open space to gain the copse, piff! came a bullet, whizzing past me ; and just as I reached the cover, piff! came another. I ducked my head and made for the thicket ; but just as I did so, my foot caught in a branch. I stumbled and pitched forward ; and trying to save myself, I grasped a bough above me ; it smashed suddenly, and down I went. Ay! down sure enough— for I went right through the furze, and into a well—one of those old, walled wells they have in these countries, with a huge bucket that fills up the whole space, and is worked by a chain. Luckily, the bucket was linked up near the top, and caught me, or I should have gone where there would have been no more heard of Pièrre Canot; as it was, I was sorely bruised by the fall, and didn't recover myself for full ten minutes after. Then I discovered that I was sitting in a large wooden trough, hooped with iron, and supported by two heavy chains that passed over a windlass, about ten feet above my head.

"I was safe enough for the matter of that; at least none were likely to discover me, as I could easily see, by the rust of the chain and the grass-grown edges, that the well had been long disused. Now the position was far from being pleasant. There stood the farm-house full of soldiers, the muskets ranging over every approach to where I lay. Of my comrades there was nothing to be seen, they had either missed the way or retreated; and so time crept on, and I pondered on what might be going forward elsewhere, and whether it would ever be my own fortune to see my comrades again.

" It might be an hour—it seemed three or four to me— after this, as I looked over the plain, I saw the caps of our infantry just issuing over the brushwood, and a glancing lustre of their bayonets, as the sun tipped them. They were advancing, but, as it seemed, slowly—halting at times, and then moving forward again—just like a force waiting for others to come up. At last they debouched into the plain; but, to my surprise, they wheeled about to the right, leaving the farm-house on their flank, as if to march beyond it. This was to lose their way totally; nothing would be easier than to carry the position of the farm, for the Germans were evidently few, had no videttes, and thought themselves in perfect security. I crept out from my ambush, and holding my cap on a stick tried to attract notice from our fellows, but none saw me. I ventured at last to shout aloud, but with no better success; so that, driven to the end of my resources, I set to and beat a 'roulade' on the drum, thundering away with all my might, and not caring what might come of it—for I was half mad with vexation as well as despair. They heard me now; I saw a staff officer gallop up to the head of the leading division and halt them; a volley came peppering from behind me, but without doing me any injury, for I was safe once more in my bucket. Then came another pause, and again I repeated my manœuvre, and to my delight perceived that our fellows was advancing at quick march. I beat harder, and the drums of the grenadiers answered me. All right now, thought I, as, springing forward, I called out—'This way, boys, the wall of the orchard has scarcely a man to defend it!' and I rattled out the ' pas-de-charge,' with all my force. One crashing fire of guns and small arms answered me from the farm-house, and then away went the Germans as hard as they could! —such running never was seen! One of the guns they carried off with them, the tackle of the other broke, and the drivers, jumping off their saddles, took to their legs at once. Our lads were over the walls, through the windows, between the stockades, everywhere in fact, in a minute, and once inside, they carried all before them. The village was taken at the point of the bayonet, and in less than an hour the whole force of the brigade was advancing in full march on the enemy's flank. There was little resistance made after that, and Kaunitz only saved his artillery by leaving his rear guard to be cut to pieces."

The cannonier nodded, as if in full assent, and Pièrre looked around him with the air of a man who has vindicated his claim to greatness.

" Of course," said he, " the despatch said little about Pièrre Canot, but a great deal about Moreau, and Kleber, and the rest of them."

While some were well satisfied that Pièrre had well established his merits as the conqueror of " Grandrengs," others quizzed him about the heroism of lying hid in a well, and owing all his glory to a skin of parchment.

" An' thou wert with the army of Italy, Pièrre," said the hussar, " thou'd have seen men march boldly to victory, and not skulk under ground like a mole."

" I am tired of your song about this army of Italy," broke in the cannonier ; " we who have served in La Vendée and the North know what fighting means as well, mayhap, as men whose boldest feats are scaling rocks and clambering up precipices. Your Bonaparte is more like one of those 'Guerilla chiefs they have in the ' Basque,' than the general of a French army."

"The man who insults the army of Italy, or its chief, insults me !" said the corporal, springing up, and casting a sort of haughty defiance around him.

" And then ?"—asked the other.

" And then—if he be a French soldier, he knows what should follow."

" Parbleu !" said the cannonier, coolly, " there would be little glory in cutting you down, and even less in being wounded by you; but if you will have it so, it's not an old soldier of the artillery will baulk your humour."

As he spoke, he slowly arose from the ground, and tightening his waist-belt, seemed prepared to follow the other. The rest sprung to their feet at the same time, but not, as I anticipated, to offer a friendly mediation between the angry parties, but in full approval of their readiness to decide by the sword a matter too trivial to be called a quarrel.

In the midst of the whispering conferences as to place and weapons—for the short straight sword of the artillery was very unlike the curved sabre of the hussar—the quick tramp of horses was heard, and suddenly the head of a squadron was seen, as, with glancing helmets and glittering equipments, they turned off the high-road and entered the wood.

"Here they come!—here come the troops!" was now heard on every side; and all question of the duel was forgotten in the greater interest inspired by the arrival of the others. The sight was strikingly picturesque; for, as they rode up, the order to dismount was given, and in an instant the whole squadron was at work picqueting and unsaddling their horses; forage was shaken out before the weary and hungry beasts, kits were unpacked, cooking utensils produced, and everyone busy in preparing for the bivouac. An infantry column followed close upon the others, which was again succeeded by two batteries of field-artillery and some squadrons of heavy dragoons; and now the whole wood, far and near, was crammed with soldiers, waggons, caissons, and camp equipage. To me the interest of the scene was never-ending—life, bustle, and gaiety on every side. The reckless pleasantry of the camp, too, seemed elevated by the warlike accompaniments of the picture—the caparisoned horses, the brass guns, blackened on many a battle-field, the weather-seamed faces of the hardy soldiers themselves, all conspiring to excite a high enthusiasm for the career.

Most of the equipments were new and strange to my eyes. I had never before seen the grenadiers of the Republican Guard, with their enormous shakos, and their long-flapped vests, descending to the middle of the thigh; neither had I seen the "Hussars de la mort," in their richly-braided uniform of black, and their long hair curled in ringlets at either side of the face. The cuirassiers, too, with their low cocked hats, and straight black feathers, as well as the "Portes Drapeaux," whose brilliant uniforms, all slashed with gold, seemed scarcely in keeping with yellow-topped boots: all were now seen by me for the first time. But of all the figures which amused me most by its singularity, was that of a woman, who, in a short frock-coat and a low-crowned hat, carried a little barrel at her side, and led an ass loaded with two similar but rather larger casks. Her air and gait were perfectly soldier-like; and as she passed the different posts and sentries, she saluted them in true military fashion. I was not long to remain in ignorance of her vocation nor her name; for scarcely did she pass a group without stopping to dispense a wonderful cordial that she carried; and then I heard the familiar title of "La Mére Madou," uttered in every form of panegyric.

She was a short, stoutly-built figure, somewhat past the middle of life, but without any impairment of activity in her movements. A pleasing countenance, with good teeth, and black eyes, a merry voice, and a ready tongue, were qualities more than sufficient to make her a favourite with the soldiers, whom I found she had followed to more than one battle-field.

"Peste!" cried an old grenadier, as he spat out the liquor on the ground. "This is one of those sweet things they make in Holland; it smacks of treacle and bad lemons."

"Ah, Grognard!" said she, laughing, "thou art more used to corn-brandy, with a clove of garlick in't, than to good curaçoa."

"What, curaçoa! Mére Madou, has got curaçoa there?' cried a grey-whiskered captain, as he turned on his saddle at the word.

"Yes, mon capitaine, and such as no burgomaster ever drank better;" and she filled out a little glass and presented it gracefully to him.

"Encore, ma bonne Mére," said he, as he wiped his thick moustache; "that liquor is another reason for ex-tending the blessings of liberty to the brave Dutch."

"Didn't I tell you so?" said she, refilling the glass; "but, holloa, there goes Gregoire at full speed. Ah, scoundrels that ye are, I see what ye've done." And so was it; some of the wild young voltigeur fellows had fastened a lighted furze-bush to the beast's tail, and had set him at a gallop through the very middle of the encamp-ment, upsetting tents, scattering cooking-pans, and tum-bling the groups, as they sat, in every direction.

The confusion was tremendous, for the picqueted horses jumped about, and some breaking loose, gallopped here and there, while others set off with half-unpacked waggons, scattering their loading as they went.

It was only when the blazing furze had dropped off that the cause of the whole mischance would suffer himself to be captured and led quietly back to his mistress. Half-crying with joy, and still wild with anger, she kissed the beast and abused her tormentors by turns.

"Cannoniers that ye are," she cried, "ma foi! you'll have little taste for fire when the day comes that ye should face it! Pauvre Gregoire, they've left thee a tail like a tirailleur's feather! Plagues light on the thieves that did it! Come here, boy," said she, addressing me, "hold the bridle; what's thy corps, lad?"

"I have none now; I only followed the soldiers from Paris."

"Away with thee, street runner; away with thee, then," said she, contemptuously; "there are no pockets to pick here; and if there were, thou'd lose thy ears for the doing it. Be off, then, back with thee to Paris and all its villanies. There are twenty thousand of thy trade there, but there's work for ye all."

"Nay, Mére, don't be harsh with the boy," said a soldier; "you can see by his coat that his heart is with us."

"And he stole that, I'll be sworn," said she, pulling me round by the arm, full in front of her. "Answer me, 'gamin,' where did'st find that old tawdry jacket?'"

"I got it in a place where, if they had hold of thee and thy bad tongue, it would fare worse with thee than thou thinkest," said I, maddened by the imputed theft and insolence together.

"And where may that be, young slip of the galleys?" cried she, angrily.

"In the 'Prison du Temple.'"

"Is that their livery, then?" said she, laughing and pointing at me with ridicule, "or is it a family dress made after thy father's?"

"My father wore a soldier's coat, and bravely, too," said I, with difficulty restraining the tears that rose to my eyes.

"In what regiment, boy?" asked the soldier who spoke before.

"In one that exists no longer," said I, sadly, and not wishing to allude to a service that would find but slight favour in republican ears.

"That must be the 24th of the Line; they were cut to pieces at 'Tongres.'"

" No—no, he's thinking of the 9th, that got so roughly handled at Fontenoy," said another.

"Of neither," said I; "I am speaking of those who have left nothing but a name behind them, the 'Garde du Corps' of the king."

"Voila!" cried Madou, clapping her hands in astonishment at my impertinence; "there's an aristocrat for you! Look at him, mes braves! it's not every day we have the grand seigneurs condescending to come amongst us! You can learn something of courtly manners from the polished descendant of our nobility. Say, boy, art a count, or a baron, or perhaps a duke?"

"Make way there—out of the road, Mére Madou," cried a dragoon, curveting his horse in such a fashion as almost to upset ass and 'cantiniére' together, "the staff is coming."

The mere mention of the word sent numbers off in full speed to their quarters; and now all was haste and bustle to prepare for the coming inspection. The Mére's endeavours to drag her beast along were not very successful; for, with the peculiar instinct of his species, the more necessity there was of speed, the lazier he became; and as every one had his own concerns to look after, she was left to her own unaided efforts to drive him forward.

"Thou'lt have a day in prison if thou'rt found here, Mére Madou," said a dragoon, as he struck the ass with the flat of his sabre.

"I know it well," cried she, passionately; " but I have none to help me. Come here, lad; be good-natured, and forget what passed. Take his bridle while I whip him on."

I was at first disposed to refuse, but her pitiful face and sad plight made me think better of it; and I seized the bridle at once; but just as I had done so, the escort gallopped forward, and the dragoons coming on the flank of the miserable beast, over he went, barrels and all, crushing me beneath him as he fell.

"Is the boy hurt?" were the last words I heard, as I fainted; but a few minutes after I found myself seated on the grass, while a soldier was staunching the blood that ran freely from a cut in my forehead.

"It is a trifle, General—a mere scratch," said a young officer to an old man on horseback beside him, "and the leg is not broken."

"Glad of it," said the old officer; "casualties are insufferable, except before an enemy. Send the lad to his regiment."

"He's only a camp-follower, Gene al. He does not belong to us."

"There, my lad, take this, then, and make thy way back to Paris," said the old general, as he threw me a small piece of money.

I looked up, and, straight before me, saw the same offic r who had given me the assignat the night before.

"General Lacoste!" cried I, in delight, for I thoug t him already a friend.

"How is this—have I an acquaintance here?" said he, smiling; "on my life! it's the young rogue I met this morning. Eh! art not thou the artillery-driver I spoke to at the barrack?"

"Yes, General, the same."

"Diantre! It seems fated, then, that we are not to part company so easily; for hadst thou remained in Paris, lad, we had most probably never met again."

"Ainsi, je suis bien *tombé*, General," said I, punning upon my accident.

He laughed heartily, less I suppose at the jest, which was a poor one, than at the cool impudence with which I uttered it; and then turning to one of the staff, said,—

"I spoke to Bertholet about this boy already; see that they take him in the 9th. I say, my lad, what's thy name?"

"Tiernay, sir."

"Ay, to be sure, Tiernay. Well, Tiernay, thou shalt be a hussar, my man. See that I get no disgrace by the appointment."

I kissed his hand fervently, and the staff rode forward, leaving me the happiest heart that beat in all that crowded host.

CHAPTER VII.

A PASSING ACQUAINTANCE.

If the guide who is to lead us on a long and devious track stops at every by-way, following out each path that seems to invite a ramble or suggest a halt, we naturally might feel distrustful of his safe conduct, and uneasy at the prospect of the road before us. In the same way may the reader be disposed to fear that he who descends to slight and trivial circumstances will scarcely have time for

events which ought to occupy a wider space in his reminiscences ; and for this reason I am bound to apologise for
the seeming transgression of my last chapter. Most true
it is, that were I to relate the entire of my life with a
similar diffuseness, my memoir would extend to a length
far beyond what I intend it to occupy. Such, however,
is very remote from my thoughts. I have dwelt, with,
perhaps, something of prolixity, upon the soldier-life and
characteristics of a past day, because I shall yet have to
speak of changes, without which the contrast would be
inappreciable ; but I have also laid stress upon an incident
trivial in itself, because it formed an event in my own
fortunes. It was thus, in fact, that I became a soldier.

Now, the man who carries a musket in the ranks may
very reasonably be deemed but a small ingredient of the
mass that forms an army ; and in our day his thoughts,
hopes, fears, and ambitions are probably as unknown and
uncared for as the precise spot of earth that yielded the
ore from which his own weapon was smelted. This is not
only reasonable, but it is right. In the time of which
I am now speaking it was far otherwise. The Republic,
in extinguishing a class, had elevated the individual ; and
now each, in whatever station he occupied, felt himself
qualified to entertain opinions and express sentiments
which, because they were his own, he presumed them to
be national. The idlers of the streets discussed the
deepest questions of politics ; the soldiers talked of war
with all the presumption of consummate generalship.
The great operations of a campaign, and the various
qualities of different commanders, were the daily subjects
of dispute in the camp. Upon one topic only were all
agreed ; and there, indeed, our unanimity repaid all previous discordance. We deemed France the only civilised
nation of the globe, and reckoned that people thrice
happy who, by any contingency of fortune, engaged our
sympathy, or procured the distinction of our presence in
arms. We were the heaven-born disseminators of freedom
throughout Europe ; the sworn enemies of kingly domi-
nation ; and the missionaries of a political creed, which
was not alone to ennoble mankind, but to render its condition eminently happy and prosperous.

There could not be an easier lesson to learn than this,
and particularly when dinned into your ears all day, and
from every rank and grade around you. It was the pro-
gramme of every message from the Directory ; it was the
opening of every general order from the General ; it was
the table-talk at your mess. The burthen of every song,

the title of every military march performed by the regi‑
mental band, recalled it; even the riding-master, as he
followed the recruit around the weary circle, whip in
hand, mingled the orders he uttered with apposite axioms
upon republican grandeur. How I think I hear it still!
as the grim old quarter-master-sergeant, with his Alsatian
accent and deep-toned voice, would call out,—

"Elbows back!—wrist lower and free from the side—
free, I say, as every citizen of a great Republ'c!—head
erect, as a Frenchman has a right to carry it!—chest full
out, like one who can breathe the air of heaven, and ask
no leave from king or despot!—down with your heel, sir;
think that you crush a tyrant beneath it!"

Such and such like were the running commentaries on
equitation, till often I forgot whether the lesson had more
concern with a seat on horseback or the great cause of
monarchy throughout Europe. I suppose, to use a popular
phrase of our own day, "the system worked well;" cer‑
tainly the spirit of the army was unquestionable. From
the grim old veteran, with snow-white moustache, to the
beardless boy, there was but one hope and wish—the glory
of France. How they understood that glory, or in what
it essentially consisted, is another and very different ques‑
tion.

Enrolled as a soldier in the ninth regiment of Hussars,
I accompanied that corps to Nancy, where, at that time, a
large cavalry school was formed, and where the recruits
from the different regiments were trained and managed
before being sent forward to their destination.

A taste for equitation, and a certain aptitude for catching
up the peculiar character of the different horses, at once
distinguished me in the riding-school, and I was at last
adopted by the riding-master of the regiment as a kind of
aide to him in his walk. When I thus became a bold and
skilful horseman, my proficiency interfered with my pro‑
motion, for instead of accompanying my regiment I was
detained at Nancy, and attached to the permanent staff of
the cavalry school there.

At first I asked for nothing better. It was a life of con‑
tinued pleasure and excitement, and while I daily acquired
knowledge of a subject which interested me deeply, I grew
tall and strong of limb, and with that readiness in danger,
and that cool collectedness in moments of difficulty that
are so admirably taught by the accidents and mischances
of a cavalry riding-school.

The most vicious and unmanageable beasts from the Li‑
mousin were often sent to us, and when any one of these

was deemed peculiarly untractable, "Give him to Tiernay," was the last appeal, before abandoning him as hopeless. I'm certain I owe much of the formation of my character to my life at this period, and that my love of adventure, my taste for excitement, my obstinate resolution to conquer a difficulty, my inflexible perseverance when thwarted, and my eager anxiety for praise, were all picked up amid the sawdust and tan of the riding-school. How long I might have continued satisfied with such triumphs, and content to be the wonder of the freshly-joined conscripts, I know not, when accident, or something very like it, decided the question.

It was a calm, delicious evening in April, in the year after I had entered the school, that I was strolling alone on the old fortified wall, which, once a strong redoubt, was the favourite walk of the good citizens of Nancy. I was somewhat tired with the fatigues of the day, and sat down to rest under one of the acacia trees, whose delicious blossom was already scenting the air. The night was still and noiseless; not a man moved along the wall; the hum of the city was gradually subsiding, and the lights in the cottages over the plain told that the labourer was turning homeward from his toil. It was an hour to invite calm thoughts, and so I fell a-dreaming over the tranquil pleasures of a peasant's life, and the unruffled peace of an existence passed amid scenes that were endeared by years of intimacy. "How happily," thought I, "time must steal on in these quiet spots, where the strife and struggle of war are unknown, and even the sounds of conflict never reach." Suddenly my musings were broken in upon by hearing the measured tramp of cavalry, as at a walk; a long column wound their way along the zig-zag approaches, which by many a redoubt and fosse, over many a drawbridge, and beneath many a strong arch, led to the gates of Nancy. The loud, sharp call of a trumpet was soon heard, and, after a brief parley, the massive gates of the fortress were opened for the troops to enter. From the position I occupied exactly over the gate, I could not only see the long, dark line of armed men as they passed, but also hear the colloquy which took place as they entered:

" What regiment? "

" Detachments of the 12th Dragoons and the 22nd Chasseurs-à-Cheval."

" Where from? "

" Valence."

" Where to? "

" The army of the Rhine."

" Pass on!"

And with the words the ringing sound of the iron-shod horses was heard beneath the vaulted entrance. As they issued from beneath the long deep arch, the men were formed in line along two sides of a wide "Place" inside the walls, where, with that despatch that habit teaches, the billets were speedily distributed, and the parties "told off" in squads for different parts of the city. The force seemed a considerable one, and with all the celerity they could employ, the billeting occupied a long time. As I watched the groups moving off, I heard the direction given to one party, "Cavalry School—Rue de Lorraine." The young officer who commanded the group took a direction exactly the reverse of the right one ; and hastening down from the rampart, I at once overtook them, and explained the mistake. I offered them my guidance to the place, which being willingly accepted, I walked along at their side.

Chatting as we went, I heard that the dragoons were hastily withdrawn from La Vendée to form part of the force under General Hoche. The young sous-lieutenant, a mere boy of my own age, had already served in two campaigns in Holland and the south of France ; had been wounded in the Loire, and received his grade of officer at the hands of Hoche himself on the field of battle.

He could speak of no other name—Hoche was the hero of all his thoughts—his gallantry, his daring, his military knowledge, his coolness in danger, his impetuosity in attack, his personal amiability, the mild gentleness of his manner, were themes the young soldier loved to dwell on ; and however pressed by me to talk of war and its chances, he inevitably came back to the one loved theme—his general.

When the men were safely housed for the night, I invited my new friend to my own quarters, where, having provided the best entertainment I could afford, we passed more than half the night in chatting. There was nothing above mediocrity in the look or manner of the youth ; his descriptions of what he had seen were unmarked by anything glowing or picturesque ; his observations did not evince either a quick or a reflective mind, and yet, over this mass of commonplace, enthusiasm for his leader had shed a rich glow, like a gorgeous sunlight on a landscape, that made all beneath it seem brilliant and splendid.

"And now," said he, after an account of the last action he had seen, "and now, enough of myself; let's talk of thee. Where hast thou been ?"

"Here!" said I, with a sigh, and in a voice that shame had almost made inaudible. "Here, here, at Nancy."

"Not always here?"

"Just so. Always here."

"And what doing, mon cher. Thou art not one of the Municipal Guard, surely?"

"No," said I, smiling sadly, "I belong to the 'Ecole d'Equitation.'"

"Ah, that's it," said he, in somewhat of confusion; "1 always thought they selected old serjeants en retraite, worn out veterans, and wounded fellows, for riding-school duty."

"Most of ours are such," said I, my shame increasing at every word—"but somehow they chose me also, and I had no will in the matter——"

"No will in the matter, parbleu! and why not? Every man in France has a right to meet the enemy in the field. Thou art a soldier, a hussar of the 9th, a brave and gallant corps, and art to be told, that thy comrades have the road to fame and honour open to them; whilst thou art to mope away life like an invalided drummer? It is too gross an indignity, my boy, and must not be borne. Away with you to-morrow at daybreak to the 'Etat Major,' ask to see the Commandant. You're in luck, too, for our colonel is with him now, and he is sure to back your request. Say that you served in the school to oblige your superiors, but that you cannot see all chances of distinction lost to you for ever by remaining there. They've given you no grade yet, I see," continued he, looking at my arm.

"None; I am still a private."

"And I a sous-lieutenant, just because I have been where powder was flashing! You can ride well, of course?"

"I defy the wildest Limousin to shake me in my saddle."

"And, as a swordsman, what are you?"

"Gros Jean calls me his best pupil."

"Ah, true! you have Gros Jean here, the best 'sabreur' in France! And here you are—a horseman, and one of Gros Jean's 'eléves'—rotting away life in Nancy! Have you any friends in the service?"

"Not one."

"Not one! Nor relations, nor connections?"

"None. I am Irish by descent. My family are only French by one generation."

"Irish! Ah! that's lucky too," said he. "Our colonel is an Irishman. His name is Mahon. You're certain of

getting your leave now. I'll present you to him to-morrow. We are to halt two days here, and before that is
over, I hope you'll have made your last caracole in the
riding-school of Nancy."

"But remember," cried I, "that although Irish by
family, I have never been there. I know nothing of either
the people or the language—and do not present me to the
general as his countryman."

"I'll call you by your name, as a soldier of the 9th
Hussars, and leave you to make out your claim as countrymen, if you please, together."

This course was now agreed upon, and after some further
talking, my friend, refusing all my offers of a bed, coolly
wrapped his cloak about him, and, with his head on the
table, fell fast asleep, long before I had ceased thinking
over his stories and his adventures in camp and battle-field.

CHAPTER VIII.

"TRONCHON."

My duties in the riding-school were always over before
mid-day, and as noon was the hour appointed by the
young lieutenant to present me to his colonel, I was ready
by that time, and anxiously awaiting his arrival. I had
done my best to smarten up my uniform, and make all my
accoutrements bright and glistening. My scabbard was
polished like silver, the steel front of my shako shone
like a mirror, and the tinsel lace of my jacket had undergone a process of scrubbing and cleaning that threatened
its very existence. My smooth chin and beardless upper
lip, however, gave me a degree of distress that all other
deficiencies failed to inflict: I can dare to say, that no
mediæval gentleman's bald spot ever cost him one-half the
misery as did my lack of moustache occasion me. "A hussar without beard, as well without spurs or sabretasche;"
a tambour major without his staff, a cavalry charger without a tail, couldn't be more ridiculous: and there was that
old serjeant of the riding-school, "Tronchon," with a
beard that might have made a mattress! How the goods
of this world are unequally distributed! thought I; still
why might he not spare me a little—a very little would

suffice—just enough to give the "air hussar" to my countenance. He's an excellent creature, the kindest old fellow
in the world. I'm certain he'd not refuse me; to be sure,
the beard is a red one, and pretty much like bell-wire in
consistence; no matter, better that than this girlish smooth
chin I now wear.

Tronchon was spelling out the "Moniteur's" account of
the Italian campaign as I entered his room, and found it excessively difficult to get back from the Alps and Appennines
to the humble request I preferred.

"Poor fellows," muttered he, "four battles in seven
days, without stores of any kind or rations—almost without bread; and here comest thou, whining because thou
hasn't a beard."

"If I were not a hussar——"

"Bah!" said he, interrupting, "what of that? Where
shouldst thou have had thy baptism of blood, boy? Art a
child, nothing more."

"I shared my quarters last night with one, not older,
Tronchon, and he was an officer, and had seen many a
battle-field."

"I know that, too," said the veteran, with an expression
of impatience—"and that General Bonaparte will give
every boy his epaulettes before an old and tried soldier."

"It was not Bonaparte. It was——"

"I care not who promoted the lad; the system is just
the same with them all. It is no longer, 'Where have you
served?—what have you seen?' but, 'Can you read glibly?
—can you write faster than speak?—have you learned to
take towns upon paper, and attack a breastwork with a
rule and a pair of compasses?' This is what they called
'la génie' 'la génie'—ha! ha! ha!" cried he, laughing
heartily; "that's the name old women used to give the
devil when I was a boy."

It was with the greatest difficulty I could get him back
from these disagreeable reminiscences to the object of my
visit, and, even then, I could hardly persuade him that I
was serious in asking the loan of a beard. The prayer of
my petition being once understood, he discussed the project gravely enough; but to my surprise he was far more
struck by the absurd figure *he* should cut with his diminished mane, than *I* with my mock moustache.

"There's not a child in Nancy won't laugh at me—
they'll cry, 'There goes old Tronchon—he's like Kleber's
charger, which the German cut the tail off, to make a shako
plume!'"

I assured him that he might as well pretend to miss one

6

tree in the forest of "Fontainebleu"—that after furnishin
a squadron like myself, his would be still the first beard in
the Republic ; and at last he yielded, and gave in.

Never did a little damsel of the nursery array her doll
with more delighted looks, and gaze upon her handiwork
with more self-satisfaction, than did old Tronchon survey
me, as, with the aid of a little gum, he decorated my lip
with a stiff line of his iron-red beard.

"Diantre!" cried he, in ecstacy, "if thou ben't something like a man after all. Who would have thought it
would have made such a change ? Thou might pass for
one that saw real smoke and real fire, any day, lad. Ay!
thou hast another look in thine eye, and another way to
carry thy head, now ! Trust me, thou'lt look a different
fellow on the left of the squadron."

I began to think so too, as I looked at myself in the
small triangle of a looking-glass which decorated Tronchon's wall, under a picture of Kellerman, his first captain.
I fancied that the improvement was most decided.   I
thought that, bating a little over-ferocity, a something
verging upon the cruel, I was about as perfect a type of
the hussar as need be. My jacket seemed to fit tighter—
my pelisse hung more jauntily—my shako sat more saucily
on one side of my head—my sabre banged more proudly
against my boot—my very spurs jangled with a pleasanter
music—and all because a little hair bristled over my lip,
and curled in two spiral flourishes across my cheek! I
longed to see the effect of my changed appearance, as I
walked down the " Place Carrière," or sauntered into the
café where my comrades used to assemble. What will
Mademoiselle Josephine say, thought I, as I ask for my
" petit vèrre," caressing my moustache thus ! Not a doubt
of it, what a fan is to a woman a beard is to a soldier !—a
something to fill up the pauses in conversation, by blandly
smoothing with the finger, or fiercely curling at the point

"And so thou art going to ask for thy grade, Maurice?'
broke in Tronchon, after a long silence.

"Not at all. I am about to petition for employment upon
active service. I don't seek promotion till I have deserved
it."

" Better still, lad. I was eight years myself in the ranks
before they gave me the stripe on my arm. Parbleu ! the
Germans had given me some three or four with the sabre
before that time."

" Do you think they'll refuse me, Tronchon ? "

"Not if thou go the right way about it, lad. Thou mustn't
fancy it's like asking leave from the captain to spend the

evening in a Guinguette, or to go to the play with thy sweetheart No, no, boy. It must be done 'en regle.' Thou'lt have to wait on the general at his quarters at four o'clock, when he 'receives,' as they call it. Thou'lt be there, mayhap, an hour, ay, two or three belike, and after all, perhaps, won't see him that day at all! I was a week trying to catch Kellerman, and, at last, he only spoke to me going down stairs with his staff,—

"'Eh, Tronchon, another bullet in thy old carcass; want a furlough to get strong again, eh ?'

"'No, colonel; all sound this time. I want to be a sergeant—I'm twelve years and four months, corporal.'

"'Slow work, too,' said he, laughing, 'ain't it, Charles?' and he pinched one of his young officers by the cheek. 'Let old Tronchon have his grade; and I say, my good fellow,' said he to me, 'don't come plaguing me any more about promotion till I'm General of Division. You hear that ?'

"Well, he's got his step since; but I never teased him after."

"And why so, Tronchon ?" said I.

" I'll tell thee, lad," whispered he, in a low, confidential tone, as if imparting a secret well worth the hearing. "They can find fellows every day fit for lieutenants and chefs d'escadron. Parbleu! they meet with them in every café, in every 'billiard' you enter; but a sergeant! Maurice, one that drills his men on parade—can dress them like a wall—see that every kit is well pack'd, and every cartouch well filled—who knows every soul in his company as he knows the buckles of his own sword-belt—that's what one should not chance upon in baste. It's easy enough to manœuvre the men, Maurice; but to make them, boy, to fashion the fellows so that they be like the pieces of a great machine, that's the real labour—that's soldiering indeed."

"And you say I must write a petition, Tronchon ?" said I, more anxious to bring him back to my own affairs than listen to these speculations of his. How shall I do it ?"

" Sit down there, lad, and I'll tell thee. I've done the thing some scores of times, and know the words as well as I once knew my 'Pater.' Parbleu, I often wish I could remember that now, just to keep me from gloomy thoughts when I sit alone of an evening."

It was not a little to his astonishment, but still more to his delight, that I told the poor fellow I could help to refresh his memory, knowing, as I did, every word of the litanies by heart; and, accordingly, it was agreed on that

I should impart religious instruction in exchange for the secular knowledge he was conferring upon me.

"As for the petition," said Tronchon, seating himself opposite to me at the table, "it is soon done; for mark me, lad, these things must always be short; if thou be long-winded, they put thee away, and tell some of the clerks to look after thee—and there's an end of it. Be brief, therefore, and next—be legible—write in a good, large round hand; just as, if thou wert speaking, thou wouldst talk with a fine, clear, distinct voice. Well then, begin thus :—'Republic of France, one and invincible!' Make a flourish round that, lad, as if it came freely from the pen. When a man writes—'France!' he should do it as he whirls his sabre round his head in a charge! Ay, just so."

"I'm ready, Tronchon, go on."

"'Mon General!' Nay, nay—General mustn't be as large as France—yes, that's better. 'The undersigned, whose certificates of service and conduct are herewith enclosed.' Stay, stop a moment, Tronchon; don't forget that I have got neither one nor t'other. No matter; I'll make thee out both. Where was I?—Ay, 'herewith enclosed; and whose wounds, as the accompanying report will show——'"

"Wounds! I never received one."

"No matter, I'll—eh—what? Feu d'enfer! how stupid I am! What have I been thinking of? Why, boy, it was a sick-furlough I was about to ask for; the only kind of petition I have ever had to write in a life long."

"And I am asking for active service."

"Ha! That came without asking for in my case."

"Then what's to be done, Tronchon?—clearly this won't do!"

He nodded sententiously an assent, and, after a moment's rumination, said,—

"It strikes me, lad, there can be no need of begging for that which usually comes unlooked for; but if thou don't choose to wait for thy billet for t'other world, but must go and seek it, the best way will be to up and tell the general as much."

"That was exactly my intention."

"If he asks thee 'Canst ride?' just say, 'Old Tronchon taught me;' he'll be one of the young hands, indeed, if he don't know that name! And, mind, lad, have no whims or caprices about whatever service he names thee for, even wer't the infantry itself! It's a hard word, that' I know it well! but a man must make up his mind for any thing and everything. Wear any coat, go anywhere, face any enemy thou'rt ordered, and have none of those new-fangled notions about this general, or that army. Be a good soldier and a good comrade. Share thy kit and thy purse to the last sous, for it will not only be generous in thee, but that so long as thou hoardest not, thou'lt never be over eager for pillage. Mind these things, and with a stout heart and a sharp sabre, Maurice, 'tu ira loin.' Yes, I tell thee again, lad, ' tu ira loin.' "

I give these three words as he said them, for they have rung in my ears throughout all my life long. In moments of gratified ambition, in the glorious triumph of success, they have sounded to me like the confirmed predictions of one who foresaw my elevation in less prosperous hours. When fortune has looked dark and lowering, they have been my comforter and support, telling me not to be downcast or depressed, that the season of sadness would soon pass away, and the road to fame and honour again open before me.

" You really think so, Tronchon? You think that I shall be something yet?"

" 'Tu ira loin,' I say," repeated he emphatically, and with the air of an oracle who would not suffer further interrogation. I therefore shook his hand cordially, and set out to pay my visit to the general.

CHAPTER IX.

A SCRAPE AND ITS CONSEQUENCES.

WHEN I reached the quarters of the Etat Major, I found the great courtyard of the " hotel " crowded with soldiers of every rank and arm of the service. Some were newly-joined recruits waiting for the orders to be forwarded to their respective regiments, some were invalids just is-sued from the hospital, some were sick and wounded on their way homeward. There were sergeants with billet rolls, and returns, and court-martial sentences. Adjutants with regimental documents hastening hither and thither. Mounted orderlies, too, continually came and went; all was bustle, movement, and confusion. Officers in staff uniforms called out the orders from the different windows, and despatches were sent off here and there with hot haste. The building was the ancient palace of the Dukes of Lorraine, and a splendid fountain of white marble in the centre of the " Cour," still showed the proud armorial bearings of that princely house. Around the sculptured base of this now were seated groups of soldiers; their war-worn looks and piled arms contrasting strangely enough with the great porcelain vases of flowering plants that still decorated the rich "plateau." Shakos, helmets, and great-coats were hung upon the orange trees. The heavy boots of the cuirassier, the white leather apron of the " sapeur," were drying along the marble benches of the terrace. The richly-traceried veining of gilt iron-work, which separated the court from the garden, was actually covered with belts, swords, bayonets, and horse gear, in every stage and process of cleaning. Within the garden itself, however, all was silent and still; two sentries, who paced backwards and forwards beneath the "grille," showing that the spot was to be respected by those whose careless gestures and reckless air betrayed how little influence the mere " genius of the place" would exercise over them.

To me the interest of everything was increasing; and whether I lingered to listen to the raw remarks of the new recruit, in wonder at all he saw, or stopped to hear the campaigning stories of the old soldiers of the army, I never wearied. Few, if any, knew whither they were going; perhaps to the north to join the army of the Sambre; perhaps to the east to the force upon the Rhine. It might be that they were destined for Italy: none cared! Meanwhile, at every moment, detachments moved off, and their places were filled by fresh arrivals—all dusty and way-worn from the march. Some had scarcely time to eat a hurried morsel, when they were called on to " fall in," and again the word " forward" was given. Such of the infantry as appeared too weary for the march were sent on in great charrettes drawn by six or eight horses, and capable of carrying forty men in each ; and of these there seemed to be no end. No sooner was one detach-ment away than another succeeded. Whatever their des-tination, one thing seemed evident, the urgency that called them was beyond the common. For a while I forgot all about myself in the greater interest of the scene ; but then came the thought that I too should have my share in this onward movement, and now I set out to seek for my young friend, the " Sous-Lieutenant." I had not asked his name, but his regiment I knew to be the 22nd Chas-seurs-à-Cheval. The uniform was light green, and easily enough to be recognised; yet nowhere was it to be seen. There were cuirassiers, and hussars, heavy dragoons, and carabiniers in abundance—everything, in short, but what I sought.

At last I asked of an old quarter-master where the 22nd were quartered, and heard, to my utter dismay, that they had marched that morning at eight o'clock. There were two more squadrons expected to arrive at noon, but the orders were that they were to proceed without further halt.

" And whither to ?" asked I.

" To Treves, on the Moselle," said he, and turned away as if he would not be questioned further. It was true that my young friend could not have been much of a patron, yet the loss of him was deeply felt by me. He was to have introduced me to his colonel, who probably might have obtained the leave I desired at once; and now I knew no one, not one even to advise me how to act. I sat down upon a bench to think, but could resolve on nothing; the very sight of that busy scene had now become a reproach to me. There were the veterans of a hundred battles hastening forward again to the field ; there were the young soldiers just flushed with recent victory; even the peasant boys were " eager for the fray;" but I alone was to have no part in the coming glory. The enthusiasm of all around only served to increase and deepen my depression. There was not one there, from the old and war-worn veteran of the ranks to the merest boy, with whom I would not gladly have exchanged fortunes. Some hours passed over in these gloomy reveries, and when I looked up from the stupor my own thoughts had thrown over me, the " Cour" was almost empty. A few sick soldiers, waiting for their billets of leave, a few recruits not yet named to any corps, and a stray orderly or two standing beside his horse, were all that remained.

I arose to go away, but in my pre-occupation of mind, nstead of turning toward the street, I passed beneath a large archway into another court of the building, some-what smaller, but much richer in decoration and orna-ment than the outer one. After spending some time ad-miring the quaint devices and grim heads which peeped out from all the architraves and friezes, my eye was taught by a low, arched doorway, in the middle of which was a small railed window, like the grille of a convent. I approached, and perceived that it led into a garden, by a long, narrow walk of clipped yew, dense and upright as a wall. The trimly-raked gravel, and the smooth surface of the hedge, showed the care bestowed on the grounds to be a wide contrast to the neglect exhibited in the mansion itself; a narrow border of hyacinths and carnations ran along either side of the walk, the gorgeous blossoms appearing in strong relief against the background of dark foliage.

The door, as I leaned against it, gently yielded to the pressure of my arm, and almost without knowing it, I found myself standing within the precincts of the garden. My first impulse, of course, was to retire and close the door again, but somehow, I never knew exactly why, I could not resist the desire to see a little more of a scene so tempting. There was no mark of footsteps on the gravel, and I thought it likely the garden was empty. On I went, therefore, at first with cautious and uncertain steps, at last with more confidence, for as I issued from the hedge-walk, and reached an open space beyond, the solitude seemed unbroken. Fruit-trees, loaded with their produce, stood in a closely-shaven lawn, through which a small stream meandered, its banks planted with daffodills and water-lilies. Some pheasants moved about through the grass, but without alarm at my presence; while a young fawn boldly came over to me, and although in seeming disappointment at not finding an old friend, continued to walk beside me as I went.

The grounds appeared of great extent; paths led off in every direction; and while, in some places, I could perceive the glittering roof and sides of a conservatory, in others the humble culture of a vegetable garden was to be seen. There was a wondrous fascination in the calm and tranquil solitude around; and coming, as it did, so immediately after the busy bustle of the "soldiering," I soon not only forgot that I was an intruder there, but suffered myself to wander "fancy free," following out the thoughts each object suggested. I believe at that moment, if the choice were given me, I would rather have been the "Adam of that Eden" than the proudest of those generals that ever led a column to victory! Fortunately, or unfortunately—it would not be easy to decide which —the alternative was not open to me. It was while I was still musing, I found myself at the foot of a little eminence, on which stood a tower whose height and position showed it had been built for the view it afforded over a vast tract of country. Even from where I stood, at its base, I could see over miles and miles of a great plain, with the main roads leading towards the north and eastward. This spot was also the boundary of the grounds, and a portion of the old boulevard of the town formed the defence against the open country beyond. It was a deep ditch, with sides of sloping sward, cropped neatly, and kept in trimmest order; but, from its depth and width, forming a fence of a formidable kind. I was peering cautiously down into the abyss, when I heard a voice so close to my ear that I started with surprise. I listened, and perceived that the speaker was directly above me; and leaning over the battlements at the top of the tower.

" You're quite right," cried he, as he adjusted a telescope to his eye, and directed his view towards the plain. He has gone wrong! He has taken the Strasbourg road, instead of the northern one."

An exclamation of anger followed these words; and now I saw the telescope passed to another hand, and to my astonishment, that of a lady.

" Was there ever stupidity like that? He saw the map like the others, and yet——Parbleu! it's too bad!"

I could perceive that a female voice made some rejoinder, but not distinguish the words; when the man again spoke—

" No, no: it's all a blunder of that old major; and here am I without an orderly to send after him. Diable! it is provoking."

" Isn't that one of your people at the foot of the tower?" said the lady, as she pointed to where I stood, praying for the earth to open and close over me; for as he moved his head to look down, I saw the epaulettes of a staff officer.

" Halloa!" cried he, " are you on duty?"

" No, sir; I was——"

Not waiting for me to finish an explanation, he went on—

" Follow that division of cavalry that has taken the Strasbourg road, and tell Major Roquelard that he has gone wrong; he should have turned off to the left at the suburbs. Lose no time, but away at once. You are mounted, of course?"

" No, sir, my horse is at quarters; but I can——"

" No, no; it will be too late," he broke in again. " Take my troop horse, and be off. You'll find him in the stable to your left."

Then turning to the lady I heard him say—

" It may save Roquelard from an arrest."

I did not wait for more, but hurried off in the direction he had pointed. A short gravel walk brought me in front of a low building, in the cottage style, but which, deco-

rated with emblems of the chase, I guessed to be the stable.
Not a groom was to be seen ; but the door being unlatched
I entered freely. Four large and handsome horses were
feeding at the racks, their glossy coats and long silken
manes showing the care bestowed upon them. Which is
the trooper? thought I, as I surveyed them all with keen
and scrutinizing eye. All my skill in such matters was unable to decide the point; they seemed all alike valuable
and handsome—in equally high condition, and exhibiting
equal marks of careful treatment. Two were stamped on
the haunches with the letters " R. F.;" and these, of
course, were cavalry horses. One was a powerful black
horse, whose strong quarters and deep chest bespoke great
action, while the backward glances of his eye indicated
the temper of a " tartar." Making choice of him without
an instant's hesitation, I threw on the saddle, adjusted
the stirrups to my own length, buckled the bridle, and
led him forth. In all my "school experience" I had
never seen an animal that pleased me so much; his well-
arched neck and slightly-dipped back showed that an
Arab cross had mingled with the stronger qualities of the
Norman horse. I sprung to my saddle with delight; to
be astride such a beast was to kindle up all the enthusiasm
of my nature, and as I grasped the reins, and urged him
forward, I was half wild with excitement.

Apparently the animal was accustomed to more gentle
treatment, for he gave a loud snort, such as a surprised or
frightened horse will give, and then bounded forward once
or twice, as if to dismount me. This failing, he reared up
perfectly straight, pawing madly, and threatening even to
fall backwards. I saw that I had, indeed, selected a
wicked one ; for in every bound and spring, in every cur-
vet and leap, the object was clearly to unseat the rider.
At one instant he would crouch, as if to lie down, and then
bound up several feet in the air, with a toss up of his
haunches that almost sent me over the head. At another
he would spring from side to side, writhing and twisting
like a fish, till the saddle seemed actually slipping away
from his lithe body. Not only did I resist all these attacks,
but vigorously continued to punish with whip and spur
the entire time—a proceeding, I could easily see, he was
not prepared for. At last, actually maddened with his inability to throw me, and enraged by my continuing to spur
him, he broke away, and dashing headlong forward, rushed
into the very thickest of the grove. Fortunately for me,
the trees were either shrubs or of stunted growth, so that
 had only to keep my saddle to escape danger ; but

suddenly emerging from this, he gained the open sward, and as if his passion became more furious as he indulged in it, he threw up his head, and struck out in full gallop. I had but time to see that he was heading for the great fosse of the boulevard, when we were already on its brink. A shout, and a cry of I know not what, came from the tower ; but I heard nothing more. Mad as the maddened animal himself, perhaps at that moment just as indifferent to life, I dashed the spurs into his flanks, and over we went, lighting on the green sward as easily as a seagull on a wave. To all seeming, the terrible leap had somewhat sobered him ; but on me it had produced the very opposite effect. I felt that I had gained the mastery, and resolved to use it. With unrelenting punishment, then, I rode him forward, taking the country as it lay straight before me. The few fences which divided the great fields were too insignificant to be called leaps, and he took them in the "sling" of his stretching gallop. He was now subdued, yielding to every turn of my wrist, and obeying every motive of my will like an instinct. It may read like a petty victory; but he who has ever experienced the triumph over an enraged and powerful horse, well knows that few sensations are more pleasurably exciting. High as is the excitement of being borne along in full speed, leaving village and spire, glen and river, bridge and mill behind you—now careering up the mountain side, with the fresh breeze upon your brow ; now diving into the dark forest, startling the hare from her cover, and sending the wild deer scampering before you—it is still increased by the sense of a victory, by feeling that the mastery is with you, and that each bound of the noble beast beneath you has its impulse in your own heart.

Although the cavalry squadrons I was despatched to overtake had quitted Nancy four hours before, I came up with them in less than an hour, and inquiring for the officer in command, rode up to the head of the division. He was a thin, gaunt-looking, stern-featured man, who listened to my message without changing a muscle.

"Who sent you with this order?" said he.

"A general officer, sir, whose name I don't know ; but who told me to take his own horse and follow you."

"Did he tell you to kill the animal, sir?" said he, pointing to the heaving flanks and shaking tail of the exhausted beast.

"He bolted with me at first, major, and having cleared the ditch of the boulevard, rode away with me."

"Why, it's Colonel Mahon's Arab, 'Aleppo,'" said another

officer ; "what could have persuaded him to mount an orderly on a beast worth ten thousand francs ?"

I thought I'd have fainted, as I heard these words ; the whole consequences of my act revealed themselves before me, and I saw arrest, trial, sentence, imprisonment, and Heaven knew what afterwards, like a panorama rolling out to my view.

"Tell the colonel, sir," said the major, "that I have taken the north road, intending to cross over at Beaumont ; that the artillery trains have cut up the Metz road so deeply cavalry cannot travel ; tell him I thank him much for his politeness in forwarding this despatch to me ; and tell him, that I regret the rules of active service should prevent my sending back an escort to place yourself under arrest for the manner in which you have ridden—you hear, sir ?"

I touched my cap in salute.

"Are you certain, sir, that you have my answer correctly ?"

"I am, sir."

"Repeat it, then."

I related the reply, word for word, as he spoke it.

"No, sir," said he as I concluded ; "I said for un-soldier-like and cruel treatment to your horse."

One of his officers whispered something in his ear, and he quietly added—

"I find that I had not used these words, but I ought to have done so ; give the message, therefore, as you heard it at first."

"Mahon will shoot him, to a certainty," muttered one of the captains.

"I'd not blame him," joined another ; "that horse saved his life at Quiberon, when he fell in with a patrol ; and look at him now !"

The major made a sign for me to retire, and I turned and set out towards Nancy, with the feelings of a convict on the way to his fate.

If I did not feel that these brief records of an humble career were "upon honour," and that the only useful lesson a life so unimportant can teach, is the conflict between opposing influences, I might possibly be disposed to blink the avowal, that, as I rode along towards Nancy, a very great doubt occurred to me as to whether I ought not to desert ! It is a very ignoble expression ; but it must out. There were not in the French service any of those igno-minious punishments which, once undergone, a man is dis-honoured for ever, and no more admissible to rank with

men of character than if convicted of actual crime; but
there were marks of degradation, almost as severe, then
in vogue, and which men dreaded with a fear nearly as
acute—such, for instance, as being ordered for service at
the Bagne·de Brest, in Toulon—the arduous duty of
guarding the galley-slaves, and which was scarcely a degree above the condition of the condemned themselves.
Than such a fate as this, I would willingly have preferred
death. It was, then, this thought that suggested desertion; but I soon rejected the unworthy temptation, and
held on my way towards Nancy.

Aleppo, if at first wearied by the severe burst, soon
rallied, while he showed no traces of his fiery temper, and
exhibited few of fatigue; and as I walked along at his
side, washing his mouth and nostrils at each fountain I
passed, and slackening his saddle-girths to give him
freedom, long before we arrived at the suburbs he had
regained all his looks and much of his spirit.

At last we entered Nancy about nightfall, and, with a
failing heart, I found myself at the gate of the Ducal
palace. The sentries suffered me to pass unmolested, and
entering, I took my way through the court-yard, towards
the small gate of the garden, which, as I had left it, was
unlatched.

It was strange enough, the nearer I drew towards the
eventful moment of my fate, the more resolute and composed my heart became. It is possible, thought I, that in
a fit of passion he will send a ball through me, as the
officer said. Be it so—the matter is the sooner ended. If,
however, he will condescend to listen to my explanation,
I may be able to assert my innocence, at least so far as
intention went. With this comforting conclusion, I descended at the stable door. Two dragoons in undress were
smoking, as they lay at full length upon a bench, and
speedily arose as I came up.

"Tell the colonel he's come, Jacques," said one, in a
loud voice, and the other retired; while the speaker, turning towards me, took the bridle from my hand, and led
the animal in, without vouchsafing a word to me.

"An active beast that," said I, affecting the easiest and
coolest indifference. The soldier gave me a look of undisguised amazement, and I continued—

"He has had a bad hand on him, I should say—some
one too flurried and too fidgetty to give confidence to a
hot-tempered horse."

Another stare was all the reply.

"In a little time, and with a little patience, I'd make him as gentle as a lamb."

"I'm afraid you'll not have the opportunity," replied he, significantly; "but the colonel, I see, is waiting for you, and you can discuss the matter together."

The other dragoon had just then returned, and made me a sign to follow him. A few paces brought us to the door of a small pavilion, at which a sentry stood, and having motioned to me to pass in, my guide left me. An orderly sergeant at the same instant appeared, and beckoning to me to advance, he drew aside a curtain, and pushing me forward, let the heavy folds close behind me; and now I found myself in a richly-furnished chamber, at the further end of which an officer was at supper with a young and handsome woman. The profusion of wax lights on the table—the glitter of plate, and glass, and porcelain —the richness of the lady's dress, which seemed like the costume of a ball—were all objects distracting enough, but they could not turn me from the thought of my own condition; and I stood still and motionless, while the officer, a man of about fifty, with dark and stern features, deliberately scanned me from head to foot. Not a word did he speak, not a gesture did he make, but sat, with his black eyes actually piercing me. I would have given anything for some outbreak of anger, some burst of passion, that would have put an end to this horrible suspense, but none came; and there he remained several minutes, as if contemplating something too new and strange for utterance. "This must have an end," thought I—"here goes;" and so, with my hand in salute, I drew myself full up, and said—

"I carried your orders, sir, and received for answer that Major Roquelard had taken the north road advisedly, as that by Beaumont was cut up by the artillery trains; that he would cross over to the Metz Chaussée as soon as possible; that he thanked you for the kindness of your warning, and regretted that the rules of active service precluded his despatching an escort of arrest along with me, for the manner in which I had ridden with the order."

"Anything more?" asked the colonel. in a voice that sounded thick and guttural with passion.

"Nothing more, sir."

"No further remark or observation?"

"None, sir—at least from the major."

"What then—from any other?"

"A captain, sir, whose name I do not know, did say something."

"What was it?"

"I forget the precise words, sir, but their purport was, that Colonel Mahon would certainly shoot me when I got back."

"And you replied?"

"I don't believe I made any reply at the time, sir."

"But you thought, sir—what were your thoughts?"

"I thought it very like what I'd have done myself in a like case, although certain to be sorry for it afterwards."

Whether the emotion had been one for some time previous restrained, or that my last words had provoked it suddenly, I cannot tell, but the lady here burst out into a fit of laughter, but which was as suddenly checked by some sharp observation of the colonel, whose stern features grew sterner and darker every moment.

"There we differ, sir," said he, "for I should not. At the same instant he pushed his plate away, to make room on the table for a small portfolio, opening which, he prepared to write.

"You will bring this paper," continued he, "to the 'Prevot Marshal.' To-morrow morning you shall be tried by a regimental court-martial, and as your sentence may probably be the galleys and hard labour——"

"I'll save them the trouble," said I, quietly drawing my sword; but scarcely was it clear of the scabbard when a shriek broke from the lady, who possibly knew not the object of my act; at the same instant the colonel bounded across the chamber, and striking me a severe blow upon the arm, dashed the weapon from my hand to the ground.

"You want the 'fusillade'—is that what you want?" cried he, as, in a towering fit of passion, he dragged me forward to the light. I was now standing close to the table; the lady raised her eyes towards me, and at once broke out into a burst of laughter; such hearty, merry laughter, that, even with the fear of death before me, I could almost have joined in it.

"What is it—what do you mean, Laure?" cried the colonel, angrily.

"Don't you see it?" said she, still holding her kerchief to her face—"can't you perceive it yourself? He has only one moustache!"

I turned hastily towards the mirror beside me, and there was the fatal fact revealed—one gallant curl disported proudly over the left cheek, while the other was left bare.

"Is the fellow mad—a mountebank?" said the colonel, whose anger was now at its white heat.

"Neither, sir," said I, tearing off my remaining moustache, in shame and passion together. "Among my other misfortunes I have that of being young; and what's worse, I was ashamed of it; but I begin to see my error, and know that a man may be old without gaining either in dignity or temper."

With a stroke of his closed fist upon the table, the colonel made every glass and decanter spring from their places, while he uttered an oath that was only current in the days of that army. "This is beyond belief," cried he. "Come, gredin, you have at least had one piece of good fortune: you've fallen precisely into the hands of one who can deal with you.—Your regiment?"

"The Ninth Hussars."

"Your name?"

"Tiernay."

"Tiernay; that's not a French name?"

"Not originally; we were Irish once."

"Irish," said he, in a different tone from what he had hitherto used. "Any relative of a certain Comte Maurice de Tiernay, who once served in the Royal Guard?"

"His son, sir."

"What—his son! Ar't certain of this, lad? You remember your mother's name then—what was it?"

"I never knew which was my mother," said I. "Mademoiselle de la Lasterie or——"

He did not suffer me to finish, but throwing his arms around my neck, pressed me to his bosom.

"You are little Maurice, then," said he, "the son of my old and valued comrade! Only think of it, Laure—I was that boy's godfather."

Here was a sudden change in my fortunes; nor was it without a great effort that I could credit the reality of it, as I saw myself seated between the colonel and his fair companion, both of whom overwhelmed me with attention. It turned out that Colonel Mahon had been a fellow-guardsman with my father, for whom he had ever preserved the warmest attachment. One of the few survivors of the "Garde du Corps," he had taken service with the Republic, and was already reputed as one of the most distinguished cavalry officers.

"Strange enough, Maurice," said he to me, "there was something in your look and manner, as you spoke to me there, that recalled your poor father to my memory; and without knowing or suspecting why, I suffered you to bandy words with me, while at another moment I would have ordered you to be ironed and sent to prison."

Of my mother, of whom I wished much to learn some-thing, he would not speak, but adroitly changed the con-versation to the subject of my own adventures, and these he made me recount from the beginning. If the lady enjoyed all the absurdities of my chequered fortune with a keen sense of the ridiculous, the colonel apparently could trace in them but so many resemblances to my fa-ther's character, and constantly broke out into exclamations of "How like him!" "Just what he would have done himself!" "His own very words!" and so on.

It was only in a pause of the conversation, as the clock on the mantle-piece struck eleven, that I was aware of the lateness of the hour, and remembered that I should be on the punishment-roll the next morning for absence from quarters.

"Never fret about that, Maurice, I'll return your name as on a special service; and to have the benefit of truth on our side, you shall be named one of my orderlies, with the grade of corporal."

"Why not make him a sous-lieutenant?" said the lady, in a half-whisper. "I'm sure he is better worth his epau-lettes than any I have seen on your staff."

"Nay, nay," muttered the colonel, "the rules of the service forbid it. He'll win his spurs time enough, or I'm much mistaken."

While I thanked my new and kind patron for his good-ness, I could not help saying that my heart was eagerly set upon the prospect of actual service; and that proud as I should be of his protection, I would rather merit it by my conduct than owe my advancement to favour.

"Which simply means that you are tired of Nancy, and riding drill, and want to see how men comport themselves where the manœuvres are not arranged beforehand. Well, so far you are right, boy. I shall, in all likelihood, be stationed here for three or four months, during which you might have advanced a stage or so towards those epau-lettes my fair friend desires to see upon your shoulders. You shall, therefore, be sent forward to your own corps. I'll write to the colonel to confirm the rank of corporal; the regiment is at present on the Moselle; and, if I mis-take not, will soon be actively employed. Come to me to-morrow before noon, and be prepared to march with the first detachments that are sent forward."

A cordial shake of the hand followed these words; and the lady having also vouchsafed me an equal token of

7

her good-will, I took my leave, the happiest fellow that
ever betook himself to quarters after hours, and as indifferent to the penalties annexed to the breach of discipline
as if the whole code of martial law were a mere fable.

CHAPTER X.

AN ARISTOCRATIC REPUBLICAN.

IF the worthy reader would wish to fancy the happiest of
all youthful beings, let him imagine what I must have
been, as, mounted upon Aleppo, a present from my godfather, with a purse of six shining louis in my pocket,
and a letter to my colonel, I set forth for Metz. I had
breakfasted with Colonel Mahon, who, amid much good
advice for my future guidance, gave me, half slily, to
understand that the days of Jacobinism had almost run
their course, and that a reactionary movement had already
set in. The Republic, he added, was as strong, perhaps
stronger, than ever, but that men had grown weary of mob
tyranny, and were, day by day, reverting to the old loyalty, in respect for whatever pretended to culture, good
breeding, and superior intelligence. "As, in a shipwreck,
the crew instinctively turn for counsel and direction to the
officers, you will see that France will, notwithstanding all
the libertinism of our age, place her confidence in the men
who have been the tried and worthy servants of former
governments. So far, then, from suffering on account of
your gentle blood, Maurice, the time is not distant when
it will do you good service; and when every association
that links you with family and fortune will be deemed an
additional guarantee of your good conduct. I mention
these things," continued he, "because your colonel is what
they call a 'Grosbleu,' that is, a coarse-minded, inveterate
republican, detesting aristocracy and all that belongs to it.
Take care, therefore, to give him no just cause for discontent, but be just as steady in maintaining your position as
the descendant of a noble house, who has not forgotten
what were once the privileges of his rank. Write to me
frequently and freely, and I'll take care that you want for
nothing, so far as my small means go, to sustain whatever
grade you occupy. Your own conduct shall decide

whether I ever desire to have any other inheritor than the son of my oldest friend in the world."

Such were his last words to me, as I set forth, in company with a large party, consisting, for the most part, of under officers and employés attached to the medical staff of the army. It was a very joyous and merry fraternity, and, consisting of ingredients drawn from different pursuits and arms of the service, infinitely amusing from contrast of character and habits. My chief associate amongst them was a young sous-lieutenant of dragoons, whose age, scarcely much above my own, joined to a joyous, reckless temperament, soon pointed him out as the character to suit me: his name was Eugene Santron. In appearance he was slightly formed, and somewhat under-sized, but with handsome features, their animation rendered sparkling by two of the wickedest black eyes that ever glistened and glittered in a human head. I soon saw that, under the mask of affected fraternity and equality, he nourished the most profound contempt for the greater number of associates, who, in truth, were, however " braves gens," the very roughest and least-polished specimens of the polite nation. In all his intercourse with them, Eugene affected the easiest tone of camaraderie and equality, never assuming in the slightest, nor making any pretensions to the least superiority on the score of position or acquirements, but on the whole consoling himself, as it were, by " playing them off " in their several eccentricities, and rendering every trait of their vulgarity and ignorance tributary to his own amusement. Partly from seeing that he made me an exception to this practice, and partly from his perceiving the amusement it afforded me, we drew closer towards each other, and before many days elapsed, had become sworn friends.

There is probably no feature of character so very attractive to a young man as frankness. The most artful of all flatteries is that which addresses itself by candour, and seems at once to select, as it were by intuition, the object most suited for a confidence. Santron carried me by a coup de main of this kind, as taking my arm one evening, as I was strolling along the banks of the Moselle, he said—

" My dear Maurice, it's very easy to see that the society of our excellent friends yonder is just as distasteful to you as to me. One cannot always be satisfied laughing at their solecisms in breeding and propriety. One grows weary at last of ridiculing their thousand absurdities; and then there comes the terrible retribution in the reflection of what the devil brought me into such company? a question that, however easily answered, grows more and more intolerable the oftener it is asked. To be sure, in my case there was little choice in the matter, for I was not in any way the arbiter of my own fortune. I saw myself converted from a royal page to a printer's devil by a kind old fellow, who saved my life by smearing my face with ink, and covering my scarlet uniform with a filthy blouse; and since that day I have taken the hint, and often found the lesson a good one—the dirtier the safer!

"We were of the old nobility of France, but as the name of our family was the cause of its extinction, I took care to change it. I see you don't clearly comprehend me, and so I'll explain myself better. My father lived unmolested during the earlier days of the Revolution, and might so have continued to the end, if a detachment of the Garde Republicaine had not been despatched to our neighbourhood of Sarre Louis, where it was supposed some lurking regard for royalty yet lingered. These fellows neither knew nor cared for the ancient noblesse of the country, and one evening a patrol of them stopped my father as he was taking his evening walk along the ramparts. He would scarcely deign to notice the insolent ' Qui va la!' of the sentry, a summons he at least thought superfluous in a town which had known his ancestry for eight or nine generations. At the repetition of the cry, accompanied by something that sounded ominous, in the sharp click of a gun-lock, he replied haughtily, ' Je suis le Marquis de Saint-Trone.'

"'There are no more Marquises in France!' was the savage answer.

"My father smiled contemptuously, and briefly said ' Saint-Trone.'

"' We have no Saints either,' cried another.

"' Be it so, my friend,' said he, with mingled pity and disgust. 'I suppose some designation may at least be left to me, and that I may call myself Trone.'

"' We are done with thrones long ago,' shouted they in chorus, ' and we'll finish you also.'

"Aye, and they kept their word, too. They shot him that same evening, on very little other charge than his own name! If I have retained the old sound of my name I have given it a more plebeian spelling, which is, perhaps, just as much of an alteration as any man need submit to for a period that will pass away so soon."

"How so, Eugene? you fancy the Republic will not endure in France. What, then, can replace it?"

" Anything, everything ; for the future all is possible. We have annihilated legitimacy, it is true, just as the Indians destroy a forest, by burning the trees, but the roots remain, and if the soil is incapable of sending up the giant stems as before, it is equally unable to furnish a new and different culture. Monarchy is just as firmly rooted in a Frenchman's heart, but he will have neither patience for its tedious growth, nor can he submit to restore what has cost him so dearly to destroy. The consequences will, therefore, be a long and continued struggle between parties, each imposing upon the nation the form of government that pleases it in turn. Meanwhile you and I, and others like us, must serve whatever is uppermost—the cleverest fellow he who sees the coming change, and prepares to take advantage of it."

" Then are you a Royalist?" asked I.

" A Royalist! What I stand by a monarch who deserted his aristocracy, and forgot his own order ; defend a throne that he had reduced to the condition of a fauteuil de Bourgeois?"

" You are then for the Republic ? "

" For what robbed me of my inheritance—what degraded me from my rank, and reduced me to a state below that of my own vassals! Is this a cause to uphold?"

" You are satisfied with military glory, perhaps," said I, scarcely knowing what form of faith to attribute to him.

" In an army where my superiors are the very dregs of the people ; where the canaille have the command, and the chivalry of France is represented by a sans-culotte!"

" The cause of the church——"

A burst of ribald laughter cut me short, and laying his hand on my shoulder he looked me full in the face ; while with a struggle to recover his gravity, he said—

" I hope, my dear Maurice, you are not serious, and that you do not mean this for earnest! Why, my dear boy, don't you talk of the Eleusinian Mysteries, the Delphic Oracle of Alchemy, Astrology—of anything, in short, of which the world, having amused itself, has, at length, grown weary ? Can't you see that the church has passed away, and these good priests have gone the same road as their predecessors? Is any acuteness wanting to show that there is an end of this superstition that has enthralled men's minds for a couple of thousand years ? No, no, their game is up, and for ever. These pious men, who despised this world, and yet had no other hold upon the minds of others than by the very craft and subtlety that world taught them—these heavenly souls, whose whole machinations revolved about earthy objects and the successes of this grovelling planet! Fight for them! No, parbleu; we owe them but little love or affection. Their whole aim in life has been to disgust one with whatever is enjoyable, and the best boon they have conferred upon humanity, that bright thought of locking up the softest eyes and fairest cheeks of France in cloisters and nunneries! I can forgive our glorious Revolution much of its wrong when I think of the Prêtre; not but that they could have knocked down the church without suffering the ruins to crush the chateau!"

Such, in brief, were the opinions my companion held, and of which I was accustomed to hear specimens every day; at first, with displeasure and repugnance; later on, with more of toleration; and at last, with a sense of amusement at the singularity of the notions, or the dexterity with which he defended them. The poison of his doctrines were the more insidious, because, mingled with a certain dash of good nature, and a reckless, careless easiness of disposition always attractive to very young men. His reputation for courage, of which he had given signal proofs, elevated him in my esteem; and, ere long, all my misgivings about him, in regard of certain blemishes, gave way before my admiration of his heroic bearing and a readiness to confront peril, wherever to be found.

I had made him the confidant of my own history, of which I told him everything, save the passages which related to the Pére Michel. These I either entirely glossed over, or touched so lightly as to render unimportant; a dread of ridicule restraining me from any mention of those earlier scenes of my life, which were alone of all those I should have avowed with pride. Perhaps it was from mere accident—perhaps some secret shame to conceal my forlorn and destitute condition may have had its share in the motive; but, for some cause or other, I gave him to understand that my acquaintance with Colonel Mahon had dated back to a much earlier period than a few days before, and, the impression once made, a sense of false shame led me to support it.

"Mahon can be a good friend to you," said Eugene; "he stands well with all parties. The Convention trust him, the sans-culottes are afraid of him, and the few men of family whom the guillotine has left look up to him as one of their staunchest adherents. Depend upon it, therefore, your promotion is safe enough, even if there were not a field open for every man who seeks the path to emi-

nence. The great point, however, is to get service with
the army of Italy. These campaigns here are as barren
and profitless as the soil they are fought over: but, in the
south, Maurice, in the land of dark eyes and tresses,
under the blue skies, or beneath the trellised vines, there
are rewards of victory more glorious than a grateful
country, as they call it, ever bestowed. Never forget, my
boy, that you or I have no cause! It is to us a matter of
indifference what party triumphs, or who is uppermost.
The government may change to-morrow, and the day
after, and so on for a month long, and yet we remain
just as we were. Monarchy, Commonwealth, Democracy
—what you will—may rule the hour, but the sous-lieutenant is but the servant who changes his master. Now, in
revenge for all this, we have one compensation—which is,
to 'live for the day.' To make the most of that brief
hour of sunshine granted us, and to taste of every pleasure—to mingle in every dissipation—and enjoy every excitement that we can. This is my philosophy, Maurice,
and just try it."

Such was the companion with whom chance threw me
in contact, and I grieve to think how rapidly his influence
gained the mastery over me.

CHAPTER XI.

"THE PASSAGE OF THE RHINE."

I PARTED from my friend Eugene at Treves, where he
remained in garrison, while I was sent forward to Cob-
lentz to join my regiment, at that time forming part of
Ney's division.

Were I to adhere in my narrative to the broad current
of great events, I should here have to speak of that grand
scheme of tactics by which Kleber, advancing from the
Lower Rhine, engaged the attention of the Austrian
Grand Duke, in order to give time and opportunity for
Hoche's passage of the river at Strasbourg, and the com-
mencement of that campaign which had for its object the
subjugation of Germany. I have not, however, the pretension to chronicle those passages which history has for
ever made memorable, even were my own share in them

of a more distinguished character. The insignificance of
my station must, therefore, be my apology if I turn from
the description of great and eventful incidents to the humble narrative of my own career.

Whatever the contents of Colonel Mahon's letter, they
did not plead very favourably for me with Colonel Hacque,
my new commanding officer; neither, to all seeming, did
my own appearance weigh anything in my favour. Raising
his eyes at intervals from the letter to stare at me, he uttered some broken phrases of discontent and displeasure;
at last he said—"What's the object of this letter, sir; to
what end have you presented it to me?"

"As I am ignorant of its contents, mon Colonel," said
I, calmly, "I can scarcely answer the question."

"Well, sir, it informs me that you are the son of a
certain Count Tiernay, who has long since paid the price
of his nobility; and that being an especial protegé of the
writer, he takes occasion to present you to me; now I ask
again, with what object?"

"I presume, sir, to obtain for me the honour which I
now enjoy—to become personally known to you."

"I know every soldier under my command, sir," said
he, rebukingly, "as you will soon learn if you remain in
my regiment. I have no need of recommendatory letters
on that score. As to your grade of corporal, it is not confirmed; time enough when your services shall have shown
that you deserve promotion. Parbleu, sir, you'll have to
show other claims than your ci-devant countship."

"Colonel Mahon gave me a horse, sir; may I be permitted to retain him as a regimental mount?" asked I,
timidly.

"We want horses—what is he like?"

"Three-quarters Arab, and splendid in action, sir."

"Then, of course, unfit for service and field manœuvres.
Send him to the Etat Major. The Republic will find a
fitting mount for you; you may retire."

And I did retire, with a heart almost bursting between
anger and disappointment. What a future did this opening present to me! What a realisation this of all my
flattering hopes!

This sudden reverse of fortune, for it was nothing less,
did not render me more disposed to make the best of my
new condition, nor see in the most pleasing light the rough
and rude fraternity among which I was thrown. The
Ninth Hussars were reputed to be an excellent service-
corps, but, off duty, contained some of the worst ingredients of the army. Play, and its consequence, duelling,

filled up every hour not devoted to regimental duty; and
low as the tone of manners and morals stood in the service
generally, "Hacque's Tapageurs," as they were called, enjoyed the unflattering distinction of being the leaders.
Self-respect was a quality utterly unknown amongst them
—none felt ashamed at the disgrace of punishment—and
as all knew that, at the approach of the enemy, prison-
doors would open, and handcuffs fall off, they affected to
think the Salle de Police was a pleasant alternative to the
fatigue and worry of duty. These habits not only stripped
soldiering of all its chivalry, but robbed freedom itself of
all its nobility. These men saw nothing but licentiousness in their newly-won liberty. Their "Equality" was
the permission to bring everything down to a base and unworthy standard; their "Fraternity," the appropriation
of what belonged to one richer than themselves.

It would give me little pleasure to recount, and the
reader, in all likelihood, as little to hear, the details of my
life among such associates. They are the passages of my
history most painful to recall, and least worthy of being
remembered; nor can I even yet write without shame the
confession, how rapidly their habits became my own. Eugene's teachings had prepared me, in a manner, for their
lessons. His scepticism extending to everything and every
one, had made me distrustful of all friendship, and suspicious of whatever appeared a kindness. Vulgar association, and daily intimacy with coarsely-minded men, soon
finished what he had begun; and in less time than it took
me to break my troop-horse to regimental drill, I had been
myself "broke in" to every vice and abandoned habit of
my companions.

It was not in my nature to do things by halves; and
thus I became, and in a brief space, too, the most inveterate Tapageur of the whole regiment. There was not a
wild prank or plot in which I was not foremost, not a breach
of discipline unaccompanied by my name or presence, and
more than half the time of our march to meet the enemy,
I passed in double irons under the guard of the Provost-
marshal.

It was at this pleasant stage of my education that our
brigade arrived at Strasbourg, as part of the corps d'armée,
under the command of General Moreau.

He had just succeeded to the command on the dismissal
of Pichegru, and found the army not only dispirited by the
defeats of the past campaign, but in a state of rudest
indiscipline and disorganisation. If left to himself, he
would have trusted much to time and circumstances for

the reform of abuses that had been the growth of many months long. But Regnier, the second in command, was made of "different stuff;" he was a harsh and stern disciplinarian, who rarely forgave a first, never a second, offence, and who, deeming the Salle de Police as an incumbrance to an army on service, which, besides, required a guard of picked men, that might be better employed elsewhere, usually gave the preference to the shorter sentence of "four paces and a fusillade." Nor was he particular in the classification of those crimes he thus expiated : from the most trivial excess to the wildest scheme of insubordination, all came under the one category. More than once, as we drew near to Strasbourg, I heard the project of a mutiny discussed, day after day. Some one or other would denounce the "scélérat Regnier," and proclaim his readiness to be the executioner; but the closer we drew to head-quarters, the more hushed and subdued became these mutterings, till at last they ceased altogether ; and a dark and foreboding dread succeeded to all our late boastings and denunciations.

This at first surprised and then utterly disgusted me with my companions. Braves as they were before the enemy, had they no courage for their own countrymen ? Was all their valour the offspring of security, or could they only be rebellious when the penalty had no terrors for them ? Alas! I was very young, and did not then know that men are never strong against the right, and that a bad cause is always a weak one.

It was about the middle of June when we reached Strasbourg, where now about forty thousand troops were assembled. I shall not readily forget the mingled astonishment and disappointment our appearance excited as the regiment entered the town. The Tapageurs, so celebrated for all their terrible excesses and insubordination, were seen to be a fine corps of soldier-like fellows, their horses in high condition, their equipments and arms in the very best order. Neither did our conduct at all tally with the reputation that preceded us. All was orderly and regular in the several billets; the parade was particularly observed ; not a man late at the night muster. What was the cause of this sudden and remarkable change? Some said that we were marching against the enemy ; but the real explanation lay in the few words of a general order read to us by our colonel the day before we entered the city :—

" The 9th Hussars have obtained the unworthy reputation of being an ill-disciplined and ill-conducted regiment, relying upon their soldier-like qualities in face of the enemy to cover the disgrace of their misconduct in quarters. This is a mistake that must be corrected. All Frenchmen are brave ; none can arrogate to themselves any prerogative of valour. If any wish to establish such a belief, a campaign can always attest it. If any profess to think so without such proof, and, acting in conformity with this impression, disobey their orders or infringe regimental discipline, I will have them shot.

"REGNIER,

"Adjutant-General."

This was, at least, a very straightforward and intelligible announcement, and as such my comrades generally acknowledged it. I, however, regarded it as a piece of monstrous and intolerable tyranny, and sought to make converts to my opinion by declaiming about the rights of Frenchmen, the liberty of free discussion, the glorious privilege of equality, and so on ; but these arguments sounded faint in presence of the drum-head; and while some slunk away from the circle around me, others significantly hinted that they would accept no part of the danger my doctrines might originate.

However I might have respected my comrades had they been always the well-disciplined body I now saw them, I confess that this sudden conversion from fear was in nowise to my taste, and rashly confounded their dread of punishment with a base and ignoble fear of death. "And these are the men," thought I, "who talk of their charging home through the dense squares of Austria—who have hunted the leopard into the sea ! and have carried the flag of France over the high Alps !"

A bold rebel, whatever may be the cause against which he revolts, will always be sure of a certain ascendancy. Men are prone to attribute power to pretension, and he who stands foremost in the breach will at least win the suffrages of those whose cause he assumes to defend. In this way it happened that exactly as my comrades fell in my esteem, I was elevated in theirs ; and while I took a very depreciating estimate of their courage, they conceived a very exalted opinion of mine.

It was altogether inexplicable to see these men, many of them the bronzed veterans of a dozen campaigns—the wounded and distinguished soldiers in many a hard-fought field, yielding up their opinions and sacrificing their convictions to a raw and untried stripling who had never yet seen an enemy.

With a certain fluency of speech I possessed also a readiness at picking up information, and arraying the scattered fragments of news into a certain consistence, which greatly imposed upon my comrades. A quick eye for manœuvres, and a shrewd habit of combining in my own mind the various facts that came before me, made me appear to them a perfect authority on military matters, of which I talked, I shame to say, with all the confidence and presumption of an accomplished general. A few lucky guesses, and a few half hints, accidentally confirmed, completed all that was wanting; and what says "Le Jeune Maurice," was the inevitable question that followed each piece of flying gossip, or every rumour that rose of a projected movement.

I have seen a good deal of the world since that time, and I am bound to confess, that not a few of the great reputations I have witnessed have stood upon grounds very similar, and not a whit more stable than my own. A bold face, a ready tongue, a promptness to support, with my right hand, whatever my lips were pledged to, and, above all, good luck, made me the king of my company; and although that sovereignty only extended to half a squadron of hussars, it was a whole universe to me.

So stood matters when, on the 23rd of June, orders came for the whole corps d'armée to hold itself in readiness for a forward movement. Rations for two days were distributed, and ammunition given out as if for an attack of some duration. Meanwhile, to obviate any suspicion of our intentions, the gates of Strasbourg, on the eastern side, were closed—all egress in that direction forbidden—and couriers and estafettes sent off towards the north, as if to provide for the march of our force in that direction. The arrival of various orderly dragoons during the previous night, and on that morning early, told of a great attack in force on Manheim, about sixty miles lower down the Rhine, and the cannonade of which some avowed that they could hear at that distance. The rumour, therefore, seemed confirmed, that we were ordered to move to the north, to support this assault.

The secret despatch of a few dismounted dragoons and some riflemen to the banks of the Rhine, however, did not strike me as according with this view, and particularly as I saw that, although all were equipped, and in readiness to move, the order to march was not given, a delay very unlikely to be incurred if we were destined to act as the reserve of the force already engaged.

Directly opposite to us, on the right bank of the river, and separated from it by a low flat of about two miles in extent, stood the fortress of Kehl, at that time garrisoned by a strong Austrian force ; the banks of the river, and the wooded islands in the stream, which communicated with the right by bridges, or fordable passes, being also held by the enemy in force.

These we had often seen, by the aid of telescopes, from the towers and spires of Strasbourg ; and now I remarked that the general and his staff seemed more than usually intent on observing their movemants. This fact, coupled with the not less significant one that no preparations for a defence of Strasbourg were in progress, convinced me that, instead of moving down the Rhine to the attack on Manheim, the plan of our general was to cross the river where we were, and make a dash at the fortress of Kehl. I was soon to receive the confirmation of my suspicion, as the orders came for two squadrons of the 9th to proceed, dismounted, to the bank of the Rhine, and, under shelter of the willows, to conceal themselves there. Taking possession of the various skiffs and fishing boats along the bank, we were distributed in small parties, to one of which, consisting of eight men under the orders of a corporal, I belonged.

About an hour's march brought us to the river-side, in a little clump of alder willows, where, moored to a stake, lay a fishing boat with two short oars in her. Lying down beneath the shade, for the afternoon was hot and sultry, some of us smoked, some chatted, and a few dozed away the hours that somehow seemed unusually slow in passing.

There was a certain dogged sullenness about my companions, which proceeded from their belief that we and all who remained at Strasbourg were merely left to occupy the enemy's attention, while greater operations were to be carried on elsewhere.

"You see what it is to be a condemned corps," muttered one ; "it's little matter what befalls the old 9th, even should they be cut to pieces."

"They didn't think so at Enghien," said another, "when we rode down the Austrian cuirassiers."

"Plain enough," cried a third, "we are to have skirmishers' duty here, without skirmishers' fortune in having a force to fall back upon."

" Eh! Maurice, is not this very like what you predicted
for us?" broke in a fourth, ironically.

" I'm of the same mind still," rejoined I, coolly : " the
general is not thinking of a retreat ; he has no intention
of deserting a well-garrisoned, well-provisioned fortress.
Let the attack on Manheim have what success it may,
Strasbourg will be held still.   I overheard Colonel Guyon
remark that the waters of the Rhine have fallen three feet
since the draught set in, and Regnier replied 'that we must
lose no time, for there will come rain and floods ere long.'
Now what could that mean but the intention to cross over
yonder ?"

" Cross the Rhine in face of the fort of Kehl !" broke
in the corporal.

" The French army have done bolder things before
now!" was my reply ; and, whatever the opinion of my
comrades, the flattery ranged them on my side.   Perhaps
the corporal felt it beneath his dignity to discuss tactics
with an inferior, or perhaps he felt unable to refute the
specious pretensions I advanced ; in any case he turned
away, and either slept, or affected sleep, while I strenuously
laboured to convince my companions that my surmise was
correct.

I repeated all my former arguments about the decrease
in the Rhine, showing that the river was scarcely two-
thirds of its habitual breadth, that the nights were now
dark, and well suited for a surprise, that the columns which
issued from the town took their departure with a pomp
and parade far more likely to attract the enemy's attention
than escape his notice, and were, therefore, the more likely
to be destined for some secret expedition, of which all this
display was but the blind.   These, and similar facts, I
grouped together with a certain ingenuity, which, if it
failed to convince, at least silenced my opponents.   And
now the brief twilight, if so short a struggle between day
and darkness deserved the name, passed off, and night
suddenly closed around us—a night black and starless, for
a heavy mass of lowering cloud seemed to unite with the
dense vapour that arose from the river, and the low-lying
grounds along side of it.   The air was hot and sultry, too,
like the precursor of a thunder-storm, and the rush of the
stream as it washed among the willows sounded preter-
naturally loud in the stillness.

A hazy, indistinct flame, the watch-fire of the enemy,
on the island of Eslar, was the only object visible in the
murky darkness.   After a while, however, we could detect

another fire on a smaller island, a short distance higher up the stream. This, at first dim and uncertain, blazed up after a while, and at length we descried the dark shadows of men as they stood around it.

It was but the day before that I had been looking on a map of the Rhine, and remarked to myself that this small island, little more than a mere rock in the stream, was so situated as to command the bridge between Eslar and the German bank, and I could not help wondering that the Austrians had never taken the precaution to strengthen it, or at least place a gun there, to enfilade the bridge. Now, to my extreme astonishment, I saw it occupied by the soldiery, who, doubtless, were artillery, as in such a position small arms would prove of slight efficiency. As I reflected over this, wondering within myself if any intimation of our movements could have reached the enemy, I heard along the ground on which I was lying the peculiar tremulous, dull sound communicated by a large body of men marching. The measured tramp could not be mistaken, and as I listened I could perceive that a force was moving towards the river from different quarters. The rumbling roll of heavy guns and the clattering noise of cavalry were also easily distinguished, and awaking one of my comrades I called his attention to the sounds.

"Parbleu!" said he, "thou'rt right; they're going to make a dash at the fortress, and there will be hot work ere morning. What say you now, corporal? has Maurice hit it off this time?"

"That's as it may be," growled the other sulkily; "guessing is easy work ever for such as thee! but if he be so clever, let him tell us why are we stationed along the river's bank in small detachments. We have had no orders to observe the enemy, nor to report upon anything that might go forward; nor do I see with what object we were to secure the fishing boats; troops could never be conveyed across the Rhine in skiffs like these!"

"I think that this order was given to prevent any of the fishermen giving information to the enemy in case of a sudden attack," replied I.

"Mayhap thou wert at the council of war when the plan was decided on," said he, contemptuously. "For a fellow that never saw the smoke of an enemy's gun, thou hast a rare audacity in talking of war!"

"Yonder is the best answer to your taunt," said I, as in a little bend of the stream beside us, two boats were seen to pull under the shelter of the tall alders, from which the clank of arms could be plainly heard; and now another larger launch swept past, the dark shadows of a dense crowd of men showing above the gunwale.

"They are embarking, they are certainly embarking" now ran from mouth to mouth. As the troops arrived at the river's bank they were speedily "told off" in separate divisions, of which some were to lead the attack, others to follow, and a third portion to remain as a reserve in the event of a repulse.

The leading boat was manned entirely by volunteers, and I could hear from where I lay, the names called aloud as the men stepped out from the ranks. I could hear that the first point of attack was the island of Eslar. So far there was a confirmation of my own guessing, and I did not hesitate to assume the full credit of my skill from my comrades. In truth, they willingly conceded all or even more than I asked for. Not a stir was heard, not a sight seen, not a movement made of which I was not expected to tell the cause and the import; and knowing that to sustain my influence there was nothing for it but to affect a thorough acquaintance with everything, I answered all their questions boldly and unhesitatingly. I need scarcely observe that the corporal in comparison sunk into downright insignificance. He had already shown himself a false guide, and none asked his opinion further, and I became the ruling genius of the hour. The embarkation now went briskly forward, several light field-guns were placed in the boats, and two or three large rafts, capable of containing two companies each, were prepared to be towed across by boats.

Exactly as the heavy hammer of the cathedral struck one, the first boat emerged from the willows, and darting rapidly forward, headed for the middle of the stream; another and another in quick succession followed, and speedily were lost to us in the gloom; and now two four-oared skiffs stood out together, having a raft, with two guns, in tow; by some mischance, however, they got entangled in a side current, and the raft swerving to one side, swept past the boats, carrying them down the stream along with it. Our attention was not suffered to dwell on this mishap, for at the same moment the flash and rattle of fire-arms told us the battle had begun. Two or three isolated shots were first heard, and then a sharp platoon fire, accompanied by a wild cheer, that we well knew came from our own fellows. One deep mellow boom of a large gun resounded amidst the crash, and a slight streak of flame, higher up the stream, showed that the shot came from th small island I have already spoken of.

" Listen, lads," said I ; " that came from the ' Fels
Insel.' If they are firing grape yonder, our poor fellows
in the boats will suffer sorely from it. By Jove, there is a
crash !"

As I was speaking, a rattling noise like the sound of
clattering timber was heard, and with it a sharp, shrill cry
of agony, and all was hushed.

" Let's at them, boys ; they can't be much above our
own number. The island is a mere rock," cried I to my
comrades.

" Who commands this party " said the corporal, " you
or I ?"

" You, if you lead us against the enemy," said I; " but
I'll take it if my comrades will follow me. There goes
another shot, lads—yes or no—now is the time to
speak."

" We're ready," cried three, springing forward with
one impulse.

At the instant I jumped into the skiff, the others took
their places, and then came a fourth, a fifth, a sixth, and a
seventh, leaving the corporal alone on the bank.

" Come along, corporal," cried I, " we'll win your
epaulettes for you ;" but he turned away without a word ;
and not waiting further, I pushed out the skiff, and sent
her skimming down the stream.

" Pull steady, boys, and silently," said I ; " we must
gain the middle of the current, and then drop down the
river without the least noise. Once beneath the trees,
we'll give them a volley, and then the bayonet. Remember, lads, no flinching ; it's as well to die here as be shot
by old Regnier to-morrow."

The conflict on the Eslar island was now, to all seeming,
at its height. The roll of musketry was incessant, and
sheets of flame, from time to time, streaked the darkness
above the river.

" Stronger and together, boys—once more—there it is
—we are in the current now ; in with you, men, and look
to your carbines ; see that the priming is safe ; every shot
soon will be worth a fusilade. Lie still now, and wait for
the word to fire."

The spreading foliage of the nut-trees was rustling over
our heads as I spoke, and the sharp skiff, borne on the
current, glided smoothly on till her bow struck the rock.
With high-beating hearts we clambered up the little cliff ;
and as we reached the top, beheld immediately beneath
us, in a slight dip of the ground, several figures around a
gun, which they were busy in adjusting. I looked **right**

and left to see that my little party were all assembled, and without waiting for more, gave the order—fire !

We were within pistol range, and the discharge was a deadly one. The terror, however, was not less complete ; for all who escaped death fled from the spot, and dashing through the brushwood, made for the shallow part of the stream, between the island and the right bank.

Our prize was a brass eight-pounder, and an ample supply of ammunition. The gun was pointed towards the middle of the stream, where the current being strongest, the boats would necessarily be delayed ; and in all likeli- hood some of our gallant comrades had already experi- enced its fatal fire. To wheel it right about, and point it on the Eslar bridge, was the work of a couple of minutes ; and while three of our little party kept up a steady fire on the retreating enemy, the others loaded the gun and prepared to fire.

Our distance from the Eslar island and bridge, as well as I could judge from the darkness, might be about two hundred and fifty yards ; and, as we had the advantage of a slight elevation of ground, our position was ad- mirable.

" Wait patiently, lads," said I, restraining, with diffi- culty, the burning ardour of my men. " Wait patiently, till the retreat has commenced over the bridge. The work is too hot to last much longer on the island ; to fire upon them there would be to risk our own men as much as the enemy. See what long flashes of flame break forth among the brushwood ; and listen to the cheering now. That was a French cheer !—and there goes another. Look !—look, the bridge is darkening already ! That was a bugle-call, and they are in full retreat. Now, lads— now !"

As I spoke, the gun exploded, and the instant after we heard the crashing rattle of the timber, as the shot struck the bridge, and splintered the wood-work in all directions.

" The range is perfect, lads," cried I. " Load and fire with all speed."

Another shot, followed by a terrific scream from the bridge, told how the work was doing. Oh ! the savage exultation, the fiendish joy of my heart, as I drank in that cry of agony, and called upon my men to load faster.

Six shots were poured in with tremendous precision and effect, and the seventh tore away one of the main supports of the bridge, and down went the densely crowded column into the Rhine ; at the same instant the guns of our launches opened a destructive fire upon the banks, which soon were swept clean of the enemy.

High up on the stream, and for nearly a mile below also, we could see the boats of our army pulling in for shore; the crossing of the Rhine had been effected, and we now prepared to follow.

CHAPTER XII.

"A GLANCE AT STAFF-DUTY."

ALTHOUGH the passage of the Rhine was but the prelude to the attack on the fortress, that exploit being accomplished, Kehl was carried at the point of the bayonet, the French troops entering the outworks pell-mell with the retreating enemy, and in less than two hours after the landing of our first detachments, the "tri-colour" waved over the walls of the fortress.

Lost amid the greater and more important successes which since that time have immortalised the glory of the French arms, it is almost impossible to credit the celebrity attached at that time to this brilliant achievement, whose highest merits probably were rapidity and resolution. Moreau had long been jealous of the fame of his great rival, Bonaparte, whose tactics, rejecting the colder dictates of prudent strategy, and the slow progress of scientific manœuvres, seemed to place all his confidence in the sudden inspirations of his genius, and the indomitable bravery of his troops. It was necessary, then, to raise the morale of the army of the Rhine, to accomplish some great feat similar in boldness and heroism to the wonderful achievements of the Italian army. Such was the passage of the Rhine at Strasbourg, effected in the face of a great enemy, advantageously posted, and supported by one of the strongest of all the frontier fortresses.

The morning broke upon us in all the exultation of our triumph, and as our cheers rose high over the field of the late struggle, each heart beat proudly with the thought of how that news would be received in Paris.

" You'll see how the bulletin will spoil all," said a young officer of the army of Italy, as he was getting his wound dressed on the field. " There will be such a long narrative of irrelevant matter—such details of this, that, and t'other—that the public will scarce know whether the placard announces a defeat or a victory.

"Parbleu!" replied an old veteran of the Rhine army, "what would you have? You'd not desire to omit the military facts of such an exploit?"

"To be sure I would," rejoined the other. "Give me one of our young general's bulletins, short, stirring, and effective.—'Soldiers! you have crossed the Rhine against an army double your own in numbers and munitions of war. You have carried a fortress, believed impregnable, at the bayonet. Already the great flag of our nation waves over the citadel you have won. Forward, then, and cease not till it floats over the cities of conquered Germany, and let the name of France be that of Empire over the continent of Europe.'"

"Ha! I like that," cried I, enthusiastically; "that's the bulletin to my fancy. Repeat it once more, mon lieutenant, that I may write it in my note-book."

"What! hast thou a note-book?" cried an old staff-officer, who was preparing to mount his horse; "let's see it, lad."

With a burning cheek and trembling hand, I drew my little journal from the breast of my jacket, and gave it to him.

"Sacre bleu!" exclaimed he, in a burst of laughter, "what have we here? Why, this is a portrait of old General Moricier, and although a caricature, a perfect likeness. And here comes a plan for manœuvring a squadron by threes from the left. This is better—it is a receipt for an 'Omelette à la Hussard;' and here we have a love-song, and a moustache-paste, with some hints about devotion, and diseased frog in horses. Most versatile genius, certainly!" and so he went on, occasionally laughing at my rude sketches and ruder remarks, till he came to a page headed "Equitation, as practised by Officers of the Staff," and followed by a series of caricatures of bad riding, in all its moods and tenses. The flush of anger which instantly coloured his face soon attracted the notice of those about him, and one of the bystanders quickly snatched the book from his fingers, and, in the midst of a group all convulsed with laughter, proceeded to expatiate upon my illustrations. To be sure, they were absurd enough. Some were represented sketching on horseback, under shelter of an umbrella; others were "taking the depth of a stream" by a "header" from their own saddles; some again were "exploring ground for an attack in line," by a measurement of the rider's own length over the head of his horse. Then there were ridiculous situations, such as "sitting down before a fortress," "taking an angle of incidence," and so on. Sorry jests all of them, but sufficient to amuse those with whose daily associations they chimed in, and to whom certain traits of portraiture gave all the zest of a personality.

My shame at the exposure, and my terror for its consequences, gradually yielded to a feeling of flattered vanity at the success of my lucubrations; and I never remarked that the staff-officer had ridden away from the group till I saw him galloping back at the top of his speed.

"Is your name Tiernay, my good fellow?" cried he, riding close up to my side, and with an expression on his features I did not half like.

"Yes, sir," replied I.

"Hussar of the Ninth, I believe?" repeated he, reading from a paper in his hand.

"The same, sir."

"Well, your talents as a draughtsman have procured you promotion, my friend; I have obtained your discharge from your regiment, and you are now my orderly—orderly on the staff, do you mind; so mount, sir, and follow me.

I saluted him respectfully, and prepared to obey his orders. Already I foresaw the downfall of all the hopes I had been cherishing, and anticipated the life of tyranny and oppression that lay before me. It was clear to me that my discharge had been obtained solely as a means of punishing me, and that Captain Discau, as the officer was called, had destined me to a pleasant expiation of my note-book. The savage exultation with which he watched me, as I made up my kit and saddled my horse —the cool malice with which he handed me back the accursed journal, the cause of all my disasters—gave me a dark foreboding of what was to follow; and as I mounted my saddle, my woeful face and miserable look brought forth a perfect shout of laughter from the bystanders.

Captain Discau's duty was to visit the banks of the Rhine and the Eslar island, to take certain measurements of distances, and obtain accurate information on various minute points respecting the late engagement, for, while a brief announcement of the victory would suffice for the bulletin, a detailed narrative of the event in all its bear-ings must be drawn up for the minister of war, and for this latter purpose various staff-officers were then employed in different parts of the field.

As we issued from the fortress, and took our way over
the plain, we struck out into a sharp gallop; but as we
drew near the river, our passage became so obstructed by
lines of baggage waggons, tumbrils, and ammunition carts,
that we were obliged to dismount and proceed on foot;
and now I was to see for the first time that dreadful
picture which, on the day after a battle, forms the reverse
of the great medal of glory. Huge litters of wounded
men, on their way back to Strasbourg, were drawn by six
or eight horses, their jolting motion increasing the agony
of sufferings that found their vent in terrific cries and
screams; oaths, yells, and blasphemies, the ravings of
madness, and the wild shouts of infuriated suffering, filled
the air on every side. As if to give the force of contrast
to this uproar of misery, two regiments of Swabian infantry marched past as prisoners. Silent, crest-fallen,
and wretched-looking, they never raised their eyes from
the ground, but moved, or halted, wheeled, or stood at ease,
as though by some impulse of mechanism; a cord coupled
the wrists of the outer files one with another, which
struck me less as a measure of security against escape,
than as a mark of indignity.

Carts and charettes with wounded officers, in which
often-times the uniform of the enemy appeared side by
side with our own, followed in long procession; and thus
were these two great currents—the one hurrying forward,
ardent, high-hearted, and enthusiastic; the other returning maimed, shattered, and dying!

It was an affecting scene to see the hurried gestures, and
hear the few words of adieu, as they passed each other.
Old comrades who were never to meet again, parted with
a little motion of the hand; sometimes a mere look was all
their leave-taking : save when, now and then, a halt would
for a few seconds bring the lines together, and then many
a bronzed and rugged cheek was pressed upon the faces
of the dying, and many a tear fell from eyes bloodshot
with the fury of the battle! Wending our way on foot
slowly along, we at last reached the river side, and having
secured a small skiff, made for the Eslar island; our first
business being to ascertain some details respecting the in-
trenchments there, and the depth and strength of the
stream between it and the left bank. Discau, who was a
distinguished officer, rapidly possessed himself of the
principal facts he wanted, and then, having given me his
portfolio, he seated himself under the shelter of a broken
waggon, and opening a napkin, began his breakfast off a
portion of a chicken and some bread,—viands which, I

own, more than once made my lips water as I watched him.

"You've eaten nothing to-day, Tiernay?" asked he, as he wiped his lips with the air of a man that feels satisfied.

"Nothing, mon capitaine," replied I.

"That's bad," said he, shaking his head ; "a soldier cannot do his duty if his rations be neglected. I have always maintained the principle : Look to the men's necessaries—take care of their food and clothing. Is there anything on that bone there ?"

"Nothing, mon capitaine."

"I'm sorry for it; I meant it for you; put up that bread, and the remainder of that flask of wine. Bourdeaux is not to be had every day. We shall want it for supper, Tiernay,"

I did as I was bid, wondering not a little why he said "we," seeing how little a share I occupied in the co-partnery.

"Always be careful of the morrow on a campaign, Tiernay—no squandering, no waste ; that's one of my principles," said he, gravely, as he watched me while I tied up the bread and wine in the napkin. "You'll soon see the advantage of serving under an old soldier."

I confess the great benefit had not already struck me, but I held my peace and waited ; meanwhile he continued—

"I have studied my profession from my boyhood, and one thing I have acquired that all experience has confirmed—the knowledge that men must neither be taxed beyond their ability nor their endurance ; a French soldier, after all, is human ; eh, is't not so ?"

"I feel it most profoundly, mon capitaine," replied I, with my hand on my empty stomach.

"Just so," rejoined he ; "every man of sense and discretion must confess it. Happily for you, too, I know it ; ay, Tiernay I know it, and practise it. When a young fellow has acquitted himself to my satisfaction during the day—not that I mean to say that the performance has not its fair share of activity and zeal—when evening comes and stable duty finished, arms burnished, and accoutrements cleaned, what do you think I say to him ?—eh, Tiernay—just guess now ?"

"Probably, sir, you tell him he is free to spend an hour at the canteen, or take his sweetheart to the theatre."

"What! more fatigue! more exhaustion to an already tired and worn-out nature!"

"I ask pardon, sir, I see I was wrong; but I had forgotten how thoroughly the poor fellow was done up. I now see that you told him to go to bed."

"To bed! to bed! Is it that he might writhe in the nightmare, or suffer agony from cramps? To bed after fatigue like this! No, no, Tiernay; that was not the schoo. in which I was brought up; we were taught to think of the men under our command; to remember that they had wants, sympathies, hopes, fears, and emotions like our own. I tell him to seat himself at the table, and with pen, ink, and paper before him, to write up the blanks. I see you don't quite understand me, Tiernay, as to the meaning of the phrase, but I'll let you into the secret. You have been kind enough to give me a peep at your note-book, and you shall in return have a look at mine. Open that volume, and tell me what you find in it."

I obeyed the direction, and read at the top of a page the words, "Skeleton, 5th Prarial," in large characters, followed by several isolated words, denoting the strength of a brigade, the number of guns in a battery, the depth of a fosse, the height of a parapet, and such like. These were usually followed by a flourish of the pen, or sometimes by the word "Bom.," which singular monosyllable always occurred at the foot of the pages.

"Well, have you caught the key to the cipher?" said he, after a pause.

"Not quite, sir," said I, pondering; "I can perceive that the chief facts stand prominently forward, in a fair round hand; I can also guess that the flourishes may be spaces left for detail; but this word "Bom." puzzles me completely."

"Quite correct, as to the first part," said he, approvingly; "and as to the mysterious monosyllable, it is nothing more than an abbreviation for 'Bombaste,' which is always to be done to the taste of each particular commanding officer."

"I perceive, sir," said I, quickly; "like the wadding of a gun, which may increase the loudness, but never affect the strength of the shot."

"Precisely, Tiernay; you have hit it exactly. Now I hope that, with a little practice, you may be able to acquit yourself respectably in this walk; and now to begin our skeleton. Turn over to a fresh page, and write as I dictate to you.'

So saying, he filled his pipe and lighted it, and disposing his limbs in an attitude of perfect ease, he
began :—

" 8th Thermidor, midnight—twelve battalions, and two
batteries of field—boats and rafts—Eslar Island—stockades—eight guns—Swabian infantry—sharp firing, and a
flourish—strong current—flourish—detachment of the
28th carried down—' Bom.' Let me see it now—all right
—nothing could be better—proceed. The 10th, 45th, and
48th landing together—more firing—flourish—first gun
captured—Bom.—bayonet charges—Bom. Bom.—three
guns taken—Bom. Bom. Bom.—Swabs in retreat—flourish.
The bridge eighty toises in length—flanking fire—heavy
loss—flourish."

" You go a little too fast, mon capitaine," said I, for a
sudden bright thought just flashed across me.

" Very well," said he, shaking the ashes of his pipe out
upon the rock, " I'll take my doze, and you may awaken
me when you've filled in those details—it will be a very fair
exercise for you ; " and with this he threw his handkerchief over his face, and without any other preparation was
soon fast asleep.

I own that, if I had not been a spectator of the action,
it would have been very difficult, if not impossible, for me
to draw up anything like a narrative of it from the meagre
details of the captain's note-book. My personal observations, however, assisted by an easy imagination, suggested
quite enough to make at least a plausible story, and I
wrote away without impediment and halt till I came to
that part of the action in which the retreat over the bridge
commenced. There I stopped. Was I to remain satisfied
with such a crude and one-sided explanation as the note-
book afforded, and merely say that the retreating forces
were harassed by a strong flank fire from our batteries?
Was I to omit the whole of the great incident, the occupation of the " Fels Insel," and the damaging discharges
of grape and round shot which plunged through the
crowded ranks, and ultimately destroyed the bridge?
Could I—to use the phrase so popular—could I, in the
" interests of truth," forget the brilliant achievement of a
gallant band of heroes who, led on by a young hussar of
the 9th, threw themselves into the " Fels Insel," routed
the garrison, captured the artillery, and directing its fire
upon the retiring enemy, contributed most essentially to
the victory. Ought I, in a word, to suffer a name so associated with a glorious action to sink into oblivion?
Should Maurice Tiernay be lost to fame out of any neg-

lect or false shame on my part? Forbid it all truth and
justice! cried I, as I set myself down to relate the whole
adventure most circumstantially. Looking up from time
to time at my officer, who slept soundly, I suffered myself
to dilate upon a theme in which somehow I felt a more than
ordinary degree of interest. The more I dwelt upon the
incident, the more brilliant and striking did it seem. Like
the appetite, which the proverb tells us comes by eating,
my enthusiasm grew under indulgence, so that, had a
little more time been granted me, I verily believe I should
have forgotten Moreau altogether, and coupled only Maurice Tiernay with the passage of the Rhine, and the capture of the fortress of Kehl. Fortunately, Captain Discau
awoke, and cut short my historic recollections by asking
me how much I had done, and telling me to read it aloud
to him.

I accordingly began to read my narrative slowly and
deliberately, thereby giving myself time to think what I
should best do when I came to that part which became
purely personal. To omit it altogether would have been
dangerous, as the slightest glance at the mass of writing
would have shown the deception. There was, then, nothing left, but to invent at the moment another version, in
which Maurice Tiernay never occurred, and the incident
of the Fels Insel should figure as unobtrusively as possible. I was always a better improvisatore than amanuen-
sis; so that without a moment's loss of time I fashioned a
new and very different narrative, and detailing the battle
tolerably accurately, minus the share my own heroism had
taken in it. The captain made a few, a very few corrections of my style, in which the "flourish" and "bom."
figured, perhaps, too conspicuously; and then told me
frankly, that once upon a time he had been fool enough to
give himself great trouble in framing these kind of reports, but that having served for a short period in the
" bureau" of the minister of war, he had learned better—
" In fact," said he, " a district report is never read! Some
hundreds of them reach the office of the minister every
day, and are safely deposited in the "archives" of the department. They have all, besides, such a family resemblance, that with a few changes in the name of the commanding officer, any battle in the Netherlands would do
equally well for one fought beyond the Alps! Since I became acquainted with this fact, Tiernay, I have bestowed
less pains upon the matter, and usually deputed the task
to some smart orderly of the staff."

So, thought I, I have been writing history for nothing;

and Maurice Tiernay, the real hero of the passage of the Rhine, will be unrecorded and unremembered, just for want of one honest and impartial scribe to transmit his name to posterity. The reflection was not a very encouraging one ; nor did it serve to lighten the toil in which I passed many weary hours, copying out my own precious manuscript. Again and again during that night did I wonder at my own diffuseness—again and again did I curse the prolix accuracy of a description that cost such labour to reiterate. It was like a species of poetical justice on me for my own amplifications; and when the day broke, and I still sat at my table writing on, at the third copy of this precious document, I vowed a vow of brevity, should I ever survive to indite similar compositions.

CHAPTER XIII.

A FAREWELL LETTER.

It was in something less than a week after that I entered upon my new career as orderly in the staff, when I began to believe myself the most miserable of all human beings. On the saddle at sunrise, I never dismounted, except to carry a measuring chain, "to step distances," mark out entrenchments, and then write away, for hours, long enormous reports, that were to be models of calligraphy, neatness and elegance—and never to be read. Nothing could be less like soldiering than the life I led ; and were it not for the clanking sabre I wore at my side, and the jingling spurs that decorated my heels, I might have fancied myself a notary's clerk. It was part of General Moreau's plan to strengthen the defences of Kehl before he advanced further into Germany ; and to this end repairs were begun upon a line of earth-works, about two leagues to the northward of the fortress, at a small village called "Ekheim." In this miserable little hole, one of the dreariest spots imaginable, we were quartered, with two companies of "sapeurs" and some of the waggon-train, trenching, digging, carting earth, sinking wells, and in fact engaged in every kind of labour save that which seemed to be characteristic of a soldier.

I used to think that Nancy and the riding-school were

the most dreary and tiresome of all destinies, but they were enjoyments and delight compared with this. Now it very often happens in life that when a man grows discontented and dissatisfied with mere monotony, when he chafes at the sameness of a tiresome and unexciting existence, he is rapidly approaching to some critical or eventful point, where actual peril and real danger assail him, and from which he would willingly buy his escape by falling back upon that wearisome and plodding life he had so often deplored before. This case was my own. Just as I had convinced myself that I was exceedingly wretched and miserable, I was to know there are worse things in this world than a life of mere uniform stupidity. I was waiting outside my captain's door for orders one morning, when at the tinkle of his little hand-bell I entered the room where he sat at breakfast, with an open despatch before him.

"Tiernay," said he, in his usual quiet tone, "here is an order from the adjutant-general to send you back under an escort to head-quarters. Are you aware of any reason for it, or is there any charge against you which warrants this?"

"Not to my knowledge, mon capitaine," said I, trembling with fright, for I well knew with what severity discipline was exercised in that army, and how any, even the slightest, infractions met the heaviest penalties.

"I have never known you to pillage," continued he, "have never seen you drink, nor have you been disobedient while under my command; yet this order could not be issued on light grounds; there must be some grave accusation against you, and in any case you must go; therefore arrange all my papers, put everything to rights, and be ready to return with the orderly."

"You'll give me a good character, mon capitaine," said I, trembling more than ever—"you'll say what you can for me, I'm sure."

"Willingly, if the general or chief were here," replied he; "but that's not so. General Moreau is at Strasbourg. It is General Regnier that is in command of the army, and unless specially applied to, I could not venture upon the liberty of obtruding my opinion upon him."

"Is he so severe, sir?" asked I, timidly.

"The general is a good disciplinarian," said he, cautiously, while he motioned with his hand towards the door: and accepting the hint, I retired.

It was evening when I re-entered Kehl, under an escort of two of my own regiment, and was conducted to the

"Salle de Police." At the door stood my old corporal, whose malicious grin, as I alighted, revealed the whole story of my arrest; and I now knew the charge that would be preferred against me—a heavier there could not be made—was, " disobedience in the field." I slept very little that night, and when I did close my eyes, it was to awake with a sudden start, and believe myself in presence of the court-martial, or listening to my sentence, as read out by the President. Towards day, however, I sunk into a heavy, deep slumber, from which I was aroused by the reveillée of the barracks.

I had barely time to dress when I was summoned before the "Tribunale Militaire"—a sort of permanent court-martial, whose sittings were held in one of the churches of the town. Not even all the terror of my own precarious position could overcome the effect of old prejudices in my mind, as I saw myself led up the dim aisle of the church towards the altar rails, within which, around a large table, were seated a number of officers, whose manner and bearing evinced but little reverence for the sacred character of the spot.

Stationed in a group of poor wretches whose wan looks and anxious glances told that they were prisoners like myself, I had time to see what was going forward around me. The President, who alone wore his hat, read from a sort of list before him the name of a prisoner and that of the witnesses in the cause. In an instant they were all drawn up and sworn. A few questions followed, rapidly put, and almost as rapidly replied to. The prisoner was called on then for his defence : if this occupied many minutes, he was sure to be interrupted by an order to be brief. Then came the command to "stand by;" and after a few seconds' consultation together, in which many times a burst of laughter might be heard, the court agreed upon the sentence, recorded and signed it, and then proceeded with the next case.

If nothing in the procedure imposed reverence or respect, there was that in the despatch which suggested terror, for it was plain to see that the Court thought more of the cost of their own precious minutes than of the years of those on whose fate they were deciding. I was sufficiently near to hear the charges of those who were arraigned, and, for the greater number, they were all alike. Pillage, in one form or another, was the universal offending, and from the burning of a peasant's cottage, to the theft of his dog or his "poulet," all came under this head.

At last came number 82—"Maurice Tiernay, hussar of the Ninth." I stepped forward to the rails.

"Maurice Tiernay," read the President, hurriedly, "accused by Louis Gaussin, corporal of the same regiment, 'of wilfully deserting his post while on duty in the field, and in the face of direct orders to the contrary; inducing others to a similar breach of discipline.' Make the charge, Gaussin."

The corporal stepped forward, and began—

"We were stationed in detachment on the bank of the Rhine, on the evening of the 23rd——"

"The Court has too many duties to lose its time for nothing," interrupted I. "It is all true. I did desert my post, I did disobey orders; and, seeing a weak point in the enemy's line, attacked and carried it with success. The charge is, therefore, admitted by me, and it only remains for the Court to decide how far a soldier's zeal for his country may be deserving of punishment. Whatever the result, one thing is perfectly clear, Corporal Gaussin will never be indicted for a similar misdemeanour."

A murmur of voices and suppressed laughter followed this impertinent and not over-discreet sally of mine, and the President, calling out, "Proven by acknowledgment," told me to "stand by." I now fell back to my former place, to be interrogated by my comrades on the result of my examination, and hear their exclamations of surprise and terror at the rashness of my conduct. A little reflection over the circumstances would probably have brought me over to their opinion, and shown me that I had gratuitously thrown away an opportunity of self-defence; but my temper could not brook the indignity of listening to the tiresome accusation and the stupid malevolence of the corporal, whose hatred was excited by the influence I wielded over my comrades.

It was long past noon ere the proceedings terminated, for the list was a full one, and at length the Court rose, apparently not sorry to exchange their tiresome duties for the pleasant offices of the dinner-table. No sentences had been pronounced, but one very striking incident seemed to shadow forth a gloomy future. Three, of whom I was one, were marched off, doubly guarded, before the rest, and confined in separate cells of the "Salle," where every precaution against escape too plainly showed the importance attached to our safe keeping.

At about eight o'clock, as I was sitting on my bed—if that inclined plane of wood, worn by the form of many a former prisoner, could deserve the name—a sergeant entered with the prison allowance of bread and water. He placed it beside me without speaking, and stood for a few seconds gazing at me.

"What age art thou, lad?" said he, in a voice of compassionate interest.

"Something over fifteen, I believe," replied I.

"Hast father and mother?"

"Both are dead!"

"Uncles or aunts living?"

"Neither."

"Hast any friends who could help thee?"

"That might depend on what the occasion for help should prove, for I have one friend in the world."

"Who is he?"

"Colonel Mahon, of the Cuirassiers."

"I never heard of him—is he here?"

"No, I left him at Nancy; but I could write to him."

"It would be too late, much too late."

"How do you mean—too late?" asked I, tremblingly.

"Because it is fixed for to-morrow evening," replied he, in a low, hesitating voice.

"What? the——the——" I could not say the word, but merely imitated the motion of presenting and firing. He nodded gravely in acquiescence.

"What hour is it to take place?" asked I.

"After evening parade. The sentence must be signed by General Berthier, and he will not be here before that time."

"It would be too late then, sergeant," said I, musing, "far too late. Still I should like to write the letter, I should like to thank him for his kindness in the past, and show him, too, that I have not been either unworthy or ungrateful. Could you let me have paper and pen, sergeant?"

"I can venture so far, lad; but I cannot let thee have a light, it is against orders; and during the day thou'lt be too strictly watched."

"No matter; let me have the paper and I'll try to scratch a few lines in the dark; and thou'lt post it for me, sergeant? I ask thee as a last favour to do this."

"I promise it," said he, laying his hand on my shoulder. After standing for a few minutes thus in silence, he started suddenly and left the cell.

I now tried to eat my supper, but although resolved on behaving with a stout and unflinching courage throughout the whole sad event, I could not swallow a mouthful. A sense of choking stopped me at every attempt, and even

the water I could only get down by gulps. The efforts I
made to bear up seemed to have caused a species of hyste-
rical excitement that actually rose to the height of intoxication, for I talked away loudly to myself, laughed and
sung. I even jested and mocked myself on this sudden
termination of a career that I used to anticipate as stored
with future fame and rewards. At intervals, I have no
doubt that my mind wandered far beyond the control of
reason, but as constantly came back again to a full consciousness of my melancholy position, and the fate that
awaited me. The noise of the key in the door silenced
my ravings, and I sat still and motionless as the sergeant
entered with the pen, ink, and paper, which he laid down
upon the bed, and then as silently withdrew.

A long interval of stupor, a state of dreary half consciousness, now came over me, from which I aroused myself with great difficulty to write the few lines I destined
for Colonel Mahon. I remember even now, long as has
been the space of years since that event, full as it has
been of stirring and strange incidents, I remember perfectly the thought which flashed across me as I sat, pen in
hand, before the paper. It was the notion of a certain
resemblance between our actions in this world with the
characters I was about to inscribe upon that paper.
Written in darkness and in doubt, thought I, how shall
they appear when brought to the light! Perhaps those
I have deemed the best and fairest shall seem but to be the
weakest or the worst! What need of kindness to forgive
the errors, and of patience to endure the ignorance! At
last I began,—"Mon Colonel,—Forgive, I pray you, the
errors of these lines, penned in the darkness of my cell,
and the night before my death. They are written to thank
you ere I go hence, and to tell you that the poor heart
whose beating will soon be still, throbbed gratefully towards
you to the last! I have been sentenced to death for a
breach of discipline of which I was guilty. Had I failed
in the achievement of my enterprise by the bullet of an
enemy, they would have named me with honour ; but I
have had the misfortune of success, and to-morrow am I
to pay its penalty. I have the satisfaction, however, of
knowing that my share in that great day can neither be
denied nor evaded ; it is already on record, and the time
may yet come when my memory will be vindicated. I
know not if these lines be legible, nor if I have crossed
or recrossed them. If they are blotted they are not my
tears have done it, for I have a firm heart and a good
courage ; and when the moment comes——" here my hand

trembled so much, and my brain grew so dizzy, that I lost the thread of my meaning, and merely jotted down at random a few words, vague, unconnected, and unintelligible, after which, and by an effort that cost all my strength, I wrote "Maurice Tiernay, late Hussar of the 9th Regiment."

A hearty burst of tears followed the conclusion of this letter; all the pent-up emotion with which my heart was charged broke out at last, and I cried bitterly. Intense passions are, happily, never of long duration, and, better still, they are always the precursors of calm. Thus, tranquil, the dawn of morn broke upon me, when the sergeant came to take my letter, and apprise me that the adjutant would appear in a few moments to read my sentence, and inform me when it was to be executed.

"Thou'lt bear up well, lad; I know thou wilt," said the poor fellow, with tears in his eyes. "Thou hast no mother, and thou'lt not have to grieve for her."

"Don't be afraid, sergeant; I'll not disgrace the old 9th. Tell my comrades I said so."

"I will. I will tell them all! Is this thy jacket, lad?"

"Yes; what do you want it for?"

"I must take it away with me. Thou art not to wear it more?"

"Not wear it, nor die in it! and why not?"

"That is the sentence, lad; I cannot help it. It's very hard, very cruel; but so it is."

"Then I am to die dishonoured, sergeant; is that the sentence?"

He dropped his head, and I could see that he moved his sleeve across his eyes; and then, taking up my jacket, he came towards me.

"Remember, lad, a stout heart; no flinching. Adieu—God bless thee." He kissed me on either cheek, and went out.

He had not been gone many minutes, when the tramp of marching outside apprised me of the coming of the adjutant, and the door of my cell being thrown open, I was ordered to walk forth into the court of the prison. Two squadrons of my own regiment, all who were not on duty, were drawn up, dismounted, and without arms; beside them stood a company of grenadiers and a half battalion of the line, the corps to which the other two prisoners belonged, and who now came forward, in shirt-sleeves like myself, into the middle of the court.

One of my fellow-sufferers was a very old soldier, whose hair and beard were white as snow; the other was a

9

middle-aged man, of a dark and forbidding aspect, who scowled at me angrily as I came up to his side, and seemed as if he scorned the companionship. I returned a glance, haughty and as full of defiance as his own, and never noticed him after.

The drum beat a roll, and the word was given for silence in the ranks—an order so strictly obeyed, that even the clash of a weapon was unheard, and, stepping in front of the line, the Auditeur Militaire read out the sentences. As for me, I heard but the words " Peine afflictive et infamante ;" all the rest became confusion, shame, and terror co-mingled; nor did I know that the ceremonial was over when the troops began to defile, and we were marched back again to our prison quarters.

CHAPTER XIV.

A SURPRISE AND AN ESCAPE.

It is a very common subject of remark in newspapers, and as invariably repeated with astonishment by the readers, how well and soundly such a criminal slept on the night before his execution. It reads like a wonderful evidence of composure, or some not less surprising proof of apathy or indifference. I really believe it has as little relation to one feeling as to the other, and is simply the natural consequence of faculties over-strained, and a brain surcharged with blood ; sleep being induced by causes purely physical in their nature. For myself, I can say that I was by no means indifferent to life, nor had I any contempt for the form of death that awaited me. As localities which have failed to inspire a strong attachment become endowed with a certain degree of interest when we are about to part from them for ever, I never held life so desirable as now that I was going to leave it; and yet, with all this, I fell into a sleep so heavy and profound, that I never awoke till late in the evening. Twice was I shaken by the shoulder ere I could throw off the heavy weight of slumber ; and even when I looked up, and saw the armed figures around me, I could have lain down once more and composed myself to another sleep.

The first thing which thoroughly aroused me, and at

once brightened up my slumbering senses, was missing my jacket, for which I searched every corner of my cell, forgetting that it had been taken away, as the nature of my sentence was declared "infamante." The next shock was still greater, when two sapeurs came forward to tie my wrists together behind my back; I neither spoke nor resisted, but in silent submission complied with each order given me.

All preliminaries being completed, I was led forward, preceded by a pioneer, and guarded on either side by two sapeurs of "the guard;" a muffled drum, ten paces in advance, keeping up a low monotonous rumble as we went.

Our way led along the ramparts, beside which ran a row of little gardens, in which the children of the officers were at play. They ceased their childish gambols as we drew near, and came closer up to watch us. I could mark the terror and pity in their little faces as they gazed at me; I could see the traits of compassion with which they pointed me out to each other, and my heart swelled with gratitude for even so slight a sympathy. It was with difficulty I could restrain the emotion of that moment, but with a great effort I did subdue it, and marched on, to all seeming, unmoved. A little further on, as we turned the angle of the wall, I looked back to catch one last look at them. Would that I had never done so! They had quitted the railings, and were now standing in a group, in the act of performing a mimic execution. One, without his jacket, was kneeling on the grass. But I could not bear the sight, and in scornful anger I closed my eyes, and saw no more.

A low whispering conversation was kept up by the soldiers around me. They were grumbling at the long distance they had to march, as the "affair" might just as well have taken place on the glacis as two miles away. How different were my feelings—how dear to me was now every minute, every second of existence; how my heart leaped at each turn of the way, as I still saw a space to traverse and some little interval longer to live!

"And mayhap after all," muttered one dark-faced fellow, "we shall have come all this way for nothing. There can be no 'fusilade' without the general's signature, so I heard the adjutant say; and who's to promise that he'll be at his quarters?"

"Very true," said another; "he may be absent, or at table."

"**At table!**" cried two or three together; "and what if
he were?"

"If he be," rejoined the former speaker, "we may go
back again for our pains! I ought to know him well; I
was his orderly for eight months, when I served in the
'Legers,' and can tell you, my lads, I wouldn't be the officer who would bring him a report or a return to sign when
once he had opened out his napkin on his knee; and it's
not very far from his dinner-hour now."

What a sudden thrill of hope ran through me! Perhaps I should be spared for another day.

"No, no, we're all in time," exclaimed the sergeant;
"I can see the general's tent from this; and there he
stands, with all his staff around him."

"Yes; and there go the other escorts—they will be up
before us if we don't make haste; quick-time, lads. Come
along, mon cher," said he, addressing me—"thou'rt not
tired, I hope?"

"Not tired!" replied I; "but remember, sergeant, what
a long journey I have before me."

"Pardie! I don't believe all that rhodomontade about
another world," said he, gruffly; "the Republic settled
that question."

I made no reply, for such words, at such a moment,
were the most terrible of tortures to me. And now we
moved on at a brisker pace, and crossing a little wooden
bridge, entered a kind of esplanade of closely-shaven turf,
at one corner of which stood the capacious tent of the
commander-in-chief, for such, in Moreau's absence, was
General Berthier. Numbers of staff-officers were riding
about on duty, and a large travelling-carriage, from which
the horses seemed recently detached, stood before the
tent.

We halted as we crossed the bridge, while the adjutant
advanced to obtain the signature to the sentence. My
eyes followed him till they swam with rising tears, and I
could not wipe them away, as my hands were fettered.
How rapidly did my thoughts travel during those few
moments. The good old Père Michel came back to me in
memory, and I tried to think of the consolation his
presence would have afforded me; but I could do no more
than think of them.

"Which is the prisoner Tiernay?" cried a young aide-
de-camp, cantering up to where I was standing.

"Here, sir," replied the sergeant, pushing me forward.

"So," rejoined the officer, angrily, "this fellow has

been writing letters, it would seem, reflecting upon the justice of his sentence, and arraigning the conduct of his judges. Your epistolary tastes are like to cost you dearly, my lad; it had been better for you if writing had been omitted in your education. Re-conduct the others, sergeant, they are respited; this fellow alone is to undergo his sentence."

The other two prisoners gave a short and simultaneous cry of joy as they fell back, and I stood alone in front of the escort.

"Parbleu! he has forgotten the signature," said the adjutant, casting his eye over the paper: "he was chattering and laughing all the time, with the pen in his hand, and I suppose fancied that he had signed it."

"Nathalie was there, perhaps," said the aide-de-camp, significantly.

"She was, and I never saw her looking better. It's something like eight years since I saw her last; and I vow she seems not only handsomer but fresher, and more youthful, to-day than then."

"Where is she going?—have you heard?"

"Who can tell? Her passport is like a firman—she may travel where she pleases. The rumour of the day says Italy."

"I thought she looked provoked at Moreau's absence; it seemed like want of attention on his part, a lack of courtesy she's not used to."

"Very true; and her reception of Berthier was anything but gracious, although he certainly displayed all his civilities in her behalf."

"Strange days we live in!" sighed the other; "when a man's promotion hangs upon the favourable word of a——"

"Hush!—take care!—be cautious!" whispered the other. "Let us not forget this poor fellow's business. How are you to settle it? Is the signature of any consequence? The whole sentence is all right and regular."

"I shouldn't like to omit the signature," said the other, cautiously; "it looks like carelessness, and might involve us in trouble hereafter."

"Then we must wait some time, for I see they are gone to dinner."

"So I perceive," replied the former, as he lighted his cigar, and seated himself on a bank. "You may let the prisoner sit down, sergeant, and leave his hands free; he looks wearied and exhausted."

I was too weak to speak, but I looked my gratitude;

and sitting down upon the grass, covered my face and wept heartily.

Although quite close to where the officers sat together chatting and jesting, I heard little or nothing of what they said. Already the things of life had ceased to have any hold upon me ; and I could have heard of the greatest victory, or listened to a story of the most fatal defeat, without the slightest interest or emotion. An occasional word or a name would strike upon my ear, but leave no impression nor any memory behind it.

The military band was performing various marches and opera airs before the tent where the general dined, and in the melody, softened by distance, I felt a kind of calm and sleepy repose that lulled me into a species of ecstacy.

At last the music ceased to play, and the adjutant, starting hurriedly up, called on the sergeant to move forward.

"By Jove !" cried he, "they seem preparing for a promenade, and we shall get into a scrape if Berthier sees us here. Keep your party yonder, sergeant, out of sight, till I obtain the signature."

And so saying, away he went towards the tent at a sharp gallop.

A few seconds, and I watched him crossing the esplanade; he dismounted and disappeared. A terrible choking sensation was over me, and I scarcely was conscious that they were again tying my hands. The adjutant came out again, and made a sign with his sword.

"We are to move on !" said the sergeant, half in doubt.

"Not at all," broke in the aide-de-camp; "he is making a sign for you to bring up the prisoner ! There, he is repeating the signal—lead him forward."

I knew very little of how—less still of why—but we moved on in the direction of the tent, and in a few minutes stood before it. The sounds of revelry and laughter —the crash of voices, and the clink of glasses—together with the hoarse bray of the brass band, which again struck up—all were co-mingled in my brain, as, taking me by the arm, I was led forward within the tent, and found myself at the foot of a table covered with all the gorgeousness of silver plate, and glowing with bouquets of flowers and fruits. In the one hasty glance I gave, before my lids fell over my swimming eyes, I could see the splendid uniforms of the guests as they sat around the board, and the magnificent costume of a lady in the place of honour next the head.

Several of those who sat at the lower end of the table

drew back their seats as I came forward, and seemed as if desirous to give the general a better view of me.

Overwhelmed by the misery of my fate, as I stood awaiting my death, I felt as though a mere word, a look, would have crushed me but one moment back; but now, as I stood there before that group of gazers, whose eyes scanned me with looks of insolent disdain, or still more insulting curiosity, a sense of proud defiance seized me, to confront and dare them with glances haughty and scornful as their own. It seemed to me so base and unworthy a part to summon a poor wretch before them, as if to whet their new appetite for enjoyment by the aspect of his misery, that an indignant anger took possession of me, and I drew myself up to my full height, and stared at them calm and steadily.

"So, then!" cried a deep soldier-like voice from the far end of the table, which I at once recognised as the general-in-chief's—" so, then, gentlemen, we have now the honour of seeing amongst us the hero of the Rhine! This is the distinguished individual by whose prowess the passage of the river was effected, and the Swabian infantry cut off in their retreat! Is it not true, sir?" said he, addressing me with a savage scowl.

"I have had my share in the achievement!" said I, with the cool air of defiance.

"Parbleu! you are modest, sir. So had every drummer-boy that beat his tattoo! But your's was the part of a great leader, if I err not?"

I made no answer, but stood firm and unmoved.

"How do you call the island which you have immortalised by your valour?"

"The Fels Insel, sir."

"Gentlemen, let us drink to the hero of the Fels Insel," said he, holding up his glass for the servant to fill it. "A bumper—a full, a flowing bumper! And let him also pledge a toast in which his interest must be so brief. Give him a glass, Contard."

The order was obeyed in a second; and I, summoning up all my courage to seem as easy and indifferent as they were, lifted the glass to my lips, and drained it off.

"Another glass now to the health of this fair lady, through whose intercession we owe the pleasure of your company," said the general.

"Willingly," said I; "and may one so beautiful seldom find herself in a society so unworthy of her!"

A perfect roar of laughter succeeded the insolence of

this speech; amid which I was half pushed, half dragged, up to the end of the table, where the general sat.

" How so, Coquin, do you dare to insult a French general, at the head of his own staff!"

" If I did, sir, it were quite as brave as to mock a poor criminal on the way to his execution!"

" That is the boy!—I know him now!—the very same lad!" cried the lady, as, stooping behind Berthier's chair, she stretched out her hand towards me.   " Come here; are you not Colonel Mahon's godson?"

I looked her full in the face; and whether her own thoughts gave the impulse, or that something in my stare suggested it, she blushed till her cheek grew crimson.

" Poor Charles was so fond of him!" whispered she in Berthier's ear; and as she spoke, the expression of her face at once recalled where I had seen her, and I now perceived that she was the same person I had seen at table with Colonel Mahon, and whom I believed to be his wife.

A low whispering conversation now ensued between the general and her, at the close of which he turned to me and said,—

" Madame Merlancourt has deigned to take an interest in you—you are pardoned. Remember, sir, to whom you owe your life, and be grateful to her for it."

I took the hand she extended towards me, and pressed it to my lips.

" Madame," said I, " there is but one favour more I would ask in this world, and with it I could think myself happy."

" But can I grant it, mon cher?" said she, smiling.

" If I am to judge from the influence I have seen you wield, madame, here and elsewhere, this petition will easily be accorded."

A slight flush coloured the lady's cheek, while that of the general became dyed red with anger. I saw that I had committed some terrible blunder, but how, or in what, I knew not.

" Well, sir," said Madame Merlancourt, addressing me with a stately coldness of manner, very different from her former tone, " let us hear what you ask, for we are already taking up a vast deal of time that our host would prefer devoting to his friends—what is it you wish?"

" My discharge from a service, madame, where zeal and enthusiasm are rewarded with infamy and disgrace; my freedom to be anything but a French soldier."

" You are resolved, sir, that I am not to be proud of my

protegé," said she, haughtily; "what words are these to speak in presence of a general and his officers?"

"I am bold, madame, as you say, but I am wronged."

"How so, sir—in what have you been injured?" cried the general, hastily, "except in the excessive condescension which has stimulated your presumption. But we are really two indulgent in this long parley. Madame, permit me to offer you some coffee under the trees. Contardo, tell the band to follow us. Gentlemen, we expect the pleasure of your society."

And so saying, Berthier presented his arm to the lady, who swept proudly past without deigning to notice me. In a few minutes the tent was cleared of all, except the servants occupied in removing the remains of the dessert, and I fell back, unremarked and unobserved, to take my way homeward to the barracks, more indifferent to life than ever I had been afraid of death.

As I am not likely to recur at any length to the somewhat famous person to whom I owed my life, I may as well state that her name has since occupied no inconsiderable share of attention in France, and her history, under the title of "Mémoires d'une Contemporaine," excited a degree of interest and anxiety in quarters which one might have fancied far above the reach of her revelations. At the time I speak of, I little knew the character of the age in which such influences were all powerful, nor how destinies very different from mine hung upon the favouritism of "La belle Nathalie." Had I known these things, and, still more, had I known the sad fate to which she brought my poor friend, Colonel Mahon, I might have scrupled to accept my life at such hands, or involved myself in a debt of gratitude to one for whom I was subsequently to feel nothing but hatred and aversion. It was indeed a terrible period, and in nothing more so than the fact, that acts of benevolence and charity were blended up with features of falsehood, treachery, and baseness, which made one despair of humanity, and think the very worst of their species.

CHAPTER XV.

SCRAPS OF HISTORY.

NOTHING displays more powerfully the force of egotism than the simple truth that, when any man sits himself down to write the events of his life, the really momentous occurrences in which he may have borne a part occupy a conspicuously small place, when each petty incident of a merely personal nature is dilated and extended beyond all bounds. In one sense, the reader benefits by this, since there are few impertinences less forgiveable than the obtrusion of some insignificant name into the narrative of facts that are meet for history. I have made these remarks in a spirit of apology to my reader; not alone for the accuracy of my late detail, but also, if I should seem in future to dwell but passingly on the truly important facts of a great campaign, in which my own part was so humble.

I was a soldier in that glorious army which Moreau led into the heart of Germany, and whose victorious career would only have ceased when they entered the capital of the Empire, had it not been for the unhappy mistakes of Jourdan, who commanded the auxiliary forces in the north. For nigh three months we advanced steadily and successfully, superior in every engagement; we only waited for the moment of junction with Jourdan's army, to declare the empire our own; when at last came the terrible tidings that he had been beaten, and that Latour was advancing from Ulm to turn our left flank, and cut off our communications with France.

Two hundred miles from our own frontiers—separated from the Rhine by that terrible Black Forest whose defiles are mere gorges between vast mountains—with an army fifty thousand strong on one flank, and the Archduke Charles commanding a force of nigh thirty thousand on the other—such were the dreadful combinations which now threatened us with a defeat not less signal than Jourdan's own. Our strength, however, lay in a superb army of seventy thousand unbeaten men, led on by one whose name alone was victory.

On the 24th of September, the order for retreat was given; the army began to retire by slow marches, prepared to contest every inch of ground, and make every available spot a battle-field. The baggage and ammunition were sent on in front, and two days' march in advance. Behind, a formidable rear-guard was ready to repulse every attack of the enemy. Before, however, entering those close defiles by which his retreat lay, Moreau determined to give one terrible lesson to his enemy. Like the hunted tiger turning upon his pursuers, he suddenly halted at Biberach, and ere Latour, who commanded the Austrians, was aware of his purpose, assailed the Imperial forces with an attack on right, centre, and left together. Four thousand prisoners and eighteen pieces of cannon were the trophies of the victory.

The day after this decisive battle our march was resumed, and the advanced-guard entered that narrow and dismal defile which goes by the name of the "Valley of Hell," when our left and right flanks, stationed at the entrance of the pass, effectually secured the retreat against molestation. The voltigeurs of St. Cyr crowning the heights as we went, swept away the light troops which were scattered along the rocky eminences, and in less than a fortnight our army debouched by Fribourg and Oppenheim into the valley of the Rhine, not a gun having been lost, not a caisson deserted, during that perilous movement.

The Archduke, however, having ascertained the direction of Moreau's retreat, advanced by a parallel pass through the Kinzigthal, and attacked St. Cyr at Nauendorf, and defeated him. Our right flank, severely handled at Emmendingen, the whole force was obliged to retreat on Huningen, and once more we found ourselves upon the banks of the Rhine, no longer an advancing army, high in hope, and flushed with victory—but beaten, harassed, and retreating!

The last few days of that retreat presented a scene of disaster such as I can never forget. To avoid the furious charges of the Austrian cavalry, against which our own could no longer make resistance, we had fallen back upon a line of country cut up into rocky cliffs and precipices, and covered by a dense pine forest. Here, necessarily broken up into small parties, we were assailed by the light troops of the enemy, led on through the various passes by the peasantry, whose animosity our own severity had excited. It was, therefore, a continual hand-to-hand struggle, in which, opposed as we were to over numbers well acquainted with every advantage of the ground, our loss was terrific. It is said that nigh seven thousand men fell—an immense number, when no general action had occurred. Whatever the actual loss, such were the circumstances of our army, that Moreau hastened to propose an armistice, on the condition of the Rhine being the boundary between the two armies, while Kehl was still to be held by the French.

The proposal was rejected by the Austrians, who at once commenced preparations for a siege of the fortress with forty thousand troops, under Latour's command. The earlier months of winter now passed in the labours of the siege, and on the morning of New-Year's Day the first attack was made; the second line was carried a few days after, and, after a glorious defence by Desaix, the garrison capitulated, and evacuated the fortress on the 9th of the month. Thus, in the space of six short months, had we advanced with a conquering army into the very heart of the Empire, and now we were back again within our own frontier; not one single trophy of all our victories remaining, two-thirds of our army dead or wounded, more than all, the prestige of our superiority fatally injured, and that of the enemy's valour and prowess as signally elevated.

The short annals of a successful soldier are often comprised in the few words which state how he was made lieutenant at such a date, promoted to his company here, obtained his majority there, succeeded to the command of his regiment at such a place, and so on. Now my exploits may even be more briefly written as regards this campaign; —for whether at Kehl, at Nauendorf, on the Etz, or at Huningen, I ended as I begun—a simple soldier of the ranks. A few slight wounds, a few still more insignificant words of praise, were all that I brought back with me; but if my trophies were small, I had gained considerably both in habits of discipline and obedience. I had learned to endure, ably and without complaining, the inevitable hardships of a campaign, and, better still, to see that the irrepressible impulses of the soldier, however prompted by zeal or heroism, may oftener mar than promote the more mature plans of his general. Scarcely had my feet once more touched French ground, than I was seized with the ague, then raging as an epidemic among the troops, and sent forward with a large detachment of sick to the Military Hospital of Strasbourg.

Here I bethought me of my patron, Colonel Mahon, and determined to write to him. For this purpose I addressed a question to the Adjutant-General's office to ascertain the colonel's address. The reply was a brief and stunning one—he had been dismissed the service. No personal calamity could have thrown me into deeper affliction; nor had I even the sad consolation of learning any of the circumstances of this misfortune. His death, even though thereby I should have lost my only friend, would have been a lighter evil than this disgrace; and coming as did the tidings when I was already broken by sickness and defeat, more than ever disgusted me with a soldier's life. It was then with a feeling of total indifference that I heard a rumour which at another moment would have filled me with enthusiasm—the order for all invalids sufficiently well to be removed, to be drafted into regiments serving in Italy. The fame of Bonaparte, who commanded that army, had now surpassed that of all the other generals; his victories paled the glory of their successes, and it was already a mark of distinction to have served under his command.

The walls of the hospital were scrawled over with the names of his victories; rude sketches of Alpine passes, terrible ravines, or snow-clad peaks, met the eye everywhere; and the one magical name, "Bonaparte," written beneath, seemed the key to all their meaning. With him war seemed to assume all the charms of romance. Each action was illustrated by feats of valour or heroism, and a halo of glory seemed to shine over all the achievements of his genius.

It was a clear, bright morning of March, when a light frost sharpened the air, and a fair, blue sky overhead showed a cloudless elastic atmosphere, that the "invalides," as we were all called, were drawn up in the great square of the hospital for inspection. Two superior officers of the staff, attended by several surgeons and an adjutant, sat at a table in front of us, on which lay the regimental books and conduct-rolls of the different corps. Such of the sick as had received severe wounds, incapacitating them for further service, were presented with some slight reward—a few francs in money, a great-coat, or a pair of shoes, and obtained their freedom. Others, whose injuries were less important, received their promotion, or some slight increase of pay, these favours being all measured by the character the individual bore in his regiment, and the opinion certified of him by his commanding officer. When my turn came and I stood forward, I felt a kind of shame to think how little claim I could prefer either to honour or advancement.

"Maurice Tiernay, slightly wounded by a sabre at Nauendorf—flesh-wound at Biberach—enterprising and

active, but presumptuous and overbearing with his comrades," read out the adjutant, while he added a few words
I could not hear, but at which the superior laughed
heartily.

"What says the doctor?" asked he, after a pause.

"This has been a bad case of ague, and I doubt if the
young fellow will ever be fit for active service—certainly
not at present."

"Is there a vacancy at Saumur?" asked the general.
"I see he has been employed in the school at Nancy."

"Yes, sir; for the third class there is one."

"Let him have it, then. Tiernay, you are appointed
as aspirant of the third class at the College of Saumur.
Take care that the report of your conduct be more creditable than what is written here. Your opportunities will
now be considerable, and if well employed, may lead to
further honour and distinction; if neglected or abused,
your chances are forfeited for ever."

I bowed and retired, as little satisfied with the admonition as elated with a prospect which converted me from
a soldier into a scholar, and, in the first verge of manhood,
threw me back once more into the condition of a mere
boy.

Eighteen months of my life—not the least happy, perhaps, since in the peaceful portion I can trace so little to
be sorry for—glided over beside the banks of the beautiful
Loire, the intervals in the hour of study being spent
either in the riding-school, or the river, where, in addition
to swimming and diving, we were instructed in pontooning
and rafting, the modes of transporting ammunition and
artillery, and the attacks of infantry by cavalry picquets.

I also learned to speak and write English and German
with great ease and fluency, besides acquiring some skill
in military drawing and engineering.

It is true that the imprisonment chafed sorely against
us, as we read of the great achievements of our armies in
various parts of the world; of the great battles of Cairo
and the pyramids, of Acre and Mount Thabor; and of
which a holiday and a fête were to be our only share.

The terrible storms which shook Europe from end to
end, only reached us in the bulletins of new victories;
and we panted for the time when we, too, should be actors
in the glorious exploits of France.

It is already known to the reader that of the country
from which my family came I myself knew nothing. The
very little I had ever learned of it from my father, was
also a mere tradition; still was I known among my com-

rades only as "the Irishman," and by that name was I
recognised, even in the record of the school, where I was
inscribed thus—"Maurice Tiernay, dit l'Irlandais." It
was on this very simple and seemingly-unimportant fact
my whole fate in life was to turn; and in this wise——
But the explanation deserves a chapter of its own, and
shall have it.

CHAPTER XVI.

"AN OLD GENERAL OF THE IRISH BRIGADE."

IN obedience to an order which arrived at Saumur one
morning in the July of 1798, I was summoned before the
commandant of the school, when the following brief colloquy ensued :—

"Maurice Tiernay," said he, reading from the record of
the school, "why are you called l'Irlandais?"

"I am Irish by descent, sir."

"Ha! by descent. Your father was then an Emigré?"

"No, sir—my great grandfather."

"Parbleu! that is going very far back. Are you aware
of the causes which induced him to leave his native
country?"

"They were connected with political troubles, I've
heard, sir. He took part against the English, my father
told me, and was obliged to make his escape to save his
life."

"You then hate the English, Maurice?"

"My grandfather certainly did not love them, sir."

"Nor can you, boy, ever forgive their having exiled
your family from country and home : every man of honour
retains the memory of such injuries."

"I can scarcely deem that an injury, sir, which has
made me a French citizen," said I, proudly.

"True, boy—you say what is perfectly true and just ;
any sacrifice of fortune or patrimony is cheap at such a
price ; still you have suffered a wrong—a deep and irreparable wrong—and as a Frenchman you are ready to
avenge it."

Although I had no very precise notion, either as to the
extent of the hardships done me, nor in what way I was

to demand the reparation, I gave the assent he seemed to expect.

"You are well acquainted with the language, I believe?" continued he.

"I can read and speak English tolerably well, sir."

"But I speak of Irish, boy—of the language which is spoken by your fellow-countrymen," said he, rebukiugly.

"I have always heard, sir, that this has fallen into disuse, and is little known, save among the peasantry in a few secluded districts."

He seemed impatient as I said this, and referred once more to the paper before him, from whose minutes he appeared to have been speaking.

"You must be in error, boy. I find here that the nation is devotedly attached to its traditions and its literature, and feels no injury deeper than the insulting substitution of a foreign tongue for their own noble language."

"Of myself I know nothing, sir; the little I have learned was acquired when a mere child."

"Ah, then you probably forget, or may never have heard the fact; but it is as I tell you. This, which I hold here, is the report of a highly-distinguished and most influential personage, who lays great stress upon the circumstance. I am sorry, Tiernay, very sorry, that you are unacquainted with the language."

He continued for some minutes to brood over this disappointment, and at last returned to the paper before him.

"The geography of the country—what kuowledge have you on that subject?"

"No more, sir, than I may possess of other countries, and merely learned from maps."

"Bad again," muttered he to himself. "Madgett calls these 'essentials;' but we shall see." Then addressing me, he said, "Tiernay, the object of my present interrogatory is to inform you that the Directory is about to send an expedition to Ireland to assist in the liberation of that enslaved people. It has been suggested that young officers and soldiers of Irish descent might render peculiar service to the cause, and I have selected you for an opportunity which will convert those worsted epaulettes into bullion."

This at least was intelligible news, and now I began to listen with more attention.

"There is a report," said he, laying down before me a very capacious manuscript, "which you will carefully peruse. Here are the latest pamphlets setting forth the state of public opinion in Ireland; and here are various maps of the coast, the harbours, and the strongholds of that country, with all of which you may employ yourself advantageously; and if, on considering the subject, you feel disposed to volunteer—for as a volunteer only could your services be accepted—I will willingly support your request by all the influence in my power."

"I am ready to do so at once, sir," said I, eagerly; "I have no need to know any more than you have told me."

"Well said, boy; I like your ardour. Write your petition and it shall be forwarded to-day. I will also try and obtain for you the same regimental rank you hold in the school"—I was a sergeant—"it will depend upon yourself afterwards to secure a further advancement. You are now free from duty; lose no time, therefore, in storing your mind with every possible information, and be ready to set out at a moment's notice."

"Is the expedition so nearly ready, sir?" asked I, eagerly.

He nodded, and with a significant admonition as to secrecy, dismissed me, bursting with anxiety to examine the stores of knowledge before me, and prepare myself with all the details of a plan in which already I took the liveliest interest. Before the week expired, I received an answer from the minister, accepting the offer of my services. The reply found me deep in those studies, which I scarcely could bear to quit even at meal-times. Never did I experience such an all-devouring passion for a theme as on that occasion. "Ireland" never left my thoughts; her wrongs and sufferings were everlastingly before me; all the cruelties of centuries—all the hard tyranny of the penal laws—the dire injustice of caste oppression—filled me with indignation and anger; while, on the other hand, I conceived the highest admiration of a people who, undeterred by the might and power of England, resolved to strike a great blow for liberty.

The enthusiasm of the people—the ardent darings of a valour whose impetuosity was its greatest difficulty—their high romantic temperament—their devotion—their gratitude—the child-like trustfulness of their natures, were all traits, scattered through the various narratives, which invariably attracted me, and drew me more strongly to their cause—more from affection than reason.

Madgett's memoir was filled with these, and he, I concluded, must know them well, being, as it was asserted, one of the ancient nobility of the land, and who now desired nothing better than to throw rank, privilege, and title into the scale, and do battle for the liberty and equality of his countrymen. How I longed to see this great

man, whom my fancy arrayed in all the attributes he so
lavished upon his countrymen, for they were not only, in
his description, the boldest and the bravest, but the handsomest people of Europe.

As to the success of the enterprise, whatever doubts I
had at first conceived, from an estimate of the immense
resources of England, were speedily solved, as I read of
the enormous preparations the Irish had made for the
struggle. The Roman Catholics, Madgett said, were three
millions, the Dissenters another million, all eager for
freedom and French alliance, wanting nothing but the
appearance of a small armed force to give them the necessary organisation and discipline. They were somewhat
deficient, he acknowledged, in fire-arms—cannon they had
none whatever; but the character of the country, which
consisted of mountains, valleys, ravines and gorges, reduced war to the mere chivalrous features of personal
encounter. What interminable descriptions did I wade
through of clubs and associations, the very names of which
were a puzzle to me—the great union of all appearing to
be a society called "Defenders," whose oath bound them
to "fidelity to the united nations of France and Ireland!"

So much for the one side. For the other, it was asserted that the English forces then in garrison in Ireland
were below contempt; the militia, being principally Irish,
might be relied on for taking the popular side; and as to
the Regulars, they were either "old men or boys," incapable of active service; and several of the regiments
being Scotch, greatly disaffected to the Government.
Then, again, as to the navy, the sailors in the English
fleet were more than two-thirds Irishmen, all Catholics,
and all disaffected.

That the enterprise contained every element of success,
then, who could doubt? The nation, in the proportion of
ten to one, were for the movement. On their side lay
not alone the wrongs to avenge, but the courage, the
energy, and the daring. Their oppressors were as weak
as tyrannical, their cause was a bad one, and their support
of it a hollow semblance of superiority.

If I read these statements with ardour and avidity, one
lurking sense of doubt alone obtruded itself on my reasonings. Why, with all these guarantees of victory, with
everything that can hallow a cause, and give it stability
and strength—why did the Irish ask for aid? If they
were, as they alleged, an immense majority—if theirs
was all the heroism and the daring—if the struggle was
to be maintained against a miserably inferior force, weak

ened by age, incapacity, and disaffection—what need had they of Frenchmen on their side? The answer to all such doubts, however, was "the Irish were deficient in organisation."

Not only was the explanation a very sufficient one, but it served in a high degree to flatter our vanity. We were, then, to be organisers of Ireland; from us were they to take the lessons of civilisation, which should prepare them for freedom—ours was the task to discipline their valour, and train their untaught intelligence. Once landed in the country, it was to our standard they were to rally; from us were to go forth the orders of every movement and measure; to us this new land was to be an El dorado. Madgett significantly hinted everywhere at the unbounded gratitude of Irishmen; and more than hinted at the future fate of certain confiscated estates. One phrase, ostentatiously set forth in capitals, asserted that the best general of the French Republic could not be anywhere employed with so much reputation and profit. There was, then, everything to stimulate the soldier in such an enterprise —honour, fame, glory, and rich rewards were all among the prizes.

It was when deep in the midst of these studies, poring over maps and reports, taxing my memory with hard names, and getting off by heart dates, distances, and numbers, that the order came for me to repair at once to Paris, where the volunteers of the expedition were to assemble. My rank of sergeant had been confirmed, and in this capacity, as "sous officier," I was ordered to report myself to General Kilmaine, the adjutant-general of the expedition, then living in the "Rue Chantereine." I was also given the address of a certain Lestaing—Rue Tarbout—a tailor, from whom, on producing a certificate, I was to obtain my new uniform.

Full as I was of the whole theme, thinking of the expedition by day, and dreaming of it by night, I was still little prepared for the enthusiasm it was at that very moment exciting in every society of the capital. For some time previous a great number of Irish emigrants had made Paris their residence; some were men of good position and ample fortune; some were individuals of considerable ability and intelligence. All were enthusiastic, and ardent in temperament—devotedly attached to their country—hearty haters of England, and proportionally attached to all that was French. These sentiments, coupled with a certain ease of manner, and a faculty of adaptation, so peculiarly Irish, made them general favourites in society; and long before the Irish question had found any favour with the public, its national supporters had won over the hearts and good wishes of all Paris to the cause.

Well pleased, then, as I was with my handsome uniform of green and gold, my small chapeau, with its plume of cock's feathers, and the embroidered shamrock on my collar, I was not a little struck by the excitement my first appearance in the street created. Accustomed to see a hundred strange military costumes—the greater number, I own, more singular than tasteful—the Parisians, I concluded, would scarcely notice mine in the crowd. Not so, however; the print-shops had already given the impulse to the admiration, and the "Irish Volunteer of the Guard" was to be seen in every window, in all the "glory of his bravery." The heroic character of the expedition, too, was typified by a great variety of scenes, in which the artist's imagination had all the credit. In one picture the "jeune Irlandais" was planting a national flag of very capacious dimensions on the summit of his native mountains; here he was storming "Le chateau de Dublin," a most formidable fortress, perched on a rock above the sea; here he was crowning the heights of "La citadelle de Cork," a very Gibraltar in strength; or he was haranguing the native chieftains, a highly picturesque group—a cross between a knight crusader and a South-sea islander.

My appearance, therefore, in the streets was the signal for general notice and admiration, and more than one compliment was uttered, purposely loud enough to reach me, on the elegance and style of my equipment. In the pleasant flurry of spirits excited by this flattery, I arrived at the general's quarters in the Rue Chantereine. It was considerably before the time of his usual receptions, but the glitter of my epaulettes, and the air of assurance I had assumed, so far imposed upon the old servant who acted as valet, that he at once introduced me into a small saloon, and after a brief pause presented me to the general, who was reclining on a sofa at his breakfast. Although far advanced in years, and evidently broken by bad health, General Kilmaine still preserved traces of great personal advantages, while his manner exhibited all that polished ease and courtesy which was said to be peculiar to the Irish gentleman of the French court. Addressing me in English, he invited me to join his meal, and on my declining, as having already breakfasted, he said, "I perceive, from your name, we are countrymen, and as your uniform tells me the service in which you are engaged, we may speak with entire confidence. Tell me then, frankly, all that you know of the actual condition of Ireland."

Conceiving that this question applied to the result of my late studies, and was meant to elicit the amount of my information, I at once began a recital of what I had learned from the books and reports I had been reading. My statistics were perfect—they had been gotten off by heart; my sympathies were, for the same reason, most eloquent; my indignation was boundless on the wrongs I deplored, and in fact, in the fifteen minutes during which he permitted me to declaim without interruption, I had gone through the whole " cause of Ireland," from Henry II. to George III.

"You have been reading Mr. Madgett, I perceive," said he, with a smile; "but I would rather hear something of your own actual experience. Tell me, therefore, in what condition are the people at this moment, as regards poverty ? "

"I have never been in Ireland, general," said I, not without some shame at the avowal coming so soon after my eloquent exhortation.

"Ah, I perceive," said he, blandly, "of Irish origin, and a relative probably of that very distinguished soldier, Count Maurice de Tiernay, who served in the Garde-du Corps."

"His only son, general," said I, blushing with eagerness and pleasure at the praise of my father.

"Indeed!" said he, smiling courteously, and seeming to meditate on my words. "There was not a better nor a braver sabre in the corps than your father—a very few more of such men might have saved the monarchy—as it was, they dignified its fall. And to whose guidance and care did you owe your early training, for I see you have not been neglected ? "

A few words told him the principal events of my early years, to which he listened with deep attention. At length he said, " And now you are about to devote your acquirements and energy to this new expedition ? "

" All, general! Everything that I have is too little for such a cause."

"You say truly, boy," said he, warmly; "would that so good a cause had better leaders. I mean," added he, hurriedly, "wiser ones. Men more conversant with the actual state of events, more fit to cope with the great difficulties before them, more ready to take advantage of circumstances, whose outward meaning will often prove deceptive. In fact, Irishmen of character and capacity,

tried soldiers and good patriots. Well, well, let us hope
the best. In whose division are you?"

"I have not yet heard, sir. I have presented myself
here to-day to receive your orders."

"There again is another instance of their incapacity,"
cried he, passionately. "Why, boy, I have no command,
nor any function. I did accept office under General
Hoche, but he is not to lead the present expedition."

"And who is, sir?"

"I cannot tell you. A week ago they talked of
Grouchy, then of Hardy; yesterday it was Humbert;
to-day it may be Bonaparte, and to-morrow yourself!
Ay, Tiernay, this great and good cause has its national
fatality attached to it, and is so wrapped up in low intrigue
and falsehood, that every minister becomes in turn disgusted with the treachery and mendacity he meets with,
and bequeaths the question to some official underling,
meet partisan for the mock patriot he treats with."

"But the expedition will sail, general?" asked I, sadly
discomfited by this tone of despondency.

He made me no answer, but sat for some time absorbed
in his own thoughts. At last he looked up, and said, "You
ought to be in the army of Italy, boy; the great teacher
of war is there."

"I know it, sir, but my whole heart is in this struggle.
I feel that Ireland has a claim on all who derived even a
name from her soil. Do you not believe that the expedition will sail?"

Again he was silent and thoughtful.

"Mr. Madgett would say yes," said he, scornfully,
"though, certes, he would not volunteer to bear it company."

"Colonel Cherin, General!" said the valet, as he flung
open the door for a young officer in a staff uniform. I
arose at once to withdraw, but the general motioned to
me to wait in an adjoining room, as he desired to speak
with me again.

Scarcely five minutes had elapsed when I was summoned
once more before him.

"You have come at a most opportune moment, Tiernay," said he; "Colonel Cherin informs me that an expedition is ready to sail from Rochelle at the first favourable
wind. General Humbert has the command; and if you
are disposed to join him I will give you a letter of presen-
tation."

Of course I did not hesitate in accepting the offer; and
while the general drew over his desk to write the letter,

I withdrew towards the window to converse with Colonel Cherin.

"You might have waited long enough," said he, laughing, "if the affair had been in other hands than Humbert's. The delays and discussions of the official people, the difficulty of anything like agreement, the want of money, and fifty other causes, would have detained the fleet till the English got scent of the whole. But Humbert has taken the short road in the matter. He only arrived at La Rochelle five days ago, and now he is ready to weigh anchor."

"And in what way has he accomplished this?" asked I, in some curiosity.

"By a method," replied he, laughing again, "which is usually reserved for an enemy's country. Growing weary of a correspondence with the minister, which seemed to make little progress, and urged on by the enthusiastic stories of the Irish refugees, he resolved to wait no longer; and so he has called on the merchants and magistrates to advance him a sum on military requisition, together with such stores and necessaries as he stands in need of."

"And they have complied?" asked I.

"Parbleu! that have they. In the first place, they had no other choice; and in the second, they are but too happy to get rid of him and his 'Legion Noir,' as they are called, so cheaply. A thousand louis and a thousand muskets would not pay for the damage of these vagabonds each night they spent in the town."

I confess that this description did not tend to exalt the enthusiasm I had conceived for the expedition; but it was too late for hesitation—too late for even a doubt. Go forward I should, whatever might come of it. And now the general had finished his letter, which, having sealed and addressed, he gave into my hand, saying—"This will very probably obtain you promotion, if not at once, at least on the first vacancy. Good bye, my lad; there may be hard knocks going where you will be, but I'm certain you'll not disgrace the good name you bear, nor the true cause for which you are fighting. I would that I had youth and strength to stand beside you in the struggle! Good bye."

He shook me affectionately by both hands; the colonel, too, bade me adieu not less cordially; and I took my leave with a heart overflowing with gratitude and delight.

CHAPTER XVII.

LA ROCHELLE.

LA ROCHELLE is a quiet little town at the bottom of a small bay, the mouth of which is almost closed up by two islands. There is a sleepy, peaceful air about the place— a sort of drowsy languor pervades everything and everybody about it, that tells of a town whose days of busy prosperity have long since passed by, and which is dragging out life, like some retired tradesman—too poor for splendour, but rich enough to be idle. A long avenue of lime-trees incloses the harbour; and here the merchants conduct their bargains, while their wives, seated beneath the shade, discuss the gossip of the place over their work. All is patriarchal and primitive as Holland itself; the very courtesies of life exhibiting that ponderous stateliness which insensibly reminds one of the land of dykes and broad breeches. It is the least "French" of any town I have ever seen in France; none of that light merriment, that gay volatility of voice and air which form the usual atmosphere of a French town. All is still, orderly, and sombre; and yet on the night in which— something more than fifty years back—I first entered it, a very different scene was presented to my eyes.

It was about ten o'clock, and by a moon nearly full, the diligence rattled along the covered ways of the old fortress, and crossing many a moat and drawbridge, the scenes of a once glorious struggle, entered the narrow streets, traversed a wide place, and drew up within the ample portals of "La Poste."

Before I could remove the wide capote which I wore, the waiter ushered me into a large salón where a party of about forty persons were seated at supper. With a few exceptions they were all military officers, and sous-officiers of the expedition, whose noisy gaiety and boisterous mirth sufficiently attested that the entertainment had begun a considerable time before.

A profusion of bottles, some empty, others in the way to become so, covered the table, amidst which lay the fragments of a common table-d'hôte supper—large dishes of cigars and basins of tobacco figuring beside the omelettes and the salad.

The noise, the crash, the heat, the smoke, and the confusion—the clinking of glasses, the singing, and the speech-making, made a scene of such turmoil and uproar, that I would gladly have retired to some quieter atmosphere, when suddenly an accidental glimpse of my uniform caught some eyes among the revellers, and a shout was raised of "Halloa, comrades! here's one of the 'Guides' among us." And at once the whole assembly rose up to greet me. For full ten minutes I had to submit to a series of salutations, which led to every form, from hand-shaking and embracing to kissing; while, perfectly unconscious of any cause for my popularity, I went through the ceremonies like one in a dream.

"Where's Kilmaine?" "What of Hardy?" "Is Grouchy coming?" "Can the Brest fleet sail?" "How many line-of-battle ships have they?" "What's the artillery force?" "Have you brought any money?" This last question, the most frequent of all, was suddenly poured in upon me, and with a fortunate degree of rapidity, that I had no time for a reply, had I even the means of making one.

"Let the lad have a seat and a glass of wine before he submits to this interrogatory," said a fine, jolly-looking old chef-d'escadron at the head of the table, while he made a place for me at his side. "Now tell us, boy, what number of the 'Guides' are to be of our party?"

I looked a little blank at the question, for in truth I had not heard of the corps before, nor was I aware that it was their uniform I was then wearing.

"Come, come, be frank with us, lad," said he; "we are all comrades here. Confound secrecy, say I."

"Ay, ay," cried the whole assembly together—"confound secrecy. We are not bandits nor highwaymen; we have no need of concealment."

"I'll be as frank as you can wish, comrades," said I; "and if I lose some importance in your eyes by owning that I am not the master of a single state secret, I prefer to tell you so, to attempting any unworthy disguise. I come here, by orders from General Kilmaine, to join your expedition; and except this letter for General Humbert, I have no claim to any consideration whatever."

The old chef took the letter from my hands and examined the seal and superscription carefully, and then passed the document down the table for the satisfaction of the rest.

While I continued to watch with anxious eyes the letter on which so much of my own fate depended, a low whispering conversation went on at my side, at the end of which the chef said,—

"It's more than likely, lad, that your regiment is not coming; but our general is not to be baulked for that. Go he will; and let the government look to themselves if he is not supported. At all events you had better see General Humbert at once; there's no saying what that dispatch may contain. Santerre, conduct him up stairs."

A smart young fellow arose at the bidding, and beckoned me to follow him.

It was not without difficulty that we forced our way up stairs, down which porters, and sailors, and soldiers were now carrying a number of heavy trunks and packing-cases. At last we gained an ante-room, where confusion seemed at its highest, crowded as it was by soldiers, the greater number of them intoxicated, and all in a state of riotous and insolent insubordination. Amongst these were a number of the townspeople, eager to prefer complaints for outrage and robbery, but whose subdued voices were drowned amid the clamour of their oppressors. Meanwhile, clerks were writing away receipts for stolen and pillaged articles, and which, signed with the name of the general, were grasped at with eager avidity. Even personal injuries were requited in the same cheap fashion, orders on the national treasury being freely issued for damaged noses and smashed heads, and gratefully received by the confiding populace.

"If the wind draws a little more to the southward before morning, we'll pay our debts with the top-sail sheet, and it will be somewhat shorter, and to the full as honest," said a man in a naval uniform.

"Where's the office of the 'Regiment des Guides?'" cried a soldier from the door at the further end of the room; and before I had time to think over the designation of rank given me, I was hurried into the general's presence.

General Humbert, whose age might have been thirty-eight or forty, was a tall, well-built, but somewhat over-corpulent man; his features frank and manly, but with a dash of coarseness in their expression, particularly about the mouth; a sabre-cut, which had divided the upper lip, and whose cicatrix was then seen through his moustache, heightening the effect of his sinister look; his carriage was singularly erect and soldier-like. but all his gestures betrayed the habits of one who had risen from the ranks, and was not unwilling to revive the recollection.

He was parading the room from end to end when I entered, stopping occasionally to look out from an open window upon the bay, where by the clear moonlight might be seen the ships of the fleet at anchor. Two officers of his staff were writing busily at a table, whence the materials of a supper had not yet been removed. They did not look up as I came forward, nor did he notice me in any way for several minutes. Suddenly he turned towards me, and snatching the letter I held in my hand, proceeded to read it. A burst of coarse laughter broke from him as he perused the lines; and then throwing down the paper on the table, he cried out,—

" So much for Kilmaine's contingent. I asked for a company of engineers and a squadron of ' Guides,' and they send me a boy from the cavalry-school of Saumur. I tell them that I want some fellows conversant with the language and the people, able to treat with the peasantry, and acquainted with their habits, and here I have got a raw youth whose highest acquirement in all likelihood is to daub a map with water-colours, or take fortifications with a pair of compasses! I wish I had some of these learned gentlemen in the trenches for a few hours. Parbleu! I think I could teach them something they don't learn from Citizen Carnot. Well, sir," said he, turning abruptly towards me, " how many squadrons of the ' Guides' are completed?"

" I cannot tell, General," was my timid answer.

" Where are they stationed?"

" Of that also I am ignorant, sir."

" Peste!" cried he, stamping his foot passionately; then suddenly checking his anger, he asked, " How many are coming to join this expedition? Is there a regiment, a division, a troop? Can you tell me with certainty that a sergeant's-guard is on the way hither?"

" I cannot, sir; I know nothing whatever about the regiment in question."

" You have never seen it?" cried he, vehemently.

" Never, sir."

" This exceeds all belief," exclaimed he, with a crash of his closed fist upon the table. " Three weeks letter-writing! Estafettes, orderlies, and special couriers to no end! And here we have an unfledged cur from a cavalry institute, when I asked for a strong reinforcement. Then what brought you here, boy?"

" To join your expedition, General."

" Have they told you it was a holiday-party that we had
planned?   Did they say it was a junketting we were bent
upon?"

" If they had, sir, I would not have come."

" The greater fool you, then, that's all," cried he,
laughing; " when I was your age I'd not have hesitated
twice between a merry-making and a bayonet-charge."

While he was thus speaking, he never ceased to sign his
name to every paper placed before him by one or other of
the secretaries.

" No, parbleu!" he went on, " La maitresse before the
mitraille any day for me.   But what's all this, Girard.
Here I'm issuing orders upon the national treasury for
hundreds of thousands without let or compunction."

The aide-de-camp whispered a word or two in a low tone.

" I know it, lad; I know it well," said the general, laughing heartily ; " I only pray that all our requisitions may
be as easily obtained in future.   Well, Monsieur le Guide,
what are we to do with you?"

" Not refuse me, I hope, General," said I, diffidently.

" Not refuse you, certainly; but in what capacity to
take you, lad, that's the question.   If you had served—if
you had even walked a campaign——"

" So I have, General—this will show you where I have
been;" and I handed him the " livret" which every soldier carries of his conduct and career.

He took the book, and casting his eyes hastily over it,
exclaimed—

" Why, what's this, lad?   You've been at Kehl, at
Emendingen, at Rorshach, at Huyningen, through all that
Black Forest affair with Moreau!   You have seen smoke,
then.   Ay! I see honourable mention of you besides, for
readiness in the field and zeal during action.   What! more
brandy, Girard.   Why our Irish friends must have been
exceedingly thirsty.   I've given them credit for something
like ten thousand ' velts' already!   No matter, the poor
fellows may have to put up with short rations for all this
yet—and there goes my signature once more.   What does
that blue light mean, Girard?" said he, pointing to a
bright blue star that shone from a mast of one of the
ships of war.

" That is the signal, General, that the embarkation of
the artillery is complete."

" Parbleu!" said he with a laugh, " it need not have
taken long; they've given in two batteries of eights, and
one of them has not a gun fit for service.   There goes a
rocket, now.   Isn't that the signal to heave short on the

anchors? Yes, to be sure. And now it is answered by the other! Ha! lads, this does look like business at last!"

The door opened as he spoke, and a naval officer entered.

"The wind is drawing round to the south, General; we can weigh with the ebb if you wish it."

"Wish it!—if I wish it! Yes, with my whole heart and soul I do! I am just as sick of La Rochelle as is La Rochelle of me. The salute that announces our departure will be a 'feu-de-joie' to both of us! Ay, sir, tell your captain that I need no further notice than that he is ready. Girard, see to it that the marauders are sent on board in irons. The fellows must learn at once that discipline begins when we trip our anchors. As for you," said he, turning to me, "you shall act upon my staff with provisional rank as sous-lieutenant: time will show if the grade should be confirmed. And now hasten down to the quay, and put yourself under Colonel Serasin's orders."

Colonel Serasin, the second in command, was, in many respects, the very opposite of Humbert. Sharp, petulant, and irascible, he seemed quite to overlook the fact, that, in an expedition which was little better than a foray, there must necessarily be a great relaxation of the rules of discipline, and many irregularities at least winked at, which, in stricter seasons, would call for punishment. The consequence was, that a large proportion of our force went on board under arrest, and many actually in irons. The Irish were, without a single exception, all drunk; and the English soldiers, who had procured their liberation from imprisonment on condition of joining the expedition, had made sufficiently free with the brandy-bottle, to forget their new alliance, and vent their hatred of France and Frenchmen in expressions whose only alleviation was, that they were nearly unintelligible.

Such a scene of uproar, discord, and insubordination never was seen. The relative conditions of guard and prisoner elicited national animosities that were scarcely even dormant, and many a bloody encounter took place between those whose instinct was too powerful to feel themselves anything but enemies. A cry, too, was raised, that it was meant to betray the whole expedition to the English, whose fleet, it was asserted, had been seen off Oleron that morning; and although there was not even the shadow of a foundation for the belief, it served to increase the alarm and confusion. Whether originating or not with the Irish, I cannot say, but certainly they took advantage of it to avoid embarking; and now began a schism which threatened to wreck the whole expedition, even in the harbour.

The Irish, as indifferent to the call of discipline as they were ignorant of French, refused to obey orders save from officers of their own country; and although Serasin ordered two companies to "load with ball and fire low," the similar note for preparation from the insurgents induced him to rescind the command and try a compromise. In this crisis I was sent by Serasin to fetch what was called the "Committee," the three Irish deputies who accompanied the force. They had already gone aboard of the Dedalus, little foreseeing the difficulties that were to arise on shore.

Seated in a small cabin next the wardroom, I found these three gentlemen, whose names were Tone, Teeling, and Sullivan. Their attitudes were gloomy and despondent, and their looks anything but encouraging as I entered. A paper on which a few words had been scrawled, and signed with their three names underneath, lay before them, and on this their eyes were bent with a sad and deep meaning. I knew not then what it meant, but I afterwards learned that it was a compact formally entered into and drawn up, that if, by the chance of war, they should fall into the enemy's hands, they would anticipate their fate by suicide, but leave to the English government all the ignominy and disgrace of their death.

They seemed scarcely to notice me as I came forward, and even when I delivered my message they heard it with a half' indifference.

"What do you want us to do, sir?" said Teeling, the eldest of the party. "We hold no command in the service. It was against our advice and counsel that you accepted these volunteers at all. We have no influence over them."

"Not the slightest," broke in Tone. "These fellows are bad soldiers and worse Irishmen. The expedition will do better without them."

"And they better without the expedition," muttered Sullivan, drily.

"But you will come, gentlemen, and speak to them," said I. "You can at least assure them that their suspicions are unfounded."

"Very true, sir," replied Sullivan, "we can do so, but with what success? No, no. If you can't maintain discipline here on your own soil, you'll make a bad hand of doing it when you have your foot on Irish ground. And, after all, I for one am not surprised at the report gaining credence."

" How so, sir?" asked I, indignantly.

" Simply that when a promise of fifteen thousand men dwindles down to a force of eight hundred; when a hundred thousand stand of arms come to be represented by a couple of thousand; when an expedition, pledged by a government, has fallen down to a marauding party; when Hoche or Kleber—— But never mind, I always swore that if you sent but a corporal's guard that I'd go with them."

A musket-shot here was heard, followed by a sharp volley and a cheer, and, in an agony of anxiety, I rushed to the deck. Although above half a mile from the shore, we could see the movement of troops hither and thither, and hear the loud words of command. Whatever the struggle, it was over in a moment, and now we saw the troops descending the steps to the boats. With an inconceivable speed the men fell into their places, and, urged on by the long sweeps, the heavy launches swept across the calm water of the bay.

If a cautious reserve prevented any open questioning as to the late affray, the second boat which came alongside revealed some of its terrible consequences. Seven wounded soldiers were assisted up the side by their comrades, and in total silence conveyed to their station between decks.

" A bad augury this!" muttered Sullivan, as his eye followed them. " They might as well have left that work for the English!"

" A swift six-oar boat, with the tricolour flag floating from a flag-staff at her stern, now skimmed along toward us, and as she came nearer we could recognise the uniforms of the officers of Humbert's staff, while the burly figure of the general himself was soon distinguishable in the midst of them.

As he stepped up the ladder, not a trace of displeasure could be seen on his broad bold features. Greeting the assembled officers with a smile, he asked how the wind was.

" All fair, and freshening at every moment," was the answer.

" May it continue!" cried he, fervently. " Welcome a hurricane, if it only waft us westward!"

The foresail filled out as he spoke, the heavy ship heaved over to the wind, and we began our voyage.

CHAPTER XVIII.

"THE BAY OF RATHFRAN."

OUR voyage was very uneventful, but not without anxiety, since, to avoid the English cruisers and the Channel-fleet, we were obliged to hold a southerly course for several days, making a great circuit before we could venture to bear up for the place of our destination. The weather alternated between light winds and a dead calm, which usually came on every day at noon, and lasted till about sunset. As to me, there was an unceasing novelty in everything about a ship; her mechanism, her discipline, her progress, furnished abundant occupation for all my thoughts, and I never wearied of acquiring knowledge of a theme so deeply interesting. My intercourse with the naval officers, too, impressed me strongly in their favour in comparison with their comrades of the land service. In the former case, all was zeal, activity, and watchfulness. The look-out never slumbered at his post; and an unceasing anxiety to promote the success of the expedition manifested itself in all their words and actions. This, of course, was all to be expected in the discharge of the duties peculiarly their own; but I also looked for something which should denote preparation and forethought in the others; yet nothing of the kind was to be seen. The expedition was never discussed even as table-talk; and for anything that fell from the party in conversation, it would have been impossible to say if our destination were China or Ireland. Not a book nor a map, not a pamphlet nor a paper that bore upon the country whose destinies were about to be committed to us, ever appeared on the tables. A vague and listless doubt how long the voyage might last was the extent of interest any one condescended to exhibit; but as to what was to follow after—what new chapter of events should open when this first had closed, none vouchsafed to inquire.

Even to this hour I am puzzled whether to attribute this strange conduct to the careless levity of national character, or to a studied and well " got up " affectation. In all probability both influences were at work ; while a third

not less powerful, assisted them—this was the gross ignorance and shameless falsehood of some of the Irish leaders
of the expedition, whose boastful and absurd histories
ended by disgusting every one. Among the projects discussed at the time, I well remember one which was often
gravely talked over, and the utter absurdity of which
certainly struck none amongst us. This was no less than
the intention of demanding the West India Islands from
England as an indemnity for the past woes and bygone
misgovernment of Ireland. If this seem barely credible
now, I can only repeat my faithful assurance of the fact,
and I believe that some of the memoirs of the time will
confirm my assertion.

The French officers listened to these and similar speculations with utter indifference; probably to many of them
the geographical question was a difficulty that stopped any
further inquiry, while others felt no further interest than
what a campaign promised. All the enthusiastic narratives, then, of high rewards and splendid trophies that
awaited us, fell upon inattentive ears, and at last the word
Ireland ceased to be heard amongst us. Play of various
kinds occupied us when not engaged on duty. There was
little discipline maintained on board, and none of that
strictness which is the habitual rule of a ship-of-war. The
lights were suffered to burn during the greater part of the
night in the cabins; gambling went on usually till daybreak; and the quarter-deck, that most reverential of
spots to every sailor-mind, was often covered by lounging
groups, who smoked, chatted, or played at chess, in all the
cool apathy of men indifferent to its claim for respect.

Now and then, the appearance of a strange sail afar off,
or some dim object in the horizon, would create a momentary degree of excitement and anxiety; but when the
"look-out" from the mast-head had proclaimed her a
"schooner from Brest," or a "Spanish fruit-vessel," the
sense of danger passed away at once, and none ever reverted to the subject.

With General Humbert I usually passed the greater
part of each forenoon,—a distinction, I must confess, I owed
to my skill as a chess-player, a game of which he was
particularly fond, and in which I had attained no small
proficiency. I was too young and too unpractised in the
world to make my skill subordinate to my chief's, and
beat him at every game with as little compunction as
though he were only my equal, till, at last, vexed at his
want of success, and tired of a contest that offered no
vicissitude of fortune, he would frequently cease playing

11

to chat over the events of the time, and the chances of the
expedition.

It was with no slight mixture of surprise and dismay
that I now detected his utter despair of all success, and
that he regarded the whole as a complete forlorn-hope.
He had merely taken the command to involve the French
Government in the cause, and so far compromise the national character that all retreat would be impossible. " We
shall be all cut to pieces or taken prisoners the day after we
land," was his constant exclamation, "and then, but not
till then, will they think seriously in France of a suitable
expedition." There was no heroism, still less was there
any affectation of recklessness, in this avowal. By nature
he was a rough, easy, good-tempered fellow, who liked his
profession less for its rewards than for its changeful scenes
and moving incidents—his one predominating feeling being
that France should give rule to the whole world, and the
principles of her Revolution be everywhere pre-eminent.
To promote this consummation the loss of an army was
of little moment. Let the cause but triumph in the end,
and the cost was not worth fretting about.

Next to this sentiment was his hatred of England, and
all that was English. Treachery, falsehood, pride, avarice,
grasping covetousness, and unscrupulous aggression, were
the characteristics by which he described the nation ; and
he made the little knowledge he had gleaned from newspapers and intercourse so subservient to this theory, that
I was an easy convert to his opinion ; so that, ere long,
my compassion for the wrongs of Ireland was associated
with the most profound hatred of her oppressors.

To be sure, I should have liked the notion that we
ourselves were to have some more active share in the liberation of Irishmen than the mere act of heralding another
and more successful expedition ; but even in this thought
there was romantic self-devotion, not unpleasing to the
mind of a boy ; but, strange enough, I was the only one
who felt it.

The first sight of land to one on sea is always an event
of uncommon interest ; but how greatly increased is the
feeling when that land is to be the scene of a perilous exploit—the cradle of his ambition, or perhaps his grave!
All my speculations about the expedition—all my day
dreams of success, or my anxious hours of dark foreboding-
ings—never brought the matter so palpably before me as
the dim outline of a distant headland, which, I was told,
was part of the Irish coast.

This was on the 8th of August, but on the following day

we stood further out to sea again, and saw no moie of it.
The three succeeding ones we continued to beat up slowly
to the northward against a head wind and a heavy sea ; but
on the evening of the 21st the sun went down in mellow
splendour, and a light air from the south springing up, the
sailors pronounced a most favourable change of weather,
—a prophecy that a starry night and a calm sea soon confirmed.

The morning of the 22nd broke splendidly—a gentle
breeze from the south-west slightly curled the blue waves,
and filled the canvas of the three frigates, as in close order they sailed along under the tall cliffs of Ireland. We
were about three miles from the shore, on which now
every telescope and glass was eagerly directed. As the
light and fleeting clouds of early morning passed away we
could descry the outlines of the bold coast, indented with
many a bay and creek, while rocky promontories and
grassy slopes succeeded each other in endless variety of
contrast. Towns, or even villages, we could see none—a
few small wretched-looking hovels were dotted over the
hills, and here and there a thin wreath of blue smoke bespoke habitation, but, save these signs, there was an air of
loneliness and solitude which increased the solemn feelings
of the scene.

All these objects of interest, however, soon gave way
before another to the contemplation of which every eye
was turned. This was a small fishing-boat, which, with a
low mast and ragged piece of canvas, was seen standing
boldly out for us : a red handkerchief was fastened to a stick
in the stern, as if for a signal, and on our shortening sail,
to admit of her overtaking us, the ensign was lowered as
though in acknowledgment of our meaning.

The boat was soon alongside, and we now perceived that
her crew consisted of a man and a boy, the former of
whom, a powerfully-built, loose fellow, of about five-and-
forty, dressed in a light blue frieze jacket and trousers,
adroitly caught at the cast of rope thrown out to him, and
having made fast his skiff, clambered up the ship's side
at once, gaily, as though he were an old friend coming
to welcome us.

"Is he a pilot?" asked the officer of the watch, addressing one of the Irish officers.

"No ; he's only a fisherman, but he knows the coast
perfectly, and says there is deep water within twenty
fathoms of the shore."

An animated conversation in Irish now ensued between
the peasant and Captain Madgett, during which a wondering

and somewhat impatient group stood around, speedily increased by the presence of General Humbert himself and
his staff.

"He tells me, General," said Madgett, "that we are
in the Bay of Killala, a good and safe anchorage, and,
during the southerly winds, the best on all the coast."

"What news has he from the shore?" asked Humbert,
sharply, as if the care of the ship was a very secondary
consideration.

"They have been expecting us with the greatest impatience, General; he says the most intense anxiety for our
coming is abroad."

"What of the people themselves? Where are the
national forces? Have they any head-quarters near this?
Eh, what says he? What is that? Why does he laugh?"
asked Humbert, in impatient rapidity, as he watched the
changes in the peasant's face.

"He was laughing at the strange sound of a foreign
language, so odd and singular to his ears," said Madgett;
but for all his readiness, a slight flushing of the cheek
showed that he was ill at ease.

"Well, but what of the Irish forces? Where are
they?"

For some minutes the dialogue continued in an animated strain between the two; the vehement tone and
gestures of each bespeaking what sounded at least like al-
tercation; and Madgett at last turned half angrily away,
saying, "The fellow is too ignorant; he actually knows
nothing of what is passing before his eyes."

"Is there no one else on board can speak this 'bara-
gouinage,'" cried Humbert, in anger.

"Yes, General, I can interrogate him," cried a young
lad named Conolly, who had only joined us on the day
before we sailed.

And now as the youth addressed the fisherman in a few
rapid sentences, the other answered as quickly, making a
gesture with his hands that implied grief, or even
despair.

"We can interpret that for ourselves," broke in Humbert; "he is telling you that the game is up."

"Exactly so, General; he says that the insurrection
has been completely put down, that the Irish forces are
scattered or disbanded, and all the leaders taken."

"The fellow is just as likely to be an English spy,"
said Madgett, in a whisper; but Humbert's gesture of
impatience showed how little trust he reposed in the
allegation.

" Ask him what English troops are quartered in this part of the country," said the general.

" A few militia, and two squadrons of dragoons," was the prompt reply.

" No artillery?"

" None."

" Is there any rumour of our coming abroad, or have the frigates been seen?" asked Humbert.

" They were seen last night from the church steeple of Killala, General," said Conolly, translating, " but believed to be English."

" Come; that is the best news he has brought us yet," said Humbert, laughing; " we shall at least surprise them a little. Ask him what men of rank or consequence live in the neighbourhood, and how are they affected towards the expedition?"

A few words, and a low dry laugh, made all the peasant's reply.

" Eh, what says he?" asked Humbert.

" He says, sir, that, except a Protestant bishop, there's nothing of the rank of gentry here."

" I suppose we need scarcely expect his blessing on our efforts," said Humbert, with a hearty laugh. " What is he saying now?—what is he looking at?"

" He says that we are now in the very best anchorage of the bay," said Conolly, " and that on the whole coast there's not a safer spot."

A brief consultation now took place between the general and naval officers, and in a few seconds the word was given to take in all sail and anchor.

" I wish I could speak to that honest fellow myself," said Humbert, as he stood watching the fisherman, who, with a peasant curiosity, had now approached the mast, and was passing his fingers across the blades of the cutlasses as they stood in the sword-rack.

" Sharp enough for the English, eh?" cried Humbert, in French, but with a gesture that seemed at once intelligible. A dry nod of the head gave assent to the remark.

" If I understand him aright," said Humbert, in a half whisper to Conolly, " we are as little expected by our friends as by our enemies; and that there is little or no force in arms among the Irish."

" There are plenty ready to fight, he says, sir, but none accustomed to discipline."

A gesture, half contemptuous, was all Humbert's reply, and he now turned away and walked the deck alone and in silence. Meanwhile the bustle and movements of the crew continued, and soon the great ships, their sails all coiled, lay tranquilly at anchor in a sea without a ripple.

"A boat is coming out from the shore, General," whispered the lieutenant on duty.

"Ask the fisherman if he knows it."

Conolly drew the peasant's attention to the object, and the man, after looking steadily for a few seconds became terribly agitated.

"What is it man—can't you tell who it is?" asked Conolly.

But although so composed before, so ready with all his replies, he seemed now totally unmanned—his frank and easy features being struck with the signs of palpable terror. At last, and with an effort that bespoke all his fears, ne muttered—"'Tis the king's boat is coming, and 'tis the Collector's on board of her!"

"Is that all?" cried Conolly, laughing, as he translated the reply to the general.

"Won't you say that I'm a prisoner, sir; won't you tell them that you 'took' me?" said the fisherman, in an accent of fervent entreaty, for already his mind anticipated the casualty of a failure, and what might betide him afterwards; but no one now had any care for him or his fortunes—all was in preparation to conceal the national character of the ships. The marines were ordered below, and all others whose uniforms might betray their country, while the English colours floated from every mast-head.

General Humbert, with Serasin and two others, remained on the poop-deck, where they continued to walk, apparently devoid of any peculiar interest or anxiety in the scene. Madgett alone betrayed agitation at this moment, his pale face was paler than ever, and there seemed to me a kind of studious care in the way he covered himself up with his cloak, so that not a vestige of his uniform could be seen.

The boat now came close under our lee, and Conolly being ordered to challenge her in English, the Collector, standing up in the stern, touched his hat, and announced his rank. The gangway-ladder was immediately lowered, and three gentlemen ascended the ship's side and walked aft to the poop. I was standing near the bulwark at the time, watching the scene with intense interest. As General Humbert stood a little in advance of the rest, the Collector, probably taking him for the captain, addressed him with some courteous expressions of welcome, and was proceed-

ing to speak of the weather, when the general gently
stopped him by asking if he spoke French.

I shall never forget the terror of face that question
evoked. At first, looking at his two companions, the Collector turned his eyes to the gaff, where the English flag
was flying; but still unable to utter a word, he stood like
one entranced.

" You have been asked if you can speak French, sir?"
said Conolly, at a sign from the general.

" No—very little—very badly—not at all; but isn't this
—am I not on board of——"

" Can none of them speak French?" said Humbert,
shortly.

" Yes, sir," said a young man on the Collector's right;
" I can make myself intelligible in that language, although
no great proficient."

" Who are you, monsieur?—are you a civilian?" asked
Humbert.

" Yes, sir. I am the son of the Bishop of Killala, and
this young gentleman is my brother."

" What is the amount of the force in this neighbourhood?"

" You will pardon me, sir," said the youth, " if I ask,
first, who it is puts this question, and under what circumstances I am expected to answer it."

" All frank and open, sir," said Humbert, good-hu-
mouredly. " I'm the General Humbert, commanding the
army for the liberation of Ireland—so much for your first
question. As to your second one, I believe that if you
have any concern for yourself, or those belonging to you,
you will find that nothing will serve your interest so much
as truth and plain dealing."

" Fortunately, then, for me," said the youth, laughing,
" I cannot betray my king's cause, for I know nothing,
nothing whatever, about the movement of troops. I
seldom go ten miles from home, and have not been even
at Ballina since last winter."

" Why so cautious about your information, then, sir,"
broke in Serasin, roughly, " since you have none to
give?"

" Because I had some to receive, sir, and was curious to
know where I was standing," said the young man, boldly.

While these few sentences were being interchanged,
Madgett had learned from the Collector, that, except a
few companies of militia and fencibles, the country was
totally unprovided with troops; but he also picked up, that
the people were so crest-fallen and subdued in courage

from the late failure of the rebellion, that it was very doubtful whether our coming would arouse them to another effort. This information, particularly the latter part of it, Madgett imparted to Humbert at once, and I thought, by his manner, and the eagerness with which he spoke, that he seemed to use all his powers to dissuade the general from a landing ; at least I overheard him more than once say—" Had we been further north, sir——"

Humbert quickly stopped him by the words—

" And what prevents us, when we have landed, sir, in extending our line north'ard?—the winds cannot surely master us, when we have our feet on the sward. Enough of all this : let these gentlemen be placed in security, and none have access to them without my orders. Make signal for the commanding-officers to come on board here. We've had too much of speculation—a little action now will be more profitable."

" So, we are prisoners, it seems !" said the young man who spoke French, as he moved away with the others, who, far more depressed in spirit, hung their heads in silence, as they descended between decks.

Scarcely was the signal for a council of war seen from the mast-head, when the different boats might be descried stretching across the bay with speed. And now all were assembled in General Humbert's cabin, whose rank and station in the service entitled them to the honour of being consulted.

To such of us as held inferior "grade," the time passed tediously enough as we paced the deck, now turning from the aspect of the silent and seemingly uninhabited cliffs along shore, to listen if no sign betokened the breaking up of the council ; nor were we without serious fears that the expedition would be abandoned altogether. This suspicion originated with some of the Irish themselves, who, however confident of success, and boastful of their country's resources before we sailed, now made no scruple of averring that everything was the exact reverse of what they had stated, for that the people were dispirited, the national forces disbanded, neither arms, money, nor organisation anywhere—in fact, that a more hopeless scheme could not be thought of than the attempt, and that its result could not fail to be defeat and ruin to all concerned.

Shall I own that the bleak and lonely aspect of the hills along shore, the dreary character of the landscape, the almost death-like stillness of the scene, aided these gloomy impressions, and made it seem as if we were about to try our fortune on some desolate spot, without one look of encouragement, or one word of welcome to greet us? The sight of even an enemy's force would have been a relief to this solitude—the stir and movement of a rival army would have given spirit to our daring, and nerved our courage, but there was something inexpressibly sad in this unbroken monotony.

A few tried to jest upon the idea of liberating a land that had no inhabitants—the emancipation of a country without people; but even French flippancy failed to be witty on a theme so linked with all our hopes and fears, and at last a dreary silence fell upon all, and we walked the deck without speaking, waiting and watching for the result of that deliberation which already had lasted above four mortal hours.

Twice was the young man who spoke French summoned to the cabin, but, from the briefness of his stay, apparently with little profit; and now the day began to wane, and the tall cliffs threw their lengthened shadows over the still waters of the bay, and yet nothing was resolved on. To the quiet and respectful silence of expectation, now succeeded a low and half-subdued muttering of discontent; groups of five or six together were seen along the deck, talking with eagerness and animation, and it was easy to see that whatever prudential or cautious reasons dictated to the leaders, their arguments found little sympathy with the soldiers of the expedition. I almost began to fear that if a determination to abandon the exploit were come to, a mutiny might break out, when my attention was drawn off by an order to accompany Colonel Charost on shore to "reconnoitre." This at least looked like business, and I jumped into the small boat with alacrity.

With the speed of four oars stoutly plied, we skimmed along the calm surface, and soon saw ourselves close in to the shore. Some little time was spent in looking for a good place to land, for although not the slightest air of wind was blowing, the long swell of the Atlantic broke upon the rocks with a noise like thunder. At last we shot into a little creek with a shelving gravelly beach, and completely concealed by the tall rocks on every side; and now we sprang out, and stood upon Irish ground!"

CHAPTER XIX.

A "RECONNAISSANCE."

FROM the little creek where we landed, a small zig-zag
path led up the sides of the cliff, the track by which the
peasants carried the sea-weed which they gathered for
manure, and up this we now slowly wended our way.
Stopping for some time to gaze at the ample bay beneath
us, the tall-masted frigates floating so majestically on its
glassy surface—it was a scene of tranquil and picturesque
beauty with which it would have been almost impossible
to associate the idea of war and invasion. In the lazy
bunting that hung listlessly from peak and mast-head—in
the cheerful voices of the sailors, heard afar off in the stillness—in the measured plash of the sea itself, and the fearless daring of the sea-gulls, as they soared slowly above
our heads—there seemed something so suggestive of peace
and tranquillity, that it struck us as profanation to disturb it.
As we gained the top and looked around us, our astonishment became even greater. A long succession of low
hills, covered with tall ferns or heath, stretched away on
every side; not a house, nor a hovel, nor a living thing to
be seen. Had the country been one uninhabited since the
Creation, it could not have presented an aspect of more
thorough desolation! No road-track, nor even a foot-
path, led through the dreary waste before us, on which, to
all seeming, the foot of man had never fallen. And as we
stood for some moments, uncertain which way to turn, a
sense of the ridiculous suddenly burst upon the party, and
we all broke into a hearty roar of laughter.
"I little thought," cried Charost, "that I should ever
emulate 'La Perouse,' but it strikes me that I am destined
to become a great discoverer."
"How so, Colonel?" asked his aide-de-camp.
"Why, it is quite clear that this same island is uninhabited; and if it be all like this, I own I'm scarcely surprised at it."
"Still, there must be a town not far off, and the residence of that bishop we heard of this morning."
A half incredulous shrug of the shoulders was all his

reply, as he sauntered along with his hands behind his back, apparently lost in thought; while we, as if instinctively partaking of his gloom, followed him in total silence.

"Do you know, gentlemen, what I'm thinking of?" said he, stopping suddenly and facing about. "My notion is, that the best thing to do here would be to plant our tricolour, proclaim the land a colony of France, and take to our boats again."

This speech, delivered with an air of great gravity, imposed upon us for an instant; but the moment after, the speaker breaking into a hearty laugh, we all joined him, as much amused by the strangeness of our situation, as by anything in his remark.

"We never could bring our guns through a soil like this, Colonel," said the aide-de-camp, as he struck his heel into the soft and clayey surface.

"If we could ever land them at all!" muttered he, half aloud; then added, "But for what object should we? Believe me, gentlemen, if we are to have a campaign here, bows and arrows are the true weapons."

"Ah! what do I see yonder?" cried the aide-de-camp; "are not those sheep feeding in that little glen?"

"Yes," cried I, "and a man herding them, too. See, the fellow has caught sight of us, and he's off as fast as his legs can carry him." And so was it: the man had no sooner seen us than he sprung to his feet and hurried down the mountain at full speed.

Our first impulse was to follow and give him chase, and even without a word we all started off in pursuit; but we soon saw how fruitless would be the attempt, for, even independent of the start he had got of us, the peasant's speed was more than the double of our own.

"No matter," said the colonel, "if we have lost the shepherd we have at least gained the sheep, and so I recommend you to secure mutton for dinner to-morrow."

With this piece of advice, down the hill he darted as hard as he could; Briolle, the aide-de-camp, and myself following at our best pace. We were reckoning without our host, however, for the animals, after one stupid stare at us, set off in a scamper that soon showed their mountain breeding, keeping all together like a pack of hounds, and really not very inferior in the speed they displayed.

A little gorge led between the hills, and through this they rushed madly, and with a clatter like a charge of cavalry. Excited by the chase, and emulous each to outrun the other, the colonel threw off his chako, and Briolle his sword, in the ardour of pursuit. We now gained on them rapidly, and though, from a winding in the glen, they had momentarily got out of sight, we knew that we were close upon them. I was about thirty paces in advance of my comrades, when, on turning an angle of the gorge, I found myself directly in front of a group of mud hovels, near which were standing about a dozen ragged, miserable-looking men, armed with pitchforks and scythes, while in the rear stood the sheep, blowing and panting from the chase.

I came to a dead stop; and although I would have given worlds to have had my comrades at my side, I never once looked back to see if they were coming; but, putting a bold face on the matter, called out the only few words I knew of Irish, "Go de-mat ha tn."

The peasants looked at each other; and whether it was my accent, my impudence, or my strange dress and appearance, or altogether, I cannot say, but after a few seconds' pause they burst out into a roar of laughter, in the midst of which my two comrades came up.

"We saw the sheep feeding on the hills yonder," said I, recovering self-possession, "and guessed that by giving them chase they'd lead us to some inhabited spot. What is this place called?"

"Shindrennin," said a man who seemed to be the chief of the party; "and, if I might make so bould, who are you, yourselves?"

"French officers; this is my colonel," said I, pointing to Charost, who was wiping his forehead and face after his late exertion.

The information, far from producing the electric effect of pleasure I had anticipated, was received with a coldness almost amounting to fear, and they spoke eagerly together for some minutes in Irish.

"Our allies evidently don't like the look of us," said Charost, laughing; "and if the truth must be told, I own the disappointment is mutual."

"'Tis too late you come, sir," said the peasant, addressing the colonel, while he removed his hat, and assumed an air of respectful deference. "'Tis all over with poor Ireland, this time."

"Tell him," said Charost, to whom I translated the speech, "that it's never too late to assert a good cause: that we have got arms for twenty thousand, if they have but hands and hearts to use them. Tell him that a French army is now lying in that bay yonder, ready and able to accomplish the independence of Ireland."

I delivered my speech as pompously as it was briefed

to me; and, although I was listened to in silence, and respectfully, it was plain my words carried little or no conviction with them. Not caring to waste more of our time in such discourse, I now inquired about the country —in what directions lay the high roads, and the relative situations of the towns of Killala, Castlebar, and Ballina, the only places of comparative importance in the neighbourhood. I next asked about the landing-places, and learned that a small fishing-harbour existed, not more than half a mile from the spot where we had landed, from which a little country road lay to the village of Palmerstown. As to the means of transporting baggage, guns, and ammunition, there were few horses to be had, but with money we might get all we wanted; indeed, the peasants constantly referred to this means of success, even to asking "What the French would give a man that was to join them?" If I did not translate the demand with fidelity to my colonel, it was really that a sense of shame prevented me. My whole heart was in the cause; and I could not endure the thought of its being degraded in this way. It was growing duskish, and the colonel proposed that the peasant should show us the way to the fishing-harbour he spoke of, while some other of the party might go round to our boat, and direct them to follow us thither. The arrangement was soon made, and we all sauntered down towards the shore, chatting over the state of the country, and the chances of a successful rising. From the specimen before me, I was not disposed to be over sanguine about the peasantry. The man was evidently disaffected towards England. He bore her neither good-will nor love; but his fears were greater than all else. He had never heard of anything but failure in all attempts against her; and he could not believe in any other result. Even the aid and alliance of France inspired no other feeling than distrust; for he said more than once, "Sure what can harm yez? Haven't ye yer ships, beyant, to take yez away, if things goes bad?"

I was heartily glad that Colonel Charost knew so little English, that the greater part of the peasant's conversation was unintelligible to him, since, from the first, he had always spoken of the expedition in terms of disparagement; and certainly what we were now to hear was not of a nature to controvert the prediction.

In our ignorance as to the habits and modes of thought of the people, we were much surprised at the greater interest the peasant betrayed when asking us about France and her prospects, than when the conversation concerned his own country. It appeared as though, in the one case, distance gave grandeur and dimensions to all his conceptions, while familiarity with home scenes and native politics had robbed them of all their illusions. He knew well that there were plenty of hardships, abundance of evils, to deplore in Ireland; rents were high, taxes and tithes oppressive, agents were severe, bailiffs were cruel; social wrongs he could discuss for hours, but of political woes, the only ones we could be expected to relieve or care for, he really knew nothing. "'Tis true," he repeated, "that what my honour said was all right, Ireland was badly treated," and so on; "liberty was an elegant thing if a body had it," and such like; but there ended his patriotism.

Accustomed for many a day to the habits of a people where all were politicians, where the rights of man and the grand principles of equality and self-government were everlastingly under discussion, I was, I confess it, sorely disappointed at this worse than apathy.

"Will they fight?—ask him that," said Charost, to whom I had been conveying a rather rose-coloured version of my friend's talk.

"Oh, be gorra! we'll fight sure enough!" said he, with a half-dogged scowl beneath his brows.

"What number of them may we reckon on in the neighbourhood?" repeated the colonel.

"'Tis mighty hard to say; many of the boys were gone over to England for the harvest; some were away to the counties inland, others were working on the roads; but if they knew, sure they'd be soon back again."

"Might they calculate on a thousand stout, effective men?" asked Charost.

"Ay, twenty, if they were at home," said the peasant, less a liar by intention than from the vague and careless disregard of truth so common in all their own intercourse with each other.

I must own that the degree of credit we reposed in the worthy man's information was considerably influenced by the state of facts before us, inasmuch as that the "elegant, fine harbour" he had so gloriously described—"the beautiful road"—"the neat little quay" to land upon, and the other advantages of the spot, all turned out to be most grievous disappointments. That the people were not of our own mind on these matters, was plain enough from the looks of astonishment our discontent provoked; and now a lively discussion ensued on the relative merits of various bays, creeks, and inlets along the coast, each of which, with some unpronounceable name or other, was seen to have a special advocate in its favour, till at last the colonel lost all patience, and jumping into the boat, ordered the men to push off for the frigate.

Evidently out of temper at the non-success of his "reconnaissance," and as little pleased with the country as the people, Charost did not speak a word as we rowed back to the ship. Our failure, as it happened, was of little moment, for another party, under the guidance of Madgett, had already discovered a good landing-place at the bottom of the Bay of Rathfran, and arrangements were already in progress to disembark the troops at daybreak. We also found that, during our absence, some of the "chiefs" had come off from shore, one of whom, named Neal Kerrigan, was destined to attain considerable celebrity in the rebel army. He was a talkative, vulgar, presumptuous fellow, who, without any knowledge or experience whatever, took upon him to discuss military measures and strategy with all the assurance of an old commander.

Singularly enough, Humbert suffered this man to influence him in a great degree, and yielded opinion to him on points even where his own judgment was directly opposed to the advice he gave.

If Kerrigan's language and bearing were directly the reverse of soldier-like, his tawdry uniform of green and gold, with massive epaulettes and a profusion of lace, were no less absurd in our eyes, accustomed as we were to the almost puritan plainness of military costume. His rank, too, seemed as undefined as his information; for while he called himself "General," his companions as often addressed him by the title of "Captain." Upon some points his counsels, indeed, alarmed and astonished us.

" It was of no use whatever," he said, " to attempt to discipline the peasantry, or reduce them to anything like habits of military obedience. Were the effort to be made, it would prove a total failure ; for they would either grow disgusted with the restraint, and desert altogether, or so infect the other troops with their own habits of disorder, that the whole force would become a mere rabble. Arm them well, let them have plenty of ammunition, and free liberty to use it in their own way and their own time, and we should soon see that they would prove a greater terror to the English than double the number of trained and disciplined troops."

In some respects this view was a correct one; but whether it was a wise counsel to have followed, subsequent events gave us ample cause to doubt.

Kerrigan. however, had a specious, reckless, go-a-head way with him, that suited well the tone and temper of Humbert's mind. He never looked too far into consequences, but trusted that the eventualities of the morrow would always suggest the best course for the day after; and this alone was so akin to our own general's mode of proceeding, that he speedily won his confidence.

The last evening on board was spent merrily on all sides. In the general cabin, where the staff and all the "chefs de brigade," were assembled, gay songs, and toasts, and speeches succeeded each other till nigh morning. The printed proclamations, meant for circulation among the people were read out, with droll commentaries; and all imaginable quizzing and jesting went on about the new government to be established in Ireland, and the various offices to be bestowed upon each. Had the whole expedition been a joke, the tone of levity could not have been greater. Not a thought was bestowed, not a word wasted upon any of the graver incidents that might ensue. All were, if not hopeful and sanguine, utterly reckless, and thoroughly indifferent to the future.

CHAPTER XX.

KILLALA.

I WILL not weary my reader with an account of our debarkation, less remarkable as it was for the "pomp and circumstance of war" than for incidents and accidents the most absurd and ridiculous—the miserable boats of the peasantry, the still more wretched cattle employed to drag our artillery and train-waggons, involving us in innumerable misfortunes and mischances. Never were the heroic illusions of war more thoroughly dissipated than by the scenes which accompanied our landing! Boats and baggage-waggons upset; here, a wild, half savage-looking fellow swimming after a cocked hat—there, a group of ragged wretches scraping sea-weed from a dripping officer of the staff; noise, uproar, and confusion everywhere; smart aides-de-camp mounted on donkeys; trim field-pieces "horsed" by a promiscuous assemblage of men, women, cows, ponies, and asses. Crowds of idle country-people thronged the little quay, and, obstructing the passages, gazed upon the whole with eyes of wonderment and surprise, but evidently enjoying all the drollery of the scene with higher relish than they felt interest in its object or success. This trait in them soon attracted all our notice, for they laughed at everything: not a caisson tumbled into the sea, not a donkey brought his rider to the ground, but one general shout shook the entire assemblage.

If want and privation had impressed themselves by every external sign on this singular people, they seemed to possess inexhaustible resources of good humour and good spirits within. No impatience or rudeness on our part could irritate them; and even to the wildest and least civilised-looking fellow around, there was a kind of native courtesy and kindliness, that could not fail to strike us.

A vague notion prevailed that we were their "friends;" and although many of them did not clearly comprehend why we had come, or what was the origin of the warm attachment between us, they were too lazy and too indifferent to trouble their heads about the matter. They were satisfied that there would be a "shindy" somewhere, and somebody's bones would get broken, and even that much was a pleasant and reassuring consideration; while others of keener mould revelled in plans of private vengeance against this landlord or that agent—small debts of hatred to be paid off in the day of general reckoning!

From the first moment nothing could exceed the tone of fraternal feeling between our soldiers and the people. Without any means of communicating their thoughts by speech, they seemed to acquire an instinctive knowledge of each other in an instant. If the peasant was poor, there was no limit to his liberality in the little he had. He dug up his half-ripe potatoes, he unroofed his cabin to furnish straw for litter, he gave up his only beast, and was ready to kill his cow, if asked, to welcome us. Much of this was from the native, warm, and impulsive generosity of their nature, and much, doubtless, had its origin in the bright hopes of future recompense inspired by the eloquent appeals of Neal Kerrigan, who, mounted on an old white mare, rode about on every side, addressing the people in Irish, and calling upon them to give all aid and assistance to "the expedition."

The difficulty of the landing was much increased by the small space of level ground which intervened between the cliffs and the sea, and of which now the thickening crowd

filled every spot. This and the miserable means of conveyance for our baggage delayed us greatly, so that, with
a comparatively small force, it was late in the afternoon
before we had all reached the shore.

We had none of us eaten since morning, and were not
sorry, as we crowned the heights, to hear the drums beat
for "cooking." In an inconceivably short time fires
blazed along the hills, around which, in motley groups,
stood soldiers and peasantry mingled together, while the
work of cooking and eating went briskly on, amid hearty
laughter and all the merriment that mutual mistakes and
misconceptions occasioned. It was a new thing for French
soldiers to bivouac in a friendly country, and find themselves the welcome guests of a foreign people; and certainly, the honours of hospitality, however limited the
means, could not have been performed with more of courtesy or good will. Paddy gave his "all," with a generosity that might have shamed many a richer donor.

While the events I have mentioned were going forward,
and a considerable crowd of fishermen and peasants had
gathered about us, still it was remarkable that, except
immediately on the coast itself, no suspicion of our arrival
had gained currency, and even the country people who
lived a mile from the shore were ignorant of who we were.
The few, who from distant heights and headlands, had
seen the ships, mistook them for English, and as all those
who were out with fish or vegetables to sell were detained
by the frigates, any direct information about us was impossible. So far, therefore, all might be said to have
gone most favourably with us. We had safely escaped
the often-menaced dangers of the channel fleet; we had
gained a secure and well-sheltered harbour; and we had
landed our force not only without opposition, but in perfect secrecy. There were, I will not deny, certain little
counterbalancing circumstances on the other side of the
account not exactly so satisfactory. The patriot forces
upon which we had calculated had no existence. There
were neither money, nor stores, nor means of conveyance
to be had; even accurate information as to the strength
and position of the English was unattainable; and as to
generals and leaders, the effective staff had but a most
sorry representative in the person of Neal Kerrigan
This man's influence over our general increased with every
hour, and one of the first orders issued after our landing
contained his appointment as an extra aide-de-camp on
General Humbert's staff.

In one capacity Neal was most useful. All the available

sources of pillage for a wide circuit of country he knew by heart, and it was plain, from the accurate character of his information, varying, as it did, from the chattels of the rich landed proprietor to the cocks and hens of the cottier, that he had taken great pains to master his subject. At his suggestion it was decided that we should march that evening on Killala, where little or more likely no resistance would be met with, and General Humbert should take up his quarters in the "Castle," as the palace of the bishop was styled. There, he said, we should not only find ample accommodation for the staff, but good stabling, well filled, and plenty of forage, while the bishop himself might be a most useful hostage to have in our keeping. From thence, too, as a place of some note, general orders and proclamations would issue, with a kind of notoriety and importance necessary at the outset of an undertaking like ours; and truly never was an expedition more loaded with this species of missive than ours—whole cart-loads of printed papers, decrees, placards, and such like, followed us. If our object had been to drive out the English by big type and a flaming letter-press, we could not have gone more vigorously to work. Fifty thousand broad-sheet announcements of Irish independence were backed by as many proud declarations of victory, some dated from Limerick, Cashel, or Dublin itself.

Here, a great placard gave the details of the new Provincial Government of Western Ireland, with the name of the "Prefect" a blank. There was another, containing the police regulations for the "arrondissements" of Connaught, "et ses dependances." Every imaginable step of conquest and occupation was anticipated and provided for in these wise and considerate protocols, from the "enthusiastic welcome of the French on the western coast" to the hour of "General Humbert's triumphal entry into Dublin!" Nor was it prose alone, but even poetry did service in our cause. Songs, not, I own, conspicuous for any great metrical beauty, commemorated our battles and our bravery; so that we entered upon the campaign as deeply pledged to victory as any force I ever heard or read of in history.

Neal, who was, I believe, originally a schoolmaster, had great confidence in this arsenal of "black and white;" and soon persuaded General Humbert that a bold face and a loud tongue would do more in Ireland than in any countra under heaven; and indeed, if his own career might by called a success, the theory deserved some consideratione A great part of our afternoon was then spent in distributing these documents to the people, not one in a hundred of whom could read, but who treasured the placards with a reverence nothing diminished by their ignorance. Emissaries, too, were appointed to post them up in conspicuous places through the country, on the doors of the chapels, at the smiths' forges, at cross-roads, everywhere, in short, where they might attract notice. The most important and business-like of all these, however, was one headed "Arms!"—"Arms!" and which went on to say that no man who wished to lift his hand for old Ireland need do so without a weapon; and that a general distribution of guns, swords, and bayonets would take place at noon the following day at the Palace of Killala.

Serasin, and, I believe, Madgett, were strongly opposed to this indiscriminate arming of the people; but Neal's counsels were now in the ascendant, and Humbert gave an implicit confidence to all he suggested.

It was four o'clock in the evening when the word to march was given, and our gallant little force began its advance movement. Still attached to Colonel Charost's staff, and being, as chasseurs, in the advance, I had a good opportunity of seeing the line of march from an eminence about half a mile in front. Grander and more imposing displays I have indeed often witnessed. As a great military "spectacle" it could not, of course, be compared with those mighty armies I had seen deploying through the defiles of the Black Forest, or spreading like a sea over the wide plain of Germany; but in purely picturesque effect, this scene surpassed all I had ever beheld at the time, nor do I think that, in after-life, I can recall one more striking.

The winding road, which led over hill and valley, now disappearing, now emerging, with the undulations of the soil, was covered by troops marching in a firm compact order; the grenadiers in front, after which came the artillery, and then the regiments of the line. Watching the dark column, occasionally saluting it as it went with a cheer, stood thousands of country-people on every hill-top and eminence, while far away in the distance the frigates lay at anchor in the bay, the guns at intervals thundering out a solemn "boom" of welcome and encouragement to their comrades.

There was something so heroic in the notion of that little band of warriors throwing themselves fearlessly into a strange land, to contest its claim for liberty with one of the most powerful nations of the world; there was a character of daring intrepidity in this bold advance, they knew

not whither, nor against what force, that gave the whole
an air of glorious chivalry.

I must own that distance lent its wonted illusion to the
scene, and proximity, like its twin-brother familiarity,
destroyed much of the "prestige" my fancy had conjured
up. The line of march, so imposing when seen from afar,
was neither regular nor well kept. The peasantry were
permitted to mingle with the troops; ponies, mules, and
asses, loaded with camp-kettles and cooking vessels, were
to be met with everywhere. The baggage-waggons were
crowded with officers, and "sous-officiers," who, disappointed in obtaining horses, were too indolent to walk.
Even the gun-carriages, and the guns themselves, were
similarly loaded, while, at the head of the infantry column,
in an old ricketty gig, the ancient mail conveyance between
Ballina and the coast, came General Humbert, Neal Kerrigan capering at his side on the old grey, whose flanks
were now tastefully covered by the tri-colour ensign of one
of the boats as a saddle-cloth.

This nearer and less enchanting prospect of my gallant
comrades I was enabled to obtain on being despatched to
the rear by Colonel Charost, to say that we were now
within less than a mile of the town of Killala, its venerable
steeple and the tall chimneys of the palace being easily
seen above the low hills in front. Neal Kerrigan passed
me as I rode back with my message, galloping to the front
with all the speed he could muster; but while I was talking
to the general he came back to say that the beating of
drums could be heard from the town, and that by the rapid
movements here and there of people, it was evident the
defence was being prepared. There was a look-out, too,
from the steeple, that showed our approach was already
known. The general was not slow in adopting his measures,
and the word was given for quick march, the artillery to
deploy right and left of the road, two companies of grenadiers forming on the flanks. "As for you, sir," said
Humbert to me, "take that horse," pointing to a mountain
pony, fastened behind the gig, "ride forward to the town,
and make a reconnaissance. You are to report to me,"
cried he, as I rode away, and was soon out of hearing.

Quitting the road, I took a foot-track across the fields,
and which the pony seemed to know well, and after a
sharp canter reached a small, poor suburb of the town, if
a few straggling wretched cabins can deserve the name; a
group of countrymen stood in the middle of the road, about
fifty yards in front of me; and while I was deliberating
whether to advance or retire, a joyous cry of "Hurra for

the French!" decided me, and I touched my cap in salute
and rode forward.

Other groups saluted me with a similar cheer, as I went
on ; and now windows were flung open, and glad cries and
shouts of welcome rang out from every side. These signs
were too encouraging to turn my back upon, so I dashed
forward through a narrow street in front, and soon found
myself in a kind of square or "Place," the doors and
windows of which were all closed, and not a human being
to be seen anywhere. As I hesitated what next to do, I
saw a soldier in a red coat rapidly turn the corner—"What
do you want here, you spy," he cried out in a loud voice,
and at the same instant his bullet rang past my ear with a
whistle. I drove in the spurs at once, and just as he had
gained a doorway, I clove his head open with my sabre—
he fell dead on the spot before me. Wheeling my horse
round, I now rode back as I had come, at full speed, the
same welcome cries accompanying me as before.

Short as had been my absence, it was sufficient to have
brought the advanced guard close up with the town, and
just as I emerged from the little suburb, a quick, sharp
firing drew my attention towards the left of the wall, and
there I saw our fellows advancing at a trot, while about
twenty red-coats were in full flight before them, the wild
cries of the country-people following them as they went.

I had but time to see thus much, and to remark that
two or three English prisoners were taken, when the
general came up. He had now abandoned the gig, and
was mounted on a large, powerful black horse, which
I afterwards learned was one of the bishop's. My tidings
were soon told, and, indeed, but indifferently attended
to, for it was evident enough that the place was our
own.

"This way, General—follow me," cried Kerrigan. "If
the light companies will take the road down to the 'Acres,'
they'll catch the yeomen as they retreat by that way, and
we have the town our own."

The counsel was speedily adopted ; and although a
dropping fire here and there showed that some slight
resistance was still being made, it was plain enough that
all real opposition was impossible.

"Forward!" was now the word ; and the chasseurs,
with their muskets "in sling," advanced at a trot up the
main street. At a little distance the grenadiers followed,
and debouching into the square, were received by an ill-
directed volley from a few of the militia, who took to
their heels after they fired. Three or four red-coats were

killed, but the remainder made their escape through the churchyard, and gaining the open country, scattered and fled as best they could.

Humbert, who had seen war on a very different scale, could not help laughing at the absurdity of the skirmish, and was greatly amused with the want of all discipline and " accord " exhibited by the English troops.

" I foresee, gentlemen," said he, jocularly, "that we may have abundance of success, but gain very little glory, in the same campaign. Now for a blessing upon our labours —where shall we find our friend the bishop ? "

" This way, General," cried Neal, leading down a narrow street, at the end of which stood a high wall, with an iron gate. This was locked, and some efforts at barricading it showed the intention of a defence; but a few strokes of a pioneer's hammer smashed the lock, and we entered a kind of pleasure-ground, neatly and trimly kept. We had not advanced many paces when the bishop, followed by a great number of his clergy—for it happened to be the period of his annual visitation—came forward to meet us.

Humbert dismounted, and removing his chapeau, saluted the dignitary with a most finished courtesy. I could see, too, by his gesture, that he presented General Serasin, the second in command ; and, in fact, all his motions were those of a well-bred guest at the moment of being received by his host. Nor was the bishop, on his side, wanting either in ease or dignity ; his manner, not without the appearance of deep sorrow, was yet that of a polished gentleman doing the honours of his house to a number of strangers.

As I drew nearer I could hear that the bishop spoke French fluently, but with a strong foreign accent. This facility, however, enabled him to converse with ease on every subject, and to hold intercourse directly with our general, a matter of no small moment to either party. It is probable that the other clergy did not possess this gift, for assuredly their manner towards us inferiors of the staff was neither gracious nor conciliating ; and as for myself, the few efforts I made to express, in English, my admiration for the coast scenery, or the picturesque beauty of the neighbourhood, were met in any rather than a spirit of politeness.

The generals accompanied the bishop into the castle, leaving myself and three or four others on the outside. Colonel Charost soon made his appearance, and a guard was stationed at the entrance gate, with a strong picket

In the garden. Two sentries were placed at the hall-door,
and the words "Quartier Général" written up over the
portico. A small garden pavilion was appropriated to the
colonel's use, and made the office of the adjutant-general,
and in less than half an hour after our arrival, eight sous-
officiers were hard at work under the trees, writing away
at billets, contribution orders, and forage rations ; while
I, from my supposed fluency in English, was engaged in
carrying messages to and from the staff to the various
shopkeepers aud tradesmen of the town, numbers of whom
now flocked around us with expressions of welcome and
rejoicing.

CHAPTER XXI.

OUR ALLIES.

I HAVE spent pleasanter, but I greatly doubt if I ever
knew busier, days, than those I passed at the Bishop's
Palace at Killala ; and now, as I look back upon the event,
I cannot help wondering that we could seriously have
played out a farce so full of absurdity and nonsense!
There was a gross mockery of all the usages of war,
which, had it not been for the serious interests at stake,
would have been highly laughable and amusing.

Whether it was the important functions of civil government, the details of police regulation, the imposition of
contributions, the appointment of officers, or the arming
of the volunteers, all was done with a pretentious affectation of order that was extremely ludicrous. The very
institutions which were laughingly agreed at over-night,
as the wine went briskly round, were solemnly ratified in
the morning, and, still more strange, apparently believed
in by those whose ingenuity devised them ; and thus the
" Irish Directory," as we styled the imaginary government, the National Treasury, the Pension Fund, were
talked of with all the seriousness of facts ! As to the
Commissariat, to which I was for the time attached, we
never ceased writing receipts and acknowledgments for
stores and munitions of war, all of which were to be
honourably acquitted by the Treasury of the Irish Republic.

No people could have better fallen in with the humour

of this delusion than the Irish. They seemed to believe everything, and yet there was a reckless, headlong indifference about them, which appeared to say, that they were equally prepared for any turn fortune might take, and if the worst should happen, they would never reproach us for having misled them. The real truth was—but we only learned it too late—all those who joined us were utterly indifferent to the great cause of Irish independence; their thoughts never rose above a row and a pillage. It was to be a season of sack, plunder, and outrage, but nothing more! That such were the general sentiments of the volunteers, I believe none will dispute. We, however, in our ignorance of the people and their language, interpreted all the harum-scarum wildness we saw as the buoyant temperament of a high-spirited nation, who, after centuries of degradation and ill-usage, saw the dawning of liberty at last.

Had we possessed any real knowledge of the country, we should at once have seen that of those who joined us, none were men of any influence or station. If, now and then, a man of any name strayed into the camp, he was sure to be one whose misconduct or bad character had driven him from associating with his equals; and, even of the peasantry, our followers were of the very lowest order. Whether General Humbert was the first to notice the fact, I know not; but Charost, I am certain, remarked it, and even thus early predicted the utter failure of the expedition.

I must confess the "Volunteers" were the least imposing of allies! I think I have the whole scene before my eyes this moment, as I saw it each morning in the Palace garden.

The enclosure, which, more orchard than garden, occupied a space of a couple of acres, was the head-quarters of Colonel Charost; and here, in a pavilion formerly dedicated to hoes, rakes, rolling-stones, and garden-tools, we were now established to the number of fourteen. As the space beneath the roof was barely sufficient for the Colonel's personal use, the officers of his staff occupied convenient spots in the vicinity. My station was under a large damson-tree, the fruit of which afforded me, more than once, the only meal I tasted from early morning till late at night; not, I must say, from any lack of provisions, for the Palace abounded with every requisite of the table, but that, such was the pressure of business, we were not able to leave off work even for half an hour during the day.

A subaltern's guard of grenadiers, divided into small

parties, did duty in the garden; and it was striking to mark the contrast between these bronzed and war-worn figures, and the reckless tatterdemalion host around us. Never was seen such a scare-crow set! Wild-looking, ragged wretches, their long, lank hair hanging down their necks and shoulders, usually bare-footed, and with every sign of starvation in their features; they stood in groups and knots, gesticulating, screaming, hurraing, and singing, in all the exuberance of a joy that caught some, at least, of its inspiration from whiskey.

It was utterly vain to attempt to keep order amongst them; even the effort to make them defile singly through the gate into the garden was soon found impracticable, without the employment of a degree of force that our adviser, Kerrigan, pronounced would be injudicious. Not only the men made their way in, but great numbers of women, and even children also; and there they were, seated around fires, roasting their potatoes in this bivouac fashion, as though they had deserted hearth and home to follow us.

Such was the avidity to get arms—of which the distribution was announced to take place here—that several had scaled the wall in their impatience, and as they were more or less in drink, some disastrous accidents were momentarily occurring, adding the cries and exclamations of suffering to the ruder chorus of joy and revelry that went on unceasingly.

The impression—we soon saw how absurd it was—the impression that we should do nothing that might hurt the national sensibilities, but concede all to the exuberant ardour of a bold people, eager to be led against their enemies, induced us to submit to every imaginable breach of order and discipline.

" In a day or two, they'll be like your own men; you'll not know them from a battalion of the line. Those fellows will be like a wall under fire."

Such and such like were the assurances we were listening to all day, and it would have been like treason to the cause to have refused them credence.

Perhaps I might have been longer a believer in this theory, had I not perceived signs of a deceptive character in these our worthy allies; many who, to our faces, wore nothing but looks of gratitude and delight, no sooner mixed with their fellows than their downcast faces and dogged expression betrayed some inward sense of disappointment.

One very general source of dissatisfaction arose from

the discovery, that we were not prepared to pay our allies! We had simply come to arm and lead them, to shed our own blood, and pledge our fortunes in their cause ; but we certainly had brought no military chest to bribe their patriotism, nor stimulate their nationality ; and this I soon saw was a grievous disappointment.

In virtue of this shameful omission on our part, they deemed the only resource was to be made officers, and thus crowds of uneducated, semi-civilised vagabonds were every hour assailing us with their claims to the epaulette. Of the whole number of these, I remember but three who had ever served at all ; two were notorious drunkards, and the third a confirmed madman, from a scalp wound he had received when fighting against the Turks. Many, however, boasted high-sounding names, and were, at least so Kerrigan said, men of the first families in the land.

Our general-in-chief saw little of them while at Killala, his principal intercourse being with the bishop and his family ; but Colonel Charost soon learned to read their true character, and from that moment conceived the most disastrous issue to our plans. The most trustworthy of them was a certain O'Donnell, who, although not a soldier, was remarked to possess a greater influence over the rabble volunteers than any of the others. He was a young man of the half-squire class, an ardent and sincere patriot, after his fashion ; but that fashion, it must be owned, rather partook of the character of class-hatred and religious animosity than the features of a great struggle for national independence. He took a very low estimate of the fighting qualities of his countrymen, and made no secret of declaring it.

"You would be better without them altogether," said he one day to Charost ; "but if you must have allies, draw them up in line, select one-third of the best, and arm them."

"And the rest?" asked Charost.

"Shoot them," was the answer.

This conversation is on record—indeed, I believe there is yet one witness living to corroborate it.

I have said that we were very hard worked ; but I must fain acknowledge that the real amount of business done was very insignificant, so many were the mistakes, misconceptions, and interruptions, not to speak of the time lost by that system of conciliation of which I have already made mention. In our distribution of arms there was little selection practised or possible. The process was a brief one, but it might have been briefer.

Thomas Colooney, of Banmayroo, was called, and not usually being present, the name would be passed on, from post to post, till it swelled into a general shout of Colooney.

" Tom Colooney, you're wanted ; Tom, run for it, man, there's a price bid for you ! Here's Mickey, his brother, maybe he'll do as well."

And so on : all this accompanied by shouts of laughter, and a running fire of jokes, which, being in the vernacular, was lost to us.

At last the real Colooney was found, maybe eating his dinner of potatoes, maybe discussing his poteen with a friend—sometimes engaged in the domestic duties of washing his shirt or his small-clothes, fitting a new crown to his hat, or a sole to his brogues—whatever his occupation, he was urged forward by his friends and the public, with many a push, drive, and even a kick, into our presence, where, from the turmoil, uproar, and confusion, he appeared to have fought his way by main force, and very often, indeed, this was literally the fact, as his bleeding nose, torn coat, and bare head attested.

" Thomas Colooney—are you the man ? " asked one of our Irish officers of the staff.

" Yis, yer honour, I'm that same ! "

" You've come here, Colooney, to offer yourself as a volunteer in the cause of your country ? "

Here a yell of " Ireland for ever ! " was always raised by the bystanders, which drowned the reply in its enthusiasm, and the examination went on :—

" You'll be true and faithful to that cause till you secure for your country the freedom of America and the happiness of France ? Kiss the cross. Are you used to firearms ? "

" Isn't he ?—maybe not ! I'll be bound he knows a musket from a mealy pratie ! "

Such and such like were the comments that rang on all sides, so that the modest " Yis, sir," of the patriot was completely lost.

" Load that gun, Tom," said the officer.

Here Colooney, deeming that so simple a request must necessarily be only a cover for something underhand—a little clever surprise or so—takes up the piece in a very gingerly manner, and examines it all round, noticing that there is nothing, so far as he can discover, unusual nor uncommon about it.

" Load that gun, I say."

Sharper and more angrily is the command given this time.

" Yis, sir, immadiately."

And now Tom tries the barrel with the ramrod, lest there should be already a charge there—a piece of forethought that is sure to be loudly applauded by the public, not the less so because the impatience of the French officers is making itself manifest in various ways.

At length he rams down the cartridge, and returns the ramrod ; which piece of adroitness, if done with a certain air of display and flourish, is unfailingly saluted by another cheer. He now primes and cocks the piece, and assumes a look of what he believes to be most soldier-like severity.

As he stands thus for scrutiny, a rather lively debate gets up as to whether or not Tom bit off the end of the cartridge before he rammed it down. The biters and anti-biters being equally divided, the discussion waxes strong. The French officers, eagerly asking what may be the disputed point, laugh very heartily on hearing it.

" I'll lay ye a pint of sperits she won't go off," cries one.

" Done! for two naggins, if he pulls strong," rejoins another.

" Devil fear the same gun," cries a third ; " she shot Mr. Sloan at fifty paces, and killed him dead."

" 'Tisn't the same gun—that's a Frinch one—a bran new one !"

" She isn't."

" She is."

" No, she isn't."

" Yes, but she is."

" What is't you say?"

" Hould your prate."

" Arrah, teach your mother to feed ducks."

" Silence in the ranks. Keep silence there. Attention, Colooney!"

" Yis, sir."

" Fire !"

" What at, sir ?" asks Tom, taking an amateur glance of the company, who look not over satisfied at his scrutiny.

" Fire in the air !"

Bang goes the piece, and a yell follows the explosion, while cries of " Well done, Tom," " Begorra, if a Protestant got that !" and so on, greet the performance.

" Stand by, Colooney!" and the volunteer falls back to make way for another and similar exhibition, occasionally varied by the humour or the blunders of the new candidate.

As to the Treasury orders, as we somewhat ludicrously

styled the cheques upon our imaginary bank, the scenes
they led to were still more absurd and complicated. We
paid liberally, that is to say in promises, for everything,
and our generosity saved us a good deal of time, for it
was astonishing how little the owners disputed our solvency when the price was left to themselves. But the
rations were indeed the most difficult matter of all; it
being impossible to convince our allies of the fact that the
compact was one of trust, and the ration was not his own
to dispose of in any manner that might seem fit.

"Sure, if I don't like to ate it—if I haven't an appetite
for it—if I'd rather have a pint of sperits, or a flannel
waistcoat, or a pair of stockings, than a piece of mate,
what harm is that to any one?"

This process of reasoning was much harder of answer
than is usually supposed, and even when replied to,
another difficulty arose in its place. Unaccustomed to
flesh diet, when they tasted they could not refrain from it,
and the whole week's rations of beef, amounting to eight
pounds, were frequently consumed in the first twenty-
four hours.

Such instances of gormandising were by no means un-
frequent, and, stranger still, in no one case, so far as I
knew, followed by any ill consequences.

The leaders were still more difficult to manage than
the people. Without military knowledge or experience of
any kind, they presumed to dictate the plan of a campaign to old and distinguished officers like Humbert and
Serasin, and when overruled by argument or ridicule, invariably fell back upon their superior knowledge of Ireland and her people, a defence for which, of course, we
were quite unprepared, and unable to oppose anything.
From these and similar causes it may well be believed
that our labours were not light, and yet somehow, with
all the vexations and difficulties around us, there was a
congenial tone of levity, an easy recklessness, and a careless freedom in the Irish character that suited us well.
There was but one single point whereupon we were not
thoroughly together, and this was religion. They were a
nation of most zealous Catholics; and as for us, the revolution had not left the vestige of a belief amongst us.

A reconnaissance in Ballina, meant rather to discover
the strength of the garrison than of the place itself,
having shown that the royal forces were inconsiderable in
number, and mostly militia, General Humbert moved forward, on Sunday morning the 26th, with nine hundred
men of our own force, and about three thousand "volun-

teers," leaving Colonel Charost and his staff, with two companies of foot, at Killala, to protect the town, and organise the new levies as they were formed.

We saw our companions defile from the town with heavy hearts. The small body of real soldiers seemed even smaller still from being enveloped by that mass of peasants who accompanied them, and who marched on the flanks or in the rear, promiscuously, without discipline or order—a noisy, half-drunken rabble, firing off their muskets at random, and yelling as they went, in savage glee and exultation. Our sole comfort was in the belief, that, when the hour of combat did arrive, they would fight to the very last. Such were the assurances of their own officers, and made so seriously and confidently, that we never thought of mistrusting them.

"If they be but steady under fire," said Charost, " a month will make them good soldiers. Ours is an easy drill, and soon learned ; but I own," he added, " they do not give me this impression."

Such was the reflection of one who watched them as they went past, and with sorrow we saw ourselves concurring in the sentiment.

CHAPTER XXII.

THE DAY OF "CASTLEBAR."

WE were all occupied with our drill at daybreak on the morning of the 27th of August, when a mounted orderly arrived at full gallop, with news that our troops were in motion for Castlebar, and orders for us immediately to march to their support, leaving only one subaltern and twenty men in "the Castle."

The worthy bishop was thunderstruck at the tidings. It is more than probable that he never entertained any grave fears of our ultimate success; still he saw that in the struggle, brief as it might be, rapine, murder, and pillage would spread over the country, and that crime of every sort would be certain to prevail during the short interval of anarchy.

As our drums were beating the " rally," he entered the garden, and with hurried steps came forward to where Colonel Charost was standing delivering his orders.

" Good day, Mons. l'Eveque," said the colonel, removing his hat, and bowing low. "You see us in a moment of haste. The campaign has opened, and we are about to march."

"Have you made any provision for the garrison of this town, Colonel?" said the bishop, in terror. "Your presence alone here restrained the population hitherto. If you leave us——"

"We shall leave you a strong force of our faithful allies, sir," said Charost; "Irishmen could scarcely desire better defenders than their countrymen."

"You forget, Colonel, that some of us here are averse to this cause, but, as non-combatants, lay claim to protection."

"You shall have it, too, Mons. l'Eveque; we leave an officer and twenty men."

"An officer and twenty men!" echoed the bishop, in dismay.

"Quite sufficient, I assure you," said Charost, coldly; "and if a hair of one of their heads be injured by the populace, trust me, sir, that we shall take a terrible vengeance."

"You do not know these people, sir, as I know them," said the bishop, eagerly. "The same hour that you march out, will the town of Killala be given up to pillage. As for your retributive justice, I may be pardoned for not feeling any consolation in the pledge, for certes neither I nor mine will live to witness it."

As the bishop was speaking, a crowd of volunteers, some in uniform and all armed, drew nearer and nearer to the place of colloquy; and although understanding nothing of what went forward in the foreign language, seemed to watch the expressions of the speakers' faces with a most keen interest. To look at the countenances of these fellows, truly one would not have called the bishop's fears exaggerated; their expression was that of demoniac passion and hatred.

"Look, sir," said the bishop, turning round, and facing the mob, "look at the men to whose safeguard you propose to leave us."

Charost made no reply; but making a sign for the bishop to remain where he was, re-entered the pavilion hastily. I could see through the window that he was reading his despatches over again, and evidently taking counsel with himself how to act. The determination was quickly come to.

"Mons. l'Eveque," said he, laying his hand on the bishop's arm, "I find that my orders admit of a choice on my part. I will, therefore, remain with you myself, and keep a sufficient force of my own men. It is not impossible, however, that in taking this step I may be perilling my own safety. You will, therefore, consent that one of your sons shall accompany the force now about to march, as a hostage. This is not an unreasonable request on my part."

"Very well, sir," said the bishop, sadly. "When do they leave?"

"Within half an hour," said Charost.

The bishop, bowing, retraced his steps through the garden back to the house. Our preparations for the road were by this time far advanced. The command said, "Light marching order, and no rations;" so that we foresaw that there was sharp work before us. Our men—part of the 12th demi-brigade, and a half company of grenadiers—were, indeed, ready on the instant; but the Irish were not so easily equipped. Many had strayed into the town; some, early as it was, were dead drunk; and not a few had mislaid their arms or their ammunition, secretly preferring the chance of a foray of their own to the prospect of a regular engagement with the Royalist troops.

Our force was still a considerable one, numbering at least fifteen hundred volunteers, besides about eighty of our men. By seven o'clock we were under march, and, with drums beating, defiled from the narrow streets of Killala into the mountain road that leads to Cloonagh; it being our object to form a junction with the main body at the foot of the mountain.

Two roads led from Ballina to Castlebar—one to the eastward, the other to the west of Lough Con. The former was a level road, easily passable by wheel carriages, and without any obstacle or difficulty whatever; the other took a straight direction over lofty mountains, and in one spot—the Pass of Barnageeragh—traversed a narrow defile, shut in between steep cliffs, where a small force, assisted by artillery, could have arrested the advance of a great army. The road itself, too, was in disrepair, the rains of autumn had torn and fissured it, while heavy sandslips and fallen rocks in many places rendered it almost impassable.

The Royalist generals had reconnoitred it two days before, and were so convinced that all approach in this direction was out of the question, that a small picket of observation, posted near the Pass of Barnageeragh, was withdrawn as useless, and the few stockades they had fixed were still standing as we marched through.

13

General Humbert had acquired all the details of these
separate lines of attack, and at once decided for the mountain road, which, besides the advantage of a surprise, was
in reality four miles shorter.

The only difficulty was the transport of our artillery,
but as we merely carried those light field-pieces called
"curricle guns," and had no want of numbers to draw
them, this was not an obstacle of much moment. With
fifty, sometimes sixty, peasants to a gun, they advanced,
at a run, up places where our infantry found the ascent
sufficiently toilsome. Here, indeed, our allies showed in
the most favourable colours we had yet seen them. The
prospect of a fight seemed to excite their spirits almost to
madness; every height they surmounted they would break
into a wild cheer, and the vigour with which they tugged
the heavy ammunition-carts through the deep and spongy
soil never interfered with the joyous shouts they gave,
and the merry songs they chaunted in rude chorus.

> " Tra, la, la! the French is comin',
> What'll now the red coats do?
> Maybe they wont get a drubbin'!
> Sure we'll lick them black and blue!

> " Ye little knew the day was near ye,
> Ye little thought they'd come so far;
> But here's the boys that never fear ye—
> Run, yer sowls, for Castlebar!"

To this measure they stepped in time, and although
the poetry was lost upon our ignorance, the rattling joy-
ousness of the air sounded pleasantly, and our men, soon
catching up the tune, joined heartily in the chorus.

Another very popular melody ran somewhat thus:—

> " Our day is now begun,
>   Says the Shan van voght,
> Our day is now begun,
>   Says the Shan van voght.
> Our day is now begun,
> And ours is all the fun!
> Be my sowl ye'd better run!
>   Says the Shan van voght!"

There were something like a hundred verses to this
famous air, but it is more than likely, from the specimen
given above, that my reader will forgive the want of
memory that leaves me unable to quote the remaining
ninety-nine; nor is it necessary that I should add, that
the merit of these canticles lay in the hoarse accord of a
thousand rude voices, heard in the stillness of a wild

mountain region, and at a time when an eventful struggle was before us: such were the circumstances which possibly made these savage rhymes assume something of terrible meaning.

We had just arrived at the entrance of Barnageeragh, when one of our mounted scouts rode up to say, that a peasant, who tended cattle on the mountains, had evidently observed our approach, and hastened into Castlebar with the tidings.

It was difficult to make General Humbert understand this fact.

" Is this the patriotism we have heard so much of? Are these the people who would welcome us as deliverers? Parbleu! I've seen nothing but lukewarmness or downright opposition since I landed! In that same town we have just quitted—a miserable hole, too, was it—what was the first sight that greeted us? a fellow in our uniform hanging from the stanchion of a window, with an inscription round his neck, to the purport that he was a traitor! This is the fraternity which our Irish friends never wearied to speak of!"

Our march was now hastened, and in less thar an hour we debouched from the narrow gorge into the open plain before the town of Castlebar. A few shots in our front told us that the advanced picket had fallen in with the enemy, but a French cheer also proclaimed that the Royalists had fallen back, and our march continued un molested. The road, which was wide and level here, traversed a flat country, without hedgerow or cover, so that we were able to advance in close column, without any precaution for our flanks; but before us there was a considerable ascent, which shut out all view of the track beyond it. Up this our advanced guard was toiling, somewhat wearied with a seven hours' march and the heat of a warm morning, when scarcely had the leading files topped the ridge, than plump went a round shot over their heads, which, after describing a fine curve. plunged into the soft surface of a newly-ploughed field. The troops were instantly retired behind the crest of the hill, and an orderly despatched to inform the general that we were in face of the enemy. He had already seen the shot and marked its direction. The main body was accordingly halted, and, defiling from the centre, the troops extended on either side into the fields. While this movement was being effected Humbert rode forward, and, crossing the ridge, reconnoitred the enemy.

It was, as he afterwards observed a stronger force than

he had anticipated, consisting of between three and four
thousand bayonets, with four squadrons of horse, and two
batteries of eight guns, the whole admirably posted on a
range of heights, in front of the town, and completely
covering it.

The ridge was scarcely eight hundred yards' distance,
and so distinctly was every object seen, that Humbert and
his two aides-de-camp were at once marked and fired at,
even in the few minutes during which the "reconnoissance"
lasted.

As the general retired the firing ceased, and now all
our arrangements were made without molestation of any
kind. They were, indeed, of the simplest and speediest.
Two companies of our grenadiers were marched to the
front, and in advance of them, about twenty paces, were
posted a body of Irish in French uniforms. This place
being assigned them, it was said, as a mark of honour, but
in reality for no other purpose than to draw on them the
Royalist artillery, and thus screen the grenadiers.

Under cover of this force came two light six-pounder
guns, loaded with grape, and intended to be discharged
at point-blank distance. The infantry brought up the
rear in three compact columns, ready to deploy into line
at a moment.

In these very simple tactics no notice whatever was
taken of the great rabble of Irish who hung upon our
flanks and rear in disorderly masses, cursing, swearing,
and vociferating in all the license of insubordination; and
O'Donnell, whose showy uniform contrasted strikingly
with the dark blue coat and low glazed cocked hat of
Humbert, was now appealed to by his countrymen as to
the reason of this palpable slight.

"What does he want? what does the fellow say?"
asked Humbert, as he noticed his excited gestures and
passionate manner.

"He is remonstrating, sir," replied I, "on the neglect
of his countrymen; he says that they do not seem treated
like soldiers; no post has been assigned, nor any order
given them."

"Tell him, sir," said Humbert, with a savage grin,
"that the discipline we have tried in vain to teach them
hitherto, we'll not venture to rehearse under an enemy's
fire; and tell him also that he and his ragged followers
are free to leave us, or, if they like better, to turn against
us, at a moment's warning."

I was saved the unpleasant task of interpreting this
civil message by Conolly, who, taking O'Donnell aside,

appeared endeavouring to reason with him, and reduce him to something like moderation.

"There, look at them, they're running like sheep!" cried Humbert, laughing, as he pointed to an indiscriminate rabble, some hundred yards off, in a meadow, and who had taken to their heels on seeing a round shot plunge into the earth near them. "Come along, sir: come with me, and when you have seen what fire is, you may go back and tell your countrymen! Serasin, is all ready? Well then, forward, march!"

"March!" was now re-echoed along the line, and steadily, as on a parade, our hardy infantry stepped out, while the drums kept up a continued roll as we mounted the hill.

The first to cross the crest of the ascent were the "Legion," as the Irish were called, who, dressed like French soldiers, were selected for some slight superiority in discipline and bearing. They had but gained the ridge, however, when a well-directed shot from a six-pounder smashed in amongst them, killing two, and wounding six or seven others. The whole mass immediately fell back on our grenadiers. The confusion compelled the supporting column to halt, and once more the troops were retired behind the hill.

"Forward, men, forward!" cried Humbert, riding up to the front, and in evident impatience at these repeated checks; and now the grenadiers passed to the front, and, mounting the height, passed over, while a shower of balls flew over and around them. A small slated house stood half way down the hill, and for this the leading files made a dash and gained it, just as the main body were, for the third time, driven back to re-form.

It was now evident that an attack in column could not succeed against a fire so admirably directed, and Humbert quickly deployed into line, and prepared to storm the enemy's position.

Up to this the conduct of the Royalists had been marked by the greatest steadiness and determination. Every shot from their batteries had told, and all promised an easy and complete success to their arms. No sooner, however, had our infantry extended into line, than the militia, unaccustomed to see an enemy before them, and unable to calculate distance, opened a useless, dropping fire, at a range where not a bullet could reach!

The ignorance of this movement, and the irregularity of the discharge, were not lost upon our fellows, most of whom were veterans of the army of the Rhine, and, with

a loud cheer of derision, our troops advanced to meet
them, while a cloud of skirmishers dashed forward and
secured themselves under cover of a hedge.

Even yet, however, no important advantage had been
gained by us, and if the Royalists had kept their ground
in support of their artillery, we must have been driven
back with loss ; but, fortunately for us, a movement we
made to keep open order was mistaken by some of the
militia officers for the preparation to outflank them, a
panic seized the whole line, and they fell back, leaving
their guns totally exposed and unprotected.

"They're running! they're running!" was the cry
along our line; and now a race was seen, which should be
first up with the artillery. The cheers at this moment
were tremendous, for our "allies," who had kept wide
aloof hitherto, were now up with us, and, more lightly,
equipped than we were, soon took the lead. The teme-
rity, however, was costly, for three several times did the
Royalist artillery load and fire; and each discharge,
scarcely at half-musket range, was terribly effective.

We were by no means prepared for either so sudden or
complete a success, and the scene was exciting in the
highest degree, as the whole line mounted the hill, cheering madly. From the crest of this rising ground we could
now see the town of Castlebar beneath us, into which the
Royalists were scampering at full speed. A preparation
for defending the bridge into the town did not escape the
watchful eyes of our general, who again gave the word
"Forward!" not by the road alone, but also by the fields
at either side, so as to occupy the houses that should command the bridge, and which, by a palpable neglect, the
others had forgotten to do.

Our small body of horse, about twenty hussars, were
ordered to charge the bridge, and had they been even
moderately well mounted, must have captured the one
gun of the enemy at once; but the miserable cattle, unable to strike a canter, only exposed them to a sharp musketry; and when they did reach the bridge, five of their
number had fallen. The six-pounder was, however, soon
taken, and the gunners sabred at their posts, while our
advanced guard coming up, completed the victory; and
nothing now remained but a headlong flight.

Had we possessed a single squadron of dragoons, few
could have escaped us, for not a vestige of discipline remained. All was wild confusion and panic. Such of the
officers as had ever seen service, were already killed or
badly wounded; and the younger ones were perfectly un-

equal to the difficult task of rallying or restoring order to a routed force.

The scene in the market-square, as we rode in, is not easily to be forgotten; about two hundred prisoners were standing in a group, disarmed, it is true, but quite unguarded, and without any preparation or precaution against escape!

Six or seven English officers, amongst whom were two majors, were gathered around General Humbert, who was conversing with them in tones of easy and jocular familiarity. The captured guns of the enemy (fourteen in all) were being ranged on one side of the square, while behind them were drawn up a strange-looking line of men, with their coats turned. These were part of the Kilkenny militia, who had deserted to our ranks after the retreat began.

Such was the "fight" of Castlebar; it would be absurd to call it a "battle;" a day too inglorious for the Royalists to reflect any credit upon us; but, such as it was, it raised the spirits of our Irish followers to a pitch of madness; and, out of our own ranks, none now doubted in the certainty of Irish independence.

Our occupation of the town lasted only a week; but, brief as the time was, it was sufficient to widen the breach between ourselves and our allies into an open and undisguised hatred. There were, unquestionably, wrongs on both sides. As for us, we were thoroughly, bitterly disappointed in the character of those we had come to liberate; and, making the egregious mistake of confounding these semi-civilised peasants with the Irish people, we deeply regretted that ever the French army should have been sent on so worthless a mission. As for them, they felt insulted and degraded by the offensive tone we assumed towards them. Not alone were they never regarded as comrades, but a taunting insolence of manner was assumed in all our dealings with them, very strikingly in contrast to that with which we conducted ourselves towards all the other inhabitants of the island, even those who were avowedly inimical to our object and our cause.

These things, with native quickness, they soon remarked. They saw the consideration and politeness with which the bishop and his family were treated; they saw several Protestant gentlemen suffered to return to their homes "on parole." They saw, too—worst grievance of all—how all attempts at pillage were restrained, or severely punished, and they asked themselves, "To what end a revolt, if neither massacre nor robbery were to follow?

If they wanted masters and rulers, sure they had the English that they were used to, and could at least understand."

Such were the causes, and such the reasonings, which gradually eat deeper and deeper into their minds, rendering them at first sullen, gloomy, and suspicious, and at last insubordinate, and openly insulting to us.

Their leaders were the first to exhibit this state of feeling. Affecting a haughty disdain for us, they went about with disparaging stories of the French soldiery; and at last went even so far as to impugn their courage!

In one of the versions of the affair of Castlebar, it was roundly asserted, that but for the Irish threatening to fire on them, the French would have turned and fled; while in another, the tactics of that day were all ascribed to the military genius of Neal Kerrigan, who, by the by, was never seen from early morning until late the same afternoon, when he rode into Castlebar on a fine bay horse that belonged to Captain Shortall of the Royal Artillery!

If the feeling between us and our allies was something less than cordial, nothing could be more friendly than that which subsisted between us and such of the Royalists as we came in contact with. The officers who became our prisoners were treated with every deference and respect. Two field-officers and a captain of carbineers dined daily with the general, and Serasin entertained several others. We liked them greatly; and I believe I am not flattering, if I say that they were equally satisfied with us. " Nos âmis l'ennemis," was the constant expression used in talking of them; and every day drew closer the ties of this comrade regard and esteem.

Such was the cordial tone of intimacy maintained between us, that I remember well, one evening at Humbert's table, an animated discussion being carried on between the general and an English staff-officer on the campaign itself—the Royalist averring, that, in marching southward at all, a gross and irreparable mistake had been made, and that if the French had occupied Sligo, and extended their wings towards the North, they would have secured a position of infinitely greater strength, and also become the centre for rallying round them a population of a very different order from the half-starved tribes of Mayo.

Humbert affected to say that the reason for his actual plan was, that twenty thousand French were daily expected to land in Lough Swilly, and that the western attack was merely to occupy time and attention, while the more formidable movement went on elsewhere,

I know not if the English believed this; I rather suspect
not. Certes, they were too polite to express any semblance of distrust of what was told them with all the air of
truth.

It was amusing, too, to see the candour with which each
party discussed the other to his face ; the French general
criticising all the faulty tactics and defective manœuvres of
the Royalists; while the English never hesitated to aver
that whatever momentary success might wait upon the
French arms, they were just as certain to be obliged to
capitulate in the end.

"You know it better than I do, General," said the Major
of Dragoons. "It may be a day or two earlier or later,
but the issue will and must be—a surrender."

"I don't agree with you," said Humbert, laughing ; "I
think there will be more than one 'Castlebar.' But let
the worst happen—and you must own that your haughty
country has received a heavy insult—your great England
has got a soufflet in the face of all Europe !"

This, which our general regarded as a great compensation—the greatest, perhaps, he could receive for all defeat—
did not seem to affect the English with proportionate dismay, nor even to ruffle the equanimity of their calm
tempers.

Upon one subject both sides were quite agreed—that the
peasantry never could aid, but very possibly would always
shipwreck, every attempt to win national independence.

"I should have one army to fight the English, and two
to keep down the Irish !" was Humbert's expression ; and
very little experience served to show that there was not
much exaggeration in the sentiment.

Our week at Castlebar taught us a good lesson in this
respect. The troops, wearied with a march that had begun
on the midnight of the day before, and with an engagement that lasted from eight till two in the afternoon, were
obliged to be under arms for several hours, to repress pillage and massacre. Our allies now filled the town, to the
number of five thousand, openly demanding that it should
be given up to them, parading the streets in riotous bands,
and displaying banners with long lists of names, doomed
for immediate destruction.

The steadiness and temper of our soldiery were severely
tried by these factious and insubordinate spirits: but discipline prevailed at last, and before the first evening closed
in, the town was quiet, and, for the time at least, danger
over.

CHAPTER XXIII.

"THE TOWN-MAJOR OF CASTLEBAR."

I AM at a loss to know whether or not I owe an apology to my reader for turning away from the more immediate object of this memoir of a life, to speak of events which have assumed an historical reputation. It may be thought ill-becoming in one who occupied the subordinate station that I did, to express himself on subjects so very far above both his experience and acquaintance; but I would premise, that in the opinions I may have formed, and the words of praise or censure dropped, I have been but retailing the sentiments of those older and wiser than myself, and by whose guidance I was mainly led to entertain not only the convictions but the prejudices of my early years.

Let the reader bear in mind, too, that I was very early in life thrown into the society of men—left self-dependent, in a great measure, and obliged to decide for myself on subjects which usually are determined by older and more mature heads. So much of excuse, then, if I seem presumptuous in saying that I began to conceive a very low opinion generally of popular attempts at independence, and a very high one of the powers of military skill and discipline. A mob, in my estimation, was the very lowest, and an army about the very highest, object I could well conceive. My short residence at Castlebar did not tend to controvert these impressions. The safety of the town and its inhabitants was entirely owing to the handful of French who held it, and who, wearied with guards, pickets, and outpost duty, were a mere fraction of the small force that had landed a few days before.

Our "allies" were now our most difficult charge. Abandoning the hopeless task of drilling and disciplining them, we confined ourselves to the more practical office of restraining pillage and repressing violence—a measure, be it said, that was not without peril, and of a very serious kind. I remember one incident, which, if not followed by grave consequences, yet appeared at the time of a very serious character.

By the accidental mis-spelling of a name, a man named

Dowall, a notorious ruffian and demagogue, was appointed "Commandant de Place," or Town-Major, instead of a most respectable shopkeeper named Downes, and who, although soon made aware of the mistake, from natural timidity took no steps to undeceive the general. Dowall was haranguing a mob of half-drunken vagabonds, when his commission was put into his hands; and accepting the post as an evidence of the fears the French entertained of his personal influence, became more overbearing and insolent than ever. We had a very gallant officer, the second major of the 12th Regiment of the Line, killed in the attack on Castlebar, and this Dowall at once took possession of poor Delaitre's horse, arms, and equipment. His coat and chako, his very boots and gloves, the scoundrel appropriated; and, as if in mockery of us and our poor friend, assumed a habit that he had, when riding fast, to place his sabre between his leg and the saddle, to prevent its striking the horse on the flanks.

I need scarcely say that, thoroughly disgusted by the unsightly exhibition, our incessant cares, and the endless round of duty we were engaged in, as well as the critical position we occupied, left us no time to notice the fellow's conduct by any other than a passing sign of anger or contempt—provocations that he certainly gave us back as insolently as we offered them. I do not believe that the general ever saw him, but I know that incessant complaints were daily made to him about the man's rapacity and tyranny, and scarcely a morning passed without a dozen remonstrances being preferred against his overbearing conduct.

Determined to have his own countrymen on his side, he issued the most absurd orders for the billeting of the rabble, the rations and allowances of all kinds. He seized upon one of the best houses for his own quarters, and three fine saddle-horses for his personal use, besides a number of inferior ones for the ruffian following he called his staff!

It was, indeed, enough to excite laughter, had not indignation been the more powerful emotion, to see this fellow ride forth of a morning—a tawdry scarf of green, with deep gold fringe, thrown over his shoulder, and a saddle-cloth of the same colour, profusely studded with gold shamrocks, on his horse; a drawn sword in his hand, and his head erect, followed by an indiscriminate rabble on foot or horseback—some with muskets, some pikes, some with sword-blades, bayonets, or even knives fastened on sticks, but all alike ferocious-looking and savage.

They affected to march in order, and, with a rude imita
tion of soldiery, carried something like a knapsack on their
shoulders, surmounted by a kettle, or tin cup, or sometimes an iron pot—a grotesque parody on the trim cooking equipment of the French soldier. It was evident,
from their step and bearing, that they thought themselves
in the very height of discipline; and this very assumption
was far more insulting to the real soldier than all the licen-
tious irregularity of the marauder. If to us they were
objects of ridicule and derision, to the townspeople they
were images of terror and dismay. The miserable shopkeeper who housed one of them lived in continual fear;
he knew nothing to be his own, and felt that his property
and family were every moment at the dictate of a ruffian
gang, who acknowledged no law, nor any rule save their
own will and convenience. D~wall's squad were indeed as
great a terror in that little town as I had seen the great
name of Robespierre in the proud city of Paris.

In my temporary position on General Serasin's staff, I
came to hear much of this fellow's conduct. The most
grievous stories were told me every day of his rapacity
and cruelty; but harassed and overworked as the general
was with duties that would have been over-much for three
or four men, I forebore to trouble him with recitals which
could only fret and distress him without affording the
slightest chance of relief to others. Perhaps this impunity
had rendered him more daring, or, perhaps, the immense
number of armed Irish, in comparison with the small force
of disciplined soldiers, emboldened the fellow; but certainly he grew day by day more presumptuous and insolent, and at last so far forgot himself as to countermand
one of General Serasin's orders, by which a guard was
stationed at the Protestant church to prevent its being
molested or injured by the populace.

General Humbert had already refused the Roman Ca-
tholic priest his permission to celebrate mass in that building, but Dowall had determined otherwise, and that, too,
by a written order, under his own hand. The French sergeant who commanded the guard of course paid little
attention to this warrant; and when Father Hennisy wanted
to carry the matter with a high hand, he coolly tore up
the paper, and threw the fragments at him. Dowall was
soon informed of the slight offered to his mandate. He
was at supper at the time, entertaining a party of his
friends, who all heard the priest's story, and, of course,
loudly sympathised with his sorrows, and invoked the
powerful leader's aid and protection. Affecting to believe

that the sergeant had merely acted in ignorance, and from not being able to read English, Dowall despatched a fellow, whom he called his aide-de-camp, a schoolmaster named Lowrie, and who spoke a little bad French, to interpret his command, and to desire the sergeant to withdraw his men, and give up the guard to a party of "the squad."

Great was the surprise of the supper party, when, after the lapse of half an hour, a country fellow came in to say that he had seen Lowrie led off to prison between two French soldiers. By this time Dowall had drank himself into a state of utter recklessness; while encouraged by his friend's praises, and the arguments of his own passions, he fancied that he might dispute ascendancy with General Humbert himself. He at once ordered out his horse, and gave a command to assemble the "squad." As they were all billeted in his immediate vicinity, this was speedily effected, and their numbers swelled by a vast mass of idle and curious, who were eager to see how the matter would end; the whole street was crowded, and when Dowall mounted, his followers amounted to above a thousand people.

If our sergeant, an old soldier of the "Sambre et Meuse," had not already enjoyed some experience of our allies, it is more than likely that, seeing their hostile advance, he would have fallen back upon the main guard, then stationed in the market-square. As it was, he simply retired his party within the church, the door of which had already been pierced for the use of musketry. This done, and one of his men being despatched to headquarters for advice and orders, he waited patiently for the attack.

I happened that night to make one of General Serasin's dinner party, and we were sitting over our wine, when the officer of the guard entered hastily with the tidings of what was going on in the town.

"Is it the Commandant de Place himself is at the head?" exclaimed Serasin, in amazement, such a thought being a direct shock to all his ideas of military discipline.

"Yes, sir," said the officer, "the soldier knows his appearance well, and can vouch for its being him."

"As I know something of him, General," said I, "I may as well mention that nothing is more likely."

"Who is he—what is he?" asked Serasin, hastily.

A very brief account—I need not say not a flattering one—told all that I knew or had ever heard of our worthy "Town Major." Many of the officers around corroborating, as I went on, all that I said, and interpolating little details of their own about his robberies and exactions.

"And yet I have heard nothing of all this before," said the general, looking sternly around him on every side.

None ventured on a reply, and what might have followed there is no guessing, when the sharp rattle of musketry cut short all discussion.

"That fire was not given by soldiers," said Serasin. "Go, Tiernay. and bring this fellow before me at once."

I bowed, and was leaving the room, when an officer, having whispered a few words in Serasin's ear, the general called me back, saying,—

"You are not to incur any risk, Tiernay; I want no struggle, still less a rescue. You understand me."

"Perfectly. General; the matter will, I trust, be easy enough!"

And so I left the room, my heart—shall I avow it?—bumping and throbbing in a fashion that gave a very poor corroboration to my words. There were always three or four horses ready saddled for duty at each general's quarters, and, taking one of them, I ordered a corporal of dragoons to follow me, and set out. It was a fine night of autumn; the last faint sunlight was yet struggling with the coming darkness, as I rode at a brisk trot down the main street towards the scene of action.

I had not proceeded far when the crowds compelled me to slacken my pace to a walk, and finding that the people pressed in upon me in such a way as to prevent anything like a defence if attacked, still more, any chance of an escape by flight, I sent the corporal forward to clear a passage, and announce my coming to the redoubted "Commandant." It was curious to see how the old dragoon's tactic effected his object, and with what speed the crowd opened and fell back, as with a flank movement of his horse he "passaged" up the street, prancing, bounding, and back-leaping, yet all the while perfectly obedient to the hand, and never deviating from the straight line in the very middle of the thoroughfare.

I could catch from the voices around me that the mob had fired a volley at the church-door, but that our men had never returned the fire, and now a great commotion of the crowd, and that swaying, surging motion of the mass, which is so peculiarly indicative of a coming event, told that something more was in preparation: and such was it; for already numbers were hurrying forward with straw-faggots, broken furniture, and other combustible material, which, in the midst of the wildest cries and shouts of

triumph, were now being heaped up against the door.
Another moment, and I should have been too late—as it
was, my loud summons to "halt," and a bold command
for the mob to fall back, only came at the very last
minute.

"Where's the commandant?" said I, in an imperious
tone.

"Who wants him?" responded a deep husky voice,
which I well knew to be Dowall's.

"The general in command of the town," said I firmly ;
"General Serasin."

"Maybe I'm as good a general as himself," was the
answer. "I never called him my superior yet! Did I,
boys?"

"Never—devil a bit—why would you?" and such like,
were shouted by the mob around us, in every accent of
drunken defiance.

"You'll not refuse General Serasin's invitation to confer
with your commandant, I hope?" said I, affecting a tone
of respectful civility, while I gradually drew nearer and
nearer to him, contriving, at the same time, by a dexte-
rous plunging of my horse, to force back the bystanders,
and thus isolate my friend Dowall.

"Tell him I've work to do here," said he, "and can't
come ; but if he's fond of a bonfire he may as well step
down this far and see one."

By this time, at a gesture of command from me, the corporal had placed himself on the opposite side of Dowall's
horse, and by a movement similar to my own, completely
drove back the dense mob, so that we had him completely
in our power, and could have sabred or shot him at any
moment.

"General Serasin only wishes to see you on duty, Commandant," said I, speaking in a voice that could be heard
over the entire assemblage ; and then dropping it to a
whisper, only audible to himself, I added,—

"Come along quietly, sir, and without a word. If you
speak, if you mutter, or if you lift a finger, I'll run my
sabre through your body."

"Forward, way, there," shouted I aloud, and the corporal, holding Dowall's bridle, pricked the horse with the
point of his sword, and right through the crowd we went
at a pace that defied following, had any the daring to
think of it.

So sudden was the act and so imminent the peril, for I
held the point of my weapon within a few inches of his
back, and would have kept my word most assuredly too,

that the fellow never spoke a syllable as we went, nor ventured on even a word of remonstrance till we descended at the general's door. Then, with a voice tremulous with restrained passion, he said,—

"If ye think I'll forgive ye this thrick, my fine boy, may the flames and fire be my portion! and if I hav'n't my revenge on ye yet, my name isn't Mick Dowall."

With a dogged, sulky resolution he mounted the stairs, but as he neared the room where the general was, and from which his voice could even now be heard, his courage seemed to fail him, and he looked back as though to see if no chance of escape remained. The attempt would have been hopeless, and he saw it.

"This is the man, General," said I, half pushing him forward into the middle of the room, where he stood with his hat on, and in attitude of mingled defiance and terror.

"Tell him to uncover," said Serasin; but one of the aides-de-camp, more zealous than courteous, stepped forward and knocked the hat off with his hand. Dowall never budged an inch, nor moved a muscle, at this insult; to look at him you could not have said that he was conscious of it.

"Ask him if it was by his orders that the guard was assailed," said the general.

I put the question in about as many words, but he made no reply.

"Does the man know where he is? does he know who I am?" repeated Serasin, passionately.

"He knows both well enough, sir," said I; "this silence is a mere defiance of us."

"Parbleu!" cried an officer, "that is the 'coquin' took poor Delaitre's equipments; the very uniform he has on was his."

"The fellow was never a soldier," said another.

"I know him well," interposed a third—"he is the very terror of the townsfolk."

"Who gave him his commission?—who appointed him?" asked Serasin.

Apparently the fellow could follow some words of French, for as the general asked this he drew from his pocket a crumpled and soiled paper, which he threw heedlessly upon the table before us.

"Why this is not his name, sir," said I; "this appointment is made out in the name of Nicholas Downes, and our friend here is called Downall."

"Who knows him? who can identify him?" asked Serasin.

" I can say that his name is Dowall, and that he worked
as a porter on the quay in this town when I was a boy,"
said a young Irishman who was copying letters and papers
at a side-table. " Yes, Dowall," said the youth, confront-
ing the look which the other gave him. " I am neither
afraid nor ashamed to tell you to your face that I know
you well, and who you are, and what you are."

I'm an officer in the Irish Independent Army now," said
Dowall, resolutely. "To the divil I fling the French commission and all that belongs to it. 'Tisn't troops that run
and guns that burst we want. Let them go back again the
way they came, we're able for the work ourselves."

Before I could translate this rude speech an officer broke
into the room, with tidings that the streets had been
cleared, and the rioters dispersed ; a few prisoners, too,
were taken, whose muskets bore trace of being recently
discharged.

" They fired upon our pickets, General," said the officer, whose excited look and voice betrayed how deeply he
felt the outrage.

The men were introduced ; three ragged, ill-looking
wretches, apparently only roused from intoxication by the
terror of their situation, for each was guarded by a soldier
with a drawn bayonet in his hand.

" We only obeyed ordhers, my lord ; we only did what
the Captain tould us," cried they, in a miserable, whining
tone, for the sight of their leader in captivity had sapped
all their courage.

" What am I here for? who has any business with me?"
said Dowall, assuming before his followers an attempt at
his former tone of bully.

" Tell him," said Serasin, " that wherever a French
general stands in full command he will neither brook insolence nor insubordination, Let those fellows be turned
out of the town, and warned never to approach the quarters
of the army under any pretence whatever. As for this
scoundrel, we'll make an example of him. Order a peloton into the yard, and shoot him."

I rendered this speech into English as the general spoke
it, and never shall I forget the wild scream of the wretch
as he heard the sentence.

" I'm an officer in the army of Ireland. I don't belong
to ye at all. You've no power over me. Oh, Captain,
darlin' ; oh, gentlemen, speak for me ! General, dear ;
General, honey, don't sintince me ! don't for the love o
God !" and in grovelling terror the miserable creatur
threw himself on his knees to beg for mercy.

14

" Tear off his epaulettes," cried Serasin ; " never let a French uniform be so disgraced."

The soldiers wrenched off the epaulettes at the command, and not satisfied with this, they even tore away the lace from the cuffs of the uniform, which now hung in ragged fragments over his trembling hands.

" Oh, sir! oh, General! oh, gentlemen, have marcy!"

" Away with him," said Serasin, contemptuously ; " it is only the cruel can be such cowards. Give the fellow his fusilade with blank cartridge, and the chances are, fear will kill him outright."

The scene that ensued is too shocking, too full of abasement to record ; there was nothing that fear of death, nothing that abject terror could suggest, that this miserable wretch did not attempt to save his life ; he wept—he begged in accents that were unworthy of all manhood—he kissed the very ground at the general's feet in his abject sorrow ; and when at last he was dragged from the room his screams were the most terrific and piercing.

Although all my compassion was changed into contempt, I felt that I could never have given the word to fire upon him, had such been my orders ; his fears had placed him below all manhood, but they still formed a barrier of defence around him. I accordingly whispered a few words to the sergeant, as we passed down the stairs, and then affecting to have forgotten something, I stepped back towards the room, where the general and his staff were sitting. The scuffling sound of feet, mingled with the crash of firearms, almost drowned the cries of the still struggling wretch ; his voice, however, burst forth into a wild cry, and then there came a pause—a pause that at last became insupportable to my anxiety, and I was about to rush down stairs, when a loud yell, a savage howl of derision and hate burst forth from the street ; and on looking out I saw a vast crowd before the door, who were shouting after a man, whose speed soon carried him out of reach. This was Dowall, who, thus suffered to escape, was told to fly from the town and never to return to it.

" Thank Heaven," muttered I, " we've seen the last of him."

The rejoicing was, however, premature.

CHAPTER XXIV.

"THE MISSION TO THE NORTH."

I HAVE never yet been able to discover whether General Humbert really did feel the confidence that he assumed at this period, or that he merely affected it, the better to sustain the spirits of those around him. If our success at Castlebar was undeniable, our loss was also great, and far more than proportionate to all the advantages we had acquired. Six officers and two hundred and forty men were either killed or badly wounded, and as our small force had really acquired no reinforcement worth the name, it was evident that another such costly victory would be our ruin.

Not one gentleman of rank or influence had yet joined us, few of the priesthood; and, even among the farmers and peasantry, it was easy to see that our recruits comprised those whose accession could never have conferred honour or profit on any cause.

Our situation was anything but promising. The rumours that reached us (and we had no other or more accurate information than rumours), told that an army of thirty thousand men, under the command of Lord Cornwallis, was in march against us; that all the insurrectionary movements of the south were completely repressed; that the spirit of the rebels was crushed, and their confidence broken, either by defeat or internal treachery. In a word, that the expedition had already failed, and the sooner we had the means of leaving the land of our disasters the better.

Such were the universal feelings of all my comrades; but Humbert, who had often told us that we were only here to " eclairer la route " for another and more formidable mission, now pretended to think that we were progressing most favourably towards a perfect success. Perhaps he firmly believed all this, or perhaps he thought that the pretence would give more dignity to the finale of an exploit which he already saw was nearly played out! I know not which is the true explanation, and am half disposed to think that he was actuated as much by one impulse as the other.

"The Army of the North" was the talisman, which we now heard of for the first time, to repair all our disasters, and ensure complete victory. "The Army of the North," whose strength varied from twenty to twenty-five, and sometimes reached even thirty thousand men, and was commanded by a distinguished Irish general, was now the centre to which all our hopes turned. Whether it had already landed, and where, of what it consisted, and how officered, not one of us knew anything; but by dint of daily repetition and discussion we had come to believe in its existence as certainly as though we had seen it under arms.

The credulous lent their convictions without any trouble to themselves whatever; the more sceptical studied the map, and fancied twenty different places in which they might have disembarked; and thus the "Army of the North" grew to be a substance and reality, as undoubted as the scenes before our eyes.

Never was such a ready solution of all difficulties discovered as this same "Army of the North." Were we to be beaten by Cornwallis, it was only a momentary check, for the Army of the North would come up within a few days and turn the whole tide of war. If our Irish allies grew insubordinate or disorderly, a little patience and the Army of the North would settle all that. Every movement projected was fancied to be in concert with this redoubted corps, and at last every trooper that rode in from Killala or Ballina was questioned as to whether his despatches did not come from the Army of the North.

Frenchmen will believe anything you like for twenty-four hours. They can be flattered into a credulity of two days, and, by dint of great artifice and much persuasion, will occasionally reach a third; but there, faith has its limit; and if nothing palpable, tangible, and real, intervene, scepticism ensues; and what with native sarcasm, ridicule, and irony, they will demolish the card edifice of credit far more rapidly than ever they raised it. For two whole days the "Army of the North" occupied every man amongst us. We toasted it over our wine; we discussed it at our quarters; we debated upon its whereabouts, its strength, and its probable destination; but on the third morning a terrible shock was given to our feelings by a volatile young lieutenant of hussars exclaiming,—

"Ma foi! I wish I could see this same 'Army of the North!'"

Now, although nothing was more reasonable than this

wish, nor was there any one of us who had not felt a similar desire, this sudden expression of it struck us all most
forcibly, and a shrinking sense of doubt spread over every
face, and men looked at each other as though to say—" Is
the fellow capable of supposing that such an army does
not exist?" It was a very dreadful moment—a terrible
interval of struggle between the broad daylight of belief
and the black darkness of incredulity; and we turned
glances of actual dislike at the man who had so unwar-
rantably shaken our settled convictions.

"I only said I should like to see them under arms,"
stammered he, in the confusion of one who saw himself
exposed to public obloquy.

This half apology came too late—the mischief was done !
and we shunned each other like men who were afraid to
read the accusation of even a shrewd glance. As for myself, I can compare my feelings only to those of the
worthy alderman, who broke out into a paroxysm of grief
on hearing that "Robinson Crusoe" was a fiction. I believe, on that sudden revulsion of feeling, I could have
discredited any and everything. If there was no Army
of the North, was I quite sure that there was any expedition
at all? Were the generals mere freebooters, the chiefs
of a marauding venture? Were the patriots anything but
a disorderly rabble eager for robbery and bloodshed? Was
Irish Independence a mere phantom? Such were among
the shocking terrors that came across my mind as I sat in
my quarters, far too dispirited and depressed to mix among
my comrades.

It had been a day of fatiguing duty, and I was not sorry,
as night fell, that I might betake myself to bed, to forget,
if it might be, the torturing doubts that troubled me.
Suddenly I heard a heavy foot upon the stair, and an orderly entered with a command for me to repair to the
head-quarters of the general at once. Never did the call
of duty summon me less willing, never found me so totally
disinclined to obey. I was weary and fatigued; but worse,
than this, I was out of temper with myself, the service,
and the whole world. Had I heard that the Royal forces
were approaching, I was exactly in the humour to have
dashed into the thick of them, and sold my life as dearly
as I could, out of desperation.

Discipline is a powerful antagonist to a man's caprices'
for with all my irritability and discontent I arose, and resuming my uniform set out for General Humbert's quarters. I followed "the orderly," as he led the way
through many a dark street and crooked alley till we

reached the square. There, too, all was in darkness, save at the mainguard, where, as usual, the five windows of the first story were a blaze of light, and the sounds of mirth and revelry, the nightly orgies of our officers, were ringing out in the stillness of the quiet hour. The wild chorus of a soldier-song, with its "rantan-plan" accompaniment of knuckles on the table, echoed through the square, and smote upon my ear with anything but a congenial sense of pleasure.

In my heart I thought them a senseless, soulless crew, that could give themselves to dissipation and excess on the very eve, as it were, of our defeat, and with hasty steps I turned away into the side street, where a large lamp, the only light to be seen, proclaimed General Humbert's quarters.

A bustle and stir, very unusual at this late hour, pervaded the passages and stairs, and it was some time before I could find one of the staff to announce my arrival, which at last was done somewhat unceremoniously, as an officer hurried me through a large chamber crowded with the staff into an inner room, where, on a small field-bed, lay General Humbert, without coat or boots, a much-worn scarlet cloak thrown half over him, and a black handkerchief tied round his head. I had scarcely seen him since our landing, and I could with difficulty recognise the burly, high-complexioned soldier of a few days back, in the worn and haggard features of the sick man before me. An attack of ague, which he had originally contracted in Holland, had relapsed upon him, and he was now suffering all the lassitude and sickness of that most depressing of all maladies.

Maps, books, plans, and sketches of various kinds scattered the bed, the table, and even the floor around him; but his attitude as I entered betrayed the exhaustion of one who could labour no longer, and whose worn-out faculties demanded rest. He lay flat on his back, his arms straight down beside him, and, with half-closed eyes, seemed as though falling off to sleep.

His first aide-de-camp, Merochamp, was standing with his back to a small turf fire, and made a sign to us to be still, and make no noise as we came in.

"He's sleeping," said he; "it's the first time he has closed his eyes for ten days."

We stood for a moment uncertain, and were about to retrace our steps, when Humbert said, in a low, weak voice,—

"No! I'm not asleep, come in."

The officer who presented me now retired, and I advanced towards the bed-side.

" This is Tiernay, General," said Merochamp, stooping down and speaking low ; " you wished to see him."

" Yes, I wanted him. Ha! Tiernay, you see me a good deal altered since we parted last; however, I shall be all right in a day or two ; it's a mere attack of ague, and will leave when the good weather comes. I wished to ask you about your family, Tiernay ; was not your father Irish ? "

" No, sir ; we were Irish two or three generations back, but since that we have belonged either to Austria or to France."

" Then where were you born ? "

" In Paris, sir, I believe, but certainly in France."

" Then I said so, Merochamp ; I knew that the boy was French."

" Still I don't think the precaution worthless," replied Merochamp ; " Teeling and the others advise it."

" I know they do," said Humbert, peevishly, " and for themselves it may be needful ; but this lad's case will be injured, not bettered by it. He is not an Irishman ; he never was at any time a British subject. Have you any certificate of birth or baptism, Tiernay ? "

" None, sir ; but I have my ' livret' for the school of Saumur, which sets forth my being a Frenchman by birth."

" Quite sufficient, boy, let me have it."

It was a document which I always carried about with me since I landed, to enable me any moment, if made prisoner, to prove myself an alien, and thus escape the inculpation of fighting against the flag of my country. Perhaps there was something of reluctance in my manner as I relinquished it, for the general said, " I'll take good care of it, Tiernay, you shall not fare the worse because it is in my keeping. I may as well tell you that some of our Irish officers have received threatening letters. It is needless to say they are without name, stating that if matters go unfortunately with us in this campaign they will meet the fate of men taken in open treason ; and that their condition of officers in our service will avail them nothing. I do not believe this. I cannot believe that they will be treated in any respect differently from the rest of us. However, it is only just that I should tell you that your name figures amongst those so denounced ; for this reason I have sent for you now You, at least, have nothing to apprehend on this score. You are as much a Frenchman as myself. I know Merochamp thinks differently from

me, and that your Irish descent and name will be quite
enough to involve you in the fate of others."

A gesture, half of assent but half of impatience, from
the aide-de-camp, here arrested the speaker.

"Why not tell him frankly how he stands?" said
Humbert, eagerly; "I see no advantage in any concealment."

Then addressing me, he went on. "I purpose, Tiernay, to give you the same option I gave the others, but
which they have declined to accept. It is this : we are
daily expecting to hear of the arrival of a force in the
north under the command of Generals Tandy and Rey."

"The Army of the North?" asked I, in some anxiety.

"Precisely; the Army of the North. Now I desire to open
a communication with them, and at the same time to do so
through the means of such officers as, in the event of any
disaster here, may have the escape to France open to
them; which this army will have, and which, I need not
say, we have no longer. Our Irish friends have declined
this mission as being more likely to compromise them if
taken; and also as diminishing and not increasing their
chance of escape. In my belief that you were placed
similarly I have sent for you here this evening, and at the
same time desire to impress upon you that your accept-
ance or refusal is purely a matter at your own volition."

"Am I to regard the matter simply as one of duty, sir?
or as an opportunity of consulting my personal safety?"

"What shall I say to this, Merochamp?" asked Humbert, bluntly.

"That you are running to the full as many risks of
being hanged for going as by staying; such is my opinion," said the aide-de-camp. "Here as a rebel, there as
a spy."

"I confess, then," said I, smiling at the cool brevity of
the speech, "the choice is somewhat embarrassing! May
I ask what you advise me to do, General?"

"I should say go, Tiernay."

"Go, by all means, lad," broke in the aide-de-camp,
who throughout assumed a tone of dictation and familiarity
most remarkable. "If a stand is to be made in this miserable country it will be with Rey's force; here the game
will not last much longer. There lies the only man capable of conducting such an expedition, and his health cannot stand up against its trials!"

"Not so, Merochamp; I'll be on horseback to-morrow
or the day after at furthest; and if I never were to take
the field again, there are others, yourself amongst the

number, well able to supply my place : but to Tiernay—
what says he?"

"Make it duty, sir, and I shall go, or remain here with
an easy conscience," said I.

"Then duty be it, boy," said he; "and Merochamp
will tell you everything, for all this discussion has wearied
me much, and I cannot endure more talking."

"Sit down here," said the aide-de-camp, pointing to a
seat at his side, "and five minutes will suffice."

He opened a large map of Ireland before us on the
table, and running his finger along the coast-line of the
western side, stopped abruptly at the bay of Lough
Swilly.

"There," said he, "that is the spot. There, too,
should have been our own landing! The whole population of the North will be with them—not such allies as
these fellows, but men accustomed to the use of arms, able
and willing to take the field. They say that five thousand
men could hold the passes of those mountains against
thirty."

"Who says this?" said I, for I own it that I had grown
marvellously sceptical as to testimony.

"Napper Tandy, who is a general of division, and one
of the leaders of this force;" and he went on : "The utmost we can do will be to hold these towns to the westward till they join us. We may stretch away thus far,"
and he moved his finger towards the direction of Leitrim,
but no further. "You will have to communicate with
them; to explain what we have done, where we are, and
how we are. Conceal nothing—let them hear fairly that
this patriot force is worth nothing, and that even to garrison the towns we take they are useless. Tell them, too,
the sad mistake we made by attempting to organise
what never can be disciplined, and let them not arm a
population, as we have done, to commit rapine and
plunder."

Two letters were already written—one addressed to
Rey, the other to Napper Tandy. These I was ordered
to destroy if I should happen to become a prisoner ; and
with the map of Ireland, pen-marked in various directions,
by which I might trace my route, and a few lines to
Colonel Charost, whom I was to see on passing at Killala,
I was dismissed. When I approached the bed-side to
take leave of the general he was sound asleep. The excitement of talking having passed away, he was pale as
death, and his lips totally colourless. Poor fellow, he
was exhausted-looking and weary, and I could not help

thinking, as I looked on him, that he was no bad emblem of the cause he had embarked in!

I was to take my troop-horse as far as Killala, after which I was to proceed either on foot, or by such modes of conveyance as I could find, keeping as nigh the coast as possible, and acquainting myself, so far as I might do, with the temper and disposition of the people as I went. It was a great aid to my sinking courage to know that there really was an '·Army of the North," and to feel myself accredited to hold intercourse with the generals commanding it.

Such was my exultation at this happy discovery, that I was dying to burst in amongst my comrades with the tidings, and proclaim, at the same time, my own high mission. Merochamp had strictly enjoined my speedy departure without the slightest intimation to any whither I was going, or with what object.

A very small cloak-bag held all my effects, and with this slung at my saddle I rode out of the town just as the church clock was striking twelve. It was a calm, starlight night, and once a short distance from the town, as noiseless and still as possible ; a gossoon, one of the numerous scouts we employed in conveying letters or bringing intelligence, trotted along on foot beside me to show the way, for there was a rumour that some of the Royalist cavalry still loitered about the passes to capture our despatch bearers, or make prisoners of any stragglers from the army.

These " gossoons," picked up by chance, and selected for no other qualification than because they were keen-eyed and swift of foot, were the most faithful and most worthy creatures we met with. In no instance were they ever known to desert to the enemy, and, stranger still, they were never seen to mix in the debauchery and excesses so common to all the volunteers of the rebel camp. Their intelligence was considerable, and to such a pitch had emulation stimulated them in the service, that there was no danger they would not incur in their peculiar duties.

My companion on the present occasion was a little fellow of about thirteen years of age, and small and slight even for that ; we knew him as " Peter," but whether he had any other name, or what, I was ignorant. He was wounded by a sabre-cut across the hand, which nearly severed the fingers from it, at the bridge of Castlebar, but, with a strip of linen bound round it, now he trotted along as happy and careless as if nothing ailed him.

I questioned him as we went, and learned that his father had been a herd in the service of a certain Sir Roger Palmer, and his mother a dairy-maid in the same house, but as the patriots had sacked and burned the "Castle," of course they were now upon the world. He was a good deal shocked at my asking what part his father took on the occasion of the attack, but for a very different reason than that which I suspected.

"For the cause, of course!" replied he, almost indignantly; "why wouldn't he stand up for ould Ireland!"

"And your mother—what did she do?"

He hung down his head, and made no answer till I repeated the question.

"Faix," said he, slowly and sadly, "she went and towld the young ladies what was goin' to be done, and if it hadn't been that the 'boys' caught Tim Hynes, the groom, going off to Foxford with a letter, we'd have had the dragoons down upon us in no time! They hanged Tim, but they let the young ladies away, and my mother with them, and off they all went to Dublin."

"And where's your father now?" I asked.

"He was drowned in the bay of Killala four days ago. He went with a party of others to take oatmeal from a sloop that was wrecked in the bay, and an English cruiser came in at the time and fired on them; at the second discharge the wreck and all upon it went down!"

He told all these things without any touch of sorrow in voice or manner. They seemed to be the ordinary chances of war, and so he took them. He had three brothers and a sister; of the former two were missing, the third was a scout; and the girl—she was but nine years old—was waiting on a canteen, and mighty handy, he said, for she knew a little French already, and understood the soldiers when they asked for a "goutte," or wanted "du feu" for their pipes.

Such, then, was the credit side of the account with Fortune, and, strange enough, the boy seemed satisfied with it; and although a few days had made him an orphan and houseless, he appeared to feel that the great things in store for his country were an ample recompense for all. Was this, then, patriotism? Was it possible that one, untaught and unlettered as he was, could think national freedom cheap at such a cost? If I thought so for a moment, a very little further inquiry undeceived me. Religious rancour, party feuds, the hate of the Saxon—a blind, ill-directed, unthinking hate—were the motives which actuated him. A terrible retribution for something upon somebody, an awful wiping out of old scores, a reversal of the lot of rich and poor, were the main incentives to his actions, and he was satisfied to stand by at the drawing of this great lottery, even without holding a ticket in it!

It was almost the first moment of calm reflective thought I had enjoyed, as I rode along thus in the quiet stillness of the night, and I own that my heart began to misgive me as to the great benefits of our expedition. I will not conceal the fact, that I had been disappointed in every expectation I had formed of Ireland.

The bleak and barren hills of Mayo, the dreary tracts of mountain and morass, were about as unworthy representatives of the boasted beauty and fertility, as were the half-clad wretches who flocked around us of that war-like people of whom we had heard so much. Where were the chivalrous chieftains with their clans behind them? Where the thousands gathering around a national standard? Where that high-souled patriotism, content to risk fortune, station—all, in the conflict for national independence? A rabble led on by a few reckless debauchees, and two or three disreputable or degraded priests, were our only allies; and even these refused to be guided by our councils, or swayed by our authority. I half suspected Serasin was right when he said—"Let the Directory send thirty thousand men and make it a French province, but let us not fight an enemy to give the victory to the 'sans culottes.'"

As we neared the pass of Barnageeragh, I turned one last look on the town of Castlebar, around which, at little intervals of space, the watch-fires of our pickets were blazing; all the rest of the place was in darkness.

It was a strange and a thrilling thought to think that there, hundreds of miles from their home, without one link that could connect them to it, lay a little army in the midst of an enemy's country, calm, self-possessed, and determined. How many, thought I, are destined to leave it? How many will bring back to our dear France the memory of this unhappy struggle?

CHAPTER XXV.

A PASSING VISIT TO KILLALA.

I FOUND a very pleasant party assembled around the bishop's breakfast-table at Killala. The bishop and his family were all there, with Charost and his staff, and some three or four other officers from Ballina. Nothing could be less constrained, more easy or more agreeable, than the tone of intimacy which in a few days had grown up between them. A cordial good feeling seemed to prevail on every subject, and even the reserve which might be thought natural on the momentous events then happening was exchanged for a most candid and frank discussion of all that was going forward, which, I must own, astonished as much as it gratified me.

The march on Castlebar, the choice of the mountain-road, which led past the position occupied by the Royalists, the attack and capture of the artillery, had all to be related by me for the edification of such as were not conversant with French; and I could observe that however discomfited by the conduct of the militia, they fully relied on the regiments of the line and the artillery. It was amusing, too, to see with what pleasure they listened to all our disparagement of the Irish volunteers.

Every instance we gave of insubordination or disobedience delighted them, while our own blundering attempts to manage the people, the absurd mistakes we fell into, and the endless misconceptions of their character and habits, actually convulsed them with laughter.

"Of course," said the bishop to us, "you are prepared to hear that there is no love lost between you, and that they are to the full as dissatisfied with you as you are dissatisfied with them?"

"Why, what can they complain of?" asked Charost, smiling; "we gave them the place of honour in the very last engagement!"

"Very true, you did so, and they reaped all the profit of the situation. Monsieur Tiernay had just told the havoc that grape and round shot scattered amongst the poor creatures. However, it is not of this they complain—it is

their miserable fare, the raw potatoes, their beds in open
fields and highways, while the French, they say, eat of the
best and sleep in blankets; they do not understand this
inequality, and perhaps it is somewhat hard to comprehend."

"Patriotism ought to be proud of such little sacrifices,"
said Charost, with an easy laugh; "besides, it is only a
passing endurance: a month hence, less, perhaps, will see
us dividing the spoils, and revelling in the conquest of
Irish independence."

"You think so, colonel?" asked the bishop, half slyly.

"Parbleu! to be sure I do—and you?"

"I'm just as sanguine," said the bishop, "and fancy
that, about a month hence, we shall be talking of all these
things as matters of history; and while sorrowing over
some of the unavoidable calamities of the event, preserving a grateful memory of some who came as enemies but
left us warm friends."

"If such is to be the turn of fortune," said Charost,
with more seriousness than before, "I can only say that
the kindly feelings will not be one-sided."

And now the conversation became an animated discussion on the chances of success or failure. Each party supported his opinion ably and eagerly, and with a degree of
freedom that was not a little singular to the bystanders.
At last, when Charost was fairly answered by the bishop
on every point, he asked,—

"But what say you to the Army of the North?"

"Simply, that I do not believe in such a force," rejoined
the bishop.

"Not believe it—not believe on what General Humbert
relies at this moment, and to which that officer yonder is
an accredited messenger! When I tell you that a most
distinguished Irishman, Napper Tandy——"

"Napper Tandy!" repeated the bishop, with a good-
humoured smile, "the name is quite enough to relieve one
of any fears, if they ever felt them. I am not sufficiently
acquainted with your language to give him the epithet he
deserves, but if you can conceive an empty, conceited man,
as ignorant of war as of politics, rushing into a revolution
for the sake of a green uniform, and ready to convulse a
kingdom that he may be called a major-general, only
enthusiastic in his personal vanity, and wanting even in
that heroic daring which occasionally dignifies weak capa-
cities—such is Napper Tandy."

"What in soldier-phrase we call a 'Blague,'" said Charost, laughing; "I'm sorry for it."

What turn the conversation was about to take I cannot guess, when it was suddenly interrupted by one of the bishop's servants rushing into the room, with a face blood-less from terror. He made his way up to where the bishop sat, and whispered a few words in his ear.

"And how is the wind blowing, Andrew?" asked the bishop, in a voice that all his self-command could not completely steady.

"From the north, or the north-west, and mighty strong, too, my lord," said the man, who trembled in every limb.

The affrighted aspect of the messenger, the excited expression of the bishop's face, and the question as to the "wind," at once suggested to me the idea that a French fleet had arrived in the bay, and that the awful tidings were neither more nor less than the announcement of our reinforcement.

"From the north-west," repeated the bishop; "then, with God's blessing, we may be spared." And so saying, he arose from the table, and with an effort that showed that the strength to do so had only just returned to him. "Colonel Charost, a word with you!" said he, leading the way into an adjoining room.

"What is it?—what has happened?—what can it be?" was asked by each in turn. And now groups gathered at the windows, which all looked into the court of the building, now crowded with people, soldiers, servants, and country-folk, gazing earnestly towards the roof of the castle.

"What's the matter, Terry?" asked one of the bishop's sons, as he threw open the window.

"'Tis the chimbley on fire, Master Robert," said the man; "the kitchen chimbley, wid those divils of Frinch!"

I cannot describe the burst of laughter that followed the explanation!

So much terror for so small a catastrophe was inconceivable; and whether we thought of Andrew's horrified face, or the worthy bishop's pious thankgiving as to the direction of the wind, we could scarcely refrain from another outbreak of mirth. Colonel Charost made his appearance at the instant, and although his step was hurried, and his look severe, there was nothing of agitation or alarm on his features.

"Turn out the guard, Truchet, without arms," said he. "Come with me, Tiernay—an awkward business enough," whispered he, as he led me along. "These fellows have set fire to the kitchen chimney, and we have three hundred barrels of gunpowder in the cave!" Nothing could be

more easy and unaffected than the way he spoke this; and
I actually stared at him, to see if his coldness was a mere
pretence, but far from it—every gesture and every word
showed the most perfect self-possession, with a prompt
readiness for action.

When we reached the court, the bustle and confusion
had reached its highest, for, as the wind lulled, large
masses of inky smoke hung, like a canopy, over head,
through which a forked flame darted at intervals, with
that peculiar furnace-like roar that accompanies a jet of
fire in confined places. At times, too, as the soot ignited,
great showers of bright sparks floated upwards, and afterwards fell, like a fiery rain, on every side. The country
people, who had flocked in from the neighbourhood, were
entirely occupied with these signs, and only intent upon
saving the remainder of the house, which they believed in
great peril, totally unaware of the greater and more imminent danger close beside them.

Already they had placed ladders against the walls, and,
with ropes and buckets, were preparing to ascend, when
Truchet marched in with his company, in fatigue-jackets,
twenty sappers with shovels accompanying them.

"Clear the court-yard, now," said Charost, "and leave
this matter to us."

The order was obeyed somewhat reluctantly, it is true,
and at last we stood the sole occupants of the spot, the
bishop being the only civilian present, he having refused
to quit the spot, unless compelled by force.

The powder was stored in a long shed adjoining the
stables, and originally used as a shelter for farming tools
and utensils. A few tarpaulins we had carried with us
from the ships were spread over the barrels, and on this
now some sparks of fire had fallen, as the burning soot had
been carried in by an eddy of wind.

The first order was, to deluge the tarpaulins with water;
and while this was being done, the sappers were ordered to
dig trenches in the garden, to receive the barrels. Every
man knew the terrible peril so near him; each felt that at
any instant a frightful death might overtake him, and yet
every detail of the duty was carried on with the coldest
unconcern; and when at last the time came to carry away
the barrels, on a species of handbarrow, the fellows stepped
in time, as if on the march, and moved in measure, a degree
of indifference which, to judge from the good bishop's countenance, evidently inspired as many anxieties for their spi-
ritual welfare as it suggested astonishment and admiration
for their courage. He himself, it must be owned, dis-

played no sign of trepidation, and in the few words he spoke, or the hints he dropped, exhibited every quality of a brave man.

At moments the peril seemed very imminent indeed. Some timber having caught fire, slender fragments of burning wood fell in masses, covering the men as they went, and falling on the barrels, whence the soldiers brushed them off with cool indifference. The dense, thick smoke, too, obscuring every object a few paces distant, added to the confusion, and occasionally bringing the going and returning parties into collision, a loud shout, or cry, would ensue; and it is difficult to conceive how such a sound thrilled through the heart at such a time. I own that more than once I felt a choking fulness in the throat, as I heard a sudden yell, it seemed so like a signal for destruction. In removing one of the last barrels from the hand-barrow, it slipped, and, falling to the ground, the hoops gave way, it burst open, and the powder fell out on every side. The moment was critical, for the wind was baffling, now wafting the sparks clear away, now whirling them in eddies around us. It was then that an old sergeant of grenadiers threw off his upper coat and spread it over the broken cask, while, with all the composure of a man about to rest himself, he lay down on it, while his comrades went to fetch water. Of course his peril was no greater than that of every one around him, but there was an air of quick determination in his act which showed the training of an old soldier. At length the labour was ended, the last barrel was committed to the earth, and the men, formed into line, were ordered to wheel and march. Never shall I forget the bishop's face as they moved past. The under-sized and youthful look of our soldiers had acquired for them a kind of depreciating estimate in comparison with the more mature and manly stature of the British soldier, to whom, indeed, they offered a strong contrast on parade; but now, as they were seen in a moment of arduous duty, surrounded by danger, the steadiness and courage, the prompt obedience to every command, the alacrity of their movements, and the fearless intrepidity with which they performed every act, impressed the worthy bishop so forcibly, that he muttered half aloud, "Thank Heaven there are but few of them!"

Colonel Charost resisted steadily the bishop's proffer to afford the men some refreshment; he would not even admit of an extra allowance of brandy to their messes. "If we become too liberal for slight services, we shall never be

15

able to reward real ones," was his answer; and the bishop was reduced to the expedient of commemorating what he could not reward. This, indeed, he did with the most unqualified praise, relating in the drawing-room all that he had witnessed, and lauding French valour and heroism to the very highest.

The better to conceal my route, and to avoid the chances of being tracked, I sailed that evening in a fishing-boat for Killybegs, a small harbour on the coast of Donegal, having previously exchanged my uniform for the dress of a sailor, so that if apprehended I should pretend to be an Ostend or Antwerp seaman, washed overboard in a gale at sea. Fortunately for me, I was not called on to perform this part, for as my nautical experiences were of the very slightest, I should have made a deplorable attempt at the impersonation. Assuredly the fishermen of the smack would not have been among the number of the "imposed upon," for a more sea-sick wretch never masqueraded in a blue jacket than I was.

My only clue, when I touched land, was a certain Father Doogan, who lived at the foot of the Bluerock Mountains, about fifteen miles from the coast, and to whom I brought a few lines from one of the Irish officers, a certain Bourke of Ballina. The road led in this direction, and so little intercourse had the shore folk with the interior, that it was with difficulty any one could be found to act as a guide thither. At last an old fellow was discovered, who used to travel these mountains formerly with smuggled tobacco and tea; and although, from the discontinuance of the smuggling trade, and increased age, he had for some years abandoned the line of business, a liberal offer of payment induced him to accompany me as guide.

It was not without great misgivings that I looked at the very old and almost decrepit creature who was to be my companion through a solitary mountain region.

The few stairs he had to mount in the little inn where I put up seemed a sore trial to his strength and chest; but he assured me that, once out of the smoke of the town, and with his foot on the "short grass of the sheep-patch," he'd be like a four-year-old; and his neighbour having corroborated the assertion, I was fain to believe him.

Determined, however, to make his excursion subservient to profit in his old vocation, he provided himself with some pounds of tobacco and a little parcel of silk handkerchiefs, to dispose of amongst the country-people, with which, and a little bag of meal slung at his back, and a walking-stick in his hand, he presented himself at my door just as day was breaking.

"We'll have a wet day I fear, Jerry," said I, looking out.

"Not a bit of it," replied he. "'Tis the spring-tides makes it cloudy there beyant; but when the sun gets up it will be a fine mornin'; but I'm thinkiu' ye'r strange in them parts;" and this he said with a keen, sharp glance under his eyes.

"Donegal is new to me, I confess," said I, guardedly.

"Yes, and the rest of Ireland, too," said he, with a roguish leer. "But come along, we've a good step before us;" and with these words he led the way down the stairs, holding the balustrade as he went, and exhibiting every sign of age and weakness. Once in the street, however, he stepped out more freely, and before we got clear of the town, walked at a fair pace, and, to all seeming, with perfect ease

CHAPTER XXVI.

A REMNANT OF "FONTENOY."

THERE was no resisting the inquisitive curiosity of my companion. The short dry cough, the little husky " ay," that sounded like anything rather than assent, which followed on my replies to his questions, and, more than all, the keen, oblique glances of his shrewd grey eyes, told me that I had utterly failed in all my attempts at mystification, and that he read me through and through.

" And so," said he, at last, after a somewhat lengthy narrative of my shipwreck, " and so the Flemish sailors wear spurs ? "

" Spurs ! of course not ; why should they ? " asked I in some astonishment.

" Well, but don't they ? " asked he again.

" No such thing ; it would be absurd to suppose it."

" So I thought," rejoined he ; " and when I looked at yer ' honour's' boots " (it was the first time he had addressed me by this title of deference), "and saw the marks on the heels for spurs, I soon knew how much of a sailor you were."

" And if not a sailor, what am I, then ? " asked I ; for in the loneliness of the mountain region where we walked, I could afford to throw off my disguise without risk.

" Ye'r a French officer of dragoons, and God bless ye ; but ye'r young to be at the trade. Arn't I right, now ? "

" Not very far from it, certainly, for I am a lieutenant of hussars," said I, with a little of that pride which we of the loose pelisse always feel on the mention of our corps.

" I knew it well all along," said he, coolly ; " the way you stood in the room, your step as you walked, and, above all, how ye believed me when I spoke of the spring-tides, and the moon only in her second quarter, I saw you never was a sailor, anyhow. And so I set a thinking what you were. You were too silent for a pedlar, and your hands were too white to be in the smuggling trade ; but when I saw your boots, I had the secret at once, and knew ye were one of the French army that landed the other day at Killala."

"It was stupid enough of me not to have remembered the boots!" said I, laughing.

"Arrah, what use would it be?" replied he; "sure ye'r too straight in the back, and your walk is too reg'lar, and your toes turns in too much, for a sailor; the very way you hould a switch in your hand would betray you!"

"So it seems, then, I must try some other disguise," said I, "if I'm to keep company with people as shrewd as you are."

"You needn't," said he, shaking his head doubtfully; "any that wants to betray ye wouldn't find it hard."

I was not much flattered by the depreciating tone in which he dismissed my efforts at personation, and walked on for some time without speaking.

"Yez came too late, four months too late," said he, with a sorrowful gesture of the hands. "When the Wexford boys was up, and the Kildare chaps, and plenty more ready to come in from the North, then, indeed, a few thousand French down here in the West would have made a differ; but what's the good in it now? The best men we had are hanged or in gaol; some are frightened; more are traitors! 'Tis too late—too late!"

"But not too late for a large force landing in the North, to rouse the island to another effort for liberty."

"Who would be the gin'ral?" asked he, suddenly.

"Napper Tandy, your own countryman," replied I, proudly.

"I wish ye luck of him,!" said he, with a bitter laugh; "'tis more like mocking us than anything else the French does be, with the chaps they sent here to be gin'rals. Sure it isn't Napper Tandy, nor a set of young lawyers like Tone and the rest of them, we wanted. It was men that knew how to drill and manage troops—fellows that was used to fightin'; so that when they said a thing, we might believe that they understhood it, at laste. I'm ould enough to remimber the "Wild Geese,' as they used to call them—the fellows that ran away from this to take sarvice in France; and I remember, too, the sort of men the French were that came over to inspect them—soldiers, real soldiers, every inch of them. And a fine sarvice it was. Volte-face!" cried he, holding himself erect, and shouldering his stick like a musket, "marche! Ha, ha! ye didn't think that was in me; but I was at the thrade long before you were born."

" How is this?" said I, in amazement; "you were not in the French army?"

" Wasn't I, though ? maybe I didnt get that stick there." And he bared his breast as he spoke, to show the cicatrix of an old flesh-wound from a Highlander's bayonet. " I was at Fontenoy!"

The last few words he uttered with a triumphant pride that I shall never forget. As for me, the mere name was magical. "Fontenoy" was like one of those great words which light up a whole page of history; and it almost seemed impossible that I should see before me a soldier of that glorious battle.

"Aye, faith!" he added, " 'tis more than fifty, 'tis nigh sixty years now since that, and I remember it as if it was yesterday. I was in the regiment 'Tourville ;' I was re-cruited for the 'Dillon,' but they scattered us about among the other corps afterwards, because we used now and then to be fighting and quarrellin' among one another. Well, it was the Dillons that gained the battle ; for after the English was in the village of Fontenoy, and the French was falling back upon the heights near the wood—arrah, what's the name of the wood? Sure, I'll forget my own name next. Aye, to be sure, Verzon—the 'Wood of Ver-zon.' Major Jodillon—that's what the French called him, but his name was Joe Dillon—turned an eight-pounder, short round into a little yard of a farm-house, and making a breach for the gun, he opened a dreadful fire on the English column. It was loaded with grape, and at half musket range, so you may think what a peppering they got. At last the column halted and lay down ; and Joe seen an officer ride off to the rear, to bring up artillery to silence our guns. A few minutes more and it would be all over with us. So Joe shouts out as loud as he could, ' Cavalry there ! tell off by threes, and prepare to charge.' I needn't tell you that the divil a horse nor a rider was within a mile of us at the time ; but the English didn't know that, and, hearin' the order, up they jumps, and we heerd the word passin', 'Prepare to receive cavalry.' They formed square at once, and the same minute we plumped into them with such a charge as tore a lane right through the middle of them. Before they could recover, we opened a platoon fire on their flank ; they staggered, broke, and at last fell back in disorder upon Aeth, with the whole of the French army after them. Such firin'— grape, round-shot, and musketry—I never seed afore, and we all shouting like divils, for it was more like a hunt nor

anything else; for ye see the Dutch never came up, but
left the English to do all the work themselves, and that's
the reason they couldn't form, for they had no supportin'
colum'.

"It was then I got that stick of the bayonet, for there
was such runnin' that we only thought of pelting after
them as hard as we could; but ye see, there's nothin' so
treacherous as a Highlander. I was just behind one, and
had my sword-point between his bladebones ready to run
him through, when he turned short about, and run his
bayonet into me under the short ribs, and that was all I
saw of the battle; for I bled till I fainted, and never knew
more of what happened. 'Tisn't by way of making little
of Frenchmen I say it, for I sarved too long wid them for
that—but sorra taste of that victory ever they'd see if it
wasn't for the Dillons, and Major Joe that commanded
them! The English knows it well, too! Maybe, they don't
do us many a spite for it to this very day!"

"And what became of you after that?"

"That same summer I came over to Scotland with the
young Prince Charles, and was at the battle of Preston-
pans afterwards! and, what's worse, I was at Culloden!
Oh, that was the terrible day. We were dead bate before
we began the battle. We were on the march from one
o'clock the night before, under the most dreadful rain ever
ye seen! We lost our way twice, and after four hours of
hard marching, we found ourselves opposite a mill-dam we
crossed early that same morning; for the guides led us all
astray! Then came ordhers to wheel about face and go
back again; and back we went, cursing the blaguards that
deceaved us, and almost faintin' with hunger. Some of us
had nothing to eat for two days, and the Prince, I seen
myself, had only a brown bannock to a wooden measure
of whiskey for his own breakfast. Well, it's no use talking; we were bate, and we retreated to Inverness that
night, and next morning we surrendered and laid down
our arms—that is the ' Regiment du Tournay ' and the
' Voltiguers de Metz,' the corps I was in myself."

"And did you return to France?"

"No; I made my way back to Ireland, and after loiter-
in' about home some time, and not liking the ways of
turning to work again, I took sarvice with one Mister
Brooke, of Castle Brooke, in Fermanagh, a young man
that was just come of age, and as great a divil, God forgive me, as ever was spawned. He was a Protestant, but
he didn't care much about one side or the other, but only

wanted divarsion and his own fun out of the world ; and
faix he took it, too ! He had plenty of money, was a fine
man to look at, and had courage to face a lion !

" The fiist place we went to was Aix-la-Chapelle, for
Mr. Brooke was named something—I forget what—to Lord
Sandwich, that was going there as an Ambassador. It
was a grand life there while it lasted. Such liveries, such
coaches, such elegant dinners every day, I never saw even
in Paris. But my master was soon sent away for a piece
of wildness he did. There was an ould Austrian there—
a Count Riedensegg was his name—and he was always
plottin' and schamin' with this, that, and the other ; buyin'
up the sacrets of others, and gettin' at their private papers
one way or the other ; and at last he begins to thry the
same game with us ; and as he saw that Mr. Brooke was
very fond of high play, and would bet anything one offered
him, the ould Count sends for a great gambler from Vienna,
the greatest villain, they say, that ever touched a card.
Ye may have heerd of him, tho' 'twas long ago that he
lived, for he was well known in them times. He was the
Baron von Breckendorf, and a great friend afterwards of
the Prince Ragint and all the other blaguards in London.

" Well, sir, the Baron arrives in great state, with despatches, they said, but sorrow other despatch he carried
nor some packs of marked cards, and a dice-box that could
throw sixes whenever ye wanted; and he puts up at the
Grand Hotel, with all his servants in fine liveries and as
much state as a prince. That very day Mr. Brooke dined
with the Count, and in the evening himself and the Baron
sits down to the cards; and, pretending to be only playin'
for silver, they were bettin' a hundred guineas on every
game.

"I always heerd that my master was cute with the
cards, and that few was equal to him in any game with
paste-board or ivory; but, be my conscience, he met his
match now, for if it was ould Nick was playin' he couldn't
do the thrick nater nor the Baron. He made everything
come up just like magic: if he wanted a seven of diamonds, or an ace of spades, or the knave of clubs, there it
was for you.

" Most gentlemen would have lost temper at seein' the
luck so dead agin' them, and everything goin' so bad; but
my master only smiled, and kept muttering to himself,
' Faix, its beautiful; by my conscience its elegant; I never
saw anybody could do it like that.' At last the Baron
stops and asks, ' What is it he's saying to himself?' ' I'll

tell you by and by,' says my master, 'when we're done playing; and so on they went, betting higher and higher, till at last the stakes wasn't very far from a thousand pounds on a single card. At the end, Mr. Brooke lost everything, and in the last game, by way of generosity, the Baron says to him, 'Double or quit?' and he tuk it.

"This time luck stood to my master, and he turned the queen of hearts; and as there was only one card could beat him, the game was all as one as his own. The Baron takes up the pack, and begins to deal. 'Wait,' says my master, leaning over the table, and talking in a whisper; 'wait,' says he; 'what are ye doin' there wid your thumb?' for sure enough he had his thumb dug hard into the middle of the pack.

"'Do you mane to insult me?' says the Baron, getting mighty red, and throwing down the cards on the table. 'Is that what you're at?'

"Go on with the deal,' says Mr. Brooke, quietly; 'but listen to me,' and here he dropped his voice to a whisper, 'as sure as you turn the king of hearts, I'll send a bullet through your skull! Go on, now, and don't rise from that seat till you've finished the game.' Faix he just did as he was bid; he turned a little two or three of diamonds, and gettin' up from the table, he left the room, and the next morning there was no more seen of him in Aix-la-Chapelle. But that wasn't the end of it; for scarce was the Baron two posts on his journey when my master sends in his name, and says he wants to speak to Count Riedensegg. There was a long time and a great debatin', I believe, whether they'd let him in or not; for the Count couldn't make if it was mischief he was after; but at last he was ushered into the bed-room where the other was in bed.

"'Count,' says he, after he fastened the door, and saw that they was alone, 'Count, you tried a dirty thrick with that dirty spalpeen of a Baron—an ould blaguard that's as well known as Freney the robber—but I forgive you for it all, for you did it in the way of business. I know well what you was afther; you wanted a peep at our despatches—there, ye needn't look cross and angry—why wouldn't ye do it, just as the Baron always took a sly glance at my cards before he played his own. Well, now, I'm just in the humour to sarve you. They're not trating me as they ought here, and I'm going away, and if you'll give me a few letthers to some of the pretty women in Vienna, Katinka Batthyani, and Amalia Gradoffsky, and one or two

men in the best set, I'll send you in return something will
surprise you.'

" It was after a long time and great batin' about the
bush, that the ould Count came in; but the sight of a
sacret cypher did the business, and he consented.

" 'There it is,' says Mr. Brooke, 'there's the whole
key to our correspondence; study it well, and I'll bring
you a sacret despatch in the evening—something that will
surprise you.'

" ' Ye will—will ye?' says the Count.

" ' On the honour of an Irish gentleman, I will,' says
Mr. Brooke.

" The Count sits down on the spot and writes the letters to all the prencesses and countesses in Vienna, saying
that Mr. Brooke was the elegantest, and politest, and most
trusty young gentleman ever he met; and telling them to
treat him with every consideration.

" ' There will be another account of me,' says the master to me, ' by the post; but I'll travel faster, and give me
a fair start, and I ask no more.'

" And he was as good as his word, for he started that
evening for Vienna, without lave or license, and that's the
way he got dismissed from his situation."

" And did he break his promise to the Count, or did he
really send him any intelligence?"

" He kept his word, like a gentleman; he promised him
something that would surprise him, and so he did. He
sent him the weddin' of Ballyporeen in cypher. It took a
week to make out, and I suppose they've never got to the
right understandin' it yet."

" I'm curious to hear how he was received in Vienna,
after this," said I. " I suppose you accompanied him to
that city?"

" Troth I did, and a short life we led there;—but here
we are now, at the end of our journey. That's Father
Doogan's down there, that small, low, thatched house in
the hollow."

" A lonely spot, too. I don't see another near it for
miles on any side."

" Nor is there. His chapel is at Murrab, about three
miles off. My eyes isn't over good; but I don't think
there's any smoke coming out of the chimley."

" You are right—there is not."

" He's not at home, then, and that's a bad job for us, for
there's not another place to stop the night in."

" But there will be surely some one in the house."

"Most likely not; 'tis a brat of a boy from Murrah does be with him when he's at home, and I'm sure he's not there now."

This reply was not very cheering, nor was the prospect itself much brighter. The solitary cabin, to which we were approaching, stood in a rugged glen, the sides of which were covered with a low furze, intermixed here and there with the scrub of what once had been an oak forest. A brown, mournful tint was over everything—sky and landscape alike; and even the little stream of clear water that wound its twining course along took the same colour from the gravelly bed it flowed over. Not a cow nor sheep was to be seen, nor even a bird; all was silent and still.

"There's few would like to pass their lives down there, then!" said my companion, as if speaking to himself.

"I suppose the priest, like a soldier, has no choice in these matters."

"Sometimes he has, though. Father Doogan might have had the pick of the county, they say; but he chose this little quiet spot here. He's a friar of some ordher abroad, and when he came over, two or three years ago, he could only spake a little Irish, and, I believe, less English; but there wasn't his equal for other tongues in all Europe. They wanted him to stop and be the head of a college somewhere in Spain, but he wouldn't. 'There was work to do in Ireland,' he said, and there he'd go, and to the wildest and laste civilised bit of it besides; and ye see that he was not far out in his choice when he took Murrah."

"Is he much liked here by the people?"

"They'd worship him, if he'd let them, that's what it is; for if he has more larnin' and knowledge in his head than ever a bishop in Ireland, there's not a child in the barony his equal for simplicity. He that knows the names of the stars, and what they do be doing, and where the world's going, and what's comin' afther her, hasn't a thought for the wickedness of this life, no more than a sucking infant! He could tell you every crop to put in your ground from this to the day of judgment, and I don't think he'd know which end of the spade goes into the ground.

While we were thus talking, we reached the door, which, as well as the windows, was closely barred and fastened. The great padlock, however, on the former, with characteristic acuteness, was locked without being hasped,

so that, in a few seconds, my old guide had undone all the
fastenings, and we found ourselves under shelter.

A roomy kitchen, with a few cooking utensils, formed
the entrance hall; and as a small supply of turf stood in
one corner, my companion at once proceeded to make a
fire, congratulating me as he went on with the fact of our
being housed, for a long-threatening thunderstorm had
already burst, and the rain was now swooping along in
torrents.

While he was thus busied, I took a ramble through the
little cabin, curious to see something of the "interior" of
one whose life had already interested me. There were
but two small chambers, one at either side of the kitchen.
The first I entered was a bed-room, the only furniture
being a common bed, or a tressel like that of an hospital,
a little coloured print of St. Michael adorning the wall
overhead. The bed-covering was cleanly, but patched in
many places, and bespeaking much poverty, and the black
"soutane" of silk that hung against the wall seemed to
show long years of service. The few articles of any pretensions to comfort were found in the sitting-room, where a
small book-shelf with some well-thumbed volumes, and a
writing-table covered with papers, maps, and a few pencil-
drawings, appeared. All seemed as if he had just quitted
the spot a few minutes before; the pencil lay across a half-
finished sketch; two or three wild plants were laid within
the leaves of a little book on botany; and a chess problem, with an open book beside it, still waited for solution
on a little board, whose workmanship clearly enough
betrayed it to be by his own hands.

I inspected everything with an interest inspired by all I
had been hearing of the poor priest, and turned over the
little volumes of his humble library, to trace, if I might,
some clue to his habits in his readings. They were all,
however, of one cast and character—religious tracts and
offices, covered with annotations and remarks, and showing by many signs the most careful and frequent perusal.
It was easy to see that his taste for drawing or for chess
were the only dissipations he permitted himself to indulge.
What a strange life of privation, thought I, alone, and
companionless as he must be! and while speculating on the
sense of duty which impelled such a man to accept a post
so humble and unpromising, I perceived that on the wall
right opposite to me there hung a picture, covered by a
little curtain of green silk.

Curious to behold the saintly effigy so carefully en-

shrined, I drew aside the curtain, and what was my astonishment to find a little coloured sketch of a boy about
twelve years old, dressed in the tawdry and much-worn
uniform of a drummer. I started. Something flashed
suddenly across my mind, that the features, the dress, the
air, were not unknown to me. Was I awake, or were my
senses misleading me? I took it down and held it to the
light, and as well as my trembling hands permitted, I
spelled out, at the foot of the drawing, the words "Le
Petit Maurice, as I saw him last." Yes: it was my own
portrait, and the words were in the writing of my dearest
friend in the world, the Père Michel. Scarce knowing
what I did, I ransacked books and papers on every side,
to confirm my suspicions, and although his name was nowhere to be found, I had no difficulty in recognising his
hand, now so forcibly recalled to my memory.

Hastening into the kitchen, I told my guide, that I must
set out to Murrah at once, that it was, above all, important
that I should see the priest immediately. It was in vain
that he told me he was unequal to the fatigue of going
further, that the storm was increasing, the mountain torrents were swelling to a formidable size, that the path
could not be discovered after dark; I could not brook the
thought of delay, and would not listen to the detail of
difficulties. "I must see him and I will," were my answers
to every obstacle. If I were resolved on one side, he was
no less obstinate on the other; and after explaining with
patience all the dangers and hazards of the attempt, and
still finding me unconvinced, he boldly declared that I
might go alone, if I would, but that he would not leave
the shelter of a roof, such a night, for any one.

There was nothing in the shape of argument I did not
essay. I tried bribery, I tried menace, flattery, intimida-
tion, all—and all with the like result. "Wherever he is
to-night, he'll not leave it, that's certain," was the only
satisfaction he would vouchsafe, and I retired beaten from
the contest, and disheartened. Twice I left the cottage,
resolved to go alone and unaccompanied, but the utter
darkness of the night, the torrents of rain that beat
against my face, soon showed me the impracticability of
the attempt, and I retraced my steps crest-fallen and discomfited. The most intense curiosity to know how and
by what chances he had come to Ireland mingled with my
ardent desire to meet him. What stores of reminiscence
had we to interchange! Nor was it without pride that I
bethought me of the position I then held, an officer of a

hussar regiment, a soldier of more than one campaign, and high on the list for promotion. If I hoped, too, that many of the good father's prejudices against the career I followed would give way to the records of my own past life, I also felt how, in various respects, I had myself conformed to many of his notions. We should be dearer, closer friends than ever. This I knew and was sure of.

I never slept the whole night through: tired and weary as the day's journey had left me, excitement was still too strong for repose, and I walked up and down, lay for half an hour on my bed, rose to look out, and peer for coming dawn! Never did hours lag so lazily. The darkness seemed to last for an eternity, and when at last day did break, it was through the lowering gloom of skies still charged with rain, and an atmosphere loaded with vapour.

"This is a day for the chimney-corner, and thankful to have it we ought to be," said my old guide, as he replenished the turf fire, at which he was preparing our breakfast. "Father Doogan will be home here afore night, I'm sure, and as we have nothing better to do, I'll tell you some of our old adventures when I lived with Mr. Brooke. 'Twill sarve to pass the time, any way."

"I'm off to Murrah, as soon as I have eaten something," replied I.

" 'Tis little you know what a road it is," said he, smiling dubiously. " 'Tis four mountain rivers you'd have to cross, two of them, at least, deeper than your head, and there's the pass of Barnascorney, where you'd have to turn the side of a mountain, with a precipice hundreds of feet below you, and a wind blowing that would wreck a seventy-four! There's never a man in the barony would venture over the same path, with a storm ragin' from the nor'-west."

"I never heard of a man being blown away off a mountain," said I, laughing contemptuously.

"Arrah, didn't ye, then? then maybe ye never lived in parts where the heaviest ploughs and harrows that can be laid in the thatch of a cabin are flung here and there, like straws, and the strongest timbers torn out of the walls, and scattered for miles along the coast, like the spars of a shipwreck."

" But so long as a man has hands to grip with—'

" How ye talk! sure, when the wind can tear the strongest trees up by the roots; when it rolls big rocks fifty and a hundred feet out of their place; when the very shingle on the mountain-side is flyin' about like dust and sand, where would your grip be? It is not only on the mountains either, but down in the plains, aye, even in the narrowest glens, that the cattle lies down under shelter of the rocks; and many's the time a sheep, or even a heifer, is swept away off the cliffs into the sea."

With many an anecdote of storm and hurricane he seasoned our little meal of potatoes. Some curious enough, as illustrating the precautionary habits of a peasantry, who, on land, experience many of the vicissitudes supposed peculiar to the sea; others too miraculous for easy credence, but yet vouched for by him with every affirmative of truth. He displayed all his powers of agreeability and amusement, but his tales fell on unwilling ears, and when our meal was over I started up and began to prepare for the road.

"So you will go, will you?" said he, peevishly. "'Tis in your country to be obstinate, so I'll say nothing more; but maybe 'tis only into throubles you'd be running, after all!"

"I'm determined on it," said I, "and I only ask you to tell me what road to take."

"There is only one, so there is no mistakin' it; keep to the sheep path, and never leave it except at the torrents; you must pass them how ye can: and when ye come to four big rocks in the plain, leave them to your left, and keep the side of the mountain for two miles 'till ye see the smoke of the village underneath you. Murrah is a small place, and ye'll have to look out sharp, or maybe ye'll miss it."

"That's enough," said I, putting some silver in his hand as I pressed it. "We'll probably meet no more; good bye, and many thanks for your pleasant company."

"No, we're not like to meet again," said he, thoughtfully, "and that's the reason I'd like to give you a bit of advice. Hear me, now, said he, drawing closer and talking in a whisper; you can't go far in this country without being known; 'tisn't your looks alone, but your voice, and your tongue, will show what ye are. Get away out of it as fast as you can! there's thraitors in every cause, and there's chaps in Ireland would rather make money as informers than earn it by honest industry! Get over to the Scotch islands; get to Isla or Barra; get anywhere out of this for the time."

"Thanks for the counsel," said I, somewhat coldly, "I'll have time to think over it as I go along;" and with these words I set forth on my journey.

CHAPTER XXVII.

"THE CRANAGH."

I WILL not weary my reader with a narrative of my mountain walk, nor the dangers and difficulties which beset me on that day of storm and hurricane. Few as were the miles to travel, what with accidents, mistakes of the path, and the halts to take shelter, I only reached Murrah as the day was declining.

The little village, which consisted of some twenty cabins, occupied a narrow gorge between two mountains, and presented an aspect of greater misery than I had ever witnessed before, not affording even the humblest specimen of a house of entertainment. From some peasants that were lounging in the street I learned that " Father Doogan " had passed through two days before in company with a naval officer, whom they believed to be French. At least " he came from one of the ships in the Lough, and could speak no English." Since that the priest had not returned, and many thought that he had gone away for ever. This story varied in a few unimportant particulars. I heard from several, and also learned that a squadron of several sail had, for three or four days, been lying at the entrance of Lough Swilly, with, it was said, large reinforcements for the "army of independence." There was then no time to be lost; here was the very force which I had been sent to communicate with; there were the troops that should at that moment be disembarking. The success of my mission might all depend now on a little extra exertion, and so I at once engaged a guide to conduct me to the coast, and having fortified myself with a glass of mountain whiskey I felt ready for the road.

My guide could only speak a very little English; so that our way was passed in almost unbroken silence; and as, for security, he followed the least frequented paths, we scarcely met a living creature as we went. It was with a strange sense of half pride, half despondency, that I bethought me of my own position there—a Frenchman

alone, and separated from his countrymen—in a wild
mountain region of Ireland, carrying about him documents that, if detected, might peril his life ; involved in a
cause that had for its object the independence of a nation ;
and that, against the power of the mightiest kingdom in
Europe. An hour earlier or later, an accident by the way,
a swollen torrent, a chance impediment of any kind that
should delay me—and what a change might that produce
in the whole destiny of the world !

The despatches I carried conveyed instructions the most
precise and accurate: the places for combined action of the
two armies—information as to the actual state of parties,
and the condition of the native forces, was contained in
them. All that could instruct the newly-come generals, or
encourage them to decisive measures, were there ; and
yet, on what narrow contingencies did their safe arrival
depend ! It was thus, in exaggerating to myself the
part I played—in elevating my humble position into all
the importance of a high trust—that I sustained my
drooping spirits, and acquired energy to carry me through
fatigue and exhaustion. During that night, and the
greater part of the following day, we walked on, almost
without halt, scarcely eating, and, except by an occasional
glass of whiskey, totally unrefreshed; and I am free to
own, that my poor guide—a bare-legged youth of about
seventeen, without any of those high-sustaining illusions
which stirred within my heart—suffered far less either
from hunger or weariness than I did. So much for motives.
A shilling or two were sufficient to equalise the balance
against all the weight of my heroism and patriotic ardour together.

A bright sun, and a sharp wind from the north, had
succeeded to the lowering sky and heavy atmosphere of
the morning, and we travelled along with light hearts and
brisk steps, breasting the side of a steep ascent, from the
summit of which, my guide told me, I should behold the
sea—the sea ! not only the great plain on which I expected
to see our armament, but the link which bound me to my
country ! Suddenly, just as I turned the angle of a cliff, it
burst upon my sight—one vast mirror of golden splendour
—appearing almost at my feet ! In the yellow gleams of a
setting sun, long columns of azure-coloured light streaked
its calm surface, and tinged the atmosphere with a warm
and rosy hue. While I was lost in admiration of the picture, I heard the sound of voices close beneath me, and,
on looking down, saw two figures who, with telescope

16

in hand, were steadily gazing on a little bay that extended
towards the west.

At first, my attention was more occupied by the strangers
than by the object of their curiosity, and I remarked that
they were dressed and equipped like sportsmen, their guns
and game-bags lying against the rock behind them.

"Do you still think that they are hovering about the
coast, Tom?" said the elder of the two, "or are you not
convinced, at last, that I am right?"

"I believe you are," replied the other; "but it certainly did not look like it yesterday evening, with their
boats rowing ashore every half hour, signals flying, and
blue lights burning; all seemed to threaten a landing."

"If they ever thought of it they soon changed their
minds," said the former. "The defeat of their comrades
in the west, and the apathy of the peasantry here, would
have cooled down warmer ardour than theirs. There they
go, Tom. I only hope that they'll fall in with Warren's
squadron, and French insolence receive at sea the lesson
we failed to give them on land."

"Not so," rejoined the younger; "Humbert's capitula-
tion, and the total break up of the expedition, ought to
satisfy even your patriotism."

"It fell far short of it, then!" cried the other. "I'd
never have treated those fellows other than as bandits and
freebooters. "I'd have hanged them as highwaymen.
Theirs was less war than rapine; but what could you expect? I have been assured that Humbert's force consisted
of little other than liberated felons and galley-slaves—the
refuse of the worst population of Europe!"

Distracted with the terrible tidings I had overheard—
overwhelmed with the sight of the ships, now glistening
like bright specks on the verge of the horizon, I forgot my
own position—my safety—everything but the insult thus
cast upon my gallant comrades.

"Whoever said so was a liar, and a base coward, to
boot!" cried I, springing down from the height and con-
fronting them both where they stood. They started back,
and, seizing their guns, assumed an attitude of defence,
and then, quickly perceiving that I was alone—for the
boy had taken to flight as fast as he could—they stood
regarding me with faces of intense astonishment.

"Yes," said I, still boiling with passion, "you are two
to one, on your own soil besides, the odds you are best
used to; and yet I repeat it that he who asperses the character of General Humbert's force is a liar."

" He's French."

" No, he's Irish," muttered the elder.

" What signifies my country, sirs," cried I, passionately, " if I demand retraction for a falsehood."

" It signifies more than you think of, young man," said the elder, calmly, and without evincing even the slightest irritation in his manner. If you be a Frenchman born, the lenity of our government accords you the privilege of a prisoner of war. If you be only French by adoption, and a uniform, a harsher destiny awaits you."

" And who says I am a prisoner yet?" asked I, drawing myself up, and staring them steadily in the face.

" We should be worse men, and poorer patriots than you give us credit for, or we should be able to make you so," said he quietly : " but this is no time for ill-temper on either side. The expedition has failed. Well, if you will not believe me, read that. There, in that paper, you will see the official account of General Humbert's surrender at Boyle. The news is already over the length and breadth of the island ; even if you only landed last night I cannot conceive how you should be ignorant of it !" I covered my face with my hands to hide my emotion ; and he went on : " If you be French you have only to claim and prove your nationality, and you partake the fortunes of your countrymen."

" And if he be not," whispered the other, in a voice which, although low, I could still detect, " why should we give him up?"

" Hush, Tom, be quiet," replied the elder, " let him plead for himself."

" Let me see the newspaper," said I, endeavouring to seem calm and collected ; and taking it at the place he pointed out, I read the heading in capitals, " CAPITULA- TION OF GENERAL HUMBERT AND HIS WHOLE FORCE." I could see no more. I could not trace the details of so horrible a disaster, nor did I ask to know by what means it occurred. My attitude and air of apparent occupation, however, deceived the other ; and the elder, supposing that I was engaged in considering the paragraph, said, " You'll see the government proclamation on the other side ; a general amnesty to all under the rank of officers in the rebel army, who give up their arms within six days. The French to be treated as prisoners of war."

" Is he too late to regain the fleet?" whispered the younger.

" Of course he is. They are already hull down ; besides, who's to assist his escape, Tom? You forget the position he stands in."

"But I do not forget it," answered I, "and you need not be afraid that I will seek to compromise you, gentlemen. Tell me where to find the nearest justice of the peace, and I will go and surrender myself."

"It is your wisest and best policy," said the elder; "I am not in the commission, but a neighbour of mine is, and lives a few miles off, and, if you like, we'll accompany you to his house."

I accepted the offer, and soon found myself descending the steep path of the mountain in perfect good-fellowship with the two strangers. It is likely enough, if they had taken any peculiar pains to obliterate the memory of our first meeting, or if they had displayed any extraordinary efforts of conciliation, that I should have been on my guard against them; but their manners, on the contrary, was easy and unaffected in every respect. They spoke of the expedition sensibly and dispassionately, and while acknowledging that there were many things they would like to see altered in the English rule of Ireland, they were very averse from the desire of a foreign intervention to rectify them.

I avowed to them that we had been grossly deceived. That all the representations made to us depicted Ireland as a nation of soldiers, wanting only arms and military stores to rise as a vast army. That the peasantry were animated by one spirit, and the majority of the gentry willing to hazard everything on the issue of a struggle. Our Killala experiences, of which I detailed some, heartily amused them, and it was in a merry interchange of opinions that we now walked along together.

A cluster of houses, too small to be called a village, and known as the "Cranagh," stood in a little nook of the bay; and here they lived. They were brothers; and the elder held some small appointment in the revenue, which maintained them as bachelors in this cheap country. In a low conversation that passed between them it was agreed that they would detain me as their guest for that evening, and on the morrow accompany me to the magistrate's house, about five miles distant. I was not sorry to accept their hospitable offer. I longed for a few hours of rest and respite before embarking on another sea of troubles. The failure of the expedition, and the departure of the fleet, had overwhelmed me with grief, and I was in no mood to confront new perils.

If my new acquaintances could have read my inmost thoughts, their manner towards me could not have displayed more kindness or good-breeding. Not pressing me with questions on subjects where the greatest curiosity would have been permissible, they suffered me to tell only so much as I wished of our late plans; and, as if purposely to withdraw my thoughts from the unhappy theme of our defeat, led me to talk of France, and her career in Europe.

It was not without surprise that I saw how conversant the newspapers had made them with European politics, nor how widely different did events appear when viewed from afar off, and by the lights of another and different nationality. Thus all that we were doing on the Continent to propagate liberal notions, and promote the spread of freedom, seemed to their eyes but the efforts of an ambitious power to crush abroad what they had annihilated at home, and extend their own influence in disseminating doctrines, all to revert, one day or other, to some grand despotism, whenever the man arose capable to exercise it. The elder would not even concede to us that we were fit for freedom.

"You are glorious fellows at destroying an old edifice," said he, "but sorry architects when comes the question of rebuilding; and as to liberty, your highest notion of it is an occasional anarchy. Like schoolboys, you will bear any tyranny for ten years, to have ten days of a 'barring out' afterward."

I was not much flattered by these opinions; and, what was worse, I could not get them out of my head all night afterwards. Many things I had never doubted about now kept puzzling and confounding me, and I began, for the first time, to know the misery of the struggle between implicit obedience and conviction.

CHAPTER XXVIII.

SOME NEW ACQUAINTANCES.

I WENT to bed at night in all apparent health; save from the flurry and excitement of an anxious mind, I was in no respect different from my usual mood; and yet when I awoke next morning, my head was distracted with a racking pain, cramps were in all my limbs, and I could not turn or even move without intense suffering. The long exposure to rain, while my mind was in a condition of extreme excitement, had brought on an attack of fever, and before evening set in, I was raving in wild delirium. Every scene I had passed through, each eventful incident of my life, came flashing in disjointed portions through my poor brain; and I raved away of France, of Germany, of the dreadful days of terror, and the fearful orgies of the "Revolution." Scenes of strife and struggle — the terrible conflicts of the streets—all rose before me; and the names of every bloodstained hero of France now mingled with the obscure titles of Irish insurrection.

What narratives of my early life I may have given— what stories I may have revealed of my strange career, I cannot tell; but the interest my kind hosts took in me grew stronger every day. There was no care nor kindness they did not lavish on me. Taking alternate nights to sit up with me, they watched beside my bed, like brothers. All that affection could give they rendered me; and even from their narrow fortunes they paid a physician, who came from a distant town to visit me. When I was sufficiently recovered to leave my bed, and sit at the window, or stroll slowly in the garden, I became aware of the full extent to which their kindness had carried them, and in the precautions for secresy I saw the peril to which my presence exposed them. From an excess of delicacy towards me, they did not allude to the subject, nor show the slightest uneasiness about the matter; but day by day some little circumstance would occur, some slight and trivial fact reveal the state of anxiety they lived in.

They were averse, too, from all discussion of late events, and either answered my questions vaguely or with a certain reserve; and when I hinted at my hope of being soon able to appear before a magistrate and establish my claim as a French citizen, they replied that the moment was an unfavourable one ; the lenity of the government had latterly been abused ; their gracious intentions misstated and perverted ; that, in fact, a reaction towards severity had occurred, and military law and courts-martial were summarily disposing of cases that a short time back would have received the mildest sentences of civil tribunals. It was clear, from all they said, that if the rebellion was suppressed, the insurrectionary feeling was not extinguished, and that England was the very reverse of tranquil on the subject of Ireland.

It was to no purpose that I repeated my personal indifference to all these measures of severity; that in my capacity as a Frenchman and an officer I stood exempt from all the consequences they alluded to. Their reply was, that in times of trouble and alarm things were done which quieter periods would never have sanctioned, and that indiscreet and over-zealous men would venture on acts that neither law nor justice could substantiate. In fact, they gave me to believe, that such was the excitement of the moment, such the embittered vengeance of those whose families or fortunes had suffered by the rebellion, that no reprisals would be thought too heavy, nor any harshness too great, for those who aided the movement.

Whatever I might have said against the injustice of this proceeding, in my secret heart I had to confess that it was only what might have been expected; and coming from a country where it was enough to call a man an aristocrat, and then cry "a la lanterne," I saw nothing unreasonable in it all.

My friends advised me, therefore, instead of preferring any formal claim to immunity, to take the first occasion of escaping to America, whence I could not fail, later on, of returning to France. At first, the counsel only irritated me, but by degrees, as I came to think more calmly and seriously of the difficulties, I began to regard it in a different light; and at last I fully concurred in the wisdom of the advice, and resolved on adopting it.

To sit on the cliffs, and watch the ocean for hours, became now the practice of my life—to gaze from daybreak almost to the falling of night over the wide expanse of sea, straining my eyes at each sail, and conjecturing to what

distant shore they were tending. The hopes which at
first sustained at last deserted me, as week after week
passed over, and no prospect of escape appeared. The
life of inactivity gradually depressed my spirits, and I fell
into a low and moping condition, in which my hours rolled
over without thought or notice. Still, I returned each
day to my accustomed spot, a lofty peak of rock that stood
over the sea, and from which the view extended for miles
on every side. There, half hid in the wild heath, I used
to lie for hours long, my eyes bent upon the sea, but my
thoughts wandering away to a past that never was to be
renewed, and a future I was never destined to experience.

Although late in the autumn, the season was mild and
genial, and the sea calm and waveless, save along the
shore, where, even in the stillest weather, the great
breakers came tumbling in with a force, independent of
storm; and listening to their booming thunder, I have
dreamed away hour after hour unconsciously. It was one
day, as I lay thus, that my attention was caught by the
sight of three large vessels on the very verge of the
horizon. Habit had now given me a certain acuteness,
and I could perceive from their height and size that they
were ships of war. For a while they seemed as if steer-
ing for the entrance of the "lough," but afterwards they
changed their course, and headed towards the west. At
length they separated, and one of smaller size, and probably a frigate from her speed, shot forward beyond the
rest, and, in less than half an hour, disappeared from
view. The other two gradually sunk beneath the horizon,
and not a sail was to be seen over the wide expanse.
While speculating on what errand the squadron might be
employed, I thought I could hear the deep and rolling
sound of distant cannonading. My ear was too practised
in the thundering crash of the breakers along shore to
confound the noises; and as I listened I fancied that I
could distinguish the sound of single guns from the louder
roar of a whole broadside. This could not mean saluting,
nor was it likely to be a mere exercise of the fleet. They
were not times when much powder was expended unpro-
fitably. Was it then an engagement? But with what or
whom? Tandy's expedition, as it was called, had long
since sailed, and must ere this have been captured or safe
in France. I tried a hundred conjectures to explain the
mystery, which now, from the long continuance of the
sounds, seemed to denote a desperately contested engagement. It was not till after three hours that the cannon-

ading ceased, and then I could descry a thick dark canopy of smoke that hung hazily over one spot in the horizon, as if marking out the scene of the struggle. With what aching, torturing anxiety I burned to know what had happened, and with which side rested the victory!

Well habituated to hear of the English as victors in every naval engagement, I yet went on hoping against Hope itself, that Fortune might for once have favoured us; nor was it till the falling night prevented my being able to trace out distant objects, that I could leave the spot and turn homewards. With wishes so directly opposed to theirs, I did not venture to tell my two friends what I had witnessed, nor trust myself to speak on a subject where my feelings might have betrayed me into unseemly expressions of my hopes. I was glad to find that they knew nothing of the matter, and talked away indifferently of other subjects. By daybreak the next morning I was at my post, a sharp nor'wester blowing, and a heavy sea rolling in from the Atlantic. Instinctively carrying my eyes to the spot where I had heard the cannonade, I could distinctly see the tops of spars, as if the upper rigging of some vessels, beyond the horizon. Gradually they rose higher and higher, till I could detect the yard-arms and cross-trees, and finally the great hulls of five vessels that were bearing towards me.

For above an hour I could see their every movement, as with all canvas spread they held on majestically towards the land, when at length a lofty promontory of the bay intervened, and they were lost to my view. I jumped to my legs at once, and set off down the cliff to reach the headland, from whence an uninterrupted prospect extended. The distance was greater than I had supposed, and in my eagerness to take a direct line to it, I got entangled in difficult gorges among the hills, and impeded by mountain torrents which often compelled me to go back a considerable distance; it was already late in the afternoon as I gained the crest of a ridge over the Bay of Lough Swilly. Beneath me lay the calm surface of the lough, landlocked and still; but further out seaward there was a sight that made my very limbs tremble, and sickened my heart as I beheld it. There was a large frigate, that, with studding-sails set, stood boldly up the bay, followed by a dismasted three-decker, at whose mizen floated the ensign of England over the French "tricolour." Several other vessels were grouped about the offing, all of them displaying English colours.

The dreadful secret was out. There had been a tremendous sea-fight, and the Hoche, of seventy-four guns, was the sad spectacle which, with shattered sides and ragged rigging, I now beheld entering the bay. Oh, the humiliation of that sight! I can never forget it. And although on all the surrounding hills scarcely fifty country-people were assembled, I felt as if the whole of Europe were spectators of our defeat. The flag I had always believed triumphant now hung ignominiously beneath the ensign of the enemy, and the decks of our noble ship were crowded with the uniforms of English sailors and marines.

The blue water surged and spouted from the shot holes as the great hull loomed heavily from side to side, and broken spars and ropes still hung over the side as she went, a perfect picture of defeat. Never was disaster more legibly written. I watched her till the anchor dropped, and then, in a burst of emotion, I turned away, unable to endure more. As I hastened homeward I met the elder of my two hosts coming to meet me, in considerable anxiety. He had heard of the capture of the Hoche, but his mind was far more intent on another and less important event. Two men had just been at his cottage with a warrant for my arrest. The document bore my name and rank, as well as a description of my appearance, and significantly alleged, that, although Irish by birth, I affected a foreign accent for the sake of concealment.

"There is no chance of escape, now," said my friend; "we are surrounded with spies on every hand. My advice is, therefore, to hasten to Lord Cavan's quarters—he is now at Letterkenny—and give yourself up as a prisoner. There is at least the chance of your being treated like the rest of your countrymen. I have already provided you with a horse and a guide, for I must not accompany you myself. Go, then, Maurice. We shall never see each other again; but we'll not forget you, nor do we fear that you will forget us. My brother could not trust himself to take leave of you, but his best wishes and prayers go with you."

Such were the last words my kind-hearted friend spoke to me; nor do I know what reply I made, as overcome by emotion, my voice became thick and broken. I wanted to tell all my gratitude, and yet could say nothing. To this hour I know not with what impression of me he went away. I can only assert, that in all the long career of vicissitudes of a troubled and adventurous life, these brothers have occupied the chosen spot of my affection, for everything that was disinterested in kindness and generous in good feeling.

They have done more; for they have often reconciled me to a world of harsh injustice and illiberality, by remembering that two such exceptions existed, and that others may have experienced what fell to my lot.

For a mile or two my way lay through the mountains, but after reaching the high road I had not proceeded far when I was overtaken by a jaunting-car, on which a gentleman was seated, with his leg supported by a cushion, and bearing all the signs of a severe injury.

" Keep the near side of the way, sir, I beg of you," cried he; "I have a broken leg, and am excessively uneasy when a horse passes close to me."

I touched my cap in salute, and immediately turned my horse's head to comply with his request.

" Did you see that, George?" cried another gentleman, who sat on the opposite side of the vehicle; "did you remark that fellow's salute? My life on't, he's a French soldier."

" Nonsense, man; he's the steward of a Clyde smack, or a clerk in a counting-house," said the first, in a voice which, though purposely low, my quick hearing could catch perfectly.

" Are we far from Letterkenny just now, sir?" said the other, addressing me.

" I believe about five miles," said I, with a prodigious effort to make my pronunciation pass muster.

" You're a stranger in these parts, I see, sir," rejoined he, with a cunning glance at his friend, while he added, lower, " Was I right, Hill?"

Although seeing that all concealment was now hopeless, I was in nowise disposed to plead guilty at once, and therefore, with a cut of my switch, pushed my beast into a sharp canter to get forward.

My friends, however, gave chase, and now the jaunting-car, notwithstanding the sufferings of the invalid, was clattering after me at about nine miles an hour. At first I rather enjoyed the malice of the penalty their curiosity was costing, but as I remembered that the invalid was not the chief offender, I began to feel compunction at the severity of the lesson, and drew up to a walk.

They at once shortened their pace, and came up beside me.

" A clever hack you're riding, sir," said the inquisitive man.

"Not so bad for an animal of this country," said I, superciliously.

"Oh, then, what kind of a horse are you accustomed to?" asked he, half insolently.

"The Limousin," said I, coolly, "what we always mount in our hussar regiments in France."

"And you are a French soldier, then," cried he, in evident astonishment at my frankness.

"At your service, sir," said I, saluting; "a lieutenant of hussars; and if you are tormented by any further curiosity concerning me, I may as well relieve you by stating that I am proceeding to Lord Cavan's head-quarters to surrender as a prisoner."

"Frank enough that!" said he of the broken leg, laughing heartily as he spoke. "Well, sir," said the other, "you are, as your countrymen would call it, ' bien venu,' for we are bound in that direction ourselves, and will be happy to have your company."

One piece of tact my worldly experience had profoundly impressed upon me, and that was, the necessity of always assuming an air of easy unconcern in every circumstance of doubtful issue. There was quite enough of difficulty in the present case to excite my anxiety, but I rode along beside the jaunting-car, chatting familiarly with my new acquaintances, and, I believe, without exhibiting the slightest degree of uneasiness regarding my own position.

From them I learned so much as they had heard of the late naval engagement. The report was that Bompard's fleet had fallen in with Sir John Warren's squadron; and having given orders for his fastest sailers to make the best of their way to France, had, with the Hoche, the Loire, and the Resolve, given battle to the enemy. These had all been captured, as well as four others which fled, two alone of the whole succeeding in their escape. I think now that, grievous as these tidings were, there was nothing of either boastfulness or insolence in the tone in which they were communicated to me. Every praise was accorded to Bompard for skill and bravery, and the defence was spoken of in terms of generous eulogy. The only trait of acrimony that showed itself in the recital was a regret that a number of Irish rebels should have escaped in the Biche, one of the smaller frigates; and several emissaries of the people, who had been deputed to the admiral, were also alleged to have been on board of that vessel.

"You are sorry to have missed your friend the priest of Murrah," said Hill, jocularly.

" Yes, by George, that fellow should have graced a gallows if I had been lucky enough to have taken him."

" What was his crime, sir?" asked I, with seeming unconcern.

"Nothing more than exciting to rebellion a people with whom he had no tie of blood or kindred! He was a Frenchman, and devoted himself to the cause of Ireland, as they call it, from pure sympathy——"

" And a dash of Popery," broke in Hill.

" It's hard to say even that; my own opinion is, that French Jacobinism cares very little for the Pope. Am I right, young gentleman—you don't go very often to confession?"

" I should do so less frequently if I were to be subjected to such a system of interrogatory as yours," said I, tartly.

They both took my impertinent speech in good part, and laughed heartily at it; and thus, half amicably, half in earnest, we entered the little town of Letterkenny, just as night was falling.

"If you'll be our guest for this evening, sir," said Hill, " we shall be happy to have your company."

I accepted the invitation, and followed them into the inn.

CHAPTER XXIX.

"THE BREAKFAST AT LETTERKENNY."

EARLY the next morning, a messenger arrived from the Cranagh, with a small packet of my clothes and effects, and a farewell letter from the two brothers. I had but time to glance over its contents when the tramp of feet and the buzz of voices in the street attracted me to the window, and on looking out I saw a long line of men, two abreast, who were marching along as prisoners, a party of dismounted dragoons keeping guard over them on either side, followed by a strong detachment of marines. The poor fellows looked sad and crest-fallen enough. Many of them wore bandages on their heads and limbs, the tokens of the late struggle. Immediately in front of the inn door stood a group of about thirty persons; they were the staff of the English force, and the officers of our fleet, all mingled together, and talking away with the greatest air of unconcern. I was struck by remarking that all our seamen, though prisoners, saluted the officers as they passed, and in the glances interchanged I thought I could read a world of sympathy and encouragement. As for the officers, like true Frenchmen they bore themselves as though it were one of the inevitable chances of war, and, however vexatious for the moment, not to be thought of as an event of much importance. The greater number of them belonged to the army, and I could see the uniforms of the staff, artillery and dragoons, as well as the less distinguished costume of the line.

Perhaps they carried the affectation of indifference a little too far, and in the lounging ease of their attitude, and the cool unconcern with which they puffed their cigars, displayed an over-anxiety to seem unconcerned. That the English were piqued at their bearing was still more plain to see; and indeed, in the sullen looks of the one, and the careless gaiety of the other party, a stranger might readily have mistaken the captor for the captive.

My two friends of the evening before were in the midst

of the group. He who had questioned me so sharply now wore a general officer's uniform, and seemed to be the chief in command. As I watched him I heard him addressed by an officer, and now saw that he was no other than Lord Cavan himself, while the other was a well-known magistrate and country gentleman, Sir George Hill.

The sad procession took almost half an hour to defile; and then came a long string of country cars and carts, with sea-chests and other stores belonging to our officers, and, last of all, some eight or ten ammunition waggons and gun-carriages, over which an English union-jack now floated in token of conquest.

There was nothing like exultation or triumph exhibited by the peasantry as this pageant passed. They gazed in silent wonderment at the scene, and looked like men who scarcely knew whether the result boded more of good or evil to their own fortunes. While keenly scrutinising the looks and bearing of the bystanders, I received a summons to meet the general and his party at breakfast.

Although the occurrence was one of the most pleasurable incidents of my life, which brought me once more into intercourse with my comrades and my countrymen, I should perhaps pass it over with slight mention, were it not that it made me witness to a scene which has since been recorded in various different ways, but of whose exact details I profess to be an accurate narrator.

After making a tour of the room, saluting my comrades, answering questions here, putting others there, I took my place at the long table, which, running the whole length of the apartment, was indiscriminately occupied by French and English, and found myself with my back to the fireplace, and having directly in front of me a man of about thirty-three or thirty-four years of age, dressed in the uniform of a chef de brigade ; light haired and blue eyed, he bore no resemblance whatever to those around him, whose dark faces and black beards proclaimed them of a foreign origin. There was an air of mildness in his manner, mingled with a certain impetuosity that betrayed itself in the rapid glances of his eye, and I could plainly mark that while the rest were perfectly at their ease, he was constrained, restless, watching eagerly everything that went forward about him, and showing unmistakeably a certain anxiety and distrust, widely differing from the gay and careless indifference of his comrades. I was curious to hear his name, and on asking, learned that he was the Chef de Brigade

Smith, an Irishman by birth, but holding a command in the French service.

I had but asked the question, when pushing back his chair from the table he arose suddenly, and stood stiff and erect, like a soldier on parade.

"Well, sir, I hope you are satisfied with your inspection of me," cried he, and sternly, addressing himself to some one behind my back. I turned and perceived it was Sir George Hill, who stood in front of the fire leaning on his stick. Whether he replied or not to this rude speech I am unable to say, but the other walked leisurely round the table and came directly in front of him. "You know me now, sir, I presume," said he, in the same imperious voice, "or else this uniform has made a greater change in my appearance than I knew of."

"Mr. Tone!" said Sir George, in a voice, scarcely above a whisper.

"Ay, sir, Wolfe Tone; there is no need of secrecy here; Wolfe Tone, your old college acquaintance in former times, but now chef de brigade in the service of France."

"This is a very unexpected, a very unhappy meeting, Mr. Tone," said Hill, feelingly; "I sincerely wish you had not recalled the memory of our past acquaintance. My duty gives me no alternative."

"Your duty, or I mistake much, can have no concern with me, sir," cried Tone, in a more excited voice.

"I ask for nothing better than to be sure of this, Mr. Tone," said Sir George, moving slowly towards the door.

"You would treat me like an emigré rentré," cried Tone, passionately, "but I am a French subject and a French officer!"

"I shall be well satisfied if others take the same view of your case, I assure you," said Hill, as he gained the door.

"You'll not find me unprepared for either event, sir," rejoined Tone, following him out of the room, and banging the door angrily behind him.

For a moment or two the noise of voices was heard from without, and several of the guests, English and French, rose from the table, eagerly inquiring what had occurred, and asking for an explanation of the scene, when suddenly the door was flung wide open, and Tone appeared between two policemen, his coat off, and his wrists enclosed in handcuffs.

"Look here, comrades," he cried in French; "this is another specimen of English politeness and hospitality

After all," added he, with a bitter laugh, "they have no designation in all their heraldry as honourable as these fetters, when worn for the cause of freedom! Good bye, comrades; we may never meet again, but don't forget how we parted!"

These were the last words he uttered, when the door was closed, and he was led forward under charge of a strong force of police and military. A postchaise was soon seen to pass the windows at speed, escorted by dragoons, and we saw no more of our comrade.

The incident passed even more rapidly than I write it. The few words spoken, the hurried gestures, the passionate exclamations, are yet all deeply graven on my memory; and I can recall every little incident of the scene, and every feature of the locality wherein it occurred. With true French levity many reseated themselves at the breakfast-table; whilst others, with perhaps as little feeling, but more of curiosity, discussed the event, and sought for an explanation of its meaning.

"Then what's to become of Tiernay," cried one, "if it be so hard to throw off this 'coil of Englishmen?' His position may be just as precarious."

"That is exactly what has occurred," said Lord Cavan; "a warrant for his apprehension has just been put into my hands, and I deeply regret that the duty should violate that of hospitality, and make my guest my prisoner."

"May I see this warrant, my lord?" asked I.

"Certainly, sir. Here it is; and here is the information on oath through which it was issued, sworn to before three justices of the peace by a certain Joseph Dowall, late an officer in the rebel forces, but now a pardoned approver of the Crown; do you remember such a man, sir?"

I bowed, and he went on.

"He would seem a precious rascal; but such characters become indispensable in times like these. After all, M. Tiernay, my orders are only to transmit you to Dublin under safe escort, and there is nothing either in my duty or in your position to occasion any feeling of unpleasantness between us. Let us have a glass of wine together."

I responded to this civil proposition with politeness, and after a slight interchange of leave-takings with some of my newly-found comrades, I set out for Derry on a jaunting car, accompanied by an officer and two policemen, affecting to think very little of a circumstance which, in reality, the more I reflected over, the more serious I deemed it.

CHAPTER XXX.

SCENE IN THE ROYAL BARRACKS.

IT would afford me little pleasure to write, and doubtless
my readers less to read, my lucubrations as I journeyed
along towards Dublin. My thoughts seldom turned from
myself and my own fortunes, nor were they cheered by
the scene through which I travelled. The season was a
backward and wet one, and the fields, partly from this
cause, and partly from the people being engaged in
the late struggle, lay untilled and neglected. Groups of
idle, lounging peasants stood in the villages, or loitered
on the high roads as we passed, sad, ragged-looking, and
wretched. They seemed as if they had no heart to resume their wonted life of labour, but were waiting for
some calamity to close their miserable existence. Strongly
in contrast with this were the air and bearing of the yeo-
manry and militia detachments with whom we occasionally
came up. Quite forgetting how little creditable to some
of them, at least, were the events of the late campaign,
they gave themselves the most intolerable airs of heroism,
and in their drunken jollity, and reckless abandonment,
threatened, I know not what—utter ruin to France and
all Frenchmen. Bonaparte was the great mark of all
their sarcasms, and, from some cause or other, seemed to
enjoy a most disproportioned share of their dislike and
derision.

At first it required some effort of constraint on my part
to listen to this ribaldry in silence ; but prudence, and a
little sense, taught me the safer lesson of "never mind-
ing," and so I affected to understand nothing that was
said in a spirit of insult or offence.

On the night of the 7th of November we drew nigh to
Dublin; but instead of entering the capital, we halted at
a small village outside of it, called Chapelizod. Here a
house had been fitted up for the reception of French prisoners, and I found myself, if not in company, at least
under the same roof, with my countrymen.

Nearer intercourse than this, however, I was not destined to enjoy, for early on the following morning I was ordered to set out for the Royal Barracks, to be tried before a court-martial. It was on a cold, raw morning, with a thin, drizzly rain falling, that we drove into the barrack yard, and drew up at the mess-room, then used for the purposes of a court. As yet none of the members had assembled, and two or three mess-waiters were engaged in removing the signs of last night's debauch, and restoring a semblance of decorum to a very racketty-looking apartment. The walls were scrawled over with absurd caricatures, in charcoal or ink, of notorious characters of the capital, and a very striking " battle piece " commemorated the " Races of Castlebar," as that memorable action was called, in a spirit, I am bound to say, of little flattery to the British arms. There were, to be sure, little compensatory illustrations here and there of French cavalry in Egypt, mounted on donkeys, or revolutionary troops on parade, ragged as scarecrows, and ill-looking as highwaymen; but a most liberal justice characterised all these frescoes, and they treated both Trojan and Tyrian alike.

I had abundant time given me to admire them, for although summoned for seven o'clock, it was nine before the first officer of the court-martial made his appearance, and he having popped in his head, and perceiving the room empty, sauntered out again, and disappeared. At last a very noisy jaunting-car rattled into the square, and a short, red-faced man was assisted down from it, and entered the mess-room. This was Mr. Peters, the Deputy Judge Advocate, whose presence was the immediate signal for the others, who now came dropping in from every side, the President, a Colonel Daly, arriving the last.

A few tradespeople, loungers, it seemed to me, of the barracks, and some half-dozen non-commissioned officers off duty, made up the public ; and I could not but feel a sense of my insignificance in the utter absence of interest my fate excited. The listless indolence and informality, too, offended and insulted me ; and when the President politely told me to be seated, for they were obliged to wait for some books or papers left behind at his quarters, I actually was indignant at his coolness.

As we thus waited, the officers gathered round the fireplace, chatting and laughing pleasantly together, discussing the social events of the capital, and the gossip of the day; everything, in fact, but the case of the individual on whose future fate they were about to decide.

At length the long-expected books made their appearance, and a few well-thumbed volumes were spread over
the table, behind which the Court took their places, Colonel
Daly in the centre, with the judge upon his left.

The members being sworn, the Judge Advocate arose,
and in a hurried, humdrum kind of voice, read out what
purported to be the commission under which I was to be
tried; the charge being, whether I had or had not acted
treacherously and hostilely to his Majesty, whose natural-
born subject I was, being born in that kingdom, and, consequently, owing to him all allegiance and fidelity. "Guilty
or not guilty, sir?"

"The charge is a falsehood; I am a Frenchman," was
my answer.

"Have respect for the Court, sir," said Peters; "you
mean that you are a French officer, but by birth an Irishman."

"I mean no such thing;—that I am French by birth, as
I am in feeling—that I never saw Ireland till within a few
months back, and heartily wish I had never seen it."

"So would General Humbert, too, perhaps," said Daly,
laughing; and the Court seemed to relish the jest.

"Where were you born, then, Tiernay?"

"In Paris, I believe."

"And your mother's name, what was it?"

"I never knew; I was left an orphan when a mere infant,
and can tell little of my family."

"Your father was Irish, then?"

"Only by descent. I have heard that we came from a
family who bore the title of ' Timmahoo'—Lord Tiernay
of Timmahoo."

"There was such a title," interposed Peters; "it was
one of King James's last creations after his flight from
the Boyne. Some, indeed, assert that it was conferred
before the battle. What a strange coincidence, to find the
descendant, if he be such, labouring in something like the
same cause as his ancestor."

"What's your rank, sir?" asked a sharp, severe-looking
man, called Major Flood.

"First Lieutenant of Hussars."

"And is it usual for a boy of your years to hold that
rank; or was there anything peculiar in your case that
obtained the promotion?"

"I served in two campaigns, and gained my grade regularly."

"Your Irish blood, then, had no share in your advancement?" asked he again.

"I am a Frenchman, as I said before," was my answer.

"A Frenchman, who lays claim to an Irish estate and an Irish title," replied Flood. "Let us hear Dowall's statement."

And now, to my utter confusion, a man made his way to the table, and, taking the book from the Judge Advocate, kissed it in token of an oath.

"Inform the Court of anything you know in connection with the prisoner," said the judge.

And the fellow, not daring even to look towards me, began a long, rambling, unconnected narrative of his first meeting with me at Killala, affecting that a close intimacy had subsisted between us, and that in the faith of a confidence, I had told him how, being an Irishman by birth, I had joined the expedition in the hope that with the expulsion of the English I should be able to re-establish my claim to my family rank and fortune. There was little coherence in his story, and more than one discrepant statement occurred in it; but the fellow's natural stupidity imparted a wonderful air of truth to the narrative, and I was surprised how naturally it sounded even to my own ears, little circumstances of truth being interspersed through the recital, as though to season the falsehood into a semblance of fact.

"What have you to reply to this, Tiernay?" asked the colonel.

"Simply, sir, that such a witness, were his assertions even more consistent and probable, is utterly unworthy of credit. This fellow was one of the greatest marauders of the rebel army: and the last exercise of authority I ever witnessed by General Humbert was an order to drive him out of the town of Castlebar."

"Is this the notorious Town Major Dowall?" asked an officer of artillery.

"The same, sir."

"I can answer, then, for his being one of the greatest rascals unhanged," rejoined he.

"This is all very irregular, gentlemen," interposed the Judge Advocate; "the character of a witness cannot be impugned by what is mere desultory conversation. Let Dowall withdraw."

The man retired, and now a whispered conversation was kept up at the table for about a quarter of an hour, in which I could distinctly separate those who befriended from those who opposed me, the major being the chief of the latter party. One speech of his which I overheard made a slight impression on me, and for the first time suggested uneasiness regarding the event.

"Whatever you do with this lad must have an immense influence on Tone's trial. Don't forget that if you acquit him, you'll be sorely puzzled to convict the other."

The colonel promptly overruled this unjust suggestion, and maintained that in my accent, manner, and appearance, there was every evidence of my French origin.

"Let Wolfe Tone stand upon his own merits," said he, "but let us not mix this case with his."

"I'd have treated every man who landed to a rope," exclaimed the major, "Humbert himself among the rest. It was pure 'brigandage,' and nothing less."

"I hope if I escape, sir, that it will never be my fortune to see you a prisoner of France," said I, forgetting all in my indignation.

"If my voice have any influence, young man, that opportunity is not likely to occur to you," was the reply.

This ungenerous speech found no sympathy with the rest, and I soon saw that the major represented a small minority in the Court.

The want of my commission, or of any document suitable to my rank or position in the service, was a great drawback; for I had given all my papers to Humbert, and had nothing to substantiate my account of myself. I saw how unfavourably this acknowledgment was taken by the Court; and when I was ordered to withdraw that they might deliberate, I own that I felt great misgivings as to the result.

The deliberation was a long, and, as I could overhear, a strongly disputed one. Dowall was twice called in for examination, and when he retired on the last occasion the discussion grew almost stormy.

As I stood thus awaiting my fate, the public, now removed from the Court, pressed eagerly to look at me; and while some thronged the doorway, and even pressed against the sentry, others crowded at the window to peep in. Among these faces, over which my eye ranged in half vacancy, one face struck me, for the expression of sincere sympathy and interest it bore. It was that of a middle-aged man of an humble walk in life, whose dress bespoke him from the country. There was nothing in his appearance to have called for attention or notice, and at any other time I should have passed him over without remark; but now, as his features betokened a feeling almost verging on anxiety, I could not regard him without interest.

Whichever way my eyes turned, however my thoughts might take me off, whenever I looked towards him I was sure to find his gaze steadily bent upon me, and with an expression quite distinct from mere curiosity. At last came the summons for me to re-appear before the Court, and the crowd opened to let me pass in.

The noise, the anxiety of the moment, and the movement of the people, confused me at first; and when I recovered self-possession, I found that the Judge Advocate was reciting the charge under which I was tried. There were three distinct counts, on each of which the Court pronounced me "Not Guilty," but at the same time qualifying the finding by the additional words—"by a majority of two;" thus showing me that my escape had been a narrow one.

"As a prisoner of war," said the President, "you will now receive the same treatment as your comrades of the same rank. Some have been already exchanged, and some have given bail for their appearance to answer any future charges against them."

"I am quite ready, sir, to accept my freedom on parole," said I; "of course, in a country where I am an utter stranger, bail is out of the question."

"I'm willing to bail him, your worship; I'll take it on me to be surety for him," cried a coarse, husky voice from the body of the Court; and at the same time a man dressed in a great coat of dark frieze pressed through the crowd and approached the table.

"And who are you, my good fellow, so ready to impose yourself on the Court?" asked Peters.

"I'm a farmer of eighty acres of land, from the Black Pits, near Baldoyle, and the adjutant there, Mr. Moore, knows me well."

"Yes," said the adjutant, "I have known you some years, as supplying forage to the cavalry, and always heard you spoken of as honest and trustworthy."

"Thank you, Mr. Moore; that's as much as I want."

"Yes; but it's not as much as we want, my worthy man," said Peters; "we require to know that you are a solvent and respectable person."

"Come out and see my place, then; ride over the land and look at my stock; ask my neighbours my character; find out if there's anything against me."

"We prefer to leave all that trouble on your shoulders," said Peters; "show us that we may accept your surety, and we'll entertain the question at once."

" How much is it? " asked he, eagerly.

" We demanded five hundred pounds for a major on the staff; suppose we say two, colonel, is that sufficient?" asked Peters of the President.

" I should say quite enough," was the reply.

" There's eighty of it, any way," said the farmer, producing a dirty roll of bank notes, and throwing them on the table; " I got them from Mr. Murphy in Smithfield this morning, and I'll get twice as much more from him for asking ; so if your honours will wait 'till I come back, I'll not be twenty minutes away."

" But we can't take your money, my man ; we have no right to touch it."

" Then what are ye talking about two hundred pounds for ?" asked he, sternly.

" We want your promise to pay in the event of this bail being broken."

" Oh, I see, it's all the same thing in the end ; I'll do it either way."

" We'll accept Mr. Murphy's guarantee for your solvency," said Peters ; " obtain that, and you can sign the bond at once."

" Faith, I'll get it, sure enough, and be here before you've the writing drawn out," said he, buttoning up his coat.

" What name are we to insert in the bond ? "

" Tiernay, sir."

" That's the prisoner's name, but we want yours."

" Mine's Tiernay, too, sir ; Pat Tiernay of the Black Pits."

Before I could recover from my surprise at this announcement he had left the court, which in a few minutes afterwards broke up, a clerk alone remaining to fill up the necessary documents and complete the bail-bond.

The colonel, as well as two others of his officers, pressed me to join them at breakfast, but I declined, resolving to wait for my namesake's return, and partake of no other hospitality than his.

It was near one o'clock when he returned, almost worn out with fatigue, since he had been in pursuit of Mr. Murphy for several hours, and only came upon him by chance at last. His business, however, he had fully accomplished ; the bail-bond was duly drawn out and signed, and I left the barrack in a state of happiness very different from the feeling with which I had entered it that day.

CHAPTER XXXI.

A BRIEF CHANGE OF LIFE AND COUNTRY.

My new acquaintance never ceased to congratulate himself on what he called the lucky accident that had led him to the barracks that morning, and thus brought about our meeting. " Little as you think of me, my dear," said he, "I'm one of the Tiernays of Timmahoo myself; faix, until I saw you, I thought I was the last of them! There are eight generations of us in the churchyard at Kells, and I was looking to the time when they'd lay my bones there, as the last of the race, but I see there's better fortune before us."

" But you have a family, I hope?"

" Sorrow one belonging to me. I might have married when I was young, but there was a pride in me to look for something higher than I had any right, except from blood I mean ; for a better stock than our own isn't to be found ; and that's the way years went over and I lost the opportunity, and here I am now an old bachelor, without one to stand to me, barrin' it be yourself."

The last words were uttered with a tremulous emotion, and, on turning towards him, I saw his eyes swimming with tears, and perceived that some strong feeling was working within him.

" You can't suppose I can ever forget what I owe you, Mr. Tiernay."

" Call me Pat, Pat Tiernay," interrupted he, roughly.

" I'll call you what you please," said I, " if you let me add friend to it."

" That's enough ; we understand one another now, no more need be said; you'll come home and live with me. It's not long, maybe, you'll have to do that same ; but when I go you'll be heir to what I have : 'tis more, perhaps, than many supposes, looking at the coat and the gaiters I am wearin'. Mind, Maurice, I don't want you, nor I don't expect you to turn farmer like myself. You need never turn a hand to anything. You'll have your horse to ride—two, if you like it. Your time will be all your own, so that you spend a little of it now and then with me, and as much diversion as ever you care for."

I have condensed into a few words the substance of a conversation which lasted till we reached Baldoyle ; and passing through that not over-imposing village, gained the neighbourhood of the sea shore, along which stretched the farm of the " Black Pits," a name derived, I was told, from certain black holes that were dug in the sands by fishermen in former times, when the salt tide washed over the pleasant fields where corn was now growing. A long, low, thatched cabin, with far more indications of room and comfort than pretension to the picturesque, stood facing the sea. There were neither trees nor shrubs around it, and the aspect of the spot was bleak and cheerless enough, a colouring a dark November day did nothing to dispel.

It possessed one charm, however ; and had it been a hundred times inferior to what it was, that one would have compensated for all else—a hearty welcome met me at the door, and the words, " This is your home, Maurice," filled my heart with happiness.

Were I to suffer myself to dwell even in thought on this period of my life, I feel how insensibly I should be led away into an inexcusable prolixity. The little meaningless incidents of my daily life, all so engraven on my memory still, occupied me pleasantly from day till night. Not only the master of myself and my own time, I was master of everything around me. Uncle Pat, as he loved to call himself, treated me with a degree of respect that was almost painful to me, and only when we were alone together did he relapse into the intimacy of equality. Two first-rate hunters stood in my stable ; a stout-built half-deck boat lay at my command beside the quay ; I had my gun and my greyhounds ; books, journals ; everything, in short, that a liberal purse and a kind spirit could confer—all but acquaintance. Of these I possessed absolutely none. Too proud to descend to intimacy with the farmers and small shopkeepers of the neighbourhood, my position excluded me from acquaintance with the gentry ; and thus I stood between both, unknown to either.

For a while my new career was too absorbing to suffer me to dwell on this circumstance. The excitement of field sports sufficed me when abroad, and I came home usually so tired at night that I could barely keep awake

to amuse Uncle Pat with those narratives of war and campaigning he was so fond of hearing. To the hunting-field
succeeded the Bay of Dublin, and I passed days, even
weeks, exploring every creek and inlet of the coast ; now
cruising under the dark cliffs of the Welsh shore, or,
while my boat lay at anchor, wandering among the solitary
valleys of Lambay ; my life, like a dream full of its own
imaginings, and unbroken by the thoughts or feelings
of others ! I will not go the length of saying that I was
self-free from all reproach on the inglorious indolence in
which my days were passed, or that my thoughts never
strayed away to that land where my first dreams of ambition were felt. But a strange fatuous kind of languor
had grown upon me, and the more I retired within myself, the less did I wish for a return to that struggle with
the world which every active life engenders. Perhaps—I
cannot now say if it were so—perhaps I resented the dis-
dainful distance with which the gentry treated me, as we
met in the hunting-field or the coursing-ground. Some
of the isolation I preferred may have had this origin, but
choice had the greater share in it, until at last my greatest
pleasure was to absent myself for weeks on a cruise,
fancying that I was exploring tracts never visited by man,
and landing on spots where no human foot had ever been
known to tread.

If Uncle Pat would occasionally remonstrate on the
score of these long absences, he never ceased to supply
means for them, and my sea store and a well-filled purse
were never wanting, when the blue Peter floated from
" La Hoche," as in my ardour I had named my cutter.
Perhaps at heart he was not sorry to see me avoid the
capital and its society. The bitterness which had succeeded the struggle for independence was now at its
highest point, and there was what, to my thinking at
least, appeared something like the cruelty of revenge
in the sentences which followed the state trials. I will
not suffer myself to stray into the debatable ground of
politics, nor dare I give an opinion on matters, where,
with all the experience of fifty years superadded, the
wisest heads are puzzled how to decide ; but my impression at the time was that lenity would have been
a safer and a better policy than severity, and that in the
momentary prostration of the country, lay the precise
conjuncture for those measures of grace and favour, which
were afterwards rather wrung from than conceded by the
English Government. Be this as it may, Dublin offered a
strange spectacle at that period. The triumphant joy of

one party—the discomfiture and depression of the other
All the exuberant delight of success here; all the bitterness of failure there. On one side festivities, rejoicings,
and public demonstrations; on the other, confinement,
banishment, or the scaffold.

The excitement was almost madness. The passion for
pleasure, restrained by the terrible contingencies of the
time, now broke forth with redoubled force, and the capi-
al was thronged with all its rank, riches, and fashion,
when its jails were crowded, and the heaviest sentences of
the law were in daily execution. The state-trials were
crowded by all the fashion of the metropolis; and the
heart-moving eloquence of Curran was succeeded by the
strains of a merry concert. It was just then, too, that
the great lyric poet of Ireland began to appear in society,
and those songs which were to be known afterwards as
"The Melodies," par excellence, were first heard in all
the witching enchantment which his own taste and voice
could lend them. To such as were indifferent to or could
forget the past, it was a brilliant period. It was the last
flickering blaze of Irish nationality, before the lamp was
extinguished for ever.

Of this society I myself saw nothing. But even in the
retirement of my humble life the sounds of its mirth and
pleasure penetrated, and I often wished to witness the
scenes which even in vague description were fascinating.
It was then, in a kind of discontent at my exclusion, that I
grew from day to day more disposed to solitude, and
fonder of those excursions which led me out of all reach
of companionship or acquaintance. In this spirit I planned
a long cruise down channel, resolving to visit the island of
Valentia, or, if the wind and weather favoured, to creep
around the south-west coast as far as Bantry or Kenmare.
A man and his son, a boy of about sixteen, formed all my
crew, and were quite sufficient for the light tackle and
easy rig of my craft. Uncle Pat was already mounted on
his pony, and ready to set out for market, as we prepared
to start. It was a bright spring morning—such a one as
now and then the changeful climate of Ireland brings forth
in a brilliancy of colour and softness of atmosphere that
are rare in even more favoured lands.

"You have a fine day of it, Maurice, and just enough
wind," said he, looking at the point from whence it came.
"I almost wish I was going with you."

"And why not come, then?" asked I. "You never will
give yourself a holiday. Do so for once, now."

"Not to-day, anyhow," said he, half sighing at his self-denial. "I have a great deal of business on my hands to-day, but the next time—the very next you're up to a long cruise, I'll go with you."

"That's a bargain, then?"

"A bargain. Here's my hand on it."

We shook hands cordially on the compact. Little knew I it was to be for the last time, and that we were never to meet again!

I was soon aboard, and with a free mainsail skimming rapidly over the bright waters of the bay. The wind freshened as the day wore on, and we quickly passed the Kish light-ship, and held our course boldly down channel. The height of my enjoyment in these excursions consisted in the unbroken quietude of mind I felt, when removed from all chance interruption, and left free to follow out my own fancies and indulge my dreamy conceptions to my heart's content. It was then I used to revel in imaginings which sometimes soared into the boldest realms of ambition, and at others strayed contemplatively in the humblest walks of obscure fortune. My crew never broke in upon these musings ; indeed, old Tom Finerty's low croning song rather aided than interrupted them. He was not much given to talking, and a chance allusion to some vessel afar off, or some headland we were passing, were about the extent of his communicativeness, and even these often fell on my ear unnoticed.

It was thus, at night, we made the Hook Tower ; and on the next day passed, in a spanking breeze, under the bold cliffs of Tramore, just catching, as the sun was sinking, the sight of Youghal Bay and the tall headlands beyond it.

"The wind is drawing more to the nor'ard," said old Tom, as night closed in, "and the clouds look dirty."

"Bear her up a point or two," said I, "and let us stand in for Cork Harbour, if it comes on to blow."

He muttered something in reply, but I did not catch the words, nor, indeed, cared I to hear them, for I had just wrapped myself in my boat-cloak, and, stretched at full length on the shingle ballast of the yawl, was gazing in rapture at the brilliancy of the starry sky above me. Light skiffs of feathery cloud would now and then flit past, and a peculiar hissing sound of the sea told, at the same time, that the breeze was freshening But old Tom had done his duty in mentioning this once, and thus having dis-burthened his conscience, he closehauled his mainsail, shifted the ballast a little to midships, and, putting up the collar of his pilot-coat, screwed himself tighter into the corner beside the tiller, and chewed his quid in quietness. The boy slept soundly in the bow, and I, lulled by the motion and the plashing waves, fell into a dreamy stupor, like a pleasant sleep. The pitching of the boat continued to increase, and twice or thrice struck by a heavy sea, she lay over, till the white waves came tumbling in over her gunwale. I heard Tom call to his boy, something about the head-sail, but for the life of me I could not or would not arouse myself from a train of thought that I was following.

"She's a stout boat to stand this," said Tom, as he rounded her off, at a coming wave, which, even thus escaped, splashed over us like a cataract. " I know many a bigger craft wouldn't hold up her canvas under such a gale."

" Here it comes, father. Here's a squall," cried the boy; and with a crash like thunder, the wind struck the sail, and laid the boat half-under.

" She'd float if she was full of water," said the old man, as the craft " righted."

" But maybe the spars wouldn't stand," said the boy, anxiously.

" 'Tis what I'm thinking," rejoined the father. " There's a shake in the mast, below the caps."

" 'Tell him it's better to bear up, and go before it," whispered the lad, with a gesture towards where I was lying.

" Troth, it's little he'd care," said the other ; " besides, he's never plazed to be woke up."

" Here it comes again," cried the boy. But this time the squall swept past ahead of us, and the craft only reeled to the swollen waves, as they tore by.

" We'd better go about, sir," said Tom to me ; "there's a heavy sea outside, and it's blowing hard now."

" And there's a split in the mast as long as my arm," cried the boy.

" I thought she'd live through any sea, Tom !" said I, laughing ; for it was his constant boast that no weather could harm her.

" There goes the spar !" shouted he, while with a loud snap the mast gave way, and fell with a crash over the side. The boat immediately came head to wind, and sea after sea broke upon her bow, and fell in great floods over us.

" Cut away the stays—clear the wreck," cried Tom, " before the squall catches her."

And although we now laboured like men whose lives depended on the exertion, the trailing sail and heavy rigging, shifting the ballast as they fell, laid her completely over ; and when the first sea struck her, over she went. The violence of the gale sent me a considerable distance out, and for several seconds I felt as though I should never reach the surface again. Wave after wave rolled over me, and seemed bearing me downwards with their weight. At last I grasped something ; it was a rope—a broken halyard ; but by its means I gained the mast, which floated alongside of the yawl as she now lay keel uppermost. With what energy did I struggle to reach her ! The space was scarcely a dozen feet, and yet it cost me what seemed an age to traverse. Through all the roaring of the breakers, and the crashing sounds of storm, I thought I could hear my comrades' voices shouting and screaming, but this was in all likelihood a mere deception, for I never saw them more !

Grasping with a death-grip the slippery keel, I hung on the boat through all the night. The gale continued to increase, and by daybreak it blew a perfect hurricane. With an aching anxiety I watched for light to see if I were near the land, or if any ship were in sight ; but when the sun rose, nothing met my eyes but a vast expanse of waves tumbling and tossing in mad confusion, while overhead some streaked and mottled clouds were hurried along with the wind. Happily for me, I have no correct memory of that long day of suffering. The continual noise, but more still, the incessant motion of sea and sky around, brought on a vertigo, that seemed like madness ; and although the instinct of self-preservation remained, the wildest and most incoherent fancies filled my brain. Some of these were powerful enough to impress themselves upon my memory for years after, and one I have never yet been able to dispel. It clings to me in every season of unusual depression or dejection ; it recurs in the half nightmare sleep of over fatigue, and even invades me when, restless and feverish, I lie for hours incapable of repose. This is the notion that my state was one of after-life punishment ; that I had died, and was now expiating a sinful life by the everlasting misery of a castaway. The fever brought on by thirst and exhaustion, and the burning sun which beamed down upon my uncovered head, soon completed the measure of this infatuation, and all sense and guidance left me.

By what instinctive impulse I still held on my grasp, I cannot explain ; but there I clung during the whole of that

long dreadful day, and the still more dreadful night, when
the piercing cold cramped my limbs, and seemed as if
freezing the very blood within me. It was no wish for
life, it was no anxiety to save myself, that now filled me.
It seemed like a vague impulse of necessity that compelled
me to hang on. It was, as it were, part of that terrible
sentence which made this my doom for ever!

An utter unconsciousness must have followed this state,
and a dreary blank, with flitting shapes of suffering, is all
that remains to my recollection.

    *   *   *   *   *   *

Probably within the whole range of human sensations,
there is not one so perfect in its calm and soothing influence as the first burst of gratitude we feel when recovering from a long and severe illness! There is not an object,
however humble and insignificant, that is not for the time
invested with a new interest. The air is balmier, flowers
are sweeter, the voices of friends, the smiles and kind
looks, are dearer and fonder than we have ever known
them. The whole world has put on a new aspect for us,
and we have not a thought that is not teeming with forgiveness and affection. Such, in all their completeness,
were my feelings as I lay on the poop-deck of a large
three-masted ship, which, with studding and top-gallant
sails all set, proudly held her course up the Gulf of St.
Lawrence.

She was a Dantzig barque, the "Hoffnung," bound for
Quebec, her only passengers being a Moravian minister
and his wife, on their way to join a small German colony
established near Lake Champlain. To Gottfried Kröller
and his dear little wife I owe not life alone, but nearly all
that has made it valuable. With means barely removed
from absolute poverty, I found that they had spared
nothing to assist in my recovery; for, when discovered,
emaciation and wasting had so far reduced me that nothing
but the most unremitting care and kindness could have
succeeded in restoring me. To this end they bestowed
not only their whole time and attention, but every little
delicacy of their humble sea-store. All the little cordials
and restoratives, meant for a season of sickness or debility,
were lavished unsparingly on me, and every instinct of
national thrift and carefulness gave way before the more
powerful influence of Christian benevolence.

I can think of nothing but that bright morning, as I lay
on a mattress on the deck, with the "Pfarrer" on one
side of me, and his good little wife, Lyschen, on the other;

he with his volume of "Wieland," and she working away
with her long knitting-needles, and never raising her head
save to bestow a glance at the poor sick boy, whose blood-
less lips were trying to mutter her name in thankfulness.
It is like the most delicious dream as I think over those
hours, when, rocked by the surging motion of the large
ship, hearing in half distinctness the words of the "Pfarrer's" reading, I followed out little fancies—now self-ori-
ginating, now rising from the theme of the poet's musings.

How softly the cloud-shadows moved over the white
sails and swept along the bright deck! How pleasantly
the water rippled against the vessel's side! With what a
glad sound the great ensign flapped and fluttered in the
breeze! There was light, and life, and motion on every
side, and I felt all the intoxication of enjoyment.

And like a dream was the portion of my life which followed. I accompanied the Pfarrer to a small settlement
near "Crown Point," where he was to take up his residence
as minister. Here we lived amid a population of about
four or five hundred Germans, principally from Pomerania,
on the shores of the Baltic, a peaceful, thrifty, quiet set
of beings, who, content with the little interests revolving
around themselves, never troubled their heads about the
great events of war or politics ; and here in all likelihood
should I have been content to pass my days, when an
accidental journey I made to Albany, to receive some
letters for the Pfarrer, once more turned the fortune of
my life.

It was a great incident in the quiet monotony of my
life, when I set out one morning, arrayed in a full suit of
coarse, glossy black, with buttons like small saucers, and a
hat whose brim almost protected my shoulders. I was,
indeed, an object of very considerable envy to some, and
I hope, also, not denied the admiring approval of some
others. Had the respectable city I was about to visit been
the chief metropolis of a certain destination which I must
not name, the warnings I received about its dangers, dissipations, and seductions, could scarcely have been more
earnest or impressive. I was neither to speak with, nor
even to look at, those I met in the streets. I was carefully to avoid taking my meals at any of the public eating-
houses, rigidly guarding myself from the contamination of
even a chance acquaintance. It was deemed as needless to
caution me against theatres or places of amusements, as to
hint to me that I should not commit a highway robbery or a
murder, and so, in sooth, I should myself have felt it.

The patriarchal simplicity in which I had lived for above
a year had not been without its effect in subduing exaggerated feeling, or controlling that passion for excitement
so common to youth. I felt a kind of drowsy, dreamy
langour over me, which I sincerely believed represented a
pious and well-regulated temperament. Perhaps in time
it might have become such. Perhaps with others, more
happily constituted, the impression would have been confirmed and fixed; but in my case it was a mere lacquer,
that the first rubbing in the world was sure to brush
off.

I arrived safely at Albany, and having presented myself
at the bank of Gabriel Shultze, was desired to call the following morning, when all the letters and papers of Gottfried Kröller should be delivered to me. A very cold invitation to supper was the only hospitality extended to me.
This I declined on pretext of weariness, and set out to
explore the town, to which my long residence in rural life
imparted a high degree of interest.

I don't know what it may now be—doubtless a great
capital, like one of the European cities; but at that time
I speak of, Albany was a strange, incongruous assemblage
of stores and wooden houses, great buildings like granaries, with whole streets of low sheds around them, where,
open to the passer-by, men worked at various trades, and
people followed out the various duties of domestic life in
sight of the public; daughters knitted and sewed; mothers
cooked and nursed their children; men ate, and worked,
and smoked, and sang, as if in all the privacy of closed
dwellings, while a thick current of population poured by,
apparently too much immersed in their own cares, or too
much accustomed to the scene, to give it more than passing notice.

It was curious how one bred and born in the great city
of Paris, with all its sights and sounds, and scenes of excitement and display, could have been so rusticated by
time as to feel a lively interest in surveying the motley
aspect of this quaint town. There were, it is true, features
in the picture very unlike the figures in "Old World"
landscape. A group of red men, seated around a fire in
the open street, or a squaw carrying on her back a baby,
firmly tied to a piece of curved bark; a southern stater,
with a spanking waggon-team, and two grinning negroes
behind, were new and strange elements in the life of a
city. Still, the mere movement, the actual busy stir and
occupation of the inhabitants, attracted me as much as any-

thing else; and the shops and stalls, where trades were carried on, were a seduction I could not resist

The strict puritanism in which I had lately lived taught me to regard all these things with a certain degree of distrust. They were the impulses of that gold-seeking passion of which Gottfried had spoken so frequently; they were the great vice of that civilisation, whose luxurious tendency he often deplored; and here, now, more than one-half around me were arts that only ministered to voluptuous tastes. Brilliant articles of jewellery; gay cloaks, worked with wampam, in Indian taste; ornamental turning, and costly weapons, inlaid with gold and silver, succeeded each other, street after street; and the very sight of them, however pleasurable to the eye, set me a moralising in a strain that would have done credit to a son of Geneva. It might have been, that in my enthusiasm I uttered half aloud what I intended for soliloquy; or perhaps some gesture, or peculiarity of manner, had the effect; but so it was: I found myself an object of notice; and my queer-cut coat and wide hat, contrasting so strangely with my youthful appearance and slender make, drew many a criticism on me.

" He ain't a Quaker, that's a fact," cried one, " for they don't wear black."

" He's a down-easter—a horse-jockey chap, I'll be bound," cried another. " They put on all manner of disguises and ' masqueroonings.' I know 'em !"

"He's a calf preacher—a young bottle-nosed Gospeller," broke in a thick, short fellow, like the skipper of a merchant ship. " Let's have him out for a preachment."

" Ay, you're right," chimed in another. " I'll get you a sugar hogshead in no time ; " and away he ran on the mission.

Between twenty and thirty persons had now collected; and I saw myself, to my unspeakable shame and mortification, the centre of all their looks and speculations. A little more aplomb or knowledge of life would have taught me coolness enough in a few words to undeceive them; but such a task was far above me now; and I saw nothing for it but flight. Could I only have known which way to take, I need not have feared any pursuer, for I was a capital runner, and in high condition; but of the locality I was utterly ignorant, and should only surrender myself to mere chance. With a bold rush, then, I dashed right through the crowd, and set off down the street, the whole crew after me. The dusk of the closing evening was in

my favour ; and although volunteers were enlisted in the
chase at every corner and turning, I distanced them, and
held on my way in advance. My great object being not
to turn on my course, lest I should come back to my starting point, I directed my steps nearly straight onward,
clearing apple-stalls and fruit-tables at a bound ; and more
than once taking a flying leap over an Indian's fire, when
the mad shout of the red man would swell the chorus that
followed me. At last I reached a network of narrow
lanes and alleys, by turning and wending through which
I speedily found myself in a quiet secluded spot, with
here and there a flickering candle-light from the windows,
but no other sign of habitation. I looked anxiously about
for an open door ; but they were all safe barred and fastened ; and it was only on turning a corner I spied what
seemed to me a little shop, with a solitary lamp over the
entrance. A narrow canal, crossed by a ricketty old
bridge, led to this ; and the moment I had crossed over, I
seized the single plank which formed the footway, and
shoved it into the stream. My retreat being thus secured,
I opened the door, and entered. It was a barber's shop ;
at least, so a great chair before a cracked old looking-glass,
with some well-worn combs and brushes, bespoke it ; but
the place seemed untenanted, and although I called aloud
several times, none came or responded to my summons.

I now took a survey of the spot, which seemed of the
poorest imaginable. A few empty pomatum pots, a case
of razors that might have defied the most determined
suicide, and a half-finished wig, on a block painted like a
red man, were the entire stock in trade. On the walls,
however, were some coloured prints of the battles of the
French army in Germany and Italy. Execrably done
things they were, but full of meaning and interest to my
eyes in spite of that. With all the faults of drawing and
all the travesties of costume, I could recognise different
corps of the service, and my heart bounded as I gazed on
the tall shakos swarming to a breach, or the loose jacket
as it floated from the hussar in a charge. All the wild
pleasures of soldiering rose once more to my mind, and I
thought over old comrades who doubtless were now earn-
ing the high rewards of their bravery in the great career
of glory. And as I did so, my own image confronted me
in the glass, as with long, lank hair, and a great bolster of
a white cravat, I stood before it. What a contrast !—how
unlike the smart hussar, with curling locks and fierce
moustache! Was I as much changed in heart as in looks?

Had my spirit died out within me? Would the proud notes of the bugle or the trumpet fall meaningless on my ears, or the hoarse cry of " Charge !" send no bursting fulness to my temples? Ay, even these coarse representations stirred the blood in my veins, and my step grew firmer as I walked the room.

In a passionate burst of enthusiasm, I tore off my slouched hat and hurled it from me. It felt like the badge of some ignoble slavery, and I determined to endure it no longer. The noise of the act called up a voice from the inner room, and a man, to all appearance suddenly roused from sleep, stood at the door. He was evidently young, but poverty, dissipation, and raggedness made the question of his age a difficult one to solve. A light-coloured moustache and beard covered all the lower part of his face, and his long blonde hair fell heavily over his shoulders.

" Well," cried he, half angrily, " what's the matter ; are you so impatient that you must smash the furniture ?"

Although the words were spoken as correctly as I have written them, they were uttered with a foreign accent ; and, hazarding the stroke, I answered him in French by apologizing for the noise.

" What! a Frenchman," exclaimed he, " and in that dress! what can that mean?"

" If you'll shut your door, and cut off pursuit of me, I'll tell you everything," said I, " for I hear the voices of people coming down that street in front."

" I'll do better," said he, quickly; " I'll upset the bridge, and they cannot come over."

" That's done already," replied I ; " I shoved it into the stream as I passed."

He looked at me steadily for a moment without speaking, and then approaching close to me, said, " Parbleu the act was very unlike your costume!" At the same time he shut the door, and drew a strong bar across it. This done, he turned to me once more,—" Now for it: who are you, and what has happened to you?"

" As to what I am," replied I, imitating his own abruptness, " my dress would almost save the trouble of explaining ; these Albany folk, however, would make a field-preacher of me, and to escape them I took to flight."

" Well, if a fellow will wear his hair that fashion, he must take the consequence," said he, drawing out my long lank locks as they hung over my shoulders. " And so you wouldn't hold forth for them ; not even give them a stave of a conventicle chant." He kept his eyes rivetted on me as he spoke, and then seizing two pieces of stick from the firewood, he beat on the table the rantan-plan of the French drum. "That's the music you know best, lad, eh? —that's the air, which, if it has not led heavenward, has conducted many a brave fellow out of this world at least: do you forget it?"

"Forget it! no," cried I; "but who are you; and how comes it that—that"——I stopped in confusion at the rudeness of the question I had begun.

"That I stand here, half-fed, and all but naked; a barber in a land where men don't shave once a month. Parbleu! they'd come even seldomer to my shop if they knew how tempted I feel to draw the razor sharp and quick across the gullet of a fellow with a well-stocked pouch."

As he continued to speak, his voice assumed a tone and cadence that sounded familiar to my ears as I stared at him in amazement.

"Not know me yet!" exclaimed he, laughing; "and yet all this poverty and squalor isn't as great a disguise as your own, Tiernay. Come, lad, rub your eyes a bit, and try if you can't recognise an old comrade."

"I know you, yet cannot remember how or where we met," said I, in bewilderment.

"I'll refresh your memory," said he, crossing his arms, and drawing himself proudly up. "If you can trace back in your mind to a certain hot and dusty day, on the Metz road, when you, a private in the Seventh Hussars, were eating an onion and a slice of black bread for your dinner, a young officer, well looking and well mounted, cantered up and threw you his brandy flask. Your acknowledgment of the civility showed you to be a gentleman; and the acquaintance thus opened sooned ripened into intimacy."

"But he was the young Marquis de Saint Trone," said I, perfectly remembering the incident.

"Or Eugene Santron, of the republican army, or the barber at Albany, without any name at all," said he, laughing. "What, Maurice, don't you know me yet?"

"What, the lieutenant of my regiment? The dashing officer of hussars?"

"Just so, and as ready to resume the old skin as ever," cried he, "and brandish a weapon somewhat longer, and perhaps somewhat sharper, too, than a razor."

We shook hands with all the cordiality of old comrades, meeting far away from home, and in a land of strangers; and although each was full of curiosity to learn the other's

history, a kind of reserve held back the inquiry, till Santron said, " My confession is soon made, Maurice ; I left
the service in the Meuse, to escape being shot.   One day,
on returning from a field manœuvre, I discovered that my
portmanteau had been opened, and a number of letters
and papers taken out.   They were part of a correspondence I held with old General Lamarre, about the restoration of the Bourbons, a subject, I'm certain, that half the
officers in the army were interested in, and, even to Bonaparte himself, deeply implicated in, too.   No matter, my
treason, as they called it, was too flagrant, and I had just
twenty minutes' start of the order which was issued for
my arrest to make my escape into Holland.   There I
managed to pass several months in various disguises, part
of the time being employed as a Dutch spy, and actually
charged with an order to discover tidings of myself, until
I finally got away in an Antwerp schooner, to New York.
From that time my life has been nothing but a struggle, a
hard one, too, with actual want, for in this land of enterprise and activity, mere intelligence, without some craft
or calling, will do nothing.

"I tried fifty things: to teach riding—and when I mounted
into the saddle, I forgot everything but my own enjoyment, and caracolled, and plunged, and passaged, till the
poor beast hadn't a leg to stand on ; fencing—and I got
into a duel with a rival teacher, and ran him through the
neck, and was obliged to fly from Halifax; French—I made
love to my pupil, a pretty looking Dutch girl, whose father
didn't smile on our affection; and so on, I descended from
a dancing-master to a waiter, a lacquais de place, and at
last settled down as a barber, which brilliant speculation I
had just determined to abandon this very night, for to-
morrow morning, Maurice, I start for New York and
France again ; ay, boy, and you'll go with me.   This is no
land for either of us."

" But I have found happiness, at least contentment,
here," said I, gravely.

" What ! play the hypocrite with an old comrade !
shame on you, Maurice," cried he. " It is these confounded locks have perverted the boy," added he, jumping
up, and before I knew what he was about, he had shorn
my hair, in two quick cuts of the scissors, close to the head.
" There," said he, throwing the cut-off hair towards me,
" there lies all your saintship ; depend upon it, boy, they'd
hunt you out of the settlement if you came back to them
cropped in this fashion."

"But you return to certain death, Santron," said I; "your crime is too recent to be forgiven or forgotten."

"Not a bit of it; Fouché, Cassaubon, and a dozen others, now in office, were deeper than I was There's not a public man in France could stand an exposure, or hazard recrimination. It's a thieves' amnesty at this moment, and I must not lose the opportunity. I'll show you letters that will prove it, Maurice ; for, poor and ill-fed as I am, I like life just as well as ever I did. I mean to be a general of division one of these days, and so will you too, lad, if there's any spirit left in you."

Thus did Santron rattle on, sometimes of himself and his own future; sometimes discussing mine; for while talking, he had contrived to learn all the chief particulars of my history, from the time of my sailing from La Rochelle for Ireland.

The unlucky expedition afforded him great amusement, and he was never weary of laughing at all our adventures and mischances in Ireland. Of Humbert, he spoke as a fourth or fifth-rate man, and actually shocked me by all the heresies he uttered against our generals, and the plan of campaign; but, perhaps, I could have borne even these better than the sarcasms and sneers at the little life of "the settlement." He treated all my efforts at defence as mere hypocrisy, and affected to regard me as a mere knave, that had traded on the confiding kindness of these simple villagers. I could not undeceive him on this head ; nor what was more, could I satisfy my own conscience that he was altogether in the wrong ; for, with a diabolical inge-nuity, he had contrived to hit on some of the most vexa-tious doubts which disturbed my mind, and instinctively to detect the secret cares and difficulties that beset me. The lesson should never be lost on us, that the devil was depicted as a sneerer ! I verily believe the powers of temptation have no such advocacy as sarcasm. Many can resist the softest seductions of vice ; many are proof against all the blandishments of mere enjoyment, come in what shape it will ; but how few can stand firm against the as-saults of clever irony, or hold fast to their convictions when assailed by the sharp shafts of witty depreciation !

I am ashamed to own how little I could oppose to all his impertinences about our village, and its habits ; or how im-possible I found it not to laugh at his absurd descriptions of a life which, without having ever witnessed, he depicted with a rare acuracy. He was shrewd enough not to push this ridicule offensively ; and long before I knew it, I found

myself regarding, with his eyes, a picture in which, but a few months back, I stood as a foreground figure. I ought to confess, that no artificial aid was derived from either good cheer, or the graces of hospitality; we sat by a miserable lamp, in a wretchedly cold chamber, our sole solace some bad cigars, and a can of flat stale cider.

"I have not a morsel to offer you to eat, Maurice, but to-morrow we'll breakfast on my razors, dine on that old looking-glass, and sup on two hard brushes and the wig!"

Such were the brilliant pledges, and we closed a talk which the flickering lamp at last put an end to.

A broken, unconnected conversation followed for a little time, but at length, worn out and wearied, each dropped off to sleep—Eugene on the straw settle, and I in the old chair—never to awake till the bright sun was streaming in between the shutters, and dancing merrily on the tiled floor.

An hour before I awoke, he had completed the sale of all his little stock in trade, and, with a last look round the spot where he had passed some months of struggling poverty, out we sallied into the town.

"We'll breakfast at Jonathan Hone's," said Santron. "It's the first place here. I'll treat you to rump-steaks, pumpkin pie, and a gin twister that will astonish you. Then, while I'm arranging for our passage down the Hudson, you'll see the hospitable banker, and tell him how to forward all his papers, and so forth, to the settlement, with your respectful compliments and regrets, and the rest of it."

"But am I to take leave of them in this fashion?" asked I.

"Without you want me to accompany you there, I think it's by far the best way," said he, laughingly. "If, however, you think that my presence and companionship will add any lustre to your position, say the word, and I'm ready. I know enough of the barber's craft now to make up a head 'en Puritan,' and, if you wish, I'll pledge myself to impose upon the whole colony."

Here was a threat there was no mistaking; and any imputation of ingratitude on my part were far preferable to the thought of such an indignity. He saw his advantage at once, and boldly declared that nothing should separate us.

"The greatest favour, my dear Maurice, you can ever expect at my hands is, never to speak of this freak of yours; or, if I do, to say that you performed the part to perfection."

My mind was in one of those moods of change when the slightest impulse is enough to sway it, and, more from this cause than all his persuasion, I yielded; and the same evening saw me gliding down the Hudson, and admiring the bold Kaatskills, on our way to New York.

CHAPTER XXXII.

"THE ATHOL TENDER."

As I cast my eyes over these pages, and see how small a portion of my life they embrace, I feel like one who, having a long journey before him, perceives that some more speedy means of travel must be adopted, if he ever hope to reach his destination. With the instinctive prosiness of age I have lingered over the scenes of boyhood, a period which, strange to say, is fresher in my memory than many of the events of few years back; and were I to continue my narrative as I have begun it, it would take more time on my part, and more patience on that of my readers, than are likely to be conceded to either of us. Were I to apologise to my readers for any abruptness in my transitions, or any want of continuity in my story, I should perhaps inadvertently seem to imply a degree of interest in my fate which they have never felt; and, on the other hand, I would not for a moment be thought to treat slightingly the very smallest degree of favour they may feel disposed to show me. With these difficulties on either hand, I see nothing for it but to limit myself for the future to such incidents and passages of my career as most impressed themselves on myself, and to confine my record to the events in which I personally took a share.

Santron and I sailed from New York on the 9th of February, and arrived in Liverpool on the 14th of March.

We landed in as humble a guise as need be. One small box contained all our effects, and a little leathern purse, with something less than three dollars, all our available wealth. The immense movement and stir of the busy town, the crash and bustle of trade, the roll of waggons, the cranking clatter of cranes and windlasses, the incessant flux and reflux of population, all eager and intent on business, were strange spectacles to our eyes as we loitered, houseless and friendless, through the streets, staring in wonderment at the wealth and prosperity of that land we were taught to believe was tottering to bankruptcy.

Santron affected to be pleased with all, talked of the "beau pillage" it would afford one day or other; but in reality this appearance of riches and prosperity seemed to depress and discourage him. Both French and American writers had agreed in depicting the pauperism and dis-content of England, and yet where were the signs of it? Not a house was untenanted, every street was thronged, every market filled; the equipages of the wealthy vied with the loaded waggons in number; and if there were not the external evidences of happiness and enjoyment the gayer population of other countries display, there was an air of well-being and comfort such as no other land could exhibit.

Another very singular trait made a deep impression on us. Here were these islanders with a narrow strait only separating them from a land bristling with bayonets. The very roar of the artillery at exercise might be almost heard across the gulf, and yet not a soldier was to be seen about! There were neither forts nor bastions. The harbour, so replete with wealth, lay open and unprotected, not even a gun-boat or a guard-ship to defend it! There was an insolence in this security that Santron could not get over, and he muttered a prayer that the day might not be distant that should make them repent it.

He was piqued with everything. While on board ship we had agreed together to pass ourselves for Canadians, to avoid all inquiries of the authorities! Heaven help us! The authorities never thought of us. We were free to go or stay as we pleased. Neither police nor passport officers questioned us. We might have been Hoche and Massena for aught they either knew or cared. Not a "Mouchard" tracked us; none even looked after us as we went. To me this was all very agreeable and reassuring; to my companion it was contumely and insult. All the ingenious fiction he had devised of our birth, parentage, and pursuits,

was a fine romance inedited, and he was left to sneer at
the self-sufficiency that would not take alarm at the
advent of two ragged youths on the quay of Liverpool.

"If they but knew who we were, Maurice," he kept
continually muttering as we went along; "if these fellows only knew whom they had in their town, what a rum-
pus it would create! How the shops would close! What
barricading of doors and windows we should see! What
bursts of terror and patriotism! Par St. Denis, I have a
mind to throw up my cap in the air and cry 'Vive la Republique,' just to witness the scene that would follow."

With all these boastings, it was not very difficult to
restrain my friend's ardour, and to induce him to defer his
invasion of England to a more fitting occasion, so that at
last he was fain to content himself with a sneering commentary on all around him; and in this amiable spirit we
descended into a very dirty cellar to eat our first dinner
on shore.

The place was filled with sailors, who, far from indulging
in the well-known careless gaiety of their class, seemed
morose and sulky, talking together in low murmurs, and
showing unmistakeable signs of discontent and dissatisfaction. The reason was soon apparent; the press-gangs
were out to take men off to reinforce the blockading force
before Genoa, a service of all others the most distasteful
to a seaman. If Santron at first was ready to flatter himself into the notion that very little persuasion would make
these fellows take part against England, as he listened
longer he saw the grievous error of the opinion, no epithet
of insult or contempt being spared by them when talking
of France and Frenchmen. Whatever national animosity
prevailed at that period, sailors enjoyed a high pre-eminence in feeling. I have heard that the spirit was encouraged by those in command, and that narratives of
French perfidy, treachery, and even cowardice, were the
popular traditions of the sea service. We certainly could
not controvert the old adage as to "listeners," for every
observation and every anecdote conveyed a sneer or an
insult on our country. There could be no reproach in
listening to these unresented, but Santron assumed a most
indignant air, and more than once affected to be overcome
by a spirit of recrimination. What turn his actions might
have taken in this wise I cannot even guess, for suddenly
a rush of fellows took place up the ladder, and in less than
a minute the whole cellar was cleared, leaving none but

the hostess and an old lame waiter along with ourselves in the place.

"You've got a protection, I suppose, sirs," said the woman, approaching us; "but still I'll advise you not to trust to it over-much; they're in great want of men just now; and they care little for law or justice when once they have them on the high seas."

"We have no protection," said I; "we are strangers here, and know no one."

"There they come, sir; that's the tramp," cried the woman; "there's nothing for it now but to stay quiet and hope you'll not be noticed. Take those knives up, will ye," said she, flinging a napkin towards me, and speaking in an altered voice, for already two figures were darkening the entrance, and peering down into the depth below, while turning to Santron she motioned him to remove the dishes from the table—a service in which, to do him justice, he exhibited a zeal more flattering to his tact than his spirit of resistance.

"Tripped their anchors already, Mother Martin?" said a large-whiskered man, with a black belt round his waist; while, passing round the tables, he crammed into his mouth several fragments of the late feast.

"You wouldn't have 'em wait for you, Captain John," said she, laughing.

"It's just what I would, then," replied he. "The Admiralty has put thirty shillings more on the bounty, and where will these fellows get the like of that? It isn't a West India service, neither, nor a coastin' cruise off Newfoundland, but all as one as a pleasure-trip up the Mediterranean, and nothing to fight but Frenchmen. Eh, younker, that tickles your fancy," cried he to Santron, who, in spite of himself, made some gesture of impatience. "Handy chaps, those, Mother Martin, where did you chance on 'em?"

"They're sons of a Canada skipper in the river yonder," said she, calmly.

"They arn't over like to be brothers," said he, with the grin of one too well accustomed to knavery to trust anything opposed to his own observation. "I suppose them's things happens in Canada as elsewhere," said he, laughing, and hoping the jest might turn her flank. Meanwhile the press-leader never took his eyes off me, as I arranged plates and folded napkins with all the skill which my early education in Boivin's restaurant had taught me.

"He is a smart one," said he, half-musingly. "I say,

boy, would you like to go as cook's aid on board a king's
ship? I know of one as would just suit you."

"I'd rather not, sir; I'd not like to leave my father,"
said I, backing up Mrs. Martin's narrative.

"Nor that brother, there; wouldn't he like it?"

I shook my head negatively.

"Suppose I have a talk with the skipper about it," said
he, looking at me steadily for some seconds. "Suppose I
was to tell him what a good berth you'd have, eh?"

"Oh, if he wished it, I'd make no objection," said I, assuming all the calmness I could.

"That chap aint your brother—and he's no sailor neither.
Show me your hands, youngster," cried he to Santron, who
at once complied with the order, and the press captain
bent over and scanned them narrowly. As he thus stood
with his back to me, the woman shook her head significantly, and pointed to the ladder. If ever a glance conveyed a whole story of terror hers did. I looked at my
companion as though to say, "Can I desert him?" and the
expression of her features seemed to imply utter despair.
This pantomime did not occupy half a minute. And now,
with noiseless step, I gained the ladder, and crept cautiously
up it. My fears were how to escape those who waited outside; but as I ascended I could see that they were loitering about in groups, inattentive to all that was going on
below. The shame at deserting my comrade so nearly
overcame me, that, when almost at the top, I was about to
turn back again. I even looked round to see him, but, as
I did so, I saw the press leader draw a pair of handcuffs
from his pocket, and throw them on the table. The instincts
of safety were too strong, and with a spring I gained the
street, and, slipping noiselessly along the wall, escaped the
"look-out." Without a thought of where I was going to,
or what to do, I ran at the very top of my speed directly
onwards, my only impulse being to get away from the spot.
Could I reach the open country I thought it would be my
best chance. As I fled, however, no signs of a suburb
appeared; the streets, on the contrary, grew narrower and
more intricate; huge warehouses, seven or eight stories
high, loomed at either side of me; and at last, on turning
an angle, a fresh sea-breeze met me, and showed that I
was near the harbour. I avow that the sight of shipping,
the tall and taper spars that streaked the sky of night, the
clank of chain cables, and the heavy surging sound of the
looming hulls, were anything but encouraging, longing as
I did for the rustling leaves of some green lane; but still

all was quiet and tranquil; a few flickering lights twinkled here and there from a cabin window, but everything seemed sunk in repose.

The quay was thickly studded with hogsheads and bales of merchandise, so that I could easily have found a safe resting-place for the night, but a sense of danger banished all wish for sleep, and I wandered out, restless and uncertain, framing a hundred plans, and abandoning them when formed.

So long as I kept company with Santron, I never thought of returning to "Uncle Pat;" my reckless spendthrift companion had too often avowed the pleasure he would feel in quartering himself on my kind friend, dissipating his hard-earned gains, and squandering the fruits of all his toil. Deterred by such a prospect I resolved rather never to revisit him than in such company. Now, however, I was again alone, and all my hopes and wishes turned towards him. A few hours' sail might again bring me beneath his roof, and once more should I find myself at home. The thought was calming to all my excitement; I forgot every danger I had passed through; I lost all memory of every vicissitude I had escaped, and had only the little low parlour in the "Black Pits" before my mind's eye; the wild, unweeded garden, and the sandy, sunny beach before the door. It was as though all that nigh a year had compassed had never occurred, and that my life at Crown Point and my return to England were only a dream. Sleep overcame me as I thus lay pondering, and when I awoke the sun was glittering in the bright waves of the Mersey, a fresh breeze was flaunting and fluttering the half-loosened sails, and the joyous sounds of seamen's voices were mingling with the clank of capstans, and the measured stroke of oars.

It was full ten minutes after I awoke before I could remember how I came there, and what had befallen me. Poor Santron, where is he now? was my first thought, and it came with all the bitterness of self-reproach.

Could I have parted company with him under other circumstances, it would not have grieved me deeply. His mocking, sarcastic spirit, the tone of depreciation which he used towards everything and everybody, had gone far to sour me with the world, and day by day I felt within me the evil influences of his teachings. How different were they from poor Gottfried's lessons, and the humble habits of those who lived beneath them! Yet I was sorry, deeply sorry, that our separation should have been thus,

and almost wished I had stayed to share his fate, whatever
it might be.

While thus swayed by different impulses, now thinking
of my old home at Crown Point, now of "Uncle Pat's"
thatched cabin, and again of Santron, I strolled down to
the wharf, and found myself in a considerable crowd of
people, who were all eagerly pressing forward to witness
the embarkation of several boats-full of pressed seamen,
who, strongly guarded and ironed, were being conveyed to
the Athol tender, a large three-master, about a mile off,
down the river. To judge from the cut faces and ban-
daged heads and arms, the capture had not been effected
without resistance. Many of the poor fellows appeared
rather suited to an hospital than the duties of active service; and several lay with bloodless faces and white lips,
the handcuffed wrists seeming a very mockery of a condition so destitute of all chance of resistance.

The sympathies of the bystanders were very varied regarding them. Some were full of tender pity and compassion; some denounced the system as a cruel and oppressive tyranny; others deplored it as an unhappy necessity;
and a few well-to-do-looking old citizens, in drab shorts and
wide-brimmed hats, grew marvellously indignant at the
recreant poltroonery of "the scoundrels who were not
proud to fight their country's battles."

As I was wondering within myself how it happened that
men thus coerced could ever be depended on in moments
of peril and difficulty, and by what magic the mere exercise of discipline was able to merge the feelings of the man
in the sailor, the crowd was rudely driven back by policemen, and a cry of "make way," "fall back there," given.
In the sudden retiring of the mass I found myself standing
on the very edge of the line along which a new body of
impressed men were about to pass. Guarded front, flank,
and rear, by a strong party of marines, the poor fellows
came along slowly enough. Many were badly wounded,
and walked lamely; some were bleeding profusely from
cuts on the face and temples, and one, at the very tail of
the procession, was actually carried in a blanket by four
sailors. A low murmur ran through the crowd at the
spectacle, which gradually swelled louder and fuller till it
burst forth into a deep groan of indignation, and a cry of
shame! shame! Too much used to such ebullitions of
public feeling, or too proud to care for them, the officer
in command of the party never seemed to hear the angry
cries and shouts around him; and I was even more struck

by his cool self-possession than by their enthusiasm. For a moment or two I was convinced that a rescue would be attempted. I had no conception that so much excitemen could evaporate innocuously, and was preparing myself to take part in the struggle when the line halted as the leading files gained the stairs, and, to my wonderment, the crowd became hushed and still. Then, one burst of excited pity over, not a thought occurred to any to offer resistance to the law, or dare to oppose the constituted authorities. How unlike Frenchmen ! thought I; nor am I certain whether I deemed the disparity to their credit !

"Give him a glass of water !" I heard the officer say, as he leaned over the litter, and the crowd at once opened to permit some one to fetch it. Before I believed it were possible to have procured it, a tumbler of water was passed from hand to hand till it reached mine, and, stepping forwards, I bent down to give it to the sick man. The end of a coarse sheet was thrown over his face, and as it was removed I almost fell over him, for it was Santron. His face was covered with a cold sweat, which lay in great drops all over it, and his lips were slightly frothed. As he looked up I could see that he was just rallying from a fainting fit, and could mark in the change that came over his glassy eye that he had recognised me. He made a faint effort at a smile, and, in a voice barely a whisper, said, "I knew thou'd not leave me, Maurice."

"You are his countryman?" said the officer, addressing me in French.

"Yes, sir," was my reply.

"You are both Canadians, then?"

"Frenchmen, sir, and officers in the service. We only landed from an American ship yesterday, and were trying to make our way to France."

"I'm sorry for you," said he, compassionately; "nor do I know how to help you. Come on board the tender, however, and we'll see if they'll not give you a passage with your friend to the Nore. I'll speak to my commanding-officer for you."

This scene all passed in a very few minutes, and before I well knew how or why, I found myself on board of a ship's long-boat, sweeping along over the Mersey, with Santron's head in my lap, and his cold, clammy fingers grasped in mine. He was either unaware of my presence or too weak to recognise me, for he gave no sign of knowing me; and during our brief passage down the river, and when lifted up the ship's side, seemed totally insensible to everything.

The scene of uproar, noise, and confusion on board the Athol is far above my ability to convey. A shipwreck, a fire, and mutiny, all combined, could scarcely have collected greater elements of discord. Two large detachments of marines, many of whom, fresh from furlough, were too drunk for duty, and were either lying asleep along the deck, or riotously interfering with everybody; a company of Sappers en route to Woolwich, who would obey none but their own officer, and he was still ashore; detachments of able-bodied seamen from the Jupiter, full of grog and prize-money; four hundred and seventy impressed men, cursing, blaspheming, and imprecating every species of calamity on their captors; added to which, a crowd of Jews, bumboat women, and slop-sellers of all kinds, with the crews of two ballast-lighters, fighting for additional pay, being the chief actors in a scene whose discord I never saw equalled. Drunkenness, suffering, hopeless misery, and even insubordination, all lent their voices to a tumult, amid which the words of command seemed lost, and all effort at discipline vain.

How we were ever to go to sea in this state, I could not even imagine; the ship's crew seemed inextricably mingled with the rioters, many of whom were just sufficiently sober to be eternally meddling with the ship's tackle; belaying what ought to be " free," and loosening what should have been " fast;" getting their fingers jammed in blocks, and their limbs crushed by spars till the cries of agony rose high above every other confusion. Turning with disgust from a spectacle so discordant and disgraceful, I descended the ladders, which led, by many a successive flight, into the dark, low-ceilinged chamber called the " sick bay," and where poor Santron was lying in, what I almost envied, insensibility to the scene around him. A severe blow from the hilt of a cutlass had caused a concussion of the brain, and, save in the momentary excitement which a sudden question might cause, left him totally unconscious. His head had been already shaved before I descended, and I found the assistant-surgeon, an Irishman, Mr. Peter Colhayne, experimenting a new mode of cupping as I entered. By some mischance of the machinery, the lancets of the cupping instrument had remained permanently fixed, refusing to obey the spring, and standing all straight outside the surface. In this dilemma, Peter's ingenuity saw nothing for it but to press them down vigorously into the scalp, and then saw them backwards the whole length of the head, a performance the originality of which, in all probability, was derived from the operation ot a harrow in agriculture. He had just completed a third track when I came in, and, by great remonstrance and no small flattery, induced him to desist. "We have glasses," said he, " but they were all broke in the cock-pit; but a tin porringer is just as good." And so saying, he lighted a little pledget of tow, previously steeped in turpentine, and, popping it into the tin vessel, clapped it on the head. This was meant to exhaust the air within, and thus draw the blood to the surface, a scientific process he was good enough to explain most minutely for my benefit, and the good results of which he most confidently vouched for.

"They've a hundred new conthrivances," said Mr. Col-hayne, " for doing that simple thing ye see there. They've pumps, and screws, and hydraulic devilments as much complicated as a watch that's always getting out of order and going wrong; but with that ye'll see what good 'twill do him ; he'll be as lively as a lark in ten minutes."

The prophecy was destined to a perfect fulfilment, for poor Santron, who lay motionless and unconscious up to that moment, suddenly gave signs of life by moving his features, and jerking his limbs to this side and that. The doctor's self-satisfaction took the very proudest form. He expatiated on the grandeur of medical science, the wonderful advancement it was making, and the astonishing progress the curative art had made even within his own time. I must own that I should have lent a more implicit credence to this pæan if I had not waited for the removal of the cupping vessel, which, instead of blood, contained merely the charred ashes of the burnt tow, while the scalp beneath it presented a blackened, seared aspect, like burned leather. Such was literally the effect of the operation ; but as from that period the patient began steadily to improve, I must leave to more scientific inquirers the task of explaining through what agency, and on what principles.

Santron's condition, although no longer dangerous, presented little hope of speedy recovery. His faculties were clouded and obscured, and the mere effort at recognition seemed to occasion him great subsequent disturbance. Colhayne, who, whatever may have been his scientific deficiencies, was good-nature and kindness itself, saw nothing for him but removal to Haslar, and we now only waited for the ship's arrival at the Nore to obtain the order for his transmisson.

If the Athol was a scene of the wildest confusion and
uproar when we tripped our anchor, we had not been six
hours at sea when all was a picture of order and propriety.
The decks were cleared of every one not actually engaged
in the ship's working, or specially permitted to remain;
ropes were coiled; boats hauled up; sails trimmed;
hatches down; sentinels paced the deck in appointed
places, and all was discipline and regularity. From the
decorous silence that prevailed, none could have supposed
so many hundred living beings were aboard, still less, that
they were the same disorderly mob who sailed from the
Mersey a few short hours before. From the surprise which
all this caused me I was speedily aroused by an order more
immediately interesting, being summoned on the poop-
deck to attend the general muster. Up they came from
holes and hatchways, a vast host, no longer brawling
and insubordinate, but quiet, submissive, and civil. Such
as were wounded had been placed under the doctor's care,
and all those now present were orderly and service-like.
With a very few exceptions they were all sailors, a few
having already served in a king's ship. The first lieutenant, who inspected us, was a grim, grey-headed man past
the prime of life, with features hardened by disappointment and long service, but who still retained an expression of kindliness and good nature. His duty he despatched with all the speed of long habit; read the name;
looked at the bearer of it; asked a few routine questions;
and then cried " stand by," even ere the answers were
finished. When he came to me he said,—

" Abraham Hackett. Is that your name, lad ? "

" No, sir. I'm called Maurice Tiernay."

" Tiernay, Tiernay," said he a couple of times over.
" No such name here."

" Where's Tiernay's name, Cottle? " asked he of a subordinate behind him.

The fellow looked down the list—then at me—then at
the list again—and then back to me, puzzled excessively
by the difficulty, but not seeing how to explain it.

" Perhaps I can set the matter right, sir," said I. " I
came aboard along with a wounded countryman of
mine—the young Frenchman who is now in the sick
bay."

" Ay, to be sure; I remember all about it now," said
the lieutenant. " You call yourselves French officers ? "

" And such are we, sir."

" Then how the devil came ye here ? Mother Martin's

cellar is, to say the least of it, an unlikely spot to select as a restaurant."

" The story is a somewhat long one, sir."

" Then I havn't time for it, lad," he broke in. " We've rather too much on hand just now for that. If you've got your papers, or anything to prove what you assert, I'll land you when I come into the Downs, and you'll, of course, be treated as your rank in the service requires. If you have not, I must only take the responsibility on myself to regard you as an impressed man. Very hard, I know, but can't help it. Stand by."

These few words were uttered with a most impetuous speed; and as all reply to them was impossible, I saw my case decided and my fate decreed, even before I knew they were under litigation.

As we were marched forwards to go below, I overheard an officer say to another,—

" Hay will get into a scrape about those French fellows; they may turn out to be officers, after all."

" What matter ?" cried the other. " One is dying ; and the other Hay means to draft on board the 'Téméraire.' Depend upon it, we'll never hear more of either of them."

This was far from pleasant tidings ; and yet I knew not any remedy for the mishap. I had never seen the officer who spoke to me ashore since we came on board. I knew of none to intercede for me ; and as I sat down on the bench beside poor Santron's cot, I felt my heart lower than it had ever been before. I was never enamoured of the sea service ; and certainly the way to overcome my dislike was not by engaging against my own country ; and yet this, in all likelihood, was now to be my fate. These were my last waking thoughts the first night I passed on board the Athol.

CHAPTER XXXIII.

A BOLD STROKE FOR FAME AND FORTUNE.

To be awakened suddenly from a sound sleep; hurried half-dressed, up a gangway; and, ere your faculties have acquired free play, be passed over a ship's side, on a dark and stormy night, into a boat wildly tossed here and there, with spray showering over you, and a chorus of loud voices about you; is an event not easily forgotten. Such a scene still dwells in my memory, every incident of it as clear and distinct as though it had occurred only yesterday. In this way was I "passed," with twelve others, on board his Majesty's frigate, Téméraire, a vessel which, in the sea service, represented what a well-known regiment did on shore, and bore the reputation of being a "condemned ship;" this depreciating epithet having no relation to the qualities of the vessel herself, which was a singularly beautiful French model, but only to that of the crew and officers; it being the policy of the day to isolate the black-guards of both services, confining them to particular crafts and corps, making, as it were, a kind of index expurga-torius, where all the rascality was available at a moment's notice.

It would be neither agreeable to my reader nor myself, if I should dwell on this theme, nor linger on a description where cruelty, crime, heartless tyranny, and reckless in-subordination made up all the elements. A vessel that floated the seas only as a vast penitentiary—the "cats," the "yardarm," and the " gangway," comprising its scheme of discipline—would scarcely be an agreeable subject: and, in reality, my memory retains of the life aboard little else than scenes of suffering and sorrow. Captain Gesbrook had the name of being able to reduce any, the most insubordinate, to discipline. The veriest rascals of the fleet, the con-summate scoundrels, one of whom was deemed pollution to an ordinary crew, were said to come from his hands models of seamanship and good conduct; and it must be owned, that if the character was deserved, it was not ob-

tained without some sacrifice. Many died under punishment; many carried away with them diseases under which
they lingered on to death; and not a few preferred suicide
to the terrible existence on board. And although a
Téméraire—as a man who had served in her was always
afterwards called—was now and then shown as an example
of sailor-like smartness and activity, very few knew how
dearly that one success had been purchased, nor by what
terrible examples of agony and woe that solitary conversion was obtained.

To me the short time I spent on board of her is a
dreadful dream. We were bound for the Mediterranean,
to touch at Malta and Gibraltar, and then join the blockading squadron before Genoa. What might have been my
fate, to what excess passionate indignation might have
carried me, revolted as I was by tyranny and injustice, I
know not, when an accident, happily for me, rescued me
from all temptation. We lost our mizen-mast, in a storm,
in the Bay of Biscay, and a dreadful blow on the head,
from the spanker-boom, felled me to the deck, with a
fracture of the skull.

From that moment I know of nothing till the time when
I lay in my cot, beside a port-hole of the main deck, gazing
at the bright blue waters that flashed and rippled beside
me, or straining my strength to rest on my elbow, when I
caught sight of the glorious city of Genoa, with its grand
mountain background, about three miles from where I lay.
Whether from a due deference to the imposing strength of
the vast fortress, or that the line of duty prescribed our
action, I cannot say, but the British squadron almost exclusively confined its operations to the act of blockade.
Extending far across the bay, the English ensign was seen
floating from many a taper mast, while boats of every
shape and size plied incessantly from ship to ship, their
course marked out at night by the meteor-like light that
glittered in them; not, indeed, that the eye often turned
in that direction, all the absorbing interest of the scene
lying in-shore. Genoa was, at that time, surrounded by
an immese Austrian force, under the command of General
Melas, who, occupying all the valleys and deep passes of
the Appennines, were imperceptible during the day; but
no sooner had night closed in, than a tremendous cannonade began, the balls describing great semicircles in the air
ere they fell to scatter death and ruin on the devoted city.
The spectacle was grand beyond description, for while the
distance at which we lay dulled and subdued the sound

of the artillery to a hollow booming, like far-off thunder, the whole sky was streaked by the course of the shot, and, at intervals, lighted up by the splendour of a great fire, as the red shot fell into and ignited some large building or other.

As, night after night, the cannonade increased in power and intensity, and the terrible effects showed themselves in flames which burst out from different quarters of the city, I used to long for morning, to see if the tri-colour still floated on the walls, and when my eye caught the well-known ensign, I could have wept with joy as I beheld it.

High up, too, on the cliffs of the rugged Appennines, from many a craggy eminence, where perhaps a solitary gun was stationed, I could see the glorious flag of France, the emblem of liberty and glory too!

In the day the scene was one of calm and tranquil beauty. It would have seemed impossible to connect it with war and battle. The glorious city, rising in terraces of palaces, lay reflected in the mirror-like waters of the bay, blue as the deep sky above them. The orange-trees, loaded with golden fruit, shed their perfume over marble fountains, amid gardens of every varied hue; bands of military music were heard from the public promenades; all the signs of joy and festivity which betokened a happy and pleasure-seeking population. But at night the "red artillery" again flashed forth, and the wild cries of strife and battle rose through the beleaguered city. The English spies reported that a famine and a dreadful fever were raging within the walls, and that all Massena's efforts were needed to repress an open mutiny of the garrison; but the mere aspect of the "proud city" seemed to refute the assertion. The gay carolling of church bells vied with the lively strains of martial music, and the imposing pomp of military array, which could be seen from the walls, bespoke a joyous confidence, the very reverse of this depression.

From the "tops," and high up in the rigging, the movements in-shore could be descried; and frequently, when an officer came down to visit a comrade, I could hear of the progress of the siege, and learn, I need not say with what delight, that the Austrians had made little or no way in the reduction of the place, and that every stronghold and bastion was still held by Frenchmen.

At first, as I listened, the names of new places and new generals confused me; but by daily familiarity with the topic, I began to perceive that the Austrians had interposed a portion of their force between Massena's division and that of Suchet, cutting off the latter from Genoa, and compelling him to fall back towards Chiavari and Borghetto, along the coast of the Gulf. This was the first success of any importance obtained ; and it was soon followed by others of equal significance, Soult being driven from ridge to ridge of the Appennines, till he was forced back within the second line of defences.

The English officers were loud in condemning Austrian slowness ; the inaptitude they exhibited to profit by a success, and the over-caution which made them, even in victory, so careful of their own safety. From what I overheard, it seemed plain that Genoa was untenable by any troops but French, or opposed to any other adversaries than their present ones.

The bad tidings—such I deemed them—came quicker and heavier. Now, Soult was driven from Monte Notte. Now, the great advance post of Monte Faccio was stormed and carried. Now, the double eagle was floating from San Tecla, a fort within cannon-shot of Genoa. A vast semicircle of bivouac fires stretched from the Appennines to the sea, and their reflected glare from the sky lit up the battlements and ramparts of the city.

"Even yet, if Massena would make a dash at them," said a young English lieutenant, "the white-coats would fall back."

"My life on't he'd cut his way through, if he knew they were only two to one !"

And this sentiment met no dissentient. All agreed that French heroism was still equal to the overthrow of a force double its own.

It was evident that all hope of reinforcement from France was vain. Before they could have begun their march southward, the question must be decided one way or other.

"There's little doing to-night," said an officer, as he descended the ladder to the sick bay. "Melas is waiting for some heavy mortars that are coming up ; and then there will be a long code of instructions from the Aulic Council, and a whole treatise on gunnery to be read, before he can use them. Trust me, if Massena knew his man, he'd be up and at him."

Much discussion followed this speech, but all more or less agreed in its sentiment. Weak as were the French, lowered by fever and by famine, they were still an overmatch for their adversaries. What a glorious avowal from the lips of an enemy was this! The words did more for my recovery than all the cares and skill of physic. Oh, if my countrymen but knew! if Massena could but hear it! was my next thought; and I turned my eyes to the ramparts, whose line was marked out by the bivouac fires, through the darkness. How short the distance seemed! and yet it was a whole world of separation. Had it been a great plain in a mountain tract, the attempt might almost have appeared practicable; at least, I had often seen fellows who would have tried it. Such were the ready roads, the royal paths to promotion; and he who trod them saved miles of weary journey. I fell asleep, still thinking on these things; but they haunted my dreams. A voice seemed ever to whisper in my ear—" If Massena but knew, he would attack them! One bold dash, and the Austrians would fall back." At one instant, I thought myself brought before a court-martial of English officers, for attempting to carry these tidings, and proudly avowing the endeavour, I fancied I was braving the accusation. At another, I was wandering through the streets of Genoa, gazing on the terrible scenes of famine I had heard of. And lastly, I was marching with a night party to attack the enemy. The stealthy footfall of the column appeared suddenly to cease; we were discovered; the Austrian cavalry were upon us! I started and awoke, and found myself in the dim, half-lighted chamber, with pain and suffering around me, and where, even in this midnight hour, the restless tortures of disease were yet wakeful.

"The silence is more oppressive to me than the roll of artillery," said one, a sick midshipman, to his comrade. "I grew accustomed to the clatter of the guns, and slept all the better for it."

"You'll scarcely hear much more of that music," replied his friend. "The French must capitulate to-morrow or next day."

"Not if Massena would make a dash at them," thought I; and with difficulty could I refrain from uttering the words aloud.

They continued to talk to each other in low whispers, and, lulled by the drowsy tones, I fell asleep once more, again to dream of my comrades and their fortunes. A heavy bang like a cannon shot awoke me; but whether this were real or not I never knew; most probably, however, it was the mere creation of my brain, for all were now in deep slumber around me, and even the marine on duty had seated himself on the ladder, and with his musket

between his legs, seemed dozing away peacefully. I looked
out through the little window beside my berth. A light
breeze was faintly rippling the dark water beneath me. It
was the beginning of a " Levanter," and scarcely ruffled
the surface as it swept along.

"Oh, if it would but bear the tidings I am full of !"
thought I. "But why not dare the attempt myself ?" While
in America I had learned to become a good swimmer.
Under Indian teaching, I had often passed hours in the
water ; and though now debilitated by long sickness, I
felt that the cause would supply me with the strength I
needed. From the instant that I conceived the thought,
till I found myself descending the ship's side, was scarcely
a minute. Stripping off my woollen shirt, and with
nothing but my loose trousers, I crept through the little
window, and lowering myself gently by the rattlin of my
hammock, descended slowly and noiselessly into the sea. I
hung on thus for a couple of seconds, half fearing the
attempt, and irresolute of purpose. Should strength fail,
or even a cramp seize me, I must be lost, and none would
ever know in what an enterprise I had perished. It would
be set down as a mere attempt at escape. This notion
almost staggered my resolution, but only for a second or
so ; and with a short prayer, I slowly let slip the rope,
and struck out to swim.

The immense efforts required to get clear of the ship's
side discouraged me dreadfully, nor probably without the
aid of the " Levanter " should I have succeeded in doing
so, the suction of the water along the sides was so powerful.
At last, however, I gained the open space, and found
myself stretching away towards shore rapidly. The night
was so dark that I had nothing to guide me save the
lights on the ramparts ; but in this lay my safety. Swimming is, after all, but a slow means of progression. After
what I judged to be an hour in the water, as I turned my
head to look back, I almost fancied that the great bowsprit
of the Téméraire was over me, and that the figure who
leaned over the taffrail was steadily gazing on me. How
little way had I made, and what a vast reach of water lay
between me and the shore !   I tried to animate my courage
by thinking of the cause, how my comrades would greet
me, the honour in which they would hold me for the exploit, and such like ; but the terror of failure damped this
ardour, and hope sank every moment lower and lower.

For some time I resolved within myself not to look
back ; the discouragement was too great ; but the impulse

to do so became all the greater, and the only means of resisting was by counting the strokes, and determining not
to turn my head before I had made a thousand. The monotony of this last, and the ceaseless effort to advance,
threw me into a kind of dreamy state, wherein mere
mechanical effort remained. A few vague impressions are
all that remain to me of what followed. I remember the
sound of the morning guns from the fleet; I remember,
too, the hoisting of the French standard at daybreak on
the fort of the Mole; I have some recollection of a bastion
crowded with people, and hearing shouts and cheers like
voices of welcome and encouragement; and then a whole
fleet of small boats issuing from the harbour, as if by one
impulse; and then there comes a bright blaze of light
over one incident, for I saw myself, dripping and almost
dead, lifted on the shoulders of strong men, and carried
along a wide street filled with people. I was in Genoa!

CHAPTER XXXIV.

"GENOA IN THE SIEGE."

Up a straight street, so steep and so narrow that it seemed a stair, with hundreds of men crowding around me, I was borne along. Now, they were sailors who carried me; now, white-bearded grenadiers, with their bronzed, bold faces; now, they were the wild-looking Faquini of the Mole, with long-tasselled red caps, and gaudy sashes around their waists. Windows were opened on either side as we went, and eager faces protruded to stare at me; and then there were shouts and cries of triumphant joy bursting forth at every moment, amidst which I could hear the ever-recurring words—"Escaped from the English fleet."

By what means, or when, I had exchanged my dripping trousers of coarse sail-cloth for the striped gear of our republican mode—how one had given me his jacket, another a cap, and a third a shirt—I knew not; but there I was, carried along in triumph, half fainting from exhaustion, and almost maddened by excitement. That I must have told something of my history—Heaven knows how incoherently and unconnectedly—is plain enough, for I could hear them repeating one to the other—"Had served with Moreau's corps in the Black Forest;" "A hussar of the Ninth;" "One of Humbert's fellows;" and so on.

As we turned into a species of "Place," a discussion arose as to whither they should convey me. Some were for the "Cavalry Barracks," that I might be once more with those who resembled my old comrades. Others, more considerate, were for the hospital; but a staff-officer decided the question by stating that the general was at that very moment receiving the report in the church of the Annunziata, and that he ought to see me at once.

"Let the poor fellow have some refreshment," cried one. "Here, take this, it's coffee." "No, no, the 'petit goutte 's better—try that flask." "He shall have my chocolate," said an old major, from the door of a café;

and thus they pressed and solicited me with a generosity
that I had yet to learn how dear it cost.

"He ought to be dressed;" "He should be in uniform;" "Is better as he is;" "The general will not
speak to him thus;" "He will;" "He must."

Such, and such like, kept buzzing around me, as with
reeling brain and confused vision they bore me up the
great steps, and carried me into a gorgeous church, the
most splendidly ornamented building I had ever beheld.
Except, however, in the decorations of the ceiling, and
the images of saints which figured in niches high up,
every trace of a religious edifice had disappeared. The
pulpit had gone—the chairs and seats for the choir, the
confessionals, the shrines, altars—all had been uprooted,
and a large table, at which some twenty officers were
seated writing, now occupied the elevated platform of the
high altar, while here and there stood groups of officers,
with their reports from their various corps or parties in
out-stations. Many of these drew near to me as I entered,
and now the buzz of voices in question and rejoinder
swelled into a loud noise, and while some were recounting
my feat with all the seeming accuracy of eye-witnesses,
others were as resolutely protesting it all to be impossible.
Suddenly the tumult was hushed, the crowd fell back, and
as the clanking muskets proclaimed a "a salute," a whispered murmur announced the "General."

I could just see the waving plumes of his staff, as they
passed up, and then, as they were disappearing in the
distance, they stopped, and one hastily returned to the
entrance of the church.

"Where is this fellow? let me see him," cried he,
hurriedly, brushing his way through the crowd. "Let
him stand down; set him on his legs."

"He is too weak, Capitaine," said a soldier.

"Place him in a chair, then," said the aide-de-camp,
for such he was. "You have made your escape from the
English fleet, my man?" continued he, addressing me.

"I am an officer, and your comrade," replied I,
proudly; for with all my debility, the tone of his address
stung me to the quick.

"In what service, pray?" asked he, with a sneering look
at my motley costume.

"Your general shall hear where I have served, and how,
whenever he is pleased to ask me," was my answer.

"Ay, parbleu," cried three or four sous-officiers in
a breath, "the general shall see him himself."

And with a jerk they hoisted me once more on their shoulders, and with a run—the regular storming tramp of the line—they advanced up the aisle of the church, and never halted till within a few feet of where the staff were gathered around the general. A few words—they sounded like a reprimand—followed; a severe voice bade the soldiers "fall back," and I found myself standing alone before a tall and very strongly-built man, with a large, red-brown beard; he wore a grey upper coat over his uniform, and carried a riding-whip in his hand.

"Get him a seat. Let him have a glass of wine," cried he quickly, as he saw the tottering efforts I was making to keep my legs. "Are you better now?" asked he, in a voice which, rough as it was, sounded kindly.

Seeing me so far restored, he desired me to recount my late adventure, which I did in the fewest words, and the most concise fashion I could. Although never interrupting, I could mark that particular portions of my narrative made much impression on him, and he could not repress a gesture of impatience when I told him that I was impressed as a seaman to fight against the flag of my own country.

"Of course, then," cried he, "you were driven to the alternative of this attempt."

"Not so, General," said I, interrupting; "I had grown to be very indifferent about my own fortunes. I had become half fatalist as to myself. It was on very different grounds, indeed, that I dared this danger. It was to tell you, for if I mistake not I am addressing General Massena, tidings of deep importance."

I said these words slowly and deliberately, and giving them all the impressiveness I was able.

"Come this way, friend," said he, and, assisting me to arise, he led me a short distance off, and desired me to sit down on the steps in front of the altar railing. "Now, you may speak freely. I am the General Massena, and I have only to say, that if you really have intelligence of any value for me, you shall be liberally rewarded; but if you have not, and if the pretence be merely an effort to impose on one whose cares and anxieties are already hard to bear, it would be better that you had perished on sea than tried to attempt it."

There was a stern severity in the way he said this, which for a moment or two actually overpowered me. It was quite clear that he looked for some positive fact, some direct piece of information on which he might implicitly

rely; and here was I now with nothing save the gossip of
some English lieutenants, the idle talk of inexperienced
young officers. I was silent. From the bottom of my
heart I wished that I had never reached the shore, to
stand in a position of such humiliation as this.

"So, then, my caution was not unneeded," said the
general, as he bent his heavy brows upon me. "Now,
sir, there is but one amende you can make for this; tell
me frankly, have others sent you on this errand, or is the
scheme entirely of your own devising? Is this an English
plot, or is there a Bourbon element in it?"

"Neither one nor the other," said I, boldly, for indignation at last gave me courage. "I hazarded my life to
tell you what I overheard among the officers of the fleet
yonder; you may hold their judgment cheap; you may
not think their counsels worth the pains of listening
to; but I could form no opinion of this, and only thought if
these tidings could reach you, you might profit by them."

"And what are they?" asked he, bluntly.

"They said that your force was wasting away by famine
and disease; that your supplies could not hold out above
a fortnight; that your granaries were empty, and your
hospitals filled."

"They scarcely wanted the gift of second sight to see
this," said he, bitterly. "A garrison in close siege for
four months may be suspected of as much."

"Yes; but they said that as Soult's force fell back upon
the city, your position would be rendered worse."

"Fell back from where?" asked he, with a searching
look at me.

"As I understood, from the Appennines," replied I,
growing more confident as I saw that he became more
attentive. "If I understood them aright, Soult held a position called the 'Monte Faccio.' Is there such a name?"

"Go on," said he, with a nod of assent.

"That this could not long be tenable without gaining
the highest fortified point of the mountain. The 'Monte
Creto' they named it."

"The attempt on which has failed!" said Massena, as if
carried away by the subject; "and Soult himself is a
prisoner! Go on."

"They added, that now but one hope remained for this
army."

"And what was that, sir?" said he, fiercely. "What
suggestion of cunning strategy did these sea-wolves intimate?"

"To cut your way through the blockade, and join Suchet's corps, attacking the Austrians at the Monte Ratte, and by the sea-road gaining the heights of Borchetta."

"Do these heroic spirits know the strength of tha same Austrian corps? did they tell you that it numbered fifty-four thousand bayonets?"

"They called them below forty thousand; and that now that Bonaparte was on his way through the Alps, perhaps by this over the Mount Cenis ——"

"What! did they say this? Is Bonaparte so near us?" cried he, placing a hand on either shoulder, as he stared me in the face.

"Yes; there is no doubt of that. The despatch to Lord Keith brought the news a week ago, and there is no secret made about it in the fleet."

"Over Mount Cenis!" repeated he to himself. "Already in Italy!"

"Holding straight for Milan, Lord Keith thinks," added I.

"No, sir, straight for the Tuilleries," cried Massena, sternly; and then correcting himself suddenly, he burst into a forced laugh. I must confess that the speech puzzled me sorely at the time, but I lived to learn its meaning, and many a time have I wondered at the shrewd foresight which even then read the ambitious character of the future Emperor.

"Of this fact, then, you are quite certain. Bonaparte is on his march hither?"

"I have heard it spoken of every day for the last week," replied I; "and it was in consequence of this that the English officers used to remark, if Massena but knew it, he'd make a dash at them, and clear his way through at once."

"They said this, did they?" said he, in a low voice, and as if pondering over it.

"Yes; one and all agreed in thinking there could not be a doubt of the result."

"Where have you served, sir?" asked he, suddenly turning on me, and with a look that showed he was resolved to test the character of the witness.

"With Moreau, sir, on the Rhine and the Schwartz Wald; in Ireland with Humbert."

"Your regiment?"

"The Ninth Hussars."

"The 'Tapageurs,'" said he, laughing. "I know them

20

and glad I am not to have their company here at this
moment; you were a lieutenant?"

"Yes, sir."

"Well, supposing that, on the faith of what you have
told me, I was to follow the wise counsel of these gentlemen, would you like the alternative of gaining your promotion in the event of success, or being shot by a peloton
if we fail."

"They seem sharp terms, sir," said I, smiling, "when
it is remembered that no individual efforts of mine can
either promote one result or the other."

"Ay, but they can, sir," cried he, quickly. "If you
should. turn out to be an Austro-English spy; if these
tidings be a character to lead my troops into danger ; if,
in reliance on you, I should be led to compromise the
honour and safety of a French army ; your life, were it
worth ten thousand times over your own value of it,
would be a sorry recompense. Is this intelligible?"

"Far more intelligible than flattering," said I, laughing ;
for I saw that the best mode to treat him was by an
imitation of his own frank and careless humour. "I have
already risked that life you hold so cheaply, to convey
this information, but I am still ready to accept the conditions you offer me, if, in the event of success, my name
appear in the despatch."

He again stared at me with his dark and piercing eyes ;
but I stood the glance with a calm conscience, and he
seemed so to read it, for he said,—

"Be it so. I will, meanwhile, test your prudence. Let
nothing of this interview transpire; not a word of it
among the officers and comrades you shall make acquaintance with. You shall serve on my own staff; go now,
and recruit your strength for a couple of days, and then
report yourself at head quarters when ready for duty.
Latrobe, look to the Lieutenant Tiernay; see that he
wants for nothing, and let him have a horse and a uniform
as soon as may be."

Captain Latrobe, the future General of Division, was
then a young gay officer of about five-and-twenty, very
good-looking, and full of life and spirits, a buoyancy which
the terrible uncertainties of the siege could not repress.

"Our general talks nobly, Tiernay" said he, as he gave
me his arm to assist me; "but you'll stare when I tell
you that 'wanting for nothing' means, having four ounces
of black bread, and ditto of blue cheese per diem; and as
to a horse, if I possessed such an animal, I'd have given a

dinner party yesterday and eaten him. You look surprised, but when you see a little more of us here, you'll begin to think that prison rations in the fleet yonder were luxuries compared to what we have. No matter: you shall take share of my superabundance, and if I have little else to offer, I'll show you a view from my window, finer than anything you ever looked on in your life, and with a sea breeze that would be glorious if it didn't make one hungry."

While he thus rattled on, we reached the street, and there calling a couple of soldiers forwards, he directed them to carry me along to his quarters, which lay in the upper town, on an elevated plateau that overlooked the city and the bay together.

From the narrow lanes, flanked with tall, gloomy houses, and steep, ill-paved streets, exhibiting poverty and privation of every kind, we suddenly emerged into an open space of grass, at one side of which a handsome iron railing stood, with a richly-ornamented gate, gorgeously gilded. Within this was a garden and a fish-pond, surrounded with statues, and further on, a long, low villa, whose windows reached to the ground, and were shaded by a deep awning of striped blue and white canvas. Camelias, orange-trees, cactuses, and magnolias, abounded everywhere; tulips and hyacinths seemed to grow wild; and there was in the half-neglected look of the spot something of savage luxuriance that heightened the effect immensely.

" This is my Paradise, Tiernay, only wanting an Eve to be perfect," said Latrobe, as he set me down beneath a spreading lime-tree. " Yonder are your English friends; there they stretch away for miles beyond that point. That's the Monte Creto, you may have heard of; and there's the Bochetta. In that valley, to the left, the Austrian outposts are stationed; and from those two heights closer to the shore, they are gracious enough to salute us every evening after sunset, and even prolong the attention sometimes the whole night through. Turn your eyes in this direction, and you'll see the ' cornice' road, that leads to la belle France, but of which we see as much from this spot as we are ever like to do. So much for the geography of our position ; and now to look after your breakfast. You have, of course, heard that we do not revel in superfluities. Never was the boasted excellence of our national cookery more severely tested, for we have successively descended from cows and sheep to goats, horses, donkeys, dogs, occasionally experimenting on hides and shoe-leather, till we ended by regarding a rat as a rarity, and deeming a mouse a delicacy of the season. As for vegetables, there would not have been a flowering plant in all Genoa, if tulip and ranunculus roots had not been bitter as aloes. These seem very inhospitable confessions, but I make them the more freely since I am about to treat you ' en Gourmet.' Come in now, and acknowledge that juniper bark isn't bad coffee, and that commissary bread is not to be thought of ' lightly.' "

In this fashion did my comrade invite me to a meal, which, even with this preface, was far more miserable and scanty than I looked for.

CHAPTER XXXV.

A NOVEL COUNCIL OF WAR.

I HAD scarcely finished my breakfast, when a group of officers rode up to our quarters to visit me. My arrival had already created an immense sensation in the city, and all kinds of rumours were afloat as to the tidings I had brought. The meagreness of the information would, indeed, have seemed in strong contrast to the enterprise and hazard of the escape, had I not the craft to eke it out by that process of suggestion and speculation in which I was rather an adept.

Little in substance as my information was, all the younger officers were in favour of acting upon it. The English are no bad judges of our position and chances, was the constant argument. They see exactly how we stand; they know the relative forces of our army, and the enemy's; and if the " cautious islanders"—such was the phrase—advised a coup de main, it surely must have much in its favour. I lay stress upon the remark, trifling as it may seem; but it is curious to know, that with all the immense successes of England on sea, her reputation, at that time, among Frenchmen, was rather for prudent and well-matured undertaking, than for those daring enterprises which are as much the character of her courage.

My visitors continued to pour in during the morning, officers of every arm and rank, some from mere idle curiosity, some to question and interrogate, and not a few to solve doubts in their mind as to my being really French, and a soldier, and not an agent of that " perfide Albion," whose treachery was become a proverb amongst us. Many were disappointed at my knowing so little. I neither could tell the date of Napoleon's passing St. Gothard, nor the amount of his force; neither knew I whether he meant to turn eastward towards the plains of Lombardy, or march direct to the relief of Genoa. Of Moreau's successes in Germany, too, I had only heard vaguely; and, of course, could recount nothing. I could overhear, ncco,

sionally, around and about me, the murmurs of dissatisfaction my ignorance called forth, and was not a little
grateful to an old artillery captain for saying, "That's the
very best thing about the lad; a spy would have had his
whole lesson by heart."

"You are right, sir," cried I, catching at the words;
"I may know but little, and that little, perhaps, value-
less and insignificant; but my truth no man shall gain-
say."

The boldness of this speech from one wasted and miserable as I was, with tattered shoes and ragged clothes,
caused a hearty laugh, in which, as much from policy as
feeling, I joined myself.

"Come here, mon cher," said an infantry colonel, as,
walking to the door of the room, he drew his telescope
from his pocket, "you tell us of a coup de main—on the
Monte Faccio, is it not?"

"Yes," replied I, promptly, "so I understand the
name."

"Well, have you ever seen the place?"

"Never."

"Well, there it is yonder;" and he handed me his glass
as he spoke; "you see that large beetling cliff, with the
olives at the foot.   There, on the summit, stands the
Monte Faccio. The road—the pathway rather, and a steep
one it is—leads up where you see those goats feeding, and
crosses in front of the crag, directly beneath the fire of the
batteries.   There's not a spot on the whole ascent where
three men could march abreast ; and wherever there is any
shelter from fire, the guns of the 'Sprona,' that small fort
to the right, take the whole position. What do you think
of your counsel now?"

"You forget, sir, it is not my counsel. I merely repeat
what I overheard."

"And do you mean to say, that the men who gave
that advice were serious, or capable of adopting it themselves?"

"Most assuredly; they would never recommend to
others what they felt unequal to themselves. I know
these English well, and so much will I say of them."

"Bah!" cried he, with an insolent gesture of his hand,
and turned away; and I could plainly see, that my praises
of the enemy were very ill-taken. In fact, my unlucky
burst of generosity had done more to damage my credit,
than all the dangerous or impracticable features of my
scheme. Every eye was turned to the bold precipice, and

the stern fortress that crowned it, and all agreed that an attack must be hopeless.

I saw, too late, the great fault I had committed, and that nothing could be more wanting in tact than to suggest to Frenchmen an enterprise which Englishmen deemed practicable, and which yet, to the former, seemed beyond all reach of success. The insult was too palpable and too direct, but to retract was impossible, and I had now to sustain a proposition which gave offence on every side.

It was very mortifying to me to see how soon all my personal credit was merged in this unhappy theory. No one thought more of my hazardous escape, the perils I encountered, or the sufferings I had undergone. All that was remembered of me was the affront I had offered to the national courage, and the preference I had implied to English bravery.

Never did I pass a more tormenting day; new arrivals continually refreshed the discussion, and always with the same results; and although some were satisfied to convey their opinions by a shake of the head or a dubious smile, others, more candid than civil, plainly intimated that if I had nothing of more consequence to tell, I might as well have stayed where I was, and not added one more to a garrison so closely pressed by hunger. Very little more of such reasoning would have persuaded myself of its truth, and I almost began to wish that I was once more back in the "sick bay" of the frigate.

Towards evening I was left alone; my host went down to the town on duty; and after the visit of a tailor, who came to try on me a staff uniform—a distinction, I after-wards learned, owing to the abundance of this class of costume, and not to any claims I could prefer to the rank —I was perfectly free to stroll about where I pleased un molested, and, no small blessing, unquestioned.

On following along the walls for some distance, I came to a part where a succession of deep ravines opened at the foot of the bastions, conducting by many a tortuous and rocky glen to the Appennines. The sides of these gorges were dotted here and there with wild hollies and fig-trees, stunted and ill-thriven, as the nature of the soil might imply. Still, for the sake of the few berries, or the sap-less fruit they bore, the soldiers of the garrison were ac-customed to creep out from the embrasures, and descend the steep cliffs, a peril great enough in itself, but terribly increased by the risk of exposure to the enemy's "Tirailleurs," as well as the consequences such indiscipline would bring down on them.

So frequent, however, had been these infractions, that little footpaths were worn bare along the face of the cliff, traversing in many a zigzag a surface that seemed like a wall. It was almost incredible that men would brave such peril for so little; but famine had rendered them indifferent to death; and although debility exhibited itself in every motion and gesture, the men would stand unshrinking and undismayed beneath the fire of a battery. At one spot, near the angle of a bastion, and where some shelter from the north winds protected the place, a little clump of orange-trees stood, and towards these, though fully a mile off, many a foot-track led, showing how strong had been the temptation in that quarter. To reach it, the precipice should be traversed, the gorge beneath and a considerable ascent of the opposite mountain accomplished; and yet all these dangers had been successfully encountered, merely instigated by hunger!

High above this very spot, at a distance of perhaps eight-hundred feet, stood the Monte Faccio—the large black and yellow banner of Austria floating from its walls, as if amid the clouds. I could see the muzzles of the great guns protruding from the embrasures; and I could even catch glances of a tall bearskin, as some soldier passed or repassed behind the parapet, and I thought how terrible would be the attempt to storm such a position. It was, indeed, true, that if I had the least conception of the strength of the fort, I never should have dared to talk of a coup de main. Still I was in a manner pledged to the suggestion. I had perilled my life for it, and few men do as much for an opinion; for this reason I resolved, come what would, to maintain my ground, and hold fast to my conviction. I never could be called upon to plan the expedition, nor could it by any possibility be confided to my guidance; responsibility could not, therefore, attach to me. All these were strong arguments, at least quite strong enough to decide a wavering judgment.

Meditating on these things, I strolled back to my quarters. As I entered the garden, I found that several officers were assembled, among whom was Colonel de Barre, the brother of the general of that name who afterwards fell at the Borodino. He was chef d'etat major to Massena, and a most distinguished and brave soldier. Unlike the fashion of the day, which made the military man affect the rough coarseness of a savage, seasoning his talk with oaths, and curses, and low expressions, De Barre had something of the petit maitre in his address, which nothing short of his well-proved courage would have saved from ridicule. His voice was low and soft, his smile perpetual; and although well-bred enough to have been dignified and easy, a certain fidgetty impulse to be pleasing made him always appear affected and unnatural. Never was there such a contrast to his chief; but indeed it was said, that to this very disparity of temperament he owed all the influence he possessed over Massena's mind.

I might have been a general of division at the very least, to judge from the courteous deference of the salute with which he approached me—a politeness the more striking, as all the others immediately fell back, to leave us to converse together. I was actually overcome with the flattering terms in which he addressed me on the subject of my escape.

"I could scarcely at first credit the story," said he, "but when they told me that you were a 'Ninth man,' one of the old Tapageurs, I never doubted it more. You see what a bad character is, Monsieur de Tiernay!" It was the first time I had ever heard the prefix to my name, and I own the sound was pleasurable. "I served a few months with your corps myself, but I soon saw there was no chance of promotion among fellows all more eager than myself for distinction. Well, sir, it is precisely to this reputation I have yielded my credit, and to which General Massena is kind enough to concede his own confidence. Your advice is about to be acted on, Mons. de Tiernay."

"The coup de main——"

"A little lower, if you please, my dear sir. The expedition is to be conducted with every secrecy, even from the officers of every rank below a command. Have the goodness to walk along with me this way. If I understand General Massena aright, your information conveys no details, nor any particular suggestions as to the attack."

"None whatever, sir. It was the mere talk of a gunroom—the popular opinion among a set of young officers."

"I understand," said he, with a bow and a smile; "the suggestion of a number of high-minded and daring soldiers, as to what they deemed practicable."

"Precisely, sir."

"Neither could you collect from their conversation anything which bore upon the number of the Austrian advance guard, or their state of preparation?"

" Nothing, sir. The opinion of the English was, I suspect, mainly founded on the great superiority of our forces
to the enemy's in all attacks of this kind."

" Our ' esprit Tapageur,' eh?" said he, laughing, and
pinching my arm familiarly, and I joined in the laugh with
pleasure. " Well, Monsieur de Tiernay, let us endeavour
to sustain this good impression. The attempt is to be made
to-night."

" To-night!" exclaimed I, in amazement: for everything within the city seemed tranquil and still.

"To-night, sir; and, by the kind favour of General
Massena, I am to lead the attack; the reserve, if we are
ever to want it, being under his own command. It is to
be at your own option on which staff you will serve."

" On yours, of course, sir," cried I, hastily. " A man
who stands unknown and unvouched for among his comrades, as I do, has but one way to vindicate his claim to
credit, by partaking the peril he counsels."

" There could be no doubt either of your judgment, or
the sound reasons for it," replied the colonel; " the only
question was, whether you might be unequal to the
fatigue."

" Trust me, sir, you'll not have to send me to the rear,"
said I, laughing.

" Then you are extra on my staff, Mons. de Tiernay."

As we walked along, he proceeded to give me the details
of our expedition, which was to be on a far stronger scale
than I anticipated. Three battalions of infantry, with
four light batteries, and as many squadrons of dragoons,
were to form the advance.

" We shall neither want the artillery, nor cavalry, except to cover a retreat," said he; " I trust, if it come to
that, there will not be many of us to protect; but such
are the general's orders, and we have but to obey them."

With the great events of that night on my memory, it
is strange that I should retain so accurately in my mind
the trivial and slight circumstances, which are as fresh
before me as if they had occurred but yesterday.

It was about eleven o'clock, of a dark but starry night,
not a breath of wind blowing, that, passing through a
number of gloomy, narrow streets, I suddenly found myself in the courtyard of the Balbé Palace. A large marble fountain was playing in the centre, around which
several lamps were lighted; by these I could see that the
place was crowded with officers, some seated at tables
drinking, some smoking, and others lounging up and down

In conversation. Huge loaves of black bread, and wicker-covered flasks of country wine, formed the entertainment; but even these, to judge from the zest of the guests, were no common delicacies. At the foot of a little marble group, and before a small table, with a map on it, sat General Massena himself, in his grey over-coat, cutting his bread with a case knife, while he talked away to his staff.

"These maps are good for nothing, Bressi," cried he. "To look at them, you'd say that every road was practicable for artillery, and every river passable, and you find afterwards that all these fine chaussees are bypaths, and the rivulets downright torrents. Who knows the Chiavari road?"

"Giorgio knows it well, sir," said the officer addressed, and who was a young Piedmontese from Massena's own village.

"Ah, Birbante!" cried the general, "are you here again?" and he turned laughingly towards a little bandy-legged monster, of less than three feet high, who, with a cap stuck jauntily on one side of his head, and a wooden sword at his side, stepped forward with all the confidence of an equal.

"Ay, here I am," said he, raising his hand to his cap, soldier fashion; "there was nothing else for it but this trade," and he placed his hand on the hilt of his wooden weapon; "you cut down all the mulberries and left us no silk-worms; you burned all the olives, and left us no oil; you trampled down our maize crops and our vines. Per Baccho! the only thing left was to turn brigand like yourself, and see what would come of it."

"Is he not cool to talk thus to a general at the head of his staff?" said Massena, with an assumed gravity.

"I knew you when you wore a different looking epaulette than that there," said Giorgio, "and when you carried one of your father's meal sacks on your shoulder, instead of all that bravery."

"Parbleu! so he did," cried Massena, laughing heartily. "That scoundrel was always about our mill, and, I believe, lived by thieving!" added he, pointing to the dwarf.

"Every one did a little that way in our village," said the dwarf; "but none ever profited by his education like yourself."

If the general and some of the younger officers seemed highly amused at the fellow's impudence and effrontery some of the others looked angry and indignant. A few

were really well born, and could afford to smile at these
recognitions; but many who sprung from an origin even
more humble than the general's could not conceal their
angry indignation at the scene.

"I see that these gentlemen are impatient of our vulgar
recollections," said Massena, with a sardonic grin; "so
now to business, Giorgio. You know the Chiavari road—
what is't like?"

"Good enough to look at, but mined in four places."

The general gave a significant glance at the staff, and
bade him go on.

"The white coats are strong in that quarter, and have
eight guns to bear upon the road, where it passes beneath
Monte Ratte."

"Why, I was told that the pass was undefended!" cried
Massena, angrily; "that a few skirmishers were all that
could be seen near it."

"All that could be seen!—so they are; but there are
eight twelve-pounder guns in the brushwood, with shot
and shell enough to be seen, and felt too."

Massena now turned to the officers near him, and conversed with them eagerly for some time. The debated
point I subsequently heard was how to make a feint attack
on the Chiavari road, to mask the coup de main intended
for the Monte Faccio. To give the false attack any colour
of reality, required a larger force and greater preparation
than they could afford, and this was now the great difficulty.
At last it was resolved that this should be a mere demon-
stration, not to push far beyond the walls, but, by all the
semblance of a serious advance, to attract as much attention as possible from the enemy.

Another and a greater embarrassment lay in the fact,
that the troops intended for the coup de main had no other
exit than the gate which led to Chiavari; so that the two
lines of march would intersect and interfere with each
other. Could we even have passed out our Tirailleurs in
advance, the support could easily follow; but the enemy
would, of course, notice the direction our advance would
take, and our object be immediately detected.

"Why not pass the skirmishers out by the embrasures,
to the left yonder," said I; "I see many a track where
men have gone already."

"It is steep as a wall," cried one.

"And there's a breast of rock in front that no foot could
scale."

"You have at least a thousand feet of precipice above

you, when you reach the glen, if ever you do reach it alive."

" And this to be done in the darkness of a night !"

Such were the discouraging comments which rattled, quick as musketry, around me.

" The lieutenant's right, nevertheless," said Giorgio. " Half the voltigeurs of the garrison know the path well already; and as to darkness—if there were a moon you dared not attempt it."

" There's some truth in that," observed an old major.

" Could you promise to guide them, Giorgio? " said Massena.

" Yes, every step of the way; up to the very walls of the fort."

" There, then," cried the general, " one great difficulty is got over already."

" Not so fast, Generale mio," said the dwarf; " I said I could, but I never said that I would."

" Not for a liberal present, Giorgio; not if I filled that leather pouch of yours with five-franc pieces, man ? "

" I might not live to spend it, and I care little for my next of kin," said the dwarf, drily.

" I don't think that we need his services, General," said I; " I saw the place this evening, and however steep it seems from the walls, the descent is practicable enough— at least I am certain that our Tirailleurs, in the Black Forest, would never have hesitated about it."

I little knew that when I uttered this speech I had sent a shot into the very heart of the magazine, the ruling passion of Massena's mind being an almost insane jealousy of Moreau's military fame; his famous campaign of Southern Germany, and his wonderful retreat upon the Rhine, being regarded as achievements of the highest order.

" I've got some of those regiments you speak of in my brigade here, sir," said he, addressing himself directly to me, " and I must own that their discipline reflects but little credit on the skill of so great an officer as General Moreau; and as to light troops, I fancy Colonel de Vallence yonder would scarcely feel it a flattery, were you to tell him to take a lesson from them."

" I have just been speaking to Colonel de Vallence, General," said Colonel de Barre. " He confirms everything Mons. de Tiernay tells us of the practicable nature of these paths; his fellows have tracked them at all hours, and neither want guidance nor direction to go."

" In that case I may as well offer my services," said

Giorgio, tightening his belt; " but I must tell you that it is too late to begin to-night—we must start immediately after nightfall. It will take from forty to fifty minutes to descend the cliff, a good two hours to climb the ascent, so that you'll not have much time to spare before daybreak."

Giorgio's opinion was backed by several others, and it was finally resolved upon that the attempt should be made on the following evening. Meanwhile, the dwarf was committed to the safe custody of a sergeant, affectedly to look to his proper care and treatment, but really to guard against any imprudent revelations that he might make respecting the intended attack.

CHAPTER XXXVI.

GENOA DURING THE SIEGE.

If the natural perils of the expedition were sufficient to suggest grave thoughts, the sight of the troops that were to form it was even a stronger incentive to fear. I could not believe my eyes, as I watched the battalions which now deployed before me. Always accustomed, whatever the hardships they were opposed to, to see French soldiers light-hearted, gay, and agile, performing their duties in a spirit of sportive pleasure, as if soldiering were but fun, what was the shock I received at sight of these care-worn, downcast, hollow-checked fellows, dragging their legs wearily along, and scarcely seeming to hear the words of command ; their clothes, patched and mended, sometimes too big, sometimes too little, showing that they had changed wearers without being altered ; their tattered shoes, tied on with strings round the ancles ; their very weapons dirty and uncared for ; they resembled rather a horde of bandits than the troops of the first army of Europe. There was, besides, an expression of stealthy, treacherous ferocity in their faces, such as I never saw before. To this pitiable condition had they been brought by starvation. Not alone the horses had been eaten, but dogs and cats ; even the vermin of the cellars and sewers was consumed as food. Leather and skins were all eagerly devoured ; and there is but too terrible reason to believe that human flesh itself was used to prolong for a few hours this existence of misery.

As they defiled into the " Piazza," there seemed a kind of effort to assume the port and bearing of their craft ; and although many stumbled, and some actually fell, from weakness, there was an evident attempt to put on a military appearance. The manner of the adjutant, as he passed down the line, revealed at once the exact position of affairs. No longer inspecting every little detail of equipment, criticising this, or remarking on that, his whole attention was given to the condition of the musket, whose lock he closely scrutinised, and then turned to the cartouch-box. The ragged uniforms, the uncouth shakos, the belts dirty and awry, never called forth a word of rebuke. Too glad, as it seemed, to recognise even the remnants of discipline, he came back from his inspection apparently will satisfied and content.

"These fellows turn out well," said Colonel de Barre, as he looked along the line ; and I started to see if the speech were an unfeeling jest. Far from it ; he spoke in all seriousness! The terrible scenes he had for months been witnessing ; the men dropping from hunger at their posts ; the sentries fainting as they carried arms, and borne away to the hospital to die; the bursts of madness that would now and then break forth from men whose agony became unendurable, had so steeled him to horrors, that even this poor shadow of military display seemed orderly and imposing.

"They are the 22nd, Colonel," replied the adjutant, proudly, " a corps that always have maintained their character, whether on parade or under fire!"

"Ah! the 22nd, are they? They have come up from Ronco, then?"

"Yes, sir ; they were all that General Soult could spare us."

"Fine-looking fellows they are," said De Barre, scanning them through his glass. "The third company is a little, a very little, to the rear—don't you perceive it?—and the flank is a thought or so restless and unsteady."

"A sergeant has just been carried to the rear ill, sir," said a young officer, in a low voice.

"The heat, I have no doubt; a 'colpo di sole,' as they tell us everything is," said De Barre. "By the way, is not this the regiment that boasts the pretty vivandière? What's this her name is?"

"Lela, sir."

"Yes, to be sure, Lela. I'm sure I've heard her toasted often enough at cafés and restaurants."

"There she is, sir, yonder, sitting on the steps of the fountain;" and the officer made a sign with his sword for the girl to come over. She made an effort to arise at the order, but tottered back, and would have fallen if a soldier had not caught her. Then suddenly collecting her strength, she arranged the folds of her short scarlet jupe, and smoothing down the braids of her fair hair, came forward, at that sliding, half-skipping pace that is the wont of her craft.

The exertion, and possibly the excitement, had flushed her cheek, so that as she came forward her look was brilliantly handsome; but as the colour died away, and a livid pallor spread over her jaws, lank and drawn in by famine, her expression was dreadful. The large eyes, lustrous anu wild-looking, gleamed with the fire of fever, while her thin nostrils quivered at each respiration.

Poor girl, even then, with famine and fever eating within her, the traits of womanly vanity still survived, and as she carried her hand to her cap in salute, she made a faint attempt at a smile!

"The 22nd may indeed be proud of their vivandière," said De Barre, gallantly.

"What hast in the 'tonnelet,' Lela?" continued he, tapping the little silver-hooped barrel she carried at her back.

"Ah, que voulez vous?" cried she, laughing, with a low, husky sound, the laugh of famine.

"I must have a glass of it to your health, ma belle Lela, if it cost me a crown piece;" and he drew forth the coin as he spoke.

"For such a toast, the liquor is quite good enough," said Lela, drawing back at the offer of money; while slinging the little cask in front, she unhooked a small silver cup, and filled it with water.

"No brandy, Lela?"

"None, colonel," said she, shaking her head; "and if I had, those poor fellows yonder would not like it so well."

"I understand," said he significantly; theirs is the thirst of fever.

A short, dry cough, and a barely perceptible nod of the head, was all her reply; but their eyes met, and any so sad an expression as they interchanged I never beheld! it was a confession in full of all each had seen of sorrow, of suffering, and of death—the terrible events three months of famine had revealed, and all the agonies of pestilence and madness.

"That is delicious water, Tiernay," said the colonel, as he passed me the cup, and thus trying to get away from the sad theme of his thoughts.

"I fetch it from a well outside the walls every morning," said Lela; "ay, and within gun-shot of the Austrian sentries, too."

"There's coolness for you, Tiernay," said the colonel; "think what the 22nd are made of when their vivandière dares to do this!"

21

"They'll not astonish him," said Lela, looking steadily at me.

"And why not, ma belle?" cried De Barre.

"He was a Tapageur, one of the 'Naughty Ninth,' as they called them."

"How do you know that, Lela? Have we ever met before?" cried I, eagerly.

"I've seen you, sir," said she, slily. "They used to call you the corporal that won the battle of Kehl. I know my father always said so."

I would have given worlds to have interrogated her further; so fascinating is selfishness, that already at least a hundred questions were presenting themselves to my mind. Who could Lela be? and who was her father? and what were these reports about me? Had I really won fame without knowing it? and did my comrades indeed speak of me with honour? All these, and many more inquiries, were pressing for utterance, as General Massena walked up with his staff. The general fully corroborated De Barre's opinion of the "22nd." They were, as he expressed, a "magnificent body." "It was a perfect pleasure to see such troops under arms." "Those fellows certainly exhibited few traces of a starved-out garrison."

Such and such like were the jesting observations bandied from one to the other, in all the earnest seriousness of truth! What more terrible evidence of the scenes they had passed through, than these convictions! What more stunning proof of the condition to which long suffering had reduced them!

"Where is our pleasant friend, who talked to us of the Black Forest last night? Ah, there he is; well, Monsieur Tiernay, do you think General Moreau's people turned out better than that after the retreat from Donaueschingen?"

There was no need for any reply, since the scornful burst of laughter of the staff already gave the answer he wanted; and now he walked forward to the centre of the piazza, while the troops proceeded to march past.

The band, a miserable group, reduced from fifty to thirteen in number, struck up a quick step, and the troops, animated by the sounds, and more still, perhaps, by Massena's presence, made an effort to step out in quick time; but the rocking, wavering motion, the clinking muskets, and uncertain gait, were indescribably painful to a soldier's eye. Their colonel, De Vallence, however, evidently did not regard them thus, for as he joined the staff, he received the general's compliments with all the good faith and composure in the world.

The battalions were marched off to barracks, and the group of officers broke up to repair to their several quarters. It was the hour of dinner, but it had been many a day since that meal had been heard of amongst them. A stray café here and there was open in the city, but a cup of coffee, without milk, and a small roll of black bread, a horrid compound of rye and cocoa, was all the refreshment obtainable ; and yet, I am bold to say that a murmur or a complaint was unheard against the general or the government. The heaviest reverses, the gloomiest hours of ill fortune, never extinguished the hope that Genoa was to be relieved at last, and that all we had to do was to hold out for the arrival of Bonaparte. To the extent of this conviction is to be attributed the wide disparity between the feeling displayed by the military and the townsfolk.

The latter, unsustained by hope, without one spark of speculation to cheer their gloomy destiny, starved, and sickened, and died in masses. The very requirements of discipline were useful in averting the despondent vacuity which comes of hunger. Of the sanguine confidence of the soldiery in the coming of their comrades, I was to witness a strong illustration on the very day of which I have been speaking.

It was about four o'clock in the afternoon, the weather had been heavy and overcast, and the heat excessive, so that all who were free from duty had either lain down to sleep, or were quietly resting within doors, when a certain stir and movement in the streets, a rare event during the hours of the siesta, drew many a head to the windows. The report ran, and like wildfire it spread through the city, that the advanced guard of Bonaparte had reached Ronco that morning, and were already in march on Genoa! Although nobody could trace this story to any direct source, each believed and repeated it ; the tale growing more consistent and fuller at every repetition. I need not weary my reader with all the additions and corrections the narrative received, nor recount how now it was Moreau with the right wing of the army of the Rhine ; now it was Kellermann's brigade ; now it was Macdonald, who had passed the Ticino ; and last of all, Bonaparte. The controversy was often even an angry one, when, finally, all speculation was met by the official report, that all that was known lay in the simple fact, that heavy guns had been

heard that morning, near Ronco, and as the Austrians held
no position with artillery there, the firing must needs be
French.

This very bare announcement was, of course, a great
"come down" for all the circumstantial detail with which
we had been amusing ourselves and each other, but yet it
nourished hope, and the hope that was nearest to all our
hearts, too! The streets were soon filled; officers and
soldiers hastily dressed, and with many a fault of costume
were all commingled, exchanging opinions, resolving
doubts, and even bandying congratulations. The starved
and hungry faces were lighted up with an expression of
savage glee. It was like the last flickering gleam of passion in men, whose whole vitality was the energy of fever!
The heavy debt they owed their enemy was at last to be
paid, and all the insulting injury of a besieged and famine-
stricken garrison to be avenged. A surging movement in
the crowd told that some event had occurred; it was Massena
and his staff, who were proceeding to a watch-tower in the
bastion, from whence a wide range of country could be
seen. This was reassuring. The general himself entertained the story, and here was proof that there was
"something in it." All the population now made for the
walls; every spot from which the view towards Ronco
could be obtained was speedily crowded, every window
filled, and all the housetops crammed. A dark mass of
inky cloud covered the tops of the Appennines, and even
descended to some distance down the sides. With what
shapes and forms of military splendour did our imaginations people the space behind that sombre curtain! What
columns of stern warriors, what prancing squadrons, what
earth-shaking masses of heavy artillery! How longingly
each eye grew weary watching—waiting for the veil to be
rent, and the glancing steel to be seen glistening bright in
the sun-rays!

As if to torture our anxieties, the lowering mass grew
darker and heavier, and rolling lazily adown the mountain,
it filled up the valley, wrapping earth and sky in one
murky mantle.

"There, did you hear that?" cried one; "that was
artillery."

A pause followed, each ear was bent to listen, and not a
word was uttered, for full a minute or more; the immense
host, as if swayed by the one impulse, strained to catch
the sounds, when suddenly, from the direction of the
mountain top, there came a rattling, crashing noise, fol-

lowed by the dull, deep booming that every soldier's heart
responds to. What a cheer then burst forth! never did I
hear—never may I hear—such a cry as that was; it was
like the wild yell of a shipwrecked crew, as some distant
sail hove in sight; and yet, through its cadence, there rang
the mad lust for vengeance! Yes, in all the agonies of
sinking strength, with fever in their hearts, and the death
sweat on their cheeks, their cry was Blood! The puny
shout, for such it seemed now, was drowned in the deafening crash that now was heard; peal after peal shook the
air, the same rattling, peppering noise of musketry continuing through all.

That the French were in strong force, as well as the
enemy, there could now be no doubt. Nothing but a
serious affair and a stubborn resistance could warrant such
a fire. It had every semblance of an attack with all arms.
The roar of the heavy guns made the air vibrate, and the
clatter of small arms was incessant. How each of us
filled up the picture from the impulses of his own fancy!
Some said that the French were still behind the mountain,
and storming the heights of the Borghetto; others thought
that they had gained the summit, but not "en force," and
were only contesting their position there; and a few, more
sanguine, of whom I was one myself, imagined that they
were driving the Austrians down the Appennines, cleaving
their ranks, as they went, with their artillery.

Each new crash, every momentary change of direction
of the sounds, favoured this opinion or that, and the excitement of partisanship rose to an immense height. What
added indescribably to the interest of the scene, was a
group of Austrian officers on horseback, who, in their
eagerness to obtain tidings, had ridden beyond their lines,
and were now standing almost within musket range of us.
We could see that their telescopes were turned to the eventful spot, and we gloried to think of the effect the scene
must have been producing on them.

"They've seen enough!" cried one of our fellows,
laughing, while he pointed to the horsemen, who, suddenly
wheeling about, galloped back to their camp at full speed.

"You'll have the drums beat to arms now; there's little
time to lose. Our cuirassiers will soon be upon them,"
cried another, in ecstacy.

"No, but the rain will, and upon us, too," said Giorgio,
who had now come up; "don't you see that it's not a
battle yonder, it's a 'borasco.' There it comes." And as
if the outstretched finger of the dwarf had been the wand

of a magician, the great cloud was suddenly torn open
with a crash, and the rain descended like a deluge, swept
along by a hurricane wind, and came in vast sheets of
water, while high over our heads, and moving onward towards the sea, growled the distant thunder. The great
mountain was now visible from base to summit, but not a
soldier, not a gun, to be seen! Swollen and yellow, the
gushing torrents leaped madly from crag to crag, and
crashing trees, and falling rocks, added their wild sounds
to the tumult.

There we stood, mute and sorrow-struck, regardless of
the seething rain, unconscious of anything save our disappointment. The hope we built upon had left us, and
the dreary scene of storm around seemed but a type of our
own future! And yet we could not turn away, but with
eyes strained and aching, gazed at the spot from where our
succour should have come.

I looked up at the watch-tower, and there was Massena
still, his arms folded, on a battlement ; he seemed to be
deep in thought. At last he arose, and drawing his cloak
across his face, descended the winding-stair outside the
tower. His step was slow, and more than once he halted,
as if to think. When he reached the walls, he walked
rapidly on, his suite following him.

" Ah, Mons. Tiernay," said he, as he passed me, " you
know what an Appennine storm is now ; but it will cool the
air and give us delicious weather ;" and so he passed on
with an easy smile.

CHAPTER XXXVII.

MONTE DI FACCIO.

THE disappointment we had suffered was not the only circumstance adverse to our expedition. The rain had now
swollen the smallest rivulets to the size of torrents; in
many places the paths would be torn away and obliterated,
and everywhere the difficulty of a night march enormously
increased. Giorgio, however, who was, perhaps, afraid of
forfeiting his reward, assured the general that these mountain streams subside even more rapidly than they rise;
that such was the dryness of the soil, no trace of rain
would be seen by sunset, and that we should have a calm,
starry night; the very thing we wanted for our enterprise.
We did not need persuasion to believe all he said—the
opinion chimed in with our own wishes, and, better still,
was verified to the very letter by a glorious afternoon.
Landward, the spectacle was perfectly enchanting; the
varied foliage of the Appennines, refreshed by the rain,
glittered and shone in the sun's rays, while in the bay, the
fleet, with sails hung out to dry, presented a grand and an
imposing sight. Better than all, Monte Faccio now appeared quite near us; we could, even with the naked eye,
perceive all the defences, and were able to detect a party
of soldiers at work outside the walls, clearing, as it seemed
some water-course that had been impeded by the storm
Unimportant as the labour was, we watched it anxiously,
for we thought that perhaps before another sunset many
a brave fellow's blood might dye that earth. During the
whole of that day, from some cause or other, not a shot
had been fired either from the land-batteries or the fleet,
and as though a truce had been agreed to, we sat watching
each other's movements peacefully and calmly.

"The Austrians would seem to have been as much deceived as ourselves, sir," said an old artillery sergeant to
me, as I strolled along the walls at nightfall. "The pickets last night were close to the glacis, but see, now they
have fallen back a gun-shot or more."

"But they had time enough since to have resumed their old position," said I, half doubting the accuracy of the surmise.

"Time enough, parbleu; I should think so too! but when the white-coats manœuvre, they write to Vienna to ask, 'What's to be done next?'"

This passing remark, in which, with all its exaggeration, there lay a germ of truth, was the universal judgment of our soldiers on those of the Imperial army; and to the prevalence of the notion may be ascribed much of that fearless indifference with which small divisions of ours attacked whole army corps of the enemy. Bonaparte was the first to point out this slowness, and to turn it to the best advantage.

"If our general ever intended a sortie, this would be the night for it, sir," resumed he; "the noise of those mountain streams would mask the sounds of a march, and even cavalry, if led with caution, might be in upon them before they were aware."

This speech pleased me, not only for the judgment it conveyed, but as an assurance that our expedition was still a secret in the garrison.

On questioning the sergeant further, I was struck to find that he had abandoned utterly all hope of ever seeing France again; such he told me was the universal feeling of the soldiery. "We know well, sir, that Massena is not the man to capitulate, and we cannot expect to be relieved." And yet with this stern, comfortless conviction on their minds—with hunger, and famine, and pestilence on every side—they never uttered one word of complaint, not even a murmur of remonstrance. What would Moreau's fellows say of us? What would the Army of the Meuse think? These were the ever-present arguments against surrender; and the judgment of their comrades was far more terrible to them than the grape-shot of the enemy.

"But do you not think, when Bonaparte crosses the Alps, he will hasten to our relief?"

"Not he, sir! I know him well. I was in the same troop with him, a bombardier at the same gun. Bonaparte will never go after small game where there's a nobler prey before him. If he does cross the Alps, he'll be for a great battle under Milan; or, mayhap, march on Venice. He's not thinking of our starved battalions here; he's planning some great campaign, depend on it. He never faced the Alps to succour Genoa."

How true was this appreciation of the great general's ambition, I need scarcely repeat; but so it was at the time; many were able to guess the bold aspirings of one who, to the nation, seemed merely one among the numerous candidates for fame and honours.

It was about an hour after my conversation with the sergeant, that an orderly came to summon me to Colonel de Barre's quarters; and with all my haste to obey, I only arrived as the column was formed. The plan of attack was simple enough. Three Voltigeur companies were to attempt the assault of the Monte Faccio, under De Barre; while, to engage attention, and draw off the enemy's force, a strong body of infantry and cavalry was to debouch on the Chiavari road, as though to force a passage in that direction. In all that regarded secrecy and despatch our expedition was perfect; and as we moved silently through the streets, the sleeping citizens never knew of our march. Arrived at the gate, the column halted, to give us time to pass along the walls and descend the glen, an operation which, it was estimated, would take forty-five minutes; at the expiration of this they were to issue forth to the feint attack.

At a quick step we now pressed forward towards the angle of the bastion, whence many a path led down the cliff in all directions. Half a dozen of our men, well acquainted with the spot, volunteered as guides, and the muskets being slung on the back, the word was given to "move on," the rallying-place being the plateau of the orange-trees I have already mentioned.

"Steep enough this," said De Barre to me, as, holding on by briars and brambles, we slowly descended the gorge; "but few of us will ever climb it again."

"You think so?" asked I, in some surprise.

"Of course, I know it," said he. "Vallence, who commands the battalions below, always condemned the scheme; rely on it, he's not the man to make himself out a false prophet. I don't pretend to tell you that in our days of monarchy there were neither jealousies nor party grudges, and that men were above all small and ungenerous rivalry; but, assuredly, we had less of them than now. If the field of competition is more open to everyone, so are the arts by which success is won; a pre-eminence in a republic means always the ruin of a rival. If we fail, as fail we must, he'll be a general."

"But why must we fail?"

"For every reason; we are not in force; we know nothing of what we are about to attack ; and, if repulsed, have no retreat behind us."

"Then why——?" I stopped, for already I saw the impropriety of my question.

"Why did I advise the attack?" said he, mildly, taking up my half-uttered question. "Simply because death outside these walls is quicker and more glorious than within them. There's scarcely a man who follows us has not the same sentiment in his heart. The terrible scenes of the last five weeks have driven our fellows to all but mutiny. Nothing, indeed, maintained discipline but a kind of tigerish thirst for vengeance—a hope that the day of reckoning would come round, and one fearful lesson teach these same white-coats how dangerous it is to drive a brave enemy to despair."

De Barre continued to talk in this strain as we descended, every remark he made being uttered with all the coolness of one who talked of a matter indifferent to him. At length the way became too steep for much converse, and slipping, and scrambling, we now only interchanged a chance word as we went. Although two hundred and fifty men were around and about us, not a voice was heard ; and, except the occasional breaking of a branch, or the occasional fall of some heavy stone into the valley, not a sound was heard. At length a long, shrill whistle announced that the first man had reached the bottom, which, to judge from the faintness of the sound, appeared yet a considerable distance off. The excessive darkness increased the difficulty of the way, and De Barre continued to repeat— "that we had certainly been misinformed, and that even in daylight the descent would take an hour."

It was full half an hour after this when we came to a small rivulet, the little boundary-line between the two steep cliffs. Here our men were all assembled, refreshing themselves with the water, still muddy from recent rain, and endeavouring to arrange equipments and arms, damaged and misplaced by many a fall.

"We've taken an hour and twenty-eight minutes," said De Barre, as he placed a fire-fly on the glass of his watch, to see the hour. "Now, men, let us make up for lost time. En avant !"

"En avant !" was quickly passed from mouth to mouth, and never was a word more spirit-stirring to Frenchmen ! With all. the alacrity of men fresh and "eager for the fray," they began the ascent, and, such was the emulous ardour to be first, that it assumed all the features of a race.

A close pine-wood greatly aided us now, and, in less time than we could believe it possible, we reached the plateau appointed for our rendezvous. This being the last spot of meeting before our attack on the fort, the final dispositions were here settled on, and the orders for the assault arranged. With daylight, the view from this terrace, for such it was in reality, would have been magnificent, for even now, in the darkness, we could track out the great thoroughfares of the city, follow the windings of the bay and harbour, and, by the lights on board, detect the fleet as it lay at anchor. To the left, and for many a mile, as it seemed, were seen twinkling the bivouac fires of the Austrian army; while directly above our heads, glittering like a red star, shone the solitary gleam that marked out the " Monte Faccio."

I was standing silently at De Barre's side, looking on this sombre scene, so full of terrible interest, when he clutched my arm violently, and whispered,—

" Look yonder; see, the attack has begun."

The fire of the artillery had flashed as he spoke, and now, with his very words, the deafening roar of the guns was heard from below.

" I told you he'd not wait for us, Tiernay. I told you how it would happen!" cried he; then suddenly recovering his habitual composure of voice and manner, he said, "Now for our part, men; forwards."

And away went the brave fellows, tearing up the steep mountain side, like an assault party at a breach. Though hidden from our view by the darkness and the dense wood, we could hear the incessant din of large and small arms; the roll of the drums summoning men to their quarters, and what we thought were the cheers of charging squadrons.

Such was the mad feeling of excitement these sounds produced, that I cannot guess what time elapsed before we found ourselves on the crest of the mountain, and not above three hundred paces from the outworks of the fort. The trees had been cut away on either side, so as to offer a species of " glacis," and this must be crossed under the fire of the batteries, before an attack could be commenced. Fortunately for us, however, the garrison was too confident of its security to dread a coup de main from the side of the town, and had placed all their guns along the bastion, towards Borghetto, and this De Barre immediately detected. A certain "alert" on the walls, however, and a quick movement of lights here and there, showed that

they had become aware of the sortie from the town, and
gradually we could see figure after figure ascending the
walls, as if to peer down into the valley beneath.

"You see what Vallence has done for us," said De
Barre, bitterly; "but for him we should have taken these
fellows, en flagrant delit, and carried their walls before
they could turn out a captain's guard."

As he spoke a heavy crashing sound was heard, and a
wild cheer. Already our pioneers had gained the gate,
and were battering away at it; another party had reached
the walls, and thrown up their rope ladders, and the attack was opened! In fact, Giorgio had led one division
by a path somewhat shorter than ours, and they had
begun the assault before we issued from the pine-wood.

We now came up at a run, but under a smart fire from
the walls, already fast crowding with men. Defiling close
beneath the wall, we gained the gate, just as it had fallen beneath the assaults of our men; a steep covered way led up
from it, and along this our fellows rushed madly, but suddenly from the gloom a red glare flashed out, and a terrible
discharge of grape swept all before it. "Lie down!" was
now shouted from front to rear, but even before the order
could be obeyed another and more fatal volley followed.

Twice we attempted to storm the ascent; but wearied
by the labour of the mountain pass—worn out by fatigue
—and, worse still, weak from actual starvation, our men
faltered! It was not fear, nor was there anything akin to
it; for even as they fell under the thick fire their shrill
cheers breathed stern defiance. They were utterly exhausted, and failing strength could do no more! De
Barre took the lead, sword in hand, and with one of those
wild appeals that soldiers never hear in vain, addressed
them; but the next moment his shattered corpse was carried to the rear. The scaling party, alike repulsed, had
now defiled to our support; but the death-dealing artillery swept through us without ceasing. Never was there
a spectacle so terrible as to see men, animated by courageous devotion, burning with glorious zeal, and yet powerless from very debility—actually dropping from the weakness of famine! The staggering step—the faint shout—
the powerless charge—all showing the ravages of pestilence and want!

Some sentiment of compassion must have engaged our
enemies' sympathy, for twice they relaxed their fire, and
only resumed it as we returned to the attack. One fearful discharge of grape, at pistol range, now seemed to have

closed the struggle ; and as the smoke cleared away, the earth was seen crowded with dead and dying. The broken ranks no longer showed discipline—men gathered in groups around their wounded comrades, and, to all seeming, indifferent to the death that menaced them. Scarcely an officer survived, and, among the dead beside me, I recognised Giorgio, who still knelt in the attitude in which he had received his death wound.

I was like one in some terrible dream, powerless and terror-stricken, as I stood thus amid the slaughtered and the wounded.

"You are my prisoner," said a gruff-looking old Croat grenadier, as he snatched my sword from my hand by a smart blow on the wrist; and I yielded without a word.

"Is it over?" said I; "is it over?"

"Yes, parbleu, I think it is," said a comrade, whose cheek was hanging down from a bayonet wound. "There are not twenty of us remaining, and they will do very little for the service of the 'Great Republic.'"

CHAPTER XXXVIII.

A ROYALIST " DE LA VIEILLE ROCHE."

On a hot and sultry day of June I found myself seated in a country cart, and under the guard of two mounted dragoons, wending my way towards Kuffstein, a Tyrol fortress, to which I was sentenced as a prisoner. A weary journey was it; for in addition to my now sad thoughts I had to contend against an attack of ague, which I had just caught, and which was then raging like a plague in the Austrian camp. One solitary reminiscence, and that far from a pleasant one, clings to this period. We had halted on the outskirts of a little village called "Broletto," for the siesta; and there, in a clump of olives, were quietly dozing away the sultry hours, when the clatter of horsemen awoke us; and on looking up, we saw a cavalry escort sweep past at a gallop. The corporal who commanded our party hurried into the village to learn the news, and soon returned with the tidings that " a great victory had been gained over the French, commanded by Bonaparte in person; that the army was in full retreat; and this was the despatch an officer of Melas' staff was now hastening to lay at the feet of the Emperor."

" I thought several times this morning," said the corporal, " that I heard artillery; and so it seems I might, for we are not above twenty miles from where the battle was fought."

" And how is the place called ? " asked I, in a tone sceptical enough to be offensive.

" Marengo," replied he; " mayhap, the name will not escape your memory."

How true was the surmise, but in how different a sense from what he uttered it! But so it was; even as late as four o'clock the victory was with the Austrians. Three separate envoys had left the field with tidings of success; and it was only late at night that the general, exhausted by a disastrous day, and almost broken-hearted, could write to tell his master that " Italy was lost."

I have many a temptation here to diverge from a line that I set down for myself in these memoirs, and from which as yet I have not wandered—I mean, not to dwell upon events wherein I was not myself an actor; but I am determined still to adhere to my rule; and leaving that glorious event behind me, plod wearily along my now sad journey.

Day after day we journeyed through a country teeming with abundance : vast plains of corn and maize, olives and vines, everywhere—on the mountains, the crags, the rocks, festooned over cliffs, and spreading their tangled networks over cottages; and yet everywhere poverty, misery, and debasement, ruined villages, and a half-naked, starving populace, met the eye at every turn. There was the stamp of slavery on all, and still more palpably was there the stamp of despotism in the air of their rulers.

I say this in a sad spirit ; for within a year from the day in which I write these lines I have travelled the self-same road, and with precisely the self-same objects before me. Changed in nothing, save what time changes, in ruin and decay! There was the dreary village as of yore ; the un-glazed windows closed with some rotten boarding, or occu-pied by a face gaunt with famine. The listless, unoccu-pied group still sat or lay on the steps before the church ; a knot of nearly naked creatures sat card-playing beside a fountain, their unsheathed knives alongside of them ; and lastly, on the wall of the one habitation which had the semblance of decency about it, there stared out the "double-headed eagle," the symbol of their shame and their slavery ! It never can be the policy of a government to retard the progress and depress the energies of a people beneath its rule. Why, then, do we find a whole nation, gifted and capable as this, so backward in civilisation? Is the fault with the rulers? or are there, indeed, people whose very development is the obstacle to their improve-ment ; whose impulses of right and wrong will submit to no discipline ; and who are incapable of appreciating true liberty? This would be a gloomy theory ; and the very thought of it suggests darker fears for a land to which my sympathies attach me more closely !

If any spot can impress the notion of impregnability it is Kuffstein. Situated on an eminence of rock over the inn, three sides of the base are washed by that rapid river, a little village occupies the fourth ; and from this the sup-plies are hoisted up to the garrison above by cranes and pulleys ; the only approach being by a path wide enough for a single man, and far too steep and difficult of access to admit of his carrying any burthen, however light. All that science and skill could do is added to the natural strength of the position, and from every surface of the vast rock itself the projecting mouths of guns and mortars show resources of defence it would seem madness to attack.

Three thousand men, under the command of General Urleben, held this fortress at the time I speak of; and by their habits of discipline and vigilance, showed that no over-security would make them neglect the charge of so important a trust. I was the first French prisoner that had ever been confined within the walls, and to the accident of my uniform was I indebted for this distinction. I have mentioned that in Genoa they gave me a staff-officer's dress and appointments, and from this casual circumstance it was supposed that I should know a great deal of Massena's movements and intentions, and that by judicious management I might be induced to reveal it.

General Urleben, who had been brought up in France, was admirably calculated to have promoted such an object were it practicable. He possessed the most winning address as well as great personal advantages; and although now past the middle of life was reputed one of the handsomest men in Austria. He at once invited me to his table, and having provided me with a delightful little chamber, from whence the view extended for miles along the inn, he sent me stores of books, journals, and newspapers, French, English, and German, showing by the very candour of their tidings a most flattering degree of confidence and trust.

If imprisonment could ever be endurable with resignation mine ought to have been so. My mornings were passed in weeding or gardening a little plot of ground outside my window, giving me ample occupation in that way, and rendering carnations and roses dearer to me, through all my after-life, than without such associations they would ever have been. Then I used to sketch for hours, from the walls, bird's-eye views, prisoner's glimpses, of the glorious Tyrol scenery below us. Early in the afternoon came dinner, and then, with the general's pleasant converse, a cigar, and a chess-board, the time wore smoothly on till nightfall.

An occasional thunder-storm, grander and more sublime than anything I have ever seen elsewhere, would now and then vary a life of calm, but not unpleasant monotony; and occasionally, too, some passing escort, on the way to or from Vienna, would give tidings of the war; but except in these, each day was precisely like the other; so that when the almanac told me it was autumn, I could scarcely believe a single month had glided over. I will not attempt to conceal the fact, that the inglorious idleness of my life, this term of inactivity at an age when hope, and vigour, and energy were highest within me, was a grievous privation; but, except in these regrets, I could almost call this time a happy one. The unfortunate position in which I started in life gave me little opportunity, or even inclination for learning. Except the little Pére Michel had taught me, I knew nothing. I need not say that this was but a sorry stock of education, even at that period, when, I must say, the sabre was more in vogue than the grammar.

I now set steadily about repairing this deficiency. General Urleben lent me all his aid, directing my studies, supplying me with books, and at times affording me the still greater assistance of his counsel and advice. To history generally, but particularly that of France, he made me pay the deepest attention, and seemed never to weary while impressing upon me the grandeur of our former monarchies, and the happiness of France when ruled by her legitimate sovereigns.

I had told him all that I knew myself of my birth and family, and frequently would he allude to the subject of my reading, by saying, "the son of an old 'Garde du Corps' needs no commentary when perusing such details as these. Your own instincts tell you how nobly these servants of a monarchy bore themselves—what chivalry lived at that time in men's hearts, and how generous and self-denying was their loyalty."

Such and such like were the expressions which dropped from him from time to time; nor was their impression the less deep when supported by the testimony of the memoirs with which he supplied me. Even in deeds of military glory the Monarchy could compete with the Republic, and Urleben took care to insist upon a fact I was never unwilling to concede—that the well-born were ever foremost in danger, no matter whether the banner was a white one or a tricolour.

" Le bon sang ne peut pas meutir " was an adage I never disputed, although certainly I never expected to hear it employed to the disparagement of those to whom it did not apply.

As the winter set in I saw less of the general. He was usually much occupied in the mornings, and at evenings he was accustomed to go down to the village, where, of late,

some French emigré families had settled—unhappy exiles,
who had both peril and poverty to contend against!
Many such were scattered through the Tyrol at that
period, both for the security and the cheapness it afforded.
Of these Urleben rarely spoke; some chance allusion,
when borrowing a book or taking away a newspaper, being
the extent to which he ever referred to them.

One morning, as I sat sketching on the walls, he came
up to me and said, "Strange enough, Tiernay, last night
I was looking at a view of this very scene, only taken from
another point of sight; both were correct, accurate in
every detail, and yet most dissimilar—what a singular
illustration of many of our prejudices and opinions! The
sketch I speak of was made by a young countrywoman of
yours—a highly-gifted lady, who little thought that
the accomplishments of her education were one day to be
the resources of her livelihood. Even so," said he, sighing, "a Marquise of the best blood of France is reduced
to sell her drawings!"

As I expressed a wish to see the sketches in question,
he volunteered to make the request if I would send some
of mine in return; and thus accidentally grew up a sort of
intercourse between myself and the strangers, which gradually extended to books and music, and, lastly, to civil
messages and inquiries of which the general was ever the
bearer.

What a boon was all this to me! What a sun-ray through
the bars of a prisoner's cell was this gleam of kindness
and sympathy! The very similarity of our pursuits, too,
had something inexpressibly pleasing in it, and I bestowed
ten times as much pains upon each sketch, now that I knew
to whose eyes it would be submitted.

"Do you know, Tiernay," said the general to me. one
day, "I am about to incur a very heavy penalty in your
behalf—I am going to contravene the strict orders of the
War Office, and take you along with me this evening down
to the village."

I started with surprise and delight together, and could
not utter a word.

"I know perfectly well," continued he, "that you will
not abuse my confidence. I ask, then, for nothing beyond
your word, that you will not make any attempt at escape;
for this visit may lead to others, and I desire, so far as
possible, that you should feel as little constraint as a
prisoner well may."

I readily gave the pledge required, and he went on—

"I have no cautions to give you, nor any counsels. Madame d'Aigreville is a Royalist."

"She is madame, then!" said I, in a voice of some disappointment.

"Yes, she is a widow, but her niece is unmarried," said he, smiling at my eagerness. I affected to hear the tidings with unconcern, but a burning flush covered my cheek, and I felt as uncomfortable as possible.

I dined that day as usual with the general; adjourning after dinner to the little drawing-room, where we played our chess. Never did he appear to me so tedious in his stories, so intolerably tiresome in his digressions, as that evening. He halted at every move—he had some narrative to recount, or some observation to make, that delayed our game to an enormous time ; and at last, on looking out of the window, he fancied there was a thunder-storm brewing, and that we should do well to put off our visit to a more favourable opportunity.

"It is little short of half a league," said he, "to the village, and in bad weather is worse than double the distance."

I did not dare to controvert his opinion, but, fortunately, a gleam of sunshine shot, the same moment, through the window, and proclaimed a fair evening.

Heaven knows I had suffered little of a prisoner's durance —my life had been one of comparative freedom and ease ; and yet, I cannot tell the swelling emotion of my heart with which I emerged from the deep archway of the fortress, and heard the bang of the heavy gate as it closed behind me. Steep as was the path, I felt as if I could have bounded down it without a fear! The sudden sense of liberty was maddening in its excitement, and I half suspect that had I been on horseback in that moment of wild delight, I should have forgotten all my plighted word and parole, though I sincerely trust that the madness would not have endured beyond a few minutes. If there be among my readers one who has known imprisonment, he will forgive this confession of a weakness, which to others of less experience will seem unworthy, perhaps dishonourable.

Dorf Kuffstein was a fair specimen of the picturesque simplicity of a Tyrol village. There were the usual number of houses, with carved galleries and quaint images in wood, the shrines and altars, the little "platz," for Sunday recreation, and the shady alley for rifle practice.

There were also the trellised walks of vines, and the

orchards, in the midst of one of which we now approached a long, low farm-house, whose galleries projected over the river. This was the abode of Madame d'Aigreville.

A peasant was cleaning a little mountain pony, from which a side-saddle had just been removed as we came up, and he, leaving his work, proceeded to ask us into the house, informing us as he went, that the ladies had just returned from a long ramble, and would be with us presently.

The drawing-room into which we were shown was a perfect picture of cottage elegance; all the furniture was of polished walnut-wood, and kept in the very best condition. It opened by three spacious windows upon the terrace above the river, and afforded a view of mountain and valley for miles on every side. An easel was placed on this gallery, and a small sketch in oils of Kuffstein was already nigh completed on it. There were books, too, in different languages, and, to my inexpressible delight, a piano!

The reader will smile, perhaps, at the degree of pleasure objects so familiar and every-day called forth; but let him remember how removed were all the passages of my life from such civilising influences—how little of the world had I seen beyond camps and barrack-rooms, and how ignorant I was of the charm which a female presence can diffuse over even the very humblest abode.

Before I had well ceased to wonder, and admire these objects, the Marquise entered.

A tall and stately old lady, with an air at once haughty and gracious, received me with a profound courtesy, while she extended her hand to the salute of the general. She was dressed in deep mourning, and wore her white hair in two braids along her face. The sound of my native language, with its native accent, made me forget the almost profound reserve of her manner, and I was fast recovering from the constraint her coldness imposed, when her niece entered the room. Mademoiselle, who was at that time about seventeen, but looked older by a year or two, was the very ideal of "brunette" beauty; she was dark-eyed and black-haired, with a mouth the most beautifully formed; her figure was light, and her foot a model of shape and symmetry. All this I saw in an instant, as she came, half-sliding, half-bounding, to meet the general; and then turning to me, welcomed me with a cordial warmth, very different from the reception of Madame la Marquise.

Whether it was the influence of her presence, whether

It was a partial concession of the old lady's own, or whether my own awkwardness was wearing off by time, I cannot say—but gradually the stiffness of the interview began to diminish. From the scenery around us we grew to talk of the Tyrol generally, then of Switzerland, and lastly of France. The Marquise came from Auvergne, and was justly proud of the lovely scenery of her birth-place.

Calmly and tranquilly as the conversation had been carried on up to this period, the mention of France seemed to break down the barrier of reserve within the old lady's mind, and she burst out in a wild flood of reminiscences of the last time she had seen her native village. "The Blues," as the revolutionary soldiers were called, had come down upon the quiet valley, carrying fire and carnage into a once peaceful district. The chateau of her family was razed to the ground; her husband was shot upon his own terrace; the whole village was put to the sword; her own escape was owing to the compassion of the gardener's wife, who dressed her like a peasant boy, and employed her in a menial station, a condition she was forced to continue so long as the troops remained in the neighbourhood. "Yes," said she, drawing off her silk mittens, "these hands still witness the hardships I speak of. These are the marks of my servitude."

It was in vain the general tried at first to sympathise, and then withdraw her from the theme; in vain her niece endeavoured to suggest another topic, or convey a hint that the subject might be unpleasing to me. It was the old lady's one absorbing idea, and she could not relinquish it. Whole volumes of the atrocities perpetrated by the revolutionary soldiery came to her recollection; each moment, as she talked, memory would recall this fact or the other, and so she continued rattling on with the fervour of a heated imagination, and the wild impetuosity of a half-crazed intellect. As for myself, I suffered far more from witnessing the pain others felt for me, than from any offence the topic occasioned me directly. These events were all "before my time." I was neither a Blue by birth nor by adoption; a child during the period of revolution, I had only taken a man's part when the country, emerging from its term of anarchy and blood, stood at bay against the whole of Europe. These consolations were, however, not known to the others, and it was at last, in a moment of unendurable agony, that Mademoiselle rose and left the room.

The general's eyes followed her as she went, and then

sought mine with an expression full of deep meaning. If I read his look aright, it spoke patience and submission; and the lesson was an easier one than he thought.

"They talk of heroism," cried she, frantically—"it was massacre! And when they speak of chivalry, they mean the slaughter of women and children!" She looked round, seeing that her niece had left the room, suddenly dropped her voice to a whisper, and said, "Think of her mother's fate, dragged from her home, her widowed, desolate home, and thrown into the Temple, outraged and insulted, condemned on a mock trial, and then carried away to the guillotine! Ay, and even then, on that spot which coming death might have sanctified, in that moment, when even fiendish vengeance can turn away and leave its victim at liberty to utter a last prayer in peace, even then, these wretches devised an anguish greater than all death could compass. You will scarcely believe me," said she, drawing in her breath, and talking with an almost convulsive effort, "you will scarcely believe me in what I am now about to tell you, but it is the truth—the simple but horrible tr' 'h. When my sister mounted the scaffold there was no (lest to administer the last rites. It was a time, indeed, when few were left; their hallowed heads had fallen in thousands before that. She waited for a few minutes, hoping that one would appear; and when the mob learned the meaning of her delay, they set up a cry of fiendish laughter, and with a blasphemy that makes one shudder to think of, they pushed forward a boy, one of those blood-stained 'gamins' of the streets, and made him gabble a mock litany! Yes, it is true: a horrible mockery of our service, in the ears and before the eyes of that dying saint."

"When? in what year? in what place was that?" cried I, in an agony of eagerness.

"I can give you both time and place, sir," said the Marquise, drawing herself proudly up, for she construed my question into a doubt of her veracity. "It was in the year 1793, in the month of August; and as for the place, it was one well seasoned to blood—the Place de Grêve at Paris."

A fainting sickness came over me as I heard these words; the dreadful truth flashed across me that the victim was the Marquise D'Estelles, and the boy, on whose infamy she dwelt so strongly, no other than myself. For the moment, it was nothing to me that she had not identified me with this atrocity; I felt no consolation in the thought that I was unknown and unsuspected. The heavy weight of the indignant accusation almost crushed me. Its falsehood I knew, and yet, could I dare to disprove it? Could I hazard the consequences of an avowal, which all my subsequent pleadings could never obliterate. Even were my innocence established in one point; what a position did it reduce me to in every other!

These struggles must have manifested themselves strongly in my looks, for the Marquise, with all her self-occupation, remarked how ill I seemed. "I see, sir," cried she, "that all the ravages of war have not steeled your heart against true piety; my tale has moved you strongly." I muttered something in concurrence, and she went on. "Happily for you, you were but a child when such scenes were happening! Not, indeed, that childhood was always unstained in those days of blood; but you were, as I understand, the son of a Garde du Corps, one of those loyal men who sealed their devotion with their life. Were you in Paris then?"

"Yes, madam," said I, briefly.

"With your mother, perhaps?"

"I was quite alone, madam; an orphan on both sides."

"What was your mother's family name?"

Here was a puzzle; but at a hazard I resolved to claim her who should sound best to the ears of La Marquise. "La Lasterie, madam," said I.

"La Lasterie de La Vignoble—a most distinguished house, sir. Provençal, and of the purest blood. Auguste de La Lasterie married the daughter of the Duke de Miriancourt, a cousin of my husband's, and there was another of them who went as ambassador to Madrid."

I knew none of them, and I supposed I looked as much.

"Your mother was, probably, of the elder branch, sir?" asked she.

I had to stammer out a most lamentable confession of my ignorance.

"Not know your own kinsfolk, sir; not your nearest of blood!" cried she, in amazement. "General, have you heard this strange avowal? or is it possible that my ears have deceived me?"

"Please to remember, madam," said I, submissively, "the circumstances in which I passed my infancy. My father fell by the guillotine."

"And his son wears the uniform of those who slew him!"

"Of a French soldier, madam, proud of the service he

belongs to; glorying to be one of the first army in
Europe."

"An army without a cause is a banditti, sir. Your
soldiers, without loyalty, are without a banner."

"We have a country; madam."

"I must protest against this discussion going further,"
said the general, blandly, while in a lower tone he whispered something in her ear.

"Very true, very true," said she; "I had forgotten all
that. Mons. de Tiernay, you will forgive me this warmth.
An old woman, who has lost nearly everything in the world,
may have the privilege of bad temper accorded her. We
are friends now, I hope," added she, extending her hand,
and, with a smile of most gracious meaning, beckoning to
me to sit beside her on the sofa.

Once away from the terrible theme of the Revolution,
she conversed with much agreeability; and her niece having reappeared, the conversation became animated and
pleasing. Need I say with what interest I now regarded
Mademoiselle; the object of all my boyish devotion; the
same whose pale features I had watched for many an hour
in the dim half light of the little chapel; her whose image
was never absent from my thoughts waking or sleeping;
and now again appearing before me in all the grace of
coming womanhood!

Perhaps to obliterate any impression of her aunt's
severity—perhaps it was mere manner—but I thought
there was a degree of anxiety to please in her bearing towards me. She spoke, too, as though our acquaintance
was to be continued by frequent meetings, and dropped
hints of plans that implied constant intercourse. Even
excursions into the neighbourhood she spoke of; when,
suddenly stopping, she said, "But these are for the season
of spring, and before that time Mons. de Tiernay will be
far away."

"Who can tell that?" said I. "I would seem to be
forgotten by my comrades."

"Then you must take care to do that which may refresh
their memory," said she, pointedly; and, before I could
question her more closely as to her meaning, the general
had risen to take his leave.

"Madame la Marquise was somewhat more tart than
usual," said he to me, as we ascended the cliff; "but you
have passed the ordeal now, and the chances are, she will
never offend you in the same way again. Great allowances must be made for those who have suffered as she

has.   Family—fortune—station—even country—all lost
to her; and even hope now dashed by many a disappointment."

Though puzzled by the last few words, I made no remark on them, and he resumed—

"She has invited you to come and see her as often as
you are at liberty; and, for my part, you shall not be
restricted in that way.   Go and come as you please, only
do not infringe the hours of the fortress; and if you can
concede a little now and then to the prejudices of the old
lady, your intercourse will be all the more agreeable to
both parties."

"I believe, General, that I have little of the Jacobin to
recant," said I, laughing.

"I should go further, my dear friend, and say, none,"
added he.   "Your uniform is the only tint of ' blue '
about you."   And thus chatting, we reached the fortress,
and said good night.

I have been particular, perhaps tiresomely so, in retailing these broken phrases and snatches of conversation;
but they were the first matches applied to a train that
was long and artfully laid.

CHAPTER XXXIX.

"A SORROWFUL PARTING."

THE general was as good as his word, and I now enjoyed the most unrestricted liberty; in fact, the officers of the garrison said truly, that they were far more like prisoners than I was. As regularly as evening came, I descended the path to the village, and, as the bell tolled out the vespers, I was crossing the little grass-plot to the cottage. So regularly was I looked for, that the pursuits of each evening were resumed as though only accidentally interrupted. The unfinished game of chess, the half-read volume, the newly-begun drawing, were taken up where we had left them, and life seemed to have centered itself in those delightful hours between sunset and midnight.

I suppose there are few young men who have not, at some time or other of their lives, enjoyed similar privileges, and known the fascination of intimacy in some household, where the affections became engaged as the intellect expanded ; and, while winning another's heart, have elevated their own. But to know the full charm of such intercourse, one must have been as I was—a prisoner—an orphan—almost friendless in the world—a very " waif " upon the shore of destiny. I cannot express the intense pleasure these evenings afforded me. The cottage was my home, and more than my home. It was a shrine at which my heart worshipped—for I was in love ! Easy as the confession is to make now, tortures would not have wrung it from me then!

In good truth, it was long before I knew it; nor can I guess how much longer the ignorance might have lasted, when General Urleben suddenly dispelled the clouds, by informing me that he had just received from the minister-of-war at Vienna a demand for the name, rank, and regiment of his prisoner, previous to the negotiation for his exchange.

"You will fill up these blanks, Tiernay," said he, " and within a month, or less, you will be once more free, and say adieu to Kuffstein."

Had the paper contained my dismissal from the service, I shame to own it would have been more welcome! The last few months had changed all the character of my life, suggested new hopes and new ambitions. The career I used to glory in had grown distasteful; the comrades I once longed to rejoin were now become almost repulsive to my imagination. The Marquise had spoken much of emigrating to some part of the new world beyond seas, and thither my fancy alike pointed. Perhaps my dreams of a future were not the less rose-coloured that they received no shadow from anything like a "fact." The old lady's geographical knowledge was neither accurate nor extensive, and she contrived to invest this land of promise with old associations of what she once heard of Pondicherry — with certain features belonging to the United States. A glorious country it would, indeed, have been, which, within a month's voyage, realised all the delights of the tropics, with the healthful vigour of the temperate zone, and where, without an effort beyond the mere will, men amassed enormous fortunes in a year or two. In a calmer mood, I might, indeed must, have been struck with the wild inconsistency of the old lady's imaginings, and looked with somewhat of scepticism on the map for that spot of earth so richly endowed; but now I believed everything, provided it only ministered to my new hopes. Laura evidently, too, believed in the "Canaan" of which, at last, we used to discourse as freely as though we had been there. Little discussions would, however, now and then vary the uniformity of this creed, and I remember once feeling almost hurt at Laura's not agreeing with me about zebras, which I assured her were just as trainable as horses, but which the Marquise flatly refused ever to use in any of her carriages. These were mere passing clouds; the regular atmosphere of our wishes was bright and transparent. In the midst of these delicious day-dreams, there came one day a number of letters to the Marquise by the hands of a courier on his way to Naples. What their contents I never knew, but the tidings seemed most joyful, for the old lady invited the general and myself to dinner, when the table was decked out with white lilies on all sides; she herself, and Laura also, wearing them in bouquets on their dresses.

The occasion had, I could see, something of a celebration about it. Mysterious hints to circumstances I knew nothing of were constantly interchanged, the whole ending with a solemn toast to the memory of the "Saint and

Martyr;" but who he was, or when he lived, I knew not
one single fact about

That evening—I cannot readily forget it—was the first
I had ever an opportunity of being alone with Laura!
Hitherto the Marquise had always been beside us; now
she had all this correspondence to read over with the
general, and they both retired into a little boudoir for the
purpose, while Laura and myself wandered out upon the
terrace, as awkward and constrained as though our situation had been the most provoking thing possible. It was on
that same morning I had received the general's message
regarding my situation, and I was burning with anxiety to
tell it, and yet knew not exactly how. Laura, too, seemed
full of her own thoughts, and leaned pensively over the
balustrade and gazed on the stream.

"What are you thinking of so seriously?" asked I,
after a long pause.

"Of long, long ago," said she, sighing, "when I was a
little child. I remember a little chapel like that yonder,
only that it was not on a rock over a river, but stood in a
small garden; and tnough in a great city, it was as lonely
and solitary as might be—the Chapelle de St. Blois."

"St. Blois, Laura!" cried I; "oh, tell me about
that!"

"Why you surely never heard of it before," said she,
smiling. "It was in a remote quarter of Paris, nigh the
outer Boulevard, and known to but a very few! It had
once belonged to our family; for in olden times there were
chateaux and country houses within that space, which then
was part of Paris, and one of our ancestors was buried
there! How well I remember it all! The dim little aisle,
supported on wooden pillars; the simple altar, with the
oaken crucifix, and the calm, gentle features of the poor
curé."

"Can you remember all this so well?" asked I,
eagerly, for the theme was stirring my very heart of
hearts.

"All—everything—the straggling—weed-grown garden, through which we passed to our daily devotions—the
congregation standing respectfully to let us walk by, for
my mother was still the great Marquise D'Estelles,
although my father had been executed, and our estates
confiscated. They who had known us in our prosperity,
were as respectful and devoted as ever; and poor old
Richard, the lame Sacristan, that used to take my mother's
bouquet from her, and lay it on the altar; how every-

thing stands out clear and distinct before my memory!
Nay, Maurice, but I can tell you more, for strangely
enough, certain things, merely trifles in themselves, make
impressions that even great events fail to do. There was
a little boy, a child somewhat older than myself, that
used to serve the mass with the Père, and he always came
to place a footstool or a cushion for my mother. Poor little
fellow, bashful and diffident he was, changing colour at
every minute, and trembling in every limb; and when he
had done his duty, and made his little reverence, with his
hands crossed on his bosom, he used to fall back into
some gloomy corner of the church, and stand watching us
with an expression of intense wonder and pleasure! Yes,
I think I see his dark eyes, glistening through the gloom,
ever fixed on me! I am sure, Maurice, that little fellow
fancied he was in love with me!"

"And why not, Laura? was the thing so very impossible? was it even so unlikely?"

"Not that," said she, archly; "but think of a mere
child; we were both mere children; and fancy him, the
poor little boy, of some humble house, perhaps—of course
he must have been that—raising his eyes to the daughter
of the great 'Marquise;' what energy of character there
must have been to have suggested the feeling! how daring
he was, with all his bashfulness!"

"You never saw him afterwards?"

"Never!"

"Never thought of him, perhaps?"

"I'll not say that," said she, smiling. "I have often
wondered to myself, if that hardihood I speak of had
borne good or evil fruit. Had he been daring or enterprising in the right, or had he, as the sad times favoured,
been only bold and impetuous for the wrong!"

"And how have you pictured him to your imagination," said I, as if merely following out a fanciful vein of
thought.

"My fancy would like to have conceived him a chivalrous adherent to our ancient royalty, striving nobly in
exile to aid the fortunes of some honoured house, or
daring, as many brave men have dared, the heroic part of
La Vendée. My reason, however, tells me, that he was
far more likely to have taken the other part."

"To which you will concede no favour, Laura; not
even the love of glory."

"Glory, like honour, should have its fountain in a
monarchy," cried she, proudly. "The rude voices of a

multitude can confer no meed of praise. Their judgments are the impulses of the moment. But why do we
speak of these things, Maurice? nor have I, who can but
breathe my hopes for a cause, the just pretension to contend with you, who shed your blood for its opposite."

As she spoke, she hurried from the balcony, and quitted
the room. It was the first time, as I have said, that we
had ever been alone together, and it was also the first
time she had ever expressed herself strongly on the subject of party. What a moment to have declared her
opinions, and when her reminiscences, too, had recalled
our infancy! How often was I tempted to interrupt that
confession, by declaring myself, and how strongly was I
repelled by the thought that the avowal might sever us
for ever. While I was thus deliberating, the Marquise,
with the general, entered the room, and Laura followed in
a few moments.

The supper that night was a pleasant one to all save
me. The rest were gay and high-spirited. Allusions,
understood by them, but not by me, were caught up
readily, and as quickly responded to. Toasts were uttered,
and wishes breathed in concert, but all was like a dream
to me. Indeed my heart grew heavier at every moment.
My coming departure, of which I had not yet spoken, lay
drearily on my mind, while the bold decision with which
Laura declared her faith showed that our destinies were
separated by an impassable barrier.

It may be supposed that my depression was not relieved by discovering that the general had already announced my approaching departure, and the news, far
from being received with anything like regret, was made
the theme of pleasant allusion, and even congratulation.
The Marquise repeatedly assured me of the delight the
tidings gave her, and Laura smiled happily towards me,
as if echoing the sentiment.

Was this the feeling I had counted on? were these the
evidences of an affection for which I had given my whole
heart? Oh, how bitterly I reviled the frivolous ingratitude of woman! how heavily I condemned their heartless, unfeeling nature! In a few days, a few hours, perhaps, I shall be as totally forgotten here, as though I had
never been, and yet these are the people who parade their
devotion to a fallen monarchy, and their affection for an
exiled house! I tried to arm myself with every prejudice
against royalism. I thought of Santron and his selfish,
sarcastic spirit. I thought of all the stories I used to

hear of cowardly ingratitude, and noble infamy, and
tried to persuade myself that the blandishments of the
well-born were but the gloss that covered cruel and unfeeling natures.

For very pride sake, I tried to assume a manner cool
and unconcerned as their own. I affected to talk of my departure as a pleasant event, and even hinted at the career
that Fortune might hereafter open to me. In this they
seemed to take a deeper interest than I anticipated, and I
could perceive that more than once the general exchanged
looks with the ladies most significantly. I fear I grew
very impatient at last. I grieve to think that I fancied a
hundred annoyances that were never intended for me,
and when we arose to take leave, I made my adieux with a
cold and stately reserve, intended to be strongly impressive and cut them to the quick.

I heard very little of what the general said as we
ascended the cliff. I was out of temper with him, and
myself, and all the world; and it was only when he recalled my attention to the fact, for the third or fourth
time, that I learned how very kindly he meant by me in
the matter of my liberation; for while he had forwarded
all my papers to Vienna, he was quite willing to set me at
liberty on the following day, in the perfect assurance that
my exchange would be confirmed.

" You will thus have a full fortnight at your own disposal, Tiernay," said he, " since the official answer cannot
arrive from Vienna before that time, and you need
not report yourself in Paris for eight or ten days
after."

Here was a boon now thrown away! For my part, I
would a thousand times rather have lingered on at Kuffstein than have been free to travel Europe from one end
to the other. My outraged pride, however, put this out
of the question. La Marquise and her niece had both
assumed a manner of sincere gratification, and I was resolved not to be behind-hand in my show of joy! I ought
to have known it, said I again and again. I ought to
have known it. These antiquated notions of birth and
blood can never co-exist with any generous sentiment.
These remnants of a worn-out monarchy can never forgive the vigorous energy that has dethroned their decre-
pitude! I did not dare to speculate on what a girl Laura
might have been under other auspices; how nobly her
ambition would have soared; what high-souled patriotism
she could have felt; how gloriously she would have

adorned the society of a regenerated nation. I thought of her as she was, and could have hated myself for the devotion with which my heart regarded her !

I never closed my eyes the entire night. I lay down and walked about alternately, my mind in a perfect fever of conflict. Pride, a false pride, but not the less strong for that, alone sustained me. The general had announced to me that I was free. Be it so; I will no longer be a burden on his hospitality. La Marquise hears the tidings with pleasure. Agreed, then—we part without regret! Very valorous resolutions they were, but come to, I must own, with a very sinking heart and a very craven spirit.

Instead of my full uniform, that morning I put on half dress, showing that I was ready for the road; a sign, I had hoped, would have spoken unutterable things to La Marquise and Laura.

Immediately after breakfast, I set out for the cottage. All the way, as I went, I was drilling myself for the interview by assuming a tone of the coolest and easiest indifference. They shall have no triumph over me in this respect, muttered I. Let us see if I cannot be as unconcerned as they are! To such a pitch had I carried my zeal for flippancy, that I resolved to ask them whether they had no commission I could execute for them in Paris or elsewhere. The idea struck me as excellent, so indicative of perfect self-possession and command. I am sure I must have rehearsed our interview at least a dozen times, supplying all the stately grandeur of the old lady and all the quiet placitude of Laura.

By the time I reached the village I was quite strong in my part, and as I crossed the Platz I was eager to begin it. This energetic spirit, however, began to waver a little as I entered the lawn before the cottage, and a most uncomfortable throbbing at my side made me stand for a moment in the porch before I entered. I used always to make my appearance unannounced, but now I felt that it would be more dignified and distant were I to summon a servant, and yet I could find none. The household was on a very simple scale, and in all likelihood the labours of the field or the garden were now employing them. I hesitated what to do, and after looking in vain around the " cour" and the stable-yard, I turned into the garden to seek for some one.

I had not proceeded many paces along a little alley, flanked by two close hedges of yew, when I heard voices, and at the same instant my own name uttered.

" You told him to use caution, Laura; that we know
little of this Tiernay beyond his own narrative——"

" I told him the very reverse, aunt. I said that he was
the son of a loyal Garde du Corps, left an orphan in infancy, and thrown by force of events into the service of the
Republic; but that every sentiment he expressed, every
ambition he cherished, and every feeling he displayed, was
that of a gentleman ; nay, further——" But I did not wait
for more, for, striking my sabre heavily on the ground to
announce my coming, I walked hurriedly forward towards
a small arbour where the ladies were seated at breakfast.

I need not stop to say how completely all my resolves
were routed by the few words I had overheard from Laura,
nor how thoroughly I recanted all my expressions concerning her. So full was I of joy and gratitude, that I hastened
to salute her before ever noticing the Marquise, or being
conscious of her presence.

The old lady, usually the most exacting of all beings,
took my omission in good part, and most politely made
room for me between herself and Laura at the breakfast-
table.

" You have come most opportunely, Monsieur de Tiernay," said she; " for not only were we just speaking of
you, but discussing whether or not we might ask of you a
favour."

" Does the question admit of a discussion, madame? "
said I, bowing.

" Perhaps not, in ordinary circumstances, perhaps not;
but——" she hesitated, seemed confused, and looked at
Laura, who went on—

" My aunt would say, sir, that we may be possibly asking too much—that we may presume too far."

" Not on my will to serve you," broke I in, for her
looks said much more than her words.

" The matter is this, sir," said the aunt: " we have a
very valued relative——"

" Friend," interposed Laura, " friend, aunt."

" We will say friend, then," resumed she ; " a friend in
whose welfare we are deeply interested, and whose regard
for us is not less powerful, has been for some years back
separated from us by the force of those unhappy circumstances which have made so many of us exiles ! No means
have existed of communicating with each other, nor of
interchanging those hopes or fears for our country's wel·
rare which are so near to every French heart ! He in

23

Germany, we in the wild Tyrol, one-half the world apart! and dare not trust to a correspondence, the utterance of those sympathies which have brought so many to the scaffold!"

"We would ask of you to see him, Monsieur de Tiernay, to know him," burst out Laura; "to tell him all that you can of France—above all, of the sentiments of the army; he is a soldier himself, and will hear you with pleasure."

"You may speak freely and frankly," continued the Marquise; "the Count is man of the world enough to hear the truth even when it gives pain. Your own career will interest him deeply; heroism has always had a charm for all his house. This letter will introduce you; and as the general informs us you have some days at your own disposal, pray give them to our service in this cause."

"Willingly, madame," replied I, "only let me understand a little better——"

"There is no need to know more," interrupted Laura; "the Count de Marsanne will himself suggest everything of which you will talk. He will speak of us, perhaps—of the Tyrol—of Kuffstein; then he will lead the conversation to France—in fact, once acquainted, you will follow the dictates of your own fancy."

"Just so, Monsieur de Tiernay; it will be a visit with as little of ceremony as possible——"

"Aunt!" interrupted Laura, as if recalling the Marquise to caution; and the old lady at once acknowledged the hint by a significant look.

I see it all, thought I. De Marsanne is Laura's accepted lover, and I am the person to be employed as go-between. This was intolerable, and when the thought first struck me, I was out of myself with passion.

"Are we asking too great a favour, Monsieur de Tiernay?" said the Marquise, whose eyes were fixed upon me during this conflict.

"Of course not, madame," said I, in an accent of almost sarcastic tone. "If I am not wrong in my impressions, the cause might claim a deeper devotion; but this is a theme I would not wish to enter upon."

"We are aware of that," said Laura, quickly; "we are quite prepared for your reserve, which is perfectly proper and becoming."

"Your position being one of unusual delicacy," chimed in the Marquise.

I bowed haughtily and coldly, while the Marquise at

tered a thousand expressions of gratitude and regard to me.

" We had hoped to have seen you here a few days longer, monsieur," said she, " but perhaps, under the circumstances, it is better as it is."

" Under the circumstances, madame," repeated I, " I am bound to agree with you ;" and I turned to say farewell.

" Rather, au revoir, Monsieur de Tiernay," said the Marquise; " friendship, such as ours, should at least be hopeful ; say then ' au revoir.'"

" Perhaps Monsieur de Tiernay's hopes run not in the same channel as our own, aunt," said Laura, " and perhaps the days of happiness that we look forward to would bring far different feelings to his heart."

This was too pointed—this was insupportably offensive ! and I was only able to mutter, " You are right, Mademoiselle ;" and then, addressing myself to the Marquise, I made some blundering apologies about haste and so forth ; while I promised to fulfil her commission faithfully and promptly.

" Shall we not hear from you ?" said the old lady, as she gave me her hand. I was about to say, " under the circumstances," better not; but I hesitated, and Laura, seeing my confusion, said, " It might be unfair, aunt, to expect it; remember how he is placed."

" Mademoiselle is a miracle of forethought and candour too," said I. " Adieu ! adieu for ever !" The last word I uttered in a low whisper.

" Adieu, Maurice," said she, equally low, and then turned away towards the window.

From that moment until the instant when, out of breath and exhausted, I halted for a few seconds on the crag below the fortress, I knew nothing ; my brain was in a whirl of mad, conflicting thought. Every passion was working within me, and rage, jealousy, love, and revenge, were alternately swaying and controlling me. Then, however, as I looked down for the last time on the village and the cottage beside the river, my heart softened, and I burst into a torrent of tears. There, said I, as I arose to resume my way, there ! one illusion is dissipated ; let me take care that life never shall renew the affliction ! Henceforth I will be a soldier, and only a soldier.

CHAPTER XL.

"THE CHATEAU OF ETTENHEIM."

NOW come to an incident in my life, which, however briefly I may speak, has left the deepest impression on my memory. I have told the reader how I left Kuffstein fully satisfied that the Count de Marsanne was Laura's lover, and that in keeping my promise to see and speak with him, I was about to furnish an instance of self-denial and fidelity that nothing in ancient or modern days could compete with.

The letter was addressed, "The Count Louis de Marsanne, Chateau d'Ettenheim, à Bade," and thither I accordingly repaired, travelling over the Arlberg to Bregenz, and across the Lake of Constance to Freyburg; my passport containing a very few words in cypher, which always sufficed to afford me free transit and every attention from the authorities. I had left the southern Tyrol in the outburst of a glorious spring, but as I journeyed northward I found the rivers frozen, the roads encumbered with snow, and the fields untilled and dreary looking. Like all countries which derive their charms from the elements of rural beauty, foliage, and verdure, Germany offers a sad coloured picture to the traveller in winter or wintry weather.

It was thus, then, that the Grand Duchy, so celebrated for its picturesque beauty, struck me as a scene of dreary and desolate wildness, an impression which continued to increase with every mile I travelled from the high road. A long unbroken flat, intersected here and there by stunted willows, traversed by a narrow earth road, lay between the Rhine and the Taunus Mountains, in the midst of which stood the village of "Ettenheim." Outside the village, about half a mile off, and on the border of a vast pine-forest, stood the Chateau.

It was originally a hunting-seat of the Dukes of Baden, but, from neglect and disuse, gradually fell into ruin, from which it was reclaimed. imperfectly enough, a year before,

and now exhibited some remnants of its former taste, along
with the evidences of a far less decorative spirit; the
lower rooms being arranged as a stable, while the stair
and entrance to the first story opened from a roomy coach-
house. Here some four or five conveyances of rude con-
struction were gathered together, splashed and unwashed,
as if from recent use; and at a small stove in a corner was
seated a peasant in a blue frock, smoking as he affected to
clean a bridle which he held before him.

Without rising from his seat he saluted me, with true
German phlegm, and gave me the " Guten Tag," with all
the grave unconcern of a "Badener." I asked if the
Count de Marsanne lived there. He said yes, but the
" Graf" was out hunting. When would he be back? By
nightfall.

Could I remain there till his return? was my next
question; and he stared at me as I put it, with some surprise. " Warum nicht," " Why not?" was at last his
sententious answer, as he made way for me beside the
stove. I saw at once that my appearance had evidently
not entitled me to any peculiar degree of deference or
respect, and that the man regarded me as his equal. It
was true I had come some miles on foot, and with a knapsack on my shoulder, so that the peasant was fully war-
ranted in his reception of me. I accordingly seated myself
at his side, and lighting my pipe from his, proceeded to
derive all the profit I could from drawing him into conversation. I might have spared myself the trouble. Whether
the source lay in stupidity or sharpness, he evaded me on
every point. Not a single particle of information could I
obtain about the Count, his habits, or his history. He
would not even tell me how long he had resided there,
nor whence he had come. He liked hunting, and so did
the other "Herren." There was the whole I could scan;
and to the simple fact that there were others with him,
did I find myself limited.

Curious to see something of the Count's "interior," I
hinted to my companion that I had come on purpose to
visit his master, and suggested the propriety of my awaiting his arrival in a more suitable place; but he turned a
deaf ear to the hint, and drily remarked that the " Graf"
would not be long a-coming now." This prediction was,
however, not to be verified; the dreary hours of the dull
day stole heavily on, and although I tried to beguile the
time by lounging about the place, the cold ungenial weather drove me back to the stove, or to the dark precinct

of the stable, tenanted by three coarse ponies of the mountain breed.

One of these was the Graf's favourite, the peasant told me; and indeed here he showed some disposition to become communicative, narrating various gifts and qualities of the unseemly looking animal, which, in his eyes, was a paragon of horse flesh. "He could travel from here to Kehl and back in a day, and has often done it," was one meed of praise that he bestowed; a fact which impressed me more as regarded the rider than the beast, and set my curiosity at work to think why any man should undertake a journey of nigh seventy miles between two such places and with such speed. The problem served to occupy me till dark, and I know not how long after. A stormy night of rain and wind set in, and the peasant, having bedded and foraged his cattle, lighted a ricketty old lantern and began to prepare for bed; for such I at last saw was the meaning of a long crib, like a coffin, half filled with straw and sheep skins. A coarse loaf of black bread, some black forest cheese, and a flask of Kleinthaler, a most candid imitation of vinegar, made their appearance from a cupboard, and I did not disdain to partake of these delicacies.

My host showed no disposition to become more communicative over his wine, and, indeed, the liquor might have excused any degree of reserve; and no sooner was our meal over than, drawing a great woollen cap half over his face, he rolled himself up in his sheep-skins, and betook himself to sleep, if not with a good conscience, at least with a sturdy volition that served just as well.

Occasionally snatching a short slumber, or walking to and fro in the roomy chamber, I passed several hours, when the splashing sound of horses' feet, advancing up the miry road, attracted me. Several times before that I had been deceived by noises which turned out to be the effects of storm, but now, as I listened, I thought I could hear voices. I opened the door, but all was dark outside; it was the inky hour before daybreak, when all is wrapped in deepest gloom. The rain, too, was sweeping along the ground in torrents. The sounds came nearer every instant, and, at last, a deep voice shouted out, "Jacob." Before I could awaken the sleeping peasant, to whom I judged this summons was addressed, a horseman dashed up to the door and rode in; another as quickly followed him, and closed the door.

"Parbleu, d'Egville," said the first who entered, "we have got a rare peppering!"

"Even so," said the other, as he shook his hat, and threw off a cloak perfectly soaked with rain; "à la guerre comme, à la guerre."

This was said in French, when, turning towards me, the former said in German, "Be active, Master Jacob; these nags have had a smart ride of it." Then, suddenly, as the light flashed full on my features, he started back, and said, "How is this—who are you?"

A very brief explanation answered this somewhat un-courteous question, and, at the same time, I placed the Marquise's letter in his hand, saying, "The Count de Marsanne, I presume."

He took it hastily, and drew nigh to the lantern to peruse it. I had now full time to observe him, and saw that he was a tall and well-built man, of about seven or eight and twenty. His features were remarkably hand-some, and, although slightly flushed by his late exertion, were as calm and composed as might be; a short black moustache gave his upper lip a slight character of scorn, but the brow, open, frank, and good-tempered in its ex-pression, redeemed this amply. He had not read many lines when, turning about, he apologised in the most cour-teous terms for the manner of my reception. He had been on a shooting excursion for a few days back, and taken all his people with him, save the peasant, who looked after the cattle. Then, introducing me to his friend, whom he called Count d'Egville, he led the way up stairs.

It would be difficult to imagine a greater contrast to the dark and dreary coach-house than the comfortable suite of apartments which we now traversed on our way to a large, well-furnished room, where a table was laid for supper, and a huge wood fire blazed brightly on the hearth. A valet, of most respectful manner, received the Count's orders to prepare a room for me, after which my host and his friend retired to change their clothes.

Although d'Egville was many years older, and of a graver, sterner fashion than the other, I could detect a degree of deference and respect in his manner towards him, which De Marsanne accepted like one well accus-tomed to receive it. It was a time, however, when, in the wreck of fortune, so many men lived in a position of mere dependence, that I thought nothing of this, nor had I even the time, as Count de Marsanne entered. From

my own preconceived notions as to his being Laura's lover,
I was quite prepared to answer a hundred impatient inquiries about the Marquise and her niece, and as we
were now alone, I judged that he would deem the time a
favourable one to talk of them. What was my surprise,
however, when he turned the conversation exclusively to
the topic of my own journey, the route I had travelled.
He knew the country perfectly, and spoke of the various
towns and their inhabitants with acuteness and tact.

His Royalist leanings did not, like those of the Marquise, debar him from feeling a strong interest respecting
the success of the Republican troops, with whose leaders
he was thoroughly acquainted, knowing all their peculiar
excellences and defaults as though he had lived in intimacy with them. Of Bonaparte's genius he was the most
enraptured admirer, and would not hear of any comparison between him and the other great captains of the day.
D'Egville at last made his appearance, and we sat down
to an excellent supper, enlivened by the conversation of our
host, who, whatever the theme, talked well and pleas-
ingly.

I was in a mood to look for flaws in his character, my
jealousy was still urging me to seek for whatever I could
find fault with, and yet all my critical shrewdness could
only detect a slight degree of pride in his manner, not
displaying itself by any presumption, but by a certain
urbanity that smacked of condescension; but even this at
last went off, and before I wished him good night I felt
that I had never met any one so gifted with agreeable
qualities, nor possessed of such captivating manners, as
himself. Even his Royalism had its fascinations, for it
was eminently national, and showed, at every moment,
that he was far more of a Frenchman than a Monarchist.
We parted without one word of allusion to the Marquise
or to Laura! Had this singular fact any influence upon
the favourable impression I had conceived of him, or was
I unconsciously grateful for the relief thus given to all my
jealous tormentings? Certain is it that I felt infinitely
happier than I ever fancied I should be under his roof,
and, as I lay down in my bed, thanked my stars that he
was not my rival!

When I awoke the next morning I was some minutes
before I could remember where I was, and as I still lay,
gradually recalling myself to memory, the valet entered
to announce the Count.

" I have come to say adieu for a few hours," said he ;

" a very pressing appointment requires me to be at Pfortz-heim to-day, and I have to ask that you will excuse my absence. I know that I may take this liberty without any appearance of rudeness, for the Marquise has told me all about you. Pray, then, try and amuse yourself till evening, and we shall meet at supper."

I was not sorry that d'Egville was to accompany him, and, turning on my side, dozed off to sleep away some of the gloomy hours of a winter's day.

In this manner several days were passed, the Count absenting himself each morning, and returning at night-fall, sometimes accompanied by D'Egville, sometimes alone. It was evident enough, from the appearance of his horses at his return, as well as from his own jaded looks, that he had ridden hard and far; but except a chance allusion to the state of the roads or the weather, it was a topic to which he never referred, nor, of course, did I ever advert. Meanwhile our intimacy grew closer and franker. The theme of politics, a forbidden subject between men so separated, was constantly discussed be-tween us, and I could not help feeling flattered at the deference with which he listened to opinions from one so much his junior, and so inferior in knowledge as myself. Nothing could be more moderate than his views of govern-ment, only provided that it was administered by the right-ful sovereign. The claim of a king to his throne he de-clared to be the foundation of all the rights of property, and which, if once shaken or disputed, would inevitably lead to the wildest theories of democratic equality. "I don't want to convert you," would he say, laughingly; "the son of an old Garde du Corps, the born gentleman, has but to live to learn. It may come a little later or a little earlier, but you'll end as a good Monarchist."

One evening he was unusually late in returning, and when he came was accompanied by seven or eight com-panions, some younger, some older, than himself, but all men whose air and bearing bespoke their rank in life, while their names recalled the thoughts of old French chivalry. I remember among them was a Coigny, a Gram-mont, and Rouchefoucauld—the last as lively a specimen of Parisian wit and brilliancy as ever fluttered along the sunny Boulevards.

De Marsanne, while endeavouring to enjoy himself and entertain his guests, was, to my thinking, more serious than usual, and seemed impatient at D'Egville's absence, for whose coming we now waited supper.

"I should not wonder if he was lost in the deep mud of those cross-roads," said Coigny.

"Or perhaps he has fallen into the Republic," said Rouchefoucauld; "it's the only thing dirtier that I know of."

"Monsieur forgets that I wear its cloth," said I, in a low whisper to him; and low as it was, De Marsanne overheard it.

"Yes, Charles," cried he, "you must apologise, and on the spot, for the rudeness."

Rouchefoucauld reddened and hesitated.

"I insist, sir," cried De Marsanne, with a tone of superiority I had never seen him assume before.

"Perhaps," said he, with a half-sneer, "Monsieur de Tiernay might refuse to accept my excuses."

"In that case, sir," interposed De Marsanne, "the quarrel will become mine, for he is my guest, and lives here under the safeguard of my honour."

Rouchefoucauld bowed submissively, and with the air of a man severely but justly rebuked; and then advancing to me said, "I beg to tender you my apology, Monsieur, for an expression which should never have been uttered by me in your presence."

"Quite sufficient, sir," said I, bowing, and anxious to conclude a scene which for the first time had disturbed the harmony of our meetings. Slight as was the incident, its effects were yet visible in the disconcerted looks of the party, and I could see that more than one glance was directed towards me with an expression of coldness and distrust.

"Here comes D'Egville at last," said one, throwing open the window to listen; the night was starlit, but dark, and the air calm and motionless. "I certainly heard a horse's tread on the causeway."

"I hear distinctly the sound of several," cried Coigny; "and, if I mistake not much, so does M. de Tiernay." This sudden allusion turned every eye towards me, as I stood still, suffering from the confusion of the late scene.

"Yes; I hear the tramp of horses, and cavalry too, I should say, by their measured tread."

"There was a trumpet call!" cried Coigny; "what does that mean?"

"It is the signal to take open order," said I, answering as if the question were addressed to myself. "It is a picket taking a 'reconnaissance.'"

"How do you know that, sir?" said Grammont, sternly.

"Ay! how does he know that?" cried several, pas
sionately, as they closed around me.

"You must ask in another tone, Messieurs," said I,
calmly, "if you expect to be answered."

"They mean to say, how do you happen to know the
German trumpet-calls, Tiernay," said De Marsanne,
mildly, as he laid his hand on my arm.

"It's a French signal," said I; "I ought to know it
well."

Before my words were well uttered the door was thrown
open, and D'Egville burst into the room, pale as death,
his clothes all mud-stained and disordered. Making his
way through the others, he whispered a few words in De
Marsanne's ear.

"Impossible!" cried the other; "we are here in the
territory of the Margrave."

"It is as I say," replied D'Egville; "there's not a
second to lose—it may be too late even now—by Heavens
it is!—they've drawn a cordon round the Chateau."

"What's to be done, gentlemen?" said De Marsanne,
seating himself calmly, and crossing his arms on his
breast.

"What do you say, sir?" cried Grammont, advancing
to me with an air of insolent menace; "you, at least,
ought to know the way out of this difficulty."

"Or, by Heaven, his own road shall be one of the
shortest, considering the length of the journey," muttered
another; and I could hear the sharp click of a pistol-cock
as he spoke the words.

"This is unworthy of you, gentlemen, and of me,"
said De Marsanne, haughtily; and he gazed around him
with a look that seemed to abash them: "nor is it a time
to hold such disputation. There is another and a very
difficult call to answer. Are we agreed?" Before he
could finish the sentence the door was burst open, and
several dragoons in French uniforms entered, and ranged
themselves across the entrance, while a colonel, with his
sabre drawn, advanced in front of them.

"This is brigandage," cried De Marsanne, passionately,
as he drew his sword, and seemed meditating a spring
through them; but he was immediately surrounded by his
friends and disarmed. Indeed nothing could be more
hopeless than resistance; more than double our number
were already in the room, while the hoarse murmur
of voices without, and the tramp of heavy feet, announced
a strong party.

At a signal from their officer, the dragoons unslung

their carbines, and held them at the cock, when the colonel called out, "Which of you, Messieurs, is the Duc D'Enghien?"

"If you come to arrest him," replied De Marsanne, "you ought to have his description in your warrant."

"Is the descendant of a Condé ashamed to own his name?" asked the colonel, with a sneer. "But we'll make short work of it, sirs; I arrest you all. My orders are peremptory, Messieurs. If you resist, or attempt to escape——" and he made a significant sign with his hand to finish. The "Duc"—for I need no longer call him De Marsanne—never spoke a word, but with folded arms calmly walked forward, followed by his little household. As we descended the stairs, we found ourselves in the midst of about thirty dismounted dragoons, all on the alert, and prepared for any resistance. The remainder of a squadron were on horseback without. With a file of soldiers on either hand, we marched for about a quarter of a mile across the fields to a small mill, where a general officer and his staff seemed awaiting our arrival. Here, too, a picket of gens-d'armes was stationed; a character of force significant enough of the meaning of the enterprise. We were hurriedly marched into the court of the mill, the owner of which stood between two soldiers, trembling from head to foot with terror.

"Which is the Duc D'Enghien?" asked the colonel of the miller.

"That is he with the scarlet vest;" and the prince nodded an assent.

"Your age, Monsieur?" asked the colonel of the prince.

"Thirty-two—that is, I should have been so much in August, were it not for this visit," said he, smiling.

The colonel wrote on rapidly for a few minutes, and then showed the paper to the general, who briefly said, "Yes, yes; this does not concern you nor me."

"I wish to ask, sir," said the prince, addressing the general, "do you make this arrest with the consent of the authorities of this country, or do you do so in defiance of them?"

"You must reserve questions like that for the court who will judge you, Monsieur de Condé," said the officer, roughly. "If you wish for any articles of dress from your quarters, you had better think of them. My orders are to convey you to Strasbourg. Is there anything so singular in the fact, sir, that you should look so much astonished?"

"There is, indeed," said the prince, sorrowfully. "I shall be the first of my house who ever crossed that frontier a prisoner."

"But not the first who carried arms against his country," rejoined the other—a taunt the Duke only replied to by a look of infinite scorn and contempt. With a speed that told plainly the character of the expedition, we were now placed, two together, on country cars, and driven at a rapid pace towards Strasbourg. Relays of cattle awaited us on the road, and we never halted but for a few minutes during the entire journey. My companion on this dreary day was the Baron de St. Jacques, the aide-de-camp to the Duke; but he never spoke once; indeed he scarcely lifted his head during the whole road.

Heaven knows it was a melancholy journey; and neither the country nor the season were such as to lift the mind from sorrow; and yet, strange enough, the miles glided over rapidly, and to this hour I cannot remember by what magic the way seemed so short. The thought that for several days back I had been living in closest intimacy with a distinguished prince of the Bourbon family; that we had spent hours together discussing themes and questions which were those of his own house; canvassing the chances and weighing the claims of which he was himself the asserter—was a most exciting feeling. How I recalled now all the modest deference of his manner—his patient endurance of my crude opinions—his generous admissions regarding his adversaries—and, above all, his ardent devotion to France, whatever the hand that swayed her destinies; and then the chivalrous boldness of his character, blended with an almost girlish gentleness—how princely were such traits!

From these thoughts I wandered on to others about his arrest and capture, from which, however, I could not believe any serious issue was to come. Bonaparte is too noble-minded not to feel the value of such a life as this. Men like the prince can be more heavily fettered by generous treatment than by all the chains that ever bound a felon. But what will be done with him? what with his followers? and lastly, not at all the pleasantest consideration, what is to come of Maurice Tiernay, who, to say the least, has been found in very suspicious company, and without a shadow of an explanation to account for it? This last thought just occurred to me as we crossed over the long bridge of boats, and entered Strasbourg.

CHAPTER XLI.

The Duc D'Enghien and his aide-de-camp were forwarded with the utmost speed to Paris; the remainder of us were imprisoned at Strasbourg. What became of my companions I know not; but I was sent on, along with a number of others, about a month later, to Nancy, to be tried by a military commission. I may mention it here as a singular fact illustrating the secrecy of the period, that it was not till long after this time I learned the terrible fate of the poor Prince de Condé. Had I known it, it is more than probable that I should have utterly despaired of my own safety. The dreadful story of Vincennes—the mock trial, and the midnight execution, are all too well known to my readers; nor is it necessary I should refer to an event on which I myself can throw no new light. That the sentence was determined on before his arrest—and that the grave was dug while the victim was still sleeping the last slumber before "the sleep that knows not waking"—the evidences are strong and undeniable. But an anecdote which circulated at the time, and which, so far as I know, has never appeared in print, would seem to show that there was complicity, at least, in the crime, and that the secret was not confined to the First Consul's breast.

On that fatal night of the 20th March, Talleyrand was seated at a card-table at Caulaincourt's house at Paris. The party was about to rise from play, when suddenly the "pendule" on the chimney-piece struck two. It was in one of those accidental pauses in the conversation when any sound is heard with unusual distinctness. Talleyrand started as he heard it, and then turning to Caulaincourt, whispered, "Yes; 'tis all over now!" words which, accidentally overheard, without significance, were yet to convey a terrible meaning when the dreadful secret of that night was disclosed.

If the whole of Europe was convulsed by the enormity

of this crime—the foulest that stains the name of Bonaparte—the Parisians soon forgot it in the deeper interest
of the great event that was now approaching—the assumption of the imperial title by Napoleon.

The excitement on this theme was so great and absorbing, that nothing else was spoken or thought of.
Private sorrows and afflictions were disregarded and
despised, and to obtrude one's hardships on the notice
of others, seemed, at this juncture, a most ineffable selfishness. That I, a prisoner, friendless, and unknown
as I was, found none to sympathise with me, or take
interest in my fate, is, therefore nothing extraordinary.
In fact, I appeared to have been entirely forgotten; and
though still in durance, nothing was said either of the
charge to be preferred against me, nor the time when
I should be brought to trial.

Giacourt, an old lieutenant of the marines, and at that
time Deputy-Governor of the Temple, was kind and
good-natured towards me, occasionally telling of the
events which were happening without, and giving me the
hope that some general amnesty would, in all likelihood,
liberate all those whose crimes were not beyond the reach
of mercy. The little cell I occupied—(and to Giacourt's
kindness I owed the sole possession of it)—looked out
upon the tall battlements of the outer walls, which excluded all view beyond, and thus drove me within myself
for occupation and employment. In this emergency, I set
about to write some notices of my life—some brief memoirs
of those changeful fortunes which had accompanied me
from boyhood. Many of those incidents which I relate
now, and many of those traits of mind or temper that
I recall, were then for the first time noted down, and thus
graven on my memory.

My early boyhood, my first experience as a soldier, the
campaign of the "Schwartz Wald," Ireland, and Genoa,
all were mentioned, and writing as I did solely for myself,
and my own eyes, I set down many criticisms on the
generals, and their plans of campaign, which, if intended
for the inspection of others, would have been the greatest
presumption and impertinence, and in this way Moreau,
Hoche, Massena, and even Bonaparte, came in for a most
candid and impartial criticism.

How Germany might have been conquered; how Ireland
ought to have been invaded; in what way Italy should
have been treated, and lastly, the grand political error of
the seizure of the Duc D'Enghien, were subjects that I dis-

cussed and determined with consummate boldness and
self-satisfaction. I am almost overwhelmed with shame,
even now, as I think of that absurd chronicle, with its
rash judgments, its crude opinions, and its pretentious de-
cisions.

So fascinated had I become with my task, that I rose
early to resume it each morning, and used to fall asleep,
cogitating on the themes for the next day, and revolving
within myself all the passages of interest I should com-
memorate. A man must have known imprisonment to
feel all the value that can be attached to any object, no
matter how mean or insignificant, that can employ the
thoughts, amuse the fancy, or engage the affections. The
narrow cell expands under such magic, the barred case-
ment is a free portal to the glorious sun and the free air;
the captive himself is but the student bending over his
allotted task. To this happy frame of mind had I come,
without a thought or a wish beyond the narrow walls at
either side of me, when a sad disaster befell me. On
awaking one morning, as usual, to resume my labour, my
manuscript was gone! the table and writing materials, all
had disappeared, and, to increase my discomfiture, the
turnkey informed me that Lieutenant Giacourt had been
removed from his post, and sent off to some inferior station
in the provinces.

I will not advert to the dreary time which followed this
misfortune, a time in which the hours passed on unmeasured
and almost unfelt. Without speculation, without a wish,
I passed my days in a stupid indolence akin to torpor.
Had the prison-doors been open, I doubt if I should have
had the energy to make my escape. Life itself ceased to
have any value for me, but somehow I did not desire
death. I was in this miserable mood when the turnkey
awoke me one day as I was dozing on my bed. "Get up,
and prepare yourself to receive a visitor," said he. "There's
an officer of the staff without, come to see you;" and as
he spoke, a young, slightly-formed man, entered, in the
uniform of a captain, who, making a sign for the turnkey
to withdraw, took his seat at my bedside.

"Don't get up, Monsieur; you look ill and weak, so
pray let me not disturb you," said he, in a voice of kindly
meaning.

"I'm not ill," said I, with an effort—but my hollow
utterance and my sunken cheeks contradicted my words
"but I have been sleeping; I usually doze at this
hour."

"The best thing a man can do in prison, I suppose," said he, smiling good-naturedly.

"No, not the best," said I, catching up his words too literally. "I used to write the whole day long, till they carried away my paper and my pens."

"It is just of that very thing I have come to speak, sir," resumed he. "You intended that memoir for publication?"

"No; never."

"Then for private perusal among a circle of friends?"

"Just as little. I scarcely know three people in the world who would acknowledge that title."

"You had an object, however, in composing it?"

"Yes; to occupy thought; to save me from—from——" I hesitated, for I was ashamed of the confession that nearly burst from me, and, after a pause, I said, "from being such as I now am!"

"You wrote it for yourself alone, then?"

"Yes."

"Unprompted; without any suggestion from another?"

"Is it here," said I, looking around my cell, "is it here that I should be likely to find a fellow-labourer?"

"No; but I mean to ask, were the sentiments your own, without any external influence, or any persuasions from others?"

"Quite my own."

"And the narrative is true?"

"Strictly so, I believe."

"Even to your meeting with the Duc D'Enghien. It was purely accidental?"

"That is, I never knew him to be the Duke till the moment of his arrest?"

"Just so; you thought he was merely a Royalist noble. Then, why did you not address a memoir to that effect to the Minister?"

"I thought it would be useless; when they made so little of a Condé, what right had I to suppose they would think much about me?"

"If he could have proved his innocence——" he stopped, and then in an altered voice said—"but as to this memoir, you assume considerable airs of military knowledge in it, and many of the opinions smack of heads older than yours."

"They are, I repeat, my own altogether; as to their presumption, I have already told you they were intended solely for my own eye."

24

"So that you are not a Royalist?"

"No."

"Never were one?"

"Never,"

"In what way would you employ yourself, if set at liberty to-day?"

I stared, and felt confused; for however easy I found it to refer to the past, and reason on it, any speculation as to the future was a considerable difficulty.

"You hesitate; you have not yet made up your mind, apparently."

"It is not that; I am trying to think of liberty, trying to fancy myself free—but I cannot!" said I, with a weary sigh; "the air of this cell has sapped my courage and my energy—a little more will finish the ruin!"

"And yet you are not much above four or five and twenty years of age?"

"Not yet twenty!" said I.

"Come, come, Tiernay—this is too early to be sick of life!" said he, and the kind tone touched me so that I burst into tears. They were bitter tears, too; for while my heart was relieved by this gush of feeling, I was ashamed at my own weakness. "Come, I say," continued he, "this memoir of yours might have done you much mischief—happily it has not done so. Give me the permission to throw it in the fire, and, instead of it, address a respectful petition to the head of the State, setting forth your services, and stating the casualty by which you were implicated in Royalism. I will take care that it meets his eye, and, if possible, will support its prayer; above all, ask for re-instalment in your grade, and a return to the service. It may be, perhaps, that you can mention some superior officer who would vouch for your future conduct."

"Except Colonel Mahon——"

"Not the Colonel Mahon who commanded the 13th Cuirassiers?"

"The same!"

"That name would little serve you," said he, coldly; "he has been placed 'en retraite' some time back; and if your character can call no other witness than him, your case is not too favourable." He saw that the speech had disconcerted me, and soon added, "Never mind—keep to the memoir; state your case, and your apology, and leave the rest to Fortune. When can you let me have it?"

"By to-morrow—to night, if necessary."

"To-morrow will do well, and so good bye. I will order them to supply you with writing materials;" and slapping me good-naturedly on the shoulder, he cried, "Courage, my lad," and departed.

Before I lay down to sleep that night, I completed my "memoir," the great difficulty of which I found to consist in giving it that dry brevity which I knew Bonaparte would require. In this, however, I believe I succeeded at last, making the entire document not to occupy one sheet of paper. The officer had left his card of address, which I found was inscribed Monsieur Bourrienne, Rue Lafitte, a name that subsequently was to be well known to the world.

I directed my manuscript to his care, and lay down with a lighter heart than I had known for many a day. I will not weary my reader with the tormenting vacillations of hope and fear which followed. Day after day went over, and no answer came to me. I addressed two notes, respectful, but urgent, begging for some information as to my demand—none came. A month passed thus, when, one morning, the Governor of the Temple entered my room with an open letter in his hand.

"This is an order for your liberation, Monsieur de Tiernay," said he; "you are free."

"Am I reinstated in my grade?" asked I, eagerly.

He shook his head, and said nothing.

"Is there no mention of my restoration to the service?"

"None, sir."

"Then what is to become of me—to what end am I liberated?" cried I, passionately.

"Paris is a great city, there is a wide world beyond it, and a man so young as you are must have few resources, or he will carve out a good career for himself."

"Say, rather, he must have few resentments, sir," cried I, bitterly, "or he will easily hit upon a bad one;" and with this, I packed up the few articles I possessed, and prepared to depart.

I remember it well: it was between two and three o'clock of the afternoon, on a bright day in spring, that I stood on the Quai Voltaire, a very small packet of clothes in a bundle in one hand, and a cane in the other, something short of three louis in my purse, and as much depression in my heart as ever settled down in that of a youth not full nineteen. Liberty is a glorious thing, and mine had been perilled often enough, to give me a hearty appreciation of its blessing; but at that moment, as I stood friendless and companionless in a great thoroughfare of a great city, I almost wished myself back again within the dreary walls of the Temple, for somehow it felt like home! It is true, one must have had a lonely lot in life before he could surround the cell of a prison with such attributes as these! Perhaps I have more of the cat-like affection for a particular spot than most men; but I do find that I attach myself to walls with a tenacity that strengthens as I grow older, and, like my brother parasite, the ivy, my grasp becomes more rigid the longer I cling.

If I know of few merely sensual gratifications higher than a lounge through Paris, at the flood-tide of its population, watching the varied hues and complexions of its strange inhabitants, displaying, as they do in feature, air, and gesture, so much more of character and purpose than other people, so also do I feel that there is something indescribably miserable in being alone, unknown, and unnoticed in that vast throng, destitute of means for the present, and devoid of hope for the future.

Some were bent on business, some on pleasure; some were evidently bent on killing time till the hour of more agreeable occupation should arrive; some were loitering along, gazing at the prints in shop-windows, or half listlessly stopping to read at book-stalls. There was not only every condition of mankind, from wealth to mendicancy, but every frame of mind, from enjoyment to utter "ennui," and yet I thought I could not hit upon any one individual who looked as forlorn and cast-away as myself; however, there were many who passed me that day who would gladly have changed fortune with me, but it would have been difficult to persuade me of the fact in the mood I then was.

At the time I speak of, there was a species of cheap ordinary held in the open air on the quay, where people of the humblest condition used to dine; I need scarcely describe the fare—the reader may conceive what it was, which, wine included, cost only four sous; a rude table without a cloth, some wooden platters, and an iron rail to which the knives and forks were chained, formed the "equipage," the cookery bearing a due relation to the elegance of these "accessories." As for the company, if not polite, it was certainly picturesque; consisting of labourers of the lowest class, the sweepers of crossings, hackney cab men out of employ, that poorest of the poor who try to earn a livelihood by dragging the Seine for lost articles, and finally, the motley race of idlers who vacillate between beggary and ballad-singing, with now and then a dash at highway robbery for a " distraction;" a class, be it said without paradox, which in Paris includes a considerable number of tolerably honest folk.

The moment was the eventful one in which France was about once more to become a monarchy, and as may be inferred from the character of the people, it was a time of high excitement and enthusiasm. The nation, even in its humblest citizen, seemed to feel some of the reflected glory that glanced from the great achievements of Bonaparte, and his elevation was little other than a grand manifestation of national self-esteem. That he knew how to profit by this sentiment, and incorporate his own with the country's glory, so that they seemed to be inseparable, is not among the lowest nor the least of the efforts of his genius

The paroxysm of national vanity, for it was indeed no less, imparted a peculiar character to the period. A vainglorious, boastful spirit was abroad; men met each other with high-sounding gratulations about French greatness and splendour, the sway we wielded over the rest of Europe, and the influence with which we impressed our views over the entire globe. Since the fall of the monarchy there had been half a dozen national fevers! There was the great Fraternal and Equality one, there was the era of classical associations, with all their train of trumpery affectation in dress and manner.

Then came the conquering spirit, with the flattering spectacle of great armies ; and now, as if to complete the cycle, there grew up that exaggerated conception of "France and her Mission," an unlucky phrase that has since done plenty of mischief, which seemed to carry the nation into the seventh heaven of overweening self-love.

If I advert to this here, it is but passingly, neither stopping to examine its causes, nor seeking to inquire the consequences that ensued from it, but, as it were, chronicling the fact as it impressed me as I stood that day on the Quai Voltaire, perhaps the only unimpassioned lounger along its crowded thoroughfare.

Not even the ordinary "a quatre sous" claimed exemption from this sentiment. It might be supposed that meagre diet and sour wine were but sorry provocatives to national enthusiasm, but even they could minister to the epidemic ardour, and the humble dishes of that frugal board masqueraded under titles that served to feed popular vanity. Of this I was made suddenly aware as I stood looking over the parapet into the river, and heard the rude voices of the labourers as they called for cutlets a la "Caire," potatoes en "Mamelouques," or roast beef a la "Monte-Notte," while every goblet of their wine was tossed off to some proud sentiment of national supremacy.

Amused by the scene, so novel in all its bearings, I took my place at the table, not sorry for the excuse to myself for partaking so humble a repast.

"Sacre bleu," cried a rough-looking fellow with a red nightcap set on one side of the head, "make room there, we have the 'aristocrates' coming down among us."

"Monsieur is heartily welcome," said another, making room for me; "we are only flattered by such proofs of confidence and esteem."

"Ay, parbleu," cried a third. "The Empire is coming, and we shall be well bred and well mannered. I intend to give up the river, and take to some more gentlemanlike trade than drudging for dead men."

"And I, I'll never sharpen anything under a rapier or a dress sword for the court," said a knife-grinder; "we have been living like 'cannaille' hitherto—nothing better."

"A l'empire, a l'empire," shouted half a dozen voices in concert; and the glasses were drained to the toast with a loud cheer.

Directly opposite to me sat a thin, pale, mild-looking man, of about fifty, in a kind of stuff robe, like the dress of a village curate. His appearance, though palpably poor, was venerable and imposing—not the less so, perhaps, from its contrast with the faces and gestures at either side of him. Once or twice, while these ebullitions of enthusiasm burst forth, his eyes met mine, and I read, or fancied that I read, a look of kindred appreciation in their mild and gentle glance. The expression was less reproachful than compassionate, as though in pity for the ignorance rather than in reprobation for the folly. Now, strangely enough, this was precisely the very sentiment of my own heart at that moment. I remembered a somewhat similar enthusiasm for republican liberty, by men just as unfitted to enjoy it; and I thought to myself, the Empire, like the Convention, or the Directory, is a mere fabulous conception to these poor fellows, who, whatever may be the regime, will still be hewers of wood and drawers of water to the end of all time.

As I was pondering over this, I felt something touch my

arm, and on turning perceived that my opposite neighbour
had now seated himself at my side, and, in a low, soft
voice, was bidding me "Good-day." After one or two
commonplace remarks upon the weather and the scene, he
seemed to feel that some apology for his presence in such
a place was needful, for he said,—

"You are here, monsieur, from a feeling of curiosity,
that, I see well enough; but I come for a very different
reason. I am the pastor of a mountain village of the
Ardêche, and have come to Paris in search of a young girl,
the daughter of one of my flock, who, it is feared, has
been carried off, by some evil influence, from her home and
her friends, to seek fortune and fame in this rich capital;
for she is singularly beautiful, and gifted too; sings divinely,
and improvises poetry with a genius that seems inspiration."

There was a degree of enthusiasm, blended with simplicity, in the poor curé's admiration of his "lost sheep" that
touched me deeply. He had been now three weeks in vain
pursuit, and was at last about to turn homeward, discomfited and unsuccessful. "Lisette" was the very soul of the
little hamlet, and he knew not how life was to be carried
on there without her. The old loved her as a daughter;
the young were rivals for her regard.

"And to me," said the pére, "whom, in all the solitude
of my lonely lot, literature, and especially poetry, consoles
many an hour of sadness or melancholy—to me, she was
like a good angel, her presence diffusing light as she
crossed my humble threshold, and elevating my thoughts
above the little crosses and accidents of daily life."

So interested had I become in this tale, that I listened
while he told every circumstance of the little locality;
and walking along at his side, I wandered out of the city,
still hearing of "La Marche," as the village was called,
till I knew the ford where the blacksmith lived, and the
miller with the cross wife, and the lame schoolmaster, and
Pierre the postmaster, who read out the Moniteur each
evening under the elms, even to Jacques Fulgeron the
"tapageur," who had served at Jemappes, and, with his
wounded hand and his waxed moustache, was the terror of
all peaceable folk.

"You should come and see us, my dear monsieur," said
he to me, as I showed some more than common interest in
the narrative. "You, who seem to study character, would
find something better worth the notice than these hardened
natures of city life. Come, and spend a week or two with

me, and if you do not like our people and their ways, I am
but a sorry physiognomist."

It is needless to say that I was much flattered by this
kind proof of confidence and good will; and finally it was
agreed upon between us that I should aid him in his search
for three days, after which, if still unsuccessful, we should
set out together for La Marche. It was easy to see that
the poor curé was pleased at my partnership in the task,
for there were several public places of resort—theatres,
" spectacles," and the like—to which he scrupled to resort,
and these he now willingly conceded to my inspection,
having previously given me so accurate a description of
La Lisette, that I fancied I should recognise her amongst
a thousand. If her long black eyelashes did not betray
her, her beautiful teeth were sure to do so; or, if I heard
her voice, there could be no doubt then; and, lastly, her
foot would as infallibly identify her as did Cinderella's.

For want of better, it was agreed upon that we should
make the Restaurant à Quatre Sous our rendezvous each
day, to exchange our confidences and report progress. It
will scarcely be believed how even this much of a pursuit
diverted my mind from its own dark dreamings, and how
eagerly my thoughts pursued the new track that was
opened to them. It was the utter listlessness, the nothing-
ness of my life, that was weighing me down; and already
I saw an escape from this in the pursuit of a good object.
I could wager that the pastor of La Marche never thought
so intensely, so uninterruptedly, of Lisette as did I for the
four and twenty hours that followed! It was not only
that I had created her image to suit my fancy, but I had
invented a whole narrative of her life and adventures
since her arrival in Paris.

My firm conviction being that it was lost time to seek
for her in obscure and out-of-the-way quarters of the city,
I thought it best to pursue the search in the thronged and
fashionable resorts of the gay world, the assemblies and
theatres. Strong in this conviction, I changed one of my
three gold pieces to purchase a ticket for the opera. The
reader may smile at the sacrifice; but when he who thinks
four sous enough for a dinner, pays twelve francs for the
liberty to be crushed in the crowded parterre of a play-
house, he is indeed buying pleasure at a costly price. It
was something more than a fifth of all I possessed in the
world, but, after all, my chief regret arose from thinking
that it left me so few remaining " throws of the dice" for
" Fortune."

I have often reflected since that day by what a mere accident I was present, and yet the spectacle was one that I have never forgotten. It was the last time the First Consul appeared in public, before his assumption of the imperial title; and at no period through all his great career was the enthusiasm more impassioned regarding him. He sat in the box adjoining the stage—Cambaceres and Lebrun, with a crowd of others, standing, and not sitting, around and behind his chair. When he appeared, the whole theatre rose to greet him, and three several times was he obliged to rise and acknowledge the salutations. And with what a stately condescension did he make these slight acknowledgments!—what haughtiness was there in the glance he threw around him! I have often heard it said, and I have seen it also written, that previous to his assumption of the crown, Bonaparte's manner exhibited the mean arts and subtle devices of a candidate on the hustings, dispensing all the flatteries and scattering all the promises that such occasions are so pro- lific of. I cannot, of course, pretend to contradict this statement positively; but I can record the impression which that scene made upon me, as decidedly the opposite of this assumption. I have repeatedly seen him since that event, but never do I remember his calm, cold fea- tures more impassively stern, more proudly collected, than on that night.

Every allusion of the piece that could apply to him was eagerly caught up. Not a phrase nor a chance word that could compliment, was passed over in silence; and if greatness and glory were accorded, as if by an instinctive reverence, the vast assemblage turned towards him, to lay their homage at his feet. I watched him narrowly, and could see that he received them all as his rightful tribute, the earnest of the debt the nation owed him. Among the incidents of that night, I remember one which actually for the moment convulsed the house with its enthusiasm. One of the officers of his suite had somehow stumbled against Bonaparte's hat, which, on entering, he had thrown carelessly beside his chair. Stooping down and lifting it up, he perceived to whom it belonged, and then remarking the mark of a bullet on the edge, he showed it significantly to a general near him. Slight and trivial as was the incident, it was instantly caught up by the par- terre. A low murmur ran quickly around; and then a sudden cheer burst forth, for some one remembered it was the anniversary of Marengo! And now the excitement became madness, and reiterated shouts proclaimed that the glory of that day was among the proudest memories of France. For once. and once only, did any trait of feeling show itself on that impassive face. I thought I could mark even a faint tinge of colour in that sallow cheek, as in recognition he bowed a dignified salute to the waving and agitated assembly.

I saw that proud face. at moments when human ambition might have seemed to have reached its limit. and yet never with a haughtier look than on that night I speak of. His foot was already on the first step of the throne, and his spirit seemed to swell with the conscious force of coming greatness.

And Lisette, all this time? Alas, I had totally forgotten her! As the enthusiasm around me began to subside, I had time to recover myself. and look about me. There was much beauty and splendour to admire. Madame Junot was there. and Mademoiselle de Bessieres. with a crowd of others less known, but scarcely less lovely. Not one, however, could I see that corresponded with my mind-drawn portrait of the peasant beauty; and I scanned each face closely and critically. There was female loveliness of every type, from the dark-eyed beauty of Spanish race, to the almost divine regularity of a Raphaelite picture. There was the brilliant aspect of fashion, too; but nowhere could I see what I sought for: nowhere detect that image which imagination had stamped as that of the beauty of "La Marche." If disappointed in my great object, I left the theatre with my mind full of all I had witnessed. The dreadful event of Ettenheim had terribly shaken Bonaparte in my esteem; yet how resist the contagious devotion of a whole nation—how remain cold in the midst of the burning zeal of all France? These thoughts brought me to the consideration of myself. Was I. or was I not, any longer a soldier of his army? or was I disqualified for joining in that burst of national enthusiasm which proclaimed that all France was ready to march under his banner? To-morrow I'll wait upon the minister of war, thought I, or I'll seek out the commanding officer of some regiment that I know, or at least a comrade; and so I went on, endeavouring to frame a plan for my guidance, as I strolled along the streets, which were now almost deserted. The shops were all closed; of the hotels, such as were yet open were far too costly for means like mine: and so. as the night was calm and balmy with the fresh air of spring, I resolved to pass it

out of doors. I loitered then along the Champs Ely-
sées; and at length stretching myself on the grass beneath the trees, lay down to sleep. "An odd bedroom
enough," thought I, "for one who has passed the evening at the opera, and who has feasted his ears at the
expense of his stomach." I remembered, too, another night
when the sky had been my canopy in Paris, when I slept
beneath the shadow of the guillotine and the Place de
Grêve. "Well," thought I, "times are at least changed
for the better since that day; and my own fortunes are
certainly not lower."

This comforting reflection closed my waking memories,
and I slept soundly till morning.

CHAPTER XLII.

THE "COUNT DE MAUREPAS," ALIAS ——.

THERE is a wide gulf between him who opens his waking eyes in a splendid chamber, and with half-drowsy thoughts speculates on the pleasures of the coming day, and him, who, rising from the dew-moistened earth, stretches his aching limbs for a second or so, and then hurries away to make his toilette at the nearest fountain.

I have known both conditions, and yet, without being thought paradoxical, I would wish to say that there are some sensations attendant on the latter and the humbler lot which I would not exchange for all the voluptuous ease of the former. Let there be but youth, and there is something of heroism, something adventurous in the notion of thus alone and unaided breasting the wide ocean of life, and, like a hardy swimmer, daring to stem the roughest breakers without one to succour him, that is worth all the security that even wealth can impart, all the conscious ease that luxury and affluence can supply. In a world and an age like ours, thought I, there must surely be some course for one young, active, and daring as I am. Even if France reject me, there are countries beyond the seas where energy and determination will open a path. "Courage, Maurice," said I, as I dashed the sparkling water over my head, "the past has not been all inglorious, and the future may prove even better."

A roll and a glass of iced water furnished my breakfast, after which I set forth in good earnest on my search. There was a sort of self-flattery in the thought that one so destitute as I was could devote his thoughts and energies to the service of another, that pleased me greatly. It was so "unselfish"—at least I thought so. Alas and alas! how egotistical are we when we fancy ourselves least so. That day I visited St. Roch and Nôtre Dame at early mass, and by noon reached the Louvre, the gallery of which occupied me till the hour of meeting the curé drew nigh.

Punctual to his appointment, I found him waiting for me
at the corner of the quay, and although disappointed at
the failure of all his efforts, he talked away with all the
energy of one who would not suffer himself to be cast
down by adverse fortune. "I feel," said he, "a kind of
instinctive conviction that we shall find her yet. There
is something tells me that all our pains shall not go unre-
warded. Have you never experienced a sensation of this
kind,—a species of inward prompting to pursue a road,
to penetrate into a pass, or to explore a way, without exactly knowing why or wherefore?"

This question, vague enough as it seemed, led me to
talk about myself and my own position; a theme which,
however much I might have shrunk from introducing,
when once opened, I spoke of in all the freedom of old
friendship.

Nothing could be more delicate than the priest's manner during all this time; nor even when his curiosity was
highest did he permit himself to ask a question or an explanation of any difficulty that occurred; and while he
followed my recital with a degree of interest that was
most flattering, he never ventured on a word or dropped
a remark that might seem to urge me to greater frankness.
"Do you know," said he, at last, "why your story has
taken such an uncommon hold upon my attention? It is
not from its adventurous character, nor from the stirring
and strange scenes you have passed through. It is because
your old pastor and guide, the Pére Delamoy, was my own
dearest friend, my school companion and playfellow from
infancy. We were both students at Louvain together;
both called to the priesthood on the same day. Think,
then, of my intense delight at hearing his dear name once
more—ay, and permit me to say it, hearing from the lips of
another the very precepts and maxims that I can recognise
as his own. Ah, yes! mon cher Maurice," cried he, grasping
my hand in a burst of enthusiasm, "disguise it how you
may, cover it up under the uniform of a 'Bleu,' bury it
beneath the shako of the soldier of the Republic, but the
head and the heart will turn to the ancient altars of the
Church and the Monarchy. It is not alone that your good
blood suggests this, but all your experience of life goes to
prove it. Think of poor Michel, self-devoted, generous
and noble-hearted; think of that dear cottage at Kuffstein, where, even in poverty, the dignity of birth and
blood threw a grace and an elegance over daily life; think
of Ettenheim and the glorious prince—the last Condé—

and who now sleeps in his narrow bed in the fosse of Vin‹
cennes!"

"How do you mean?" said I, eagerly; for up to this
time I knew nothing of his fate.

"Come along with me, and you shall know it all," said
he; and, rising, he took my arm, and we sauntered along
out of the crowded street, till we reached the Boulevards.
He then narrated to me every incident of the midnight
trial, the sentence, and the execution. From the death-
warrant that came down ready-filled from Paris, to the
grave dug while the victm was yet sleeping—he forgot
nothing; and I own that my very blood ran cold at the
terrible atrocity of that dark murder. It was already
growing dusk when he had finished, and we parted hurriedly, as he was obliged to be at a distant quarter of Paris
by eight o'clock, again agreeing to meet, as before, on the
Quai Voltaire.

From that moment till we met the following day, the
Duc D'Enghien was never out of my thoughts, and I was
impatient for the priest's presence that I might tell him
every little incident of our daily life at Ettenheim, the
topics we used to discuss, and the opinions he expressed
on various subjects. The eagerness of the curé to listen
stimulated me to talk on, and I not only narrated all that
I was myself a witness of, but various other circumstances
which were told to me by the Prince himself; in particular,
an incident he mentioned to me one day of being visited
by a stranger who came, introduced by a letter from a very
valued friend; his business being to propose to the Duke
a scheme for the assassination of Bonaparte. At first the
Prince suspected the whole as a plot against himself, but
on further questioning he discovered that the man's intentions were really such as he professed them, and offered
his services in the conviction that no price could be deemed
too high to reward him. It is needless to say that the
offer was rejected with indignation, and the Prince dismissed the fellow with the threat of delivering him up to
the government of the French Consul. The pastor heard
this anecdote with deep attention, and, for the first time,
diverging from his line of cautious reserve, he asked me
various questions as to when the occurrence had taken
place, and where—if the Prince had communicated the
circumstance to any other than myself, and whether he
had made it the subject of any correspondence. I knew
little more than I had already told him: that the offer
was made while residing at Ettenheim, and during the

preceding year, were facts, however, that I could remember.

" You are surprised, perhaps," said he, " at the interest
I feel in all this ; but strangely enough, there is here in
Paris at this moment one of the great ' Seigneurs' of the
Ardêche ; he has come up to the capital for medical advice,
and he was a great, perhaps the greatest, friend of the poor
Duke. What if you were to come and pay him a visit
with me, there is not probably one favour the whole world
could bestow he would value so highly. You must often
have heard his name from the Prince; has he not frequently spoken of the Count de Maurepas ? " I could not
remember having ever heard the name. " It is historical
however," said the curé, " and even in our own days has
not derogated from its ancient chivalry. Have you not
heard how a noble of the Court rode postilion to the king's
carriage on the celebrated escape from Varennes ? Well,
even for curiosity sake, he is worth a visit, for this is the
very Count Henri de Maurepas, now on the verge of the
grave ! "

If the good curé had known me all my life, he could
not more successfully have baited a trap for my curiosity.
To see and know remarkable people, men who had done
something out of the ordinary route of every-day life, had
been a passion with me from boyhood. Hero-worship was,
indeed, a great feature in my character, and has more or
less influenced all my career, nor was I insensible to the
pleasure of doing a kind action. It was rare, indeed, that
one so humbly placed could ever confer a favour, and I
grasped with eagerness the occasion to do so. We agreed,
then, on the next afternoon, towards nightfall, to meet at
the quay, and proceed together to the Count's residence.
I have often reflected, since that day, that Lisette's name
was scarcely ever mentioned by either of us during this
interview; and yet, at the time, so pre-occupied were my
thoughts, I never noticed the omission. The Chateau of
Ettenheim, and its tragic story, filled my mind to the exclusion of all else.

I pass over the long and dreary hours that intervened,
and come at once to the time, a little after sunset, when
we met at our accustomed rendezvous.

The curé had provided a " fiacre " 'for the occasion, as
the Count's residence was about two leagues from the city,
on the way to Belleville. As we trotted along, he gave
me a most interesting account of the old noble, whose life
had been one continued act of devotion to the monarchy.

" It will be difficult," said he, " for you to connect the
poor, worn out, shattered wreck before you, with all that
was daring in deed and chivalrous in sentiment ; but the
' Maurepas ' were well upheld in all their glorious renown,
by him who is now to be the last of the race ! You will
see him reduced by suffering and sickness, scarcely able
to speak, but be assured that you will have his gratitude
for this act of true benevolence. Thus chatting we rattled
along over the paved highway, and at length entered upon
a deep clay road which conducted us to a spacious park,
with a long straight avenue of trees, at the end of which
stood what, even in the uncertain light, appeared a spacious chateau. The door lay open, and as we descended,
a servant in plain clothes received us, and, after a whispered word or two from the curé, ushered us along through
a suite of rooms into a large chamber furnished like a
study. There were book-shelves well filled, and a writing-
table covered with papers and letters, and the whole floor
was littered with newspapers and journals.

A lamp, shaded by a deep gauze cover, threw a half
light over everything, nor was it until we had been nearly
a couple of minutes in the room that we became aware of the
presence of the Count, who lay upon a sofa, covered up in a
fur pelisse, although the season was far advanced in spring.

His gentle " Good evening, Messieurs," was the first
warning we had of his presence, and the curé, advancing
respectfully, presented me as his young friend, Monsieur
de Tiernay.

" It is not for the first time that I hear that name," said
the sick man, with a voice of singular sweetness. It is
chronicled in the annals of our monarchy. Ay sir, I knew
that faithful servant of his king, who followed his master
to the scaffold."

" My father," cried I, eagerly.

" I knew him well," continued he, " I may say, without
vaunting, that I had it in my power to befriend him, too.
He made an imprudent marriage; he was unfortunate in
the society his second wife's family threw him amongst.
They were not his equals in birth, and far beneath him in
sentiment and principle. Well, well," sighed he, " this is
not a theme for me to speak of, nor for you to hear; tell
me of yourself. The curé says that you have had more
than your share of worldly vicissitudes. There, sit down,
and let me hear your story from your own lips."

He pointed to a seat at his side, and I obeyed him at
once; for, somehow, there was an air of command even in

the gentlest tones of his voice, and I felt that his age and his sufferings were not the only claims he possessed to in - fluence those around him.

With all the brevity in my power, my story lasted till above an hour, during which time the Count only inter- rupted me once or twice by asking to which Colonel Ma- hon I referred, as there were two of the name ; and again by inquiring in what circumstances the emigré familiy, were living as to means, and whether they appeared to derive any of their resources from France. These were points I could give no information upon, and I plainly perceived that the Count had no patience for a conjecture, and that, where positive knowledge failed, he instantly passed on to something else. When I came to speak of Ettenheim his attention became fixed, not suffering the minutest circumstance to escape him, and even asking for the exact description of the locality, and its distance from the towns in the neighbourhood.

The daily journeys of the Prince, too, interested him much, and once or twice he made me repeat what the peasant had said of the horse being able to travel from Strasbourg without a halt. I vow it puzzled me why he should dwell on these points in preference to others of far more interest, but I set them down to the caprices of ill- ness, and thought no more of them. His daily life, his conversation, the opinions he expressed about France, the questions he used to ask, were all matters he inquired into, till, finally, we came to the anecdote of the meditated as- sassination of Bonaparte. This he made me tell him twice over, each time asking me eagerly whether, by an effort of memory, I could not recall the name of the man who had offered his services for the deed. This I could not ; indeed I knew not if I had ever heard it.

" But the Prince rejected the proposal ?" said he, peer- ing at me beneath the dark shadow of his heavy brow; " he would not hear of it ?"

" Of course not," cried I ; " he even threatened to de- nounce the man to the government."

" And do you think that he would have gone thus far, sir ?" asked he, slowly.

" I am certain of it. The horror and disgust he ex- pressed when reciting the story were a guarantee for what he would have done."

" But yet Bonaparte has been a dreadful enemy to his race," said the Count.

" It is not a Condé can right himself by a murder," said I, as calmly.

25

" How I like that burst of generous Royalism, young man ! " said he, grasping my hand and shaking it warmly. " That steadfast faith in the honour of a Bourbon is the very heart and soul of loyalty ! "

Now, although I was not, so far as I knew of, anything of a Royalist—the cause had neither my sympathy nor my wishes—I did not choose to disturb the equanimity of a poor sick man by a needless disclaimer, nor induce a discussion which must be both unprofitable and painful.

" How did the fellow propose the act ? had he any accomplices ? or was he alone ? "

" I believe quite alone."

" Of course suborned by England ? Of that there can be no doubt."

" The Prince never said so."

" Well, but, it is clear enough, the man must have had means ; he travelled by a very circuitous route ; he had come from Hamburg probably ? "

" I never heard."

" He must have done so. The ports of Holland, as those of France, would have been too dangerous for him. Italy is out of the question."

I owned that I had not speculated so deeply in the matter.

" It was strange," said he, after a pause, " that the Duke never mentioned who had introduced the man to him."

" He merely called him a valued friend."

" In other words, the Count D'Artois," said the Count ; " did it not strike you so ? "

I had to confess it had not occurred to me to think so.

" But reflect a little," said he. " Is there any other living who could have dared to make such a proposal but the Count ? Who, but the head of his house, could have presumed on such a step ? No inferior could have had the audacity ! It must have come from one so highly placed that crime paled itself down to a mere measure of expediency under the loftiness of the sanction. What think you ? "

" I cannot, I will not think so," was my answer. " The very indignation of the Prince's rejection refutes the supposition."

" What a glorious gift is unsuspectfulness," said he, feelingly. " I am a rich man, and you I believe are not so ; and yet, I'd give all my wealth, ay, ten times told, not for your vigour of health, not for the lightness of your heart, nor the elasticity of your spirits, but for that one small quality, defect though it be, that makes you trustful and credulous."

I believe I would just as soon that the old gentleman had thought fit to compliment me upon any other quality. Of all my acquisitions there was not one I was so vain of as my knowledge of life and character. I had seen, as I thought, so much of life! I had peeped at all ranks and conditions of men, and it was rather hard to find an old country gentleman, a "Seigneur de Village," calling me credulous and unsuspecting!

I was much more pleased when he told the curé that a supper was ready for us in the adjoining room, at which he begged we would excuse his absence; and truly a most admirable little meal it was, and served with great elegance.

"The Count expects you to stop here; there is a chamber prepared for you," said the curé as we took our seats at table. "He has evidently taken a fancy to you. I thought, indeed I was quite certain, he would. Who can tell what good fortune this chance meeting may lead to, Monsieur Maurice! A votre sante, mon cher!" cried he, as he clinked his champagne glass against mine, and I at last began to think that destiny was about to smile on me.

"You should see his chateau in the Ardèche; this is nothing to it! There is a forest, too, of native oak, and a 'Chasse' such as royalty never owned!"

Mine were delightful dreams that night; but I was sorely disappointed on waking to find that Laura was not riding at my side through a forest-alley, while a crowd ot "Piqueurs" and huntsmen galloped to and fro, making the air vibrate with their joyous bugles. Still, I opened my eyes in a richly-furnished chamber, while a lacquais handed me my coffee on a silver stand, and in a cup of costliest Sevres.

CHAPTER XLIII.

A FOREST RIDE.

WHILE I was dressing, a note was handed to me from the curé, apologising for his departure without seeing me, and begging, as a great favour, that I would not leave the chateau till his return. He said that the Count's spirits had benefited greatly by our agreeable converse, and that he requested me to be his guest for some time to come. The postscript added a suggestion that I should write down some of the particulars of my visit to Ettenheim, but particularly of that conversation alluding to the meditated assassination of Bonaparte.

There were many points in the arrangement which I did not like. To begin, I had no fancy whatever for the condition of a dependant, and such my poverty would at once stamp me. Secondly, I was averse to this frequent intercourse with men of the Royalist party, whose restless character and unceasing schemes were opposed to all the principles of those I had served under; and finally, I was growing impatient under the listless vacuity of a life that gave no occupation, nor opened any view for the future. I sat down to breakfast in a mood very little in unison with the material enjoyments around me. The meal was all that could tempt appetite; and the view from the open window displayed a beautiful flower-garden, imperceptibly fading away into a maze of ornamental planting, which was backed again by a deep forest, the well-known wood of Belleville. Still I ate on sullenly, scarce noticing any of the objects around me. I will see the Count, and take leave of him, thought I suddenly; I cannot be his guest without sacrificing feeling in a dozen ways.

"At what hour does Monsieur rise?" asked I, of the obsequious valet who waited behind my chair.

"Usually at three or four in the afternoon, sir; but to-day he has desired me to make his excuses to you. There will be a consultation of doctors here; and the likelihood is, that he may not leave his chamber."

"Will you convey my respectful compliments, then, to him, and my regrets that I had not seen him before leaving the chateau?"

"The Count charged me, sir, to entreat your remaining here till he had seen you. He said you had done him infinite service already, and indeed it is long since he has passed a night in such tranquillity."

There are few slight circumstances which impress a stranger more favourably than any semblance of devotion on the part of a servant to his master. The friendship of those above one in life is easier to acquire than the attachment of those beneath. Love is a plant whose tendrils strive ever upwards. I could not help feeling struck at the man's manner as he spoke these few words; and insensibly my mind reverted to the master who had inspired such sentiments.

"My master gave orders, sir," continued he, "that we should do everything possible to contribute to your wishes; that the carriage, or, if you prefer them, saddle-horses, should be ready at any hour you ordered. The wood has a variety of beautiful excursions; there is a lake, too, about two leagues away; and the ruins of Monterraye are also worth seeing."

"If I had not engagements in Paris," muttered I, while I affected to mumble over the conclusion of the sentence to myself.

"Monsieur has seldom done a greater kindness than this will be," added he, respectfully; "but if Monsieur's business could be deferred for a day or two, without inconvenience——"

"Perhaps that might be managed," said I, starting up, and walking to the window, when, for the first time, the glorious prospect revealed itself before me. How delicious, after all, would be a few hours of such a retreat!— a morning loitered away in that beautiful garden; and then, a long ramble through the dark wood till sunset. Oh, if Laura were but here; if she could be my companion along those leafy alleys! If not with, I can at least think of her, thought I; seek out spots she would love to linger in, and points of view she would enjoy with all a painter's zest. And this poor Count, with all his riches, could not derive in a whole lifetime the enjoyment that a few brief hours would yield to us! So is it almost ever in this world: to one man the appliances, to another the faculties, for enjoyment.

"I am so glad Monsieur has consented," said the valet joyously.

"Did I say so? I don't know that I said any thing."

"The Count will be so gratified," added he; and hurried away to convey the tidings.

Well, be it so. Heaven knows my business in Paris will scarcely suffer by my absence; my chief occupation there being to cheat away the hours till meal-time. It is an occupation I can easily resume a few days hence. I took a book, and strolled out into the garden; but I could not read. There is a gush of pleasure felt at times from the most familiar objects, which the most complicated machinery of enjoyment often fails to equal; and now the odour of moss-roses and geraniums, the rich perfume of orange-flowers, the plash of fountains and the hum of the summer insects, steeped my mind in delight; and I lay there in a dream of bliss that was like enchantment. I suppose I must have fallen asleep; for my thoughts took every form of wildness and incoherency. Ireland; the campaign; the Bay of Genoa; the rugged height of Kuffstein, all passed before my mind, peopled with images foreign to all their incidents. It was late in the afternoon that I aroused myself, and remembered where I was; the shadows of the dark forest were stretching over the plain; and I determined on a ride beneath their mellow shade. As if in anticipation of my wishes, the horses were already saddled, and a groom stood awaiting my orders. Oh, what a glorious thing it is to be rich! thought I, as I mounted; from what an eminence does the wealthy man view life! No petty cares nor calculations mar the conceptions of his fancy. His will, like his imagination, wanders free and unfettered. And so thinking, I dashed spurs into my horse, and plunged into the dense wood. Perhaps I was better mounted than the groom, or perhaps the man was scarcely accustomed to such impetuosity. Whatever the reason, I was soon out of sight of him. The trackless grass of the alley, and its noiseless turf, made pursuit difficult in a spot where the paths crossed and recrossed in a hundred different directions; and so I rode on for miles and miles without seeing more of my follower.

Forest riding is particularly seductive; you are insensibly led on to see where this alley will open, or how that path will terminate. Some of the spirit of discovery seems to seal its attractions to the wild and devious track, untrodden as it looks; and you feel all the charm of adventure as you advance. The silence, too, is most striking; the noiseless footfall of the horse, and the unbroken stillness, add indescribable charm to the scene, and the least imaginative cannot fail to weave fancies and fictions as he goes.

Near as it was to a great city, not a single rider crossed my path ; not even a peasant did I meet. A stray bundle of faggots, bound and ready to be carried away, showed that the axe of the woodman had been heard within the solitude ; but not another trace told that human footstep had ever pressed the sward.

Although still a couple of hours from sunset, the shade of the wood was dense enough to make the path appear uncertain, and I was obliged to ride more cautiously than before. I had thought that by steadily pursuing one straight track, I should at last gain the open country, and easily find some road that would reconduct me to the chateau ; but now I saw no signs of this. " The alley " was, to all appearance, exactly as I found it—miles before. A long aisle of beech-trees stretched away in front and behind me ; a short, grassy turf was beneath my feet : and not an object to tell me how far I had come, or whither I was tending. If now and then another road crossed the path, it was in all respects like this one. This was puzzling ; and to add to my difficulty, I suddenly remembered that I had never thought of learning the name of the chateau, and well knew that to ask for it as the residence of the Count de Maurepas would be a per-fect absurdity. There was something so ludicrous in the situation, that I could not refrain from laughing at first ; but a moment's reconsideration made me regard the inci-dent more gravely. In what a position should I stand, if unable to discover the chateau. The curé might have left Paris before I could reach it ; all clue to the Count might thus be lost ; and although these were but impro-bable circumstances, they came now very forcibly before me, and gave me serious uneasiness.

"I have been so often in false positions in life, so fre-quently implicated where no real blame could attach to me, that I shall not be in the least surprised if I be arrested as a horse-stealer!" The night now began to fall rapidly, so that I was obliged to proceed at a slow pace ; and at length, as the wood seemed to thicken, I was forced to get off, and walk beside my horse. I have often found myself in situations of real peril, with far less anxiety than I now felt ; my position seemed at the time inexpli-cable and absurd. I suppose, thought I, that no man was ever lost in the wood of Belleville ; he must find his way out of it sooner or later ; and then there can be no great

difficulty in returning to Paris. This was about the
extent of the comfort I could afford myself; for, once
back in the capital, I could not speculate on a single step
further.

I was at last so weary with the slow and cautious progression I was condemned to, that I half determined to
picket my horse to a tree, and lie down to sleep till daylight. While I sought out a convenient spot for my
bivouac, a bright twinkling light, like a small star, caught
my eye. Twice it appeared, and vanished again, so that
I was well assured of its being real, and no phantom of
my now over-excited brain. It appeared to proceed from
the very densest part of the wood, and whither, so far as
I could see, no path conducted. As I listened to catch
any sounds, I again caught sight of the faint star, which
now seemed at a short distance from the road where I
stood. Fastening my horse to a branch, I advanced
directly through the brushwood for about a hundred
yards, when I came to a small open space, in which stood
one of those modest cottages, of rough timber, wherein,
at certain seasons, the gamekeepers take refuge. A low,
square, log hut, with a single door, and an unglazed window, comprised the whole edifice, being one of the humblest, even of its humble kind, I had ever seen. Stealing
cautiously to the window, I peeped in. On a stone, in
the middle of the earthern floor, a small iron lamp stood,
which threw a faint and fickle light around. There was
no furniture of any kind; nothing that bespoke the place
as inhabited; and it was only as I continued to gaze that
I detected the figure of a man, who seemed to be sleeping
on a heap of dried leaves, in one corner of the hovel. I
own that, with all my anxiety to find a guide, I began to
feel some scruples about obtruding on the sleeper's privacy. He was evidently no " Garde de Chasse," who are
a well-to-do sort of folk, being usually retired sous·
officiers of the army. He might be a poacher, a robber,
or perhaps a dash of both together—a trade I had often
heard of as being resorted to by the most reckless and
abandoned of the population of Paris, when their crimes
and their haunts became too well known in the capital.

I peered eagerly through the chamber, to see if he were
armed; but not a weapon of any kind was to be seen. I
next sought to discover if he were quite alone; and although one side of the hovel was hidden from my view, I
was well assured that he had no comrade. Come, said I
to myself, man to man, if it should come to a struggle, is

fair enough; and the chances are, I shall be able to defend myself.

His sleep was sound and heavy, like that after fatigue; so that I thought it would be easy for me to enter the hovel, and secure his arms, if he had such, before he should awake. I may seem to my reader, all this time, to have been inspired with an undue amount of caution and prudence, considering how evenly we were matched; but I would remind him, that it was a period when the most dreadful crimes were of daily occurrence. Not a night went over without some terrible assassination; and a number of escaped galley-slaves were known to be at large in the suburbs and outskirts of the capital. These men, under the slightest provocation, never hesitated at murder; for their lives were already forfeited, and they scrupled at nothing which offered a chance of escape. To add to the terror their atrocities excited, there was a rumour current at the time that the Government itself made use of these wretches for its own secret acts of vengeance; and many implicitly believed that the dark assassinations of the "Temple" had no other agency. I do not mean to say that these fears were well founded, or that I myself partook of them; but such were the reports commonly circulated, and the impunity of crime certainly favoured the impression. I know not if this will serve as an apology for the circumspection of my proceeding, as cautiously pushing the door, inch by inch, I at length threw it wide open. Not the slightest sound escaped as I did so; and yet, certainly before my hand quitted the latch, the sleeper had sprung to his knees; and with his dark eyes glaring wildly at me, crouched like a beast about to rush upon an enemy.

His attitude and his whole appearance at that moment are yet before me. Long black hair fell in heavy masses at either side of his head; his face was pale, haggard, and hunger-stricken; a deep, drooping moustache descended from below his chin, and almost touched his collar-bones, which were starting from beneath the skin; a ragged cloak, that covered him as he lay, had fallen off, and showed that a worn shirt and a pair of coarse linen trousers were all his clothing. Such a picture of privation and misery I never looked upon before nor since.

"Qui va là?" cried he, sternly, and with the voice of one not unused to command; and although the summons showed his soldier-training, his condition of wretchedness suggested deep misgivings.

" Qui va là ?" shouted he again, louder and more determinedly.

" A friend—perhaps a comrade," said I, boldly.

" Advance, comrade, and give the countersign," replied he, rapidly, and like one repeating a phrase of routine ; and then, as if suddenly remembering himself, he added, with a low sigh, " There is none !" His arms dropped heavily as he spoke, and he fell back against the wall, with his head drooping on his chest.

There was something so unutterably forlorn in his look, as he sat thus, that all apprehension of personal danger from him left me at the moment, and advancing frankly, I told him how I had lost my way in the wood, and by a mere accident chanced to descry his light as I wandered along in the gloom.

I do not know if he understood me at first, for he gazed half vacantly at my face while I was speaking, and often stealthily peered around to see if others were coming ; so that I had to repeat more than once that I was perfectly alone. That the poor fellow was insane seemed but too probable ; the restless activity of his wild eye, the suspicious watchfulness of his glances, all looked like madness, and I thought that he had probably made his escape from some military hospital, and concealed himself within the recesses of the forest. But even these signs of overwrought excitement began to subside soon ; and as though the momentary effort at vigilance had been too much for his strength, he now drew his cloak about him, and lay down once more.

I handed him my brandy-flask, which still contained a little, and he raised it to his lips with a slight nod of recognition. Invigorated by the stimulant, he supped again and again, but always cautiously, and with prudent reserve.

"You have been a soldier ?" said I, taking my seat at his side.

" I am a soldier," said he, with a strong emphasis on the verb.

"I too have served," said I ; " although, probably, neither as long nor as creditably as you have."

He looked at me fixedly for a second or two, and then dropped his eyes without a reply.

" You were probably with the Army of the Meuse ?" said I, hazarding the guess, from remembering how many of that army had been invalided by the terrible attacks of ague contracted in North Holland.

"I served on the Rhine," said he, briefly; "but I made the campaign of Jemappes, too. I served the King also—King Louis," cried he, sternly. "Is that avowal candid enough; or do you want more?"

Another Royalist, thought I, with a sigh. Whichever way I turn they meet me—the very ground seems to give them up.

"And could you find no better trade than that of a Mouchard?" asked he, sneeringly.

"I am not a Mouchard—I never was one. I am a soldier like yourself; and, mayhap, if all were to be told, scarcely a more fortunate one."

"Dismissed the service—and for what?" asked he, bluntly.

"If not broke, at least not employed," said I, bitterly.

"A Royalist?"

"Not the least of one, but suspected."

"Just so. Your letters—your private papers ransacked, and brought in evidence against you. Your conversations with your intimates noted down and attested—every word you dropped in a moment of disappointment or anger; every chance phrase you uttered when provoked, all quoted; wasn't that it?"

As he spoke this, with a rapid and almost impetuous utterance, I, for the first time, noticed that both the expressions and the accent implied breeding and education. Not all his vehemence could hide the evidences of former cultivation.

"How comes it," asked I, eagerly, "that such a man as you are is to be found thus? You certainly did not always serve in the ranks?"

"I had my grade," was his short, dry reply.

"You were a quarter-master—perhaps a sous-lieutenant?" said I, hoping by the flattery of the surmise to lead him to talk further.

"I was the colonel of a dragoon regiment," said he, sternly; "and that neither the least brave nor the least distinguished in the French army."

Ah! thought I, my good fellow, you have shot your bolt too high this time; and in a careless, easy way, I asked, "What might have been the number of your corps?"

"How can it concern you?" said he, with a savage vehemence. "You say that you are not a spy. To what end these questions? As it is, you have made this hovel, which has been my shelter for some weeks back, no longer

of any service to me. I will not be tracked. I will not
suffer espionage, by Heaven!" cried he, as he dashed his
clenched fist against the ground beside him. His eyes, as
he spoke, glared with all the wildness of insanity, and
great drops of sweat hung upon his damp forehead.

"Is it too much," continued he, with all the vehemence
of passion, "is it too much that I was master here? Are
these walls too luxurious? Is there the sign of foreign
gold in this tasteful furniture and the splendour of these
hangings? Or is this"—and he stretched out his lean
and naked arms as he spoke—"is this the garb—is this
the garb of a man who can draw at will on the coffers of
royalty? Ay!" cried he, with a wild laugh, "if this is
the price of my treachery, the treason might well be
pardoned."

I did all I could to assuage the violence of his manner.
I talked to him calmly and soberly of myself and of him,
repeating over and over the assurance that I had neither
the will nor the way to injure him. "You may be poor,"
said I, "and yet scarcely poorer than I am—friendless,
and have as many to care for you as I have. Believe me,
comrade, save in the matter of a few years the less on one
side, and some services the more on the other, there is
little to choose between us."

These few words, wrung from me in sorrowful sincerity,
seemed to do more than all I had said previously, and he
moved the lamp a little to one side that he might have a
better view of me as I sat; and thus we remained for
several minutes staring steadfastly at each other, without a
word spoken on either side. It was in vain that I sought
in that face, livid and shrunk by famine—in that straggling
matted hair, and that figure enveloped in rags, for any
traces of former condition. Whatever might once have
been his place in society, now he seemed the very lowest
of that miserable tribe whose lives are at once the miracle
and shame of our century.

"Except that my senses are always playing me false,"
said he, as he passed his hand across his eyes, "I could
say that I have seen your face before. What was your
corps?"

"The Ninth Hussars, 'the Tapageurs,' as they called
them."

"When did you join—and where?" said he, with an
eagerness that surprised me.

"At Nancy," said I, calmly.

"You were there with the advanced guard of Moreau's

corps," said he, hastily; "you followed the regiment to the Moselle."

"How do you know all this?" asked I, in amazement.

"Now for your name; tell me your name," cried he, grasping my hand in both of his—"and I charge you by all you care for here or hereafter, no deception with me. It is not a head that has been tried like mine can bear a cheat."

"I have no object in deceiving you; nor am I ashamed to say who I am," replied I. "My name is Tiernay—Maurice Tiernay."

The word was but out, when the poor fellow threw himself forward, and grasping my hands, fell upon and kissed them.

"So, then," cried he, passionately, "I am not friendless—I am not utterly deserted in life—you are yet left to me, my dear boy!"

This burst of feeling convinced me that he was deranged; and I was speculating in my mind how best to make my escape from him, when he pushed back the long and tangled hair from his face, and staring wildly at me, said, "You know me now—don't you? Oh, look again, Maurice, and do not let me think that I am forgotten by all the world."

"Good heavens!" cried I, "it is Colonel Mahon!"

"Ay, 'Le Beau Mahon,'" said he, with a burst of wild laughter; "Le Beau Mahon, as they used to call me long ago. Is this a reverse of fortune, I ask you?" and he held out the ragged remnants of his miserable clothes. "I have not worn shoes for nigh a month. I have tasted food but once in the last thirty hours! I, that have led French soldiers to the charge full fifty times, up to the very batteries of the enemy, am reduced to hide and skulk from place to place like a felon, trembling at the clank of a gendarme's boot, as never the thunder of an enemy's squadron made me. Think of the persecution that has brought me to this, and made me a beggar and a coward together!"

A gush of tears burst from him at these words, and he sobbed for several minutes like a child.

Whatever might have been the original source of his misfortunes, I had very little doubt that now his mind had been shaken by their influence, and that calamity had deranged him. The flighty uncertainty of his manner, the incoherent rapidity with which he passed from one topic to another, increased with his excitement, and he passed alternately from the wildest expressions of delight at our meeting, to the most heart-rending descriptions of his own sufferings. By great patience and some ingenuity, I learned that he had taken refuge in the wood of Belleville, where the kindness of an old soldier of his own brigade—now a Garde de Chasse—had saved him from starvation. Jacques Caillon was continually alluded to in his narrative. It was Jacques sheltered him when he came first to Belleville. Jacques had afforded him a refuge in the different huts of the forest, supplying him with food—acts not alone of benevolence, but of daring courage, as Mahon continually asserted. If it were but known, "they'd give him a peloton and eight paces." The theme of Jacques' heroism was so engrossing, that he could not turn from it; every little incident of his kindness, every stratagem of his inventive good nature, he dwelt upon with eager delight, and seemed half to forget his own sorrows in recounting the services of his benefactor. I saw that it would be fruitless to ask for any account of his past calamity, or by what series of mischances he had fallen so low. I saw—I will own with some chagrin—that, with the mere selfishness of misfortune, he could not speak of anything save what bore upon his own daily life, and totally forgot me and all about me.

The most relentless persecution seemed to follow him from place to place. Wherever he went, fresh spies started on his track, and the history of his escapes was unending. The very faggot-cutters of the forest were in league against him, and the high price offered for his capture had drawn many into the pursuit. It was curious to mark the degree of self-importance all these recitals imparted, and how the poor fellow, starving and almost naked as he was, rose into all the imagined dignity of martyrdom, as he told of his sorrows. If he ever asked a question about Paris, it was to know what people said of himself and of his fortunes. He was thoroughly convinced that Bonaparte's thoughts were far more occupied about him than on that empire now so nearly in his grasp, and he continued to repeat with a proud delight, "He has caught them all but me! I am the only one who has escaped him!" These few words suggested to me the impression that Mahon had been engaged in some plot or conspiracy; but of what nature, how composed, or how discovered, it was impossible to arrive at.

"There!" said he, at last, "there is the dawn breaking! I must be off. I must now make for the thickest part of the wood till nightfall. There are hiding-places there known to none save myself. The bloodhounds cannot track me where I go."

His impatience became now extreme. Every instant seemed full of peril to him now; every rustling leaf and every waving branch a warning. I was unable to satisfy myself how far this might be well-founded terror, or a vague and causeless fear. At one moment I inclined to this—at another, to the opposite impression. Assuredly nothing could be more complete than the precautions he took against discovery. His lamp was concealed in the hollow of a tree; the leaves that formed his bed he scattered and strewed carelessly on every side; he erased even the foot-tracks on the clay; and then gathering up his tattered cloak, prepared to set out.

"When are we to meet again, and where?" said I, grasping his hand.

He stopped suddenly, and passed his hand over his brow, as if reflecting. "You must see Caillon; Jacques will tell you all," said he, solemnly. "Good bye. Do not follow me. I will not be tracked;" and with a proud gesture of his hand he motioned me back.

Poor fellow! I saw that any attempt to reason with him would be in vain at such a moment; and determining to seek out the Garde de Chasse, I turned away slowly and sorrowfully.

"What have been my vicissitudes of fortune compared to his?" thought I. "The proud colonel of a cavalry regiment, a beggar and an outcast!" The great puzzle to me was, whether insanity had been the cause or the consequence of his misfortunes. Caillon will, perhaps, be able to tell me his story, said I to myself; and thus ruminating, I returned to where I had picketed my horse three hours before. My old dragoon experiences had taught me how to "hobble" a horse, as it is called, by passing the bridle beneath the counter before tying it, and so I found him just as I left him.

The sun was now up, and I could see that a wide track led off through the forest straight before me. I accordingly mounted, and struck into a sharp canter. About an hour's riding brought me to a small clearing, in the midst of which stood a neat and picturesque cottage, over the door of which was painted the words "Station de Chasse—No. 4." In a little garden in front, a man was working in his shirt sleeves, but his military trousers at once proclaimed him the "Garde." He stopped as I came up, and eyed me sharply.

"Is this the road to Belleville?" said I.

"You can go this way, but it takes you two miles of a round," replied he, coming closer, and scanning me keenly.

"You can tell me, perhaps, where Jacques Caillon, Garde de Chasse, is to be found?"

"I am Jacques Caillon, sir," was the answer, as he saluted in soldier fashion, while a look of anxiety stole over his face.

"I have something to speak to you about," said I, dismounting, and giving him the bridle of my horse. "Throw him some corn, if you have got it, and then let us talk together;" and with this I walked into the garden, and seated myself on a bench.

If Jacques be an old soldier, thought I, the only way is to come the officer over him; discipline and obedience are never forgotten, and whatever chances I may have of his confidence will depend on how much I seem his superior. It appeared as if this conjecture was well founded, for as Jacques came back, his manner betrayed every sign of respect and deference. There was an expression of almost fear in his face as, with his hand to his cap, he asked "What were my orders?"

The very deference of his air was disconcerting, and so, assuming a look of easy cordiality, I said,—

"First, I will ask you to give me something to eat; and, secondly, to give me your company for half an hour."

Jacques promised both, and learning that I preferred my breakfast in the open air, proceeded to arrange the table under a blossoming chestnut-tree.

"Are you quite alone here?" asked I, as he passed back and forward.

"Quite alone, sir; and except a stray faggot-cutter or a chance traveller who may have lost his way, I never see a human face from year's end to year's end. It's a lonely thing for an old soldier, too," said he, with a sigh.

"I know more than one who would envy you, Jacques," said I; and the words made him almost start as I spoke them. The coffee was now ready, and I proceeded to make my breakfast with all the appetite of a long fast.

There was indeed but little to inspire awe, or even deference, in my personal appearance—a threadbare undress frock and a worn-out old foraging cap were all the marks of my soldierlike estate; and yet, from Jacques's manner, one might have guessed me to be a general at the least. He attended me with the stiff propriety of the

parade, and when, at last, induced to take a seat, he did
so full two yards off from the table, and arose almost
every time he was spoken to. Now it was quite clear that
the honest soldier did not know me either as the hero of
Kehl, of Ireland, or of Genoa. Great achievements as
they were, they were wonderfully little noised about the
world, and a man might frequent mixed companies every
day of the week, and never hear of one of them. So far,
then, was certain, it could not be my fame had imposed on
him, and, as I have already hinted, it could scarcely be
my general appearance. Who knows, thought I, but I
owe all this obsequious deference to my horse? If Jacques
be an old cavalry-man, he will have remarked that the
beast is of great value, and doubtless argue to the worth
of the rider from the merits of his " mount." If this explanation was not the most flattering, it was, at all events,
the best I could hit on ; and with a natural reference to
what was passing in my own mind, I asked him if he had
looked to my horse.

" Oh, yes, sir," said he, reddening suddenly, " I have
taken off the saddle, and thrown him his corn."

What the deuce does his confusion mean, thought I ;
the fellow looks as if he had half a mind to run away,
merely because I asked him a simple question.

" I've had a sharp ride," said I, rather by way of saying something, " and I shouldn't wonder if he was a little
fatigued."

" Scarcely so, sir," said he, with a faint smile ; " he's old,
now, but it's not a little will tire him."

" You know him, then ? " said I, quickly.

" Ay, sir, and have known him for eighteen years. He
was in the second squadron of our regiment ; the Major
rode him two entire campaigns !"

The reader may guess that his history was interesting
to me, from perceiving the impression the reminiscence
made on the relator, and I inquired what became of him
after that.

" He was wounded by a shot at Neuwied, and sold into
the train, where they couldn't manage him ; and after
three years, when horses grew scarce, he came back into
the cavalry. A serjeant-major of lancers was killed on
him at ' Zwei Brucken.' That was the fourth rider he
brought mishap to, not to say a farrier whom he dashed to
pieces in his stable."

Ah, Jack, thought I, I have it ; it is a piece of old-
soldier superstition about this mischievous horse has in-

26

spired all the man's respect and reverence; and, if a little
disappointed in the mystery, I was so far pleased at having discovered the clue.

"But I have found him quiet enough," said I; "I
never backed him till yesterday, and he has carried me
well and peaceably."

"Ah, that he will now, I warrant him; since the day a
shell burst under him at Waitzen he never showed any
vice. The wound nearly left the ribs bare, and he was
for months and months invalided; after that he was sold
out of the cavalry, I don't know where or to whom. The
next I saw of him was in his present service."

"Then you are acquainted with the present owner?"
asked I, eagerly.

"As every Frenchman is!" was the curt rejoinder.

"Parbleu! it will seem a droll confession, then, when I
tell you, that I myself do not even know his name."

The look of contempt these words brought to my companion's face could not, it seemed, be either repressed or
concealed, and although my conscience acquitted me of
deserving such a glance, I own that I felt insulted by it.

"You are pleased to disbelieve me, Master Caillon,"
said I, sternly, "which makes me suppose that you are
neither so old nor so good a soldier as I fancied; at least
in the corps I had the honour to serve with, the word of
an officer was respected like an 'order of the day.'"

He stood erect, as if on parade, under this rebuke, but
made no answer.

"Had you simply expressed surprise at what I said, I
would have given you the explanation frankly and freely;
as it is, I shall content myself with repeating what I said
—I do not even know his name."

The same imperturbable look and the same silence met
me as before.

"Now, sir, I ask you how this gentleman is called,
whom I, alone of all France, am ignorant of?"

"Monsieur Fouché," said he, calmly.

"What! Fouché, the Minister of Police?"

This time at least, my agitated looks seemed to move
him, for he replied, quietly,—

"The same, sir. The horse has the brand of the 'Ministere' on his haunch."

"And where is the Ministere?" cried I, eagerly.

"In the Rue des Victoires, Monsieur."

"But he lives in the country, in a chateau near this
very forest."

" Where does he not live, Monsieur? At Versailles, at St. Germain, in the Luxembourg, in the Marais, at Neuilly, the Battignolles. I have carried despatches to him in every quarter of Paris. Ah, Monsieur, what secret are you in possession of, that it was worth while to lay so subtle a trap to catch you?"

This question, put in all the frank abruptness of a sudden thought, immediately revealed everything before me.

" Is it not as I have said?" resumed he, still looking at my agitated face; "is it not as I have said—Monsieur is in the web of the Mouchards?"

" Good heavens! is such baseness possible?" was all that I could utter.

" I'll wager a piece of five francs I can read the mystery," said Jacques. " You served on Moreau's staff, or with Pichegru in Holland; you either have some of the general's letters, or you can be supposed to have them. at all events; you remember many private conversations held with him on politics; you can charge your memory with a number of strong facts; and you can, if needed, draw up a memoir of all your intercourse. I know the system well, for I was a Mouchard myself."

" You a police spy, Jacques?"

" Ay, sir; I was appointed without knowing what services were expected from me, or the duties of my station. Two months' trial, however, showed that I was 'incapable,' and proved that a smart sous-officier is not necessarily a scoundrel. They dismissed me as impracticable, and made me Garde de Chasse; and they were right, too. Whether I was dressed up in a snuff-brown suit, like a bourgeois of the Rue St. Denis; whether they attired me as a farmer from the provinces, a retired maitre-de-poste, an old officer, or the conducteur of a diligence, I was always Jacques Caillon. Through everything, wigs and beards, lace or rags, jackboots or sabots, it was all alike; and while others could pass weeks in the Pays Latin as students, country doctors, or 'notaires de village,' I was certain to be detected by every brat that walked the streets."

" What a system! And so these fellows assume every disguise?" asked I, my mind full of my late rencontre.

" That they do, Moniesur. There is one fellow, a Provençal by birth, has played more characters than ever did Brunet himself. I have known him as a lacquais de place, a cook to an English nobleman, a letter-carrier, a flower-girl, a cornet-a-piston in the opera, and a curé from the Ardèche."

"A curé from the Ardèche!" exclaimed I. "Then I am a ruined man."

"What! has Monsieur fallen in with Paul?" cried he, laughing. "Was he begging for a small contribution to repair the roof of his little chapel, or was it a fire that had devastated his poor village? Did the altar want a new covering, or the curé a vestment? Was it a canopy for the Fête of the Virgin, or a few sous towards the 'Orphelines de St. Jude?'"

"None of these," said I, half angrily, for the theme was no jesting one to me. "It was a poor girl that had been carried away."

"Lisette, the miller's daughter, or the schoolmaster's niece?" broke he in, laughing. "He must have known you were new to Paris, Monsieur, that he took so little trouble about a deception. And you met him at the 'Charette rouge' in the Marais?"

"No; at a little ordinary in the Quai Voltaire."

"Better again. Why half the company there are Mouchards. It is one of their rallying-points, where they exchange tokens and information. The labourers, the beggars, the fishermen of the Seine, the hawkers of old books, the venders of gilt ornaments, are all spies; the most miserable creature that implored charity behind your chair as you sat at dinner has, perhaps, his ten francs a day on the roll of the Prefecture! Ah, Monsieur! if I had not been a poor pupil of that school, I'd have at once seen that you were a victim, and not a follower; but I soon detected my error—my education taught me at least so much!"

I had no relish for the self-gratulation of honest Jacques, uttered, as it was, at my own expense. Indeed I had no thought for anything but the entanglement into which I had so stupidly involved myself; and I could not endure the recollection of my foolish credulity, now that all the paltry machinery of the deceit was brought before me. All my regard, dashed as it was with pity for the poor curé; all my compassionate interest for the dear Lisette; all my benevolent solicitude for the sick Count, who was neither more nor less than Mons. Fouché himself, were anything but pleasant reminiscences now, and I cursed my own stupidity with an honest sincerity that greatly amused my companion.

"And is France come to this?" cried I, passionately.

and trying to console myself by inveighing against the Government.

"Even so, sir," said Jacques. "I heard Monsieur de Talleyrand say as much the other day, as I waited behind his chair. It is only 'dɑns les bonnes maisons,' said he, 'that servants ever listen at the doors;' depend upon it, then, that a secret police is a strong symptom that we are returning to a monarchy."

It was plain that even in his short career in the police service, Caillon had acquired certain shrewd habits of thought, and some power of judgment, and so I freely communicated to him the whole of my late adventure from the moment of my leaving the Temple to the time of my setting out for the Chateau.

"You have told me everything but one, Monsieur," said he, as I finished. "How came you ever to have heard the name of so humble a person as Jacques Caillon, for you remember you asked for me as you rode up?"

"I was just coming to that point, Jacques; and, as you will see, it was not an omission in my narrative, only that I had not reached so far."

I then proceeded to recount my night in the forest, and my singular meeting with poor Mahon, which he listened to with great attention and some anxiety.

"The poor Colonel!" said he, breaking in, "I suppose he s a hopeless case; his mind can never come right again."

"But if the persecution were to cease; if he were at liberty to appear once more in the world——"

"What if there was no persecution, sir?" broke in Jacques. "What if the whole were a mere dream, or fancy? He is neither tracked nor followed. It is not such harmless game the bloodhounds of the Rue des Victoires scent out."

"Was it, then, some mere delusion drove him from the service?" said I, surprised.

"I never said so much as that," replied Jacques; "Colonel Mahon has foul injury to complain of, but his present sufferings are the inflictions of his own terror; he fancies that the whole power of France is at war with him; that every engine of the Government is directed against him; with a restless fear he flies from village to village, fancying pursuit everywhere; even kindness now he is distrustful of, and the chances are, that he will quit the forest this very day, merely because he met you there."

From being of all men the most open-hearted and frank, he had become the most suspicious; he trusted nothing

nor any one; and if for a moment a burst of his old
generous nature would return, it was sure to be followed
by some excess of distrust that made him miserable almost
to despair. Jacques was obliged to fall in with this
humour, and only assist him by stealth and by stratagem;
he was even compelled to chime in with all his notions
about pursuit and danger, to suggest frequent change of
place, and endless precautions against discovery.

" Were I for once to treat him frankly, and ask him to
share my home with me," said Jacques, " I should never
see him more."

" What could have poisoned so noble a nature?" cried
I; " when I saw him last he was the very type of generous
confidence."

" Where was that, and when?" asked Jacques.

"It was at Nancy, on the march for the Rhine."

" His calamities had not fallen on him then. He was a
proud man in those days, but it was a pride that well
became him; he was the colonel of a great regiment, and
for bravery had a reputation second to none."

" He was married, I think?"

" No, sir; he was never married."

As Jacques said this, he arose, and moved slowly away,
as though he would not be questioned further. His mind,
too, seemed full of its own crowding memories, for he
looked completely absorbed in thought, and never noticed
my presence for a considerable time. At last he appeared
to have decided some doubtful issue within himself, and
said,—

" Come, sir, let us stroll into the shade of the wood, and
I'll tell you in a few words the cause of the poor colonel's
ruin—for ruin it is! Even were all the injustice to be
revoked to-morrow, the wreck of his heart could never be
repaired."

We walked along, side by side, for some time, before
Jacques spoke again, when he gave me, in brief and simple
words, the following sorrowful story. It was such a type
of the age, so pregnant with the terrible lessons of the
time, that although not without some misgivings, I repeat
it here as it was told to myself, premising that however
scant may be the reader's faith in many of the incidents of
my own narrative—and I neither beg for his trust in me,
nor seek to entrap it—I implore him to believe that what
I am now about to tell was a plain matter of fact, and, save
in the change of one name, not a single circumstance is
owing to imagination.

CHAPTER XLIV.

AN EPISODE OF '94.

WHEN the French army fell back across the Sambre, after the battle of Mons, a considerable portion of the rear, who covered the retreat, were cut off by the enemy, for it became their onerous duty to keep the allied forces in check, while the Republicans took measures to secure and hold fast the three bridges over the river. In this service many distinguished French officers fell, and many more were left badly wounded on the field; among the latter was a young captain of dragoons, who, with his hand nearly severed by a sabre cut, yet found strength enough to crawl under cover of a hedge, and there lie down in the fierce resolve to die where he was, rather than surrender himself as a prisoner.

Although the allied forces had gained the battle, they quickly foresaw that the ground they had won was untenable; and scarcely had night closed in when they began their preparations to fall back. With strong pickets of observation to watch the bridges, they slowly withdrew their columns towards Mons, posting the artillery on the heights around Grandrengs. From these movements, the ground of the late struggle became comparatively deserted, and before day began to dawn, not a sound was heard over its wide expanse, save the faint moan of a dying soldier, or the low rumble of a cart, as some spoiler of the dead stole stealthily along. Among the demoralising effects of war, none was more striking than the number of the peasantry who betook themselves to this infamous trade; and who, neglecting all thoughts of honest industry, devoted themselves to robbery and plunder. The lust of gain did not stop with the spoil of the dead, but the wounded were often found stripped of everything, and in some cases the traces of fierce struggle, and the wounds of knives and hatchets, showed that murder had consummated the iniquity of these wretches.

In part from motives of pure humanity, in part from

feelings of a more interested nature—for the terror to what this demoralisation would tend, was now great and wide-spread—the nobles and gentry of the land instituted a species of society to reward those who might succour the wounded, and who displayed any remarkable zeal in their care for the sufferers after a battle. This generous philanthropy was irrespective of country, and extended its benevolence to the soldiers of either army; of course, personal feeling enjoyed all its liberty of preference, but it is fair to say, that the cases were few where the wounded man could detect the political leanings of his benefactor.

The immense granaries, so universal in the Low Countries, were usually fitted up as hospitals, and many rooms of the chateau itself were often devoted to the same purpose, the various individuals of the household, from the "seigneur" to the lowest menial, assuming some office in the great work of charity; and it was a curious thing to see how the luxurious indolence of chateau life became converted into the zealous activity of useful benevolence; and not less curious to the moralist to observe how the emergent pressure of great crime so instinctively, as it were, suggested this display of virtuous humanity.

It was a little before daybreak that a small cart drawn by a mule drew up beside the spot where the wounded dragoon sat, with his shattered arm bound up in his sash, calmly waiting for the death that his sinking strength told could not be far distant. As the peasant approached him, he grasped his sabre in the left hand, resolved on making a last and bold resistance; but the courteous salutation, and the kindly look of the honest countryman, soon showed that he was come on no errand of plunder, while, in the few words of bad French he could muster, he explained his purpose.

"No, no, my kind friend," said the officer, "your labour would only be lost on me. It is nearly all over already! A little further on in the field, yonder, where that copse stands, you'll find some poor fellow or other better worth your care, and more like to benefit by it. Adieu!"

But neither the farewell, nor the abrupt gesture that accompanied it, could turn the honest peasant from his purpose. There was something that interested him in this very disregard of life, as well as in the personal appearance of the sufferer, and, without further colloquy, he lifted the half fainting form into the cart, and disposing the straw comfortably on either side of him, set out homeward. The wounded man was almost indifferent to what happened, and never spoke a word nor raised his head as they went along. About three hours' journey brought them to a large old-fashioned chateau beside the Sambre, an immense straggling edifice which, with a façade of nearly a hundred windows, looked out upon the river. Although now in disrepair and neglect, with ill-trimmed alleys and grass-grown terraces, it had been once a place of great pretensions, and associated with some of the palmiest days of Flemish hospitality. The Chateau d'Overbecque was the property of a certain rich merchant of Antwerp, named D'Aerschot, one of the oldest families of the land, and was, at the time we speak of, the temporary abode of his only son, who had gone there to pass the honeymoon. Except that they were both young, neither of them yet twenty, two people could not easily be found so discrepant in every circumstance and every quality. He the true descendant of a Flemish house, plodding, commonplace, and methodical, hating show and detesting expense. She a lively, volatile girl, bursting with desire to see and be seen, fresh from the restraint of a convent at Bruges, and anxious to mix in all the pleasures and dissipations of the world. Like all marriages in their condition, it had been arranged without their knowledge or consent; circumstances of fortune made the alliance suitable; so many hundred thousand florins on one side were wedded to an equivalent on the other, and the young people were married to facilitate the " transaction."

That he was not a little shocked at the gay frivolity of his beautiful bride, and she as much disappointed at the staid demureness of her stolid-looking husband, is not to be wondered at; but their friends knew well that time would smooth down greater discrepancies than even these; and if ever there was a country, the monotony of whose life could subdue all to its own leaden tone, it was Holland in old days. Whether engaged in the active pursuit of gain in the great cities, or enjoying the luxurious repose of chateau life, a dull, dreary uniformity pervaded everything—the same topics, the same people, the same landscape, recurred day after day; and save what the season induced, there was nothing of change in the whole round of their existence. And what a dull honeymoon was it for that young bride at the old Chateau of Overbecque! To toil along the deep sandy roads in a lumbering old coach with two long-tailed black horses—to halt at some little eminence, and strain the eyes over a long unbroken flat, where a windmill, miles off, was an object of interest—to

loiter beside the bank of a sluggish canal, and gaze on
some tasteless excrescence of a summerhouse, whose owner
could not be distinguished from the wooden effigy that sat
pipe in mouth, beside him—to dine in the unbroken silence
of a funeral feast, and doze away the afternoon over the
"Handelsblatt," while her husband smoked himself into
the seventh heaven of a Dutch Elysium—poor Caroline!
this was a sorry realisation of all her bright dreamings!
It ought to be borne in mind, that many descendants of
high French families, who were either too proud or too
poor to emigrate to England or America, had sought refuge
from the Revolution in the convents of the Low Countries;
where, without entering an order, they lived in all the discipline of a religious community. These ladies, many of
whom had themselves mixed in all the elegant dissipations
of the court, carried with them the most fascinating reminiscences of a life of pleasure, and could not readily forget
the voluptuous enjoyments of Versailles, and the graceful
caprices of "La Petit Trianon." From such sources as
these the young pupils drew all their ideas of the world,
and assuredly it could have scarcely worn colours more
likely to fascinate such imaginations.

What a shortcoming was the wearisome routine of Overbecque to a mind full of all the refined follies of Marie
Antoinette's court! Even war and its chances offered a
pleasurable contrast to such dull monotony, and the young
bride hailed with eagerness the excitement and bustle of
the moving armies—the long columns which poured along
the high road, and the clanking artillery, heard for miles
off! Monsieur D'Aerschot, like all his countrymen who
held property near the frontier, was too prudent to have
any political bias. Madame was, however, violently French.
The people who had such admirable taste in "toilette,"
could scarcely be wrong in the theories of government; and
a nation so invariably correct in dress, could hardly be
astray in morals. Besides this, all their notions of morality
were as pliant and as easy to wear as their own well-fitting
garments. Nothing was wrong but what looked ungrace-
fully; everything was right that sat becomingly on her
who did it—a short code, and wonderfully easy to learn.
If I have dealt somewhat tediously on these tendencies of
the time, it is that I may pass the more glibly over the consequences, and not pause upon the details by which the
young French captain's residence at Overbecque gradually
grew, from the intercourse of kindness and good offices,
to be a close friendship with his host, and as much of

regard and respectful devotion as consisted with the position of his young and charming hostess.

He thought her, as she certainly was, very beautiful; she rode to perfection, she sung delightfully; she had all the volatile gaiety of a happy child, with the graceful ease of coming womanhood. Her very passion for excitement gave a kind of life and energy to the dull old chateau, and made her momentary absence felt as a dreary blank.

It is not my wish to speak of the feelings suggested by the contrast between her husband and the gay and chivalrous young soldier, nor how little such comparisons tended to allay the repinings at her lot. Their first effect was, however, to estrange her more and more from D'Aerschot, a change which he accepted with the most Dutch indifference. Possibly, piqued by this, or desirous of awakening his jealousy, she made more advances towards the other, selecting him as the companion of her walks, and passing the greater part of each day in his society. Nothing could be more honourable than the young soldier's conduct in this trying position. The qualities of agreeability which he had previously displayed to requite, in some sort, the hospitality of his hosts, he now gradually restrained, avoiding as far as he could, without remark, the society of the young Countess, and even feigning indisposition, to escape from the peril of her intimacy.

He did more—he exerted himself to draw D'Aerschot more out, to make him exhibit the shrewd intelligence which lay buried beneath his native apathy, and display powers of thought and reflection of no mean order. Alas! these very efforts on his part only increased the mischief, by adding generosity to his other virtues! He now saw all the danger in which he was standing, and, although still weak and suffering, resolved to take his departure. There was none of the concealed vanity of a coxcomb in this knowledge. He heartily deplored the injury he had unwittingly done, and the sorry return he had made for all their generous hospitality.

There was not a moment to be lost; but the very evening before, as they walked together in the garden, she had confessed to him the misery in which she lived by recounting the story of her ill-sorted marriage. What it cost him to listen to that sad tale with seeming coldness—to hear her afflictions without offering one word of kindness; nay, to proffer merely some dry, harsh counsels of patience and submission, while he added something very like rebuke for her want of that assiduous affection which should have been given to her husband!

Unaccustomed to even the slightest censure, she could scarcely trust her ears as she heard him. Had she humiliated herself, by such a confession, to be met by advice like this? And was it he that should reproach her for the very faults his own intimacy had engendered? She could not endure the thought, and she felt that she could hate, just at the very moment when she knew she loved him!

They parted in anger—reproaches, the most cutting and bitter, on her part; coldness, far more wounding, on his! Sarcastic compliments upon his generosity, replied to by as sincere expressions of respectful friendship. What hypocrisy and self-deceit together! And yet deep beneath all lay the firm resolve for future victory. Her wounded self-love was irritated, and she was not one to turn from an unfinished purpose. As for him, he waited till all was still and silent in the house, and then seeking out D'Aerschot's chamber, thanked him most sincerely for all his kindness, and affecting a hurried order to join his service, departed. While in her morning dreams she was fancying conquest, he was already miles away on the road to France.

* * * * * * *

It was about three years after this, that a number of French officers were seated one evening in front of a little café in Freyburg. The town was then crammed with troops moving down to occupy the passes of the Rhine, near the Lake of Constance, and every hour saw fresh arrivals pouring in, dusty and wayworn from the march. The necessity for a sudden massing of the troops in a particular spot compelled the generals to employ every possible means of conveyance to forward the men to their destination, and from the lumbering old diligence with ten horses, to the light charette with one, all were engaged in this pressing service.

When men were weary, and unable to march forward, they were taken up for twelve or fourteen miles, after which they proceeded on their way, making room for others, and thus forty and even fifty miles were frequently accomplished in the same day.

The group before the café were amusing themselves criticising the strange appearance of the new arrivals, many of whom certainly made their entry in the least military fashion possible. Here came a great country waggon, with forty infantry soldiers all sleeping on the straw. Here followed a staff-officer trying to look quite at his ease in a donkey-cart. Unwieldy old bullock-carts were filled with men, and a half-starved mule tottered along with a drummer-boy in one pannier, and camp-kettles in the other.

He who was fortunate enough to secure a horse for himself, was obliged to carry the swords and weapons of his companions, which were all hung around and about him on every side, together with helmets and shakos of all shapes and sizes, whose owners were fain to cover their head with the less soldierlike appendages of a night-cap or a handkerchief. Nearly all who marched carried their caps on their muskets, for in such times as these all discipline is relaxed, save such as is indispensable to the maintenance of order; and so far was freedom conceded, that some were to be seen walking barefoot in the ranks, while their shoes were suspended by a string on their backs. The rule seemed to be " Get forward—it matters not how—only get forward !"

And with French troops, such relaxation of strict discipline is always practicable ; the instincts of obedience return at the first call of the bugle or the first roll of the drum ; and at the word to "fall in !" every symptom of disorder vanishes, and the mass of seeming confusion becomes the steady and silent phalanx.

Many were the strange sights that passed before the eyes of the party at the café, who, having arrived early in the day, gave themselves all the airs of ease and indolence before their wayworn comrades. Now laughing heartily at the absurdity of this one, now exchanging some good-humoured jest with that, they were in the very full current of their criticism, when the sharp, shrill crack of a postilion's whip informed them that a traveller of some note was approaching. A mounted courier, all slashed with gold lace, came riding up the street at the same moment, and a short distance behind followed a handsome equipage, drawn by six horses, after which came a heavy " fourgon," with four.

One glance showed that the whole equipage betokened a wealthy owner. There was all that cumbrous machinery of comfort about it that tells of people who will not trust to the chances of the road for their daily wants. Every appliance of ease was there ; and even in the self-satisfied air of the servants who lounged in the "rumble" might be read habits of affluent prosperity. A few short years back, and none would have dared to use such an equipage. The sight of so much indulgence would have awakened the fiercest rage of popular fury ; but already the high fever of democracy was gradually subsiding, and, bit by bit, men were found reverting to old habits and old usages. Still each new indication of these tastes met a certain amount of reprobation. Some blamed openly, some condemned in secret; but all felt that there was at least impolicy in a display which would serve as pretext for the terrible excesses that were committed under the banner of " Equality."

" If we lived in the days of princes," said one of the officers, " I should say there goes one now. Just look at all the dust they are kicking up yonder; while, as if to point a moral upon greatness, they are actually stuck fast in the narrow street, and unable, from their own unwieldiness, to get further."

" Just so," cried another; " they want to turn down towards the ' Swan,' and there isn't space enough to wheel the leaders."

" Who or what are they?" asked a third.

" Some commissary-general, I'll be sworn," said the first. " They are the most shameless thieves going; for they are never satisfied with robbery, if they do not exhibit the spoils in public."

" I see a bonnet and a lace veil," said another, rising suddenly, and pushing through the crowd. " I'll wager it's a ' danseuse' of the Grand Opera."

" Look at Merode!" remarked the former, as he pointed to the last speaker. " See how he thrusts himself forward there. Watch, and you'll see him bow and smile to her, as if they had been old acquaintances."

The guess was so far unlucky, that Merode had no sooner come within sight of the carriage-window, than he was seen to bring his hand to the salute, and remain in an attitude of respectful attention till the equipage moved on.

" Well, Merode, who is it?—who are they?" cried several together, as he fell back among his comrades.

" It's our new adjutant-general, parbleu!" said he, " and he caught me staring in at his pretty wife."

" Colonel Mahon!" said another, laughing; " I wish you joy of your gallantry, Merode." " And, worse still," broke in a third, " she is not his wife. She never could obtain the divorce to allow her to marry again. Some said it was the husband—a Dutchman, I believe—refused it; but the simple truth is, she never wished it herself."

" How not wish it?" remarked three or four in a breath.

"Why should she? Has she not every advantage the
position could give her, and her liberty into the bargain?
If we were back again in the old days of the Monarchy, I
agree with you she could not go to court; she would receive no invitations to the 'petits soupers' of the Trianon,
nor be asked to join the discreet hunting-parties at Fontainebleu; but we live in less polished days; and if we
have little virtue, we have less hypocrisy."

"Voila!" cried another, "only I, for one, would never
believe that we are a jot more wicked or more dissolute
than those powdered and perfumed scoundrels that played
courtier in the King's bedchamber."

"There, they are getting out, at the 'Tour d'Argent!'"
cried another. "She is a splendid figure, and what magnificence in her dress!"

"Mahon waits on her like a lacquais," muttered a grim
old lieutenant of infantry.

"Rather like a well-born cavalier, I should say," interposed a young hussar. "His manner is all that it ought
to be—full of devotion and respect."

"Bah!" said the former; "a soldier's wife, or a soldier's mistress—for it's all one—should know how to climb
up to her place on the baggage-waggon, without three lazy
rascals to catch her sleeve or her petticoats for her."

"Mahon is as gallant a soldier as any in this army," said
the hussar; "and I'd not be in the man's coat who dis-
paraged him in anything."

"By St. Denis!" broke in another, "he's not more
brave than he is fortunate. Let me tell you, it's no slight
luck to chance upon so lovely a woman as that, with such
an immense fortune, too."

"Is she rich?"

"Enormously rich. He has nothing. An emigré of
good family, I believe, but without a sous; and see how
he travels yonder!"

While this conversation was going forward, the new
arrivals had alighted at the chief inn of the town, and
were being installed in the principal suite of rooms, which
opened on a balcony over the "Place." The active preparations of the host to receive such distinguished guests—
the hurrying of servants here and there—the blaze of
wax-lights that shone half way across the street beneath
—and, lastly, the appearance of a regimental band to play
under the windows—were all circumstances well calculated to sustain and stimulate that spirit of sharp criticism
which the group around the café were engaged in.

The discussion was, however, suddenly interrupted by
the entrance of an officer, at whose appearance every one
arose and stood in attitudes of respectful attention.
Scarcely above the middle size, and more remarkable for
the calm and intellectual cast of his features, than for that
air of military pride then so much in vogue amongst the
French troops, he took his place at a small table near the
door, and called for his coffee. It was only when he was
seated, and that by a slight gesture he intimated his
wishes to that effect, that the others resumed their places,
and continued the conversation, but in a lower, more subdued tone.

" What distinguished company have we got yonder ? "
said he, after about half an hour's quiet contemplation of
the crowd before the inn, and the glaring illumination
from the windows.

" Colonel Mahon, of the Fifth Cuirassiers, General,"
replied an officer.

" Our Republican simplicity is not so self-denying a
system, after all, gentlemen," said the general, smiling
half sarcastically. " Is he very rich ? "

" His mistress is, General," was the prompt reply.

" Bah ! " said the general, as he threw his cigar away,
and, with a contemptuous expression of look, arose and
walked away.

" Parbleu ! he's going to the inn," cried an officer, who
peered out after him ; " I'll be sworn Mahon will get a
heavy reprimand for all this display and ostentation."

" And why not ? " said another. " Is it when men are
arriving half dead with fatigue, without rations, without
billets, glad to snatch a few hours' rest on the stones of the
Place, that the colonel of a regiment should travel with all
the state of an eastern despot ? "

" We might as well have the Monarchy back again,"
said an old weather-beaten captain ; " I say far better,
for their vices sat gracefully and becomingly on those
essenced scoundrels, whereas they but disfigure the plainness of our daily habits."

" All this is sheer envy, comrades," broke in a young
major of hussars, " sheer envy ; or, what is worse, downright hypocrisy. Not one of us is a whit better or more
moral than if he wore the livery of a king, and carried a
crown on his shako instead of that naked damsel that
represents French Liberty. Mahon is the luckiest fellow
going, and, I heartily believe, the most deserving of his
fortune ! And see if General Moreau be not of my

opinion.   There he is on the balcony, and she is leaning
on his arm."

"Parbleu! the major is right!" said another; "but, for
certain, it was not in that humour he left us just now; his
lips were closely puckered up, and his fingers were
twisted into his sword-knot—two signs of anger and displeasure there's no mistaking."

"If he's in a better temper, then," said another, "it
was never the smiles of a pretty woman worked the
change.   There's not a man in France so thoroughly indifferent to such blandishments."

"Tant pis pour lui," said the major; "but they're
closing the window-shutters, and we may as well go
home."

CHAPTER XLV.

THE CABINET OF A CHEF-DE-POLICE.

WHATEVER opinion may be formed of the character of the celebrated conspiracy of Georges and Pichegru, the mode of its discovery, and the secret rules by which its plans were detected, are among the great triumphs of police skill. From the hour when the conspirators first met together in London, to that last fatal moment when they expired in the Temple, the agents of Fouché never ceased to track them.

Their individual tastes and ambitions were studied; their habits carefully investigated; everything that could give a clue to their turn of thought or mind well weighed; so that the Consular Government was not only in possession of all their names and rank, but knew thoroughly the exact amount of complicity attaching to each, and could distinguish between the reckless violence of Georges and the more tempered, but higher ambition of Moreau. It was a long while doubtful whether the great general would be implicated in the scheme. His habitual reserve—a habit less of caution than of constitutional delicacy—had led him to few intimacies, and nothing like even one close friendship; he moved little in society; he corresponded with none, save on the duties of the service. Fouché's well-known boast of, "Give me two words of a man's writing and I'll hang him," were then scarcely applicable here.

To attack such a man unsuccessfully, to arraign him on a weak indictment, would have been ruin; and yet Bonaparte's jealousy of his great rival pushed him even to this peril, rather than risk the growing popularity of his name with the army.

Fouché, and, it is said also, Talleyrand, did all they could to dissuade the First Consul from this attempt, but he was fixed and immutable in his resolve, and the Police Minister at once addressed himself to his task with all his accustomed cleverness.

High play was one of the great vices of the day. It

was a time of wild and varied excitement, and men sought even in their dissipations, the whirlwind passions that stirred them in active life. Moreau, however, was no gambler; it was said that he never could succeed in learning a game. He, whose mind could comprehend the most complicated question of strategy, was obliged to confess himself conquered by ecarté! So much for the vaunted intellectuality of the play table! Neither was he addicted to wine. All his habits were temperate, even to the extent of unsociality.

A man who spoke little, and wrote less, who indulged in no dissipations, nor seemed to have taste for any, was a difficult subject to treat; and so Fouché found, as, day after day, his spies reported to him the utter failure of all their schemes to entrap him. Lajolais, the friend of Pichegru, and the man who betrayed him, was the chief instrument the Police Minister used to obtain secret information. Being well born, and possessed of singularly pleasing manners, he had the entrée of the best society of Paris, where his gay, easy humour made him a great favourite. Lajolais, however, could never penetrate into the quiet domesticity of Moreau's life, nor make any greater inroad on his intimacy than a courteous salutation as they passed each other in the garden of the Luxembourg. At the humble restaurant where he dined each day for two francs, the " General," as he was distinctively called, never spoke to any one. Unobtrusive and quiet, he occupied a little table in a recess of the window, and arose the moment he finished his humble meal. After this he was to be seen in the garden of the Luxembourg, with a cigar and a book, or sometimes without either, seated pensively under a tree for hours together.

If he had been conscious of the " espionage" established over all his actions, he could scarcely have adopted a mor guarded or more tantalising policy. To the verbal communications of Pichegru and Armand Polignac, he returned vague replies; their letters he never answered at all, and Lajolais had to confess that, after two months of close pursuit, the game was as far from him as ever!

" You have come to repeat the old song to me, Monsieur Lajolais," said Fouché one evening, as his wily subordinate entered the room; " you have nothing to tell me, eh?"

" Very little, Monsieur le Ministre, but still something. I have at last found out where Moreau spends all his evenings. I told you that about half-past nine o'clock every

night all lights were extinguished in his quarters, and,
from the unbroken stillness, it was conjectured that he had
retired to bed. Now it seems that about an hour later, he
is accustomed to leave his house, and crossing the Place
de l'Odeon, to enter the little street, called the 'Allée de
Caire,' where, in a small house next but one to the corner,
resides a certain officer, 'en retraite'—a Colonel Mahon
of the Cuirassiers."

"A Royalist?"

"This is suspected, but not known. His politics, however, are not in question here; the attraction is of a different order."

"Ha! I perceive; he has a wife or a daughter."

"Better still, a mistress. You may have heard of the
famous Caroline de Stassart, that married a Dutchman
named D'Aerschot."

"Madame Laure, as they called her," said Fouché,
laughing.

"The same. She has lived as Mahon's wife for some
years, and was as such introduced into society; in fact,
there is no reason, seeing what society is in these days,
that she should not participate in all its pleasures."

"No matter for that," broke in Fouché; "Bonaparte
will not have it so. He wishes that matters should go
back to the old footing, and wisely remarks, that it is
only in savage life that people or vices go without clothing."

"Be it so, monsieur. In the present case no such step
is necessary. I know her maid, and from her I have
heard that her mistress is heartily tired of her protector.
It was originally a sudden fancy, taken when she knew
nothing of life—had neither seen anything, nor been herself seen. By the most wasteful habits she has dissipated
all, or nearly all, her own large fortune, and involved
Mahon heavily in debt; and they are thus reduced to a
life of obscurity and poverty—the very things the least
endurable to all her notions."

"Well, does she care for Moreau?" asked Fouché,
quickly; for all stories to his ear only resolved themselves
into some question of utility or gain.

"No, but he does for her. About a year back she did
take a liking to him. He was returning from his great
German campaign, covered with honours and rich in fame;
but as her imagination is captivated by splendour, while
her heart remains perfectly cold and intact, Moreau's
simple, unpretending habits quickly effaced the memory

of his hard-won glory, and now she is quite indifferent to him."

"And who is her idol now, for, of course, she has one?" asked Fouché.

"You would scarcely guess," said Lajolais.

"Parbleu! I hope it is not myself," said Fouché, laughing.

"No, Monsieur le Ministre, her admiration is not so well placed. The man who has captivated her present fancy is neither good-looking nor well-mannered; he is short and abrupt of speech, careless in dress, utterly indifferent to woman's society, and almost rude to them."

"You have drawn the very picture of a man to be adored by them," said Fouché, with a dry laugh.

"I suppose so," said the other with a sigh; "or General Ney would not have made this conquest."

"Ah! it is Ney, then. And he, what of him?"

"It is hard to say. As long as she lived in a grand house of the Rue St. Georges, where he could dine four days a week, and, in his dirty boots and unbrushed frock, mix with all the fashion and elegance of the capital; while he could stretch full length on a Persian ottoman, and brush the cinders from his cigar against a statuette by Canova, or a gold embroidered hanging; while in the midst of the most voluptuous decorations he alone could be dirty and uncared for, I really believe that he did care for her, at least, so far as ministering to his own enjoyments; but in a miserable lodging of the 'Allée de Caire,' without equipage, lackeys, liveried footmen——"

"To be sure," interrupted Fouché, "one might as well pretend to be fascinated by the beauty of a landscape the day after it has been desolated by an earthquake. Ney is right! Well, now, Monsieur Lajolais, where does all this bring us to?"

"Very near to the end of our journey, Monsieur le Ministre. Madame, or Mademoiselle, is most anxious to regain her former position; she longs for all the luxurious splendour she used to live in. Let us but show her this rich reward, and she will be our own!"

"In my trade, Monsieur Lajolais, generalities are worth nothing. Give me details; let me know how you would proceed."

"Easily enough, sir; Mahon must first of all be disposed of, and perhaps the best way will be to have him arrested for debt. This will not be difficult, for his bills are everywhere. Once in the Temple, she will never think more of him. It must then be her task to obtain the most complete influence over Moreau. She must affect the deepest interest in the Royalist cause: I'll furnish her with all the watch-words of the party, and Moreau, who never trusts a man, will open all his confidence to a woman."

"Very good, go on!" cried Fouché, gathering fresh interest as the plot began to reveal itself before him.

"He hates writing; she will be his secretary, embodying all his thoughts and suggestions; and, now and then, for her own guidance, obtaining little scraps in his hand. If he be too cautious here, I will advise her to remove to Geneva for change of air; he likes Switzerland, and will follow her immediately."

"This will do; at least it looks practicable," said Fouché, thoughtfully; "is she equal to the part you would assign her?"

"Ay, sir, and to a higher one, too! She has considerable ability, and great ambition; her present narrow fortune has irritated and disgusted her; the moment is most favourable for us."

"If she should play us false," said Fouché, half aloud.

"From all I can learn, there is no risk of this; there is a headlong determination in her, when once she has conceived a plan, from which nothing turns her; overlooking all but her object, she will brave anything, do anything, to attain it."

"Bonaparte was right in what he said of Necker's daughter," said Fouché, musingly, "and there is no doubt it adds wonderfully to a woman's head, that she has no heart. And now, the price, Master Lajolais; remember that our treasury received some deadly wounds lately—what is to be the price?"

"It may be a smart one; she is not likely to be a cheap purchase."

"In the event of success—I mean of such proof as may enable us to arrest Moreau, and commit him to prison——" He stopped as he got thus far, and paused for some seconds—"Bethink you, then, Lajolais," said he, "what a grand step this would be, and how terrible the consequences if undertaken on rash or insufficient grounds. Moreau's popularity with the army is only second to one man's! His unambitious character has made him many friends; he has few, very few, enemies."

"But you need not push matters to the last—an implied, but not a proven guilt, would be enough; and you can pardon him!"

"Ay, Lajolais, but who would pardon us?" cried Fouché, carried beyond all the bounds of his prudence, by the thought of a danger so imminent. "Well, well, let us come back; the price—will that do?" And taking up a pen he scratched some figures on a piece of paper.

Lajolais smiled dubiously, and added a unit to the left of the sum.

"What! a hundred and fifty thousand francs!" cried Fouché.

"And a cheap bargain, too," said the other; "for after all, it is only the price of a ticket in the lottery, of which the great prize is General Ney!"

"You say truly," said the Minister; "be it so."

"Write your name there, then," said Lajolais, "beneath those figures; that will be warranty sufficient for my negotiation, and leave the rest to me."

"Nature evidently meant you for a Chef-de-Police, Master Lajolais."

"Or a Cardinal, Mons. le Ministre," said the other, as he folded up the paper, a little insignificant slip, scrawled over with a few figures, and an almost illegible word; and yet pregnant with infamy to one, banishment to another, ruin and insanity to a third.

This sad record need not be carried further. It is far from a pleasant task to tell of baseness unredeemed by one trait of virtue—of treachery, unrepented even by regret. History records Moreau's unhappy destiny—the pages of private memoir tell of Ney's disastrous connection; our own humble reminiscences speak of poor Mahon's fate, the least known of all, but the most sorrowful victim of a woman's treachery!

CHAPTER XLVI.

A GLANCE AT THE " PREFECTURE DE POLICE."

POOR Mahon's melancholy story made a deep impression upon me, and I returned to Paris execrating the whole race of spies and "Mouchards," and despising, with a most hearty contempt, a government compelled to use such agencies for its existence. It seemed to me so utterly impossible to escape the snares of a system so artfully interwoven, and so vain to rely on innocence as a protection, that I felt a kind of reckless hardihood as to whatever might betide me, and rode into the Cour of the Prefecture with a bold indifference as to my fate that I have often wondered at since.

The horse on which I was mounted was immediately recognised as I entered; and the obsequious salutations that met me showed that I was regarded as one of the trusty followers of the Minister; and in this capacity was I ushered into a large waiting-room, where a considerable number of persons were assembled, whose air and appearance, now that necessity for disguise was over, unmistakeably pronounced them to be spies of the police. Some, indeed, were occupied in taking off their false whiskers and moustaches; others were removing shades from their eyes; and one was carefully opening what had been the hump on his back in search of a paper he was anxious to discover.

I had very little difficulty in ascertaining that these were all the very lowest order of "Mouchards," whose sphere of duty rarely led beyond the Fauxbourg or the Battignolles, and indeed soon saw that my own appearance amongst them led to no little surprise and astonishment.

" You are looking for Nicquard, Monsieur?" said one, " but he has not come yet."

"No ; Monsieur wants to see Boule-de-Fer," said another.

" Here's José can fetch him," cried a third.

" He'll have to carry him, then," growled out another,
" for I saw him in the Morgue this morning!"

" What! dead?" exclaimed several together.

" As dead as four stabs in the heart and lungs can make
a man! He must have been meddling where he had no
business, for there was a piece of a lace ruffle found in his
fingers."

" Ah, voila!" cried another, " that comes of mixing in
high society."

I did not wait for the discussion that followed, but stole
quietly away as the disputants were waxing warm. Instead of turning into the Cour again, however, I passed
out into a corridor, at the end of which was a door of
green cloth. Pushing open this, I found myself in a
chamber, where a single clerk was writing at a table.

" You're late to-day, and he's not in a good humour,"
said he, scarcely looking up from his paper, " go in!"

Resolving to see my adventure to the end, I asked no
further questions, but passed on to the room beyond.
A person who stood within the doorway withdrew as I
entered, and I found myself standing face to face with the
Marquis de Maurepas, or, to speak more properly, the
Minister Fouché. He was standing at the fireplace as
I came in, reading a newspaper, but no sooner had he
caught sight of me than he laid it down, and, with his
hands crossed behind his back, continued steadily staring
at me.

" Diable!" exclaimed he, at last, "how came you
here?"

" Nothing more naturally, sir, than from the wish to
restore what you were so good as to lend me, and express my sincere gratitude for a most hospitable reception."

" But who admitted you?"

" I fancy your saddle-cloth was my introduction, sir, for
it was speedily recognised. Gesler's cap was never held
in greater honour."

" You are a very courageous young gentleman, I must
say—very courageous, indeed," said he, with a sardonic
grin that was anything but encouraging.

" The better chance that I may find favour with Monsieur de Fouché," replied I.

" That remains to be seen, sir," said he, seating himself
in his chair, and motioning me to a spot in front of it.
" Who are you?"

" A lieutenant of the Ninth Hussars, sir; by name
Maurice Tiernay."

"I don't care for that," said he, impatiently; "what's your occupation?—how do you live?—with whom do you associate?"

"I have neither means nor associates. I have been liberated from the Temple but a few days back; and what is to be my future, and where, are facts of which I know as little as does Monsieur de Fouché of my past history."

"It would seem that every adventurer, every fellow destitute of home, family, fortune, and position, thinks that his natural refuge lies in this Ministry, and that I must be his guardian."

"I never thought so, sir."

"Then why are you here? What other than personal reasons procures me the honour of this visit?"

"As Monsieur de Fouché will not believe in my sense of gratitude, perhaps he may put some faith in my curiosity, and excuse the natural anxiety I feel to know if Monsieur de Maurepas has really benefited by the pleasure of my society."

"Hardi, Monsieur, bien hardi," said the Minister, with a peculiar expression of irony about the mouth that made me almost shudder. He rang a little hand-bell as he spoke, and a servant made his appearance.

"You have forgotten to leave me my snuff-box, Geoffroy," said he mildly to the valet, who at once left the room, and speedily returned with a magnificently-chased gold box, on which the initials of the first Consul were embossed in diamonds.

"Arrange those papers, and place those books on the shelves," said the Minister. And then turning to me, as if resuming a previous conversation, went on—

"As to that memoir of which we were speaking t'other night, Monsieur, it would be exceedingly interesting just now; and I have no doubt that you will see the propriety of confiding to me what you already promised to Monsieur de Maurepas. That will do, Geoffroy; leave us."

The servant retired, and we were once more alone.

"I possess no secrets, sir, worthy the notice of the Minister of Police," said I, boldly.

"Of that I may presume to be the better judge," said Fouché calmly. "But waiving this question, there is another of some importance. You have, partly by accident, partly by a boldness not devoid of peril, obtained some little insight into the habits and details of this Ministry; at least, you have seen enough to suspect more, and misrepresent what you cannot comprehend. Now,

sir, there is an almost universal custom in all secret socie-
ties of making those who intrude surreptitiously within
their limits, to take every oath and pledge of that society,
and to assume every responsibility that attaches to its
voluntary members——"

"Excuse my interrupting you, sir ; but my intrusion
was purely involuntary ; I was made the dupe of a police
spy."

"Having ascertained which," resumed he, coldly,
"your wisest policy would have been to have kept the
whole incident for yourself alone, and neither have uttered one syllable about it, nor ventured to come here,
as you have done, to display what you fancy to be your
power over the Minister of Police. You are a very young
man, and the lesson may possibly be of service to you ;
and never forget that to attempt a contest of address with
those whose habits have taught them every wile and subtlety of their fellow-men will always be a failure. This
Ministry would be a sorry engine of government if men
of your stamp could outwit it."

I stood abashed and confused under a rebuke which
at the same time I felt to be but half deserved.

"Do you understand Spanish ?" asked he, suddenly.

"No, sir, not a word."

"I'm sorry for it ; you should learn that language
without loss of time. Leave your address with my secretary, and call here by Monday or Tuesday next."

"If I may presume so far, sir," said I, with a great effort to seem collected, "I would infer that your intention
is to employ me in some capacity or other. It is, therefore, better I should say at once, I have neither the
ability nor the desire for such occupation. I have always
been a soldier. Whatever reverses of fortune I may
meet with, I would wish still to continue in the same
career. At all events, I could never become a—a——"

"Spy. Say the word out ; its meaning conveys nothing
offensive to my ears, young man. I may grieve over the
corruption that requires such a system ; but I do not confound the remedy with the disease."

"My sentiments are different, sir," said I resolutely, as
I moved towards the door. "I have the honour to wish
you a good morning."

"Stay a moment, Tiernay," said he, looking for something amongst his papers; "there are, probably, situations where all your scruples could find accommodation,
and even be serviceable, too."

" I would rather not place them in peril, Mons. Le Ministre."

"There are people in this city of Paris who would not despise my protection, young man; some of them to the full as well supplied with the gifts of fortune as Mons. Tiernay."

"And, doubtless, more fitted to deserve it!" said I, sarcastically; for every moment now rendered me more courageous.

"And, doubtless, more fitted to deserve it," repeated he after me, with a wave of the hand in token of adieu.

I bowed respectfully, and was retiring, when he called out in a low and gentle voice,—

"Before you go, Mons. de Tiernay, I will thank you to restore my snuff-box."

"Your snuff-box, sir?" cried I, indignantly, "what do I know of it?"

"In a moment of inadvertence, you may, probably, have placed it in your pocket," said he, smiling; "do me the favour to search there."

"This is unnecessary insult, sir," said I fiercely; "and you forget that I am a French officer!"

"It is of more consequence that you should remember it," said he calmly; "and now, sir, do as I have told you."

"It is well, sir, that this scene has no witness," said I, boiling over with passion, "or, by Heaven, all the dignity of your station should not save you."

"Your observation is most just," said he, with the same coolness. "It is as well that we are quite alone; and for this reason I beg to repeat my request. If you persist in a refusal, and force me to ring that bell——"

"You would not dare to offer me such an indignity," said I, trembling with rage.

"You leave me no alternative, sir," said he, rising, and taking the bell in his hand. "My honour is also engaged in this question. I have preferred a charge——"

"You have," cried I, interrupting, "and for whose falsehood I am resolved to hold you responsible."

"To prove which you must show your innocence."

"There, then—there are my pockets; here are the few things I possess. This is my pocket-book—my purse. Oh, heavens, what is this?" cried I, as I drew forth the gold box, along with the other contents of my pocket; and then staggering back, I fell, overwhelmed with shame and sickness, against the wall. For some seconds I neither saw nor heard anything ; a vague sense of ineffable dis-grace—of some ignominy that made life a misery, was over me, and I closed my eyes with the wish never to open them more."

" The box has a peculiar value in my eyes, sir," said he , "it was a present from the First Consul, otherwise I might have hesitated——"

" Oh, sir, you cannot, you dare not, suppose me guilty of a theft. You seem bent on being my ruin ; but, for mercy's sake, let your hatred of me take some other shape than this. Involve me in what snares, what conspiracies you will, give me what share you please in any guilt, but spare me the degradation of such a shame ! "

He seemed to enjoy the torments I was suffering, and actually revel in the contemplation of my misery ; for he never spoke a word, but continued steadily to stare me in the face.

" Sit down here, Monsieur," said he, at length, while he pointed to a chair near him ; " I wish to say a few words to you, in all seriousness, and in good faith also."

I seated myself, and he went on.

" The events of the last two days must have made such an impression on your mind that even the most remark-able incidents of your life could not compete with. You fancied yourself a great discoverer, and that by the happy conjuncture of intelligence and accident, you had actually fathomed the depths of that wonderful system of police, which, more powerful than armies or councils, is the real government of France ! I will not stop now to convince you that you have not wandered out of the very shallowest channels of this system. It is enough that you have been admitted to an audience with me, to suggest an opposite conviction, and give to your recital, when you repeat the tale, a species of importance. Now, sir, my counsel to you is, never to repeat it, and for this reason : nobody possessed of common powers of judgment will ever believe you ! not one, sir ! No one would ever believe that Mon-sieur Fouché had made so grave a mistake, no more than he would believe that a man of good name and birth, a French officer, could have stolen a snuff-box. You see, Monsieur de Tiernay, that I acquit you of this shameful act. Imitate my generosity, sir, and forget all that you have witnessed since Tuesday last. I have given you good advice, sir ; if I find that you profit by it, we may see more of each other."

Scarcely appreciating the force of his parable, and think-

ing of nothing save the vindication of my honour, I muttered a few unmeaning words, and withdrew, glad to escape
a presence which had assumed, to my terrified senses, all
the diabolical subtlety of Satanic influence. Trusting that
no future accident of my life should ever bring me within
such precincts, I hurried from the place as though it were
contaminated and plague-stricken.

CHAPTER XLVII.

"THE VILLAGE OF SCHWARTZ-ACH."

I WAS destitute enough when I quitted the "Temple," a
few days back; but my condition now was sadder still, for,
in addition to my poverty and friendlessness, I had imbibed a degree of distrust and suspicion that made me
shun my fellow-men, and actually shrink from the contact
of a stranger. The commonest show of courtesy, the
most ordinary exercise of politeness, struck me as the
secret wiles of that police whose machinations, I fancied, were still spread around me. I had conceived a
most intense hatred of civilisation, or, at least, of what I
rashly supposed to be the inherent vices of civilised life.
I longed for what I deemed must be the glorious independence of a savage. If I could but discover this Paradise beyond seas, of which the Marquise raved so much ·
if I only could find out that glorious land which neithei
knew secret intrigues nor conspiracies, I should leave
France for ever, taking any condition, or braving any mischances fate might have in store for me.

There was something peculiarly offensive in the treat-

ment I had met with. Imprisoned on suspicion, I was liberated without any "amende;" neither punished like a
guilty man, nor absolved as an innocent one. I was sent
out upon the world as though the state would not own nor
acknowledge me; a dangerous practice, as I often thought,
if only adopted on a large scale. It was some days before
I could summon resolution to ascertain exactly my position: at last I did muster up courage, and under pretence
of wishing to address a letter to myself, I applied at the
Ministry of War for the address of Lieutenant Tiernay,
of the 9th Hussars. I was one of a large crowd similarly engaged, some inquiring for sons that had fallen in
battle, or husbands or fathers in far-away countries. The
office was only open each morning for two hours, and consequently, as the expiration of the time drew nigh, the eagerness of the inquirers became far greater, and the contrast
with the cold apathy of the clerks the more strongly
marked. I had given way to many, who were weaker
than myself, and less able to buffet with the crowd about
them; and at last, when, wearied by waiting, I was drawing nigh the table, my attention was struck by an old, a
very old man, who, with a beard white as snow, and long
moustaches of the same colour, was making great efforts to
gain the front rank. I stretched out my hand, and caught
his, and by considerable exertion at last succeeded in
placing him in front of me.

He thanked me fervently, in a strange kind of German,
a patois I had never heard before, and kissed my hand
three or four times over in his gratitude; indeed, so absorbed was he for the time in his desire to thank me, that
I had to recall him to the more pressing reason of his presence, and warn him that but a few minutes more of the
hour remained free.

"Speak up," cried the clerk, as the old man muttered
something in a low and very indistinct voice; "speak up,
and remember, my friend, that we do not profess to give
information further back than the times of 'Louis Qua-
torze.'"

This allusion to the years of the old man was loudly
applauded by his colleagues, who drew nigh to stare at the
cause of it.

"Sacre bleu! he is talking Hebrew," said another, "and
asking for a friend who fell at Ramoth Gilead."

"He is speaking German," said I, peremptorily, "and
asking for a relative whom he believes to have embarked
with the expedition to Egypt."

"Are you a sworn interpreter, young man?" asked an older and more consequential-looking personage.

I was about to return a hasty reply to this impertinence, but I thought of the old man, and the few seconds that still remained for his inquiry, and I smothered my anger, and was silent.

"What rank did he hold?" inquired one of the clerks, who had listened with rather more patience to the old man. I translated the question for the peasant, who, in reply, confessed that he could not tell. The youth was his only son, and had left home many years before, and never written. A neighbour, however, who had travelled in foreign parts, had brought tidings that he had gone with the expedition to Egypt, and was already high in the French army.

"You are not quite certain that he did not command the army of Egypt?" said one of the clerks, in mockery of the old man's story.

"It is not unlikely," said the peasant, gravely; "he was a brave and a bold youth, and could have lifted two such as you with one hand, and hurled you out of that window."

"Let us hear his name once more," said the elder clerk, "it is worth remembering."

"I have told you already. It was Karl Kleber."

"The General—General Kleber!" cried three or four in a breath.

"Mayhap," was all the reply.

"And are you the father of the great general of Egypt?" asked the elder, with an air of deep respect.

"Kleber is my son; and so that he is alive and well, I care little if a general or simple soldier."

Not a word was said in answer to this speech, and each seemed to feel reluctant to tell the sad tidings. At last the elder clerk said, "You have lost a good son, and France one of her greatest captains. The General Kleber is dead."

"Dead!" said the old man, slowly.

"In the very moment of his greatest glory, too, when he had won the country of the Pyramids, and made Egypt a colony of France."

"When did he die?" said the peasant.

"The last accounts from the East brought the news; and this very day the Council of State has accorded a pension to his family of ten thousand livres."

"They may keep their money. I am all that remains,

and have no want of it; and I should be poorer still before I'd take it."

These words he uttered in a low, harsh tone, and pushed his way back through the crowd.

One moment more was enough for my inquiry.

"Maurice Tiernay, of the 9th—destitué," was the short and stunning answer I received.

"Is there any reason alleged—is there any charge imputed to him?" asked I, timidly.

"Ma foi! you must go to the Minister of War with that question. Perhaps he was paymaster, and embezzled the funds of the regiment; perhaps he liked Royalist gold better than Republican silver; or perhaps he preferred the company of the baggage-train and the 'ambulances,' when he should have been at the head of his squadron."

I did not care to listen longer to this impertinence, and making my way out I gained the street. The old peasant was still standing there, like one stunned and overwhelmed by some great shock, and neither heeding the crowd that passed, nor the groups that halted occasionally to stare at him.

"Come along with me," said I, taking his hand in mine. "Your calamity is a heavy one, but mine is harder to bear up against."

He suffered himself to be led away like a child, and never spoke a word as we walked along towards the "barrière," beyond which, at a short distance, was a little ordinary, where I used to dine. There we had our dinner together, and as the evening wore on, the old man rallied enough to tell me of his son's early life, and his departure for the army. Of his great career I could speak freely, for Kleber's name was, in soldier esteem, scarcely second to that of Bonaparte himself. Not all the praises I could bestow, however, were sufficient to turn the old man from his stern conviction, that a peasant in the "Lech Thal" was a more noble and independent man than the greatest general that ever marched to victory.

"We have been some centuries there," said he, "and none of our name has incurred a shadow of disgrace. Why should not Karl have lived like his ancestors?"

It was useless to appeal to the glory his son had gained —the noble reputation he had left behind him. The peasant saw in the soldier but one who hired out his courage and his blood, and deemed the calling a low and unworthy one. I suppose I was not the first who, in the effort to convince another, found himself shaken in his own convic-

28

tions; for I own before I lay down that night many of the old man's arguments assumed a force and power that I could not resist, and held possession of my mind even after I fell asleep. In my dreams I was once more beside the American lake, and that little colony of simple people, where I had seen all that was best of my life, and learned the few lessons I had ever received of charity and good nature.

From what the peasant said, the primitive habits of the Lech Thal must be almost alike those of that little colony, and I willingly assented to his offer to accompany him in his journey homeward. He seemed to feel a kind of satisfaction in turning my thoughts away from a career that he held so cheaply, and talked enthusiastically of the tranquil life of the Bregenzer-wald.

We left Paris the following morning, and, partly by diligence, partly on foot, reached Strasbourg in a few days; thence we proceeded by Kehl to Freyburg, and, crossing the Lake of Constance at Rorshach, we entered the Bregenzer-wald on the twelfth morning of our journey. I suppose that most men preserve fresher memory of the stirring and turbulent scenes of their lives than of the more peaceful and tranquil ones, and I shall not be deemed singular when I say, that some years passed over me in this quiet spot, and seemed as but a few weeks. The old peasant was the "Vorsteher," or ruler of the village, by whom all disputes were settled, and all litigation of a humble kind decided—a species of voluntary jurisdiction maintained to this very day in that primitive region. My occupation there was as a species of secretary to the court, an office quite new to the villagers, but which served to impress them more reverentially than ever in favour of this rude justice. My legal duties over, I became a vine-dresser, a wood-cutter, or a deer-stalker, as season and weather dictated. My evenings being always devoted to the task of a schoolmaster. A curious seminary was it, too, embracing every class from childhood to advanced age, all eager for knowledge, and all submitting to the most patient discipline to attain it. There was much to make me happy in that humble lot. I had the love and esteem of all around me; there was neither a harassing doubt for the future, nor the rich man's contumely to oppress me; my life was made up of occupations which alternately engaged mind and body, and, above all and worth all besides, I had a sense of duty, a feeling that I was doing that which was useful to my fellow-men; and however

great may be a man's station in life, if it want this element,
the humblest peasant that rises to his daily toil has a nobler
and a better part.

As I trace these lines, how many memories of the spot
are rising before me!—scenes I had long forgotten—faces
I had ceased to remember! And now I see the little
wooden bridge—a giant tree, guarded by a single rail, that
crossed the torrent in front of our cottage ; and I behold
once more the little waxen image of the Virgin over the
door, in whose glass shrine at nightfall a candle ever
burned! and I hear the low hum of the villagers' prayer
as the Angelus is singing, and see on every crag or cliff
the homebound hunter kneeling in his deep devotion!

Happy people, and not less good than happy! Your
bold and barren mountains have been the safeguard of
your virtue and your innocence! Long may they prove
so, and long may the waves of the world's ambition be
stayed at their rocky feet!

I was beginning to forget all that I had seen of life, or,
if not forget, at least to regard it as a wild and troubled
dream, when an accident, one of those things we always
regard as the merest chances, once more opened the flood-
gates of memory, and sent the whole past in a strong current through my brain.

In this mountain region the transition from winter to
summer is effected in a few days. Some hours of a scorch-
ing sun and south wind swell the torrents with melted
snow ; the icebergs fall thundering from cliff and crag, and
the sporting waterfall once more dashes over the precipice.
The trees burst into leaf, and the grass springs up green
and fresh from its wintry covering; and from the dreary
aspect of snow-capped hills and leaden clouds, Nature
changes to fertile plains and hills, and a sky of almost unbroken blue.

It was of a glorious evening in April, when all these
changes were passing, that I was descending the mountain
above our village after a hard day's chamois hunting.
Anxious to reach the plain before nightfall, I could not,
however, help stopping from time to time to watch the
golden and ruby tints of the sun upon the snow, or see the
turquoise blue which occasionally marked the course of a
rivulet through the glaciers. The Alp-horn was sounding
from every cliff and height, and the lowing of the cattle
swelled into a rich and mellow chorus. It was a beautiful
picture, realising in every tint and hue, in every sound
and cadence, all that one can fancy of romantic sim-

plicity, and I surveyed it with a swelling and a grateful heart.

As I turned to resume my way, I was struck by the sound of voices speaking, as I fancied, in French, and before I could settle the doubt with myself, I saw in front of me a party of some six or seven soldiers, who, with their muskets slung behind them, were descending the steep path by the aid of sticks.

Weary-looking and foot-sore as they were, their dress, their bearing, and their soldierlike air, struck me forcibly, and sent into my heart a thrill I had not known for many a day before. I came up quickly behind them and could overhear their complaints at having mistaken the road, and their maledictions, uttered in no gentle spirit, on the stupid mountaineers who could not understand French.

"Here comes another fellow, let us try him," said one, as he turned and saw me near. "Schwartz-Ach, Schwartz-Ach," added he, addressing me, and reading the name from a slip of paper in his hand.

"I am going to the village," said I in French, "and will show the way with pleasure."

"How! what! are you a Frenchman, then?" cried the corporal, in amazement.

"Even so," said I.

"Then by what chance are you living in this wild spot? How, in the name of wonder, can you exist here?"

"With venison like this," said I, pointing to a chamois buck on my shoulder, "and the red wine of the Lech Thal, a man may manage to forget Veray's and the Dragon "Vert," particularly as they are not associated with a bill and a waiter!"

"And perhaps you are a Royalist," cried another, "and don't like how matters are going on at home?"

"I have not that excuse for my exile," said I, coldly.

"Have you served, then?"

I nodded.

"Ah, I see," said the corporal, "you grew weary of parade and guard mounting."

"If you mean that I deserted," said I, "you are wrong there; and now let it be my turn to ask a few questions. What is France about? Is the Republic still as great and victorious as ever?"

"Sacre bleu, man, what are you thinking of? We are an Empire some years back, and Napoleon has made as many kings as he has got brothers and cousins to crown.

"And the army, where is it?"

" Ask for some half dozen armies, and you'll still be short of the mark. We have one in Hamburg, and another in the far North, holding the Russians in check ; we have garrisons in every fortress of Prussia and the Rhine Land; we have some eighty thousand fellows in Poland and Gallicia ; double as many more in Spain ; Italy is our own, and so will be Austria ere many days go over."

Boastfully as all this was spoken, I found it to be not far from truth, and learned, as we walked along, that the Emperor was, at that very moment, on the march to meet the Archduke Charles, who, with a numerous army, was advancing on Ratisbon, the little party of soldiers being portion of a force despatched to explore the passes of the " Vorarlberg," and report on how far they might be practicable for the transmission of troops to act on the left flank and rear of the Austrian army. Their success had up to this time been very slight, and the corporal was making for Schwartz-Ach, as a spot where he hoped to rendezvous with some of his comrades. They were much disappointed on my telling them that I had quitted the village that morning, and that not a soldier had been seen there. There was, however, no other spot to pass the night in, and they willingly accepted the offer I made them of a shelter and a supper in our cottage.

CHAPTER XLVIII.

A VILLAGE "SYNDICUS."

I SAT up all night listening to the soldiers' stories of war and campaigning. Some had served with Soult's army in the Asturias; some made part of Davoust's corps in the north of Europe; one had just returned from Friedland, and amused us with describing the celebrated conference at Tilsit, where he had been a sentinel on the river side, and presented arms to the two Emperors as they passed. It will seem strange, but it is a fact, that this slight incident attracted towards him a greater share of his comrades' admiration than was accorded to those who had seen half the battle-fields of modern war.

He described the dress, the air, the general bearing of the emperors; remarking that although Alexander was taller, and handsomer, and even more soldier-like than our own emperor, there was a something of calm dignity and conscious majesty in Napoleon that made him appear immeasurably the superior. Alexander wore the uniform of the Russian guard, one of the most splendid it is possible to conceive: the only thing simple about him was his sword, which was a plain sabre with a tarnished gilt scabbard, and a very dirty sword-knot; and yet every moment he used to look down at it and handle it with great apparent admiration; "and well might he," added the soldier—"Napoleon had given it to him but the day before."

To listen even to such meagre details as these was to light up again in my heart the fire that was only smouldering, and that no life of peasant labour or obscurity could ever extinguish. My companions quickly saw the interest I took in their narratives, and certainly did their utmost to feed the passion—now with some sketch of a Spanish marauding party, as full of adventure as a romance; now with a description of northern warfare, where artillery thundered on the ice, and men fought behind entrenchments of deep snow.

From the North Sea to the Adriatic, all Europe was now

in arms. Great armies were marching in every direction; some along the deep valley of the Danube, others from the rich plains of Poland and Silesia; some were passing the Alps into Italy, and some again were pouring down for the Tyrol "Jochs," to defend the rocky passes of their native land against the invader. Patriotism and glory, the spirit of chivalry and conquest, all were abroad, and his must indeed have been a cold heart which could find within it no response to the stirring sounds around. To the intense feeling of shame which I at first felt at my own life of obscure inactivity, there now succeeded a feverish desire to be somewhere and do something to dispel this worse than lethargy. I had not resolution to tell my comrades that I had served : I felt reluctant to speak of a career so abortive and unsuccessful ; and yet I blushed at the halt pitying expressions they bestowed upon my life of inglorious adventure.

"You risk life and limb here in these pine-forests, and hazard existence for a bear or a chamois goat," cried one, "and half the peril in real war would perhaps make you a chef d'escadron or even a general."

"Ay," said another, "we serve in an army where crowns are military distinctions, and the epaulette is only the first step to a kingdom."

"True," broke in a third, "Napoleon has changed the whole world, and made soldiering the only trade worth following. Massena was a drummer-boy within my own memory, and see him now! Ney was not born to great wealth and honours. Junot never could learn his trade as a cobbler, and for want of better has become a general of division."

"Yes; and," said I, following out the theme, "under that wooden roof yonder, through that little diamond-paned window the vine is trained across, a greater than any of the last three first saw the light. It was there Kleber, the conqueror of Egypt, was born."

"Honour to the brave dead!" said the soldiers from their places around the fire, and carrying their hands to the salute. "We'll fire a salvo to him to-morrow before we set out!" said the corporal. "And so Kleber was born there!" said he, resuming his place, and staring with admiring interest at the dark outline of the old house, as it stood out against the starry and cloudless sky.

It was somewhat of a delicate task for me to prevent my companions offering their tribute of respect, but which the old peasant would have received with little gratitude.

seeing that he had never yet forgiven the country nor the
service for the loss of his son. With some management
I accomplished this duty, however, promising my services
at the same time to be their guide through the Bregenzer
Wald, and not to part with them till I had seen them safely
into Bavaria.

Had it not been for my thorough acquaintance with the
Tyroler dialect, and all the usages of Tyrol life, their
march would have been one of great peril, for already the
old hatred against their Bavarian oppressors was beginning to stir the land, and Austrian agents were traversing
the mountain districts in every direction, to call forth that
patriotic ardour which, ill-requited as it has been, has more
than once come to the rescue of Austria.

So sudden had been the outbreak of this war, and so
little aware were the peasantry of the frontier of either its
object or aim, that we frequently passed recruits for both
armies on their way to head-quarters on the same day;
honest Bavarians, who were trudging along the road with
pack on their shoulders, and not knowing, nor indeed
much caring, on which side they were to combat. My
French comrades scorned to report themselves to any German officer, and pushed on vigorously in the hope of meeting with a French regiment. I had now conducted my
little party to Immenstadt, at the foot of the Bavarian
Alps; and, having completed my compact, was about to
bid them good-bye.

We were seated around our bivouac fire for the last
time, as we deemed it, and pledging each other in a parting glass, when suddenly our attention was attracted to a
bright red tongue of flame that suddenly darted up from
one of the Alpine summits above our head. Another and
another followed, till at length every mountain peak for
miles and miles away displayed a great signal fire! Little
knew we that behind that giant range of mountains, from
the icy crags of the Glockner, and from the snowy summit
of the Orteler itself, similar fires were summoning all
Tyrol to the combat; while every valley resounded with
the war-cry of "God and the Emperor!" We were still in
busy conjecture what all this might portend, when a small
party of mounted men rode past us at a trot. They carried
carbines slung over their peasant frocks, and showed un-
mistakably enough that they were some newly-raised and
scarcely-disciplined force. After proceeding about a hundred yards beyond us, they halted, and drew up across
the road, unslinging their pieces as if to prepare for action.

"Look at those fellows, yonder," said the old corporal, as he puffed his pipe calmly and deliberately; "they mean mischief, or I'm much mistaken. Speak to them, Tiernay; you know their jargon."

I accordingly arose and advanced towards them, touching my hat in salute as I went forward. They did not give me much time, however, to open negotiations, for scarcely had I uttered a word, when bang went a shot close beside me; another followed; and then a whole volley was discharged, but with such haste and ill direction that not a ball struck me. Before I could take advantage of this piece of good fortune to renew my advances, a bullet whizzed by my head, and down went the left-hand horse of the file, at first on his knees, and then, with a wild plunge into the air, he threw himself stone dead on the road, the rider beneath him. As for the rest, throwing off carbines and cartouche-boxes, they sprung from their horses, and took to the mountains with a speed that showed how far more they were at home amidst rocks and heather than when seated on the saddle. My comrades lost no time in coming up; but while three of them kept the fugitives in sight, covering them all the time with their muskets, the others secured the cattle, as in amazement and terror they stood around the dead horse.

Although the 'peasant had received no other injuries than a heavy fall and his own fears inflicted, he was overcome with terror, and so certain of death that he would do nothing but mumble his prayers, totally deaf to all the efforts I made to restore his courage.

"That comes of putting a man out of his natural bent," said the old corporal. "On his native mountains, and with his rifle, that fellow would be brave enough; but making a dragoon of him is like turning a Cossack into a foot soldier. One thing is clear enough, we've no time to throw away here; these peasants will soon alarm the village in our rear, so that we had better mount and press forward."

"But in what direction?" cried another; "who knows if we shall not be rushing into worse danger?"

"Tiernay must look to that," interposed a third. "It's clear he can't leave us now; his retreat is cut off, at all events."

"That's the very point I was thinking of, lads," said L "The beacon fires show that the 'Tyrol is up,' and safely as I have journeyed hither I know well I dare not venture to retrace my road; I'd be shot in the first Dorf I entered.

On one condition, then, I'll join you; and short of that, however, I'll take my own path, come what may of it."

"What's the condition, then?" cried three or four together.

"That you give me the full and absolute command of this party, and pledge your honour, as French soldiers, to obey me in everything, till the day we arrive at the head quarters of a French corps."

"What, obey a Pekin! take the mot d'ordre from a civilian that never handled a firelock!" shouted three or four, in derision.

"I have served, and with distinction, too, my lads," said I, calmly; "and if I have not handled a firelock, it is because I wielded a sabre, as an officer of Hussars. It is not here, nor now, that I am going to tell why I wear the epaulette no longer. I'll render account of that to my superiors and yours! If you reject my offer, (and I don't press you to accept it,) let us at least part good friends. As for me, I can take care of myself." As I said this, I slung over my shoulder the cross-belt and carbine of one of the fugitives, and selecting a strongly-built, short-legged black horse as my mount, I adjusted the saddle, and sprung on his back.

"That was done like an old hussar, anyhow," said a soldier, who had been a cavalry man, "and I'll follow you whatever the rest may do." He mounted as he spoke, and saluted as if on duty. Slight as the incident was, its effect was magical. Old habits of discipline revived at the first signal of obedience, and the corporal having made his men fall in, came up to my side for orders.

"Select the best of these horses," said I, "and let us press forward at once. We are about eighteen miles from the village of Wangheim; by halting a short distance outside of it, I can enter alone, and learn something about the state of the country, and the nearest French post. The cattle are all fresh, and we can easily reach the village before daybreak."

Three of my little "command" were tolerable horsemen, two of them having served in the artillery train, and the third being the dragoon I have alluded to. I accordingly threw out a couple of these as an advanced picket, keeping the last as my aide-de-camp at my side. The remainder formed the rear, with orders, if attacked, to dismount at once, and fire over the saddle, leaving myself and the others to manœuvre as cavalry. This was the only way to give confidence to those soldiers who in the ranks would have marched up to a battery, but on horse-back were totally devoid of self-reliance. Meanwhile I imparted such instructions in equitation as I could, my own old experience as a riding-master well enabling me to select the most necessary and least difficult of a horseman's duties. Except the old corporal, all were very creditable pupils; but he, possibly deeming it a point of honour not to discredit his old career, rejected everything like teach-ing, and openly protested that, save to run away from a victorious enemy, or follow a beaten one, he saw no use in cavalry.

Nothing could be in better temper, however, nor more amicable than our discourses on this head; and as I let drop, from time to time, little hints of my services on the Rhine and in Italy, I gradually perceived that I grew higher in the esteem of my companions, so that ere we rode a dozen miles together, their confidence in me became complete.

In return for all their anecdotes of "blood and field," I told them several stories of my own life, and, at least, convinced them that if they had not chanced upon the very luckiest of mankind, they had, at least, fallen upon one who had seen enough of casualties not to be easily baffled, and who felt in every difficulty a self-confidence that no amount of discomfiture could ever entirely ob-literate. No soldier can vie with a Frenchman in tempering respect with familiarity; so that while preserving towards me all the freedom of the comrade, they recognised in every detail of duty the necessity of prompt obedience, and followed every command I gave with implicit submission.

It was thus we rode along, till in the distance I saw the spire of a village church, and recognised what I knew to be Dorf Wangheim. It was yet an hour before sunrise, and all was tranquil around. I gave the word to trot, and after about forty minutes' sharp riding, we gained a small pine-wood, which skirted the village. Here I dismounted my party, and prepared to make my entrée alone into the Dorf, carefully arranging my costume for that purpose, sticking a large bouquet of wild flowers in my hat, and assuming as much as I could of the Tyrol look and lounge in my gait. I shortened my stirrups, also, to a most awk-ward and inconvenient length, and gripped my reins into a heap in my hand.

It was thus I rode into Wangheim, saluting the people as I passed up the street, and with the short dry greeting of "Tag," and a nod as brief, playing Tyroler to the top of my bent. The "Syndicus," or the ruler of the village, lived in a good-sized house in the "Platz," which, being market-day, was crowded with people, although the articles for sale appeared to include little variety, almost everyone leading a calf by a straw rope, the rest of the population contenting themselves with a wild turkey, or sometimes two, which, held under the arms, added the most singular element to the general concert of human voices around. Little stalls for rustic jewellery and artificial flowers, the latter in great request, ran along the sides of the square, with here and there a booth where skins and furs were displayed, more, however, as it appeared, to give pleasure to a group of sturdy jägers, who stood around, recognising the track of their own bullets, than from any hope of sale. In fact, the business of the day was dull, and an experienced eye would have seen at a glance that turkeys were "heavy," and calves "looking down." No wonder that it should be so; the interest of the scene being concentrated on a little knot of some twenty youths, who, with tickets containing a number in their hats, stood before the Syndic's door. They were fine-looking, stalwart, straight fellows; and became admirably the manly costume of their native mountains; but their countenances were not without an expression of sadness, the reflection, as I soon saw, of the sadder faces around them. For so they stood, mothers, sisters, and sweethearts, their tearful eyes turned on the little band. It puzzled me not a little at first to see these evidences of a conscription in a land where hitherto the population had answered the call to arms by a levy "en masse," while the air of depression and sadness seemed also strange in those who gloried in the excitement of war. The first few sentences I overheard revealed the mystery. Wangheim was Bavarian; although strictly a Tyrol village, and Austrian Tyrol, too, it had been included within the Bavarian frontier, and the orders had arrived from Munich at the Syndicate to furnish a certain number of men by a certain day. This was terrible tidings; for although they did not as yet know that the war was against Austria, they had heard that the troops were for foreign service, and not for the defence of home and country, the only cause which a Tyroler deems worthy of battle. As I listened, I gathered that the most complete ignorance prevailed as to the service or the destination to which they were intended. The Bavarians had merely issued their mandates to the various villages of the border, and neither sent emissaries nor officers to carry them out.

Having seen how the "land lay," I pushed my way through the crowd, into the hall of the Syndicate, and by dint of a strong will and stout shoulder, at length gained the audience chamber ; where, seated behind an elevated bench, the great man was dispensing justice. I advanced boldly, and demanded an immediate audience in private, stating that my business was most pressing, and not admitting of delay. The Syndic consulted for a second cr two with his clerk, and retired, beckoning me to follow.

" You're not a Tyroler," said he to me, the moment we were alone.

" That is easy to see, Herr Syndicus," replied I. " I'm an officer of the staff, in disguise, sent to make a hasty inspection of the frontier villages, and report upon the state of feeling that prevails amongst them, and how they stand affected towards the cause of Bavaria."

" And what have you found, sir ? " said he, with native caution ; for a Bavarian Tyroler has the quality in a perfection that neither a Scotchman nor a Russian can pretend to.

" That you are all Austrian at heart," said I, determined to dash at him with a frankness that I knew he could not resist. " There's not a Bavarian amongst you. I have made the whole tour of the Vorarlberg ; through the Bregenzer-wald, down the valley of the Lech, by Immenstadt, and Wangheim ; and it's all the same. I have heard nothing but the old cry of ' Gott, und der Kaiser !' "

" Indeed !" said he, with an accent beautifully balanced between sorrow and astonishment.

" Even the men in authority, the Syndics, like yourself, have frankly told me how difficult it is to preserve allegiance to a government by whom they have been so harshly treated. I'm sure I have the ' grain question,' as they call it, and the ' Frei wechsel' with South Tyrol, off by heart," said I, laughing. " However, my business lies in another quarter. I have seen enough to show me that, save the outcasts from home and family, that class so rare in the Tyrol, that men call adventurers, we need look for no willing recruits here ; and you'll stare when I say that I'm glad of it—heartily glad of it."

The Syndic did, indeed, stare, but he never ventured a word in reply.

" I'll tell you why, then, Herr Syndicus. With a man like yourself one can afford to be open-hearted. Wangheim, Luttrich, Kempenfeld, and all the other villages at the foot of these mountains, were never other than Austrian. Diplomatists and map-makers coloured them pale blue, but they were black and yellow underneath; and what's more to the purpose, Austrian they must become again. When the real object of this war is known, all Tyrol will declare for the House of Hapsburg. We begin to perceive this ourselves, and to dread the misfortunes and calamities that must fall upon you and the other frontier towns by this divided allegiance; for when you have sent off your available youth to the Bavarians, down will come Austria to revenge itself upon your undefended towns and villages."

The Syndic apparently had thought of all these things exactly with the same conclusions, for he shook his head gravely, and uttered a low faint sigh.

"I'm so convinced of what I tell you," said I, "that no sooner have I conducted to head-quarters the force I have under my command——"

"You have a force, then, actually under your orders?" cried he, starting.

"The advanced guard is picketed in yonder pine-wood, if you have any curiosity to inspect them; you'll find them a little disorderly, perhaps, like all newly-raised levies, but I hope not discreditable allies for the great army."

The Syndic protested his sense of the favour, but begged to take all their good qualities on trust.

I then went on to assure him that I should recommend the Government to permit the range of frontier towns to preserve a complete neutrality; by scarcely any possibility could the war come to their doors; and that there was neither sound policy nor humanity in sending them to seek it elsewhere. I will not stop to recount all the arguments I employed to enforce my opinions, nor how learnedly I discussed every question of European politics. The Syndic was amazed at the vast range of my acquirements, and could not help confessing it.

My interview ended by persuading him not to send on his levies of men till he had received further instructions from Munich; to supply my advanced guards with the rations and allowances intended for the others; and lastly, to advance me the sum of one hundred and seventy crown thalers, on the express pledge that the main body of my "marauders," as I took opportunity to style them, should take the road by Kempen and Durcheim, and not touch on the village of Wangheim at all.

When discussing this last point, I declared to the Syndic

that he was depriving himself of a very imposing sight; that the men, whatever might be said of them in point of character, were a fine-looking, daring set of rascals, neither respecting laws nor fearing punishment, and that our band, for a newly-formed one, was by no means contemptible. He resisted all these seducing prospects, and counted down his dollars with the air of a man who felt he had made a good bargain. I gave him a receipt in all form, and signed Maurice Tiernay at the foot of it as stoutly as though I had the Grand Livre de France at my back.

Let not the reader rashly condemn me for this fault, nor still more rashly conclude that I acted with a heartless and unprincipled spirit in this transaction. I own that a species of Jesuistry suggested the scheme, and that while pro- viding for the exigencies of my own comrades, I satisfied my conscience by rendering a good service in return. The course of war, as I suspected it would, did sweep past this portion of the Bavarian Tyrol without inflicting any heavy loss. Such of the peasantry as joined the army fought under Austrian banners, and Wangheim and the other border villages had not to pay the bloody penalty of a divided allegiance. I may add, too, for conscience' sake, that while travelling this way many years after, I stopped a day at Wangheim to point out its picturesque scenery to a fair friend who accompanied me. The village inn was kept by an old, venerable-looking man, who also dis- charged the functions of "Vorsteher"—the title Syndicus was abolished. He was, although a little cold and reserved at first, very communicative after a while, and full of stories of the old campaigns of France and Austria, amongst which he related one of a certain set of French freebooters that once passed through Wangheim, the Cap- tain having actually breakfasted with himself, and per- suaded him to advance a loan of nigh two hundred thalers on the faith of the Bavarian Government.

"He was a good-looking, dashing sort of fellow," said he, "that could sing French love-songs to the piano and jodle 'Tyroler Lieder' for the women. My daughter took a great fancy to him, and wore his sword-knot for many a day after, till we found that he had cheated and betrayed us. Even then, however, I don't think she gave him up, though she did not speak of him as before. This is the fellow's writing," added he, producing a much-worn and much-crumpled scrap of paper from his old pocket-book, "and there's his name. I have never been able to make out clearly whether it was Thierray or Lierray"

"I know something about him," said I, "and, with your permission, will keep the document and pay the debt. Your daughter is alive still?"

"Ay, and married, too, at Bruck, ten miles from this."

"Well, if she has thrown away the old sword-knot, tell her to accept this one in memory of the French Captain, who was not, at least, an ungrateful rogue;" and I detached from my sabre the rich gold tassel and cord which I wore as a general officer.

This little incident I may be pardoned for interpolating from a portion of my life, of which I do not intend to speak further, as with the career of the Soldier of Fortune I mean to close these memoirs of Maurice Tiernay.

CHAPTER XLIX.

"A LUCKY MEETING."

THE reader will probably not complain if, passing over the manifold adventures and hair-breadth 'scapes of my little party, I come to our arrival at Ingoldstadt, where the head-quarters of General Vandamme were stationed. It was just as the recall was beating that we rode into the town, where, although nearly eight thousand men were assembled, our somewhat singular cavalcade attracted no small share of notice. Fresh rations for "man and beast" slung around our very ragged clothing, and four Austrian grenadiers tied by a cord, wrist to wrist, as prisoners behind us, we presented, it must be owned, a far more picturesque than soldier-like party.

Accepting all the attentions bestowed upon us in the most flattering sense, and affecting not to perceive the ridicule we were exciting on every hand, I rode up to the "Etat Major" and dismounted. I had obtained from "my prisoners" what I deemed a very important secret, and was resolved to make the most of it by asking for an immediate audience of the general.

"I am the Officier d'Ordonnance," said a young lieutenant of dragoons, stepping forward; "any communications you have to make must be addressed to me."

"I have taken four prisoners, Monsieur le Lieutenant," said I, "and would wish to inform General Vandamme on certain matters they have revealed to me."

"Are you in the service?" asked he, with a glance at my incongruous equipment.

"I have served, sir," was my reply.

"In what army of brigands was it then?" said he, laughing, "for, assuredly, you do not recall to my recollection any European force that I know of."

"I may find leisure and inclination to give you the fullest information on this point at another moment, sir; for the present, my business is more pressing. Can I see General Vandamme?"

29

"Of course you cannot, my worthy fellow! If you had served, as you say you have, you could scarcely have made so absurd a request. A French general of division does not give audience to every tatterdemalion who picks up a prisoner on the high road."

"It is exactly because I have served that I do make the request," said I, stoutly.

"How so, pray?" asked he, staring at me.

"Because I know well how often young staff-officers, in their self-sufficiency, overlook the most important points, and, from the humble character of their informants, frequently despise what their superiors, had they known it, would have largely profited by. And, even if I did not know this fact, I have the memory of another one scarcely less striking, which was, that General Massena himself admitted me to an audience when my appearance was not a whit more imposing than at present."

"You knew General Massena, then? Where was it, may I ask?"

"In Genoa, during the siege."

"And what regiment have you served in?"

"The Ninth Hussars."

"Quite enough, my good fellow. The Ninth were on the Sambre while that siege was going on," said he, laughing sarcastically.

"I never said that my regiment was at Genoa. I only asserted that I was," was my calm reply, for I was anxious to prolong the conversation, seeing that directly over our heads, on a balcony, a number of officers had just come out to smoke their cigars after dinner, amongst whom I ecognised two or three in the uniform of generals.

"And now for your name; let us have that," said he, seating himself, as if for a lengthy cross-examination.

I stole a quick glance over head, and seeing that two of the officers were eagerly listening to our colloquy, said aloud,—

"I'll tell you no more, sir. You have already heard quite enough to know what my business is. I didn't come here to relate my life and adventures."

"I say, Lestocque," cried a large, burly man, from above, "have you picked up Robinson Crusoe, there?"

"He's far more like the man Friday, mon General,' said the young lieutenant, laughing, "although even a savage might have more deference for his superiors."

"What does he want, then?" asked the other.

"An audience of yourself, mon General—nothing less."

"Have you told him how I am accustomed to reward people who occupy my time on false pretences, Lestocque?" said the general, with a grin. "Does he know that the Salle de Police first, and the Prevot afterwards, comprise my gratitude?"

"He presumes to say, sir, that he knows General Massena," said the lieutenant.

"Diable! He knows me, does he say—he knows me? Who is he—what is he?" said a voice I well remembered. and at the same instant the brown, dark visage of General Massena peered over the balcony.

"He's a countryman of yours, Massena," said Vandamme, laughing. "Eh, are you not a Piedmontais?"

Up to this moment I had stood silently listening to the dialogue around me, without the slightest apparent sign of noticing it. Now, however, as I was directly addressed, I drew myself up to a soldier-like attitude, and replied,—

"No, sir. I am more a Frenchman than General Vandamme, at least."

"Send that fellow here; send him up, Lestocque, and have a corporal's party ready for duty," cried the general, as he threw the end of his cigar into the street, and walked hastily away.

It was not the first time in my life that my tongue had brought peril on my head; but I ascended the stairs with a firm step, and if not with a light, at least with a resolute heart, seeing how wonderfully little I had to lose, and that few men had a smaller stake in existence than myself.

The voices were loud, and in tones of anger, as I stepped out upon the terrace.

"So we are acquaintances, it would appear, my friend?" said Massena, as he stared fixedly at me.

"If General Massena cannot recall the occasion of our meeting," said I, proudly, "I'll scarcely remind him of it."

"Come, come," said Vandamme, angrily, "I must deal with this 'gailliard' myself. Are you a French soldier?"

"I was, sir; an officer of cavalry."

"And were you broke? did you desert? or what was it?" cried he, impatiently.

"I kept better company than I believe is considered

cafe in these days, and was accidentally admitted to the acquaintance of the Prince de Condé——"

"That's it!" said Vandamme, with a long whistle; "that's the mischief, then. You are a Vendéen?"

"No, sir; I was never a Royalist, although, as I have said, exposed to the very society whose fascinations might have made me one."

"Your name is Tiernay, monsieur, or I mistake much?" said a smart-looking young man in civilian dress.

I bowed an assent, without expressing any sentiment of either fear or anxiety.

"I can vouch for the perfect accuracy of that gentleman's narrative," said Monsieur de Bourrienne, for I now saw it was himself. "You may possibly remember a visitor——"

"At the Temple," said I, interrupting him. "I recollect you perfectly, sir, and thank you for this recognition."

Monsieur de Bourrienne, however, did not pay much attention to my gratitude, but proceeded, in a few hurried words, to give some account of me to the bystanders.

"Well, it must be owned that he looks devilish unlike an officer of hussars," said Massena, as he laughed, and made others laugh, at my strange equipment.

"And yet you saw me in a worse plight, General," said I coolly.

"How so—where was that?" cried he.

"It will be a sore wound to my pride, General," said I, slowly, "if I must refresh your memory."

"You were not at Valenciennes," said he, musing. "No, no; that was before your day. Were you on the Meuse, then? No. Nor in Spain? I've always had hussars in my division; but I confess I do not remember all the officers."

"Will Genoa not give the clue, sir?" said I, glancing at him a keen look.

"Least of all," cried he. "The cavalry were with Soult. I had nothing beyond an escort in the town."

"So there's no help for it," said I, with a sigh. "Do you remember a half-drowned wretch that was laid down at your feet in the Annunziata Church one morning during the siege?"

"A fellow who had made his escape from the English fleet, and swam ashore? What! are you—By Jove! so it is, the very same. Give me your hand, my brave fellow. I've often thought of you, and wondered what had befallen you. You joined that unlucky attack on Monte

Faccio; and we had warm work ourselves on hand the day after. I say, Vandamme, the first news I had of our columns crossing the Alps were from this officer—for officer he was, and shall be again, if I live to command a French division."

Massena embraced me affectionately, as he said this; and then turning to the others, said,—

" Gentlemen, you see before you the man you have often heard me speak of—a young officer of hussars, who, in the hope of rescuing a division of the French army, at that time shut up in a besieged city, performed one of the most gallant exploits on record. Within a week after he led a storming party against a mountain fortress; and I don't care if he lived in the intimacy of every Bourbon Prince, from the Count D'Artois downwards, he's a good Frenchman, and a brave soldier. Bourrienne, you're starting for head-quarters? Well, it is not at such a moment as this, you can bear these matters in mind; but don't forget my friend Tiernay; depend upon it he'll do you no discredit. The Emperor knows well both how to employ and how to reward such men as him."

I heard these flattering speeches like one in a delicious dream. To stand in the midst of a distinguished group, while Massena thus spoke of me, seemed too much for reality, for praise had indeed become a rare accident to me; but from such a quarter it was less eulogy than fame. How hard was it to persuade myself that I was awake, as I found myself seated at the table, with a crowd of officers, pledging the toasts they gave, and drinking bumpers in friendly recognition with all around me.

Such was the curiosity to hear my story, that numbers of others crowded into the room, which gradually assumed the appearance of a theatre. There was scarcely an incident to which I referred, that some one or other of those present could not vouch for; and whether I alluded to my earlier adventures in the Black Forest, or the expedition of Humbert, or to the later scenes of my life, I met corroboration from one quarter or another. Away as I was from Paris and its influences, in the midst of my comrades, I never hesitated to relate the whole of my acquaintance with Fouché,—a part of my narrative which, I must own, amused them more than all the rest. In the midst of all these intoxicating praises, and of a degree of wonder that might have turned wiser heads, I never forgot that I was in possession of what seemed to myself at least a very important military fact—no less than the mistaken movement of an Austrian general, who had marched his division so far to the southward as to leave an interval of several miles between himself and the main body of the Imperial forces. This fact I had obtained from the grenadiers I had made prisoners, and who were stragglers from the corps I alluded to.

The movement in question was doubtless intended to menace the right flank of our army, but every soldier of Napoleon well knew that so long as he could pierce the enemy's centre such flank attacks were ineffectual, the question being already decided before they could be undertaken.

My intelligence, important as it appeared to myself, struck the two generals as of even greater moment; and Massena, who had arrived only a few hours before from his own division to confer with Vandamme, resolved to take me with him at once to head-quarters.

"You are quite certain of what you assert, Tiernay?" said he; "doubtful information, or a mere surmise, will not do with him before whom you will be summoned. You must be clear on every point, and brief—remember that—not a word more than is absolutely necessary."

I repeated that I had taken the utmost precautions to assure myself of the truth of the men's statement, and had ridden several leagues between the Austrian left and the left centre. The prisoners themselves could prove that they had marched from early morning till late in the afternoon without coming up with a single Austrian post.

The next question was to equip me with a uniform—but what should it be? I was not attached to any corps, nor had I any real rank in the army. Massena hesitated about appointing me on his own staff without authority, nor could he advise me to assume the dress of my old regiment. Time was pressing, and it was decided—I own to my great discomfiture—that I should continue to wear my Tyroler costume till my restoration to my former rank was fully established.

I was well tired, having already ridden thirteen leagues of a bad road, when I was obliged to mount once more, and accompany General Massena in his return to head-quarters. A good supper, and some excellent Bordeaux, and, better than either, a light heart, gave me abundant energy; and after the first three or four miles of the way I felt as if I was equal to any fatigue

As we rode along, the general repeated all his cautions to me in the event of my being summoned to give information at head-quarters; the importance of all my replies being short, accurate, and to the purpose; and, above all, the avoidance of anything like an opinion or expression of my own judgment on passing events. I promised faithfully to observe all his counsels, and not bring discredit on his patronage.

CHAPTER L.

THE MARCH ON VIENNA.

ALL General Massena's wise counsels, and my own steady resolves to profit by them, were so far thrown away, that, on our arrival at Abensberg, we found that the Emperor had left it four hours before, and pushed on to Ebersfield, a village about five leagues to the eastward. A despatch, however, awaited Massena, telling him to push forward with Oudinot's corps to Newstadt, and, with his own division, which comprised the whole French right, to manœuvre so as to menace the Archduke's base upon the Iser.

Let my reader not fear that I am about to inflict on him a story of the great campaign itself, nor compel him to seek refuge in a map from the terrible array of hard names of towns and villages for which that district is famous. It is enough for my purpose that I recall to his memory the striking fact, that when the French sought victory by turning and defeating the Austrian left, the Austrians were exactly in march to execute a similar movement on the French left wing. Napoleon, however, gave the first "check," and "mated" his adversary ere he could open his game. By the almost lightning speed of his manœuvres, he moved forward from Ratisbon with the great bulk of his army; and at the very time that the Archduke believed him to be awaiting battle around that city, he was far on his march to Landshut.

General Massena was taking a hurried cup of coffee, and dictating a few lines to his secretary, when a dragoon officer galloped into the town with a second despatch, which, whatever its contents, must needs have been momentous, for in a few minutes the drums were beating and trumpets sounding, and all the stirring signs of an immediate movement visible. It was yet an hour before daybreak, and dark as midnight; torches, however, blazed everywhere, and by their flaring light the artillery-trains and waggons drove through the narrow street of the village, shaking the frail old houses with their rude trot. Even in a retreating army, I have scarcely witnessed such a spectacle of uproar, confusion, and chaos; but still, in less than an hour the troops had all defiled from the town, the advanced guard was already some miles on its way; and, except a small escort of lancers before the little inn where the general still remained, there was not a soldier to be seen. It may seem absurd to say it, but I must confess that my eagerness to know what was "going on" in front, was divided by a feeling of painful uneasiness at my ridiculous dress, and the shame I experienced at the glances bestowed on me by the soldiers of the escort. It was no time, however, to speak of myself or attend to my own fortunes, and I loitered about the court of the inn wondering if, in the midst of such stirring events, the general would chance to remember me. If I had but a frock and a shako, thought I, I could make my way. It is this confounded velvet jacket and this absurd and tapering hat, will be my ruin. If I were to charge a battery, I'd only look like a merry-andrew after all; men will not respect what is only laughable. Perhaps after all, thought I, it matters little; doubtless Massena has forgotten me, and I shall be left behind like a broken limber. At one time I blamed myself for not pushing on with some detachment—at another I half resolved to put a bold face on it, and present myself before the general; and between regrets for the past and doubts for the future, I at last worked myself up to a state of anxiety little short of fever.

While I walked to and fro in this distracted mood, I perceived, by the bustle within doors, that the general was about to depart; at the same time several dismounted dragoons appeared leading saddle-horses, tightening girths, and adjusting curb-chains, all tokens of a start. While I looked on these preparations, I heard the clatter of a horse's hoofs close behind, and the spluttering noise of a struggle. I turned and saw it was the general himself, who had just mounted his charger, but before catching his right stirrup the horse had plunged, and was dragging the "orderly" across the court by the bridle. Seeing, in an instant, that the soldier's effort to hold on was only depriving General Massena of all command of the horse, who must probably have fallen on his flank, I jumped forward, caught the stirrup, and slipped it over the general's foot, and then, with a sharp blow on the soldier's wrist, compelled him to relax his grasp. So suddenly were the two movements effected, that in less time than I take to relate it, all was over, and the general, who, for a heavy man, was a good rider, was fast seated in his saddle. I had now no time, however, to bestow on him, for the dragoon, stung by the insult of a blow, and from a peasant, as he deemed it, rushed at me with his sabre.

"Halte la!" cried Massena in a voice of thunder; "it was that country fellow saved me from a broken bone, which your infernal awkwardness might have given me. Throw him a couple of florins for me," cried he to his aide-de-camp, who just rode in; "and do you, sir, join your ranks; I must look for another orderly."

"I am right glad to have been in the way, General," said I, springing forward, and touching my hat.

"What, Tiernay—this you?" cried he. "How is this? have I forgotten you all this time? What's to be done now? You ought to have gone on with the rest, Monsieur. You should have volunteered with some corps, eh?"

"I hoped to have been attached to yourself, General. I thought I could, perhaps, have made myself useful."

"Yes, yes, very true; so you might, I've no doubt; but my staff is full, I've no vacancy. What's to be done now? Lestocque, have we any spare cattle?"

"Yes, General; we've your own eight horses, and two of Cambronne's."

"Ah, poor fellow, he'll not want them more. I suppose Tiernay may as well take one of them, at least."

"There's an undress uniform, too, of Cambronne's would fit Monsieur de Tiernay," said the officer, who, I saw, had no fancy for my motley costume alongside of him.

" Oh, Tiernay doesn't care for that; he's too old a soldier to bestow a thought upon the colour of his jacket,"
said Massena.

" Pardon me, General, but it is exactly one of my weak-
nesses; and I feel that until I get rid of these trappings I
shall never feel myself a soldier."

" I thought you had been made of other stuff," muttered
the general, " and particularly since there's like to be little
love-making in the present campaign." And with that he
rode forward, leaving me to follow when I could.

" These are Cambronne's keys," said Lestocque, " and
you'll find enough for your present wants in the saddle-
bags. Take the grey, he's the better horse, and come up
with us as fast as you can."

I saw that I had forfeited something of General Massena's good opinion by my dandyism; but I was consoled
in a measure for the loss, as I saw the price at which I
bought the forfeiture. The young officer, who had fallen
three days before, and was a nephew of the General Cambronne, was a lieutenant in Murat's celebrated corps, the
Lancers of " Berg," whose uniform was the handsomest in
the French army. Even the undress scarlet frock and
small silver helmet were more splendid than many full
parade uniforms; and as I attired myself in these brilliant
trappings, I secretly vowed that the Austrians should see
them in some conspicuous position ere a month was over.
If I had but one sigh for the poor fellow to whose " ga-
lanterie" I succeeded, I had many a smile for myself as I
passe and repassed before the glass, adjusting a belt or
training an aigrette to fall more gracefully. While thus
occupied, I felt something heavy clink against my leg, and
opening the sabertasch, discovered a purse containing upwards of forty golden Napoleons and some silver. It was
a singular way to succeed to a " heritage" I thought, but,
with the firm resolve to make honest restitution, I replaced
the money where I found it, and descended the stairs, my
sabre jingling and my spurs clanking, to the infinite admiration of the hostess and her handmaiden, who looked on
my transformation as a veritable piece of magic.

I'm sure Napoleon himself had not framed one-half as
many plans for that campaign as I did while I rode along.
By a close study of the map, and the aid of all the oral
information in my power, I had at length obtained a tolerably accurate notion of the country; and I saw, or I
thought I saw, at least, half a dozen distinct ways of annihi-
lating the Austrians. I have often since felt shame, even

to myself, at the effrontery with which I discussed the great manœuvres going forward, and the unblushing coolness with which I proffered my opinions and my criticisms; and I really believe that General Massena tolerated my boldness rather for the amusement it afforded him than from any other cause.

"Well, Tiernay," said he, as a fresh order reached him, with the most pressing injunction to hurry forward, "we are to move at once on Moosburg—what does that portend?"

"Sharp work, General," replied I, not noticing the sly malice of the question; "the Austrians are there in force."

"Do your grenadiers say so?" asked he, sarcastically.

"No, General; but as the base of the operations is the Iser, they must needs guard all the bridges over the river, as well as protect the high road to Vienna by Landshut."

"But you forget that Landshut is a good eight leagues from that!" said he, with a laugh.

"They'll have to fall back there, nevertheless," said I, coolly, "or they suffer themselves to be cut off from their own centre."

"Would you believe it," whispered Massena to a colonel at his side, "the fellow has just guessed our intended movement?"

Low as he spoke, my quick ears caught the words, and my heart thumped with delight as I heard them. This was the Emperor's strategy—Massena was to fall impetuously on the enemy's left at Moosburg, and drive them to a retreat on Landshut; when, at the moment of the confusion and disorder, they were to be attacked by Napoleon himself, with a vastly superior force. The game opened even sooner than expected, and a few minutes after the conversation I have reported, our "Tirailleurs" were exchanging shots with the enemy. These sounds, however, were soon drowned in the louder din of artillery, which thundered away at both sides till nightfall. It was a strange species of engagement, for we continued to march on the entire time, the enemy as steadily retiring before us, while the incessant cannonade never ceased.

Although frequently sent to the front with orders, I saw nothing of the Austrians; a low line of bluish smoke towards the horizon, now and then flashing into flame, denoted their position, and as we were about as invisible to them, a less exciting kind of warfare would be difficult to conceive. Neither was the destruction important; many

of the Austrian shot were buried in the deep clay in our
front; and considering the time, and the number of pieces
in action, our loss was insignificant. Soldiers, if they be
not the trained veterans of a hundred battles, grow very
impatient in this kind of operation; they cannot conceive
why they are not led forward, and wonder at the over caution of the general.   Ours were mostly young levies, and
were consequently very profuse of their comments and
complaints.

"Have patience, my brave boys," said an old sergeant to
some of the grumblers; "I've seen some service, and I
never saw a battle open this way that there wasn't plen;y
of fighting ere it was over."

A long row range of hills bounds the plain to the west
of Moosburg, and on these, as night closed, our bivouac
fires were lighted, some of them extending to nearly half
a mile to the left of our real position, and giving the
Austrians the impression that our force was stationed in
that direction.   A thin drizzly rain, cold enough to be
sleet, was falling; and as the ground had been greatly cut
up by the passage of artillery and cavalry, a less comfortable spot to bivouac in could not be imagined.   It was difficult, too, to obtain wood for our fires, and our prospects
for the dark hours were scarcely brilliant.   The soldiers
grumbled loudly at being obliged to sit and cook their
messes at the murky flame of damp straw, while the fires
at our left blazed away gaily without one to profit by them.
Frenchmen, however, are rarely ill-humoured in face of
the enemy, and their complaints assumed all the sarcastic
drollery which they so well understand, and even over their
half-dressed supper they were beginning to grow merry,
when staff-officers were seen traversing the lines at full
speed in all directions.

"We are attacked—the Austrians are upon us!" cried
two or three soldiers, snatching up their muskets.

"No, no, friend," replied a veteran, "it's the other way,
we are going at them."

This was the true reading of the problem; orders were
sent to every brigade to form in close column of attack;
artillery and cavalry to advance under their cover, and
ready to deploy at a moment's notice.

Moosburg lay something short of two miles from us,
having the Iser in front, over which was a wooden bridge,
protected by a strong flanking battery.   The river was not
passable, nor had we any means of transporting artillery
across it; so that to this spot our main attack was at once

directed. Had the Austrian general, Heller, who was
second in command to the Archduke Louis, either cut off
the bridge, or taken effectual measures to oppose its passage, the great events of the campaign might have assumed
a very different feature. It is said, however, that an entire
Austrian brigade was encamped near Freising, and that the
communication was left open to save them.

Still it must be owned that the Imperialists took few precautions for their safety; for, deceived by our line of
watch-fires, the pickets extended but a short distance into
the plain; and when attacked by our light cavalry, many
of them were cut off at once; and of those who fell back,
several traversed the bridge, with their pursuers at their
heels. Such was the impetuosity of the French attack,
that although the most positive orders had been given by
Massena that not more than three guns and their caissons
should traverse the bridge together, and even these at a
walk, seven or eight were seen passing at the same instant,
and all at a gallop, making the old framework so rock and
tremble, that it seemed ready to come to pieces. As often
happens, the hardihood proved our safety. The Austrians
counting upon our slow transit, only opened a heavy fire
after several of our pieces had crossed, and were already
in a position to reply to them. Their defence, if somewhat
late, was a most gallant one, and the gunners continued to
fire on our advancing columns till we captured the block
house and sabred the men at their guns. Meanwhile the
Imperial Cuirassiers, twelve hundred strong, made a succession of furious charges upon us, driving our light cavalry
away before them, and for a brief space making the fortune
of the day almost doubtful. It soon appeared, however,
that these brave fellows were merely covering the retreat
of the main body, who in all haste were falling back on
the villages of Furth and Arth. Some squadrons of Kellerman's heavy cavalry gave time for our light artillery to
open their fire, and the Austrian ranks were rent open
with terrific loss.

Day was now dawning, and showed us the Austrian army
in retreat by the two great roads towards Landshut.
Every rising spot of ground was occupied by artillery, and
in some places defended by stockades, showing plainly
enough that all hope of saving the guns was abandoned,
and that they only thought of protecting their flying columns from our attack. These dispositions cost us heavily,
for as we were obliged to carry each of these places before
we could advance, the loss in this hand-to-hand encounter

was very considerable. At length, however, the roads
became so blocked up by artillery, that the infantry were
driven to defile into the swampy fields at the road-side, and
here our cavalry cut them down unmercifully, while
grape tore through the dense masses at half musket
range.

Had discipline or command been possible, our condition might have been made perilous enough, since, in the
impetuosity of attack, large masses of our cavalry got
separated from their support, and were frequently seen
struggling to cut their way out of the closing columns of
the enemy. Twice or thrice it actually happened that
officers surrendered the whole squadron as prisoners, and
were rescued by their own comrades afterwards. The whole
was a scene of pell-mell confusion and disorder ; some,
abandoning positions when successful defence was possible ; others, obstinately holding their ground when destruction was inevitable. Few prisoners were taken ; indeed, I believe, quarter was little thought of by either
side. The terrible excitement had raised men's passions
to the pitch of madness, and each fought with all the animosity of hate.

Massena was always in the front, and, as was his custom, comporting himself with a calm steadiness that he
rarely displayed in the common occurrences of every-day
life. Like the English Picton, the crash and thunder of
conflict seemed to soothe and assuage the asperities of an
irritable temper, and his mind appeared to find a congenial sphere in the turmoil and din of battle. The awkward
attempt of a French squadron to gallop in a deep marsh,
where men and horses were rolling indiscriminately together, actually gave him a hearty fit of laughter, and he
issued his orders for their recall, as though the occurrence
were a good joke. It was while observing this incident,
that an orderly delivered into his hands some maps and
papers that had just been captured from the fourgon of a
staff-officer. Turning them rapidly over, Massena chanced
upon the plan of a bridge, with marks indicative of points
of defence at either side of it, and the arrangements for
mining it if necessary. It was too long to represent the
bridge of Moosburg, and must probably mean that of
Landshut ; and so thinking, and deeming that its possession might be important to the Emperor, he ordered me to
take a fresh horse, and hasten with it to the head-quarters. The orders I received were vague enough.

"You'll come up with the advance guard some eight

or nine miles to the northward; you'll chance upon some of the columns near Fleisheim."

Such were the hurried directions I obtained, in the midst of the smoke and din of a battle; but it was no time to ask for more precise instructions, and away I went.

In less than twenty minutes' sharp riding I found myself in a little valley, enclosed by low hills, and watered by a small tributary of the Danube, along whose banks cottages were studded in the midst of what seemed one great orchard, since for miles the white and pink blossoms of fruit-trees were to be seen extending. The peasants were at work in the fields, and the oxen were toiling along with the heavy waggons, or the scarcely less cumbersome plough, as peacefully as though bloodshed and carnage were not within a thousand miles of them. No high road penetrated this secluded spot, and hence it lay secure, while ruin and devastation raged at either side of it. As the wind was from the west, nothing could be heard of the cannonade towards Moosburg, and the low hills completely shut out all signs of the conflict. I halted at a little wayside forge to have a loose shoe fastened, and in the crowd of gazers who stood around me, wondering at my gay trappings and gaudy uniform, not one had the slightest suspicion that I was other than Austrian. One old man asked me if it were not true that the "French were coming?" and another laughed, and said, "They had better not;" and there was all they knew of that terrible struggle—the shock that was to rend in twain a great empire.

Full of varied thought on this theme I mounted and rode forward. At first, the narrow roads were so deep and heavy, that I made little progress; occasionally, too, I came to little streams, traversed by a bridge of a single plank, and was either compelled to swim my horse across or wander long distances in search of a ford. These obstructions made me impatient, and my impatience but served to delay me more, and all my efforts to push directly forwards only tended to embarrass me. I could not ask for guidance, since I knew not the name of a single village or town, and to have inquired for the direction in which the troops were stationed might very possibly have brought me into danger.

At last, and after some hours of toilsome wandering, I reached a small wayside inn, and resolving to obtain some information of my whereabouts, I asked whither the road led that passed through a long, low, swampy plain, and disappeared in a pine-wood.

" To Landshut," was the answer.

" And the distance ? "

" Three German miles," said the host; " but they are worse than five; for since the new line has been opened this road has fallen into neglect. Two of the bridges are broken, and a landslip has completely blocked up the passage at another place."

" Then how am I to gain the new road? "

Alas! there was nothing for it but going back to the forge where I had stopped three hours and a half before, and whence I could take a narrow bridle-path to Fleisheim, that would bring me out on the great road. The very thought of retracing my way was intolerable ; many of the places I had leaped my horse over would have been impossible to cross from the opposite side ; once I narrowly escaped being carried down by a mill-race ; and, in fact, no dangers nor inconveniences of the road in front of me could equal those of the course I had just come. Besides all this, to return to Fleisheim would probably bring me far in the rear of the advancing columns, while if I pushed on towards Landshut I might catch sight of them from some rising spot of ground.

" You will go, I see," cried the host, as he saw me set out. " Perhaps you're right; the old adage says, ' It's often the roughest road leads to the smoothest fortune.' "

Even that much encouragement was not without its value. I spurred into a canter with fresh spirits. The host of the little inn had not exaggerated ; the road was execrable. Heavy rocks and mounds of earth had slipped down with the rains of winter, and remained in the middle of the way. The fallen masonry of the bridges had driven the streams into new channels with deep pools among them ; broken waggons and ruined carts marked the misfortunes of some who had ventured on the track ; and except for a well-mounted and resolute horseman the way was impracticable. I was well nigh overcome by fatigue and exhaustion, as clambering up a steep hill, with the bridle on my arm, I gained the crest of the ridge, and suddenly saw Landshut—for it could be no other—before me. I have looked at many new pictures and scenes, but I own I never beheld one that gave me half the pleasure. The ancient town, with its gaunt old belfries, and still more ancient castle, stood on a bend of the Inn, which was here crossed by a long wooden bridge, supported on boats, a wide track of shingle and gravel on either side showing the course into which the melting snows often swelled the stream. From the point where I stood I could see into the town. The Platz, the old gardens of the nunnery, the terrace of the castle, all were spread out before me ; and to my utter surprise there seemed little or no movement going forward. There were two guns in position at the bridge ; some masons were at work on the houses, beside the river, piercing the walls for the use of musketry, and an infantry battalion was under arms in the marketplace. These were all the preparations I could discover against the advance of a great army. But so it was ; the Austrian spies had totally misled them, and while they believed that the great bulk of the French lay around Ratisbon, the centre of the army, sixty-five thousand strong, and led by Napoleon himself, was in march to the southward.

That the attack on Moosburg was still unknown at Landshut seemed certain ; and I now perceived that, notwithstanding all the delays I had met with, I had really come by the most direct line ; whereas, on account of the bend of the river, no Austrian courier could have brought tidings of the engagement up to that time. My attention was next turned towards the direction whence our advance might be expected ; but although I could see nearly four miles of the road, not a man was to be descried along it.

I slowly descended the ridge, and, passing through a meadow, was approaching the high road, when suddenly I heard the clattering of a horse at full gallop coming along the causeway. I mounted at once, and pushed forward to an angle of the road, by which I was concealed from all view. The next instant, a Hungarian hussar turned the corner at top speed.

"What news?" cried I, in German; "are they coming?"

"Ay, in force," shouted he, without stopping.

I at once drew my pistol, and levelled at him. The man's back was towards me, and my bullet would have pierced his skull. It was my duty, too, to have shot him, for moments were then worth days, or even weeks. I couldn't pull the trigger, however, and I replaced my weapon in the holster. Another horseman now swept past without perceiving me, and quickly behind him came a half squadron of hussars, all riding in mad haste and confusion. The horses, though "blown," were not sweated, so that I conjectured they had ridden fast though not far. Such was the eagerness to press on, and so intent were they on the thought of their own tidings, that none saw me, and the whole body swept by and disappeared. I waited a few minutes to listen, and as the clattering to-

30

wards Landshut died away, all was silent. Trusting to my knowledge of German to save me, even if I fell in with the enemy, I now rode forward at speed in the direction of our advance. The road was straight as an arrow for miles, and a single object coming towards me was all I could detect. This proved to be a hussar of the squadron, whose horse, being dead lame, could not keep up with the rest, and now the poor fellow was making the best of his way back as well as he was able. Of what use, thought I, to make him my prisoner; one more or less at such a time can be of slight avail; so I merely halted him to ask how near the French were. The man could only speak Hungarian, but made signs that the lancers were close upon us, and counselled me to make my escape into the town with all speed. I intimated by a gesture that I could trust to my horse, and we parted. He was scarcely out of sight when the bright gleam of brass helmets came into view towards the west, and then I could make out the shining cuirasses of the "Corps de Guides," as, mounted on their powerful horses, they came galloping along.

"I thought I was foremost," said a young officer to me as he rode up. "How came you in advance?"

"Where's the 'Etat Major?'" cried I, in haste, and not heeding his question. "I have a despatch for the Emperor."

"Follow the road," said he, "and you'll come up with them in half an hour."

And with these hurried words we passed each other. A sharp pistol report a moment after told me what had befallen the poor Hungarian; but I had little time to think of his fate. Our squadrons were coming on at a sharp pace, while in their rear the jingling clash of horse-artillery resounded. From a gentle rise of the road I could see a vast distance of country, and perceive that the French columns extended for miles away — the great chaussée being reserved for the heavy artillery, while every by-road and lane were filled with troops of all arms hurrying onward. It was one of those precipitous movements by which Napoleon so often paralysed an enemy at once, and finished a campaign by one daring exploit.

At such a time it was in vain for me to ask in what direction the staff might be found. All were eager and intent on their own projects; and as squadron after squadron passed, I saw it was a moment for action rather than for thought. Still I did not like to abandon all hope of succeeding after so much of peril and fatigue, and seeing that it was impossible to advance against the flood of horse and artillery that formed along the road, I jumped my horse into a field at the side, and pushed forward. Even here, however, the passage was not quite clear, since many, in their eagerness to get forward, had taken to the same line, and, with cheering cries and wild shouts of joy, were galloping on. My showy uniform drew many an eye towards me, and at last a staff-officer cried out to me to stop, pointing with his sabre as he spoke to a hill a short distance off, where a group of officers were standing.

This was General Moulon and his staff, under whose order the advanced-guard was placed.

"A despatch—whence from?" cried he hastily, as I rode up.

"No, sir; a plan of the bridge of Landshut, taken from the enemy this morning at Moosburg."

"Are they still there?" asked he.

"By this time they must be close upon Landshut; they were in full retreat when I left them at daybreak.

"We'll be able to speak of the bridge without this," said he, laughing, and turning toward his staff, while he handed the sketch carelessly to some one beside him; "and you'll serve the Emperor quite as well, sir, by coming with us as hastening to the rear."

I professed myself ready and willing to follow his orders, and away I went with the staff, well pleased to be once more on active service.

Two cannon shots, and a rattling crash of small arms, told us that the combat had begun; and as we rose the hill, the bridge of Landshut was seen on fire in three places. Either from some mistake of his orders, or not daring to assume a responsibility for what was beyond the strict line of duty, the French commander of the artillery placed his guns in position along the river's bank, and prepared to reply to the fire now opening from the town, instead of at once dashing onward within the gates. Moulon hastened to repair the error; but by the delay in pushing through the dense masses of horse, foot, and artillery that crowded the passage, it was full twenty minutes ere he came up. With a storm of oaths on the stupidity of the artillery colonel, he ordered the firing to cease, commanding both the cavalry and the train waggons to move right and left, and give place for a grenadier battalion, who were coming briskly on with their musket at the sling.

The scene was now a madly-exciting one. The chevaux-de-frize at one end of the bridge was blazing; but beyond it, on the bridge, the Austrian engineer and his men were scattering combustible material, and with hempen torches touching the new-pitched timbers. An incessant roll of musketry issued from the houses on the river side, with now and then the deeper boom of a large gun, while the roar of voices, and the crashing noise of artillery passing through the streets, swelled into a fearful chorus. The French sappers quickly removed the burning chevaux-de-frize, and hurled the flaming timbers into the stream; and scarcely was this done, when Moulon, dismounting, advanced, cheering, at the head of his grenadiers. Charging over the burning bridge, they rushed forward; but their way was arrested by the strong timbers of a massive portcullis, which closed the passage. This had been concealed from our view by the smoke and flame; and now, as the press of men from behind grew each instant more powerful, a scene of terrible suffering ensued. The enemy, too, poured down a deadly discharge, and grape-shot tore through us at pistol-range. The onward rush of the columns to the rear defied retreat, and in the mad confusion, all orders and command were unheard or unheeded. Not knowing what delayed our advance, I was busily engaged in suppressing a fire at one of the middle buttresses, when, mounting the parapet, I saw the cause of our halt. I happened to have caught up one of the pitched torches at the instant, and the thought at once struck me how to employ it. To reach the portcullis, no other road lay open than the parapet itself—a wooden railing, wide enough for a footing, but exposed to the whole fire of the houses. There was little time for the choice of alternatives. even had our fate offered any, so I dashed on, and, as the balls whizzed and whistled around me, reached the front.

It was a terrible thing to touch the timbers against which our men were actually flattened, and to set fire to the bars around which their hands were clasped; but I saw that the Austrian musketry had already done its work on the leading files, and that not one man was living amongst them. By a blunder of one of the sappers, the portcullis had been smeared with pitch like the bridge; and as I applied the torch, the blaze sprung up, and, encouraged by the rush of air between the beams, spread in a second over the whole structure. Expecting my death-wound at every instant, I never ceased my task, even when it had become no longer necessary, impelled by a kind of insane persistence to destroy the barrier. The wind carrying the flame inward, however, had compelled the Austrians to fall back, and before they could again open a collected fire on us, the way was open, and the grenadiers, like enraged tigers, rushed wildly in.

I remember that my coat was twice on fire as, carried on my comrades' shoulders, I was borne along into the town. I recollect, too, the fearful scene of suffering that ensued, the mad butchery at each doorway as we passed, the piercing cries for mercy, and the groan of dying agony.

War has no such terrible spectacle as a town taken by infuriated soldiery, and even amongst the best of natures a relentless cruelty usurps the place of every chivalrous feeling. When or how I was wounded I never could ascertain ; but a round shot had penetrated my thigh, tearing the muscles into shreds, and giving to the surgeon who saw me the simple task of saying, " Enlevez le— point d'espoir."

I heard thus much, and I have some recollection of a comrade having kissed my forehead, and there ended my reminiscences of Landshut. Nay, I am wrong ; I cherish another and a more glorious one.

It was about four days after this occurrence that the surgeon in charge of the military hospital was obliged to secure by ligature a branch of the femoral artery which had been traversed by the ball through my thigh. The operation was a tedious and difficult one, for round shot, it would seem, have little respect for anatomy, and occasionally displace muscles in a sad fashion. I was very weak after it was over, and orders were left to give a spoonful of Bordeaux and water from time to time during the evening, a direction which I listened to attentively, and never permitted my orderly to neglect. In fact, like a genuine sick man's fancy, it caught possession of my mind that this wine and water was to save me ; and in the momentary rally of excitement it gave, I thought I tasted health once more. In this impression I never awoke from a short doze without a request for my cordial, and half mechanically would make signs to wet my lips as I slept.

It was near sunset, and I was lying with unclosed eyes, not asleep, but in that semi-conscious state that great bodily depression and loss of blood induce. The ward was unusually quiet, the little buzz of voices that generally mingled through the accents of suffering were hushed, and I could hear the surgeon's well-known voice as he spoke to some persons at the further end of the chamber.

By their stopping from time to time, I could remark that they were inspecting the different beds, but their voices were low and their steps cautious and noiseless.

" Tiernay—this is Tiernay," said some one reading my name from the paper over my head. Some low words which I could not catch followed, and then the surgeon replied,—

" There is a chance for him yet, though the debility is greatly to be feared."

I made a sign at once to my mouth, and after a second's delay the spoon touched my lips, but so awkwardly was it applied, that the fluid ran down my chin ; with a sickly impatience I turned away, but a mild low voice, soft as a woman's, said,—

" Allons!—Let me try once more ;" and now the spoon met my lips with due dexterity.

" Thanks," said I, faintly, and I opened my eyes.

" You'll soon be about again, Tiernay," said the same voice ; as for the person, I could distinguish nothing, for there were six or seven around me ; " and if I know anything of a soldier's heart, this will do just as much as the doctor."

As he spoke he detached from his coat a small enamel cross, and placed it in my hand, with a gentle squeeze of the fingers, and then saying " au revoir," moved on.

" Who's that ?" cried I, suddenly, while a strange thrill ran through me.

" Hush !" whispered the surgeon, cautiously ; " hush ! it is the Emperor."

CHAPTER LL

"SCHÖNBRUNN" IN 1809.

ABOUT two months afterwards, on a warm evening of summer, I entered Vienna in a litter, along with some twelve hundred other wounded men, escorted by a regiment of cuirassiers. I was weak and unable to walk. The fever of my wound had reduced me to a skeleton; but I was consoled for everything by knowing that I was a captain on the Emperor's own staff, and decorated by himself with the Cross of "the Legion." Nor were these my only distinctions, for my name had been included among the lists of the "Officiers d'Elite;" a new institution of the Emperor, enjoying considerable privileges and increase of pay.

To this latter elevation, too, I owed my handsome quarters in the "Raab" Palace at Vienna, and the sentry at my door, like that of a field-officer. Fortune, indeed, began to smile upon me, and never are her flatteries more welcome than in the first hours of returning health, after a long sickness. I was visited by the first men of the army; marshals and generals figured among the names of my intimates, and invitations flowed in upon me from all that were distinguished by rank and station.

Vienna, at that period, presented few features of a city occupied by an enemy. The guards, it is true, on all arsenals and forts, were French, and the gates were held by them; but there was no interruption to the course of trade and commerce. The theatres were open every night, and balls and receptions went on with only redoubled frequency. Unlike his policy towards Russia, Napoleon abstained from all that might humiliate the Austrians. Every possible concession was made to their natural tastes and feelings, and officers of all ranks in the French army were strictly enjoined to observe a conduct of conciliation and civility on every occasion of intercourse with the citizens. Few general orders could be more palatable to Frenchmen, and they set about the task of cultivating the good esteem of the Viennese with a most honest desire for success. Accident, too, aided their efforts not a little; for it chanced that a short time before the battle of Aspern, the city had been garrisoned by Croat and Wallachian regiments, whose officers, scarcely half civilised, and with all the brutal ferocity of barbarian tribes, were most favourably supplanted by Frenchmen in the best of possible tempers with themselves and the world.

It might be argued, that the Austrians would have shown more patriotism in holding themselves aloof, and avoiding all interchange of civilities with their conquerors. Perhaps, too, this line of conduct would have prevailed to a greater extent, had not those in high places set an oppo-site example. But so it was; and in the hope of obtain-ing more favourable treatment in their last extremity, the princes of the Imperial House, and the highest nobles of the land, freely accepted the invitations of our marshals, and as freely received them at their own tables.

There was something of pride, too, in the way these great families continued to keep up the splendour of their households, large retinues of servants and gorgeous equi-pages, when the very empire itself was crumbling to pieces. And to the costly expenditure of that fevered interval may be dated the ruin of some of the richest of the Austrian nobility. To maintain a corresponding style, and to re-ceive the proud guests with suitable magnificence, enormous " allowances " were made to the French generals; while in striking contrast to all the splendour, the Emperor Na-poleon lived at Schönbrunn with a most simple household and restricted retinue.

" Berthier's " Palace, in the " Graben," was, by its superior magnificence, the recognised centre of French society; and thither flocked every evening all that was most distinguished in rank of both nations. Motives of policy, or at least the terrible pressure of necessity, filled these salons with the highest personages of the empire; while as if accepting, as inevitable, the glorious ascendancy of Napoleon, many of the French emigré families emerged from their retirement to pay their court to the favoured lieutenants of Napoleon. Marmont, who was highly con-nected with the French aristocracy, gave no slight aid to this movement; and it was currently believed at the time, was secretly entrusted by the Emperor with the task of accomplishing what in modern phrase is styled, a "fusion."

The real source of all these flattering attentions on the Austrian side, however, was the well-founded dread of the partition of the empire; a plan over which Napoleon was then hourly in deliberation, and to the non-accomplishment of which he ascribed, in the days of his last exile, all the calamities of his fall. Be this as it may, few thoughts of the graver interests at stake disturbed the pleasure we felt in the luxurious life of that delightful city; nor can I, through the whole of a long and varied career, call to mind any period of more unmixed enjoyment.

Fortune stood by me in everything. Marshal Marmont required as the head of his Etat-major an officer who could speak and write German, and, if possible, who understood the Tyrol dialect. I was selected for the appointment; but then there arose a difficulty. The etiquette of the service demanded that the Chef d'etat-major should be at least a lieutenant-colonel, and I was but a captain.

"No matter," said he; "you are officier d'elite, which always gives brevet rank, and so one step more will place you where we want you. Come with me to Schönbrunn to-night, and I'll try and arrange it."

I was still very weak and unable for any fatigue, as I accompanied the marshal to the quaint old palace which, at about a league from the capital, formed the head-quarters of the Emperor. Up to this time I had never been presented to Napoleon, and had formed to myself the most gorgeous notions of the state and splendour that should surround such majesty. Guess then my astonishment, and, need I own, disappointment, as we drove up a straight avenue, very sparingly lighted, and descended at a large door, where a lieutenant's guard was stationed. It was customary for the marshals and generals of division, to present themselves each evening at Schönbrunn, from six to nine o'clock, and we found that eight or ten carriages were already in waiting when we arrived. An officer of the household recognised the marshal as he alighted, and as we mounted the stairs whispered a few words hurriedly in his ear, of which I only caught one, "Komorn," the name of the Hungarian fortress on the Danube where the Imperial family of Vienna and the cabinet had sought refuge.

"Diantre!" exclaimed Marmont, "bad news! My dear Tiernay, we have fallen on an unlucky moment to ask a favour! The despatches from Komorn are, it would seem, unsatisfactory. The Tyrol is far from quiet. Kuffstein, I think that's the name, or some such place, is attacked by a large force, and likely to fall into their hands from assault."

"That can scarcely be, sir," said I, interrupting; "I know Kuffstein well. I was two years a prisoner there; and, except by famine, the fortress is inaccessible."

"What! are you certain of this?" cried he, eagerly; "is there not one side on which escalade is possible?"

"Quite impracticable on every quarter, believe me, sir A hundred men of the line and twenty gunners might hold Kuffstein against the world."

"You hear what he says, Lefebre," said Marmont to the officer; "I think I might venture to bring him up?" The other shook his head doubtfully, and said nothing. "Well, announce me then," said the marshal; "and, Tiernay, do you throw yourself on one of those sofas there, and wait for me."

I did as I was bade, and, partly from the unusual fatigue and in part from the warmth of a summer evening, soon fell off into a heavy sleep. I was suddenly awoke by a voice saying, "Come along, captain, be quick, your name has been called twice!" I sprung up and looked about me, without the very vaguest notion of where I was. "Where to? Where am I going?" asked I, in my confusion. "Follow that gentleman," was the brief reply; and so I did in the same dreamy state that a sleep-walker might have done. Some confused impression that I was in attendance on General Marmont was all that I could collect, when I found myself standing in a great room densely crowded with officers of rank. Though gathered in groups and knots chatting, there was, from time to time, a sort of movement in the mass that seemed communicated by some single impulse; and then all would remain watchful and attentive for some seconds, their eyes turned in the direction of a large door at the end of the apartment. At last this was thrown suddenly open, and a number of persons entered, at whose appearance every tongue was hushed, and the very slightest gesture subdued. The crowd meanwhile fell back, forming a species of circle round the room, in front of which this newly-entered group walked. I cannot now remember what struggling efforts I made to collect my faculties, and think where I was then standing; but if a thunderbolt had struck the ground before me, it could not have given me a more terrific shock than that I felt on seeing the Emperor himself address the general officer beside me.

I cannot pretend to have enjoyed many opportunities of royal notice. At the time I speak of, such distinction was altogether unknown to me; but even when most highly favoured in that respect, I have never been able to divest myself of a most crushing feeling of my inferiority—a sense at once so humiliating and painful, that I longed to be away and out of a presence where I might dare to look at him who addressed me, and venture on something beyond mere replies to interrogatories. This situation, good reader, with all your courtly breeding and aplomb to boot, is never totally free of constraint; but imagine what it can be when, instead of standing in the faint sunshine of a royal smile, you find yourself cowering under the stern and relentless look of anger, and that anger an Emperor's.

This was precisely my predicament, for in my confusion I had not noticed how, as the Emperor drew near to any individual to converse, the others, at either side, immediately retired out of hearing, preserving an air of obedient attention, but without in any way obtruding themselves on the royal notice. The consequence was, that as his Majesty stood to talk with Marshal Oudinot, I maintained my place, never perceiving my awkwardness till I saw that I made one of three figures isolated in the floor of the chamber. To say that I had rather have stood in face of an enemy's battery, is no exaggeration. I'd have walked up to a gun with a stouter heart than I felt at this terrible moment; and yet there was something in that sidelong glance of angry meaning that actually nailed me to the spot, and I could not have fallen back to save my life. There were, I afterwards learned, no end of signals and telegraphic notices to me from the officers in waiting. Gestures and indications for my guidance abounded, but I saw none of them. I had drawn myself up in an attitude of parade stiffness—neither looked right nor left—and waited as a criminal might have waited for the fall of the axe that was to end his sufferings for ever.

That the Emperor remained something like two hours and a half in conversation with the marshal, I should have been quite ready to verify on oath; but the simple fact was, that the interview occupied under four minutes; and then General Oudinot backed out of the presence, leaving me alone in front of his Majesty.

The silence of the chamber was quite dreadful, as, with his hands clasped behind his back, and his head slightly thrown forward, the Emperor stared steadily at me. I am more than half ashamed of the confession; but what between the effect of long illness and suffering, the length of time I had been standing, and the emotion I experienced, I felt myself growing dizzy, and a sickly faintness began to creep over me, and but for the support of my sabre, I should actually have fallen.

"You seem weak; you had better sit down," said the Emperor, in a soft and mild voice.

"Yes, Sire, I have not quite recovered yet," muttered I, indistinctly; but before I could well finish the sentence, Marmont was beside the Emperor, and speaking rapidly to him.

"Ah, indeed!" cried Napoleon, tapping his snuff-box, and smiling. "This is Tiernay, then. Parbleu! we have heard something of you before."

Marmont still continued to talk on; and I heard the words, Rhine, Genoa, and Kuffstein distinctly fall from him. The Emperor smiled twice, and nodded his head slowly, as if assenting to what was said.

"But his wound?" said Napoleon, doubtingly.

"He says that your Majesty cured him when the doctor despaired," said Marmont. "I'm sure, Sire, he has equal faith in what you still could do for him."

"Well, sir," said the Emperor, addressing me, "if all I hear of you be correct, you carry a stouter heart before the enemy than you seem to wear here. Your name is high in Marshal Massena's list; and General Marmont desires to have your services on his staff. I make no objection; you shall have your grade."

I bowed without speaking; indeed, I could not have uttered a word, even if it had been my duty.

"They have extracted the ball, I hope?" said the Emperor to me, and pointing to my thigh.

"It never lodged, Sire; it was a round shot," said I.

"Diable! a round shot! You're a lucky fellow, Colonel Tiernay," said he, laying a stress on the title, "a very lucky fellow."

"I shall ever think so, Sire, since your Majesty has said it," was my answer.

"I was not a lieutenant-colonel at your age," resumed Napoleon; "nor were you either, Marmont. You see, sir, that we live in better times; at least, in times when merit is better rewarded." And with this he passed on; and Marmont, slipping my arm within his own, led me away, down the great stair, through crowds of attendant orderlies and groups of servants. At last we reached our carriage, and in half an hour re-entered Vienna, my heart wild with excitement, and burning with zealous ardour to do something for the service of the Emperor.

The next morning I removed to General Marmont's

quarters; and for the first time put on the golden aigrette of Chef d'etat-major, not a little to the astonishment of all who saw the "boy colonel," as, half in sarcasm, half in praise, they styled me. From an early hour of the morning till the time of a late dinner, I was incessantly occupied. The staff duties were excessively severe, and the number of letters to be read and replied to almost beyond belief. The war had again assumed something of importance in the Tyrol. Hofer and Spechbacher were at the head of considerable forces, which in the fastnesses of their native mountains were more than a match for any regular soldiery. The news from Spain was gloomy: England was already threatening her long-planned attack on the Scheldt. Whatever real importance might attach to these movements, the Austrian cabinet made them the pretext for demanding more favourable conditions; and Metternich was emboldened to go so far as to ask for the restoration of the Empire in all its former integrity.

These negotiations between the two cabinets at the time assumed the most singular form which probably was ever adopted in such intercourse; all the disagreeable intelligences and disastrous tidings being communicated from one side to the other with the mock politeness of friendly relations. As, for instance, the Austrian cabinet would forward an extract from one of Hofer's descriptions of a victory; to which the French would reply by a bulletin of Eugene Beauharnois, or, as Napoleon on one occasion did, by a copy of a letter from the Emperor Alexander, filled with expressions of friendship, and professing the most perfect confidence in his "brother of France." So far was this petty and most contemptible warfare carried, that every little gossip and every passing story was pressed into the service, and if not directly addressed to the cabinet, at least conveyed to its knowledge by some indirect channel.

It is probable I should have forgotten this curious feature of the time, if not impressed on my memory by personal circumstances too important to be easily obliterated from memory. An Austrian officer arrived one morning from Komorn, with an account of the defeat of Lefebre's force before Schenatz, and of a great victory gained by Hofer and Spechbacher over the French and Bavarians. Two thousand prisoners were said to have been taken, and the French driven across the Inn, and in full retreat on Kuffstein. Now, as I had been confined at Kuffstein, and could speak of its impregnable character from actual observation, I was immediately sent off with despatches, about some indifferent matter, to the cabinet, with injunctions to speak freely about the fortress, and declare that we were perfectly confident of its security. I may mention incidentally, and as showing the real character of my mission, that a secret despatch from Lefebre had already reached Vienna, in which he declared that he should be compelled to evacuate the Tyrol, and fall back into Bavaria.

"I have provided you with introductions that will secure your friendly reception," said Marmont to me. "The replies to these despatches will require some days, during which you will have time to make many acquaintances about the court, and if practicable to effect a very delicate object."

This, after considerable injunctions as to secrecy and so forth, was no less than to obtain a miniature, or a copy of a miniature, of the young Archduchess, who had been so dangerously ill during the siege of Vienna, and whom report represented as exceedingly handsome. A good-looking young fellow, a colonel, of two or three and twenty, with unlimited bribery, if needed, at command, should find little difficulty in the mission; at least, so Marmont assured me; and from his enthusiasm on the subject, I saw, or fancied I saw, that he would have had no objection to be employed in the service himself. For while professing how absurd it was to offer any advice or suggestion on such a subject to one like myself, he entered into details, and sketched out a plan of campaign, that might well have made a chapter of "Gil Blas." It would possibly happen, he reminded me, that the Austrian court would grow suspectful of me, and not exactly feel at ease were my stay prolonged beyond a day or two; in which case it was left entirely to my ingenuity to devise reasons for my remaining; and I was at liberty to despatch couriers for instructions, and await replies, to any extent I thought requisite. In fact, I had a species of general commission to press into the service whatever resources could forward the object of my mission, success being the only point not to be dispensed with.

"Take a week, if you like—a month, if you must, Tiernay," said he to me at parting; "but, above all, no failure! mind that—no failure!"

CHAPTER LII.

" KOMORN FORTY YEARS AGO."

I DOUBT if our great Emperor dated his first despatch from Schönbrunn with a prouder sense of elevation, than did I write "Komorn" at the top of my first letter to Marshal Marmont, detailing, as I had been directed, every incident of my reception. I will not pretend to say that my communication might be regarded as a model for diplomatic correspondence ; but having since that period seen something of the lucubrations of great envoys and plenipos, I am only astonished at my unconscious imitation of their style ; blending, as I did, the objects of my mission with every little personal incident, and making each trivial circumstance bear upon the fortune of my embassy.

I narrated my morning interview with Prince Metternich, whose courteous but haughty politeness was not a whit shaken by the calamitous position of his country, and who wished to treat the great events of the campaign as among the transient reverses which war deals out, on this side to-day, on that to-morrow. I told that my confidence in the impregnable character of Kuffstein only raised a smile, for it had already been surrendered to the Tyrolese ; and I summed up my political conjectures by suggesting that there was enough of calm confidence in the minister's manner to induce me to suspect that they were calculating on the support of the northern powers, and had not given up the cause for lost. I knew for certain that a Russian courier had arrived and departed since my own coming ; and although the greatest secrecy had attended the event, I ascertained the fact, that he had come from St. Petersburg, and was returning to Moscow, where the Emperor Alexander then was. Perhaps I was a little piqued, I am afraid I was, at the indifference manifested at my own presence, and the little, or indeed no importance, attached to my prolonged stay. For when I informed Count Stadion that I should await some tidings from Vienna before returning thither, he very politely expressed his pleasure at the prospect of my company, and proposed that we should have some partridge shooting, for which the country along the Danube is famous. The younger brother of this minister, Count Ernest Stadion, and a young Hungarian magnate, Palakzi, were my constant companions. They were both about my own age, but had only joined the army that same spring, and were most devoted admirers of one who had already won his epaulettes as a colonel in the French service. They showed me every object of interest and curiosity in the neighbourhood, arranged parties for riding and shooting, and, in fact, treated me in all respects like a much-valued guest—well repaid, as it seemed, by those stories of war and battle-fields which my own life and memory supplied.

My improved health was already noticed by all, when Metternich sent me a most polite message, stating, that if my services at Vienna could be dispensed with for a while longer, it was hoped I would continue to reside where I had derived such benefit, and breathe the cheering breezes of Hungary for the remainder of the autumn.

It was full eight-and-twenty years later that I accidentally learned to what curious circumstance I owed this invitation. It chanced that the young Archduchess, who was ill during the siege, was lingering in a slow convalescence, and to amuse the tedious hours of her sick couch, Madame Palakzi, the mother of my young friend, was accustomed to recount some of the stories which I, in the course of the morning, happened to relate to her son. So guardedly was all this contrived and carried on, that it was not, as I have said, for nearly thirty years after that I knew of it; and then, the secret was told me by the chief personage herself, the Grand Duchess of Parma.

Though nothing could better have chimed in with my plans than this request, yet, in reality, the secret object of my mission appeared just as remote as on the first day of my arrival. My acquaintances were limited to some half dozen gentlemen in waiting, and about an equal number of young officers of the staff, with whom I dined, rode, hunted, and shot; never seeing a single member of the imperial family, nor, stranger still, one lady of the household. In what Turkish seclusion they lived! when they ventured out for air and exercise, and where, were questions that never ceased to torture me. It was true that all my own excursions had been on the left bank of the river, towards which side the apartment I occupied

looked; but I could scarcely suppose that the right presented much attraction, since it appeared to be an impe-
netrable forest of oak; besides that the bridge which formerly connected it with the island of Komorn had been
cut off during the war. Of course, this was a theme on
which I could not dare to touch; and as the reserve of
my companions was never broken regarding it, I was
obliged to be satisfied with my own guesses on the subject.

I had been about two months at Komorn when I was
invited to join a shooting party on the north bank of the
river at a place called Ercacs, or, as the Hungarians pro-
nounce it, Ercacsh, celebrated for the black cock, or the
auerhahn, one of the finest birds of the east of Europe.
All my companions had been promising me great things,
when the season for the sport should begin, and I was
equally anxious to display my skill as a marksman. The
scenery, too, was represented as surpassingly fine, and I
looked forward to the expedition, which was to occupy
a week, with much interest. One circumstance alone
damped the ardour of my enjoyment: for some time
back exercise on horseback had become painful to me, and
some of those evil consequences which my doctor had
speculated on, such as exfoliation of the bone, seemed
now threatening me. Up to this the inconvenience had
gone no further than an occasional sharp pang after a
hard day's ride, or a dull uneasy feeling which prevented
my sleeping soundly at night. I hoped, however, by time,
that these would subside, and the natural strength of my
constitution carry me safely over every mischance. I was
ashamed to speak of these symptoms to my companions.
lest they should imagine that I was only screening myself
from the fatigues of which they so freely partook; and so
I continued, day after day, the same habit of severe exercise; while feverish nights, and a failing appetite, made
me hourly weaker. My spirits never flagged, and perhaps in this way damaged me seriously; supplying a false
energy long after real strength had begun to give way.
The world, indeed, "went so well" with me in all other
respects, that I felt it would have been the blackest ingratitude against Fortune to have given way to anything
like discontent or repining. It was true, I was far from
being a solitary instance of a colonel at my age; there
were several such in the army, and one or two even
younger; but they were unexceptionably men of family
influence, descendants of the ancient nobility of France,
for whose chivalric names and titles the Emperor had con-

ceived the greatest respect; and never, in all the pomp of
Louis the Fourteenth's court, were a Gramont, a Guise, a
Rochefoucauld, or a Tavanne more certain of his favourable notice. Now, I was utterly devoid of all such pretensions; my claims to gentle blood, such as they were,
derived from another land, and I might even regard
myself as the maker of my own fortune.

How little thought did I bestow on my wound, as I
mounted my horse on that mellow day of autumn! How
indifferent was I to the pang that shot through me as I
touched the flank with my leg! Our road led through a
thick forest, but over a surface of level sward, along which
we galloped in all the buoyancy of youth and high spirits.
An occasional trunk lay across our way, and these we
cleared at a leap; a feat which I well saw my Hungarian
friends were somewhat surprised to perceive gave me no
trouble whatever. My old habits of the riding-school
had made me a perfect horseman; and rather vain of my
accomplishment I rode at the highest fences I could
find. In one of these exploits an acute pang shot through
me, and I felt as if something had given way in my leg.
The pain for some minutes was so intense that I could
with difficulty keep the saddle, and even when it had par-
tially subsided the suffering was very great.

To continue my journey in this agony was impossible;
and yet I was reluctant to confess that I was overcome by
pain. Such an acknowledgment seemed unsoldier-like and
unworthy, and I determined not to give way. It was no
use; the suffering brought on a sickly faintness that completely overcame me. I had nothing for it but to turn
back; so, suddenly affecting to recollect a despatch that I
ought to have sent off before I left, I hastily apologised
to my companions, and with many promises to overtake
them by evening, I returned to Komorn.

A Magyar groom accompanied me to act as my guide;
and attended by this man, I slowly retraced my steps towards the fortress, so slowly, indeed, that it was within an
hour of sunset as we gained the crest of the little ridge,
from which Komorn might be seen, and the course of the
Danube as it wound for miles through the plain.

I is always a grand and imposing scene, one of those
vast Hungarian plains, with waving woods and golden
corn-fields, bounded by the horizon on every side, and
marked by those immense villages of twelve or even
twenty thousand inhabitants. Trees, rivers, plains, even
the dwellings of the people, are on a scale with which

nothing in the Old World can vie. But even with this great landscape before me, I was more struck by a small object which caught my eye as I looked towards the fortress. It was a little boat, covered with an awning, and anchored in the middle of the stream, and from which I could hear the sound of a voice, singing to the accompaniment of a guitar. There was a stern and solemn quietude in the scene; the dark fortress, the darker river, the deep woods casting their shadows on the water, all presented a strange contrast to that girlish voice and tinkling melody, so light-hearted and so free.

The Magyar seemed to read what was passing in my mind, for he nodded significantly, and touching his cap in token of respect, said it was the young Archduchess Maria Louisa, who, with one or two of her ladies, enjoyed the cool of the evening on the river. This was the very same princess for whose likeness I was so eager, and by whom I never could obtain the slightest tidings. With what an interest that bark became invested from that moment! I had more than suspected, I had divined, the reasons of General Marmont's commission to me, and could picture to myself the great destiny that in all likelihood awaited her who now, in sickly dalliance, moved her hand in the stream, and scattered the sparkling drops in merry mood over her companions. Twice or thrice a head of light brown hair peeped from beneath the folds of the awning, and I wondered within myself if it were on that same brow that the greatest diadem of Europe was to sit.

So intent was I on these fancies, so full of the thousand speculations that grew out of them, that I paid no attention to what was passing, and never noticed an object on which the Hungarian's eyes were bent in earnest contemplation. A quick gesture and a sudden exclamation from the man soon attracted me, and I beheld, about a quater of a mile off, an enormous timber raft descending the stream at headlong speed. That the great mass had become unmanageable, and was carried along by the impetuosity of the current, was plain enough, not only from the zig-zag course it took, but from the wild cries and frantic gestures of the men on board. Though visible to us from the eminence on which we stood, a bend of the stream still concealed it from those in the boat. To apprise them of their danger, we shouted with all our might, gesticulating at the same time, and motioning to them to put in to shore. It was all in vain; the roar of the river,

which here is almost a torrent, drowned our voices, and
the little boat still held her place in the middle of the
stream. Already the huge mass was to be seen emerging
from behind a wooden promontory of the river side, and
now their destruction seemed inevitable. Without waiting to reach the path, I spurred my horse down the steep
descent, and half falling, and half plunging, gained the
bank. To all seeming now they heard me, for I saw the
curtain of the awning suddenly move, and a boatman's
red cap peer from beneath it. I screamed and shouted
with all my might, and called out "The raft—the raft!"
till my throat felt bursting. For some seconds the progress of the great mass seemed delayed, probably by having become entangled with the trees along the shore ; but
now, borne along by its immense weight, it swung round
the angle of the bank, and came majestically on, a long,
white wave marking its course as it breasted the water.

They see it ! they see it ! Oh, good heavens ! are they
paralysed with terror, for the boatman never moves ! A
wild shriek rises above the roar of the current, and yet
they do nothing. What prayers and cries of entreaty,
what wild imprecations I uttered, I know not ; but I am
sure that reason had already left me, and nothing remained
in its place except the mad impulse to save them, or perish.
There was then so much of calculation in my mind that I
could balance the chances of breasting the stream on horseback, or alone, and this done, I spurred my animal over
the bank into the Danube. A horse is a noble swimmer
when he has courage, and a Hungarian horse rarely fails
in this quality.

Heading towards the opposite shore, the gallant beast
cleared his track through the strong current, snorting
madly, and seeming to plunge at times against the rushing
waters. I never turned my eyes from the skiff all this
time, and now could see the reason of what had seemed
their apathy. The anchor had become entangled, fouled
among some rocks or weeds of the river, and the boatman's effort to lift it were all in vain. I screamed and
yelled to the man to cut the rope, but my cries were unheard, for he bent over the gunwale, and tugged and tore
with all his might. I was more than fifty yards higher
up the stream, and rapidly gaining the calmer water under
shore, when I tried to turn my horse's head down the current ; but the instinct of safety rebelled against all control, and the animal made straight for the bank. There
was then but one chance left, and taking my sabre in my

mouth, I sprang from his back into the stream. In all the terrible excitement of that dreadful moment I clung to one firm purpose. The current would surely carry the boat into safety, if once free; I had no room for any thought but this. The great trees along shore, the great fortress, the very clouds over head, seemed to fly past me, as I was swept along; but I never lost sight of my purpose; and now almost within my grasp, I see the boat and the three figures, who are bending down over one that seems to have fainted. With my last effort, I cry again to cut the rope, but his knife has broken at the handle! I touch the side of the skiff, I grasp the gunwale with one hand, and seizing my sabre in the other, I make one desperate cut. The boat swings round to the current, the boatman's oars are out—they are saved. My "thank God!" is like the cry of a drowning man—for I know no more.

CHAPTER LIII.

A LOSS AND A GAIN.

To apologise to my reader for not strictly tracing out each day of my history, would be, in all likelihood, as great an impertinence as that of the tiresome guest who, having kept you two hours from your bed by his uninteresting twaddle, asks you to forgive him at last for an abrupt departure. I am already too full of gratitude for the patience that has been conceded to me so far, to desire to trifle with it during the brief space that is now to link us together. And believe me, kind reader, there is more in that same tie than perhaps you think, especially where the intercourse had been carried on, and, as it were, fed from month to month. In such cases the relationship between him who writes and him who reads assumes something like acquaintanceship, heightened by a greater desire on one side to please, than is usually felt in the routine business of every-day life. Nor is it a light reward, if one can think that he has relieved a passing hour of solitude or discomfort, shortened a long wintry night, or made a rainy day more endurable. I speak not here of the greater happiness in knowing that our inmost thoughts have found their echo in far-away hearts, kindling noble emotions, and warming generous aspirations, teaching courage and hope, by the very commonest of lessons; and showing that, in the moral as in the vegetable world, the bane and antidote grow side by side; and, as the eastern poet has it, "He who shakes the tree of sorrow, is often sowing the seeds of joy." Such are the triumphs of very different efforts from mine, however, and I come back to the humble theme from which I started.

If I do not chronicle the incidents which succeeded to the events of my last chapter, it is, in the first place, because they are most imperfectly impressed upon my own memory; and, in the second, they are of a nature which, whether in the hearing or the telling, can afford little pleasure; for what if I should enlarge upon a text which

runs but on suffering and sickness, nights of feverish
agony, days of anguish, terrible alternations of hope and
fear, ending, at last, in the sad, sad certainty that skill has
found its limit? The art of the surgeon can do no more,
and Maurice Tiernay must consent to lose his leg! Such
was the cruel news I was compelled to listen to as I awoke
one morning dreaming and for the first time since my accident, of my life in Kuffstein. The injuries I had received
before being rescued from the Danube had completed the
mischief already begun, and all chance of saving my limb
had now fled. I am not sure if I could not have heard a
sentence of death with more equanimity than the terrible
announcement that I was to drag out existence maimed
and crippled—to endure the helplessness of age with the
warm blood and daring passions of youth, and, worse than
all, to forego a career that was already opening with such
glorious prospects of distinction.

Nothing could be more kindly considerate than the mode
of communicating this sad announcement; nor was there
omitted anything which could alleviate the bitterness of
the tidings. The undying gratitude of the Imperial
family; their heartfelt sorrow for my suffering; the pains
they had taken to communicate the whole story of my adventure to the Emperor Napoleon himself, were all insisted on; while the personal visits of the Archdukes, and
even the Emperor himself, at my sick bed, were told to
me with every flattery such acts of condescension could
convey. Let me not be thought ungrateful, if all these
seemed but a sorry payment for the terrible sacrifice I was
to suffer; and that the glittering crosses which were already sent to me in recognition, and which now sparkled
on my bed, appeared a poor price for my shattered and
wasted limb; and I vowed to myself that to be once more
strong and in health I'd change fortunes with the humblest
soldier in the grand army.

After all, it is the doubtful alone can break down the
mind and waste the courage. To the brave man, the inevitable is always the endurable. Some hours of solitude
and reflection brought this conviction to my heart, and I
recalled the rash refusal I had already given to submit to
the amputation, and sent word to the doctors that I was
ready. My mind once made up, a thousand ingenious
suggestions poured in their consolations. Instead of in-
curring my misfortune as I had done, my mischance might
have originated in some commonplace or inglorious accident. In lieu of the proud recognitions I had earned, I
might have now the mere sympathy of some fellow-suf-

ferer in an hospital; and instead of the "Cross of St. Stephen" and the "valour medal" of Austria, my reward might have been the few sous per day allotted to an invalided soldier.

As it was, each post from Vienna brought me nothing but flattering recognitions; and one morning a large sealed letter from Duroc conveyed the Emperor's own approval of my conduct, with the cross of commander of the Legion of Honour. A whole life of arduous services might have failed to win such prizes, and so I struck the balance of good and evil fortune, and found I was the gainer!

Among the presents which I received from the Imperial family was a miniature of the young Archduchess, whose life I saved, and which I at once despatched by a safe messenger to Marshal Marmont, engaging him to have a copy of it made and the original returned to me. I concluded that circumstances must have rendered this impossible, for I never beheld the portrait again, although I heard of it among the articles bequeathed to the Duc de Reichstadt at St. Helena. Maria Louisa was, at that time, very handsome; the upper lip and mouth were, it is true, faulty, and the Austrian heaviness marred the expression of these features; but her brow and eyes were singularly fine, and her hair of a luxuriant richness rarely to be seen.

Count Palakzi, my young Hungarian friend, and who had scarcely ever quitted my bedside during my illness, used to jest with me on my admiration of the young Archduchess, and jokingly compassionate me on the altered age we lived in, in contrast to those good old times when a bold feat or a heroic action was sure to win the hand of a fair princess. I half suspect that he believed me actually in love with her, and deemed that this was the best way to treat such an absurd and outrageous ambition. To amuse myself with his earnestness, for such had it become, on the subject, I affected not to be indifferent to his allusions, and assumed all the delicate reserve of devoted admiration. Many an hour have I lightened by watching the fidgetty uneasiness the young count felt at my folly; for now instead of jesting, as before, he tried to reason me out of this insane ambition, and convince me that such pretensions were utter madness.

I was slowly convalescing, about five weeks after the amputation of my leg, when Polakzi entered my room one morning with an open letter in his hand. His cheek was flushed, and his air and manner greatly excited.

"Would you believe it, Tiernay," said he, "Stadion

writes me word from Vienna, that Napoleon has asked for the hand of the young Archduchess in marriage, and that the Emperor has consented."

"And am I not considered in this negotiation?" asked I, scarcely suppressing a laugh.

"This is no time nor theme for jest," said he, passionately; "nor is it easy to keep one's temper at such a moment. A Hapsburgher princess married to a low Corsican adventurer! to the ——"

"Come, Polakzi," cried I, "these are not words for me to listen to; and having heard them, I may be tempted to say, that the honour comes all of the other side; and that he who holds all Europe at his feet ennobles the dynasty from which he selects his empress."

"I deny it—fairly and fully deny it!" cried the passionate youth. "And every noble of this land would rather see the provinces of the empire torn from us, than a princess of the Imperial House degraded to such an alliance!"

"Is the throne of France, then, so low?" said I, calmly.

"Not when the rightful sovereign is seated on it," said he. "But are we, the subjects of a legitimate monarchy, to accept as equals the lucky accidents of your Revolution? By what claim is a soldier of fortune the peer of King or Kaiser? I for one, will never more serve a cause so degraded; and the day on which such humiliation is our lot shall be the last of my soldiering;" and so saying, he rushed passionately from the room, and disappeared.

I mention this little incident here, not as in any way connecting itself with my own fortunes, but as illustrating what I afterwards discovered to be the universal feeling entertained towards this alliance. Low as Austria then was — beaten in every battle — her vast treasury confiscated—her capital in the hands of an enemy—her very existence as an empire threatened; the thought of this insult—for such they deemed it—to the Imperial House, seemed to make the burden unendurable; and many who would have sacrificed territory and power for a peace, would have scorned to accept it at such a price as this.

I suppose the secret history of the transaction will never be disclosed; but living as I did, at the time, under the same roof with the royal family, I inclined to think that their counsels were of a divided nature; that while the Emperor and the younger Archdukes gave a favourable

ear to the project, the Empress and the Archduke Charles
as steadily opposed it. The gossip of the day spoke of
dreadful scenes between the members of the Imperial
House, and some have since asserted that the breaches
of affection that were then made never were reconciled in
after-life.

With these events of state or private history I have no
concern. My position and my nationality of course excluded me from confidential intercourse with those capable
of giving correct information; nor can I record anything
beyond the mere current rumours of the time. This
much, however, I could remark, that all whom conviction,
policy, or perhaps bribery, inclined to the alliance, were
taken into court favour, and replaced in the offices of the
household, those whose opinions were adverse. A total
change, in fact, took place in the persons of the royal
suite, and the Hungarian nobles, many of whom filled the
" Hautes Charges," as they are called, now made way for
Bohemian grandées, who were understood to entertain
more favourable sentiments towards France. Whether in
utter despair of the cause for which they had suffered so
long and so much, or that they were willing to accept this
alliance with the oldest dynasty of Europe as a compromise, I am unable to say; but so was it. Many of the
emigré nobility of France, the unflinching, implacable
enemies of Bonaparte, consented to bury their ancient
grudges, and were now seen accepting place and office in
the Austrian household. This was a most artful flattery
of the Austrians, and was peculiarly agreeable to Napoleon, who longed to legalise his position by a reconciliation
with the old followers of the Bourbons, and who dreaded
their schemes and plots far more than he feared all the
turbulent violence of the " Faubourg." In one day no
fewer than three French nobles were appointed to places
of trust in the household, and a special courier was sent
off to Gratz to convey the appointment of maid of honour
to a young French lady who lived there in exile.

Each of my countrymen, on arriving, came to visit me.
They had all known my father by name, if not personally,
and most graciously acknowledged me as one of themselves—a flattery they sincerely believed above all price.

I had heard much of the overweening vanity and con-
ceit of the Legitimatists, but the reality far exceeded all
my notions of them. There was no pretence, no affectation whatever about them. They implicitly believed that
in "accepting the Corsican," as the phrase went, they

were displaying a condescension and self-negation unparalleled in history. The tone of superiority thus assumed of course made them seem supremely ridiculous to my eyes—I, who had sacrificed heavily enough for the Empire, and yet felt myself amply rewarded. But apart from these exaggerated ideas of themselves, they were most amiable, gentle mannered, and agreeable.

The ladies and gentlemen of what was called the "Service," associated all together, dining at the same table, and spending each evening in a handsome suite appropriated to themselves. Hither some one or other of the Imperial family occasionally came to play his whist, or chat away an hour in pleasant gossip; these distinguished visitors never disturbing in the slightest degree the easy tone of the society, nor exacting any extraordinary marks of notice or attention.

The most frequent guest was the Archduke Louis, whose gaiety of temperament and easy humour induced him to pass nearly every evening with us. He was fond of cards, but liked to talk away over his game, and make play merely subsidiary to the pleasure of conversation. As I was but an indifferent "whister," but a most admirable auditor, I was always selected to make one of his party.

It was on one of the evenings when we were so engaged, and the Archduke had been displaying a more than ordinary flow of good spirits and merriment, a sudden lull in the approving laughter, and a general subsidence of every murmur, attracted my attention. I turned my head to see what had occurred, and perceived that all the company had risen, and were standing with eyes directed to the open door.

"The Archduchess, your Imperial Highness!" whispered an aide-de-camp to the Prince, and he immediately rose from the table, an example speedily followed by the others. I grasped my chair with one hand, and with my sword in the other, tried to stand up, an effort which hitherto I had never accomplished without aid. It was all in vain—my debility utterly denied the attempt. I tried again, but overcome by pain and weakness, I was compelled to abandon the effort, and sink down on my seat, faint and trembling. By this time the company had formed into a circle, leaving the Archduke Louis alone in the middle of the room; I, to my increasing shame and confusion, being seated exactly behind where the Prince stood.

There was a hope for me still; the Archduchess might pass on through the rooms without my being noticed. And this seemed likely enough, since she was merely proceeding to the apartments of the Empress, and not to delay with us. This expectation was soon destined to be extinguished; for, leaning on the arm of one of her ladies, the young Princess came straight over to where Prince Louis stood. She said something in a low voice, and he turned immediately to offer her a chair; and there was I seated, very pale, and very much shocked at my apparent rudeness. Although I had been presented before to the young Archduchess, she had not seen me in the uniform of the Corps de Guides (in which I now served as colonel), and never recognised me. She therefore stared steadily at me, and turned towards her brother as if for explanation.

"Don't you know him?" said the Archduke, laughing; "it's Colonel de Tiernay, and if he cannot stand up, you certainly should be the last to find fault with him. Pray sit quiet, Tiernay," added he, pressing me down on my seat; "and if you won't look so terrified, my sister will remember you."

"We must both be more altered than I ever expect if I cease to remember M. de Tiernay," said the Archduchess, with a most courteous smile. Then leaning on the back of a chair, she bent forward and inquired after my health. There was something so strange in the situation: a young, handsome girl condescending to a tone of freedom and intimacy with one she had seen but a couple of times, and from whom the difference of condition separated her by a gulf wide as the great ocean, that I felt a nervous tremor I could not account for. Perhaps, with the tact that Royalty possesses as its own prerogative, or, perhaps, with mere womanly intuition, she saw how the interview agitated me, and, to change the topic, she suddenly said,—

"I must present you to one of my ladies, Colonel de Tiernay, a countrywoman of your own. She already has heard from me the story of your noble devotion, and now only has to learn your name. Remember you are to sit still."

As she said this, she turned, and drawing her arm within that of a young lady behind her, led her forward.

"It is to this gentleman I owe my life, Mademoiselle D'Estelles."

I heard no more, nor did she either; for, faltering, she uttered a low, faint sigh, and fell into the arms of those behind her.

"What's this, Tiernay!—how is all this?" whispered Prince Louis; "are you acquainted with Mademoiselle?"

But I forgot everything ; the presence in which I stood, the agony of a wounded leg and all, and with a violent effort sprung from my seat.

Before I could approach her, however, she had risen from the chair, and, in a voice broken and interrupted, said,—

"You are so changed, M. de Tiernay—so much changed —that the shock overpowered me. We became acquainted in the Tyrol, Madame," said she to the Princess, "where Monsieur was a prisoner."

What observation the Princess made in reply I could not hear, but I saw that Laura blushed deeply. To hide her awkwardness perhaps it was, that she hurriedly entered into some account of our former intercourse, and I could observe that some allusion to the Prince de Condé dropped from her.

"How strange, how wonderful is all that you tell me !" said the Princess, who bent forward and whispered some words to Prince Louis ; and then, taking Laura's arm, she moved on, saying in a low voice, "Au revoir, Monsieur," as she passed.

"You are to come and drink tea in the Archduchess's apartments, Tiernay," said Prince Louis ; "you'll meet your old friend, Mademoiselle D'Estelles, and of course you have a hundred recollections to exchange with each other."

The Prince insisted on my accepting his arm, and, as he assisted me along, informed me that old Madame d'Aigreville had been dead about a year, leaving her niece an immense fortune—at least a claim to one—only wanting the sanction of the Emperor Napoleon to become valid ; for it was one of the estreated but not confiscated estates of La Vendée. Every word that dropped from the Prince extinguished some hope within me. More beautiful than ever, her rank recognised, and in possession of a vast fortune, what chance had I, a poor soldier of fortune, of success ?

"Don't sigh, Tiernay," said the Prince, laughing ; "you've lost a leg for us, and we must lend you a hand in return ;" and with this we entered the salon of the Archduchess.

CHAPTER LIV.

MAURICE TIERNAY'S "LAST WORD AND CONFESSION."

I HAVE been very frank with my readers in these memoirs
of my life. If I have dwelt somewhat vain-gloriously on
passing moments of success, it must be owned that I have
not spared my vanity and self-conceit, when either betrayed me into any excess of folly. I have neither
blinked my humble beginnings, nor have I sought to
attribute to my own merits those happy accidents which
made me what I am. I claim nothing but the humble
character—a Soldier of Fortune. It was my intention to
have told the reader somewhat more than these twenty
odd years of my life embrace. Probably, too, my subsequent career, if less marked by adventure, was more
pregnant with true views of the world and sounder lessons
of conduct; but I have discovered to my surprise that
these revelations have extended over a wider surface than
I ever destined them to occupy, and already I tremble for
the loss of that gracious attention that has been vouchsafed me hitherto. I will not trust myself to say how
much regret this abstinence has cost me ;—enough if I
avow that in jotting down the past I have lived my youth
over again, and in tracing old memories, old scenes, and
old impressions, the smouldering fire of my heart has shot
up a transient flame so bright as to throw a glow even over
the chill of my old age.

It is, after all, no small privilege to have lived and
borne one's part in stirring times ; to have breasted the
ocean of life when the winds were up and the waves ran
high ; to have mingled, however humbly, in eventful
scenes, and had one's share in the mighty deeds that were
to become history afterwards. It is assuredly in such
trials that humanity comes out best, and that the character of man displays all its worthiest and noblest attributes.
Amid such scenes I began my life, and, in the midst of
similar ones, if my prophetic foresight deceive me not, I
am like to end it.

Having said this much of and for myself, I am sure the
reader will pardon me if I am not equally communicative
with respect to another, and if I pass over the remainder
of that interval which I spent at Komorn. Even were
love-making—which assuredly it is not—as interesting to
the spectator as to those engaged—I should scruple to
recount events which delicacy should throw a veil over;

nor am I induced, even by the example of the wittiest periodical writer of the age, to make a "feuilleton" of my own marriage. Enough that I say, despite my shattered form, my want of fortune, my unattested pretension to rank or station, Mademoiselle D'Estelles accepted me, and the Emperor most graciously confirmed her claims to wealth, thus making me one of the richest and the very happiest among the Soldiers of Fortune.

The Pére Delamoy, now superior of a convent at Pisa, came to Komorn to perform the ceremony ; and if he could not altogether pardon those who had uprooted the ancient monarchy of France, yet he did not conceal his gratitude to him who had restored the church and rebuilt the altar.

There may be some who may deem this closing abrupt, and who would wish for even a word about the bride, her bouquet, and her blushes. I cannot afford to gratify so laudable a curiosity, at the same time that a lurking vanity induces me to say, that any one wishing to know more about the " personnel " of my wife or myself, has but to look at David's picture, or the engraving made from it, of the Emperor's marriage. There they will find, in the left hand corner, partly concealed behind the Grand Duke de Berg, an officer of the Guides, supporting on his arm a young and very beautiful girl, herself a bride. If the young lady's looks are turned with more interest on her companion than upon the gorgeous spectacle, remember that she is but a few weeks married. If the soldier carry himself with less of martial vigour or grace, pray bear in mind that cork legs had not attained the perfection to which later skill has brought them.

I have the scene stronger before me than painting can depict, and my eyes fill as I now behold it in my memory !

THE END.